Intimate Relationships

SIXTH EDITION

Rowland S. Miller
Sam Houston State University

Mc Graw Hill

Connect
Learn
Succeed™

The McGraw·Hill Companies

Connect
Learn
Succeed™

INTIMATE RELATIONSHIPS, SIXTH EDITION

Published by McGraw-Hill, a business unit of The McGraw-Hill Companies, Inc., 1221 Avenue of the Americas, New York, NY 10020. Copyright © 2012 by The McGraw-Hill Companies, Inc. All rights reserved. Previous editions © 2009, 2007, and 2002. Printed in the United States of America. No part of this publication may be reproduced or distributed in any form or by any means, or stored in a database or retrieval system, without the prior written consent of The McGraw-Hill Companies, Inc., including, but not limited to, in any network or other electronic storage or transmission, or broadcast for distance learning.

Some ancillaries, including electronic and print components, may not be available to customers outside the United States.

This book is printed on acid-free paper.

1 2 3 4 5 6 7 8 9 0 DOC/DOC 1 0 9 8 7 6 5 4 3 2 1

ISBN 978-0-07-811715-2
MHID 0-07-811715-1

Vice President & Editor-in-Chief: *Michael Ryan*
Vice President of Specialized Publishing: *Janice M. Roerig-Blong*
Publisher: *Michael Sugarman*
Sponsoring Editor: *Debra B. Hash*
Director of Marketing & Sales: *Jennifer J. Lewis*
Project Manager: *Melissa M. Leick*
Design Coordinator: *Margarite Reynolds*
Cover Designer: *Studio Montage, St. Louis, Missouri*

Cover Image: *Fototeca Storica Nazionale/Getty Images*
Buyer: *Sherry L. Kane*
Media Project Manager: *Sridevi Palani*
Compositor: *Laserwords Private Limited*
Typeface: 10/12 Palatino
Printer: R.R Donnelley

All credits appearing on page or at the end of the book are considered to be an extension of the copyright page.

Library of Congress Cataloging-in-Publication Data
Miller, Rowland S.
    Intimate relationships / Rowland S. Miller.—6th ed.
        p. cm.
    ISBN 978-0-07-811715-2 (alk. paper)
        1. Family life education. 2. Interpersonal relations.   I. Title.
HQ10.B735 2011
306.707—dc23

2011027470

www.mhhe.com

Contents

PREFACE   xi

1. The Building Blocks of Relationships   1

    THE NATURE AND IMPORTANCE OF INTIMACY   2

    The Nature of Intimacy   2
    The Need to Belong   4

    THE INFLUENCE OF CULTURE   6

    Sources of Change   11

    THE INFLUENCE OF EXPERIENCE   14

    THE INFLUENCE OF INDIVIDUAL DIFFERENCES   19

    Sex Differences   20
    Gender Differences   22
    Personality   27
    Self-Esteem   28

    THE INFLUENCE OF HUMAN NATURE   32

    THE INFLUENCE OF INTERACTION   36

    THE DARK SIDE OF RELATIONSHIPS   36

    FOR YOUR CONSIDERATION   37

    CHAPTER SUMMARY   38

2. Research Methods   40

    THE SHORT HISTORY OF RELATIONSHIP SCIENCE   41

    DEVELOPING A QUESTION   44

    OBTAINING PARTICIPANTS   45

CHOOSING A DESIGN   49

Correlational Designs   49
Experimental Designs   51
Developmental Designs   52

SELECTING A SETTING   54

THE NATURE OF OUR DATA   55

Self-Reports   55
Observations   59
Physiological Measures   61
Archival Materials   62

THE ETHICS OF SUCH ENDEAVORS   62

INTERPRETING AND INTEGRATING RESULTS   64

A FINAL NOTE   66

FOR YOUR CONSIDERATION   66

CHAPTER SUMMARY   67

3.   Attraction   70

THE FUNDAMENTAL BASIS OF ATTRACTION   70

PROXIMITY: LIKING THOSE NEAR US   71

Convenience: Proximity Is Rewarding, Distance Is Costly   72
Familiarity: Repeated Contact   73
The Power of Proximity   73

**PHYSICAL ATTRACTIVENESS: LIKING THOSE
WHO ARE LOVELY**   74

Our Bias for Beauty: "What Is Beautiful Is Good"   75
Who's Pretty?   77
An Evolutionary Perspective on Physical Attractiveness   81
Culture Counts, Too   84
Looks Matter   85
The Interactive Costs and Benefits of Beauty   86
Matching in Physical Attractiveness   88

RECIPROCITY: LIKING THOSE WHO LIKE US   89

SIMILARITY: LIKING THOSE WHO ARE LIKE US   92

What Kind of Similarity?   92
Do Opposites Attract?   93
Why Is Similarity Attractive?   100

BARRIERS: LIKING THOSE WE CANNOT HAVE 100

SO, WHAT DO MEN AND WOMEN WANT? 101

FOR YOUR CONSIDERATION 102

CHAPTER SUMMARY 103

4. Social Cognition 105

FIRST IMPRESSIONS (AND BEYOND) 106

THE POWER OF PERCEPTIONS 112

Idealizing Our Partners 112
Attributional Processes 113
Memories 116
Relationship Beliefs 117
Expectations 120
Self-Perceptions 125

IMPRESSION MANAGEMENT 129

Strategies of Impression Management 130
Impression Management in Close Relationships 130

SO, JUST HOW WELL DO WE KNOW OUR PARTNERS? 132

Knowledge 134
Motivation 134
Partner Legibility 134
Perceiver Ability 135
Threatening Perceptions 136
Perceiver Influence 137
Summary 137

FOR YOUR CONSIDERATION 138

CHAPTER SUMMARY 138

5. Communication 141

NONVERBAL COMMUNICATION 143

Components of Nonverbal Communication 144
Nonverbal Sensitivity 153

VERBAL COMMUNICATION 155

Self-Disclosure 155
Gender Differences in Verbal Communication 161

DYSFUNCTIONAL COMMUNICATION
AND WHAT TO DO ABOUT IT   166

Miscommunication   166
Saying What We Mean   168
Active Listening   170
Being Polite and Staying Cool   170
The Power of Respect and Validation   172

FOR YOUR CONSIDERATION   173

CHAPTER SUMMARY   173

6.   Interdependency   175

SOCIAL EXCHANGE   175

Rewards and Costs   176
What Do We Expect from Our Relationships?   176
How Well Could We Do Elsewhere?   177
Four Types of Relationships   179
CL and CL$_{alt}$ as Time Goes By   182

THE ECONOMIES OF RELATIONSHIPS   183

Rewards and Costs Are Different   187
Rewards and Costs as Time Goes By   191

ARE WE REALLY THIS GREEDY?   196

The Nature of Interdependency   196
Exchange versus Communal Relationships   197
Equitable Relationships   200
Summing Up   204

THE NATURE OF COMMITMENT   204

The Consequences of Commitment   208

FOR YOUR CONSIDERATION   209

CHAPTER SUMMARY   210

7.   Friendship   212

THE NATURE OF FRIENDSHIP   213

Attributes of Friendships   213
The Rules of Friendship   219

FRIENDSHIP ACROSS THE LIFE CYCLE   220

Childhood   221
Adolescence   222

Young Adulthood   222
Midlife   224
Old Age   224

DIFFERENCES IN FRIENDSHIP   226

Gender Differences in Same-Sex Friendships   227
Individual Differences in Friendship   229

FRIENDSHIP DIFFICULTIES   230

Shyness   231
Loneliness   236

FOR YOUR CONSIDERATION   242

CHAPTER SUMMARY   242

8.   Love   244

A BRIEF HISTORY OF LOVE   245

TYPES OF LOVE   246

The Triangular Theory of Love   246
Romantic, Passionate Love   251
Companionate Love   258
Compassionate Love   260
Styles of Loving   261

INDIVIDUAL AND CULTURAL DIFFERENCES IN LOVE   263

Culture   263
Attachment Styles   264
Age   265
Men and Women   266

DOES LOVE LAST?   267

Why Doesn't Romantic Love Last?   267
So, What Does the Future Hold?   269

FOR YOUR CONSIDERATION   271

CHAPTER SUMMARY   271

9.   Sexuality   273

SEXUAL ATTITUDES   274

Attitudes about Casual Sex   274
Attitudes about Same-Sex Sexuality   275
Cultural Differences in Sexual Attitudes   277

SEXUAL BEHAVIOR   278

Sex for the First Time   278
Sex in Committed Relationships   280
Infidelity   282
Sexual Desire   289
Safe, Sensible Sex   291

SEXUAL SATISFACTION   294

Sexual Communication   297
Sexual Satisfaction and Relationship Satisfaction   299

SEXUAL COERCION   300

FOR YOUR CONSIDERATION   302

CHAPTER SUMMARY   303

10.   Stresses and Strains   305

PERCEIVED RELATIONAL VALUE   305

HURT FEELINGS   307

OSTRACISM   310

JEALOUSY   312

Two Types of Jealousy   313
Who's Prone to Jealousy?   313
Who Gets Us Jealous?   315
What Gets Us Jealous?   316
Responses to Jealousy   320
Coping Constructively with Jealousy   322

DECEPTION AND LYING   323

Lying in Close and Casual Relationships   323
Lies and Liars   325
So, How Well Can We Detect a Partner's Deception?   326

BETRAYAL   328

Individual Differences in Betrayal   329
The Two Sides to Every Betrayal   330
Coping with Betrayal   331

FORGIVENESS   332

FOR YOUR CONSIDERATION   334

CHAPTER SUMMARY   335

11. Conflict 337

THE NATURE OF CONFLICT 337

What Is Conflict? 337
The Frequency of Conflict 339

THE COURSE OF CONFLICT 341

Instigating Events 341
Attributions 343
Engagement and Escalation 344
The Demand/Withdraw Pattern 349
Negotiation and Accommodation 351
Dealing with Conflict: Four Types of Couples 353

THE OUTCOMES OF CONFLICT 356

Ending Conflict 356
Can Fighting Be Good for a Relationship? 357

FOR YOUR CONSIDERATION 360

CHAPTER SUMMARY 361

12. Power and Violence 362

POWER AND INTERDEPENDENCE 363

Sources of Power 363
Types of Resources 365
Men, Women, and the Control of Resources 366
The Process of Power 368
The Outcome of Power 375
The Two Faces of Power 376

VIOLENCE IN RELATIONSHIPS 377

The Prevalence of Violence 377
Types of Couple Violence 378
Gender Differences in Intimate Violence 381
Correlates of Violence 381
The Rationales of Violence 386
Why Don't They All Leave? 388

FOR YOUR CONSIDERATION 389

CHAPTER SUMMARY 389

13. The Dissolution and Loss of Relationships   391

THE CHANGING RATE OF DIVORCE   392

The Prevalence of Divorce   392
Why Has the Divorce Rate Increased?   392

THE PREDICTORS OF DIVORCE   398

Levinger's Barrier Model   398
Karney and Bradbury's Vulnerability-Stress-Adaptation Model   399
Results from the PAIR Project   401
Results from the Early Years of Marriage Project   403
People's Personal Perceptions of Their Problems   404
Specific Predictors of Divorce   405

BREAKING UP   408

Breaking Up with Premarital Partners   408
Steps to Divorce   411

THE AFTERMATH OF BREAKUPS   412

Postdissolution Relationships   412
Getting Over It   414
Divorce Is Different   416
The Children of Divorce   419

FOR YOUR CONSIDERATION   422

CHAPTER SUMMARY   422

14. Maintaining and Repairing Relationships   424

MAINTAINING AND ENHANCING RELATIONSHIPS   426

Staying Committed   426
Staying Content   431

REPAIRING RELATIONSHIPS   433

Do It Yourself   433
Preventive Maintenance   435
Marital Therapy   436

IN CONCLUSION   442

FOR YOUR CONSIDERATION   443

CHAPTER SUMMARY   443

REFERENCES   R-1
CREDITS   C-1
NAME INDEX   I-1
SUBJECT INDEX   I-16

Preface to the 6ᵗʰ Edition

Welcome to *Intimate Relationships!* I'm delighted that you are holding this book in your hands. I've been deeply honored by the high regard this book has enjoyed, and am very pleased to provide you a thorough update of the remarkable work being done in relationship science. This is a busy, dynamic field, so there's much that's new in this edition. Still, my aim is unchanged: The book can be of genuine interest to the general public, but I have sought primarily to provide college audiences with broad, reader-friendly coverage of relationship science that observes rigorous standards of scholarship but that preserves the personal appeal of its subject matter. My hope is that you'll not be able to find a more accessible, more engaging, or more complete overview of the modern science of close relationships.

What's New to This Edition

This edition contains 713 new references, nearly all of them from the last three years. As a result, there is new or substantially expanded discussion of many topics, including:

Culture	Sexual satisfaction
Boredom	The biology of love
Facebook	Compassionate love
Self-control	Conflict negotiations
Speed-dating	Abstinence education
Lie detection	Intimate partner violence
Gay marriage	Affectionate communication
Marital equality	Trajectories of dissatisfaction
Social networks	Perceived partner responsiveness
Couple conflict styles	Approach and avoidance motivations

For instructors, a new Instructor's Manual and Test Bank as well as new Power-Point slides that outline each chapter are available online at: www.mhhe.com/millerint6e.

What Hasn't Changed

If you're familiar with the 5th edition of this book, you'll find things in the same places. Vital influences on close relationships are still introduced in chapter 1, and when they are later mentioned throughout the book, footnotes remind readers where to find definitions that will refresh their memories.

The book is said to be a good read. I'm glad. I am genuinely privileged to be able to describe relationship science to you; the field is fascinating and exciting, and I am proud to participate in it. I hope that shows.

I also remain deeply grateful to Sharon Brehm, the original creator of this book and to Dan Perlman, my past co-author, who enticed me into doing it in the first place. Both are wonderful, generous colleagues.

I'm happy you're here, and I hope you enjoy the book.

CHAPTER 1

The Building Blocks of Relationships

THE NATURE AND IMPORTANCE OF INTIMACY ◆ The Nature of Intimacy ◆ The Need to Belong ◆ THE INFLUENCE OF CULTURE ◆ Sources of Change ◆ THE INFLUENCE OF EXPERIENCE ◆ THE INFLUENCE OF INDIVIDUAL DIFFERENCES ◆ Sex Differences ◆ Gender Differences ◆ Personality ◆ Self-Esteem ◆ THE INFLUENCE OF HUMAN NATURE ◆ THE INFLUENCE OF INTERACTION ◆ THE DARK SIDE OF RELATIONSHIPS ◆ FOR YOUR CONSIDERATION ◆ CHAPTER SUMMARY

How's this for a vacation? Imagine yourself in a nicely appointed suite with a pastoral view. You've got cable, video games, wireless Web access, plenty of books and magazines, and all the supplies for your favorite hobby. Delightful food and drink are provided, and you have your favorite entertainments at hand. But there's a catch: No one else is around. You're completely alone. You have almost everything you want except for other people. You have no phone or e-mail, and you can't visit any blogs or Facebook pages. Text messaging and tweets are unavailable. No one else is even in sight, and you cannot interact with anyone else in any way.

How's that for a vacation? A few of us would enjoy the solitude for a while, but most of us would quickly find it surprisingly stressful to be completely detached from other people (Schachter, 1959). Most of us need others even more than we realize, and there's a reason prisons sometimes use *solitary confinement* as a form of punishment: Human beings are a very social species. People suffer when they are deprived of close contact with others, and at the core of our social nature is our need for intimate relationships.

Our relationships with others are a central aspect of our lives. They may bring us great joy when they go well, but cause great sorrow when they go poorly. Our relationships are indispensable and vital, so it's useful to understand how our relationships get started, how they operate, and how, sometimes, they end in a haze of anger and pain.

This book will promote your own understanding of close relationships. It draws on psychology, sociology, communication studies, and family studies, and it reports what behavioral scientists have learned about relationships through careful research. The book offers a different, more scientific view of relationships than you'll find in magazines or the movies; it's more reasoned, more cautious, and often less romantic. You'll also find that this book is not a how-to manual. There are many insights awaiting you in the pages ahead, but you'll need to bring your own values and personal experiences to bear on the information presented here. The purpose of this book is to introduce you to the scientific study of close relationships by guiding you through the diverse foci of relationship science.

To set the stage for the discoveries to come, we'll first define our subject matter. What are intimate relationships? Why do they matter so much? Then, we'll consider the fundamental building blocks of close relationships: the cultures we inhabit, the experiences we encounter, the personalities we possess, the human origins we all share, and the interactions we conduct. In order to understand relationships, we must first comprehend who we are, *where* we are, and how we got there.

THE NATURE AND IMPORTANCE OF INTIMACY

Relationships come in all shapes and sizes. People have parents and may have children; they have colleagues at work or classmates at school; they encounter cashiers, physicians, and office staff; they have friends; and they have lovers. This book concentrates on just the last two types of partnerships, which exemplify *intimate* relationships. Our primary focus is on intimate relationships between adults.

The Nature of Intimacy

What, then, is intimacy? The answer can depend on whom you ask because intimacy is a multifaceted concept with several different components (Prager & Roberts, 2004). However, both researchers (Ben-Ari & Lavee, 2007) and laypeople (Marston et al., 1998) agree that intimate relationships differ from more casual associations in at least six specific ways: **knowledge, caring, interdependence, mutuality, trust,** and **commitment.**

First, intimate partners have extensive personal, often confidential, *knowledge* about each other. They share information about their histories, preferences, feelings, and desires that they do not reveal to most of the other people they know. Intimate partners also *care* about each other, feeling more affection for one another than they do for most others. Intimacy increases when people believe that their partners know, understand, and appreciate them (Reis et al., 2004).

The lives of intimate partners are also intertwined: What each partner does affects what the other partner wants to do and can do. *Interdependence* between intimates—the extent to which they need and influence each other—is frequent (they often affect each other), strong (they have meaningful impacts on each other), diverse (they influence each other in many different ways), and enduring (they influence each other over long periods of time). When relationships are interdependent, one's behavior affects one's partner as well as oneself (Berscheid et al., 2004).

As a result of these close ties, people who are intimate also consider themselves to be a couple instead of two entirely separate individuals. They exhibit a high degree of *mutuality*, which means that they recognize the overlap between their lives and think of themselves as "us" instead of "me" and "her" (or "him") (Fitzsimons & Kay, 2004). In fact, that change in outlook—from "I" to "us"—often signals the subtle but significant moment in a developing relationship when new partners first acknowledge their attachment to each other (Agnew et al., 1998). Indeed, researchers sometimes assess the amount of intimacy in a close relationship by simply asking partners to rate the extent to which they "overlap." The Inclusion of Other in the Self Scale (see Figure 1.1) is a straightforward measure of mutuality that does a remarkably good job of distinguishing between intimate and more casual relationships (Agnew et al., 2004).

A quality that makes these close ties tolerable is *trust*, the expectation that an intimate partner will treat one fairly and honorably (Simpson, 2007). People expect that no undue harm will result from their intimate relationships, and they expect their partners to be responsive to their needs and concerned for their welfare (Reis et al., 2004). When such trust is lost, people often become wary and reduce the openness and interdependence that characterize closeness (Jones et al., 1997).

Finally, intimate partners are ordinarily *committed* to their relationships. That is, they expect their partnerships to continue indefinitely, and they invest the time, effort, and resources that are needed to realize that goal. Without such commitment, people who were once very close may find themselves less and less interdependent and knowledgeable about each other as time goes by.

None of these components is absolutely required for intimacy to occur, and each may exist when the others are absent. For instance, spouses in a stale, unhappy marriage may be very interdependent, closely coordinating the practical details of their daily lives but living in a psychological vacuum devoid of much affection, openness, or trust. Such partners would certainly be more intimate than mere acquaintances are, but they would undoubtedly feel less close to one another than they used to (for instance, when they decided to marry), when more of the components were present. In general, our most satisfying and meaningful intimate relationships include all six of these defining

FIGURE 1.1. **The Inclusion of Other in the Self Scale**
How intimate is a relationship? Asking people to pick the picture that portrays a particular partnership does a remarkably good job of assessing the closeness they feel.
Source: Aron et al., 1992.

Please circle the picture below that best describes your **current** relationship with your partner.

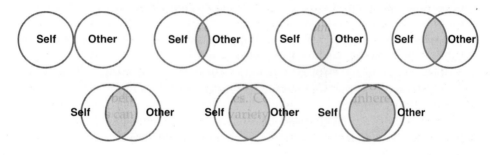

characteristics (Fletcher et al., 2000a). Still, intimacy can exist to a lesser degree when only some of them are in place. And as unhappy marriages demonstrate, intimacy can also vary enormously over the course of a long relationship.

Thus, there is no one kind of intimate relationship. Indeed, a fundamental lesson about relationships is a very simple one: They come in all shapes and sizes. This variety is a source of great complexity, but it can also be a source of endless fascination. (And that's why I wrote this book!)

The Need to Belong

Our focus on intimate relationships means that we will not consider a wide variety of the interactions that you have with others each day. For instance, we won't examine the relationships you have with most of your classmates. Should we be so particular? Is such a focus justified? The answers, of course, are yes. Although our casual interactions with strangers, acquaintances, and others can be very influential (Fingerman, 2009), there's something special about intimate relationships. In fact, a powerful and pervasive drive to establish intimacy with others may be a basic part of our human nature. According to theorists Roy Baumeister and Mark Leary (1995), we *need* frequent, pleasant interactions with intimate partners in lasting, caring relationships if we're to function normally. There is a human **need to belong** in close relationships, and if the need is not met, a variety of problems follows.

Our need to belong is presumed to necessitate "regular social contact with those to whom one feels connected" (Baumeister & Leary, 1995, p. 501). In order to fulfill the need, we are driven to establish and maintain close relationships with other people; we require interaction and communion with those who know and care for us. We don't need a lot of close relationships, just a few; when the need to belong is satiated, our drive to form additional relationships is reduced. (Thus, when it comes to relationships, quality is more important than quantity.) It also doesn't matter much *who* our partners are; as long as they provide us stable affection and acceptance, our need can be satisfied. Thus, when an important relationship ends, we are often able to find replacement partners who—though they may be quite different from our previous partners—are nonetheless able to satisfy our need to belong (Spielmann et al., 2011).

Some of the support for this theory comes from the ease with which we form relationships with others and from the tenacity with which we then resist the dissolution of our existing social ties. Indeed, when a valued relationship is in peril, we may find it hard to think about anything else. The potency of the need to belong may also be why being entirely alone for a long period of time is so stressful (Schachter, 1959); anything that threatens our sense of connection to other people can be hard to take (Leary, 2010a).

In fact, some of the strongest evidence supporting a need to belong comes from studies of the biological benefits we accrue from close ties to others. In general, people live happier, healthier, longer lives when they're closely connected to others than they do when they're on their own (Koball et al., 2010). Holding a lover's hand reduces the brain's response to threatening situations (Coan et al.,

2006), and pain seems less potent when one simply looks at a photograph of a loving partner (Master et al., 2009). Wounds even heal faster when others accept and support us (Gouin et al., 2010). In contrast, people with insufficient intimacy in their lives are at risk for a wide variety of health problems (Cohen, 2004). When they're lonely, college students have weaker immune responses, leaving them more likely to catch a cold or flu (Pressman et al., 2005). Across the life span, people who have few friends or lovers have much higher mortality rates than do those who are closely connected to caring partners; in one extensive study, people who lacked close ties to others were *2 to 3 times* more likely to die over a 9-year span (Berkman & Glass, 2000). And losing one's existing ties to others is damaging, too: Elderly widows and widowers are much more likely to die in the first few months after the loss of their spouses than they would have been had their marriages continued (Elwert & Christakis, 2008).

The quality of our connections to others also affects our mental and physical health (Kim & McKenry, 2002) (see Figure 1.2). Day by day, people who have pleasant interactions with others who care for them are more satisfied with their lives than are those who lack such social contact (Nezlek et al., 2002). And around the world, people who get and stay married are generally happier than are those who are less committed to an intimate partnership (Diener et al., 2000). Happy, contented partnerships lead to greater well-being than unhappy ones do, of course; nevertheless, most people feel more fulfilled even in an

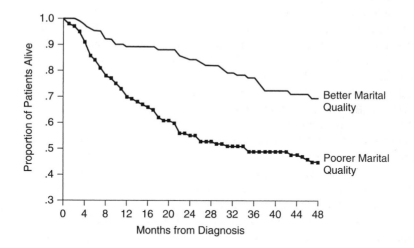

FIGURE 1.2. **Satisfying intimacy and life and death**
Here's a remarkable example of the manner in which satisfying intimacy is associated with better health. In this investigation, middle-aged patients with congestive heart failure were tracked for several years after their diseases were diagnosed. Forty-eight months later, *most* of the patients with less satisfying marriages had died whereas most of the people who were more happily married were still alive. This pattern occurred both when the initial illnesses were relatively mild and more severe, so it's a powerful example of the link between happy intimacy and better health.
Source: Coyne et al., 2001.

unhappy relationship than they do when they're completely alone (Dush & Amato, 2005). Other problems such as depression, alcoholism, eating disorders, and schizophrenia are also more likely to afflict those who have inadequate ties to others (Segrin, 1998). On the surface (as I'll explain in detail in chapter 2), such patterns do not necessarily mean that shallow, superficial relationships *cause* such problems; after all, people who are prone to schizophrenia may find it difficult to form loving relationships in the first place. Nevertheless, it does appear that a lack of intimacy can both cause such problems and make them worse (Eberhart & Hammen, 2006). In general, our well-being seems to depend on how well we satisfy the need to belong.

Why should we need intimacy so much? Why are we such a social species? One possibility is that the need to belong *evolved* over eons, gradually becoming a natural tendency in all human beings (Baumeister & Leary, 1995). That argument goes this way: Because early humans lived in small tribal groups surrounded by a difficult environment full of saber-toothed tigers, people who were loners were less likely than gregarious humans to have children who would grow to maturity and reproduce. In such a setting, a tendency to form stable, affectionate connections to others would have been evolutionarily *adaptive*, making it more likely that one's children would survive and thrive. As a result, our species slowly came to be characterized by people who cared deeply about what others thought of them and who sought acceptance and closeness from others. Admittedly, this view—which represents a provocative way of thinking about our modern behavior (and about which I'll have more to say later in this chapter)—is speculative. Nevertheless, whether or not this evolutionary account is entirely correct, there is little doubt that almost all of us now care deeply about the quality of our attachments to others. We are also at a loss, prone to illness and maladjustment, when we have insufficient intimacy in our lives. We know that food, water, and shelter are essential for life, but the need to belong suggests that intimacy with others is essential for a good, long life as well (Kenrick et al., 2010).

Now, let's examine the major influences that will determine what sort of relationships we construct when we seek to satisfy the need to belong. We'll start with a counterpoint to our innate need for intimacy: the changing cultures that provide the norms that govern our intimate relationships.

THE INFLUENCE OF CULTURE

I know it seems like ancient history—smart phones and Facebook and AIDS didn't exist—but let's look back at 1960, which may have been around the time that your grandparents were deciding to marry. If they were a typical couple, they would have married in their early twenties, before she was 21 and before he was 23.[1] They probably would not have lived together, or

---

[1] These and the following statistics were obtained from the U.S. Census Bureau at www.census.gov, the U.S. National Center for Health Statistics at www.cdc.gov/nchs, the Pew Research Center at pewsocialtrends.org, and the Population Reference Bureau at www.prb.org.

"cohabited," without being married because almost no one did at that time. And it's also unlikely that they would have had a baby without being married; 95 percent of the children born in the United States in 1960 had parents who were married to each other. Once they settled in, your grandmother probably did not work outside the home—most women didn't—and when her kids were preschoolers, it's quite likely that she stayed home with them all day; most women did. It's also likely that their children—in particular, your mom or dad—grew up in a household in which both of their parents were present at the end of the day.

Now, however, things are different. The last several decades have seen dramatic changes in the cultural context in which we conduct our close relationships. Indeed, you shouldn't be surprised if your grandparents are astonished by the cultural landscape that *you* face today. In the United States,

- Fewer people are marrying than ever before. Back in 1960, almost everyone (94 percent) married at some point in their lives, but more people remain unmarried today. Demographers now predict that only 85% of young adults will ever marry (and that proportion is even lower in Europe [Cherlin, 2009]). Include everyone who is separated, divorced, widowed, or never married, and only about *half* (52 percent) of the adult population of the United States is presently married (Mather & Lavery, 2010). That's an all-time low.

- People are waiting longer to marry. On average, a woman is more than 26 years old when she marries for the first time, and a man is 28, and these are the oldest such ages in American history (Jayson, 2010). That's much older than your grandparents probably were when they got married (see Figure 1.3). A great many Americans (46 percent) reach their mid-30s without marrying.

- People routinely live together even when they're not married. Cohabitation was very rare in 1960—only 5 percent of all adults ever did it—but it is now ordinary. Most of your classmates—over 60 percent of them—will at some time live with a lover without being married (Roberts, 2010).

- People often have babies even when they're not married. This was an uncommon event in 1960; only 5 percent of the babies born in the United States that year had unmarried mothers. Some children were *conceived* out of wedlock, but their parents usually got married before they were born. Not these days. In 2009, *41 percent* of the babies born in the United States had unmarried mothers, and this was the highest rate ever recorded (Taylor, 2010). The proportions of births outside of marriage are even higher in Northern and Western Europe (Haub, 2010).

- Almost one-half of all marriages end in divorce, a failure rate that's two times higher than it was when your grandparents married. In recent years, the divorce rate has been slowly decreasing for couples with college degrees—which is probably good news if you're reading this book!—but it remains high and unchanged for people with less education (Cherlin, 2010). In 2009 in the United States, there were half as many divorces as marriages (Tejada-Vera &

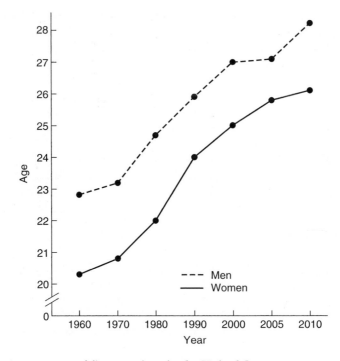

FIGURE 1.3. **Average age of first marriage in the United States.**
American men and women are waiting longer to get married than ever before.

Sutton, 2010). So because not all lasting marriages are happy ones, the best guess is that an American couple getting married this year is more likely to divorce sometime down the road than to live happily ever after.[2]

- Many children (40 percent) live in a single-parent home before they turn 12 (Taylor, 2010). As a result of the higher divorce, cohabitation, and unmarried-birth rates, many U.S. children see a variety of adults come and go through their homes (Cherlin, 2010).
- Most preschool children have mothers who work outside the home. In 1960, more than three-quarters of U.S. mothers stayed home all day when their children were too young to go to school, but only 40 percent of them do so now (Taylor, 2010). Even if a child lives with both parents, neither of them is likely to be a full-time caregiver at home all day.

These remarkable changes suggest that our shared assumptions about the role that marriage and parenthood will play in our lives have changed substantially in recent years. Once upon a time, everybody got married within a few years of leaving high school and, happy or sad, they tended to stay with their original partners. Pregnant people felt they *had* to get married, and cohabitation was

[2]This is a depressing fact, but your chances for a happy marriage (should you choose to marry) are likely to be better than those of most other people. You're reading this book, and your interest in relationship science is likely to improve your chances considerably.

Compared with marriages that took place a generation ago, today's newlyweds are older, more likely to have children from a previous marriage, and more likely to be committed to their careers as well as to their families.

known as "living in sin." But not so anymore. Marriage is now a *choice*, even if a baby is on the way, and increasing numbers of us are putting it off or not getting married at all. If we do marry, we're less likely to consider it a solemn, lifelong commitment (Cherlin, 2009). In general, recent years have seen enormous change in the cultural norms that used to encourage people to get, and stay, married (Amato et al., 2007).

Do these changes matter? Indeed, they do. Cultural standards provide a foundation for our relationships (Acitelli et al., 2011); they shape our expectations and define the patterns we think to be normal. Let's consider, in particular, the huge rise in the prevalence of cohabitation that has occurred in recent years. Most high school seniors now believe that it is a "good idea" for a couple to live together before they get married so that they can find out if they "really get along" (Bachman et al., 2001). Such attitudes make cohabitation a reasonable choice and indeed, most people now cohabit before they ever marry. However, when people do not already have firm plans to marry, cohabitation does not make it more likely that a subsequent marriage (if one occurs) will be successful; instead, such cohabitation *increases* a couple's risk that they will later divorce (Jose et al., 2010). There are probably several reasons for this. First, on average, couples who choose to cohabit are less committed to each other than are those who marry—they are, after all, keeping their options open (Wiik et al., 2009)—so they encounter more problems and uncertainties than married people do (Hsueh et al., 2009). They experience more conflict (Stanley et al., 2010), jealousy (Gatzeva & Paik, 2011), infidelity (Thornton et al., 2007), and physical aggression (Rhoades et al., 2009a), so cohabitation is more

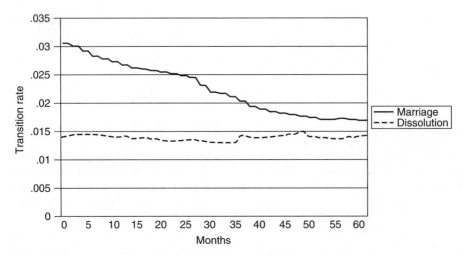

FIGURE 1.4.   **The outcomes of cohabitation over time.**
Here's what became of 2,746 cohabiting couples in the United States over a span of 5 years. As time passed, couples were less likely to marry, but no less likely to break up. After living together for 5 years, cohabiting couples were just as likely to break up as they were when they moved in together. (The transition rate describes the percentage of couples who either broke up or got married each month. The numbers seem low, but they reflect the proportion of couples who quit cohabiting each month, so the proportions add up and become sizable as months go by.)
Source: Wolfinger, 2005.

tumultuous and volatile than marriage usually is. As a result, the longer that people cohabit, the less enthusiastic about marriage—and the more accepting of divorce—they become. Take a look at Figure 1.4: As time passes, cohabitating couples gradually become *less* likely to ever marry but no less likely to split up; 5 years down the road, cohabitating couples are just as likely to break up as they were when they moved in together. (Marriage is fundamentally different. The longer a couple is married, the less likely they are to ever divorce [Wolfinger, 2005]). Overall, then, casual cohabitation that is intended to test the partners' compatibility seems to undermine the positive attitudes toward marriage, and the determination to make a marriage work, that support marital success (Rhoades et al., 2009b). These deleterious effects are milder if a couple is planning to marry when they move in together, but cohabitation can be slightly corrosive even when the partners are already engaged (Jose et al., 2010). Thus, despite its popularity, widespread acceptance of cohabitation as a "trial marriage" is one reason why, compared to 1960, fewer people get married and fewer marriages last.[3]

---

[3] Most people don't know this, so here's an example of an important pattern we'll encounter often: Popular opinion assumes one thing, but relationship science finds another. Instances such as these demonstrate the value of careful scientific studies of close relationships. Ignorance isn't bliss. Intimate partnerships are complex, and accurate information is especially beneficial when common sense and folk wisdom would lead us astray.

Sources of Change

Thus, the norms that govern our intimate relationships differ from those experienced by prior generations, and there are several reasons for this. One set of influences involves *economics.* Societies tend to harbor more single people, tolerate more divorces, and support a later age of marriage the more industrialized and affluent they become (South et al., 2001), and levels of socioeconomic development have increased around the world. Education and financial resources allow people to be more independent, so that women in particular are less likely to marry than they used to be (Dooley, 2010). More recently, the global economic recession also has had noticeable effects. Cohabitation increased noticeably as couples began living together to save money (Yen, 2010c), but marriage rates dropped among the very poor, who were reluctant to marry without a steady income (Yen, 2010b).

Over the years, the *individualism*—that is, the support of self-expression and the emphasis on personal fulfillment—that characterizes Western cultures has also become more pronounced (Twenge & Campbell, 2010). (Americans are, for instance, increasingly likely to give their children unusual names that make them stand out [Twenge et al., 2010].) Arguably, this focus on self-realization has led us to expect more personal gratification from our intimate partnerships—more pleasure and delight, and fewer hassles and sacrifices—than our grandparents did. And unlike prior generations (who often stayed together for the "sake of the kids"), we feel justified in ending our partnerships to seek contentment elsewhere if we become dissatisfied (Cherlin, 2009). Eastern cultures promote a more collective sense of self in which people feel more closely tied to their families and social groups, and the divorce rates in such cultures (such as Japan) are much lower than they are in the United States (Cherlin, 2009).

New *technology* matters, too. Modern reproductive technologies allow single women to bear children fathered by men picked from a catalog at a sperm bank whom the women have never met (Ali, 2007)! Women can also control their fertility, having children only when they choose, and American women are having fewer children than they used to. The number of American families with children at home is at an all-time low (Gillum, 2009). Modern communication technologies are also transforming the ways in which we conduct our relationships; check out the box on the next page.[4]

However, an even more important—but more subtle—influence on the norms that govern relationships may be the relative numbers of young men and women in a given culture. Societies in which men are more numerous than women tend to have very different standards than those in which women outnumber men. I'm describing a culture's **sex ratio,** a simple count of the number of men for every 100 women in a specific population. When the sex ratio is

---

[4] Please try to avoid your usual temptation to skip past the boxes. Many of them will be worth your time. Trust me.

"Baby, Why Are You Still 'Single' on Facebook?"

Really, once upon a time, smart phones and Facebook did not exist. These remarkable technologies are excellent examples of the manner in which culture can influence relationships because they have created entirely new modes of interaction with potential partners. Online, we have boundless reach to distant partners, the freedom to reveal or conceal whatever we want, and time to sit and think about what we want to say. Qualities that have a huge influence on face-to-face relationships, such as physical attractiveness and geographical proximity, are often less consequential in online partnerships (at least at first), and shy people who wouldn't dare to approach others in person may be more sociable and outgoing online (Baker & Oswald, 2010).

The technologies have also changed the way we conduct our relationships. Most U.S. teenagers have profiles on social networking sites such as Facebook (Madden, 2010), and they routinely use the sites to define the nature of their current partnerships. Your grandmother may have publicized her attachment to your grandfather by wearing his letter jacket around town; nowadays, people publicly declare their interest in a new relationship by changing their status from "single" to "in a relationship." They also prioritize their friendships by engaging in more high-tech communication with some partners than with others; friends who exchange a lot of text messages consider their relationships to be more intimate than do those who merely interact face-to-face (Igarashi et al., 2005). If things go sour, caller ID allows us to avoid contact with an ex-partner, and we can complete a breakup by returning to "single" status and deleting our past partner's number from our cell phones—all without the messy business of actually discussing our feelings with our discarded mates. All of this is very different from the manner in which our grandparents conducted their intimate relationships. The reach of these technologies is remarkable. Collections of 250 Facebook "friends" are typical (Walther & Ramirez, 2009), and American teens spend an average of 7½ hours a day online (Lewin, 2010). Will all this activity undermine our face-to-face friendships? It doesn't appear so (Wang & Wellman, 2010), but technology is certainly changing how, and with whom, we maintain relationships.

high, there are more men than women; when it is low, there are fewer men than women.

The baby boom that followed World War II caused the U.S. sex ratio, which was very high in 1960, to plummet to low levels at the end of that decade. For a time after the war, more babies were born each year than in the preceding year; this meant that when the "boomers" entered adulthood, there were fewer older men than younger women, and the sex ratio dropped. However, when birthrates began to slow and fewer children entered the demographic pipeline, each new flock of women was smaller than the preceding flock of men, and the U.S. sex ratio crept higher in the 1990s. Since then, reasonably stable birthrates among "boomer" parents have resulted in fairly equal numbers of marriage-able men and women today.

These changes may have been more important than most people realize. Cultures with high sex ratios (in which there aren't enough women) tend to support traditional, old-fashioned roles for men and women (Secord, 1983). The women stay home raising children while the men work outside the home. Such cultures also tend to be sexually conservative. The ideal newlywed is a virgin bride, unwed pregnancy is shameful, and open cohabitation is rare. Women marry at an early age (Kruger et al., 2010), and divorce is discouraged. In contrast, cultures with low sex ratios (in which there are too few men) tend to be less traditional and more permissive. Women are encouraged to work and support themselves, and they are allowed (if not encouraged) to have sexual relationships outside of marriage. If a pregnancy occurs, unmarried motherhood is an option (Harknett, 2008). The specifics vary with each historical period, but this general pattern has occurred throughout history (Guttentag & Secord, 1983). Ancient Rome, which was renowned for its sybaritic behavior? A low sex ratio. Victorian England, famous for its prim and proper ways? A high sex ratio. The Roaring Twenties, a footloose and playful decade? A low sex ratio. And in more recent memory, the "sexual revolution" and the advent of "women's liberation" in the late 1960s? A very low sex ratio.

Theorists Marcia Guttentag and Paul Secord (1983) argued that such cultural changes are not accidental. In their view, a society's norms evolve to promote the interests of its most powerful members, those who hold economic, political, and legal power. In the cultures I just mentioned, those people have been men. As a result, the norms governing relationships usually change to favor the interests of men as the numbers of available men and women change.

This is a daring assertion. After all, recent decades have seen enormous improvement in the status of U.S. women, and few of us would want to change that. But let's think it through. When sex ratios are high, there aren't enough women to go around. If a man is lucky enough to attract a woman, he'll want to keep her. And (a) encouraging women to be housewives who are financially dependent on their husbands and (b) discouraging divorce are ways to do just that (and that's the way things were in 1960). On the other hand, when sex ratios are low, there are plenty of women, and men may be less interested in being tied down to just one of them. Thus, women work and delay marriage, and couples divorce more readily if dissatisfaction sets in.

Thus, the remarkable changes in the norms for U.S. relationships since 1960 may be due, in part, to dramatic fluctuations in U.S. sex ratios. Indeed, we may already be seeing the effects of the higher sex ratios of the late 1990s. The U.S. divorce rate, which *doubled* from 1967 to 1980, has leveled off and has even dropped somewhat, and politicians now care about "family values." With roughly equal numbers of men and women now approaching marriageable age, it's likely that the cultural pendulum will swing back to sexual norms that are less permissive than those of the 1980s but not as restrained as those of 1960.

I should note that Guttentag and Secord's (1983) explanation of the operation of sex ratios—that things work to the advantage of men—is speculative. However, there is a rough but real link between a culture's proportions of men and women and its relational norms, and it serves as a compelling example of the manner in which culture can affect our relationships. To a substantial degree, what we expect and what we accept in our dealings with others can spring from the standards of the time and place in which we live.

THE INFLUENCE OF EXPERIENCE

Our relationships are also affected by the histories and experiences we bring to them, and there may be no better example of this than the global orientations toward relationships known as **attachment styles.** Years ago, developmental researchers (e.g., Bowlby, 1969) realized that infants displayed various patterns of attachment to their major caregivers (usually their mothers). The prevailing assumption was that whenever they were hungry, wet, or scared, some children found responsive care and protection to be reliably available, and they learned that other people were trustworthy sources of security and kindness. As a result, such children developed a **secure** style of attachment: They happily bonded with others and relied on them comfortably, and the children readily developed relationships characterized by relaxed trust.

Other children encountered different situations. For some, attentive care was unpredictable and inconsistent. Their caregivers were warm and interested on some occasions but distracted, anxious, or unavailable on others. These children thus developed fretful, mixed feelings about others known as **anxious-ambivalent** attachments. Being uncertain of when (or if) a departing caregiver would return, such children became nervous and clingy, displaying excessive neediness in their relationships with others.

Finally, for a third group of children, care was provided reluctantly by rejecting or hostile adults. Such children learned that little good came from depending on others, and they withdrew from others with an **avoidant** style of attachment. Avoidant children were often suspicious of and angry at others, and they did not easily form trusting, close relationships.

The important point, then, is that researchers believed that early interpersonal experiences shaped the course of one's subsequent relationships. Indeed, attachment processes became a popular topic of research because the different styles were so obvious in many children. When they faced a strange, intimidating environment, for instance, secure children ran to their mothers, calmed down, and then set out to bravely explore the unfamiliar new setting (Ainsworth et al., 1978). Anxious-ambivalent children cried and clung to their mothers, ignoring the parents' reassurances that all was well.

These patterns were impressive, but relationship researchers really began to take notice of attachment styles when Cindy Hazan and Phillip Shaver (1987) demonstrated that similar orientations toward close relationships could also be observed among *adults.* They surveyed readers of Denver's newspaper, the *Rocky*

Are You Prejudiced Against Singles?

Here's a term you probably haven't seen before: *singlism*. It refers to prejudice and discrimination against those who choose to remain single and opt not to devote themselves to a primary romantic relationship. Many of us assume that people who are 40 years old and have never married are probably lonely and immature. We seem to take it for granted that normal people want to be a part of a romantic couple, so we find it odd when anyone chooses instead to stay single (Morris & Kemp, 2011). The result is a culture that offers benefits to married couples and puts singles at a disadvantage with regard to such things as Social Security benefits, insurance rates, and service in restaurants (DePaulo, 2006).

Intimacy is good for us, and married people live longer than unmarried people do. A study of 67,000 adults in the United States found that, compared to married people of the same age and social class, divorced people were 27 percent more likely to die over a 9-year span, and those who had been widowed were 40 percent more likely—but those who had never married were 58 percent more likely to die (Kaplan & Kronick, 2006). Results like these lead some relationship researchers to straightforwardly recommend a happy marriage as a desirable goal in life. And most single people *do* want to have romantic partners; only a few singles (4 percent) prefer being unattached to being in a steady romantic relationship (Poortman & Liefbroer, 2010). Still, we make an obvious mistake if we casually assume that singles are unhealthy loners. Some singles have an active social life and close, supportive friendships that provide them all the intimacy they desire, and they remain uncoupled because they celebrate their freedom and self-sufficiency. Not everyone, they assert, wants or needs a constant companion or soulmate (DePaulo, 2011). So, what do you think? Is there something wrong or missing in people who are content to remain single? If you think there is, where did that belief come from?

Mountain News, and found that most people said that they were relaxed and comfortable depending on others; that is, they sounded secure in their intimate relationships. However, a substantial minority (about 40 percent) said they were *in*secure; they either found it difficult to trust and to depend on their partners, or they nervously worried that their relationships wouldn't last. In addition, the respondents reported childhood memories and current attitudes toward love and romance that fit their styles of attachment. Secure people generally held positive images of themselves and others, and remembered their parents as loving and supportive. In contrast, insecure people viewed others with uncertainty or distrust, and remembered their parents as inconsistent or cold.

With provocative results like these, attachment research quickly became one of the hottest fields in relationship science (e.g., Cassidy & Shaver, 2010). And researchers promptly realized that there seemed to be *four*, rather than three, patterns of attachment in adults. In particular, theorist Kim Bartholomew (1990) suggested that there were two different reasons why people might wish to avoid being too close to others. In one case, people could want relationships with others but be wary of them, fearing rejection and mistrusting them. In the other case, people could be independent and self-reliant, genuinely preferring autonomy and freedom rather than close attachments to others.

Thus, Bartholomew (1990) proposed four general categories of attachment style (see Table 1.1). The first, a **secure** style, remained the same as the secure style identified in children. The second, a **preoccupied** style, was a new name for anxious ambivalence. Bartholomew renamed the category to reflect the fact that, because they nervously depended on others' approval to feel good about themselves, such people were preoccupied with, and worried about, the status of their relationships.

The third and fourth styles reflected two different ways to be "avoidant." **Fearful** people avoided intimacy with others because of their fears of rejection. Although they wanted others to like them, they worried about the risks of relying on others. In contrast, people with a **dismissing** style felt that intimacy with others just wasn't worth the trouble. Dismissing people rejected interdependency with others because they felt self-sufficient, and they didn't care much whether others liked them or not.

It's also now generally accepted that two broad themes underlie and distinguish these four styles of attachment (Roisman, 2009). First, people differ in their *avoidance of intimacy*, which affects the ease and trust with which they accept interdependent intimacy with others. People who are comfortable and relaxed in close relationships are low in avoidance, whereas those who feel uneasy when others get close to them are high in avoidance. Furthermore, people differ in their *anxiety about abandonment*, the dread that others will find them unworthy and leave them. Secure people take great comfort in closeness with others and do not worry that others will mistreat them; as a result, they gladly seek intimate, interdependent relationships. In contrast, with all three

TABLE 1.1. Examples of Bartholomew's (1990) Four Categories of Attachment Style

Secure	It is easy for me to become emotionally close to others. I am comfortable depending on others and having others depend on me. I don't worry about being alone or having others not accept me.
Preoccupied	I want to be completely emotionally intimate with others, but I often find that others are reluctant to get as close as I would like. I am uncomfortable being without close relationships, but I sometimes worry that others don't value me as much as I value them.
Fearful	I am uncomfortable getting close to others. I want emotionally close relationships, but I find it difficult to trust others completely or to depend on them. I worry that I will be hurt if I allow myself to become too close to others.
Dismissing	I am comfortable without close emotional relationships. It is very important to me to feel independent and self-sufficient, and I prefer not to depend on others or have others depend on me.

Source: Bartholomew, 1990.

of the other styles, people are burdened with anxiety or discomfort that leaves them less at ease in close relationships. Preoccupied people want closeness but anxiously fear rejection. Dismissing people don't worry about rejection but don't like closeness. And fearful people get it from both sides, being uncomfortable with intimacy *and* worrying it won't last. (See Figure 1.5.)

Importantly, the two themes of avoidance of intimacy and anxiety about abandonment are *continuous* dimensions that range from low to high. This means that, although it's convenient to talk about attachment styles as if they were discrete, pure categories that do not overlap, it's not really accurate to do so (Fraley & Waller, 1998). When they are simply asked to pick which one of the four paragraphs in Table 1.1 fits them best, most people—usually around 60 percent—describe themselves as being securely attached (Mickelson et al., 1997).[5] However, if someone has moderate anxiety about abandonment and middling avoidance of intimacy, which category fits him or her best? The use of any of the four categories is rather arbitrary in the middle ranges of anxiety and avoidance where the boundaries of the categories meet.

So don't treat the neat classifications in Figure 1.5 too seriously. The more sophisticated way to think about attachment is that there seem to be two important themes that shape people's global orientations toward relationships with others. (Samples of the items that are currently used to measure anxiety and avoidance are provided in the box on page 59 in chapter 2.) Both are important,

FIGURE 1.5. **The dimensions underlying attachment.**

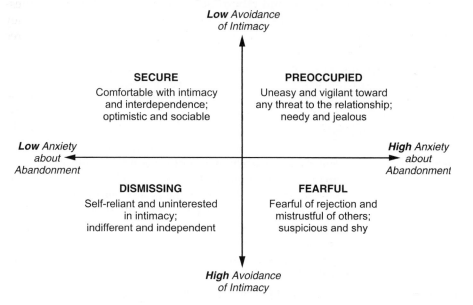

[5]These data are from the United States. Elsewhere, secure styles are more common than any of the other three styles but secure people are outnumbered by the other three groups combined. Thus, in most regions of the world, more people are insecure than secure (Data from Schmitt, 2008).

and if you compare high scorers on either dimension to low scorers on that dimension, you're likely to see meaningful differences in the manner in which those people conduct their relationships. Indeed, recent studies of attachment (e.g., Birnie & Lydon, 2011) tend to describe people with regard to their relative standing on the two dimensions of anxiety and avoidance instead of labeling them as secure, preoccupied, fearful, or dismissing.

Nevertheless, the four labels are so concise that they are still widely used, so stay sharp. Before 1990, researchers spoke of only three attachment styles: secure, avoidant, and anxious-ambivalent. Now they routinely speak of four styles, but they treat them as convenient labels for sets of anxiety and avoidance scores, not as distinctly different categories that have nothing in common. The biggest distinction may be between people who are "secure" and those who are not (being those who have high anxiety about abandonment or high avoidance of intimacy, or both). And for now, the important point is that attachment styles appear to be orientations toward relationships that are largely *learned* from our experiences with others. They are prime examples of the manner in which the proclivities and perspectives we bring to a new relationship emerge in part from our experiences in prior partnerships.

Let's examine this idea more closely. Any relationship is shaped by many different influences—that's the point of this chapter—and both babies and adults affect through their own behavior the treatment they receive from others. As any parent knows, for instance, babies are born with various temperaments and arousal levels. Some newborns have an easy, pleasant temperament, whereas others are fussy and excitable, and inborn differences in personality and emotionality make some children easier to parent than others. Thus, the quality of parenting a baby receives can depend, in part, on the child's own personality and behavior; in this way, people's attachment styles are influenced by the traits with which they were born, and our genes shape our styles (Picardi et al., 2011).

However, our experiences play even larger roles in shaping the styles we bring to subsequent relationships. The levels of acceptance or rejection we receive from our parents are huge influences early on (Rohner & Khaleque, 2010). Expectant mothers who are glad to be pregnant are more likely to have secure toddlers a year later than are mothers-to-be who are hesitant and uncertain (Miller et al., 2009). Once their babies are born, mothers who enjoy intimacy and who are comfortable with closeness tend to be more attentive and sensitive caregivers (Selcuk et al., 2010), so secure moms tend to have secure children whereas insecure mothers tend to have insecure children (Holman et al., 2009). Indeed, when mothers with difficult, irritable babies are trained to be sensitive and responsive parents, their toddlers are much more likely to end up securely attached to them than they would have been in the absence of such training (van den Boom, 1994). And a mother's influence on the attachment styles of her children does not end in preschool (Berant et al., 2008). The parenting adolescents receive as seventh graders predicts how they will behave in their own romances and friendships when they are young adults; teenagers who have nurturing and supportive relationships with their parents have richer relationships with their lovers and friends years later (Cui et al., 2002). There's no doubt that youngsters import the lessons they learn at home into their subsequent relationships with others (Zayas et al., 2011).

We're not prisoners of our experiences as children, however, because our attachment styles continue to be shaped by the experiences we encounter as adults (Zhang, 2009). Being learned, attachment styles can be *un*learned, and over time, attachment styles can and do change (Chopik et al., 2011). A bad breakup can make a formerly secure person insecure, and a good relationship can gradually make an avoidant person less wary of intimacy (Birnie & Lydon, 2011). As many as a third of us may encounter real change in our attachment styles over a 2-year period (Davila & Cobb, 2004).

Nevertheless, once they have been established, attachment styles can also be stable and long-lasting as they lead people to create new relationships that reinforce their existing tendencies (Scharfe & Cole, 2006). By remaining aloof and avoiding interdependency, for instance, fearful people may never learn that some people can be trusted and closeness can be comforting—and that perpetuates their fearful style. In the absence of dramatic new experiences, people's styles of attachment can persist for decades (Fraley, 2002).

Thus, our global beliefs about the nature and worth of close relationships appear to be shaped by our experiences within them. By good luck or bad, our earliest notions about our own interpersonal worth and the trustworthiness of others emerge from our interactions with our major caregivers and start us down a path of either trust or fear. But that journey never stops, and later obstacles or aid from fellow travelers may divert us and change our routes. Our learned styles of attachment to others may either change with time or persist indefinitely, depending on our interpersonal experiences.

THE INFLUENCE OF INDIVIDUAL DIFFERENCES

Once they are formed, attachment styles also exemplify the idiosyncratic personal characteristics that people bring to their partnerships with others. We're all individuals with singular combinations of experiences and traits, and the differences among us can influence our relationships. In romantic relationships, for instance, some pairings of attachment styles in the two partners are better—that is, more satisfying and stable—than others (Jones & Cunningham, 1996). Consider the mismatch that results when a preoccupied person falls in love with a dismissing partner; one of them may be unnerved by the other's emotional distance while the other may be annoyed by the first's clingy intrusiveness. Both partners are likely to be less at ease than they would be with lovers who were more secure.

Of course, the possibility that we can get along better with some people than with others is no surprise; we all know that. In this section of the chapter, we'll move beyond that simple truth in two ways. First, we'll explore the nature of individual differences, which are often gradual and subtle instead of abrupt. Then, we'll see how influential individual differences can be. We'll consider four different types of individual variation: sex differences, gender differences, personalities, and self-esteem.

Sex Differences

At this moment, you're doing something rare. You're reading an academic text-book about relationship science, and that's something most people will never do. This is probably the *first* serious text you've ever read about relationships, too, and that means that we need to confront—and hopefully correct—some of the stereotypes you may hold about the differences between men and women in intimate relationships.

This may not be easy. Many of us are used to thinking that men and women have very different approaches to intimacy—that, for instance, "men are from Mars, women are from Venus." In a well-known book with that title, the author asserted that:

> men and women differ in all areas of their lives. Not only do men and women communicate differently but they think, feel, perceive, react, respond, love, need, and appreciate differently. They almost seem to be from different planets, speaking different languages and needing different nourishment. (Gray, 1992, p. 5)

Wow! Men and women sound like they're members of different species. No wonder heterosexual relationships are sometimes problematic!

But the truth is more subtle. Human traits obviously vary across a wide range, and (in most cases) if we graph the number of people who possess a certain talent or ability, we'll get a distinctive chart known as a *normal curve*. Such curves describe the frequencies with which particular levels of some trait can be found in people, and they demonstrate that (a) most people have talents or abilities that are only slightly better or worse than average and (b) extreme levels of most traits, high or low, are very rare. Consider height, for example: A few people are very short or very tall, but the vast majority of us are only an inch or two shorter or taller than the average for our sex.

Why should we care about this? Because many lay stereotypes about men and women portray the sexes as having very different ranges of inter-ests, styles, and abilities. As one example, men are often portrayed as being more interested in sex than women are (see the box on page 24), and the images of the sexes that people hold often seem to resemble the situation pictured in Figure 1.6. The difference between the average man and the average woman is

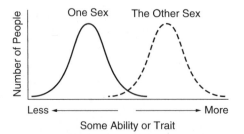

FIGURE 1.6. **An imaginary sex difference.**
Popular stereotypes portray the sexes as being very different, with almost no overlap between the styles and preferences of the two sexes. This is *not* the way things really are.

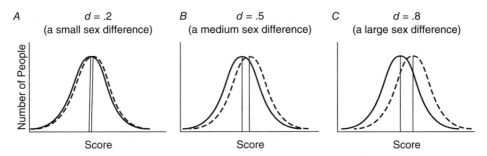

FIGURE 1.7 **Actual sex differences take the form of overlapping normal curves.**
The three graphs depict small, medium, and large sex differences, respectively. (To keep them simple, they portray the ranges of attitudes or behavior as being the same for both sexes. This isn't always the case in real life.)

presumed to be large, and there is almost no overlap between the sexes at all. But, despite the "Mars" and "Venus" stereotypes, this is *not* the way things really are. As we'll see in chapter 9, men do tend to have higher sex drives, on average, than women do. Nevertheless, *actual* sex differences take the form of the graphs shown in Figure 1.7, which depict ranges of interests and talents that *overlap* to a substantial extent (Hyde, 2007).

The three graphs in Figure 1.7 illustrate sex differences that are considered by researchers to be small, medium, and large, respectively. Formally, they differ with respect to a *d* statistic that specifies the size of a difference between two groups.[6] In the realm of sexual attitudes and behavior, graph A depicts the different ages of men and women when they first have intercourse (men tend to be slightly younger), graph B illustrates the relative frequencies with which they masturbate (men masturbate more often), and graph C depicts a hypothetical difference that is larger than any that is known to actually exist. That's right. A sprawling analysis of recent studies of human sexuality involving 1,419,807 participants from 87 different countries failed to find *any* difference in the sexual attitudes and behavior of men and women that was as large as that pictured in graph C (Petersen & Hyde, 2010). Obviously, the real-life examples that do exist look nothing like the silly stereotype pictured in Figure 1.6. More specifically, these examples make three vital points about psychological sex differences:

- Some differences are real but quite small. (Don't be confused by researchers' terminology; when they talk about a "significant" sex difference, they're usually referring to a "*statistically* significant"—that is, numerically reliable—difference, and it may not be large at all.) Almost all of the differences between men and women that you will encounter in this book fall in the small to medium range.

---

[6]To get a *d* score in these cases, you compute the difference between the average man and the average woman, and divide it by the average variability of the scores *within* each sex (which is the standard deviation of those scores). The resulting *d* value tells you how large the sex difference is compared to the usual amount by which men and women differ among themselves

- The range of behavior and opinions among members of a given sex is always *huge* compared to the average difference between the sexes. Men are more accepting of casual, uncommitted sex than women are (Petersen & Hyde, 2010), but that certainly doesn't mean that all men like casual sex. Some men like to have sex with strangers, but other men don't like that at all, and the two groups of men resemble each other much less than the average man and the average woman do. Another way to put this is that despite this sex difference in sexual permissiveness, a highly permissive man has more in common with the average *woman* on this trait than he does with a low-scoring *man*.
- The overlap in behavior and opinions is so large that many members of one sex will always score higher than the average member of the other sex. With a sex difference of medium size (with men higher and a *d* value of .5), one-third of all women will still score higher than the average man. What this means is that if you're looking for folks who like casual sex, you shouldn't just look for *men* because you heard that "men are more accepting of casual sex than women are"; you should look for permissive *people*, many of whom will be women despite the difference between the sexes.

The bottom line is that men and women usually overlap so thoroughly that they are much more similar than different on most of the dimensions and topics of interest to relationship science (Hyde, 2007). It's completely misguided to suggest that men and women come from different planets because it simply isn't true. "Research does *not* support the view that men and women come from different cultures, let alone separate worlds" (Canary & Emmers-Sommer, 1997, p. vi). According to the careful science of relationships you'll study in this book, it's more accurate to say that "men are from North Dakota, and women are from South Dakota" (Dindia, 2006, p. 18). (Or, as a bumper sticker I saw one day suggests: "Men are from Earth. Women are from Earth. Deal with it.")

Thus, sex differences in intimate relationships tend to be much less noteworthy and influential than laypeople often think. Now that you're reading a serious text on intimate relationships, you need to think more carefully about sex differences and interpret them more reasonably. There are interesting sex differences that are meaningful parts of the fabric of relationships, and we'll encounter several of them in the chapters that follow. But they occur in the context of even broader similarities between the sexes, and the differences are always modest when they are compared to the full range of human variation. It's more work, but also more sophisticated and accurate, to think of individual differences, not sex differences, as the more important influences on interpersonal interaction. People differ among themselves whether they are male or female (as in the case of attachment styles), and these variations are usually much more consequential than sex differences are.

Gender Differences

I need to complicate things further by distinguishing between sex differences and *gender* differences in close relationships. When people use the terms carefully, the term *sex differences* refers to biological distinctions between men and women that spring naturally from their physical natures. In contrast, *gender differences* refer to social and psychological distinctions that are created by our cultures and upbringing (Wood & Eagly, 2009). For instance, when they are parents, women are mothers and men are fathers—that's a sex difference—but the common belief that women are more loving, more nurturant parents than men reflects a gender difference. Many men are capable of just as much tenderness and compassion toward the young as any woman is, but if we expect and encourage women to be the primary caregivers of our children, we can create cultural gender differences in parenting styles that are not natural or inborn at all.

Distinguishing sex and gender differences is often tricky because the social expectations and training we apply to men and women are often confounded with their biological sex (Wood & Eagly, 2010). For instance, because women lactate and men do not, people often assume that predawn feedings of a new-born baby are the mother's job—even when the baby is being fed formula from a bottle that was warmed in a microwave! It's not always easy to disentangle the effects of biology and culture in shaping our interests and abilities. Nevertheless, the distinction between sex and gender differences is important because some influential differences between men and women in relationships—gender differences—are largely *taught* to us as we grow up.

The best examples of this are our **gender roles,** the patterns of behavior that are culturally expected of "normal" men and women. Men, of course, are supposed to be "masculine," which means that they are expected to be assertive, self-reliant, decisive, and competitive. Women are expected to be "feminine," or warm, sensitive, emotionally expressive, and kind. They're the *opposite* sexes to most people, and to varying degrees men and women are expected to specialize in different kinds of social behavior all over the world (Kite et al., 2008). However, people inherit only about a quarter to a third of their tendencies to be assertive or kind; most of these behaviors are learned (Cleveland et al., 2001; Lippa & Hershberger, 1999). In thoroughgoing and pervasive ways, cultural processes of socialization and modeling (rather than biological sex differences) lead us to expect that all men should be tough and all women should be tender (Reid et al., 2008).

Nevertheless, those stereotypes don't describe real people as well as you might think; only *half* of us have attributes that fit these gender role expectations cleanly (Bem, 1993). Instead of being just "masculine" or "feminine," a sizable minority of people—about 35 percent—are both assertive *and* warm, sensitive *and* self-reliant. Such people possess both sets of the competencies that are stereotypically associated with being male and with being female and are said to be **androgynous.** If androgyny sounds odd to you, you're probably just using a stereotyped vocabulary: On the surface, being "masculine" sounds incompatible with also being "feminine." In fact, because those terms are confusing, relationship researchers often use alternatives, referring to the "masculine" task-oriented talents as **instrumental** traits and to the "feminine" social and emotional skills as **expressive** traits. And it's not all that remarkable to find both sets of traits in the same individual. An androgynous person would be one who could effectively, emphatically stand up for himself or herself in a heated salary negotiation but who could then go home and sensitively,

Combating Simplistic Stereotypes

Here's a joke that showed up in my e-mail one day:

How to Impress a Woman:
Compliment her. Cuddle her. Kiss her. Caress her. Love her. Comfort her. Protect her. Hug her. Hold her. Spend money on her. Wine and dine her. Listen to her. Care for her. Stand by her. Support her. Go to the ends of the earth for her.

How to Impress a Man:
Show up naked. Bring beer.

It's a cute joke. But it may not be harmless. It reinforces the stereotypes that women seek warmth and tenderness in their relationships whereas men simply seek unemotional sex. In truth, men and women differ little in their desires in close relationships; they're not "opposite" sexes at all (Hyde, 2007). Although individuals of both sexes may differ substantially from each other, the differences between the average man and the average woman are rather small. Both women *and* men generally want their intimate partners to provide them with lots of affection and warmth (Tran et al., 2008).

But so what? What are the consequences of wrongly believing that men are all alike, having little in common with women? Pessimism and hopelessness, for two (Metts & Cupach, 1990). People who really believe that the sexes are very different are less likely to try to repair their heterosexual relationships when conflicts occur (as they inevitably do). Thinking of the other sex as a bunch of aliens from another world is not only inaccurate but also can be damaging, forestalling efforts to understand a partner's point of view and preventing collaborative problem-solving. For that reason, I'll try to do my part to avoid perpetuating wrongful impressions by comparing men and women to the *other* sex, not the *opposite* sex, for the remainder of this book. Words matter (Smith et al., 2010), so I invite you to use similar language when you think and talk about the sexes.

compassionately comfort a preschool child whose pet parakeet had died. A lot of people, those who specialize in either instrumental *or* expressive skills, would feel at home in one of those situations but not both. Androgynous people would be comfortable and capable in both domains (Cheng, 2005).

In fact, the best way to think of instrumentality and expressiveness is as two separate sets of skills that may range from low to high in either women or men (Choi et al., 2007). Take a look at Table 1.2. Traditional women are high in expressiveness but low in instrumentality; they're warm and friendly but not assertive or dominant. Men who fulfill our traditional expectations are high in instrumentality but low in expressiveness and are stoic, "macho" men. Androgynous people are both instrumental and expressive. The rest of us—about 15 percent—are either high in the skills typically associated with the other sex (and are said to be "cross-typed") or low in both sets of skills (and are said to be "undifferentiated"). Equal proportions of men and women fall into the androgynous, cross-typed, and undifferentiated categories, so, as with sex differences, it's simplistic and inaccurate to think of men and women as wholly distinct groups of people with separate, different traits (Bem, 1993).

TABLE 1.2 Gender Roles

Instrumental Traits	Expressive Traits
Assertiveness	Warmth
Self-Reliance	Tenderness
Ambition	Compassion
Leadership	Kindness
Decisiveness	Sensitivity to Others

Our culture encourages men to be highly instrumental and women to be highly expressive, but which of these talents do you *not* want in an intimate companion?

In any case, gender differences are of particular interest to relationship researchers because, instead of making men and women more compatible, they "may actually be responsible for much of the *incompatibility*" that causes relationships to fail (Ickes, 1985, p. 188). From the moment they meet, for instance, traditional men and women enjoy and like each other less than androgynous people do. In a classic experiment, Ickes and Barnes (1978) paired men and women in couples in which (a) both partners fit the traditional gender roles or (b) one or both partners were androgynous. The two people were introduced to each other and then simply left alone for 5 minutes sitting on a couch while the researchers covertly videotaped their interaction. The results were striking. The traditional couples talked less, looked at each other less, laughed and smiled less, and afterward reported that they liked each other less than did the other couples. (Think about it: Stylistically, what do a masculine man and a feminine woman have in common?) When an androgynous man met a traditional woman, an androgynous woman met a traditional man, or two androgynous people got together, they got along much better than traditional men and women did.

More importantly, the disadvantage faced by traditional couples does not disappear as time goes by. Surveys of marital satisfaction demonstrate that such couples—who have marriages in which both spouses adhere to stereotyped gender roles—are generally *less* happy with their marriages than nontraditional couples are (Helms et al., 2006). With their different styles and different domains of expertise, masculine men and feminine women simply do not find as much pleasure in each other as less traditional, less stereotyped people do (Marshall, 2010).

Perhaps this should be no surprise. When human beings devote themselves to intimate partnerships, they want affection, warmth, and understanding (Reis et al., 2000). People who are low in expressiveness—who are not very warm, tender, sensitive people—do not readily provide such warmth and tenderness; they are not very affectionate (Miller et al., 2003). As a result, men or women who have spouses who are low in expressiveness are chronically less satisfied than are those whose partners are more sensitive, understanding, and kind (Steiner-Pappalardo & Gurung, 2002). For this reason, traditional gender roles do men a disservice, depriving them of skills that would make them more rewarding husbands.

On the other hand, people who are low in instrumentality—who are low in assertiveness and personal strength—tend to have low self-esteem and to be less well adjusted than those who have better task-oriented skills (Stake & Eisele, 2010). People feel better about themselves when they are competent and effective at "taking care of business" (Reis et al., 2000), so traditional gender roles also do women a disservice, depriving them of skills that would facilitate more accomplishments and achievements. Such roles also seem to cost women money; around the world, traditional women earn less on the job than their nontraditional co-workers do (Stickney & Konrad, 2007).

The upshot of all this is that both instrumentality and expressiveness are valuable traits, and the happiest, best-adjusted, most effective, mentally healthy people possess both sets of skills (Stake & Eisele, 2010). In particular, the most desirable spouses, those who are most likely to have contented, satisfied partners, are people who are both instrumental and expressive (Marshall, 2010). And in fact, when they're given a choice, most people say that they'd prefer androgynous dating partners or spouses to those who are merely masculine or feminine (Green & Kenrick, 1994).

So, it's ironic that we still tend to put pressure on those who do not rigidly adhere to their "proper" gender roles. Women who display as much competitiveness and assertiveness as men risk being perceived as pushy, impolite, and uppity (Parks-Stamm et al., 2008), and they are more likely to encounter sexual harassment on the job (Berdahl, 2007). If anything, however, gender expectations are stricter for men than for women (Vandello et al., 2008); girls can be tomboys and nobody frets too much, but if a boy is too feminine, people worry (Sandnabba & Ahlberg, 1999). U.S. gender roles are changing slowly but surely; in particular, U.S. women are becoming more instrumental with each new generation (Twenge, 2009), and young adults of both sexes are gradually becoming more egalitarian and less traditional in their views of men and women (Bryant, 2003). Nonetheless, even if they limit our individual potentials and are right only half the time, gender stereotypes persist. Today we still expect and encourage men to be instrumental and women to be expressive (Heilman & Wallen,

Instrumental, masculine people often feel ill at ease when they are asked to provide warm, sensitive support to others.

© *Reprinted with permission of King Features Syndicate.*

2010), and such expectations are important complications for many of our close relationships.

Personality

Some consequential differences among people (such as attachment styles and gender differences) are affected by experience and may change over a few years' time, but other individual differences are more stable and lasting. Personality traits influence people's behavior in their relationships across their entire lifetimes (Roberts et al., 2007) with only gradual change over long periods of time (Roberts & Mroczek, 2008).

Personality researchers have identified a handful of central traits that characterize people all over the world (McCrae & Costa, 1997), and most of them seem to affect the quality of the relationships people have. On the positive side, extraverted, agreeable, and conscientious people have happier relationships than do those who score lower on those traits (Malouff et al., 2010). Extraverted people are outgoing and agreeable people are friendly, so they tend to be likeable. Conscientious people work hard and are organized, and they tend to follow the rules, so they weren't very popular in high school (van der Linden et al., 2010)—but, once they grow up, they make dependable, trustworthy intimate partners. "People who are less conscientious exceed their

---

The Big Five Personality Traits

A small cluster of fundamental traits does a good job of describing the broad themes in behavior, thoughts, and emotions that distinguish one person from another (McCrae & Costa, 2010). These key characteristics are called the Big Five traits by personality researchers, and most—but not all—of them appear to be very influential in intimate relationships. Which one of these would you assume does not matter much?

Openness to experience—the degree to which people are imaginative, unconventional, and artistic versus conforming, uncreative, and stodgy.

Extraversion—the extent to which people are outgoing, gregarious, assertive, and sociable versus cautious, reclusive, and shy.

Conscientiousness—the extent to which people are industrious, dependable, and orderly versus unreliable and careless.

Agreeableness—the degree to which people are compassionate, cooperative, and trusting versus suspicious, selfish, and hostile.

Neuroticism—the degree to which people are prone to high levels of negative emotion such as worry, anxiety, and anger.

The five traits are listed in order from the least important to the most influential, so the first one, openness, seems to be a minor player in close relationships. Openness is not totally inert (Donnellan et al., 2004), but the other four all make a much larger difference (Malouff et al., 2010).

credit limit . . . cancel plans, curse, oversleep, and break promises" (Jackson et al., 2010, p. 507), so they tend to be unreliable companions.

The most important of the Big Five traits, however, is the one that has a negative impact: neuroticism (Malouff et al., 2010). Neurotic people are prone to anger and anxiety, and those unhappy tendencies tend to result in touchy, pessimistic, and argumentative interactions with others (Suls & Martin, 2005). In fact, a remarkable study that tracked 300 couples over a span of 45 years found that a full 10 percent of the satisfaction and contentment spouses would experience in their marriages could be predicted from measures of their neuroticism when they were still engaged (Kelly & Conley, 1987). The less neurotic the partners were, the happier their marriages turned out to be. Everyone has good days and bad days, but some of us have *more* bad days (and fewer good ones) than other people—and those unlucky folks are especially likely to have unhappy, disappointing relationships.

Working alongside the global influences of the Big Five traits are other more specific personality variables that regulate our relationships, and I'll mention several in later chapters. For now, let's note that people's personalities affect their relationships more than their relationships affect their personalities (Asendorpf & Wilpers, 1998). Whether or not people ever marry, for instance, seems at least in part to be in their genes (Johnson et al., 2004). Some people are born with personalities that make them more likely than others to marry later in life, and these tendencies are not much affected by the experiences that they encounter. However, even our enduring personality traits can be shaped to a degree by our relationships (Lehnart et al., 2010). Dissatisfying and abusive relationships can gradually make us more anxious and neurotic, and warm, rewarding partnerships may make us more agreeable over time. But these effects are subtle, and our relationships have much bigger effects on the last individual difference we will consider: the self-evaluations we bring to our transactions with others.

Self-Esteem

Most of us like ourselves, but some of us do not. Our evaluations of ourselves constitute our **self-esteem,** and when we hold favorable judgments of our skills and traits, our self-esteem is high; when we doubt ourselves, self-esteem is low. Because people with high self-esteem are generally healthier and happier than are those with low self-regard (Crocker & Luhtanen, 2003), it's widely assumed that it's good to feel good about yourself (Swann & Bosson, 2010).

But how do people come to like themselves? A provocative, leading theory argues that self-esteem is a subjective gauge, a **sociometer,** that measures the quality of our relationships with others (Leary & Baumeister, 2000). When others like us, we like ourselves; when other people regard us positively and value their relationships with us, self-esteem is high. However, if we don't interest others—if others seem not to care whether or not we are part of their lives—self-esteem is low. Self-esteem operates in this manner, according to sociometer theory, because it is an evolved mechanism that serves our need to belong. This argument suggests that, because their reproductive success depended on

An Individual Difference That's Not Much of a Difference: Sexual Orientation

I haven't mentioned gays or lesbians until now, and that's because there hasn't been much to say. Only about 6 percent of men and 11 percent of women have had sex with a member of the same sex (Roberts, 2006a), and smaller numbers of people—less than 3 percent—consider themselves to be "homosexual" (Savin-Williams, 2006). Obviously, people who label themselves as "heterosexual" are far more numerous than bisexuals, gays, and lesbians. However, other than their relative numbers, heterosexuals and homosexuals are resoundingly similar on most of the topics we encounter in this book. For instance, gays and lesbians exhibit the same attachment styles in the same proportions as heterosexual men and women do (Roisman et al., 2008), and they, too, are happier with romantic partners of high (rather than low) expressivity (Kurdek & Schmitt, 1986).

There *are* some potentially important differences between same-sex and other-sex relationships. Gay men tend to be more expressive than heterosexual men, on average, and lesbians tend to be more instrumental than other women, so gays and lesbians are less likely to adhere to traditional gender roles than heterosexuals are (Lippa, 2005). Gays and lesbians also tend to be better educated and to be more liberal (Herek et al., 2010). But the big difference between same-sex and other-sex relationships is that a gay couple is composed of two *men* and a lesbian couple of two *women*. To the extent that there are meaningful differences in the way men and women conduct their relationships, same-sex couples may behave differently than heterosexual couples do, not because of their sexual orientations but because of the sexes of the people involved. For instance, when their relationships are new, gay men have sex more often than heterosexual couples do, and lesbian couples have sex less often than heterosexual couples do (Blumstein & Schwartz, 1983). The more men there are in a partnership, the more often the couple has sex—but that's probably because men have higher sex drives than women do, *not* because there's anything special about gay men (Vohs et al., 2004).

Except for the sex and gender differences that may exist, same-sex and other-sex partnerships operate in very similar manners (Diamond, 2006). Gays and lesbians fall in love the same way, for instance, and they feel the same passions, experience the same doubts, and feel the same commitments as heterosexuals do (Kurdek, 2006a). Where differences in relationship functioning do exist, they tend to be small, but gays and lesbians are the clear winners. They have *better* relationships than heterosexuals do (Kurdek, 2005). They divide up household chores more fairly, experience less conflict, and feel more compatible, more intimate, and more satisfied with their lovers (Balsam et al., 2008). (Given the social disapproval same-sex couples still face in many places, their contentment is remarkable. But remember, there are no sex differences in same-sex relationships. How much do you think that contributes to the success of their relationships?)

Still, there's no reason to write two different books on *Intimate Relationships*; intimacy operates the same way in both same-sex and other-sex partnerships. I'll certainly mention sexual orientation where it's appropriate, but it won't come up very often because the processes of close relationships are very similar in same-sex and heterosexual couples (Peplau & Fingerhut, 2007)—and there's often not much else to say.

staying in the tribe and being accepted by others, early humans became sensitive to any signs of exclusion that might precede rejection by others. Self-esteem became a psychological gauge that alerted people to declining acceptance by others, and dislike or disinterest from others gradually caused people to dislike themselves (Leary, 2010).

This perspective nicely fits most of what we know about the origins and operation of self-esteem. There's no question, for instance, that people feel better about themselves when they think they're attractive to the other sex (Brase & Guy, 2004). And the regard we receive from others clearly affects our subsequent self-evaluations (Stinson et al., 2010). In particular, events that involve interpersonal rejection damage our self-esteem in a way that other disappointments do not. Leary and his colleagues demonstrated this point in a clever study in which research participants were led to believe that they would be excluded from an attractive group either through bad luck—they had been randomly selected to be sent home—or because they had been voted out by the other members of the group (Leary et al., 1995). Even though the same desirable opportunity was lost in both situations, the people who had been personally rejected felt much worse about themselves than did those whose loss was impersonal. It's also interesting to note that public events that others witness affect people's self-esteem more than do private events that are otherwise identical but are known only to the individuals themselves. In this and several other respects, whether we realize it or not, our self-evaluations seem to be much affected by what we think others think of us (Koch & Shepperd, 2008), and this is true around the world (Denissen et al., 2008).

Here is further evidence, then, that we humans are a very social species: It's very hard to like ourselves (and, indeed, it would be unrealistic to do so) if others don't like us, too. In most cases, people with chronically low self-esteem have developed their negative self-evaluations through an unhappy history of failing to receive sufficient acceptance and appreciation from other people.

And sometimes, this is very unfair. Some people are victimized by abusive relationships through no fault of their own, and, despite being likable people with fine social skills, they develop low self-esteem as a result of mistreatment from others. What happens when those people enter new relationships with kinder, more appreciative partners? Does the new feedback they receive slowly improve their self-esteem?

Not necessarily. A compelling program of research by Sandra Murray and her colleagues has demonstrated that people with low self-esteem sometimes sabotage their relationships by underestimating their partners' love for them (Murray et al., 2001) and perceiving disregard when none exists (Murray et al., 2002). Take a look at Table 1.3. People with low self-regard find it hard to believe that they are well and truly loved by their partners (Murray et al., 1998) and, as a result, they tend not to be optimistic that their loves will last. "Even in their closest relationships," people with low self-esteem "typically harbor serious (but unwarranted) insecurities about their partners' feelings for them" (Holmes & Wood, 2009, p. 250). This leads them to overreact to their partners' occasional bad moods (Bellavia & Murray, 2003); they feel more rejected, experience more hurt, and get more angry than do those with higher self-esteem.

And these painful feelings make it harder for them to behave constructively in response to their imagined peril. Whereas people with high self-regard draw closer to their partners and seek to repair the relationship when frustrations arise, people with low self-esteem defensively distance themselves, stay surly, and behave badly (Murray, Bellavia et al., 2003). They also feel even worse about themselves (Murray, Griffin et al., 2003).

All of this occurs, Murray (2008) believes, because we take large risks when we come to depend on others. Close ties to an intimate partner allow us to enjoy rich rewards of support and care, but they also leave us vulnerable to devastating betrayal and rejection if our partners prove to be untrustworthy. Because they are confident about their partners' love and regard for them,

TABLE 1.3 How My Partner Sees Me

Sandra Murray and her colleagues use this scale in their studies of self-esteem in close relationships. People with high self-esteem believe that their partners hold them in high regard, but people with low self-esteem worry that their partners do not like or respect them as much. What do you think your partner thinks of you?

In many ways, your partner may see you in roughly the same way you see yourself. Yet in other ways, your partner may see you differently than you see yourself. For example, you may feel quite shy at parties, but your partner might tell you that you really seem quite relaxed and outgoing on these occasions. On the other hand, you and your partner may both agree that you are quite intelligent and patient.

For each trait or attribute that follows, please indicate *how you think that your partner sees you.* For example, if you think that your partner sees the attribute "self-assured" as moderately characteristic of you, you would choose "5."

Respond using the scale below. Please enter your response in the blank to the left of each trait or attribute listed.

1	2	3	4	5	6	7	8	9
Not at All Characteristic		Somewhat Characteristic		Moderately Characteristic		Very Characteristic		Completely Characteristic

My partner sees me as . . .

_____	Kind and Affectionate	_____	Tolerant and Accepting
_____	Critical and Judgmental	_____	Thoughtless
_____	Self-Assured	_____	Patient
_____	Sociable/Extraverted	_____	Rational
_____	Intelligent	_____	Understanding
_____	Lazy	_____	Distant
_____	Open and Disclosing	_____	Complaining
_____	Controlling and Dominant	_____	Responsive
_____	Witty and Humorous	_____	Immature
_____	Moody	_____	Warm

people with high self-esteem draw closer to their partners when difficulties arise. In contrast, people with low self-esteem have lasting doubts about their partners' regard and reliability, so when times get tough, they withdraw from their partners in an effort to protect themselves. We all need to balance connect-edness with self-protection, Murray suggests, but people with low self-esteem put their fragile egos before their relationships.

As a result, the self-doubts and thin skins of people with low self-esteem lead them to make mountains out of molehills. They wrongly perceive small bumps in the road as worrisome signs of declining commitment in their partners. Then, they respond with obnoxious, self-defeating hurt and anger that cut them off from the reassurance they crave. By comparison, people with high self-esteem correctly shrug off the same small bumps and remain confident of their partners' accep-tance and positive regard. The unfortunate net result is that once it is formed, low self-esteem may be hard to overcome; even after 10 years of marriage, people with low self-esteem still tend to believe that their spouses love and accept them less than those faithful spouses really do (Murray et al., 2000).

Thus, our self-esteem appears to both result from and then subsequently influence our interpersonal relationships (Carmichael et al., 2007). What we think of ourselves seems to depend, at least in part, on the quality of our connec-tions to others. And those self-evaluations affect our ensuing interactions with new partners, who provide us further evidence of our interpersonal worth. In fundamental ways, what we know of ourselves emerges from our partnerships with others and matters thereafter.

THE INFLUENCE OF HUMAN NATURE

Now that we have surveyed several individual characteristics that distinguish people from one another, we can address the possibility that our relationships display some underlying themes that reflect the animal nature shared by all humankind. Our concern here is with evolutionary influences that have shaped close relationships over countless generations, instilling in us certain tenden-cies that are found in everyone (Confer et al., 2010).

Evolutionary psychology starts with three fundamental assumptions. First, *sexual selection* has helped make us the species we are today (Flinn & Alexander, 2007). You've probably heard of *natural* selection, which refers to the advan-tages conferred on animals that cope more effectively than others with preda-tors and physical challenges such as food shortages. Sexual selection involves advantages that result in greater success at reproduction. And importantly:

> Contrary to what many people have been taught, evolution has nothing to do with the survival of the fittest. It is not a question of whether you live or die. The key to evolution is reproduction. Whereas all organisms eventually die, not all organisms reproduce. Further, among those that do reproduce, some leave more descendants than others. (Ash & Gallup, 2008, p. 313)

This point of view holds that motives such as the need to belong have presumably come to characterize human beings because they were *adaptive,* conferring some sort of reproductive advantage to those who possessed them. As I suggested earlier, the early humans who sought cooperative closeness with others were probably more likely than asocial loners to have children who grew up to have children of their own. Over time, then, to the extent that the desire to affiliate with others is heritable (and it is; Tellegen et al., 1988), sexual selection would have made the need to belong more prevalent, with fewer and fewer people being born without it. In keeping with this example, evolutionary principles assert that any universal psychological mechanism exists in its present form because it consistently solved some problem of survival or reproduction in the past (Confer et al., 2010).

Second, evolutionary psychology suggests that men and women should differ from one another only to the extent that they have historically faced different reproductive dilemmas (Geary, 2010). Thus, men and women should behave similarly in close relationships except in those instances in which different, specialized styles of behavior would allow better access to mates or promote superior survival of one's offspring. Are there such situations? Let's answer that question by posing two hypothetical queries:

> If, during one year, a man has sex with 100 different women, how many children can he father? (The answer, of course, is "lots, perhaps as many as 100.")

> If, during one year, a woman has sex with 100 different men, how many children can she have? (Probably just one.)

Obviously, there's a big difference in the minimum time and effort that men and women have to invest in each child they produce. For a man, the minimum requirement is a single ejaculation; given access to receptive mates, a man might father hundreds of children during his lifetime. But a woman can have children only until her menopause, and each child she has requires an enormous investment of time and energy. These biological differences in men's and women's obligatory **parental investment** in their children may have supported the evolution of different strategies for selecting mates (Geary, 2000). Conceivably, given their more limited reproductive potential, women in our ancestral past who chose their mates carefully reproduced more successfully (with more of their children surviving to have children of their own) than did women who were less thoughtful and deliberate in their choices of partners. In contrast, men who promiscuously pursued every available sexual opportunity may have reproduced more successfully. If they flitted from partner to partner, their children may have been less likely to survive, but what they didn't offer in quality (of parenting) they could make up for in quantity (of children). Thus, today—as this evolutionary account predicts—women do choose their sexual partners more carefully than men do. They insist on smarter, friendlier, more prestigious, and more emotionally stable partners than men will accept (Kenrick et al., 1990), and they are less interested in casual, uncommitted sex than men are (Schmitt, 2005). Perhaps this sex difference evolved over time.

Another reproductive difference between the sexes is that a woman always knows for sure whether or not a particular child is hers. By comparison, a man suffers **paternity uncertainty;** unless he is completely confident that his mate has been faithful to him, he cannot be absolutely certain that her child is his (Buss & Schmitt, 1993). Perhaps because of that, even though women cheat less than men do (Tsapelas et al., 2011), men are more preoccupied with worries about their partners' infidelity than women are (Schützwohl, 2006). This difference, too, may have evolved over time.

An evolutionary perspective also makes a distinction between *short-term* and *long-term* mating strategies (Buss & Schmitt, 1993). Men and women both seem to pursue different sorts of attributes in the other sex when they're having a brief fling than when they're entering a longer, more committed relationship. In particular, men have a greater desire than women do for sexual liaisons of short duration; they are more interested in brief affairs with a variety of partners, and when they enter new relationships, they're ready to have sex sooner than women are (Schmitt, 2005). As a result, when they're on the prowl, men are attracted to women who seem to be sexually available and "easy" (Schmitt et al., 2001). However, if they think about settling down, the same men who consider promiscuous women to be desirable partners in casual relationships often prefer chaste women as prospective spouses (Buss, 2000). Men also tend to seek wives who are young and pretty. When they're thinking long-term, men value physical attractiveness more than women do, and as men age, they marry women increasingly younger than themselves (Kenrick & Keefe, 1992).

Women exhibit different patterns. When women select short-term mates—particularly when they have extramarital affairs (Greiling & Buss, 2000)—they seek sexy, charming, dominant men with lots of masculine appeal. But when they evaluate potential husbands, they look for good financial prospects, men with incomes and resources who presumably can provide a safe environment for their children, even when those men aren't the sexiest guys in the pack (Gangestad & Simpson, 2000). In general, women care more than men do about the financial prospects and status of their long-term partners (Buss, 2012).

The effort to delineate human nature by identifying patterns of behavior that are found in all of humanity is one of the compelling aspects of the evolutionary perspective. In fact, the different preferences I just mentioned—with men valuing good looks and women valuing good incomes—have been found in dozens of cultures, everywhere they have been studied around the world (Buss, 2012).[7] However, an evolutionary perspective does not imply that culture is unimportant.

---

[7]Here's a chance for you to rehearse what you learned earlier in this chapter about sex differences. Men and women differ in the importance they attach to physical attractiveness and income, but that does not mean that women don't care about looks and men don't care about money. And as we'll see in chapter 3, men and women mostly want the *same* things, such as warmth, emotional stability, and generous affection, from their romantic partners. The sex differences we just described are real, but people do not want looks and money at the expense of other valuable characteristics that men and women both want (Li, 2008). Finally, before I finish this footnote, do you see how differential parental investment may promote the sex differences we've mentioned here? Think about it, and we'll return to this point in chapter 3.

Indeed, a third basic assumption of evolutionary psychology is that cultural influences determine whether evolved patterns of behavior are adaptive—and cultural change occurs faster than evolution does (Kanazawa, 2010). Thus, our species displays patterns of behavior that *were* adaptive eons ago, but not all of those inherited tendencies may fit the modern environments we inhabit now. For instance, cavemen may have reproduced successfully if they tried to mate with every possible partner, but modern men may not: In just the last two generations, we have seen (a) the creation of reproductive technologies—such as birth control pills—that allow women complete control of their fertility and (b) the spread of a lethal virus that is transmitted through sexual contact (the human immunodeficiency virus that causes AIDS). These days, a desire for multiple partners is probably less adaptive for men than it was millions of years ago. Conceivably, modern men may reproduce more successfully if they display a capacity for commitment and monogamy that encourages their partners to allow a pregnancy to occur. But the human race is still evolving. Sexual selection will ultimately favor styles of behavior that fit our new environment, but it will take several thousand generations for such adaptations to occur. (And how will our cultures have changed by then?)

Thus, an evolutionary perspective provides a fascinating explanation for common patterns in modern relationships (Eastwick, 2009): Certain themes and some sex differences exist because they spring from evolved psychological mechanisms that were useful long ago. We are not robots who are mindlessly enacting genetic directives, and we are not all alike (Michalski & Shackelford, 2010), but we do have inherited habits that are triggered by the situations we encounter. Moreover, our habits may fit our modern situations to varying degrees. Behavior results from the interplay of both personal and situational influences, but some common reactions in people result from evolved human nature itself:

> The pressures to which we have been exposed over millennia have left a mental and emotional legacy. Some of these emotions and reactions, derived from the species who were our ancestors, are unnecessary in a modern age, but these vestiges of a former existence are indelibly printed in our make-up. (Winston, 2002, p. 3)

This is a provocative point of view that has attracted both acclaim and criticism. On the one hand, the evolutionary perspective has prompted intriguing new discoveries, most of which are consistent with the ideas it asserts (Buss, 2012). On the other hand, assumptions about the primeval social environments from which human nature emerged are necessarily speculative. In addition, an evolutionary model is not the only reasonable explanation for many of the patterns at issue. For instance, women may have to pick their mates more carefully than men do because cultures routinely allow women less control over financial resources (Wood & Eagly, 2007); arguably, women have to be concerned about their spouses' incomes because it's hard for them to earn as much money themselves (Wood & Eagly, 2002). If women filled similar roles and had social status as high as men's, some of the gender differences I have described might be much reduced (Eagly & Diekman, 2003).

In any case, there *are* notable patterns in human relationships that appear everywhere, regardless of culture, and I'll describe several of them in later chapters. Whether it evolved or was a social creation (or both), there is a human nature, and it affects our intimate relationships.

THE INFLUENCE OF INTERACTION

The final building block of relationships is the interaction that the two partners share. So far, there's been much to say about the idiosyncratic experiences and personalities that individuals bring to a relationship, but it's time to acknowledge that relationships are often much more than the sum of their parts. Relationships emerge from the *combination* of their participants' histories and talents (Robins et al., 2000), and those amalgamations may be quite different from the simple sum of the individuals who create them. Chemists are used to thinking this way; when they mix two elements (such as hydrogen and oxygen), they often get a compound (such as water) that doesn't resemble either of its constituent parts. In a similar fashion, the relationship two people create results from contributions from each of them but may only faintly resemble the relationships they share with other people.

Consider the levels of trust you feel toward others. Even if you're a secure and trusting person, you undoubtedly trust some people more than others because trust is a two-way street that is influenced both by your dispositions and those of your partners (Simpson, 2007). Moreover, it emerges from the dynamic give-and-take of you and your partners day by day; trust is a fluid *process* rather than a static, changeless thing, and it ebbs and flows in all of your relationships.

Every intimate relationship is like this. Individually, two partners inevitably encounter fluctuating moods and variable health and energy; then, when they interact, their mutual influence on one another may produce a constantly changing variety of outcomes. Over time, of course, unmistakable patterns of interaction will often distinguish one relationship from another (Zayas et al., 2002). Still, at any given moment, a relationship may be an inconstant entity, the product of shifting transactions of complex people.

Overall, then, relationships are constructed of diverse influences that may range from the fads and fashions of current culture to the basic nature of the human race. Working alongside those generic influences are various idiosyncratic factors such as personality and experience, some of them learned and some of them inherited. And ultimately, two people who hail from the same planet but who may otherwise be different—to a degree—in every other respect, begin to interact. The result may be frustrating or fulfilling, but the possibilities are always fascinating—and that's what relationships are made of.

THE DARK SIDE OF RELATIONSHIPS

I began this chapter by asserting the value of intimacy to human beings, so, to be fair, I should finish it by admitting that intimacy has potential costs as well. We need intimacy—we suffer without it—but distress and displeasure sometimes result from our dealings with others. Indeed, relationships can be disappointing in so many ways that whole books can, and have been, written about their pitfalls (Cupach & Spitzberg, 2011)! When they're close to others, people may fear that their sensitive secrets will be revealed or turned against them. They may dread the loss of autonomy and personal control that comes with interdependency (Baxter, 2004), and they may worry about being abandoned by those on whom they rely. They recognize that there is dishonesty in relationships and that people sometimes confuse sex with love (Firestone & Catlett, 1999). And in fact, most of us (56 percent) have had a very troublesome relationship in the last five years (Levitt et al., 1996), so these are not empty fears.

As you might expect after our discussion of attachment styles, some people fear intimacy more than others do (Greenberg & Goldman, 2008). Indeed, some of us anxiously expect that others will reject us, and we live on edge waiting for the relational axe to fall (Romero-Canyas et al., 2009). But whether our fears are overstated or merely realistic, we're all likely to experience unexpected, frustrating costs in our relationships on occasion (Miller, 1997b). And the deleterious consequences of disappointment and distress in our close relationships on our physical health can be substantial (Whisman et al., 2010).

So why take the risk? Because we are a social species. We need each other. We prematurely wither and die without intimate connections to other people. Relationships can be complex, but they are essential parts of our lives, so they are worth understanding as thoroughly as possible. I'm glad you're reading this book, and I'll try to facilitate your understanding in the chapters that follow.

FOR YOUR CONSIDERATION

Mark and Wendy met during their junior years in college, and they instantly found a lot to like in each other. Wendy was pretty and very feminine and rather meek, and Mark liked the fact that he was able to entice her to have sex with him on their second date. Wendy was susceptible to his charms because she unjustly doubted her desirability, and she was excited that a dominant, charismatic man found her attractive. They started cohabitating during their senior years and married 6 months after graduation. They developed a traditional partnership, with Wendy staying home when their children were young and Mark applying himself to his career. He succeeded in his profession, winning several lucrative promotions, but Wendy began to feel that he was married more to his work than to her. She wanted him to talk to her more, and he began to wish that she was eating less and taking better care of herself.

In your opinion, what does the future hold for Mark and Wendy? How happy will they be with each other in another 10 years? Why?

CHAPTER SUMMARY

The Nature and Importance of Intimacy

This book focuses on adult friendships and romantic relationships.

The Nature of Intimacy. Intimate relationships differ from more casual associations in at least six specific ways: *knowledge, caring, interdependence, mutuality, trust,* and *commitment.*

The Need to Belong. Humans display a need to belong, a drive to maintain regular interaction with affectionate, intimate partners. Severe consequences may follow if the need remains unfulfilled over time.

The Influence of Culture

Cultural norms regarding relationships in the United States have changed dramatically over the last 50 years. Fewer people are marrying than ever before, and those who do marry wait longer. People routinely cohabit, and that often makes a future divorce more, not less, likely.

Sources of Change. Economic changes, increasing individualism, and new technology contribute to cultural change. So does the *sex ratio;* cultures with high sex ratios are characterized by traditional roles for men and women, whereas low sex ratios are correlated with more permissive behavior.

The Influence of Experience

Children's interactions with their caregivers produce different styles of attachment. Four styles—*secure, preoccupied, fearful,* and *dismissing*—which differ in *avoidance of intimacy* and *anxiety about abandonment*, are now recognized.

These orientations are mostly learned. Thus, our beliefs about the nature and worth of close relationships are shaped by our experiences within them.

The Influence of Individual Differences

There's wide variation in people's abilities and preferences, but individual differences are usually gradual and subtle instead of abrupt.

Sex Differences. Despite lay beliefs that men and women are quite different, most sex differences are quite small. The range of variation among members of a given sex is always large compared to the average difference between the sexes, and the overlap of the sexes is so substantial that many members of one sex will always score higher than the average member of the other sex. Thus, the sexes are much more similar than different on most of the topics of interest to relationship science.

Gender Differences. *Gender* differences refer to social and psychological distinctions that are taught to people by their cultures. Men are expected to be dominant and assertive, women to be warm and emotionally expressive—but a third of us are *androgynous* and possess both *instrumental,* task-oriented skills and *expressive,* social and emotional talents. Men and women who adhere to traditional gender roles do not like each other, either at first meeting or later during a marriage, as much as less stereotyped, androgynous people do.

Personality. Personality traits are stable tendencies that characterize people's thoughts, feelings, and behavior across their whole lives. Extraversion, agreeableness, and conscientiousness help produce pleasant relationships, but neuroticism undermines one's contentment.

Self-Esteem. What we think of ourselves emerges from our interactions with others. The *sociometer* theory argues that if others regard us positively, self-esteem is high, but if others don't want to associate with us, self-esteem is low. People who have low self-esteem undermine and sabotage their close relationships by underestimating their partners' love for them and overreacting to imagined threats.

The Influence of Human Nature

An evolutionary perspective assumes that sexual selection shapes humankind, influenced, in part, by sex differences in *parental investment* and *paternity uncertainty*. The sexes pursue different mates when they're interested in a long, committed relationship than they do when they're interested in a short-term affair. The evolutionary perspective also assumes that cultural influences determine whether inherited habits are still adaptive—and some of them may not be.

The Influence of Interaction

Relationships result from the combinations of their participants' histories and talents, and thus are often more than the sum of their parts. Relationships are fluid processes rather than static entities.

The Dark Side of Relationships

There are potential costs, as well as rewards, to intimacy. So why take the risk? Because we are a social species, and we need each other.

CHAPTER 2

Research Methods

THE SHORT HISTORY OF RELATIONSHIP SCIENCE ✦ DEVELOPING A QUESTION
✦ OBTAINING PARTICIPANTS ✦ CHOOSING A DESIGN ✦ Correlational
Designs ✦ Experimental Designs ✦ Developmental
Designs ✦ SELECTING A SETTING ✦ THE NATURE OF OUR DATA ✦ Self-
Reports ✦ Observations ✦ Physiological Measures ✦ Archival
Materials ✦ THE ETHICS OF SUCH ENDEAVORS ✦ INTERPRETING
AND INTEGRATING RESULTS ✦ A FINAL NOTE
✦ FOR YOUR CONSIDERATION ✦ CHAPTER SUMMARY

I bet you dread a chapter on research methods. You probably regard it as a distraction to be endured before getting to "the good stuff." Love, sex, and jealousy, for instance, are appealing topics, but research designs and procedures are not at the top of your list.

Nevertheless, for several reasons, some basic knowledge of the methods of inquiry is especially valuable for consumers of relationship science. For one thing, more charlatans and imposters compete for your attention in this field than in most others. Bookstores and websites are full of ideas offered by people who don't really study relationships at all but who (a) base suggestions and advice on their own idiosyncratic experiences or (b) even worse, simply make them up (Honeycutt, 1996). Appreciating the difference between trustworthy, reliable information and simple gossip can save you money and disappointment. Furthermore, misinformation about relationships is more likely to cause people real inconvenience than are misunderstandings in other sciences. People who misunderstand the nature of the solar system, for instance, are much less likely to take action that will be disadvantageous to them than are people who are misinformed about the effects of divorce on children. Studies of relationships often have real human impact in everyday life (Bradbury, 2002).

Indeed, this book speaks more directly to topics that affect you personally than most other texts you'll ever read. Because of this, you have a special responsibility to be an informed consumer who can distinguish flimsy whimsy from solid truths.

This isn't always easy. As we'll see in this chapter, there may be various ways to address a specific research question, and each may have its own particular advantages and disadvantages. Reputable scientists gather and evaluate information systematically and carefully, but no single technique may provide the indisputable answers they seek. A thoughtful understanding of relationships often requires us to combine information from many studies, evaluating diverse facts with judicious discernment. This chapter provides the overview of the techniques of relationship science that you need to make such judgments.

Only basic principles are described here, but they should help you decide what evidence to accept and what to question. Hopefully, when we're finished you'll be better equipped to distinguish useful research evidence from useless anecdotes or mere speculation. For even more information, don't hesitate to consult other sources such as Robins et al. (2009) and Leary (2011).

THE SHORT HISTORY OF RELATIONSHIP SCIENCE

Isaac Newton identified some of the basic laws of physics more than 400 years ago (back in 1687). Biology and chemistry have been around for just as long. The systematic study of human relationships, on the other hand, is a recent invention that is so new and so recent that you can actually talk, if you want, with most of the scientists who have ever studied human intimacy! This is no small matter. Because relationship science has a short history, it is less well known than most other sciences, and for that reason, it is less well understood. Very few people outside of colleges and universities appreciate the extraordinary strides this new discipline has made in the last 45 years.

Until the mid-twentieth century, relationships were pondered mainly by philosophers and poets. They had lots of opinions—doesn't everybody?—but those views were only opinions, and many of them were wrong. So, the first efforts of behavioral scientists to conduct empirical observations of real relationships were momentous developments. Relationship science can be said to have begun in the 1930s with a trickle of historically important studies of children's friendships (e.g., Moreno, 1934) and courtship and marriage (e.g., Waller, 1937). However, relatively few relationship studies were done before World War II. After the war, several important field studies, such as Whyte's (1955) *Street Corner Society* and Festinger, Schachter, and Back's (1950) study of student friendships in campus housing, attracted attention and respect. Still, relationships did not become a broad focus of research until an explosion of studies put the field on the scientific map in the 1960s and 1970s.

One of the most influential developments during that period was the new emphasis on laboratory experiments in social psychology. In a quest for precision that yielded unambiguous results, researchers began studying specific influences on relationships that they were able to control and manipulate. For instance, in a prominent line of research on the role of attitude similarity in liking, Donn Byrne and his colleagues (e.g., Byrne & Nelson, 1965) asked people to inspect an attitude survey that had supposedly been completed by a stranger in another room. Then, they asked the participants how much they liked the stranger. What the participants didn't know was that the researchers had prepared the survey either to agree or disagree with the participants' own attitudes (which had been assessed earlier). This manipulation of attitude similarity had clear effects: Apparent agreement caused people to like the stranger more than disagreement did.

Procedures like these demonstrated that some of the sources of liking could be understood through lab experiments, and their methodological rigor satisfied researchers' desires for clarity and concision. They legitimized and popularized the study of interpersonal attraction, making it an indispensable part of psychology textbooks for the first time. In retrospect, however, these investigations often did a poor job of representing the natural complexity of real relationships. The participants in many of Byrne's experiments never actually met that other person or interacted with him or her in any way. Indeed, in the procedure we have been discussing, a meeting couldn't occur because the stranger didn't actually exist! In this "phantom stranger" technique, people were merely reacting to check marks on a piece of paper and were the only real participants in the study. The researchers were measuring attraction to someone who wasn't even there. Byrne and his colleagues chose this method, limiting their investigation to one carefully controlled aspect of relationship development, to study it conclusively. However, they also created a rather sterile situation that lacked the immediacy and drama of chatting with someone face-to-face on a first date.

But don't underestimate the importance of studies like these: They demonstrated that relationships could be studied scientifically, and they suggested that such investigations had enormous promise. They really brought relationship science to the attention of fellow scholars for the first time. And in the decades since, through the combined efforts of family scholars, psychologists, sociologists, and communication researchers, relationship science has grown and evolved to encompass new methods of considerable complexity and sophistication. Today, relationship science:

- often uses diverse samples of people drawn from all walks of life and from around the world,
- examines varied types of family, friendship, and romantic relationships,
- frequently studies those relationships over long periods of time,
- studies both the pleasant and unpleasant aspects of relationships, and
- often follows relationships in their natural settings.

Here are some examples of how the field currently operates:

- At Northwestern University, Eli Finkel and his colleagues (Eastwick et al., 2010) conduct "speed-dating" studies in which singles rotate through short conversations with 10 different potential romantic partners. Participants spend 4 minutes chatting with someone, record their reactions to the interaction, and then move on to someone new. The dating prospects are real; if both members of a couple indicate that they would like to see each other again, the researchers give them access to a website where they can exchange messages. But the researchers are also able to inspect the building blocks of real romantic chemistry as people pursue new mates. (Watch http://www.youtube.com/watch?v=4hOKtyQMZeE for further detail.)

- At the University of Texas at Arlington, William Ickes and his colleagues study spontaneous, unscripted interactions between people (who have sometimes just met) by leaving them alone on a comfortable couch for a few minutes while their conversation is covertly videotaped (Ickes, 2009). The camera is actually hidden in another room across the hall and can't be seen even if you're looking directly at it, so there's no clue that anyone is watching (see Figure 2.1). Afterward, participants can review the tapes of their interaction in private cubicles where they are invited to report what they were thinking—and what they thought their partners were thinking— at each point in the interaction. The method thus provides an objective videotaped record of the interaction, and participants' thoughts and feelings and perceptions of one another can be obtained, too. (Visit this lab at http://www.uta.edu/psychology/faculty/ickes/social_lab/)
- At the University of Arizona, Matthias Mehl and his colleagues capture brief slices of social life by equipping people with small recorders that they carry during the day (Mehl & Robbins, 2011). The tiny devices record all the sounds in the immediate vicinity for 30-second intervals about 70 times a day. The resulting soundtrack indicates how often people are alone, how frequently

FIGURE 2.1. **Schematic diagram of William Ickes's lab at the University of Texas at Arlington.**
Participants in a typical study will be left alone on a couch (1)—the only place to sit—in a spacious room. A microphone hidden under a coffee table (2) and a video camera completely out of sight in another room (3) record their conversation. Afterward, the participants may offer insights into what they were thinking during their interaction when they watch their videotape in individual viewing rooms (4 and 5).

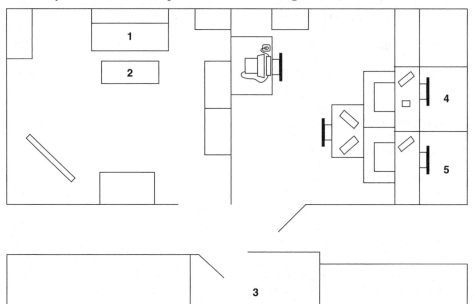

they interact with others, and whether their conversations are pleasant or argumentative. This technique allows researchers to listen in on real life as it naturally unfolds. (You can do some eavesdropping of your own at http://dingo.sbs.arizona.edu/~mehl/EAR.htm)

- In Seattle (http://www.gottman.com/research/family/), John Gottman and his colleagues invite married couples to a pleasant setting where they may take several hours revisiting the disagreement that caused their last argument. They know that they are being videotaped, but after a while they typically become so absorbed in the interaction that they forget the cameras. The researchers may even take physiological measurements such as heart rate and electrodermal responses from the participants. Painstaking second-by-second analysis of the biological, emotional, and behavioral reactions they observe allow the researchers to predict with 93 percent accuracy which of the couples will, and which will not, divorce years later (Gottman & Levenson, 2000).

- In the Early Years of Marriage Project run by Terri Orbuch and her colleagues (Birditt et al., 2010), 199 white couples and 174 black couples from the area surrounding Detroit, Michigan, have been interviewed every few years since they were married in 1986. The project is taking specific note of the influences of social and economic conditions on marital satisfaction, and it allows comparisons of the outcomes encountered by white and black Americans. In 2002, 16 years after the project began, 36 percent of the white couples and 55 percent of the black couples had already divorced (Orbuch & Brown, 2006). Entire marriages are being tracked from start to finish as time goes by. (Visit the project at http://projects.isr.umich.edu/eym/)

I hope that you're impressed by the creativity and resourcefulness embodied in these methods of research. (I am!) But as notable as they are, they barely scratch the surface in illustrating the current state of relationship science. Although still young, the field is now supported by hundreds of scholars around the world who hail from diverse scientific disciplines and whose work appears in several different professional journals devoted entirely to personal relationships. If you're a student, you probably have access to the *Journal of Marriage and Family,* the *Journal of Social and Personal Relationships,* and the journal simply entitled *Personal Relationships.* You can also check out the International Association for Relationship Research, the world's largest organization of relationship scientists, at http://www.iarr.org.

DEVELOPING A QUESTION

How do these scholars study relationships? The first step in any scientific endeavor is to ask a question, and in a field like this one, some questions emerge from *personal experience.* Relationship researchers have an advantage over many other scientists in being unusually close to their subject matter; their own experiences in close relationships can alert them to important processes, and they are sometimes hip deep in the very swamps they are trying to drain (Miller,

2008)! Broader *social problems* also suggest questions for careful study. For instance, the huge increase in the U.S. divorce rate from 1960 to 1980 resulted in a considerable amount of research on divorce as social scientists took note of the culture's changes.

Questions also come from *previous research:* Studies that answer one question may raise new ones. And still other questions are suggested by *theories* that strive to offer explanations for relational events. Useful theories both account for existing facts and make new predictions, and studies often seek to test those predictions. Research on intimate relationships involves questions that spring from all of these sources; scientists will put together their personal observations, their recognition of social problems, their knowledge of previous research, and their theoretical perspectives to create the questions they ask (Fiske, 2004).

The questions themselves are usually of two broad types. First, researchers may seek to *describe* events as they naturally occur. In this case, their goal is to delineate the patterns they observe as fully and accurately as they can. Alternatively, researchers can seek to establish the *causal connections* between events to determine which events have meaningful effects on subsequent outcomes and which do not. This distinction has important ramifications for consumers of relationship research. First, different studies have different goals, and discerning consumers judge investigations with respect to their intended purposes. If an exploratory study seeks mainly to describe a newly noticed phenomenon, we shouldn't criticize it for leaving us uncertain about the causes and the effects of that phenomenon; those are different questions to be addressed later, after we specify what we're talking about. Second, and more importantly, thoughtful consumers resist the temptation to draw causal connections from studies with descriptive goals. Only certain research designs allow any insight into the causal connections between events, and clever consumers do not jump to unwarranted conclusions that the research results do not support. I'll return to this point later in this chapter.

OBTAINING PARTICIPANTS

So, whose relationships are studied? Relationship researchers usually recruit participants in one of two ways. The first approach is to use anyone who is readily available and who consents to participate; this is a **convenience sample** because it is (comparatively) convenient for the researcher to obtain. University professors who study intimate relationships often work with college students who are required to be research participants as part of their course work. Researchers may also advertise their studies to recruit volunteers from the community. Although some specific characteristics must sometimes be met (so that a study may focus, for instance, only on dating partners who have known each other for less than 2 months), researchers who use convenience samples are usually glad to get the help of everyone they can.

In contrast, projects that use a **representative sample** strive to ensure that, collectively, their participants resemble the entire population of people who are of interest. A truly representative study of marriage, for example, would need to include married people of all sorts—all ages, all nationalities, and all socio-economic levels. That's a tall order, and it may even be impossible because, if nothing else, the people who voluntarily consent to participate in a research study may be somewhat different from those who refuse to participate (see the box on the next page). Still, some studies have obtained samples that are representative of (volunteers in) the adult population of individual countries or other delimited groups. And studies that are straightforward enough to be conducted over the Internet can attract very large samples that are much more diverse than those found on any one campus or even in any one country (Gosling et al., 2010).

On the one hand, there is no question that if we seek general principles that apply to most people, representative samples are better than convenience samples. A convenience sample always allows the unhappy possibility that the results we obtain are idiosyncratic, applying only to people who are just like our participants—students at a certain university, or people from a particular area of the country. And although relationship science is now conducted around the world, most of the studies we'll encounter in this book have come from cultures that are Western, well-educated, industrialized, relatively rich, and democratic—so their participants are a little *weird*. (Get it?) In fact, people from "weird" cultures do sometimes behave differently than those who live in less developed nations (Heinrich et al., 2010). Attitudes, to be sure, can vary considerably from one group to the next. On the other hand, many processes studied by relationship researchers are basic enough that they don't differ substantially across demographic groups; people all over the world, for instance, share similar standards about the nature of physical beauty (see chapter 3). To the extent that research examines fundamental aspects of the ways humans react to each other, convenience samples may not be disadvantageous.

Let's consider a specific example. Back In 1978, Russell Clark sent men and women out across the campus of Florida State University to proposition members of the other sex. Individually, they approached unsuspecting people and randomly assigned them to one of three invitations (see Table 2.1); some people were simply asked out on a date, whereas other people were asked to

TABLE 2.1. "Would You Go to Bed with Me Tonight?"

In Clark and Hatfield's (1989) studies, college students walking across campus encountered a stranger of the other sex who said, "Hi, I've noticed you around campus, and I find you very attractive," and then offered one of the following three invitations. What percentage of the students accepted the various offers?

Invitations	*Percentages Saying "Yes"*	
	Men	Women
"Would you go out with me tonight?"	50	56
"Would you come over to my apartment tonight?"	69	6
"Would you go to bed with me tonight?"	75	0

have sex! The notable results were that no woman accepted the offer of sex from a stranger, but 75 percent of the men did—and that was more men than accepted the date!

This was a striking result, but so what? The study involved a small convenience sample on just one campus. Perhaps the results told us more about the odd desperation of men at FSU than they did about men and women in general. In fact, Clark had trouble getting the study published because of reviewers' concerns about the generality of the results. So, in 1982, he and Elaine Hatfield tried again; they repeated the study at FSU and got the same results (Clark & Hatfield, 1989).

Well, still so what? It was 4 years later, but the procedure had still been tried only in Tallahassee. If you give this example some thought, you'll be able to generate several reasons why the results might apply only to one particular time and one particular place.

I'd like to suggest a different perspective. Let's not fuss too much about the exact percentage of college men in Florida or elsewhere who would consent to sex with a stranger. That's exactly the kind of specific attitude that may vary some from one demographic group to another. Instead of endlessly criticizing or, even worse, dismissing the results of the Clark and Hatfield (1989) studies,

The Challenge of Volunteer Bias in Relationship Research

Regardless of whether investigators use convenience or representative sampling, they still face the problem of **volunteer bias:** Of the people invited to participate, those who do may differ from those who don't. In one illustration of this problem, Karney et al. (1995) simply asked 3,606 couples who had applied for marriage licenses in Los Angeles County whether they would participate in a longitudinal study of their relationships. Only 18 percent of the couples said that they would, and that's a typical rate in procedures of this sort. But their marriage licenses, which were open to the public, provided several bits of information about them (e.g., their addresses, their ages, and their jobs). The volunteers differed from those who refused to participate in several ways; they were better educated, employed in higher-status jobs, and more likely to have cohabited. If the researchers had

carried out a complete study with these people, would these characteristics have affected their results?

The answer may depend on what questions are asked, but volunteer bias can color the images that emerge from relationship research. People who volunteer for studies dealing with sexual behavior, for instance, tend to be younger, more sexually experienced, and more liberal than nonvolunteers (Wiederman, 2004). Subtle bias can occur even when people are *required* to be research participants, as college students often are. Conscientious students participate earlier in the semester than slackers do, and students who select face-to-face lab studies are more extraverted than those who stay home and participate online (Witt et al., 2011). Volunteer biases such as these can limit the applicability of research results among those who did not participate in a particular study.

The people in a representative sample reflect the demographic characteristics (sex, age, race, etc.) of the entire population of people that the researchers wish to study.

let's recognize their limitations but not miss their point: Men were generally more accepting of casual sex than women were. When somebody actually asked, men were much more likely to accept a sexual invitation from a stranger than women were. Stated generally, that's exactly the conclusion that has now been drawn from subsequent investigations involving more than 20,000 participants from every major region of the world (Schmitt & the International Sexuality Description Project, 2003), and Clark and Hatfield were among the very first to document this sex difference. Their method was simple, and their sample was limited, but they were onto something, and their procedure detected a basic pattern that really does seem to exist.[1]

So, it's absolutely true that the Clark and Hatfield (1989) studies were not perfect. That's a judgment with which Clark and Hatfield (2003) themselves agree! But as long as their results are considered thoughtfully and judiciously, even small studies using convenience samples like these can make important contributions to relationship science. Representative samples provide desirable

[1] For instance, in May and June, 2009, 38 percent of the men but only 2 percent of the women in urban areas of Denmark accepted identical invitations to have sex with a stranger (Hald & Høgh-Olesen, 2010).

reassurance that scientific results can be widely applied, but representative samples are difficult—and expensive—to obtain. Even if researchers are able to contact a representative group of people, they may not be able to afford the payment and other expenses required to ask more than just a few questions of their participants.

Relationship science often presents dilemmas such as these: Choices must be made, but no flawless option is available. In such cases, our confidence in our collective understanding of relationships rests on a gradual accumulation of knowledge with varied methods (Reis, 2002). Any single study may have some imperfections, but those weaknesses may be answered by another study's strengths. With a series of investigations, each approaching a problem from a different angle, we gradually delineate the truth. As a thoughtful consumer of relationship science, you should try to think the way the scientists do: No one study is perfect. Be cautious. Diverse methods are valuable. Wisdom takes time. But the truth is out there, and we're getting closer all the time.

CHOOSING A DESIGN

Now that we have formulated a research question and obtained some participants, we need to arrange our observations in a way that will answer our question. This section describes different research designs that routinely appear in relationship science.

Correlational Designs

A **correlation** allows us to answer the questions, "Do two events, x and y, change together? That is, are variations in x and y related in some way?" Correlations are numbers that can range from -1.00 to $+1.00$. The larger (the absolute value of) a correlation is, the more highly related two events are. If x and y are perfectly *positively* correlated (which means they go up and down together—as x goes up, so does y; as y goes down, so does x), we obtain a correlation of $+1.00$. If x and y are perfectly *negatively* correlated (so that they change in opposite directions—as x goes up, y goes down; as x goes down, y goes up), the correlation is -1.00. When x and y have no relationship at all, their correlation is 0. Some examples of these patterns are shown in Figure 2.2.

The question of whether two events change together is enormously important and very common. Consider a question we'll answer in chapter 3: Do people who think they share similar attitudes and values tend to like each other? A correlational study designed to answer that question would typically assess naturally occurring patterns of perceived similarity and attraction in a large number of couples without trying to influence or manipulate the couples' behavior in any way. The participants' feelings would be carefully measured, and a reliable connection between similarity and attraction would help us understand the nature of contentment in new relationships.

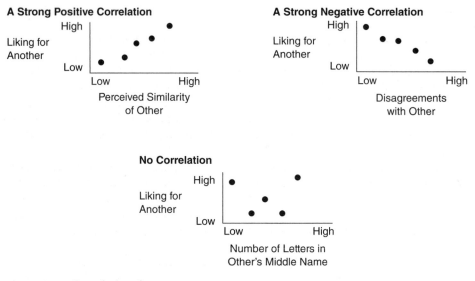

FIGURE 2.2. **Correlational patterns.**

On the other hand, even if there were a correlation between attraction and perceived similarity, there'd be a lot we wouldn't know. Indeed, unsophisticated consumers often misinterpret the results of correlational designs. A correlation tells us that an association exists between two things, but it does **not** tell us *why* those things are related. Correlations do not tell us about the causal connections between events. Be careful not to assume too much when you encounter a correlation; many different plausible causal connections may all be possible when a correlation exists. Here are three straightforward possibilities:

- *x* may cause *y*—in the example of similarity and attraction, it might be that perceived similarity leads to greater liking. *Or,*
- *y* may cause *x*—so that liking someone causes us to assume that we have a lot in common with him or her. *Or,*
- some other influence, a third variable, may cause both *x* and *y,* and the only reason *x* and *y* are related is because of their common cause. The two events *x* and *y* may not affect each other at all, and something else, such as others' good looks, may cause us to like them and to assume that they are just like us.

Any of these three, along with many other more complex chains of events, may be possible when *x* and *y* are correlated. If all we have is a correlation, all we know is that two events are related. We don't know what causal connections are involved.[2]

---

[2]I should note, however, that if we have *lots* of correlations involving a number of variables, or if we have taken our measurements on several occasions over a span of time, sophisticated statistical analyses can usually rule out some of the possible causal connections that make correlational findings ambiguous. We should be careful not to assume that simple correlations involve causal connections, but advanced statistical techniques often make it possible to draw some defensible conclusions about cause and effect within correlational designs.

Experimental Designs

When it's possible, the way to investigate causal connections is to use an experimental design. **Experiments** provide straightforward information about causes and their effects because experimenters create and control the conditions they study. In a true experiment, researchers intentionally manipulate one or more variables and randomly assign participants to the different conditions they have created to see how those changes affect people. Thus, instead of just asking "Do x and y change together?" experimenters ask "If we change x, what happens to y?"

Let's illustrate the difference between an experiment and a correlational study by reconsidering Donn Byrne's classic work on attitude similarity and attraction (e.g., Byrne & Nelson, 1965). Had Byrne simply measured partners' attitudes and their liking for each other, he would have obtained a positive correlation between similarity and liking, but he wouldn't have been sure why they were related.

What Byrne did instead was an experiment. Once his participants arrived at his lab, he flipped a coin to determine randomly who would encounter a similar stranger and who would encounter one who didn't agree with them at all. He *controlled* that apparent agreement or disagreement, and it was the only difference between the two situations in which participants found themselves. With this procedure, when Byrne observed higher liking for the similar stranger, he could reasonably conclude that the greater agreement had *caused* the higher liking. How? Because the participants were randomly assigned to the two situations, the different degrees of liking could not be due to differences in the people who encountered each situation; on average, the two groups of participants were identical. Moreover, they all had identical experiences in the experiment except for the apparent similarity of the stranger. The only reasonable explanation for the different behavior Byrne observed was that similarity leads to liking. His experiment clearly showed that the manipulated cause, attitude similarity, had a noticeable effect, higher liking.

Experiments provide clearer, more definitive tests of causal connections than other designs do. Done well, they clearly delineate cause and effect. Why, then, do researchers ever do anything else? The answer lies in the fact that experimenters must be able to control and manipulate the events they wish to study. Byrne could control the information that his participants received about someone they had never met, but he couldn't manipulate other important factors in intimate relationships. We still can't. (How do you create full-fledged experiences of romantic love in a laboratory?) You can't do experiments on events you cannot control.

So, correlational and experimental designs each have their own advantages. With a correlational design, we can study compelling events in the real world—commitment to a relationship, passionate love, unsafe sex—and examine the links among them. But correlational designs are limited in what they can tell us about the causal relationships among events. With an experimental design, we can examine causal connections, but we are limited in what we can study. Once again, there is no perfect solution—and that is another reason to study the same topic in different ways, with different research designs.

Developmental Designs

Developmental designs study the manner in which behavior or events change over time. There are three major types of such designs.

Cross-Sectional Designs

The most common type of developmental design, a **cross-sectional design,** compares people at one stage in a developmental process to other people at another stage. If we wished to examine risk factors for divorce at different stages of marriage, for instance, we could ask divorcing couples who have been married for various lengths of time about their chief complaints. We might find an association between the duration of marriages and the reasons they fail.

As this example suggests, cross-sectional designs are correlational designs, so we should be careful about the conclusions we draw from them. If we compare people who had been married for 25 years to those who were married for only 5, we're not only comparing people who were married for different lengths of time, but we're also comparing people who grew up in different circumstances, about 20 years apart. For all we know, their complaints about marriage haven't changed with the years, and their concerns just reflect the different eras in which the marriages started.

As you can see, the correlations that result from cross-sectional designs are always open to a specific kind of ambiguity: the different social, cultural, and political events our participants have experienced. Whenever age seems to be involved in relationships outcomes, we have to question whether it is really age that is involved or a variation in the backgrounds of our different age groups.

Longitudinal Designs

Cross-sectional designs confuse age with history. However, if we recruit people who are all the same age and follow them over time as they get older, we have a study in which the participants' history is the same but their age

In a cross-sectional design, researchers obtain responses from people from different age groups. To see whether musical preferences differ with age, for example, we could ask 20-year-olds and 60-year-olds to evaluate various entertainers.

changes. This is a **longitudinal design,** in which the same people are followed with repeated measurements over a period of time. If we repeatedly monitor the complaints of married couples who joined our study as newlyweds and who continue to participate as they grow older—as Terri Orbuch (Orbuch & Brown, 2006) is doing with the Early Years of Marriage Project—we will be using a longitudinal design.

These designs do a better job of disentangling history and age than cross-sectional designs do, but they're still not perfect. Dramatic changes in the surrounding culture can still be mistaken for the effects of age and experience. What if we find, as time goes by, that fights over money become more frequent? If we're collecting data during an economic recession, what appears in our study to be a typical developmental change in marital concerns could really be a temporary cultural shift that doesn't affect most marriages at all!

If we are very persistent and clever, we could generally rule out historical influences by combining longitudinal and cross-sectional designs. We could start out with two groups, people who are 20 and another group of people who are 40, and follow both groups until they reach their middle fifties. If, at age 55, members of both groups developed the same complaints about their marriages, then we might really begin to believe that we had discovered a general trend.

Of course, a study like this wouldn't be easy. In fact, there would be enormous logistical difficulties involved in conducting a single investigation that takes 35 years! One of the bigger problems facing longitudinal designs is **participant attrition,** the loss of participants over time. People move away and cannot be located, or they get busy or bored and just don't want to continue participating in the study. And the longer the study goes on, the greater these problems become. Long-term longitudinal studies sometimes end up with a small and select group of people who have stayed with the study from start to finish. Indeed, even if the study started with a representative sample, it may not have one when it's finished.

Retrospective Designs

Given the difficulties of staying in touch with our participants over the course of a longitudinal study, why don't we track changes over time by just asking people about their past experiences? We can, of course, and many studies of intimate relationships use **retrospective designs** that ask people to describe events from the past. Sometimes, long periods of time are involved ("What major arguments did you have before you got married?"); sometimes very short periods are studied ("How pleasant were your interactions with your partner over the last 24 hours?").

Retrospective designs are very flexible. If we are worried about historical influences, we can ask people of different ages to think back to the same younger age and see whether they recall similar experiences. Indeed, if people had perfect memories, retrospective designs would be extremely useful. Unfortunately, of course, memories are imperfect, and they become increasingly inaccurate when we ask people about events that took place long ago

(Frye & Karney, 2004). Whenever we rely on retrospective reports, we cannot know whether we are getting a clear picture of the past or one that has been contaminated by more recent events.

Overall, then, this brief look at developmental designs supports the point that's becoming our theme: No one type of study is perfect, but each of them has its uses. The focus on change over time provided by developmental designs is particularly valuable in relationship science; our partnerships with others are often long-term events, and we need to understand how they may change as time goes by.

SELECTING A SETTING

We're making progress. We've developed our research question, recruited our participants, and chosen our design. Now, we have to select a setting in which to conduct our investigation. The usual choices include (a) a laboratory or (b) a natural, everyday environment, such as a couple's home. Either choice has advantages and disadvantages. (But you're getting used to that, aren't you?) The lab offers the advantage of greater control over extraneous, unwanted influences. Researchers can regulate the exact experiences their participants will have and arrange the physical environment itself to fit the purposes of the study. Natural settings offer the advantage of obtaining more typical behavior, because people usually feel more comfortable and relaxed in their ordinary surroundings. The disadvantages of these two settings are mirror images of their benefits. A laboratory may elicit artificial behavior that differs from what people usually do. On the other hand, natural settings may be hard to manage and full of distractions.

Wherever a study takes place, some behaviors are difficult to study because they are rare, or unpleasant, or very intimate (or all three). One way to overcome these difficulties is to have subjects **role-play** the behavior we're trying to understand—to act "as if" they were jealous, for instance, or were having an argument, or were trying to entice someone into bed. Role-play studies vary a great deal in how realistic they are. At one extreme, participants may be asked to read a story involving the relevant behavior and to imagine those events happening to them. Such *scenarios* are always less vivid than the real events would be, and they allow people to respond in a cool, collected fashion that may be quite different from the impulsive and emotional reactions they display when such events really take place. At the other extreme, studies known as *simulations* ask people to act out a particular role in a hypothetical situation. For example, an investigator might ask a couple to pretend that they are angry with each other and then observe how they behave. This strategy is more engrossing, but participants still know that they are only pretending. Role-play studies are an ethically defensible way of studying emotionally charged topics, but people may do what they think they *should* do in these situations rather than what they really *would* do if the events actually occurred. Once again, there are both advantages and disadvantages to consider.

High-Tech Role-Playing

An intriguing new tool in relationship science is the use of *immersive virtual environments* (or IVEs) to study human interaction (Blascovich & McCall, 2010). In an IVE study, participants interact with three-dimensional computer representations of other people; they wear headsets that control what they see, and as they move through space in an empty room, the visual feedback they receive responds to their actual movements. It's like really being inside an elaborate video game.

Of course, participants know that the things they see aren't really happening. Nevertheless, an IVE can be an absorbing experience that generates behavior that resembles people's actions in real life (Kane et al., 2009). And the technique allows researchers precise control over the appearance, actions, and reactions of the virtual partners with whom the participants interact. Researchers can create exactly the same situation over and over, or they can vary the situation in subtle ways that would be hard to regulate with real-life actors and assistants. Verisimilitude versus control: Here's another research tool with important advantages and disadvantages, and we'll probably be hearing more about it in the years to come.

THE NATURE OF OUR DATA

Now, just what type of information will we be actually collecting? Are we recording others' judgments and perceptions of a relationship, or are we inspecting specific interactions ourselves? Two major types of research measures are described here: (a) people's own reports about their thoughts, feelings, and behaviors and (b) observations of others' behavior. We'll also examine some variations on these themes. No matter what data we use, our measures should have psychometric **validity** and **reliability.** That is, we should really be measuring the events we're trying to measure (that's validity), and, if those events aren't changing, we should get the same scores time after time (that's reliability).

Self-Reports

The most common means of studying intimate relationships is to ask people about their experiences. Such responses are **self-reports,** and they can be obtained in a variety of formats: through written questionnaires, verbal interviews, or even unstructured diaries in which participants write about whatever comes to mind. The common theme linking such techniques is that people are telling us about their experiences—we're not watching them ourselves.

Self-report data have important benefits. For one thing, they allow us to "get inside people's heads" and understand personal points of view that may not be apparent to outside observers. Self-report data are also inexpensive and easy to obtain. Investigators do not need elaborate equipment; they need only paper, pencils, and willing participants. Consider, for instance, the short self-report measure provided in Table 2.2: Those seven questions do a remarkably good job of assessing people's satisfaction with their close relationships. For most purposes, there's no reason to ask more elaborate questions or use other means to distinguish satisfied lovers from those who are less content because this handful of straightforward questions works just fine (Hendrick et al., 1998). Self-report measures can be both very efficient and very informative. Still (and this probably isn't a surprise!), self-reports may also present potential problems. Here are three things to worry about.

Participants' Interpretations of the Questions

Self-reports always occur in response to a researcher's instructions or questions. If the participants misinterpret what the researcher means or

TABLE 2.2 The Relationship Assessment Scale

Circle the answer below each question that best describes your current romantic relationship.

1. **How well does your partner meet your needs?**

1	2	3	4	5
not at all	somewhat	moderately well	very well	extremely well

2. **In general, how satisfied are you with your relationship?**

1	2	3	4	5
not at all	somewhat	moderately	very	extremely

3. **How good is your relationship compared to most?**

1	2	3	4	5
not at all	somewhat	moderately	very	extremely

4. **How often do you wish you hadn't gotten into this relationship?**

1	2	3	4	5
never	rarely	occasionally	often	very often

5. **To what extent has your relationship met your original expectations?**

1	2	3	4	5
not at all	somewhat	moderately well	very well	extremely well

6. **How much do you love your partner?**

1	2	3	4	5
not at all	somewhat	moderately	very much	extremely

7. **How many problems are there in your relationship?**

1	2	3	4	5
none	a few	some	many	very many

To determine your score, reverse the ratings you provided on items 4 and 7. If you circled a 1, change it to a 5; if you answered 2, make it a 4; 4 becomes 2, and 5 becomes 1. Then add up your answers. The higher your score, the more content you are with your relationship.

Source: Hendrick, Dicke, & Hendrick, 1998.

intends, their subsequent self-reports can be misleading. For instance: "With how many people have you had sex?" When men answer that question, they tend to include partners with whom they have had oral sex but no intercourse, whereas women tend to count only those partners with whom they have had intercourse (Gute et al., 2008). This is one reason why men routinely report that they have had sex with more members of the other sex than women do.[3] In fact, undetected problems with people's comprehension of terms describing sexual behavior may be a major problem in sexuality research (Wiederman, 2004).

Difficulties in Recall or Awareness

Even when people understand our questions, they may not be able to answer them correctly. For one thing, they may lack insight into their actions, so that what they think is going on isn't entirely accurate. For instance, according to their self-reports, physical attractiveness in a mate matters less to women than it does to men; women say looks are less important to them than men do. However, when they encounter and evaluate several potential partners at once in speed-dating studies, looks *do* matter just as much to women as they do to men (Eastwick & Finkel, 2008)—and for both sexes, looks are the most important influence on who likes whom (Luo & Zhang, 2009). On occasion, what people can tell us about their preferences and behavior doesn't coincide well with what they actually say and do.

Faulty memories can also be a problem. Self-reports are most accurate when people describe specific, objective events that have occurred recently. They are more likely to be inaccurate when we ask them about things that happened long ago (Feeney & Cassidy, 2003). Specific details may be forgotten— in one study (Mitchell, 2010), 50 percent of a large sample of divorced people did not correctly report in which month they were divorced—and past feelings are especially likely to be misremembered. In particular, if a passionate romance ends in pain and discontent, the disappointed lovers are likely to have a very hard time remembering how happy and enthusiastic they felt months earlier when they had just fallen in love (Grote & Frieze, 1998).

Bias in Participants' Reports

A final major worry involves the possibility of systematic bias or distortion in people's reports. One example of this (which we'll encounter again in chapter 4) is the **self-serving bias** that leads people to overestimate their responsibility for positive events in their relationships and to underestimate their blame for the bad times. People like to think of themselves in a positive light, so they tend to take the credit for their successes but duck the fault for their failures. If nothing else, domestic partners think they do a larger share of the housework than they really do (Ross & Sicoly, 1979)! Mistakes like this are not dishonest when they reflect people's genuine, but idiosyncratic, views.

---

[3] This provocative sex difference is explored in more detail in the box on page 283.

Nevertheless, self-reports obtain participants' personal perceptions of a situation, and those may differ in predictable ways from the judgments of other observers.

A more serious problem occurs when people are reluctant to tell the truth as they see it. The best known example of this is the **social desirability bias,** which refers to distortion that results from people's wishes to make good impressions on others. Participants are often reluctant to admit anything that makes them look bad or that portrays them in an undesirable light. For instance, concerns about social acceptance may make some people hesitate to honestly report their same-sex attractions and behavior to researchers; as a result, there is continuing argument about the real prevalence of same-sex sexual orientations (Tourangeau & Yan, 2007). In another instance, 4 percent of those who had been divorced a few years earlier—the researchers knew this because they had seen the divorce decrees on file at county courthouses—claimed that they had not been divorced (Mitchell, 2010). Procedures that guarantee participants' anonymity—such as allowing them to take surveys online instead of face-to-face (Brown & Vanable, 2009)—help reduce social desirability problems such as these, but bias is always a concern when studies address sensitive issues.

Assessing Attachment Styles

Studies of attachment have become a major theme in relationship science, and I'll mention attachment in every chapter to come. Where do all these findings come from? In most cases, research participants have described their feelings about close relationships on a questionnaire. Now that we've considered some of the nuances of self-report data, let's inspect the tool that's most often used to assess attachment styles.

The 12 items presented here are drawn from a longer questionnaire created by Kelly Brennan and her colleagues (1998), and they obtain results that are very similar to those obtained with the longer scale (Wei et al., 2007). I've labeled the two dimensions of attachment to which the items pertain; of course, those labels do not appear on the actual survey, and the items are mixed together.

Respondents are asked to rate the extent of their agreement or disagreement with each item on a seven-point scale ranging from 1 (*disagree strongly*) to 7 (*agree strongly*). Note that you'd report high levels of anxiety or avoidance by agreeing with some items and disagreeing with others; this is a common tactic that is used to encourage thoughtful answers and to help researchers detect careless responses.

Researchers typically derive two scores from the scale, an *anxiety* score and an *avoidance* score, and then determine how those two scores predict different relational outcomes. People with a secure style of attachment, as you may recall, would have low scores on both dimensions.[4]

---

[4] Do you need a reminder regarding attachment styles? Go back to p. 16 in chapter 1.

Items measuring
Anxiety about Abandonment:

1. I worry that romantic partners won't care about me as much as I care about them.
2. My desire to be close sometimes scares people away.
3. I need a lot of reassurance that I am loved by my partner.
4. I find that my partner(s) don't want to get as close as I would like.
5. I get frustrated when romantic partners are not available when I need them.
6. I do not often worry about being abandoned.

Items measuring
Avoidance of Intimacy:

1. I want to get close to my partner, but I keep pulling back.
2. I am nervous when partners get too close to me.
3. I try to avoid getting too close to my partner.
4. I usually discuss my problems and concerns with my partner.

5. It helps to turn to my romantic partner in times of need.
6. I turn to my partner for many things, including comfort and reassurance.

To get your own score on these items, *reverse* your score on the sixth Anxiety item and on numbers 4, 5, and 6 of the Avoidance items. A score of 1 becomes a 7, a 3 becomes a 5, a 6 becomes a 2, and so on. An average score on the Anxiety items is 22; a score below 15 is pretty low, and a score above 29 is pretty high. Average Avoidance is 15, with 9 being noticeably low and 21 being notably high (Wei et al., 2007).

Do the answers that people give to questions such as these really matter? Yes, they do. There are other means of assessing attachment that involve extensive interviews, but they are not often used because these items do such a fine job of identifying meaningful individual differences (Mikulincer & Shaver, 2007). Despite possible biases, vocabulary problems, and all the other potential problems with self-reports, these items delineate different global orientations to intimate relationships that are very influential, as we will see throughout this book.

Observations

Another way to collect information about intimate relationships is to observe behavior directly. Scientific observations are rarely casual undertakings. Researchers either measure behavior with sophisticated tools or carefully train their colleagues to make observations that are accurate, reliable, and often quite detailed.

Some studies involve direct observations of ongoing behavior whereas others use recordings from which observations are made at a later time. One method of observation, called **experience-sampling,** uses intermittent, short periods of observation to capture samples of behavior that actually occur over longer periods of time. In experience-sampling, investigators may randomly sample short spans of time when a target behavior is likely to occur, perhaps scattering several periods of observation through different times on different days. The work being done by Matthias Mehl (Mehl & Robbins, 2011) with small recorders that fit in a pocket is a fine example of this technique. The devices are called electronically activated recorders, or EARs. (Get it?) They switch on for brief periods at regular intervals during the day and capture the sounds of whatever interactions participants are having at the time. You won't be surprised to learn that when EARs capture a lot of surly emotions such as anger and contempt in couples' conversations, the partners are less content and their relationship is more fragile 6 months later (Slatcher & Ranson, 2011).

The observations that result from a procedure such as this can take several forms. Researchers sometimes make *ratings* that characterize the events they witness in relatively global (and usually subjective) terms. For example, an argument might be rated with regard to the extent to which it is "constructive and problem solving" or "argumentative and hostile." Alternatively, observers may employ *coding procedures* that focus on very specific behaviors such as the amount of time people speak during an interaction, the number of smiles they display, or the number of times they touch each other. These perceptions are typically more objective than ratings are, and they can sometimes be mechanized to be even more impartial. For instance, James Pennebaker has developed software that counts various types of words people use when they write or speak, and it allows an automatic analysis of the content of people's conversations. (And it's bad news when partners use the word "you" too frequently; such people tend to be less satisfied with their relationships than those who use "you" less often [Tausczik & Pennebaker, 2010].)

Other technologies provide additional measures of behavior. Another innovation is the use of eye-tracking methodology to assess people's visual interest in others (Lykins et al., 2006). In an eye-tracking study, participants don headgear that focuses tiny video cameras on their eyes. Then, when they inspect various images, their eye movements indicate what they're looking at, and for how long. We'd be able to tell, for instance, whether you prefer blondes or brunettes by presenting two images differing only in hair color side-by-side: You'd spend more time scrutinizing the image you find more alluring.

Observations such as these generally avoid the disadvantages of self-reports. Trained observers are usually immune to misinterpretations of the researchers' intent, and recorders don't have faulty memories or self-serving biases. On the other hand, we need self-reports if we're to understand people's personal perceptions of their experiences. Observational studies can also be expensive, sometimes requiring costly equipment and consuming hours and hours of observers' time. One remarkable study filmed every waking moment of the interactions of 32 different families over the course of one week, and the 1,540 hours of resulting video have required thousands of hours of careful inspection to code and categorize (Carey, 2010).

Observational research can also suffer from the problem of **reactivity:** People may change their behavior when they know they are being observed. (A camera in your living room would probably change some of your behavior—at least until you got used to it.) Participants may be just as concerned with creating a good impression when they know others are watching as they are when they answer an interviewer's questions. For that reason, researchers are always glad to conduct observations that cannot possibly alter the behaviors they're studying—and in one such investigation, relationship scientists are monitoring the Facebook profiles of 1,640 students at a particular university as their college years go by (Lewis et al., 2008). They're tracking the public information in the profiles to determine how the users' tastes and values influence the friendships they form. The researchers have specific, serious aims—this is not informal browsing—and they can't have unwanted influence on the behavior they're studying because the participants do not know that they are being watched! We will undoubtedly be seeing more formal studies of social networking on the Web in the years to come. (Do you find this troubling? Why?)

Physiological Measures

We can also avoid any problems with reactivity if we observe behavior that people cannot consciously control, and physiological measures of people's autonomic and biochemical reactions often do just that. Physiological measures assess such responses as heart rate, muscle tension, genital arousal, brain activity, and hormone levels to determine how our physical states are associated with our social behavior.

Some investigations examine the manner in which physiology shapes our interactions with others. For instance, the level of the neuropeptide oxytocin in your blood helps to determine how empathic and trusting you are (Campbell, 2010); remarkably, if you're given a dose of oxytocin, you'll be temporarily less suspicious of others (MacDonald & MacDonald, 2010). There are also physiological foundations to our attachment styles. Stronger autonomic reactions to social stressors, including the release of hormones such as adrenalin, are found in insecure people than in secure ones; social threats that create uneasy arousal in anxious and avoidant people often leave secure people cool and calm (Diamond & Fagundes, 2010)

Other studies consider how interactions change our physical states. Forgiveness is good for us (as we'll see in chapter 10); in particular, people who envision granting forgiveness to an offender experience lower heart rates and less muscle tension than do those who nurse a grudge (Witvliet et al., 2008). And still other studies seek to map the physiological markers of social behavior. For example, the structures in our brains that appear to regulate love and lust are being identified by researchers (see Aron, 2010) who invite participants to experience those states while their brains are being examined with fMRI (functional magnetic resonance imaging). fMRI images show which parts of the brain are consuming more nutrients and are therefore more active than others—and as it turns out, warm romantic affection and yearning sexual desire appear to be controlled by different parts of our brains. (Are you surprised?)

Physiological measures are often expensive, but their use is increasing because they allow relationship researchers to explore the physical foundations of our social behavior. They are a good example of the manner in which relationship science is becoming more complex and sophisticated all the time.

Archival Materials

Historical **archives** also avoid the problem of reactivity. Personal documents such as photographs and diaries, public media such as newspapers and magazines, and governmental records such as marriage licenses and census information can all be valuable sources of data about relationships, and when these are dated, they become "archival" information. In one study that examined the correlation between past physical attractiveness and current income, researchers rated people's attractiveness in old university yearbook photos to determine whether people who were good-looking years ago were making more money now (Frieze et al., 1991). (What did they find? See chapter 3!)

Archival materials are "nonreactive" because inspection of archival data does not change the behaviors being studied. They are also typically inexpensive to use. They can be limited, however, because they may not contain all the information a researcher would really like to have.

THE ETHICS OF SUCH ENDEAVORS

Studies using archival materials often run no risk at all of embarrassing anyone, but research on relationships does occasionally require investigators to ask questions about sensitive topics or to observe private behavior. Should we pry into people's personal affairs?

This really isn't an issue I pose lightly. Although it's enormously valuable and sorely needed, relationship science presents important ethical dilemmas. Just asking people to fill out questionnaires describing their relationships may have subtle but lasting effects on those partnerships (Zhaoyang & Cooper, 2011). When we ask people to specify what they get out of a relationship or to rate their love for their partners, for instance, we focus their attention on delicate matters they may not have thought much about. We encourage them to evaluate their relationships, and stimulate their thinking. Moreover, we arouse their natural curiosity about what their partners may be saying in response to the same questions. In general, a researcher's innocent inquiries run the risk of alerting people to relationship problems or frustrations they didn't know they had.

Simulations and other observational studies may have even more impact. Consider John Gottman's (Gottman & Levenson, 2000) method of asking spouses to revisit the issue that caused their last argument: He doesn't encourage people to quarrel and bicker, but some of them do. Spouses that disagree sourly and bitterly are at much greater risk for divorce than are spouses who disagree with grace and humor, and Gottman's work has illuminated the specific styles of behavior that forecast trouble ahead. This work is extremely important. But does it do damage? Should we actually invite couples to return to a disagreement that may erode their satisfaction even further?

The answer to that question isn't simple. Relationship scientists ordinarily are very careful to safeguard the welfare of their participants (Kimmel, 2004).

Detailed information is provided to potential participants before a study begins so that they can make an informed decision about whether or not to participate. Their consent to participate is voluntary and can be withdrawn at any time. After the data are collected, the researchers provide prompt feedback that explains any experimental manipulations and describes the larger purposes of the investigation. Final reports regarding the outcomes of the study are often made available when the study is complete. In addition, when ticklish matters are being investigated, researchers may provide information about where participants can obtain couples' counseling should they wish to do so; psychological services may even be offered for free.

As you can see, relationship science is based on compassionate concern for the well-being of its participants. People are treated with respect, thanked warmly for their efforts, and may even be paid for their time. They may also enjoy their experiences and benefit from them (Zhaoyang & Cooper, 2011). In a longitudinal study of marriages, for instance, participants who made frequent self-reports felt more competent as spouses than did those in a control condition who provided only minimal data; paying closer attention to how things were going was evidently advantageous (Veroff et al., 1992). So, at least some of the time, participation in relationship studies can be interesting and enlightening. Still, should we be trying to study such private and intimate matters as close relationships?

The answer from here is absolutely yes. There's another side to the issue of ethics I haven't yet mentioned: science's ethical imperative to gain knowledge that can benefit humanity. Ignorance can be wasteful. For instance, the U.S. Department of Health and Human Services is currently spending a pile of money to fund a Healthy Marriage Initiative that is intended to teach African Americans skills that will help them sustain their marriages. Black Americans are targets of this marriage-enrichment program because, compared to whites, they are less likely to marry and more likely to divorce (Orbuch & Brown, 2006). One of the assumptions underlying the Initiative is that the marriages of African Americans will be more stable if they come to value marriage more—so taxpayers' dollars are being spent on classes that try to convince blacks to respect and appreciate matrimony. The problem here—as is apparent to relationship scientists (Karney & Bradbury, 2005)—is that African Americans value marriage just as much as anyone else. They *want* to be married even more than whites do, but they don't get married when they face bleak economic prospects. In particular, black women do not want to marry men who don't have steady jobs (Gibson-Davis, 2009). When they do marry, their marriages are less stable on average because they more often encounter financial difficulties (Hardie & Lucas, 2010), and *any* couple that has to struggle with worries over money tends to be less content. Thus, the relative fragility of African-American marriages seems to have more to with social class than with individual attitudes (Karney & Bradbury, 2005).

So it's pretty silly to expect that values education will change anything. A government program that seeks to improve relationships would probably do better to fund effective training for better jobs or to increase the minimum wage than to try to teach people to respect marriage (Gibson-Davis, 2009). And clearly, if we seek to promote human well-being, we need good information as well as good intentions. In a culture that offers us bizarre examples of "love" on TV shows such as *Rock of Love* and *The Bachelorette*—and in which real marriages are more likely to be failures than to be successes (Cherlin, 2009)—it would be unethical *not* to try to understand how relationships work. Intimate relationships can be a source of the grandest, most glorious pleasure human beings experience, but they can also be a source of terrible suffering and appalling destructiveness. It is inherently ethical, relationship scientists assert, to try to learn how the joy might be increased and the misery reduced.

INTERPRETING AND INTEGRATING RESULTS

This isn't a statistics text (and I know you're pleased by that), but there are a few more aspects of the way relationship scientists do business that the thoughtful consumer of the field should understand. Most relationship studies subject the data they obtain to statistical analysis to determine whether their results are statistically "significant." This is a calculation of how likely it is that the results (e.g., the observed correlations or the effects of the manipulated variables in an experiment) could have occurred by chance. If it's quite unlikely that the results could be due to chance, we have a "significant" result. All of the research results reported in this book are significant results. You can also be confident that the studies that have obtained these results have passed critical inspection by other scientists. This does not mean, however, that every single specific result I may mention is unequivocally, positively true: Some of them might have occurred by chance, reflecting the influence of odd samples of people or unwanted mistakes of various sorts. Remember, too, that the results we'll encounter always describe patterns that are evident in the behavior of *groups* of people—and because of differences among individuals (see chapter 1), those patterns will apply to particular individuals to varying degrees. Please do not be so naïve as to think that research results that *do*, in fact, apply to most people must be wrong because you know someone to whom those results do not seem to apply. I'll need you to be more sophisticated and reasonable than that.

With those cautions in place, let's note that the data obtained in relationship studies can also present unique challenges and complexities. Here are three examples:

Paired, interdependent data. Most statistical procedures assume that the scores of different participants are independent and not connected in any way—that is, one person's responses are not influenced by anyone else's—but that's not true when both members of a couple are involved. Wilma's satisfaction with her relationship with Fred is very likely to be influenced by whether or not Fred is happy too, so her satisfaction is *not* independent of his. Responses obtained from relationship partners are often interdependent, and special statistical procedures are advisable for analyzing such data (e.g., Kashy et al., 2006).

Different levels of analysis. Relationship researchers must also choose between two entirely different levels of analysis, one focusing on the individuals who make up couples and the other focusing on the couples themselves (Kashy et al., 2006). For instance, researchers may examine how an individual's attachment style affects the interactive outcomes he or she obtains, or they may examine how the styles of two different partners combine to affect the quality of their relationship. The first of these questions analyzes individuals, but the second analyzes dyads, and relationship scholars must be careful to ensure that their procedures fit the level of analysis of interest to them.

Three sources of influence. Furthermore, relationships emerge from the individual contributions of the separate partners *and* from the unique effects of how they combine as a pair. For example, imagine that Betty and Barney have a happy marriage. One reason for this may be the fact that Barney is an especially pleasant fellow who gets along well with everyone, including Betty. Alternatively (or, perhaps, in addition), Betty may be the one who's easy to live with. However, Betty and Barney may also have a better relationship with each other than they could have with anyone else because of the unique way their individual traits combine; the whole may be more than the sum of its parts. Relationship researchers often encounter phenomena that result from the combination of all three of these influences, the two individual partners and the idiosyncratic partnership they share. Sophisticated statistical analyses are required to study all of these components at once (Kenny & Ledermann, 2010), another indication of the complexity of relationship science.

So what's my point here? I've noted that studies of close relationships tackle intricate matters and that statistical significance testing involves probabilities, not certainties. Should you take everything I say with a grain of salt, doubting me at every turn? Well, yes and no. I want you to be more thoughtful and less gullible, and I want you to appreciate the complexities underlying the things you're about to learn. Remember to think like a scientist: No study is perfect, but the truth is out there. We put more faith in patterns of results that are obtained by different investigators working with different samples of participants. We are also more confident when results are replicated with diverse methods.

For these reasons, scientists now do frequent **meta-analyses,** which are studies that statistically combine the results from several prior studies (Roberts et al., 2007). In a meta-analysis, an investigator compiles all existing studies of a particular phenomenon and combines their results to identify the themes they contain. If the prior studies all produce basically the same result, the meta-analysis makes that plain; if there are discrepancies, the meta-analysis may reveal why.

With tools like this at its disposal, relationship science has made enormous strides despite its short history and the complexity of its subject matter. And despite my earlier cautions, most of the things I have to tell you in this text are dependable facts, reliable results you can see for yourself if you do what the researchers did. Even more impressively, most of them are facts that had not been discovered when your parents were born.

A FINAL NOTE

In my desire to help you be more discerning, I've spent most of this chapter noting various pros and cons of diverse procedures, usually concluding that no single option is the best one in all cases. I hoped to encourage you to be more thoughtful about the complexities of good research. But in closing, let me reassure you that relationship science is in better shape than all of these uncertainties may make it seem. When relationship science began, the typical study was a cross-sectional investigation that obtained self-reports from a convenience sample of college students (Cooper & Sheldon, 2002).[5] Many studies are still of that sort. However, researchers are now routinely studying more diverse samples with sophisticated designs that employ more complex measures, and the variety of methods with which researchers now study relationships is a *strength,* not a weakness (Ickes, 2000). Furthermore, the field's judicious ability to differentiate what it does and does not yet know is a mark of its honesty and its developing maturity and wisdom.

People like easy answers. They like their information cut-and-dried. Many people actually prefer simple nonsense—such as the idea that men come from Mars and women come from Venus—to the scientific truth, if the truth is harder to grasp. However, as a new consumer of the science of relationships, you have an obligation to prefer facts to gossip, even if you have to work a little harder to make sense of their complexities. Don't mistake scientific caution for a lack of quality. To the contrary, I want to leave you with the thought that it demonstrates scientific respectability to be forthright about the strengths and weaknesses of one's discipline. It's more often the frauds and imposters who claim they are always correct than the cautious scientists, who are really trying to get it right.

FOR YOUR CONSIDERATION

Chris and Jill had to participate in research studies if they wanted to pass the Introductory Psychology course they were taking together, so they signed up for a study of "Relationship Processes." They had been dating for 2 months,

---

[5] There are several terms in this sentence that you may not have known before you started this chapter—but you do now. Pat yourself on the back.

and the study was seeking "premarital romantic couples," and they liked the fact that they would be paid $5 if they both participated. So, they attended a session with a dozen other couples in which they were separated and seated on opposite sides of a large room. They read and signed a permission form that noted they could quit anytime they wanted and then started to work on a long questionnaire.

Some of the questions were provocative. They were asked how many different people they had sex with in the last year and how many people they wanted to have sex with in the next 5 years. Then, they were asked to answer the same questions again, this time as they believed the other would. Chris had never pondered such questions before, and he realized, once he thought about it, that he actually knew very little about Jill's sexual history and future intentions. That night, he was a little anxious, wondering and worrying about Jill's answers to those questions.

In your opinion, was this research procedure ethical? Would you like to complete a similar questionnaire? Why?

CHAPTER SUMMARY

The Short History of Relationship Science

The scientific study of relationships is a recent endeavor that has come of age only in the last 30 years. The field has now grown to include the longitudinal study of all types of relationships in their natural settings around the world.

Developing a Question

Research questions come from a number of sources, including personal experience, recognition of social problems, the results of prior research, and theoretical predictions. The questions themselves are usually of two types: They seek to describe events or to delineate causal connections among variables.

Obtaining Participants

Convenience samples are composed of participants who are easily available. *Representative samples* are more costly, but they better reflect the population of interest. Both types of samples can suffer from *volunteer bias*.

Choosing a Design

Correlational Designs. A *correlation* describes the strength and direction of an association between two variables. Correlations are inherently ambiguous because events can be related for a variety of reasons.

Experimental Designs. Experiments control and manipulate situations to delineate cause and effect. Experiments are very informative, but some events cannot be studied experimentally for practical or ethical reasons.

Developmental Designs. These designs study changes in behavior over time. *Cross-sectional designs* compare participants from different age groups or time periods. *Longitudinal* research follows the same group of participants across time; *participant attrition,* the loss of participants as time goes by, can be problematic. *Retrospective designs* rely on participants' recall of past events, but people's memories can be inaccurate.

Selecting a Setting

Research can be conducted in laboratories or in real-world settings such as a couple's home. These settings can promote more natural behavior, but control over extraneous variables is reduced. *Role-play* studies allow researchers to examine emotional events in an ethical manner but may not indicate what people really do in such situations.

The Nature of Our Data

Self-Reports. With self-reports, participants describe their own thoughts, feelings, and behavior, but they may misunderstand the researchers' questions, have faulty memories, and be subject to *self-serving* and *social desirability biases.*

Observations. In *experience-sampling,* brief observations are made intermittently. Observations avoid the problems of self-reports, but they are expensive to conduct, and participants' behavior may change when they know they are being observed.

Physiological Measures. Measurements of people's biological changes indicate how our physical states are associated with our social interactions.

Archival Materials. Historical records are nonreactive and allow researchers to compare the present with the past.

The Ethics of Such Endeavors

Participation in relationship research may change people's relationships by encouraging them to think carefully about the situations they face. As a result, researchers take pains to protect the welfare of their participants.

Interpreting and Integrating Results

Statistical analysis determines the likelihood that results could have occurred by chance. When this likelihood is very low, the results are said to be *significant.* Some such results may still be due to chance, however, so the thoughtful consumer does not put undue faith in any one study. *Meta-analysis* can lend confidence to conclusions by statistically combining results from several studies.

A Final Note

Scientific caution is appropriate, but it should not be mistaken for weakness or imprecision. Relationship science is in great shape.

CHAPTER 3

Attraction

The Fundamental Basis of Attraction ◆ Proximity: Liking Those Near Us ◆ Convenience: Proximity Is Rewarding, Distance Is Costly ◆ Familiarity: Repeated Contact ◆ The Power of Proximity ◆ Physical Attractiveness: Liking Those Who Are Lovely ◆ Our Bias for Beauty: "What Is Beautiful Is Good" ◆ Who's Pretty? ◆ An Evolutionary Perspective on Physical Attractiveness ◆ Culture Counts, Too ◆ Looks Matter ◆ The Interactive Costs and Benefits of Beauty ◆ Matching in Physical Attractiveness ◆ Reciprocity: Liking Those Who Like Us ◆ Similarity: Liking Those Who Are Like Us ◆ What Kind of Similarity? ◆ Do Opposites Attract? ◆ Why Is Similarity Attractive? ◆ Barriers: Liking Those We Cannot Have ◆ So, What Do Men and Women Want? ◆ For Your Consideration ◆ Chapter Summary

You're alone in a classroom, beginning to read this chapter, when the door opens and a stranger walks in. Is this someone who appeals to you? Might you have just encountered a potential friend or lover? Remarkably, you probably developed a tentative answer to those questions more quickly than you were able to read this sentence (Willis & Todorov, 2006). What's going on? Where did your judgment come from? This chapter considers these issues. Psychologically, the first big step toward a relationship is always the same: interpersonal *attraction*, the desire to approach someone. Feelings of attraction don't guarantee that a relationship will develop, but they do open the door to the possibility. I'll examine several major influences that shape our attraction to others, starting with a basic principle about how attraction works.

THE FUNDAMENTAL BASIS OF ATTRACTION

The most fundamental assumption about interpersonal attraction is that we are attracted to others whose presence is rewarding to us (Clore & Byrne, 1974). Two different types of **rewards** influence attraction: noticeable *direct* rewards we obviously receive from our interaction with others, and more subtle *indirect* benefits of which we're not always aware, that are merely associated with someone else. Direct rewards refer to all the evident pleasures people provide us. When they shower us with interest and approval, we're usually gratified by the attention and acceptance. When they are witty and beautiful, we enjoy their pleasing characteristics. And when they give us money or good advice, we are clearly better off. Most of the time, the more direct rewards that people provide us, the more attracted we are to them.

But attraction also results from a variety of subtle influences that are only indirectly related to the obvious kindness, good looks, or pleasing personalities of those we meet. For instance, most of us like ourselves, and anything about new acquaintances that connect them to us, however tangentially, may make them seem more likable. Consider a fellow named Dennis who is fond of his name; because of the shared first letter, "it might not be too far-fetched [for] Dennis to gravitate toward cities such as Denver, careers such as dentistry, and romantic partners such as Denise" (Pelham et al., 2005, p. 106). In fact, that's what happens: People are disproportionately likely to fall in love with someone who has a name that resembles their own (Jones et al., 2004). Rewards like these are indirect and mild, and we sometimes don't even consciously notice them—but they do illustrate just how diverse and varied the rewards that attract us to others can be.

We may also gain indirect benefits from particular partners when, without deliberately doing so, we pursue partners who make it more likely that our *children* will thrive and survive to have children of their own (Buss, 2012). As we'll see, we're often attracted to others who offer advantages that would be beneficial to our potential offspring, even when having children is the furthest thing from our minds.

Indeed, most of us simply think that we're attracted to someone if he or she is an appealing person, but it's really more complex than that. Attraction does involve the perceived characteristics of the person who appeals to us, but it also depends on our individual needs, preferences, and desires, and on the situation in which we find ourselves (Graziano & Bruce, 2008). Attraction is based on rewarding experiences with another person, but those pleasant experiences can come about in a variety of ways, and we're not necessarily always aware of all of the influences that shape our choices. So, let's begin our survey of influences on attraction with one that's usually more important than we think.

PROXIMITY: LIKING THOSE NEAR US

We might get to know someone online, but isn't interaction more rewarding when we can hear others' voices, see their smiles, and actually hold their hands? Most of the time, relationships are more rewarding when they involve people who are near one another (who are physically, as well as psychologically, close). Indeed, our physical **proximity** to others often determines whether or not we ever meet them in the first place. More often than not, our friendships and romances grow out of interactions with those who are nearby.

In fact, there is a clear connection between physical proximity and interpersonal attraction, and a few feet can make a big difference. Think about your Relationships classroom: Who have you gotten to know since the semester started? Who is a new friend? It's likely that the people you know and like best sit near you in class. When they are assigned seats in a classroom, college students are much more likely to become friends with those sitting near them than with those sitting across the room, even when the room is fairly small (Back et al., 2008a).

A similar phenomenon occurs in student housing complexes. In a classic study, Festinger, Schachter, and Back (1950) examined the friendships among students living in campus housing at the Massachusetts Institute of Technology. Residents were randomly assigned to rooms in 17 different buildings that were all like the one in Figure 3.1. People who lived close to each other were much more likely to become friends than they were with those whose rooms were further apart. Indeed, the chances that residents would become friends were closely related to the distances between their rooms (see Table 3.1). Remarkably, the same result was also obtained from one building to the next: People were more likely to know and like residents of other buildings that were close to their own. Obviously, even small distances have a much larger influence on our relationships than most people realize. Whenever we choose the exact place where we will live or work or go to school, we also take a major step toward determining who the significant others in our lives are likely to be.

Convenience: Proximity Is Rewarding, Distance Is Costly

Why does proximity have such influence? One answer is that when others are nearby, it's easy to enjoy whatever rewards they offer. Everything else being equal, a partner who is nearby has a big advantage over one who is far away: The expense and effort of interacting with a distant partner—such as pricey gas and hours on the road—make a distant relationship more costly overall than one that is closer to home (Baldinger, 2008). Distant relationships are less rewarding, too; an expression of love in a text message is less pleasant than an actual kiss on the cheek. Thus, long-distance romantic relationships are generally less satisfying than are romances with partners who are nearby (Sahlstein, 2006).

The only notable thing about this result is that anyone should find it surprising. However, lovers who have to endure a period of separation may blithely believe, because their relationship has been so rewarding up to that point, that some time apart will not adversely affect their romance. If so, they may be surprised by the difference distance makes. When a relationship that enjoys the convenience of proximity becomes inconvenient due to distance, it may suffer more than anyone suspected. Even those who are already married

FIGURE 3.1. **A student apartment building at MIT.**
In the study by Festinger et al. (1950), residents were randomly assigned to rooms in buildings like these.
Source: Myers, D,. 1993.

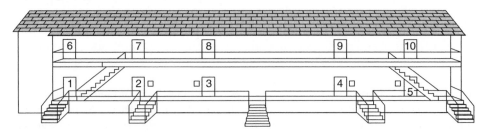

TABLE 3.1. Friendship Choices in Campus Housing at MIT

Two hundred seventy people living in buildings like that pictured in Figure 3.1 were asked to list their three closest companions. Among those living on the same floor of a given building, here's how often the residents named someone living:

1 door away	41% of the time
2 doors away	22%
3 doors away	16%
4 doors away	10%

Only 88 feet separated residents living four doors apart, at opposite ends of the same floor, but they were only one-quarter as likely to become friends as were people living in adjacent rooms. Similar patterns were obtained from one floor to the next, and from building to building in the housing complex, so it was clear that small distances played a large part in determining who would and who would not be friends.

are more likely to divorce when they have to spend time apart (Poortman, 2005). Absence does *not* seem to make the heart grow fonder.

Familiarity: Repeated Contact

Proximity also makes it more likely that two people will cross paths often and become more familiar with each other. Folk wisdom suggests that "familiarity breeds contempt," but research evidence disagrees. Instead of being irritating, repeated contact with—or **mere exposure** to—someone usually increases our liking for him or her (Zajonc, 2001). Even if we have never talked to them, we tend to like people whose faces we recognize more than those whose faces are unfamiliar to us.

Moreland and Beach (1992) provided an interesting example of the mere exposure effect when they had college women attend certain classes either 15 times, 10 times, or 5 times during a semester. These women never talked to anyone and simply sat there, but they were present in the room frequently, sometimes, or rarely. Then at the end of the semester, the real students were given pictures of the women and asked for their reactions. The results were very clear: The more familiar the women were, the more the students were attracted to them. And they were all liked better than women the students had never seen at all (See Figure 3.2.)

Thus, because proximity often leads to familiarity, and familiarity leads to liking, frequent contact with someone not only makes interaction more convenient, but also may make that person more attractive (Reis et al., 2011). As another example, it may not be surprising, then, that those of us who actually know gays and lesbians have more positive attitudes toward them than do those who don't (think that they) have any contact with gays or lesbians (Vonofakou et al., 2007).

The Power of Proximity

Of course, the power of proximity to increase attraction has limits. Constant exposure to anything—a favorite food or song, or perhaps even a lover—can be boring when saturation sets in (Bornstein, 1989). Familiarity enhances

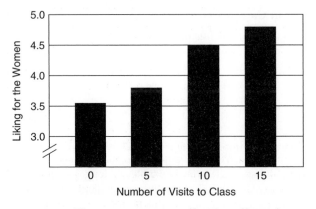

FIGURE 3.2. **The mere exposure effect in college classrooms.**
Even though they never interacted with anyone, other students liked the women more
the more often they visited a class.
Source: Data from Moreland & Beach, 1992.

attraction, but overexposure does not. And close proximity to obnoxious, disagreeable people does not necessarily get us to like them better (Ebbesen et al.,
1976). The best conclusion to make about proximity is that it accentuates our
feelings about others. We like most people better when they're nearby, but if
they annoy us, proximity may just make things worse.

Indeed, a study in a condominium complex in California (Ebbesen et al.,
1976) found that although most of the residents' friends lived nearby, most of
their enemies did, too! Only rarely did people report that they really disliked
someone who lived several buildings away from them. Instead, they despised
fellow residents who were close enough to annoy them often—by playing
music too loudly, letting pets run wild, and so on. Proximity can even ruin relationships that seemed to be working fine when the partners were apart. (See
the box on the next page). We tend to be attracted to those who are near us, but
if our contact with them is disappointing or unpleasant, we may like them *less*
than we would have had they kept their distance.

PHYSICAL ATTRACTIVENESS: LIKING THOSE WHO ARE LOVELY

After proximity brings people together, what's the first thing we're likely to
notice about those we meet? Their looks, of course. And, although we all know
that there is much more to people than their external appearance, looks count.
Physical attractiveness has a substantial influence on the first impressions that
people form of one another. In general, right or wrong, we tend to assume
that good-looking people are more likable, better people than those who are
unattractive (Brewer & Archer, 2007).

Long-Distance Dating and Mating

Back in chapter 1, I suggested that technology can affect relationships, and a superb example of that lies in the access to distant partners that we now take for granted online. It's now commonplace for romances to begin online. A dating website is the second-most-common way (after meeting through friends) that heterosexual couples get started, and it's the most frequent way gays and lesbians find partners. These days, one in every four (23 percent) heterosexual couples and most gay and lesbian couples (61 percent) meet online (Rosenfeld, 2010). It becomes easier all the time to find far-flung others who appear to have similar interests (DeAndrea et al., 2011).

I said "appear to have" because there's always a lot of *ambiguity* to deal with when people meet online. People put their best foot (and face) forward when they're writing personal profiles and posting pictures, so what you see on the Web is not necessarily what you get when you finally meet someone face-to-face (Hall et al., 2010). Indeed, on average, when people who have met online do get together in person for the first time, the knowledge they have about each other goes up, but their perceived similarity to, and their liking for, each other goes *down* (Norton et al., 2007). Evidently, when we find out who our online partners actually are—as opposed to who we *thought* they were—our attraction to them often declines (Ramirez & Zhang, 2007).

Something similar routinely occurs in long-distance relationships if the partners are reunited after some time apart. Technology makes it cheaper and easier than it used to be to maintain a relationship over long distances (McKenna, 2008), and long-distance romances are often fairly stable as long as "out of sight" doesn't become "out of mind" and the partners start dating others who are close at hand (Sahlstein, 2006). One reason that they last is because the partners tend to communicate carefully when they're apart; they steer clear of touchy topics and stick to good news about themselves (Stafford, 2010). As a result, they're likely to construct idealized images that portray each other as absolutely worth waiting for (Stafford & Merolla, 2007). But then, when they are finally reunited, those illusions are sometimes lost; neither partner is able to meet the other's lofty (and sometimes unrealistic) expectations, and disappointment ensues. There may be other unexpected nuisances, too; some autonomy and free time are lost when their lovers are in town, so unanticipated conflict may occur (Stafford et al., 2006). Altogether, although proximity makes most romantic relationships more rewarding, people who have maintained a long-distance romance may find a reunion to be surprisingly stressful: One-third of the long-distance dating partners who get back together break up within 3 months of their reunion (Stafford et al., 2006).

Our Bias for Beauty: "What Is Beautiful Is Good"

Imagine that you are given a photograph of a stranger's face and, using only that information, you're asked to guess at the personality and prospects the person possesses. Studies of judgments such as these routinely find that physically attractive people are presumed to be interesting, sociable people who are likely

TABLE 3.2. What Is Beautiful Is Good

Both male and female research participants judged that physically attractive people were more likely than unattractive people to have the following characteristics:

Kind	Interesting
Strong	Poised
Outgoing	Sociable
Nurturant	Exciting date
Sensitive	Good character
Sexually warm and responsive	

These same judges also believed that, compared to those who were unattractive, physically attractive people would have futures that involved:

More prestige	Happier marriages
More social and professional success	More fulfilling lives

Source: Dion et al., 1972.

to encounter personal and professional success in life and love (see Table 3.2). In general, we seem to use the crude stereotype that what is beautiful is good; we assume that attractive people have desirable traits that complement their desirable appearances (Lemay et al., 2010). And we seem to make these judgments automatically, without any conscious thought; a beautiful face triggers a positive evaluation the moment we see it (Cheng et al., 2003).

We don't expect good-looking strangers to be wonderful in every respect, however; the more attractive they are, the more promiscuous we think them to be (Brewer & Archer, 2007). (Is this just wishful thinking? It may be. One reason that we like to think that pretty people are outgoing and kind is because we're attracted to them, and we want them to like us in return [Lemay et al., 2010]. Hope springs eternal.) Still, there's no question that attractive people make better overall impressions on strangers than less attractive people do, and this tends to be true all over the world. In Korea, for example, pretty people are presumed to be sociable, intelligent, and socially skilled, just as they are in the United States. However, in keeping with Korea's collectivist culture (which emphasizes group harmony), attractive people are also presumed to be concerned with the well-being of others, a result that is not obtained in the West (Wheeler & Kim, 1997). What is beautiful is desirable around the world, but the specific advantages attributed to lovely people depend somewhat on the specific values of a culture.

The bias for beauty may also lead people to confuse beauty with talent. In the workplace, physically attractive people make more money and are promoted more often than are those with average looks. On average, compared to those who are moderately good-looking, attractive employees earn 5 percent more and unattractive folks earn 9 percent less (Salter, 2005). Your intelligence is likely to influence your future earnings more than your looks do, but your looks will probably still matter some no matter how smart you are (Judge et al., 2009). Indeed, on campus, attractive professors get better teaching evaluations from their students than unattractive instructors do (Hamermesh & Parker,

2005). The more attractive U.S. politicians are, the more competent they are judged to be (Olivola & Todorov, 2010). Attractive people even make better impressions in court; good-looking culprits convicted of misdemeanors in Texas get lower fines than they would have received had they been less attractive (Downs & Lyons, 1991).

But are the interactions and relationships of beautiful people really any different from those of people who are less pretty? I'll address that question shortly. First, though, we need to assess whether we all tend to agree on who is pretty and who is not.

Who's Pretty?

Consider this: On the first day of a college class, researchers invite you to join a circle that, including you, contains four men and four women. All of the others are strangers. Your task is to take a close look at each person and to rate (secretly!) his or her physical attractiveness while they all judge you in return. What would you expect? Would all four members of the other sex in your group agree about how attractive you are? Would you and the other three people of the same sex give each of the four others exactly the same rating? David Marcus and I did a study just like this to determine the extent to which beauty is in the "eye of the beholder" (Marcus & Miller, 2003). We did find some mild disagreement among the observers that presumably resulted from individual tastes. Judgments of beauty were somewhat idiosyncratic—but not much. The take-home story of our study was the overwhelming consensus among people about the physical beauty of the strangers they encountered. Our participants clearly shared the same notions of who is and who isn't pretty.

Moreover, this consensus exists across ethnic groups: Asians, Hispanics, and black and white Americans all tend to agree with each other about the attractiveness of women from all four groups (Cunningham et al., 1995). Even more striking is the finding that newborn infants exhibit preferences for faces like those that adults find attractive, too (Slater et al., 2000); when they are much too young to be affected by social norms, babies spend more time gazing at attractive than unattractive faces.

What faces are those? There's little doubt that women are more attractive if they have "baby-faced" features such as large eyes, a small nose, a small chin, and full lips (Jones, 1995). The point is not to look childish, however, but to appear feminine and youthful; beautiful women combine those baby-faced features with signs of maturity such as prominent cheekbones, narrow cheeks, and a broad smile (Cunningham et al., 2002). Women who present all these features are thought to be attractive all over the world (Jones, 1995).

Male attractiveness is more complex. Men who have strong jaws and broad foreheads—who look strong and dominant—are usually thought to be handsome (Rhodes, 2006). (Envision George Clooney.) On the other hand, when average male faces are made slightly more feminine and baby-faced through computer imaging, the "feminized" faces—which look warm and friendly—are attractive, too. (Envision Tobey Maguire.) Remarkably, which facial style is more attractive to women depends on their menstrual cycles; they find rugged, manly features more appealing when they are fertile, just before they ovulate, but they're more attracted to youthful boyishness the rest of the month (Little et al., 2002).

In any case, good-looking faces in both sexes have features that are neither too large nor too small. Indeed, they are quite average. If you use computer imaging software to create composite images that combine the features of individual faces, the *average* faces that result are more attractive than nearly all of the faces that make up the composite (Rubenstein et al., 2002). This is true not only in the United States but also in China, Nigeria, India, and Japan (Rhodes et al., 2002). (For a delightful set of examples from Germany, go to www.beautycheck.de.)

However, this doesn't mean that gorgeous people have bland, ordinary looks. The images that result from this averaging process are actually rather unusual. Their features are all proportional to one another; no nose is too big, and no eyes are too small, and there is nothing about such faces that is exaggerated, underdeveloped, or odd. Averaged faces are also *symmetrical* with the two sides of the face being mirror images of one another; the eyes are the same size, the cheeks are the same width, and so on. Facial symmetry is attractive in its own right, whether or not a face is "average" (Fink et al., 2006). In fact, if you take a close look at identical twins, whose faces are very similar, you'll probably think that the twin with the more symmetric face is the more attractive of the two (Mealey et al., 1999). Both symmetry and "averageness" make their own contribution to facial beauty; even in a group of symmetrical images, faces are more appealing the more average they become (Rhodes et al., 1999). Thus, beautiful faces combine the best features of individual faces in a balanced, well-proportioned whole.

Of course, some bodies are more attractive than others, too. Men find women's shapes most alluring when they are of normal weight, neither too

Which of these two faces is more appealing to you? They are composite images of the *same* face that have been altered to include feminine or masculine facial features, and if you're a woman, your answer may depend on the current phase of your menstrual cycle. Most women find the more masculine face on the right to be more attractive when they are fertile, but they consider the more feminine face on the left to be more appealing during the rest of the month. Picture A is a 50% feminized male composite; B is a 50% masculinized male composite.
Source: Little et al., 2002; Anthony Little (www.alittlelab.com)

A   B

heavy nor too slender, and their waists are noticeably narrower than their hips (Furnham et al., 2005). The most attractive **waist-to-hip ratio,** or WHR, is a curvy 0.7 in which the waist is 30 percent smaller than the hips (see Figure 3.3 on the next page); this "hourglass" shape appeals to men around the world (Singh et al., 2010).[1] This appears to be a fundamental preference; even men who have been blind from birth prefer a low WHR in women's bodies when they assess their shapes by touch (Karremans et al., 2010). In most cases, women who are overweight are judged to be less attractive than slender and normal women are, but thin women are *not* more attractive to men than women of normal weight (Swami et al., 2007). Men also like larger, as opposed to smaller, breasts, but their size is less important than their proportion to the rest of a woman's body; a curvy 0.75 waist-to-bust ratio is very appealing (Voracek & Fisher, 2006), and larger breasts don't enhance a woman's appeal if they are paired with a stocky body (Furnham et al., 2006). In addition, a woman's WHR has more influence on men's judgments of her attractiveness than her breast size does (Dixson et al., 2011).[2]

Once again, male attractiveness is more complex. Men's bodies are most attractive when their waists are only slightly narrower than their hips, with a WHR of 0.9. Broad shoulders and muscles are also attractive; men with higher

Look what happens when 2, 8, or 32 real faces are morphed together into composite images. When more faces are combined, the resulting image portrays a face that is not odd or idiosyncratic in any way and that has features and dimensions that are more and more typical of the human race. The result is a more attractive image. "Average" faces are attractive faces.
Source: Rubenstein et al., 2002.

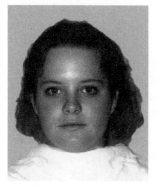

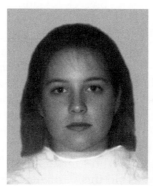

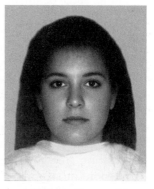

| a. 2-Face Composite | b. 8-Face Composite | c. 32-Face Composite |

[1]If you want to measure your own WHR, find the circumference of your waist at its narrowest point and divide that figure by the circumference of your hips at their broadest point, including your buttocks. Your butt is included in your "waist-to-hip" ratio.

[2]I can also report that when men get 5 seconds to inspect full-body frontal images of naked women, the first things they look at are the breasts and waist (Dixson et al., 2011). The face comes later. (But if you're a woman, you already know that.)

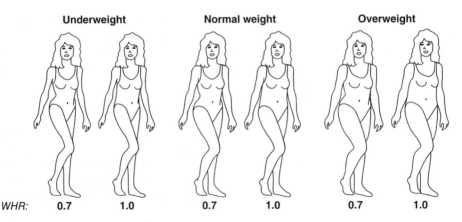

Underweight   Normal weight   Overweight

WHR: 0.7   1.0   0.7   1.0   0.7   1.0

FIGURE 3.3. **Waist-to-hip ratios.**
These six figures differ in two different ways. Two of them depict women who are thinner than normal, two depict women who are heavier than normal, and the middle two portray women of normal weight. In addition, three of the figures depict women whose waists have a circumference that is 70 percent that of their hips (so that their waist-to-hip ratios are 0.7), whereas the other three have waists that are the same circumference as their hips. When men rated these drawings, the figures with the smaller waist-to-hip ratios were always preferred to those who were less curvy, and the 0.7 figure of normal weight was liked best of all.
Source: Adapted from Singh, 1993.

shoulder-to-hip ratios (around 1.2) and bigger muscles have sex with more women and at earlier ages than do men who have narrower shoulders (Hughes & Gallup, 2003) or smaller muscles (Lassek & Gaulin, 2009)—and this, too, is true around the world (Frederick et al., 2011). However, a nice shape doesn't attract a woman to a man unless he has other resources as well; a man's WHR affects women's evaluations of him only when he earns a healthy salary (Singh, 1995). A man is not all that attractive to women if he is handsome but poor.

Judgments of physical attractiveness are evidently multifaceted, and several other characteristics also influence those perceptions. Both men and women tend to prefer heterosexual partnerships in which he is taller than she is (Salska et al., 2008), so tall men get more responses from women to their online profiles than short men do. A guy who's short—say, 5' 4"—can get as many responses on a dating website as a fellow who's much taller—say, 6' 1"—but only if he earns more money. A lot more. In this particular case, the shorter man would have to earn $221,000 more each year to be as interesting to women (Hitsch et al., 2010). Speaking of money, tall people also get more respect and higher incomes at work; independently of a person's age or sex, each inch of height amounts to $789 more in pay, on average, in the United States and Great Britain each year (Judge & Cable, 2004). Across various occupations, for instance, men who are 6' 1" earn $3,156 more each year than do men who are 5' 9".

A potential partner's smell matters more to women than to men (Herz & Inzlicht, 2002). Nevertheless, men prefer the natural scents of pretty women to those of women who are less attractive (Thornhill et al., 2003). In a typical study of this sort, people shower using unscented soap before they go to bed and then sleep in the same T-shirt for several nights. Then, research participants who have never met those people take a big whiff of those shirts and select the scents that are most appealing to them. Symmetrical, attractive people evidently smell better than asymmetrical, less attractive people do because strangers prefer the aromas of attractive people to the smells of those who are more plain (Thornhill et al., 2003). Remarkably, heterosexual men think women smell better when they're about to ovulate than at other times of the month (Gildersleeve et al., 2011), but they don't much like the smell of gay men, who have aromas that are more attractive to other gay guys than to straight men (Martins et al., 2005). I am not making this up, so there are evidently subtle influences at work here.

Women are also more attractive to men when they have longer rather than shorter hair (Knapp-Kline et al., 2005). In studies of this sort, men evaluate a woman whose hair—through the magic of computer imaging—varies in length from picture to picture. They're more interested in dating women who (appear to) have long hair, in part because they think that the women are less likely to be engaged or married and more willing to have sex on a first date (Boynton, 2008). Long hair doesn't work as well on a man's chest; women prefer men with smoother, less hairy chests to those who are more hirsute (Dixson et al., 2010).

Women also like smart guys (which should be good news for most of the men reading this book). In one intriguing study, researchers gave men intelligence tests and then filmed them throwing a Frisbee, reading news headlines aloud, and pondering the possibility of life on Mars. When women watched the videos, the smarter the men were, the more appealing they were (Prokosch et al., 2009). This may be one reason that, when they are trying to impress a woman, men use a more elaborate vocabulary—that is, bigger words—than they do in ordinary discourse (Rosenberg & Tunney, 2008).

Finally, both men and women are attracted to potential partners who are wearing something red. Research participants of both sexes found strangers of the other (but not the same) sex to be more attractive and sexually appealing when they were pictured in red rather than green or blue shirts—and men were more ready to take action by asking women for dates and spending a lot on them when the women were wearing red (Elliot et al., 2010; Elliott & Niesta, 2008). Valentines are red for a reason.

An Evolutionary Perspective on Physical Attractiveness

I've just mentioned a lot of details, so you may not have noticed, but people's preferences for prettiness generally fit the assumptions of evolutionary psychology. Consider these patterns:

- Cultures differ in several respects, but people all over the world still tend to agree on who is and who is not attractive (Cunningham et al., 1995; Jones, 1995). That's one reason that the winners of international beauty pageants usually seem gorgeous no matter where they're from.

- Babies are born with preferences for the same faces that adults find attractive (Slater et al., 2000). Some reactions to good looks may be inherited.
- Men with attractive faces have healthier, more mobile sperm than uglier men do (Soler et al., 2003). (They are also more successful, effective quarterbacks—they get higher passer ratings—in the National Football League [Williams et al., 2010].)
- People with symmetrical faces also tend to have symmetrical bodies and to enjoy better mental and physical health—and therefore make better mates—than do people with asymmetrical faces (Perilloux et al., 2010). Symmetric women have higher levels of estradiol (which probably makes them more fertile (Jasieńska et al., 2006), and symmetric people of both sexes are smarter (Luxen & Buunk, 2006) and get sick less often (Thornhill & Gangestad, 2006) than do those whose faces and bodies have odd proportions.
- Hormones influence waist-to-hip ratios by affecting the distribution of fat on people's bodies. With their particular mix of estradiol and progesterone, women with WHRs near the attractive norm of 0.7 get pregnant more easily and tend to enjoy better physical health than do women with fewer curves (Jasieńska et al., 2004). A man with an attractive WHR of 0.9 is likely to be in better health than another man with a plump belly (Payne, 2006). So, both sexes are most attracted to the physical shapes that signal the highest likelihood of good health in the other sex. Moreover, children born to women with low WHRs tend to have higher cognitive test scores than those whose mothers are stocky (Lassek & Gaulin, 2008).
- Younger women are more likely than older women to have long hair, and hair quality is correlated with physical health. So, the long hair that men prefer is associated with qualities that make a woman a good mate (Hinsz et al., 2001).

There is remarkable agreement from one culture to the next about who is, and who is not, attractive. People who are judged to be lovely in other countries will typically be attractive to us, as well.

- Ultimately, all things considered, attractive people in the United States reproduce more successfully—they have more children—than do those who are less attractive (Jokela, 2009).
- Everybody likes good looks, but physical attractiveness matters most to people who live in equatorial regions of the world where there are many parasites and pathogens that can endanger good health (Gangestad & Buss, 1993). In such areas, unblemished beauty may be an especially good sign that someone is in better health—and will make a better mate—than someone whose face is in some way imperfect (Fink et al., 2001).
- There are subtle but provocative changes in women's preferences that accompany their monthly menstrual cycles (Gangestad et al., 2010b). Women are only fertile for the few days that precede their ovulation each month (see Figure 3.4), and during that period, women find some characteristics in men to be more appealing than they seem during the rest of the month. When they are fertile, women prefer more masculine faces, deeper voices, the scents of more symmetrical men, and bolder, more arrogant, more charismatic behavior than they do when they are infertile (Thornhill & Gangestad, 2008). Thus, women are attracted to assertive, cocky men—that is, those who are "more likely to behave like cads than be good dads"

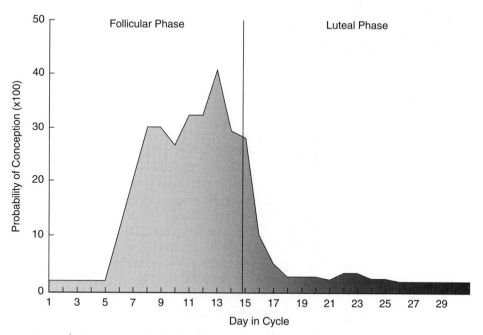

FIGURE 3.4. **Women's probability of conception during the menstrual cycle.**
Women are fertile during the few days just before they ovulate at the end of the follicular phase of their menstrual cycles. During that period, they prefer more masculine faces and bolder, more cocky behavior in men than they do during the rest of the month.
Source: From Jöchle, 1973. Total N = 1800.

(Perrett, 2010, p. 104)—when they are most likely to conceive a child, but they prefer warmer, kinder, less pushy men the rest of the month. These cyclic changes do not occur if women are not ovulating (because, for instance, they are using birth control pills) (Smith et al., 2009).

- Finally—and as you can see, this is getting to be quite a list—women make themselves more attractive to men when they are fertile each month. They wear red more often (Gonzales & Luévano, 2011) and dress more provocatively, wearing sexier clothes that show more skin (Schwarz & Hassebrauck, 2008). They're also more flirtatious (Haselton & Gangestad, 2006). They're more willing to accept an invitation to slow dance with a stranger (Guéguen, 2009), and they become more interested in casual sex (Gangestad et al., 2010a). In fact, women who perform lap dances in strip clubs make considerably more money when they're fertile than at other times of the month (Miller et al., 2007). All of this is not lost on men: When they smell T-shirts that have been worn by fertile women, their testosterone levels rise (Miller & Maner, 2010), and they start thinking sexy thoughts (Miller & Maner, 2011).[3]

These patterns convince some theorists that standards of physical beauty have an evolutionary basis (e.g., Buss, 2012). Presumably, early humans who successfully sought fertile, robust, and healthy mates were more likely to reproduce successfully than were those who simply mated at random. As a result, the common preference of modern men for symmetrical, baby-faced, low-WHR partners and of modern (fertile) women for symmetrical, masculine, and dynamic men may be evolved inclinations that are rooted more in their human natures than in their particular cultural heritage.

Culture Counts, Too

On the other hand, there's no doubt that standards of attractiveness are also affected by changing economic and cultural conditions. Have you seen those Renaissance paintings of women who look fat by modern standards? During hard times, when a culture's food supply is unreliable and people are hungry, slender women are actually *less* desirable than heavy women are (Nelson & Morrison, 2005). Around the world, only during times of plenty are slender women considered to be attractive (Swami et al., 2010). Indeed, as economic prosperity spread through the United States during the twentieth century, women were expected to be slimmer and slimmer so that *Playboy* Playmates and Miss America contestants are now skinnier, on average, than they were when you were born (Pettijohn & Jungeberg, 2004). In fact, the average Playmate is now so slender she meets the weight criterion for having an eating disorder (Owen & Laurel-Seller, 2000).

---

[3] Once again, and as always, I am not making any of this up. More importantly, aren't these findings remarkable? We recognize that animal behavior is regulated by estrous cycles. Similar such cycles are more subtle in humans, but they may exist nonetheless (Thornhill & Gangestad, 2008).

Norms can differ across ethnic groups as well (influenced in part, perhaps, by different patterns of economic well-being). Black and Latina women in the United States are more accepting of some extra weight than white women are, and indeed, black and Latino men like heavier women than white men do (Glasser et al., 2009). (But watch out: They still prefer the same curvaceous 0.7 WHR that is universally appealing to men [Singh & Luis, 1995]. In fact, even those Renaissance paintings depicted women with 0.7 WHRs.)

These findings suggest that human nature and environmental conditions work together to shape our collective judgments of who is and who isn't pretty. We're usually attracted to people who appear to be good mates, but what looks good depends somewhat on the conditions we inhabit. Still, beauty is not just in the eye of the beholder. There is remarkable agreement about who's gorgeous and who's ugly around the world.

Looks Matter

When a stranger walks into the room, you'll know with a glance how attractive he or she is (Willis & Todorov, 2006). Does that matter? Indeed, it does. Let's consider what happens when people on the prowl meet potential new mates. Researchers have examined the behavior of more than 10,000 customers of HurryDate, a dating service that stages speed-dating events in which participants have brief conversations with up to 25 different potential partners. (After each conversation, participants record a "yes" or a "no" with regard to their interest in seeing more of the person they've just met; if two people say "yes" about each other, HurryDate sends them the good news, and grants each of them access to the other's profile online. The two of them take it from there.)[4] People get a chance to quickly exchange any information they want. And what seems to drive their selections? For both sexes, it's outward appearance. "HurryDate participants are given 3 minutes in which to make their judgments, but they could mostly be made in 3 seconds" (Kurzban & Weeden, 2005, p. 240). Men are attracted to women who are slender, young, and physically attractive, and women are attracted to men who are tall, young, and physically attractive. Of all the things people could learn about each other in a few minutes of conversation, the one that matters most is physical attractiveness. This is a routine finding in speed-dating studies.

Another investigation assessed participants' Big 5 personality traits, attachment styles, political attitudes, and other values and interests and also found that the best predictor of interest in a new partner after a brief first meeting was the person's physical attractiveness. As you'd expect, friendly, outgoing people tended to be well liked, but nothing else about someone was as important after a brief meeting as his or her looks (Luo & Zhang, 2009).

Of course, speed-dating events can be a bit hectic—have you ever introduced yourself to 25 different potential partners in a busy hour and a half?—and

---

[4] This is not a recommendation for HurryDate, but you can see how the service advertises itself at www.hurrydate.com.

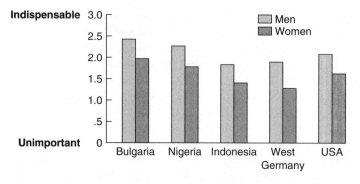

FIGURE 3.5. **Desire for physical attractiveness in a romantic partner.**
Around the world, according to their self-reports, men care about a partner's looks
more than women do.
Source: Data from Buss & Schmitt, 1993. Copyright © 1993 by the American Psychological Association.
Adapted with permission.

people may shop for partners more thoughtfully when they're able to take their
time (Lenton & Francesconi, 2010). In particular, when they ponder the question, men all over the world report higher interest in having a physically attractive romantic partner than women do (see Figure 3.5). On singles websites,
men are more likely than women to come right out and specify that they're
looking for an attractive mate (Iyengar, 2007), and men are more influenced
by looks than women are when they decide whom to contact (Hitsch et al.,
2010). Women know that men are judging them by their looks, which may be
why 91 percent of the cosmetic surgery performed in the United States in 2010
was done on women (American Society of Plastic Surgeons, 2011).

Nevertheless, women behave online just like men in being increasingly
likely to contact someone the more handsome he is (Hitsch et al., 2010). And,
despite the different emphasis men and women (say they) put on good looks,
there's no sex difference in how much physical attractiveness affects our liking
for someone we've actually just met (Eastwick & Finkel, 2008). When people
get together, looks matter. Physical attractiveness is the most potent influence
on how much the two sexes will initially like each other.

The Interactive Costs and Benefits of Beauty

So, what effects do our looks have on our interactions with others? As you
might expect, beautiful women get more dates than plain women do (Reis et al.,
1980). Moreover, people tend to enjoy their interactions with attractive women;
they talk more and are more involved, and they feel that the interactions are of
higher quality. They also give lovely waitresses better tips (Lynn, 2009). Handsome men fare well, too, receiving more smiles, talk, and positive feelings from
others than unattractive men do (Ickes, 2009).

However, men's attractiveness may play an even larger part in influencing
their access to the other sex than women's looks do (Reis et al., 1982). There is

actually no correlation overall between a woman's beauty and the amount of time she spends interacting with men. Attractive women do get more dates, but plain women spend plenty of time interacting with men in group settings where others are present. In contrast, men's looks *are* correlated with the number and length of the interactions they have with women. Unattractive men have fewer interactions of any sort with fewer women than good-looking guys do. In this sense, then, physical attractiveness has a bigger effect on the social lives of men than it does on women.

Being more popular, attractive people tend to be less lonely, more socially skilled, and a little happier than the rest of us (Feingold, 1992), and they're able to have sex with a wider variety of people if they want (Weeden & Sabini, 2007). Physical attractiveness may even account for as much as 10 percent of the variability in people's adjustment and well-being over their lifetimes (Burns & Farina, 1992). But being attractive has disadvantages, too. For one thing, others lie to pretty people more often. People are more willing to misrepresent their interests, personalities, and incomes to get a date with an attractive person than they are to fabricate an image for a plain partner (Rowatt et al., 1999). As a result, realizing that others are often "brown-nosing," or trying to ingratiate themselves, gorgeous people may cautiously begin mistrusting or discounting some of the praise they receive from others.

Consider this clever study: Attractive or unattractive people receive a written evaluation of their work from a person of the other sex who either does or does not know what they look like (Major et al., 1984). In every case, each participant receives a flattering, complimentary evaluation. (Indeed, everyone gets exactly the same praise.) How did the recipients react to this good news? Attractive men and women trusted the praise more and assumed that it was more sincere when it came from someone who *didn't* know they were good-looking. They were evidently used to getting insincere compliments from people who were impressed by their looks. On the other hand, unattractive people found the praise more compelling when the evaluator *did* know they were plain; sadly, they probably weren't used to compliments from people who were aware of their unappealing appearances.

So, gorgeous people are used to pleasant interactions with others, but they tend not to trust other people as much as less attractive people do (Reis et al., 1982). In particular, others' praise may be ambiguous. If you're very attractive, you may never be sure whether people are complimenting you because they respect your abilities or because they like your looks.

Finally, the effects that physical attractiveness will have on your social life may depend, in part, on whether you settle in a rural or urban environment. In densely populated areas in the United States, women with low WHRs are more closely connected to others and more satisfied with their lives than women with thicker waists are—but in lightly settled rural areas, there's no such pattern (Plaut et al., 2009). Physical attractiveness probably matters more when people have many different potential partners from whom to choose. Given the option, people prefer attractive partners to less lovely companions. There are places, however, where few options exist, and looks matter less (Anderson et al., 2008).

Attachment Styles and Speed-Dates

In general, when people ponder potential partners, they're more attracted to others with secure attachment styles than to those who are insecure. People with pre-occupied styles (who are anxious about abandonment) are preferred to those who are fearful or dismissing (who are avoidant of intimacy), but none of them are as attractive as those who are secure (Mikulincer & Shaver, 2007). Relaxed comfort in close relationships is evidently a desirable trait that we like in our partners no matter what our own styles may be.

What goes wrong when we meet people with insecure styles? Speed-dating research has studied this question, and it turns out that people who are anxious about abandonment make poorer impressions on others right from the start (McClure et al., 2010). They seem fretful, nervous, submissive, and withdrawn, and those they meet are unlikely to consider them desirable dates. The acute salience of potential rejection probably makes speed-dating situations especially daunting to those with anxious styles of attachment, and preoccupied people are not at their best in such situations.

What about those with avoidant styles? We're not yet sure; avoidant people don't come to speed-dating events (Schindler et al., 2010)!

Matching in Physical Attractiveness

I've spent several pages discussing physical attractiveness—which is an indication of its importance—but there is one last point to make about its influence at the beginning of a relationship. We all may want gorgeous partners, but we're likely to end up paired off with others who are only about as attractive as we are (Hitsch et al., 2010). Partners in established romantic relationships tend to have similar levels of physical attractiveness; that is, their looks are well matched, and this pattern is known as **matching.**

The more serious and committed a relationship becomes, the more obvious matching usually is. People sometimes share casual dates with others who are better-looking than they, but they are unlikely to go steady with, or become engaged to, someone who is "out of their league" (White, 1980b). What this means is that, even if everybody wants a physically attractive partner, only those who are also good-looking are likely to get them. None of the really good-looking people want to pair off with us folks of average looks, and we, in turn, don't want partners who are "beneath us," either (Lee et al., 2008).

Thus, it's not very romantic, but similarity in physical attractiveness may operate as a screening device. If people generally value good looks, matching will occur as they settle for the best-looking partner who will have them in return (Montoya, 2008). As a result, husbands and wives tend to be noticeably similar in physical attractiveness (Little et al., 2006). Down the road, physical attractiveness may not have as much impact on a marriage as it did when it brought the couple together (McNulty et al., 2008), but a close relationship may not get started if two people don't look a lot alike (Straaten et al., 2009).

RECIPROCITY: LIKING THOSE WHO LIKE US

The matching phenomenon suggests that, to enjoy the most success in the relationship marketplace, we should pursue partners who are likely to return our interest. In fact, most people do just that. When we ponder possible partners, most of us rate our realistic interest in others—and the likelihood that we will approach them and try to start a relationship—using a formula like this (Shanteau & Nagy, 1979):

$$\begin{array}{ccc}
\text{A Potential} & \text{His/Her} & \text{His/Her Probability} \\
\text{Partner's Desirability} = \text{Physical Attractiveness} \times \text{of Accepting You}
\end{array}$$

Everything else being equal, the better-looking people are, the more desirable they are. However, this formula suggests that his or her physical attractiveness is multiplied by our judgments of how likely it is that someone will like us in return to determine his or her overall appeal. Do the math. If someone likes us a lot but is rather ugly, that person probably won't be our first choice for a date. If someone else is gorgeous but doesn't like us back, we won't waste our time. The most appealing potential partner is often someone who is moderately attractive and who seems to offer a reasonably good chance of accepting us (perhaps *because* he or she isn't gorgeous).

Our expectations regarding the probability of others' acceptance have much to do with our **mate value,** or overall attractiveness as a reproductive partner. People with high mate values are highly sought by others, and as a result, they're able to insist on partners of high quality. And they do (Edlund & Sagarin, 2010). For instance, women who are very good-looking have very high standards in men; they don't just want a kind man who would be a good father, or a sexy man who has good economic prospects; they want *all* of those desirable characteristics in their partners (Buss & Shackelford, 2008). If their mate values are high enough, they might be able to attract such perfect partners—but if they're overestimating their desirability and overreaching, continual rejection will likely lead them to adjust their perceptions of their mate values and change the perceived probability of their acceptance by others (Greitemeyer, 2010).

Indeed, our histories of acceptance and rejection from others have taught us what to expect when we approach new potential partners (Kavanagh et al., 2010). Compared to the rest of us, people who are shy (Wenzel & Emerson, 2009) or who have low self-esteem (Cameron et al., 2010) nervously expect more rejection from others, and so they pursue less desirable partners. But most of us are reluctant to risk rejection when we are unsure that others will accept us. A clever demonstration of this point emerged from a study in which college men had to choose where to sit to watch a movie (Bernstein et al., 1983). They had two choices: squeeze into a small cubicle next to a very attractive woman, or sit in an adjacent cubicle—alone—where there was plenty of room. The key point is that some of the men believed that the *same* movie was playing on both monitors, whereas other men believed that *different* movies were showing on the two screens. Let's consider the guys' dilemma. Presumably, most of them wanted to become acquainted with the beautiful woman. However, when only one movie was available, squeezing in next to her entailed some risk of rejection; their intentions would be obvious, and there was some chance that the woman would tell them to "back off." However, when two different movies were available, they were on safer ground. Sitting next to the woman could mean that they just wanted to see that particular movie, not that they were attracted to her, and a rebuff from her would be rude. In fact, only 25 percent of the men dared to sit next to the woman when the same movie was on both monitors, but 75 percent did so when two movies were available and their intentions were more ambiguous. Moreover, we can be sure that the men were taking advantage of the uncertain situation to move in on the woman—instead of really wanting to see that particular movie—because the experimenters kept changing which movie played on which screen. Three-fourths of the men squeezed in with the gorgeous woman no matter which movie was playing there!

In general, then, people seem to take heed of the likelihood that they will be accepted and liked by others, and they are more likely to approach those who offer acceptance than rejection. The *best* acceptance, however, comes from potential partners who are selective and choosy and who don't offer acceptance to everyone. In speed-dating situations, for example, people who are eager to go out with everyone they meet are liked less by others—and make fewer matches—than those who are more discriminating; people who say "yes" to everybody get few "yesses" in return, whereas those who record interest in only a select few are more enticing to those they pick (Eastwick et al., 2007). These results jive nicely, by the way, with classic studies of what happens when people play "hard to get." Because people like to be liked, pretending to be aloof and only mildly interested in someone is a dumb way to try to attract him or her. Playing hard to get doesn't work. What does work is being *selectively* hard to get—that is, being a difficult catch for everyone *but* the person you're trying to attract (Walster et al., 1973). Those who can afford to say "no" to most people but who are happy to say "yes" to us are the most alluring potential partners of all.

Still, everything else being equal, it's hard *not* to like those who like us (Curtis & Miller, 1986). Imagine that the first thing you hear about a new transfer student is that he or she has noticed you and really likes you; don't you feel positively toward him or her in return?

This tendency to like those who like us is obviously consistent with the reward model of attraction. It also fits another perspective known as **balance theory** that suggests that people desire consistency among their thoughts, feelings, and social relationships (Heider, 1958). When two people like each other, their feelings fit together well and can be said to be "balanced." This is also true when two people dislike each other, but not when a person likes someone else but is disliked in return. What happens when there are three people involved? In one study that addressed this question, college students encountered an experimenter who was either pleasant or rude to them (Aronson

What's a Good Opening Line?

You're shopping for groceries, and you keep crossing paths with an attractive person you've seen somewhere on campus who smiles at you warmly when your eyes meet. You'd like to meet him or her. What should you say? You need to do more than just say, "Hi," and wait for a response, don't you? Perhaps some clever food-related witticism is the way to go: "Is your dad a baker? You've sure got a nice set of buns."

Common sense suggests that such attempts at humor are good opening lines. Indeed, various books invite you to use their funny pickup lines to increase your chances of getting a date (e.g., Dweck & Ivey, 1998). Be careful with such purchases, however; they may lead you astray. Careful research has compared the effectiveness of various types of opening lines, and a cute or flippant remark may be among the *worst* things to say.

Let's distinguish cute lines from "innocuous" openers (such as just saying, "Hi" or "How're you doing?") and "direct" lines that honestly communicate your interest (such as "Hi, I'm a little embarrassed about this, but I'd like to get to know you"). When women evaluate lines like these by watching videotapes of men who use them, they like the cute lines much less than the other two types (Kleinke & Dean, 1990). More importantly, when a guy actually uses one of these lines on a woman in a singles bar, the innocuous and direct openers get a favorable response 70 percent of the time compared to a success rate of only 24 percent for the cute lines (Cunningham, 1989). A line that is sexually forward (such as "I may not be Fred Flintstone, but I bet I can make your bed rock") usually does even worse (Cooper et al., 2007). There's no comparison: Simply saying hello is a much smarter strategy than trying to be cute or forward.

Why, then, do people write books full of flippant pickup lines? Because they're men. When a *woman* uses a cute line on a *man* in a singles bar, it usually works—but that's because any opening line from a woman works well with a man; in Cunningham's (1989) study, saying "Hi" succeeded every time. Men like women to make the first move (Enke, 2011), and they don't seem to care what opening lines women use—and this may lead them to overestimate women's liking for cute openers in return.

& Cope, 1968). After that, the experimenter's supervisor walked in and was either pleasant or rude to the experimenter! The students then had an opportunity to do a favor for the supervisor. How did they react? The students were more generous toward the supervisor when he or she had been either nice to the pleasant experimenter or mean to the unpleasant experimenter—that is, when the two interactions seemed balanced. This study and the rest of the research evidence generally support the notion that we prefer balance among our relationships. For that reason, then, we tend to like someone when we learn that he or she shares our dislike for someone else (Bosson et al., 2006); before we ever meet them, we often expect that our enemies' enemies will be our friends.

SIMILARITY: LIKING THOSE WHO ARE LIKE US

It's rewarding to meet people who like us. It's also enjoyable to find others who are *just* like us and who share the same background, interests, and tastes. Indeed, one of the most basic principles of interpersonal attraction is the rule of similarity: Like attracts like. The old cliché that "birds of a feather flock together" is absolutely correct (Fehr, 2008). Consider these examples:

- At the University of Michigan, previously unacquainted men were given free rooms in a boardinghouse in exchange for their participation in a study of developing friendships (Newcomb, 1961). At the end of the semester, the men's closest friendships were with those housemates with whom they had the most in common.
- At Purdue University, researchers intentionally created blind dates between men and women who held either similar social and political attitudes or dissimilar views (Byrne et al., 1970). Each couple spent 45 minutes at the student union getting to know each other over soft drinks. After the "dates," similar couples liked each other more than dissimilar couples did.
- At Kansas State University, 13 men spent 10 days jammed together in a simulated fallout shelter, and their feelings about each other were assessed along the way (Griffit & Veitch, 1974). The men got along fine with those with whom they had a lot in common, but would have thrown out of the shelter, if they could, those who were the least similar to themselves.

As these examples suggest, similarity is attractive.

What Kind of Similarity?

But what kinds of similarities are we talking about? Well, almost any kind. Whether they are lovers or friends, happy relationship partners resemble each other more than random strangers do on almost any measure. First, there's *demographic* similarity in age, sex, race, education, religion, and social class (Hitsch et al., 2010). Most of your best friends in high school were probably of the same age, sex, and race. People are even more likely than you'd expect to marry someone whose last name begins with the same last letter as their own (Jones et al., 2004)!

Then there's similarity in *attitudes and values*. There is a straightforward link between the proportion of the attitudes two people share and their attraction to each other (see Figure 3.6): the more agreement, the more liking (Byrne & Nelson, 1965). Take note of this pattern. Attraction doesn't level off after a certain amount of similarity is reached, and there's no danger in having "too much in common." Instead, where attitudes are concerned, the more similar two people are, the more they like each other. For whom did you vote in the last election? It's likely you and your best friend cast similar ballots. Even your casual "friends" on Facebook tend to share your tastes in books, movies, and music (Lewis et al., 2008).

Finally, partners may have similar *personalities*. People with similar styles and traits usually get along well when they encounter each other; for instance, the first meetings of two gregarious people or two shy people are typically

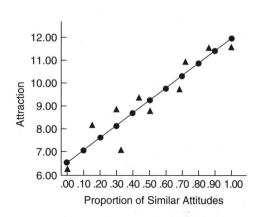

FIGURE 3.6. **The relationship between attitude similarity and attraction.**
The more two people agree with each other, the more they like each other.
Source: Adapted from Byrne & Nelson, 1965.

Attraction is strongly influenced by similarity. People who are similar in background characteristics, personality, physical attractiveness, and attitudes are more likely to be attracted to each other than are those who are dissimilar.

more enjoyable than the first conversation of a gregarious person and a shy person is (Cuperman & Ickes, 2009). Then, as time goes by, people with similar personalities—in one study, more than 800 U.S. Air Force recruits who got to know dozens of others well during basic training (Tenney et al., 2009)—like each other more than dissimilar people do. Ultimately, if they decide to marry, spouses with similar personalities have happier marriages than do those with different styles (Gaunt, 2006).

Do Opposites Attract?

The more similar two people are to one another, the more they like each other. Why, then, do many people believe that "opposites attract"? Are there instances in which people become more attracted to each other the less they have in common? In general, the answer is "no". There are some nuances at work, but people are not routinely more content with dissimilar, rather than similar, partners. However, there *are* several important subtleties in the way similarity operates that may mislead people into thinking that opposites do sometimes attract.

Matching Is a Broad Process

We've already seen that people tend to pair off with others who are similar to them in physical attractiveness. On the other hand, notable mismatches in looks sometimes occur; one famous example occurred back in 1994, when Anna

Nicole Smith, a 26-year-old *Playboy* Playmate of the Year, married J. Howard Marshall II, an 89-year-old billionaire. In such cases, the partners are clearly dissimilar in many ways, and "opposites" may seem to attract. That's a rather unsophisticated view, however, because such partners are really just matching in a broader sense, trading looks for money and vice versa. They may have different assets, but such partners are still seeking good matches with others who have similar standing overall in the interpersonal marketplace. People usually end up with others of similar mate value (Brase & Guy, 2004), but the specific rewards they offer each other may be quite different.

This sort of thing goes on all the time. A study of 6,485 users of an online dating service found that very homely—okay, ugly—men (those in the bottom 10 percent of attractiveness among men) needed $186,000 more in annual income in order to attract as much attention from women as fine-looking fellows (that is, those in the top 10 percent); nevertheless, if they did make that much more money, ugly guys received just as many inquiries as handsome men did (Hitsch et al., 2010).

Indeed, it's not very romantic, but fame, wealth, health, talent, and looks all appear to be commodities that people use to attract more desirable partners than they might otherwise entice. If we think of matching as a broad process that involves both physical attractiveness and various other assets and traits, it's evident that people usually pair off with others of similar status, and like attracts like.

In fact, trade-offs like these are central ideas in evolutionary psychology. Because men are more likely to reproduce successfully when they mate with healthy, fertile women, sexual selection has presumably promoted men's interest in youthful and beautiful partners (Buss, 2012). Youth is important because women are no longer fertile after they reach menopause in middle age. Beauty is meaningful because, as we've already seen, it is roughly correlated with some aspects of good health (Thornhill & Gangestad, 2006). Thus, men especially value good looks in women (see Figure 3.5), and, as they age, around the world, they seek wives who are increasingly younger than they are (Dunn et al., 2010): Men who marry in their twenties pair off with women who are two years younger than they are, on average, but if a man marries in his fifties, he's likely to seek a wife 15 years younger than he.

Women don't need to be as concerned about their partners' youth because men normally retain their capacity for reproduction as long as they live. Instead, given their vastly greater parental investment in their offspring,[5] women should seek mates who can shelter and protect them during the long period of pregnancy and nursing; they should prefer powerful, high-status men with resources who can provide for the well-being of mother and child. In fact, as Figure 3.7 illustrates, women *do* care more about their partners' financial prospects than men do (Gustavsson et al., 2008), and men who flash their cash attract more sexual partners than stingy men do (Kruger, 2008). Furthermore, women's preferences for the age of their mates do not change as they

---

[5] If a reminder regarding *parental investment* will be welcome, look back at p. 33.

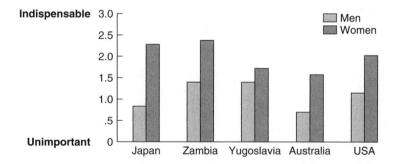

FIGURE 3.7. **Desire for good financial prospects in a romantic partner.**
Around the world, women care more about a partner's financial prospects than men do.
Source: Data from Buss & Schmitt, 1993. Copyright © 1993 by the American Psychological Association. Adapted with permission.

age; women prefer to marry men who are a few years older throughout their entire lives (Dunn et al., 2010).

Thus, matching based on the exchange of feminine youth and beauty for masculine status and resources is commonplace (Mathes & Kozak, 2008). Still, is it the result of evolutionary pressures? Advocates of a cultural perspective argue that women pursue desirable resources through their partners because they are so often denied direct access to political and economic power on their own (Wood & Eagly, 2007). Indeed, in the United States—a culture in which smart women have access to career opportunities of their own—the more intelligent a woman is, the lower her desire is for wealth and status in a romantic partner (Stanik & Ellsworth, 2010).

So, the origins of the feminine-beauty-for-masculine-money trade-off remain uncertain. But in any case, the bottom line here is that matching is a broad process that involves multiple resources and traits. When "opposites" seem to attract, people may be trading one asset for another in order to obtain partners of similar social status, and it's their similar mate values, not any apparent "opposites," that make them attractive to each other.

Discovering Dissimilarities Can Take Time

Another source of confusion lies in the fact that it takes a while for two people to get to know each other well enough to understand fully what they do and do not have in common. After 3 quick minutes of interaction during a speed-dating event, the actual similarities that two people share do not influence how much they like each other (Luo & Zhang, 2009); as we've seen, immediate attraction depends more on looks than anything else. However, the better looking others are, the more likely we are to expect (or is it hope?) that they have attitudes and values that are similar to ours (Morry, 2007). We tend to think that we have a lot in common with a pretty person—but we're often mistaken, and correcting such misperceptions can take time. If they begin dating, a couple's shared interests, attitudes, and values will become

---

Interethnic Relationships

Most of our intimate relationships are likely to be with others of the same race. Nevertheless, marriages between spouses from different ethnic groups are far more common than they used to be. About 13 percent of the married couples in the United States are of mixed race or ethnicity (Burton et al., 2010), and those couples raise an interesting question: If similarity attracts, what's going on? The answer is actually straightforward: Nothing special. If you ignore the fact of their dissimilar ethnicity, interethnic couples appear to be influenced by the same motives that guide everyone else. The partners tend to be similar in age, education, and attractiveness, and their relationships, like most, are based on common interests and personal compatibility (Shibazaki & Brennan, 1998). A few things distinguish people who date partners from other cultural groups: Compared to their peers, they've had closer contact with other ethnicities (King & Bratton, 2007), and, if they're white, they tend not to be conservative politically (Eastwick et al., 2009). In general, however, interethnic partners are just as satisfied as other couples (Troy et al., 2006) and they have the same chances for marital success as their peers (Zhang & Van Hook, 2009). Their relationships operate the same way: Two people who are more alike than different decide to stay together because they're happy and they fall in love.

---

influential (Luo, 2009), but it often takes a while for the partners to figure that out.

This process was evident in Newcomb's (1961) study of developing friendships among men sharing a boardinghouse. Soon after they met, the men liked best the housemates who they thought were most like them; thus, at first, their friendships were influenced mostly by **perceived similarity.** As the semester progressed, however, the actual similarities the men shared with each other played a larger and larger role in their friendships. When they got to know each other better, the men clearly preferred those who really were similar to them, although this was not always the case at first.

Even when we feel we know our partners well, there may be surprises ahead. According to Bernard Murstein's (1987) **stimulus-value-role** theory, we gain three different broad types of information about a new partner that influence developing relationships. When partners first meet, their attraction to each other is primarily based on "stimulus" information involving obvious attributes such as age, sex, and, of course, looks. Thereafter, during the "value" stage, attraction depends on similarity in attitudes and beliefs as people learn whether they like the same kinds of pizzas, movies, and vacations (see Figure 3.8). Only later does "role" compatibility become important as partners finally find out if they agree on the basics of parenting, careers, and housecleaning, among other life tasks. The point is that partners can be perfectly content with each other's tastes in politics and entertainment without ever realizing that they disagree fundamentally about where they'd like to live and how many kids—if any!—they want to have. Important dissimilarities sometimes

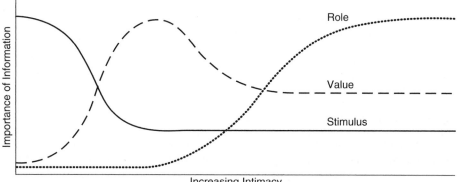

FIGURE 3.8. **Three different phases of relationship development.**
Murstein's (1987) *stimulus-value-role* theory suggests that developing relationships are influenced by three different types of information as time goes by and the partners learn more about each other.
Source: Data from Murstein, 1987.

become apparent only after couples have married; such spouses may stay together despite their differences, but it's not because opposites attract.

The influence of time and experience is also apparent in **fatal attractions** (Felmlee, 2001). These occur when a quality that initially attracts one person to another gradually becomes one of the most obnoxious, irritating things about that partner. For instance, partners who initially seem spontaneous and fun may later seem irresponsible and foolish, and those who appear strong may later seem domineering. Those who initially welcome a partner's high level of attention and devotion may come to resent such behavior when it later seems too possessive. In such cases, the annoying trait is no secret, but people fail to appreciate how their judgments of it will change with time. Importantly, such fatal qualities are often different from one's own; they may seem admirable and desirable at first—so that a spendthrift who's always broke may initially admire a tightwad who counts every penny—but over time people realize that such opposites aren't attractive (Rick et al., 2011).

Perceived versus Real Similarity: Misperception Lingers

A third subtlety lies in the fact that we rarely get to know our partners as well as we think we do. Even after years of friendship—or marriage!—partners usually think they have more in common with each other than they really do (Goel et al., 2010). They overestimate the similarities they share. What makes this provocative is that there is a higher correlation between *perceived* similarity and relationship satisfaction than there is between *real* similarity and relational bliss (Selfhout et al., 2009). To some degree, even when they're married, people maintain illusory images of their partners that portray them as similar soulmates—they're in love with the people they *think* their partners are (Montoya & Horton, 2004)—and they might be disappointed to learn the true extent of their disagreements about various issues.

This tendency to form pleasant images of our partners can help maintain relationships, as we'll see in chapter 4. On the other hand, to the extent that it involves any misperception, the tendency can also help explain why opposites sometimes seem to attract. If they try hard enough, people may perceive similarity where it does not exist and be attracted to others who are actually quite different from them. Perceived similarity can bring people together, at least for a while, even when their dissimilarity is apparent to everyone else.

You May Be the Person I Want to Become

People also admire those who possess skills and talents they wish they had. Another nuance in the operation of similarity lies in our attraction to others who are the sorts of people we want to become. We tend to like those who are similar to our *ideal selves,* that is, who exhibit desirable qualities that we want to, but may not yet, possess. This tendency is complex because it's threatening and unpleasant when people surpass our ideals and make us look bad by comparison (Herbst et al., 2003). However, as long as others are only a little better than us—so that they offer us implicit encouragement instead of humiliation—we may be attracted to those who are actually a little different from us (for now) (Klohnen & Luo, 2003). Let's not overstate this subtlety. The most appealing partners of all may be those who are similar to us in most dimensions but who fit our attainable ideals in others (Figueredo et al., 2006). Such people are hardly our "opposites." But as long as the differences are not too great, we may prefer a partner who is someone we'd like to become to one who more closely resembles who we really are now.

Dissimilarity May Decrease over Time

Moreover, relationships can change people (Ruvolo & Ruvolo, 2000). As time goes by, the members of a couple often come to share more similar attitudes (Gonzaga et al., 2010). Some of this decrease in dissimilarity probably occurs automatically as a couple shares compelling experiences, but some of it also occurs as the partners consciously seek compatibility and contentment (Becker & Lois, 2010). Thus, opposites don't attract, but some opposites may gradually fade if a couple stays together for some other reason. And over time, newfound similarity may help keep partners together even when they didn't start off having much in common.

Some Types of Similarity Are More Important than Others

A further nuance is that some similarities may be quite influential whereas other similarities—or opposites—may be rather innocuous. In particular, it's especially rewarding to have someone agree with us on issues that are very important to us. Religion is often one such issue; shared beliefs are quite satisfying to a couple when they are highly religious, but they have little effect— and even disagreement is immaterial—when neither of the partners actively observes a faith (Lutz-Zois et al., 2006). Thus, opposites don't attract, but they also may not matter if no one attaches much importance to them.

Housework and gender roles appear to be among the similarities that *do* routinely matter. Cohabiting couples who disagree with each other about the division of household labor are more likely to break up than are those who share similar views (Hohmann-Marriott, 2006), and spouses who share such work are more satisfied than those who divide it unequally (Amato et al., 2007). And husbands and wives who are more similar in their gender roles—not less, as a traditional outlook would lead us to expect—are more happily married than those who differ from one another in their styles and skills (Gaunt, 2006). In particular, compared to spouses who are more alike, macho husbands and feminine wives (who clearly have different gender roles) feel less understood, share less companionship, and experience less love and contentment in their marriages as time goes by (Helms et al., 2006).

On the other hand, satisfied partners often have personalities that differ from one another to some extent.[6] Obvious similarity in attitudes and values may be more important than similarity in personality (Watson et al., 2004), a point that brings us to our last subtlety regarding similarity and its effects.

One Way "Opposites" May Attract: Complementarity

Finally, there are times when different types of behavior can fit together well. We like responses from others that help us reach our goals. When two partners have different skills, each is usually happy to allow the other to take the lead on those tasks at which the other is more talented (Beach et al., 2001). Such behavior is said to *complement* our own, and **complementarity**— reactions that provide a good fit to our own—can be attractive. Most complementary behaviors are actually similar actions; people who are warm and agreeable, for instance, are happiest when they are met with warmth and good humor in return. However, one reliable form of complementarity involves different behaviors from two partners: dominance and submission (Markey et al., 2010). When people feel very sure of themselves, they want their partners to heed their advice; on other occasions, when people need help and advice, they want their partners to give it (Markey et al., 2003). In this manner, "opposites" may occasionally attract.

Effective, desirable complementarity can take time to develop. A couple of weeks after they move in together, for instance, there's no sign of any complementarity in the interactions of new college roommates; they're still establishing their routine, and they have not yet developed patterns of behavior that fit the other's style. After 15 weeks, however, complementarity is evident: People with cold, aloof roommates are keeping their distance, too; those with warm, agreeable roommates are being friendly and amiable in return; and those with submissive roommates are taking charge of things and calling the shots (Markey & Kurtz, 2006). A similar pattern emerges in contented romances; the partners who report the most love and the least conflict are those who are similar in warmth but dissimilar in dominance (Markey & Markey, 2007). When one partner really wants to take the lead, he or she is happiest when the other is willing to follow.

---

[6] This statement better describes couples in the United States, a country that celebrates individualism, than those in China. Unlike their U.S. counterparts, husbands and wives in China typically have quite similar personalities (Chen et al., 2009). Which pattern do you think is more advantageous?

I shouldn't overstate this case. People like others with similar personalities more than they like those who are different, and even dominant people like other assertive folks more than they like those who are chronically servile and submissive (Markey & Markey, 2007). On the other hand, when you really want something, it's nice when your partner lets you have your way. (And if you're both generous, understanding, and self-confident enough, you can take turns rewarding each other in this fashion.) The bottom line appears to be that we like partners who entertain and support us but we don't like partners who frustrate or impede us, and the blend of similarities and differences that form an optimal mix may vary from couple to couple (Baxter & West, 2003). Moreover, personal growth and novel activities are both rewarding, so we like people with interests that are different from (although not incompatible with) our own when we're confident that we'll get along well (Aron et al., 2006). The important thing to remember is that similar partners probably supply us what we want more often than anyone else can.

Why Is Similarity Attractive?

It's usually reassuring and rewarding to meet others who are just like us. Encountering similarity in others can be comforting, reminding us that we're okay the way we are. We also tend to approve of those who are similar to us; they agree with us, after all, so they usually impress us with their fine judgment and good sense (Montoya & Horton, 2004). But perhaps most importantly, when we have a lot in common, we expect to get along well with others; we expect them to like us, and that makes them likable (Singh et al., 2007). As we've seen, there are several reasons why opposites may seem to attract, but in fact birds of a feather do flock together. Similarity is rewarding; opposition is not.

BARRIERS: LIKING THOSE WE CANNOT HAVE

A final influence on attraction involves the common tendency for people to struggle to overcome barriers that keep them from what they want. The theory of psychological **reactance** states that when people lose their freedom of action or choice, they strive to regain that freedom (Brehm & Brehm, 1981). As a result, we may want something more if we are threatened with losing it.

This principle can apparently affect our feelings about our partners in relationships. Among unmarried adolescents, researchers sometimes observe an interesting pattern called the **Romeo and Juliet effect:** The more their parents interfere with their romances, the more love the teens feel for their partners (Driscoll et al., 1972). This pattern doesn't occur all the time (Leslie et al., 1986), but it does suggest that parents should think twice before they forbid their teenagers to see certain partners. If they create a state of reactance, the parents may unintentionally make the forbidden partners seem more attractive. The best course of action in such cases may be for the parents to express their displeasure mildly and not meddle further.

Another kind of barrier occurs every night when bars close and everybody has to go home. If you're looking for a date, you may find that the potential partners in a bar seem more and more attractive as closing time approaches and you face the prospect of leaving alone. In fact, when time is running out, unattached bar patrons consider the available members of the other sex to be better-looking than they seemed to be earlier in the evening (Pennebaker et al., 1979). This phenomenon doesn't involve "beer goggles," or intoxication; it occurs even if people haven't been drinking (Gladue & Delaney, 1990). However, it occurs only among those who are seeking company they don't yet have; those who are already committed to close relationships don't exhibit this pattern (Madey et al., 1996). Thus, the "closing-time effect" appears to be another case of desired-but-forbidden fruit seeming especially sweet.

SO, WHAT DO MEN AND WOMEN WANT?

We are nearly at the end of our survey of major influences on attraction, but one important point remains. As we've seen, men and women differ in the value they place on a partner's physical attractiveness and income. I don't want those results to leave you with the wrong impression, however, because despite those differences, men and women generally seek the same qualities in their relational partners (Li et al., 2011). Let's look more closely at what men and women want.

Around the world, there are three themes in the criteria with which people evaluate potential mates (Tran et al., 2008). If we had our way, almost all of us would have partners who offered

- *warmth and loyalty*, being trustworthy, kind, supportive, and understanding;
- *attractiveness and vitality*, being good-looking, sexy, and outgoing; and
- *status and resources*, being financially secure and living well.

All of these characteristics are desirable, but they're not of equal importance, and their prominence depends on whether we're seeking a relatively casual, short-term fling or a more committed long-term romance.

Both men and women are less picky when they're evaluating partners for short-term liaisons than for lasting unions (Fletcher et al., 2004). For instance, both sexes will accept lower intelligence, warmth, and earning potential in a lover with whom they have a casual fling than they would require in a spouse (Buunk et al., 2002). In particular, when they are contemplating short-term affairs, women will accept men who aren't especially kind, dependable, or understanding as long as their lovers are muscular, sexy, and "hot" (Frederick & Haselton, 2007). Even a few facial scars that would not make a husband more attractive can add to a lover's allure (Burriss et al., 2009).

But women clearly recognize that attractive, dominant, masculine men who might make compelling lovers often make unreliable long-term mates (Boothroyd et al., 2007). When they are picking husbands, women consider a man's good character to be more important than his good looks. They attach more importance to the criteria of warmth and loyalty and status and resources than to the criterion of attractiveness and vitality when they are thinking long term (Fletcher et al., 2004). Prestige and accomplishments become more important than dominance and daring (Kruger & Fitzgerald, 2011). When she can't have it all, the average woman prefers a man who is kind, understanding, and well to do—but not particularly handsome—to a good-looking but poor one, or a rich and good-looking but cold and disloyal one (Li, 2008).

Men have different priorities. Like women, they value warmth and loyalty, but unlike women, they attach more importance to attractiveness and vitality in a long-term partner than to status and resources (Fletcher et al., 2004). The average guy prefers a kind, beautiful woman without any money to wealthy women who are gorgeous grouches or women who are sweet but ugly (Li, 2008).

Of course, we typically have to accept some trade-offs like these when we're seeking intimate partners. Fulfilling all of our diverse desires by finding (and winning!) the perfect mate is hard to do. If we insist that our partners be kind and understanding *and* gorgeous *and* rich, we're likely to stay frustrated for a long time. So, when they're evaluating potential mates, men typically check first to make sure that a woman has at least average looks, and then they seek as much warmth, kindness, honesty, openness, stability, humor, and intelligence as they can get (Li et al., 2002). Great beauty is desirable to men, but it's not as important as high levels of warmth and loyalty are (with status and resources coming in a distant third). Women usually check first to make sure that a man has at least some money or prospects, and then they, too, seek as much warmth, kindness, honesty, openness, stability, humor, and intelligence as they can get (Li et al., 2002). Wealth is desirable to women, but it's not as important as high levels of warmth and loyalty, and looks are in third place.

Gays and lesbians behave similarly, wanting the same things that heterosexual men and women do (Felmlee et al., 2010). And although most of the research results described in this chapter were obtained in the United States, people all over the world concur; a global sample of 218,000 Internet users ranked intelligence, humor, kindness, and dependability as the top four traits they sought in a relationship partner (Lippa, 2007), and studies in Brazil (Castro & Lopes, 2010), Russia (Pearce et al., 2010), and Singapore (Li et al., 2011) all yielded similar results.

So, add all this up, and attraction isn't so mysterious after all. Men attend to looks and women attend to resources, but everybody seems to want partners who are amiable, agreeable, loving, and kind, and men and women do not differ in this regard. As long as she's moderately pretty and he has some money, both sexes want as much warmth and loyalty as they can get. To the extent there is any surprise here, it's in the news that women don't simply want strong, dominant men; they want their fellows to be warm and kind and capable of commitment, too (Jensen-Campbell et al., 1995). If you're an unemotional, stoic macho male, take note: Women will be more impressed if you develop some affectionate warmth to go with your strength and power.

FOR YOUR CONSIDERATION

Rasheed introduced himself to Rebecca because she was really hot, and he was mildly disappointed when she turned out to be a little suspicious, self-centered, and vain. On the other hand, she was really hot, so he asked her out anyway. Because she was impressed with his designer clothes and bold style, Rebecca was intrigued by Rasheed, but after a few minutes she thought him a little pushy and arrogant. Still, he had tickets to an expensive concert, so she accepted his invitation to go out on a date.

In your opinion, what does the date—and the future—hold for Rebecca and Rasheed? Why?

CHAPTER SUMMARY

The Fundamental Basis of Attraction

We are attracted to people whose presence is rewarding to us.

Proximity: Liking Those Near Us

We select our friends, and our enemies, from those around us.

Convenience: Proximity Is Rewarding, Distance Is Costly. Relationships with distant partners are ordinarily less satisfying than they would be if the partners were nearby.

Familiarity: Repeated Contact. In general, familiarity breeds attraction. Even brief, *mere exposure* to others usually increases our liking for them.

The Power of Proximity. Close proximity accentuates our feelings about others for better or for worse.

Physical Attractiveness: Liking Those Who Are Lovely

Our Bias for Beauty: "What Is Beautiful Is Good." We assume that attractive people have other desirable personal characteristics.

Who's Pretty? Symmetrical faces with average features are especially beautiful. *Waist-to-hip ratios* of 0.7 are very appealing in women whereas a WHR of 0.9 is attractive in a man if he has money.

An Evolutionary Perspective on Physical Attractiveness. Cross-cultural agreement about beauty, cyclical variations in women's preferences, and the link between attractiveness and good health are all consistent with the assumptions of evolutionary psychology.

Culture Counts, Too. Standards of beauty also fluctuate with changing economic and cultural conditions.

Looks Matter. When people first meet, nothing else affects attraction as much as their looks do.

The Interactive Costs and Benefits of Beauty. Physical attractiveness has a larger influence on men's social lives than on women's. Attractive people doubt the praise they receive from others, but they're still happier than unattractive people are.

Matching in Physical Attractiveness. People tend to pair off with others of similar levels of beauty.

Reciprocity: Liking Those Who Like Us

People are reluctant to risk rejection. Most people calculate others' overall desirability by multiplying their physical attractiveness by their probability of reciprocal liking. This is consistent with *balance theory*, which holds that people desire consistency among their thoughts, feelings, and relationships.

Similarity: Liking Those Who Are Like Us

Birds of a feather flock together. People like those who are similar to them.

What Kind of Similarity? Happy relationship partners resemble each other in demographic origin, attitudes and values, and personality traits.

Do Opposites Attract? Opposites do not attract, but the belief that they do may persist for several reasons. First, matching is a broad process; fame, wealth, health, talent, and looks are all commodities people use to attract others. Second, it takes time for *perceived similarity* to be replaced by a more accurate understanding of the attributes we share with others. Misperceptions may persist for some time. Third, people are also attracted to those who are mildly different from themselves but similar to their ideal selves. People also tend to become more similar over time, and some types of similarity are more important than others. Finally, we may occasionally appreciate behavior from a partner that differs from our own but that complements our actions and helps us to reach our goals.

Why Is Similarity Attractive? Similarity in others is reassuring. We also judge similar others positively and assume they like us.

Barriers: Liking the Ones We Cannot Have

The theory of psychological *reactance* suggests that people strive to restore lost freedom. The theory explains the *Romeo and Juliet effect* as well as the tendency for potential partners to seem more attractive at bars' closing time.

So, What Do Men and Women Want?

People evaluate potential partners with regard to (a) warmth and loyalty, (b) attractiveness and vitality, and (c) status and resources. For lasting romances, women want men who are warm and kind and who are not poor, and men want women who are warm and kind and who are not unattractive. Thus, everybody wants intimate partners who are amiable, agreeable, and loving.

CHAPTER 4

Social Cognition

FIRST IMPRESSIONS (AND BEYOND) ◆ THE POWER OF PERCEPTIONS ◆ Idealizing Our Partners ◆ Attributional Processes ◆ Memories ◆ Relationship Beliefs ◆ Expectations ◆ Self-Perceptions ◆ IMPRESSION MANAGEMENT ◆ Strategies of Impression Management ◆ Impression Management in Close Relationships ◆ SO, JUST HOW WELL DO WE KNOW OUR PARTNERS? ◆ Knowledge ◆ Motivation ◆ Partner Legibility ◆ Perceiver Ability ◆ Threatening Perceptions ◆ Perceiver Influence ◆ Summary ◆ FOR YOUR CONSIDERATION ◆ CHAPTER SUMMARY

Imagine that you're home in bed, sick with a killer flu, and your lover doesn't call you during the day to see how you're doing. You're disappointed. Why didn't your partner call? Does he or she not love you enough? Is this just another frustrating example of his or her self-centered lack of compassion? Or is it more likely that your loving, considerate partner didn't want to risk waking you from a nap? There are several possible explanations, and you can choose a forgiving rationale, a blaming one, or something in between. And importantly, the choice may really be up to you; the facts of the case may allow several different interpretations. But whatever you decide, your judgments are likely to be consequential. At the end of the day, your perceptions will have either sustained or undermined the happiness of your relationship.

We'll focus on judgments like these in this chapter on **social cognition,** a term that refers generally to the processes of perception and judgment with which we make sense of our social worlds (Moskowitz, 2005). Our primary concern will be with the way we *think* about our relationships. We'll explore how our judgments of our partners and their behavior set the stage for the events that follow. We'll consider our own efforts to influence and control what our partners think of us. And we'll ponder just how well two people are likely to know each other, even in an intimate relationship. Throughout the chapter, I'll emphasize the fact that our perceptions and interpretations of our partnerships are of enormous importance: What we think helps to determine what we *feel*, and then how we *act*. This wouldn't be a problem if our judgments were always correct. However, there are usually a variety of reasonable ways to interpret an event (as my opening example suggests), and we can make mistakes even when we're confident that we have arrived at the truth. Indeed, some of those mistakes may begin the moment we meet someone, as studies of first impressions reveal.

FIRST IMPRESSIONS (AND BEYOND)

First impressions matter. The judgments we form of others after a brief first meeting often have enormous staying power, with our initial perceptions continuing to be influential months later. This fact may be obvious if we dislike someone so much after an initial interaction that we avoid any further contact with him or her (Denrell, 2005); in such cases, our first impressions are the only impressions we ever get. However, first impressions continue to be influential even when we do see more of a new acquaintance. When researchers formally arranged get-acquainted conversations between new classmates, the initial impressions the students formed continued to influence their feelings about each other 9 weeks later (Sunnafrank & Ramirez, 2004).

Conceivably, some first impressions may last because they are discerning and correct. Sometimes it doesn't take us long to accurately decide who's nice and who's not, and if we're right, we may never need to revise our initial perceptions. On the other hand, first impressions can be remarkably persistent even when they're erroneous (Harris & Garris, 2008). Right or wrong, first impressions linger, and that's why they matter so much. Let's consider how they operate.

We start judging people from the moment we meet them. And by "moment," I mean the first twenty-fifth of a second. That's all it takes—only 39 milliseconds[1]—for us to determine whether a stranger's face looks angry (Bar et al., 2006). After more patient deliberation lasting one-tenth of a second,[2] we have formed judgments of a stranger's attractiveness, likeability, and trustworthiness that are the same as those we hold after a minute's careful inspection of the person's face (Willis & Todorov, 2006). Then, after watching the stranger chat with someone of the other sex for only 5 seconds, we've already decided how extraverted, conscientious, and intelligent he or she is (Carney et al., 2007). We jump to conclusions very, very quickly.

Our snap judgments are influenced by the fact that everyone we meet fits some category of people about whom we already hold stereotyped first impressions. This may sound like a daring assertion, but it really isn't. Think about it: Everyone is either male or female, and (as we saw in chapter 1), gender-role stereotypes lead us to expect different behavior from men and women. Furthermore, at a glance, we can tell whether someone is beautiful or plain, and (as we saw in chapter 3), we assume that pretty people are likeable people. Dozens of other distinctions may come into play: young/old, black/white, pierced/unpierced, country/urban, and many more. The specifics of these stereotypes may vary from one perceiver to the next, but they operate similarly in anyone: Stereotypes supply us with preconceptions about what people are like (Freeman et al., 2010). The judgments that result are often quite incorrect

---

[1]A millisecond is a thousandth of a second. So, after 39 milliseconds have passed, there's still 96.1 percent of a second yet to come before one full second has passed.

[2]I'm not kidding, but I am being playful.

(Olivola & Todorov, 2010), but they're hard to avoid: Stereotypes influence us automatically, even when we are unaware of using them (Devine & Monteith, 1999). So, some initial feelings about others may spring up unbidden even when we want to be impartial and open minded.

Then, if we do interact with someone, we continue jumping to conclusions as our interaction unfolds. Please take a moment—seriously, take your time and read the next line slowly—and consider someone who is

envious, stubborn, critical, impulsive, industrious, and intelligent.

Would you want this person as a co-worker? Probably not much. Now, please take another moment to size up someone else who is

intelligent, industrious, impulsive, critical, stubborn, and envious.

More impressive, yes? This person isn't perfect, but he or she seems competent and ambitious. The point, of course, is that the two descriptions offer the same

When we meet others for the first time, we rarely form impressions of them in an unbiased, even-handed manner. Instead, various stereotypes and primacy effects influence our interpretations of the behavior we observe.

information in a different *order,* and that's enough to engender two different impressions (Asch, 1946). Our judgments of others are influenced by a **primacy effect,** a tendency for the first information we receive about others to carry special weight, along with our instant impressions and our stereotypes, in shaping our overall impressions of them.

Primacy effects provide one important indication of why first impressions matter so much: Right or wrong, our quick first judgments of others influence our interpretations of the later information we encounter. Once a judgment forms, it affects how we use the data that follow—often in subtle ways that are difficult to detect. John Darley and Paget Gross (1983) demonstrated this when they showed Princeton students a videotape that established the social class of a young girl named "Hannah." Two different videos were prepared, and some people learned that Hannah was rather poor, whereas others found that she was pretty rich; she either played in a deteriorating, paved schoolyard and returned home to a dingy, small duplex or played on expansive, grassy fields and went home to a large, lovely house. The good news is that when Darley and Gross asked the participants to guess how well Hannah was doing in school, they did not assume the rich kid was smarter than the poor kid; the two groups both assumed she was getting average grades (see Figure 4.1). After that, however, the researchers showed the participants a tape of Hannah taking an aptitude test and doing an inconsistent job, answering some difficult questions correctly but blowing some easy ones. Everyone saw the same tape, but—and here's the bad news—they interpreted it very differently depending on their impressions of her social class. People who thought that Hannah was poor cited her mistakes and judged her as performing *below* average whereas those who thought she was rich noted her successes and rated her as considerably *better* than average. Perceivers equipped with different preconceptions about Hannah's social class interpreted the *same* sample of her behavior in very different ways and came to very different conclusions. And note how subtle this process was: They didn't leap to biased assumptions about Hannah simply by knowing her social class, making an obvious mistake that might easily be noticed. Instead, their knowledge of her social class lingered in their minds and contaminated their interpretations of her later actions. And they probably made their biased judgments with confidence, feeling fair and impartial. Both groups could point to a portion of her test performance—the part that fit their preconceptions—and feel perfectly justified in making the judgments they did, never realizing that people with other first impressions were watching the same videotape and reaching contradictory conclusions.

Thus, first impressions affect our interpretations of the subsequent information we encounter about others. They also affect our choices of the new information we seek. When we want to test a first impression about someone, we're more likely to pursue information that will confirm that belief than to inquire after data that could prove it wrong. That is, people ordinarily display a **confirmation bias:** They seek information that will prove them right more often than they look for examples that would prove them wrong (Snyder, 1981). For instance, imagine that you're instructed to interview a fellow student to find out if he or she is a sociable extravert, and you're handed a list of possible

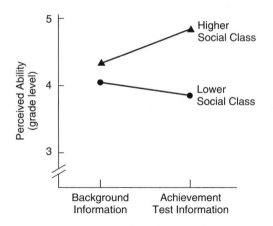

FIGURE 4.1. **Our preconceptions control our interpretations of information about others.**
People equipped with different expectations about the social class of a fourth-grade girl drew very different conclusions about her performance on an achievement test, although they all witnessed the very *same* performance. Those who thought they were watching a rich kid judged her to be performing an entire grade better than did those who thought they were watching a girl from a more modest background.
Data from Darley & Gross, 1983.

questions to ask. Some of the questions are neutral (e.g., "What are the good and bad points of acting friendly and open?") but others are slanted toward eliciting introverted responses ("What do you dislike about loud parties?") while still others are likely to get extraverted answers ("What do you do when you want to liven things up at a party?"). How would you conduct the interview? If you're like most people, you'd select questions that probe for evidence that your expectation is correct.

That's just what happened when researchers asked some people to find out if a stranger was extraverted, but asked others to find out if the person was introverted (Snyder & Swann, 1978b). The two groups of interviewers adopted two very different lines of investigation, asking questions that made it likely that they'd get examples of the behaviors they expected to find. In fact, the interviews were so biased that audiences listening to them on tape actually believed that the strangers really were rather extraverted or introverted, depending on the interviewers' preconceptions.

Indeed, the problem with confirmatory strategies is that they elicit one-sided information about others that fits our preconceptions—and as a result, we too rarely confront unequivocal evidence that our first impressions are wrong. Thus, not only may we cling to snap judgments that are incorrect, but we may also think we're right about others more often than we are (Ames et al., 2010). Indeed, most people are **overconfident** in their beliefs about others, making more mistakes than they realize. Here's an example. After you begin dating a new romantic partner, you're likely to become confident that you understand his or her sexual history as time goes by. You'll probably feel

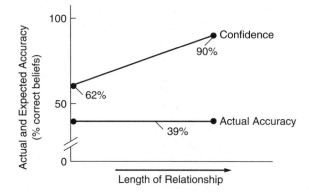

FIGURE 4.2. **Accuracy and (over) confidence in developing relationships.**
At the beginning of their relationships, people felt that they knew more about the sexual histories of their new partners than they really did. Then, as time went by, they became quite certain that they were familiar with all the facts, when in truth, their actual accuracy did not improve.
Data from Swann & Gill, 1997.

increasingly certain, for instance, that you know how many other lovers your partner has had, or whether or not he or she has a sexually transmitted infection. Remarkably, however, you're not likely to be as well-informed as you think. Studies at the University of Texas at Austin found that people could not estimate the risk that a new acquaintance was HIV-positive as well as they thought they could (Swann et al., 1995). They were overconfident when a new relationship began, and as the relationship developed, they only got *worse* (Swann & Gill, 1997). With greater familiarity, they became more certain that they understood their new partners well, but their accuracy did not change (see Figure 4.2).

So, first impressions matter because the first things we learn (a) direct our attention to certain types of new information and (b) influence our interpretations of those new facts. The net result is that we do not process information about others in an unbiased, evenhanded manner. Instead, our existing notions, whether they're simple stereotypes or quick first impressions, affect how we access and use the new data we encounter. We are usually unaware of how readily we overlook evidence that we could be wrong. We're not tentative. Armed with only some of the facts—those that tend to support our case—we put misplaced faith in our judgments of others, being wrong more often than we realize.

Now, of course, we come to know our partners better with time and experience. One of the hallmarks of intimacy is personal knowledge about a partner, and first impressions certainly change as people gain familiarity with each other (Kammrath et al., 2007). However—and this is the fundamental point I wish to make—*existing beliefs are influential* at every stage of a relationship. Even flimsy first impressions typically change less easily than they logically should because of the manner in which they influence subsequent thinking. And what happens when a relationship develops and you have a lot of information about an intimate partner? These patterns continue. People may see what they want to see and hold confident judgments that aren't always right.

Indeed, existing beliefs about lovers and friends are undoubtedly even more powerful than first impressions about new acquaintances. We have enormous amounts of information about our intimate partners but—because they matter so much to us—we sometimes find it hard to see them clearly. For instance, who are the better judges of how long your current romantic relationship will last, you or your parents? Remarkably, when university students, their room-mates, and their parents were all asked to forecast the future of the students' dating relationships, the parents made better predictions than the students did, and the roommates did better still (MacDonald & Ross, 1999). You'd think that people would be the best judges of their own relationships, but the students focused on the strengths of their partnerships and ignored the weaknesses; as a result, they confidently and optimistically predicted that the relationships would last longer than they usually did. Parents and roommates were more dispassionate and evenhanded, and although they were less confident in their predictions, they were more accurate in predicting what the future would hold. In fact, the most accurate predictions of all regarding the future of a heterosexual relationship often come from the friends of the woman involved (Loving, 2006). If her friends approve of a partnership, it's likely to continue, but if they think the relationship is doomed, it probably is (Etcheverry & Agnew, 2004).

Thus, the same overconfidence, confirmatory biases, and preconceptions that complicate our perceptions of new acquaintances operate in established relationships as well. Obviously, we're not clueless about our relationships. When

We Don't Always Know Why We Think What We Do

Consider this: When you show up for a psychology study, the researcher asks you to hold her cup of hot coffee for about 20 seconds while she records your name on a clipboard. Then, you're asked to form an impression of a stranger who is described in a brief vignette. Would your warm hands lead you to intuit that the stranger is a warm and generous person? Would you have liked the stranger less if you had been holding a cup of iced coffee instead?

Remarkably, the answer to both of those questions is yes. Warm hands led research participants to think warmer thoughts about a stranger than cool hands did (Williams & Bargh, 2008), and there are two aspects of this phenomenon that are intriguing. First, our impressions of others can be shaped by a variety of influences, and some of them have nothing to do with the person who's being judged. Second, the people in this study were completely unaware that the temporary temperature of their hands was swaying their judgment. We don't always know *why* we hold the opinions we do, and on occasion, our impressions of others are unwarranted. Both points are valuable lessons for a discerning student of social cognition.

we thoughtfully evaluate our partnerships with a deliberate, cautious frame of mind, we make more accurate predictions about their futures than we do when we're in a romantic mood. But it's hard to be dispassionate when we're devoted to a relationship and want it to continue. When people are trying to keep their relationships intact, they are particularly prone to confirmation biases that support their optimistic misperceptions of their partners (Gagné & Lydon, 2004).

So, our perceptions of our relationships are often less detached and straightforwardly accurate than we think they are. And, for better or for worse, they have considerable impact on our subsequent feelings and behavior in our relationships, as we'll see in the following section.

THE POWER OF PERCEPTIONS

Our judgments of our relationships and our partners seem to come to us naturally, as if there were only one reasonable way to view the situations we encounter. Little do we realize that we're often *choosing* to adopt the perspectives we use, and we facilitate or inhibit our satisfaction with our relationships by the choices we make.

Idealizing Our Partners

What are you looking for in an ideal romantic relationship? As we saw in chapter 3, most of us would like to have a partner who is warm and trustworthy, loyal and passionate, attractive and exciting, and rich and powerful, and our satisfaction depends on how well our lovers approach those ideals (Tran et al., 2008). What we usually get, however, is something less. How, then, do we ever stay happy with the real people we attract?

One way is to construct charitable, generous perceptions of our partners that emphasize their virtues and minimize their faults. People often judge their lovers with **positive illusions** that portray their partners in the best possible light (Holmes, 2004). Such "illusions" are a mix of realistic knowledge about our partners and idealized perceptions of them. They do not ignore a partner's real liabilities; they just consider such faults to be less significant than other people perceive them to be (Murray & Holmes, 1999). Satisfied spouses perceive their partners' deficiencies as circumscribed, specific drawbacks that are less important and influential than their many assets and advantages are (Neff & Karney, 2003). They have all the facts, but they interpret them differently than everyone else (Gagné & Lydon, 2003). They idealize their partners, judging them more positively than other people do, and even more positively than the partners judge themselves (Conley et al., 2009).

Isn't it a little dangerous to hold a lover in such high esteem? Won't people inevitably be disappointed when their partners fail to fulfill such positive perceptions? The answers may depend on just how unrealistic our positive illusions are (Neff & Karney, 2005). If we're genuinely fooling ourselves, imagining desirable qualities in a partner that he or she does not possess, we may be dooming ourselves to disillusionment (Tomlinson et al., 2010). Newlyweds do grow less satisfied if their new spouses turn out to be less wonderful than they were thought to be (Watson & Humrichouse, 2006). On the other hand, if we're aware of all the facts but are merely interpreting them in a kind, benevolent fashion, such "illusions" can be very beneficial. When we idealize our partners, we're predisposed to judge their behavior in positive ways, and we are more willing to commit ourselves to maintaining the relationship (Luo et al., 2010). It bolsters our self-esteem to be loved by others who we perceive to be so desirable (Murray et al., 2000). And we can slowly convince our partners that they actually are the wonderful people we believe them to be because our high regard improves their self-esteem, too (Murray et al., 1996). Add it all up, and idealized images of romantic partners are associated with greater satisfaction, love, and trust, and longer-lasting relationships as time goes by (Miller et al., 2006).

In addition, there's a clever way in which we protect ourselves from disillusionment: Over time, as we come to know our partners well, we tend to revise our opinions of what we want in an ideal partner so that our standards fit the partners we've got (Fletcher et al., 2000). To a degree, we conveniently decide that the qualities our partners have are the ones we want.

Thus, by choosing to look on the bright side—perceiving our partners as the best they can be—and by editing our ideals and hopes so that they fit the realities we face, we can increase the chances that we'll be happy with our present partners. Indeed, our partners generally know that we're idolizing them, and they usually want us to (Boyes & Fletcher, 2007)—and if we receive such positive, charitable perceptions in return, everybody wins.

Attributional Processes

Our delight or distress is also affected by the manner in which we choose to explain our partners' behavior. The explanations we generate for why things happen—and in particular why a person did or did not do something—are called **attributions.** An attribution identifies the causes of an event, emphasizing the impact of some influences and minimizing the role of others. Studies of such judgments are important because there are usually several possible explanations for most events in our lives, and they can differ in meaningful ways. We can emphasize influences that are either *internal* to someone, such as the person's personality, ability, or effort, or *external,* implicating the situation or circumstances the person faced. For instance (as you've probably noticed), students who do well on exams typically attribute their success to internal causes (such as their preparation and talent) whereas those who do poorly blame external factors (such as a tricky, unfair test) (Forsyth & Schlenker, 1977). The causes of events may also be rather *stable* and lasting, as our abilities are, or *unstable* and transient, such as moods that come and go. Moreover, causes can be said to be *controllable*, so that we can manage or influence them, or *uncontrollable*, so that there's nothing we can do about them. With all of these distinctions in play, diverse explanations for a given event may be plausible. And in a close relationship in which interdependent partners may *both* be partly responsible for much of what occurs, judgments of cause and effect can be especially complicated.

Nevertheless, three broad patterns routinely emerge from studies of attributions in relationships. First, despite their intimate knowledge of each other, partners are affected by robust **actor/observer effects:** They generate different explanations for their own behavior than they do for the similar actions they observe in their partners (Malle, 2006). People are often acutely aware of the external pressures that have shaped their own behavior, but they overlook how the same circumstances affect others; as a result, they acknowledge external influences when they explain their own actions, but they make internal attributions (for instance, to others' personalities) when other people behave exactly the same way. What makes this phenomenon provocative in close relationships is that it leads the partners to overlook how *they* often personally provoke the behavior they observe in each other. During an argument, if one partner thinks, "she infuriates me so when she does that," the other is likely to be thinking, "he's so temperamental. He needs to learn to control himself." This bias is so pervasive that two people in almost any interaction are reasonably likely to agree about what each of them did but to disagree about why each of them did it (Robins et al., 2004). And to complicate things further, the two partners are unlikely to be aware of the discrepancies in their attributions; each person is likely to believe that the other sees things his or her way. When partners make a conscious effort to try to understand the other's point of view, the actor/observer discrepancy gets smaller (Arriaga & Rusbult, 1998), but it rarely vanishes completely (Malle, 2006). The safest strategy is to assume that even your closest partners seldom comprehend all your reasons for doing what you do.

Second, despite genuine affection for each other, partners are also likely to display **self-serving biases** in which they readily take credit for their successes but try to avoid the blame for their failures. People like to feel responsible for the good things that happen to them, but they prefer external excuses when things go wrong. Thus, although they won't tell their partners (Miller & Schlenker, 1985), they usually think that they personally deserve much of the credit when their relationships are going well, but they're not much to blame if a partnership is faltering (Thompson & Kelley, 1981). One quality that makes this phenomenon interesting is that people expect others to be self-serving, but they don't feel that they are themselves (Kruger & Gilovich, 1999). Most of us readily recognize overreaching ownership of success and flimsy excuses for failure when they come from other people, but we think that our own similar, self-serving perceptions are sensible and accurate (Pronin et al., 2002). This occurs in part because we are aware of—and we give ourselves credit for—our own good intentions, even when we fail to follow through on them, but we judge other people only by what they do, not what they may have intended to do (Kruger & Gilovich, 2004).

This is a provocative phenomenon, so let's consider how it works. Imagine that Fred goes to sleep thinking, "I bet Wilma would like breakfast in bed in the morning." He intends to do something special for her, and he proudly gives himself credit for being a thoughtful partner. But when he oversleeps and has to dash off to work without actually having done anything generous, he's likely to continue feeling good about himself: After all, he had kind intentions. In contrast, Wilma can only judge Fred by his actions; she's not a party to what he was thinking, and she has no evidence in this instance that he was thoughtful at all. Their different sources of information may lead Fred to consider himself a better, more considerate partner than Wilma (or anyone else) perceives him to be. (Remember those thank-you notes you were intending to write but never did? You probably give yourself some credit for wanting to get around to them, but all your disappointed grandmother knows is that you never thanked her, and you're behaving like an impolite ingrate!)

Subtle processes like these make self-serving explanations of events routine in social life. It's true that loving partners are less self-serving toward each other than they are with other people (Sedikides et al., 1998). Nevertheless, self-serving biases exist even in contented relationships. In particular, when they fight with each other, spouses tend to believe that the argument is mostly their partner's fault (Schutz, 1999). And if they have extramarital affairs, people usually consider their own affairs to be innocuous dalliances, but they consider their spouse's affairs to be grievously hurtful (Buunk, 1987).

Thus, partners' idiosyncratic perspectives allow them to feel that they have better excuses for their mistakes than their friends and lovers do. They also tend to believe that their partners are the source of most disagreements and conflict. Most of us feel that *we're* pretty easy to live with, but *they're* hard to put up with sometimes. Such perceptions are undoubtedly influential, and, indeed, a third important pattern is that the general pattern of a couple's attributions helps determine how satisfied they will be with their relationship (Fincham et al., 2000). Happy people make attributions for their partners' behavior that are *relationship enhancing*. Positive actions by the partner are judged to be intentional, habitual, and indicative of the partner's fine character; that is, happy couples make controllable, stable, and internal attributions for each other's positive behavior. They also tend to discount one another's transgressions, seeing them as accidental, unusual, and circumstantial; thus, negative behavior is excused with uncontrollable, unstable, and external attributions.

Through such attributions, satisfied partners magnify their partner's kindnesses and minimize their cruelties, and, as long as a partner's misbehavior really *is* just an occasional misstep, these benevolent explanations keep the partners happy (McNulty 2010). But dissatisfied partners do just the opposite, exaggerating the bad and minimizing the good (Fincham, 2001). Unhappy people make *distress-maintaining* attributions that regard a partner's negative actions as deliberate and routine and positive behavior as unintended and accidental. (See Figure 4.3.) Thus, whereas satisfied partners judge each other in kindly ways that are likely to keep them happy, distressed couples perceive each other in an unforgiving fashion that can keep them dissatisfied no matter how each behaves. When distressed partners *are* nice to one another, each is likely to write off the other's thoughtfulness as a temporary, uncharacteristic

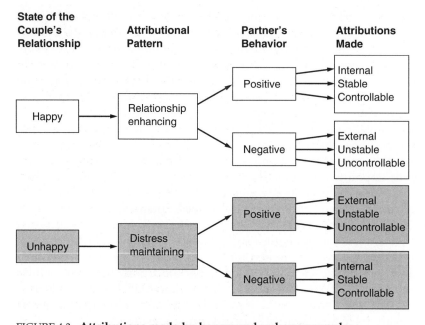

FIGURE 4.3. **Attributions made by happy and unhappy couples.**
Relationship-enhancing attributions give partners credit for thoughtful, generous
actions and excuse undesirable behavior as a temporary aberration. Distress-
maintaining attributions do just the opposite; they blame partners for undesirable
conduct but give them no credit for the nice things they do. Data from Brehm and
Kassin ©1990.

lull in the negative routine. When kindnesses seem accidental and hurts seem
deliberate, satisfaction is hard to come by.

Where does such a self-defeating pattern come from? Attachment styles are
influential. People with secure styles tend to tolerantly employ relationship-
enhancing attributions, but insecure people are more pessimistic (Pearce & Halford, 2008). People who are high in neuroticism are also more likely than others
to make distress-maintaining attributions, but disappointments of various sorts
may cause anyone to gradually adopt a pessimistic perspective (Karney & Bradbury, 2000). One thing is clear: Maladaptive attributions can lead to cantankerous behavior and ineffective problem solving, and they can cause dissatisfaction
that would not have occurred otherwise (Sillars et al., 2010). With various points
of view at their disposal, people can choose to explain a partner's behavior in
ways that are endearing and forgiving, or pessimistic and pejorative—and the
success of their relationship may ultimately hang in the balance.

Memories

Our perceptions of the current events in our relationships are obviously influential. So are our memories of the things that have happened in the past.

We usually assume that our memories are faithful representations of past
events. In particular, we're likely to trust vivid recollections because they seem

so certain and detailed. But years of research (see Della Sala, 2010) have clearly demonstrated that we edit and update our memories—even seemingly vivid ones—as new events unfold, so that what we remember about the past is always a mix of what happened then and what we know now. Psychologists use the term **reconstructive memory** to describe the manner in which our memories are continually revised and rewritten as new information is obtained.

Reconstructive memory influences our relationships. For one thing, partners' current feelings about each other influence what they remember about their shared past (McFarland & Ross, 1987). If they're presently happy, people tend to forget past disappointments; but if they're unhappy and their relationship is failing, they underestimate how happy and loving they used to be. These tricks of memory help us adjust to the situations we encounter, but they often leave us feeling that our relationships have always been more stable and predictable than they really were—and that can promote damaging overconfidence.

The good news is that by misremembering their past, partners can remain optimistic about their future. At any given point in time, contented lovers are likely to recall that they have had some problems in the past but that things have recently gotten better, so they are happier now than they used to be (Karney & Frye, 2002). What's notable about this pattern is that, if you follow couples over time, they'll tell you this over and over even when their satisfaction with each other is gradually eroding instead of increasing (Frye & Karney, 2004). Evidently, by remembering recent improvement in their partnerships that has not occurred, people remain happier than they might otherwise be. Like other perceptions, our memories influence our subsequent behavior and emotions in our intimate relationships (Simpson et al., 2010).

Relationship Beliefs

People also enter their partnerships with established beliefs about what relationships are like. These are organized in mental structures called *schemas* that provide a filing system for our knowledge about relationships and that, importantly, provide us coherent assumptions about how they work (Solomon & Theiss, 2007). One set of interrelated beliefs that is often evident in our relationship schemas is **romanticism,** the view that love should be the most important basis for choosing a mate (Weaver & Ganong, 2004). People who are high in romanticism believe that (a) each of us has only one perfect, "true" love; (b) true love will find a way to overcome any obstacle; and (c) love is possible at first sight. These beliefs apparently provide a rosy glow to a new relationship—romantic people experience more love, satisfaction, and commitment in the first few months of their romantic partnerships than unromantic people do—but these beliefs tend to erode as time goes by (Sprecher & Metts, 1999). Real relationships rarely meet such lofty expectations.

At least romantic beliefs appear to be fairly benign. The same cannot be said for some other beliefs that are clearly disadvantageous. Certain beliefs that people have about the nature of relationships are *dysfunctional;* that is, they appear to have adverse effects on the quality of relationships, making it less likely that the partners will be satisfied (Goodwin & Gaines, 2004). What ideas could people have that could have such deleterious effects? Here are six:

- *Disagreements are destructive.* Disagreements mean that my partner doesn't love me enough. If we loved each other sufficiently, we would never fight about anything.
- *"Mindreading" is essential.* People who really care about each other ought to be able to intuit each other's needs and preferences without being told what they are. My partner doesn't love me enough if I have to tell him or her what I want or need.
- *Partners cannot change.* Once things go wrong, they'll stay that way. If a lover hurts you once, he or she will hurt you again.
- *Sex should be perfect every time.* Sex should always be wonderful and fulfilling if our love is pure. We should always want, and be ready for, sex.
- *Men and women are different.* The personalities and needs of men and women are so dissimilar, you really can't understand someone of the other sex.
- *Great relationships just happen.* You don't need to work at maintaining a good relationship. People are either compatible with each other and destined to be happy together or they're not.

Most of these beliefs were identified by Roy Eidelson and Norman Epstein (1982) years ago, and since then, several studies have shown that they put people at risk for distress and dissatisfaction in close relationships (e.g., Knee et al., 2003). These beliefs are unrealistic. When disagreements do occur—as they always do—they seem momentous to people who hold these views (Franiuk et al., 2004). Any dispute implies that their love is imperfect. Worse, people with these perspectives do not behave constructively when problems arise. Believing that people can't change and that true loves just happen, such people don't try to solve problems but just avoid them (Franiuk et al., 2002), and they report more interest in ending the relationship than in making an effort to repair it (Knee et al., 2003).

In their work on relationship beliefs, Chip Knee and his colleagues refer to perspectives like these as **destiny beliefs** because they assume that two people are either well suited for each other and destined to live happily ever after, or they're not (Knee & Bush, 2008). Destiny beliefs take an inflexible view of intimate partnerships (see Table 4.1). They suggest that if two people are meant to be happy, they'll know it as soon as they meet; they'll not encounter early doubts or difficulties, and once two soulmates find each other, a happy future is ensured. This is the manner in which Hollywood often portrays love in romantic comedies—and people who watch such movies do tend to believe that true loves are meant to be (McCarthy, 2009).

Different views, which you rarely see at the movies, assume that happy relationships are the result of hard work (Knee & Bush, 2008). According to **growth beliefs**, good relationships are believed to develop gradually as the partners work at surmounting challenges and overcoming obstacles, and a basic presumption is that with enough effort, almost any relationship can succeed.

As you might expect, these different views of relationships generate different outcomes when difficulties arise (and as it turns out, Hollywood isn't doing us any favors). When couples argue or a partner misbehaves, people who hold growth beliefs remain more committed to the relationship and more optimistic that any damage can be repaired than do those who do not hold such views (Knee et al., 2004). And people who hold growth beliefs can discuss their lovers' imperfections with equanimity; in contrast, people who hold destiny beliefs become hostile when they are asked to confront their partners' faults (Knee et al., 2001).

Clearly, some relationship beliefs are more adaptive than others (Miller et al., 2008). Left to themselves, these perspectives tend to be stable and lasting (Franiuk et al., 2002), but they can change with education and insight (Sharp & Ganong, 2000). Indeed, if you recognize any of your own views among the dysfunctional beliefs on the prior page, I hope that these findings are enlightening. Unrealistic assumptions can be so idealistic and starry eyed

TABLE 4.1. Destiny and Growth Beliefs

Chip Knee (1998) measured destiny and growth perspectives with these items. Respondents were asked to rate their agreement or disagreement with each item using this scale:

1	2	3	4	5	6	7
strongly disagree						*strongly agree*

1. Potential relationship partners are either compatible or they are not.

2. The ideal relationship develops gradually over time.

3. A successful relationship is mostly a matter of finding a compatible partner right from the start.

4. Challenges and obstacles in a relationship can make love even stronger.

5. Potential relationship partners are either destined to get along or they are not.

6. A successful relationship is mostly a matter of learning to resolve conflicts with a partner.

7. Relationships that do not start off well inevitably fail.

8. A successful relationship evolves through hard work and resolution of incompatibilities.

As you undoubtedly surmised, the odd-numbered items assess a destiny orientation and the even-numbered items assess a growth orientation. A scale with these items and 14 more is now used in destiny and growth research (Knee et al., 2003), but these classic items are still excellent examples of the two sets of beliefs. Do you agree with one set of ideas more than the other?

Source: Knee, 1998.

Attachment Styles and Perceptions of Partners

Relationship beliefs can vary a lot from person to person, and another individual difference that's closely tied to the way people think about their partnerships is attachment style (Shaver & Mikulincer, 2010). People with different styles are thought to have different "mental models" of relationships; they hold different beliefs about what relationships are like, expect different behavior from their partners, and form different judgments of what their partners do. I've already noted that secure people are more likely than those with insecure styles to employ relationship-enhancing attributions (Pearce & Halford, 2008); they're also less likely to hold maladaptive relationship beliefs (Stackert & Bursik, 2003). Secure people trust their partners more (Mikulincer, 1998), believe that their partners are more supportive (Collins & Feeney, 2004), and have more positive expectations about what the future holds (Rowe & Carnelley, 2003). They're also more

likely than insecure people to remember positive things that have happened in the past (Miller & Noirot, 1999). Even their dreams are different; when they're dreaming, compared to those who are insecure, secure people portray others as being more available and supportive and as offering greater comfort (Mikulincer et al., 2009). In general, then, people with secure styles are more generous, optimistic, and kindly in their judgments of others than insecure people are.

Attachment styles *can* change, as we saw in chapter 1, but no matter what style people have, they tend to remember past events and their past perspectives on relationships as being consistent with what they're thinking *now* (Feeney & Cassidy, 2003). Happily, if positive experiences in a rewarding relationship help us gradually develop a more relaxed and trusting outlook on intimacy with others, we may slowly forget that we ever felt any other way.

that no relationship measures up to them, and distress and disappointment are certain to follow.

Expectations

When relationship beliefs are inaccurate, they *stay* wrong. In contrast, people can also have more specific expectations about the behavior of others that are initially false but that become true (Rosenthal, 2006). I'm referring here to **self-fulfilling prophecies,** which are false predictions that become true because they lead people to behave in ways that make the erroneous expectations come true. Self-fulfilling prophecies are extraordinary examples of the power of perceptions because the events that result from them occur only because people expect them to, and then act as if they will.

Let's examine Figure 4.4 together to detail how this process works. As a first step in a self-fulfilling prophecy, a person whom we'll call the *perceiver forms an expectancy* about someone else—the *target*—that predicts how the target will behave. Various information about the target, such as his or her age,

FIGURE 4.4. **A self-fulfilling prophecy.**
Originally false expectations in a perceiver (*P*) can seem to come true when he or she interacts with someone else, his or her target (*T*).

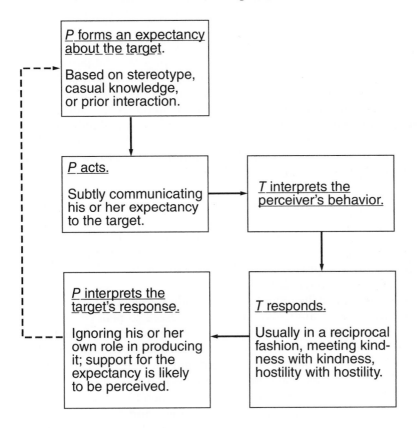

sex, race, physical attractiveness, or social class may affect the perceiver's judgments in ways of which the perceiver is unaware.

Then, in an important second step, the *perceiver acts*, usually in a fashion that is in accord with his or her expectations. Indeed, it may be hard for the perceiver to avoid subtly communicating what he or she really thinks about the target (Biesanz et al., 2001). Perceivers with favorable expectations, for instance, interact longer and more often with their targets, sharing more eye contact, sitting closer, smiling more, asking more questions, and encouraging more responses than do perceivers who have less positive expectations (Rosenthal, 2006).

The recipient of the perceiver's behavior is likely to notice all of this, and the *target's interpretation* will influence his or her response (Stukas & Snyder, 2002). In most cases, however, when the *target responds* in the fourth step, it will be in a manner that is similar to the perceiver's behavior toward him or her. Enthusiasm is usually met with interest (Snyder et al., 1977), hostility with counterattacks (Snyder & Swann, 1978a), and flirtatiousness with allurement (Ridge & Reber, 2002). Thus, the perceiver usually elicits from the target the behavior he or she expected, and that may be nothing like the way the target would have behaved if the perceiver hadn't expected it.

But such is the nature of a self-fulfilling prophecy that, as the *perceiver interprets the target's response* in the last step in the process, the perceiver is unlikely to recognize the role that he or she played in producing it (McNulty & Karney, 2002). The actor-observer effect will lead the perceiver to attribute the target's behavior to the target's personality or mood. And after all, the perceiver found in the target the behavior he or she expected; what better evidence is there that the perceiver's expectations were correct? (This is another reason that we tend to be overconfident in our judgments of others; when we make our false expectations come true, we never realize that we were ever wrong!)

Here, then, is another fundamental reason that our perceptions of others are so influential. They not only influence our interpretations of the information we gain but also guide our behavior toward others. We often get what we expect from others, and that is sometimes behavior that would not have occurred without our prompting—but we're rarely aware of how our expectations have created their own realities.

Mark Snyder and his colleagues (1977) provided an elegant example of this when they led men at the University of Minnesota to believe that they were chatting on the phone with women who were either very attractive or quite unattractive. The experimenters gave each man a fake photograph of the woman with whom he'd be getting acquainted and then recorded the ensuing conversations to see what happened. The men had higher expectations when they thought they'd be talking to gorgeous women than they did when they anticipated a conversation with a plain partner, and they were much more eager and interested when the interactions began; listeners rated them, for instance, as more sociable, warm, outgoing, and bold. The men's (often erroneous) judgments of the women were clearly reflected in their behavior toward them. How did the women respond to such treatment? They had no knowledge of having been labeled as gorgeous or homely, but they did know that they were talking to a man who sounded either enthusiastic or aloof. As a result, the men got what they expected: The women who were presumed to be attractive really did sound more alluring, reacting to their obviously interested partners with warmth and appeal of their own. By comparison, the women who talked with the relatively detached men who thought they were unattractive sounded pretty drab. In both cases, the men got out of the women the behavior they expected whether or not their expectations were accurate.

Because they guide our actions toward others, our expectations are not inert. Another fascinating example of this was obtained when researchers sent people to chat with strangers after leading them to expect that the strangers would probably either like or dislike them (Curtis & Miller, 1986). Participants in the study were told that, to study different types of interactions, the researchers had given a stranger bogus advance information about them, and they could anticipate either a friendly or unfriendly reaction from the stranger when they met. In truth, however, none of the strangers had been told anything at all about the participants, and the false expectations that the interaction would go well or poorly existed only in the minds of the participants themselves. (Imagine yourself in this intriguing position: You *think* someone you're about to meet already likes or dislikes you, but the other person really doesn't know anything about you at all.) What happened? People got what they expected. Expecting to be liked, people greeted others in an engaging, open, positive way—they behaved in a likeable manner—and really *were* liked by the strangers they met. However, those who expected to be disliked were cautious and defensive and were much less forthcoming, and they actually got their partners to dislike them. Once again, false expectations created their own behavioral reality—and positive expectations were beneficial and advantageous, but negative expectations were not.

Indeed, over time, people who chronically hold different sorts of expectations about others may create different sorts of social worlds for themselves (Stinson et al., 2009). For instance, a program of research by Geraldine Downey and her colleagues has demonstrated that people who tend to worry about rejection from others often behave in ways that make such rejection more likely (Romero-Canyas et al., 2009). People who are high in *rejection sensitivity* tend to anxiously perceive snubs from others when none are intended. Then they overreact, fearfully displaying more hostility and defensiveness than others would (Romero-Canyas et al., 2010). Their behavior is obnoxious, and as a result, both they and their partners tend to be dissatisfied with their close relationships.

The flip side of rejection sensitivity may be *optimism*, the tendency to expect good things to happen. People who are chronically optimistic enjoy more satisfying close relationships than do those who are less hopeful because their positive expectations have beneficial effects on their partnerships (Carver & Scheier, 2009). They perceive their partners to be more supportive than pessimists do (Srivastava et al., 2006), and they report that they're able to solve problems with their partners cooperatively and creatively and well (Assad et al., 2007). Their expectations that they can resolve their difficulties evidently lead them to address any problems with hopeful confidence and energy that actually do make the problems more manageable.

With time and experience, we undoubtedly learn the truth about some of our false expectations about others. Some prophecies that initially fulfill themselves dissipate over time as people become more familiar with each other. On the other hand, if people continue to act in accord with their early expectations, some self-fulfilling prophecies can persist for years (Smith et al., 1999). Altogether, then, our perceptions of our partners, the attributions we make, and the beliefs and expectations we bring to our relationships can exert a powerful influence on the events that follow. Our judgments of each other matter (Holmes, 2002). And those of us who expect others to be trustworthy, generous, and loving may find that others actually *are* good to us more often than those with more pessimistic perspectives find others being kind to them.

Nonconscious Social Cognition

If you stop and think, you'll probably recognize most of the elements of social cognition that we have discussed so far. Some attributions, beliefs, and expectations may be habitual: They operate almost automatically without any deliberation or contemplation. But they are still conscious processes; if we turn our attention to them, we can identify them, and we know they're at work.

Our close relationships can have some effects on us, however, of which we are completely unaware. We can learn lessons from our intimate connections to others that influence our actions later on in ways that we may never notice (Chen et al., 2007).

For instance, particular relationships with others are sometimes characterized by recurring themes. Your father, for example, may have constantly urged you to get good grades in school. Now, if something subtly reminds you of your father—and you like him—you may persevere longer at a difficult task than you would have had you not been reminded of him (Fitzsimons & Finkel, 2010). You may act as if your father were standing behind you, urging you on. On the other hand, if you *didn't* like your father and you're reminded of him, you may do something that he would *not* have wanted you to do (Chartrand et al., 2007). What makes these patterns provocative is that the "reminders" can be his name flashed in front of your eyes so quickly that you cannot be sure what you saw (Shah, 2003). In such a case, you may have no conscious thought of your Dad and may not realize that

you've been subliminally reminded of him, but your past experiences with him may nevertheless guide your present behavior.

In addition, we unwittingly but routinely import old experiences into our new relationships. When the new people we meet resemble our past partners, we tend to behave toward them in ways that reflect the lessons we've learned (and the baggage we're carrying) (Brumbaugh & Fraley, 2007). If new acquaintances resemble those who treated us badly, we may unintentionally behave more coolly toward these people without realizing it. Those actions may elicit less friendly reactions from them, and we may begin to create new unpleasant relationships that resemble our unhappy past experiences without our past partners ever coming consciously to mind (Berenson & Andersen, 2006).

Happily, nonconscious influences can work for us, too. If a new acquaintance resembles someone with whom you shared good times, your interactions may get off to an especially good start. Although you may not consciously be reminded of your prior partner, you may, without meaning to, be warmer, more cheerful, and more sociable than you usually are (Kraus & Chen, 2010).

Thus, we're not aware of all the ways that our memories and expectations can influence our social outcomes. Without our knowledge, some encounters with others can trigger nonconscious tendencies learned in past relationships that we do not even realize exist.

Self-Perceptions

A last example of the power of our perceptions lies in the judgments we form of *ourselves*. Our discussion of self-esteem in chapter 1 noted that our self-evaluations are potent influences on our interactions. People who have high self-esteem are usually confident that their friendly overtures toward others will be met with warmth in return, but people with low self-esteem are less certain that they can get others to like them (Baldwin & Keelan, 1999). Consequently, people who doubt themselves tend to doubt their intimate partners, and they are typically less secure in their relationships than are people with higher self-esteem (Mikulincer & Shaver, 2007).

But self-esteem is just one part of our broader **self-concepts,** which encompass all of the beliefs and feelings we have about ourselves. Our self-concepts include a wide array of self-knowledge along with our self-esteem, and all the components of the self-concept are intimately tied to our relationships with others.

During social interaction, our self-concepts try to fulfill two different functions (Kwang & Swann, 2010). On the one hand, people seek feedback from others that will *enhance* their self-concepts and allow them to think of themselves as desirable, attractive, competent people. We like to hear good things about ourselves, and we try to associate with others who will help us support positive self-images.

On the other hand, because it's unsettling to encounter information that contradicts our beliefs, we also want feedback that sustains our existing self-concepts (Swann et al., 2008). For better or worse, our self-concepts play vital roles in organizing our views of the world; they make life predictable and support coherent expectations about what each day will bring. Without a stable, steady self-concept, social life would be a confusing, chaotic jumble, and being constantly confronted with information that contradicts our self-images would be unnerving. For that reason, people also seek feedback from others that is consistent with what they already think about themselves and that *verifies* their existing self-concepts (Stinson et al., 2010).

These two motives, **self-enhancement**—the desire for positive, complimentary feedback—and **self-verification**—the desire for feedback that is consistent with one's existing self-concept—go hand-in-hand for people who like themselves and who have positive self-concepts. When such people associate with others who compliment and praise them, they receive feedback that is simultaneously self-enhancing and self-verifying. But life is more complex for people who genuinely consider themselves to be unskilled and unlovable. Positive evaluations from others make them feel good but threaten their negative self-images; negative feedback and criticism affirm their self-concepts but feel bad.

How do both motives coexist in people with negative self-concepts? One answer is that people with poor self-concepts like global praise that suggests that their partners are happy with them, but they prefer self-verifying feedback about their specific faults (Neff & Karney, 2005). Partners who accurately recognize your deficiencies but who like you anyway appear to satisfy both motives (Lackenbauer et al., 2010). Self-enhancement also appears to be a more automatic, relatively nonconscious response that is primarily emotional whereas self-verification emerges from deliberate and conscious cognition. What this means is that people with poor self-concepts *like* praise and compliments from others, but once they get a chance to *think* about them, they don't believe or trust such feedback (Swann et al., 1990).

Okay, so what? The relevance of these phenomena to the study of relationships lies in the fact that if people are choosing relationship partners carefully, they'll seek intimate partners who *support their existing self-concepts,* good or bad (Swann et al., 2008). Here's an example: Imagine that after a semester of sharing a double room in a college dorm, you're asked if you want to change roommates. You have a positive self-concept, and your roommate likes you and tells you so. Do you want to leave? Probably not. But if your roommate *dis*liked you and constantly disparaged you, you'd probably want out. You'd not want to live with someone who disagreed with you about who you are because it would be wearying and unpleasant to have to face such a contrary point of view all the time.

Now imagine that you have a lousy self-concept and you're paired with a roommate who constantly tells you that there's no reason to doubt yourself. Such encouragement feels great, and you want more, right? Wrong. The motive to protect and maintain our existing self-concepts is so strong that people with negative self-concepts want to *escape* roommates who perceive them positively; they'd rather have roommates who dislike them (Swann & Pelham, 2002). Such disapproval is unpleasant, but at least it reassures the recipients that the world is a predictable place.

Things get more complicated in romantic relationships. When people choose dating partners, self-enhancement is an important motive; everybody seeks partners who like and accept them. Thus, even people with poor self-concepts pursue casual partners who provide positive feedback (Swann et al., 2002). However, in more interdependent, committed relationships such as marriages, self-verification rises to the fore—a phenomenon called the *marriage shift*—and people want feedback that supports their self-concepts (Swann et al., 1994). (See Figure 4.5.) If people with negative self-images find themselves married to spouses who praise and appreciate them, they'll gradually find ways to avoid their spouses as much as possible:

> Imagine a man who receives what he construes to be undeserved praise from his wife. Although such praise may make him feel optimistic and happy at first, the positive glow will recede if he concludes that his wife could not possibly believe what she said. . . . [or] he may decide that she is a fool. In either case, overly favorable evaluations from someone who knows one well may foster a sense of uneasiness, inauthenticity, and distrust of the person who delivered them. (Swann, 1996, p. 118)

On the other hand, if their spouses belittle them, people with negative self-concepts will stay close at hand. (And of course, it's the other way around for those who have positive self-concepts.)

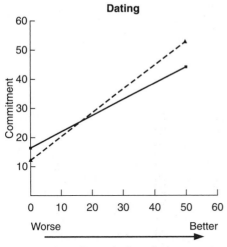

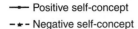

—•— Positive self-concept

—▲— Negative self-concept

FIGURE 4.5. **The marriage shift in self-verification.**
Self-enhancement is obvious in dating partnerships; we feel closer to dating partners who approve of us than to those who think we're flawed. But once people marry, self-verification rises to the fore. People with negative self-concepts actually feel closer to spouses who *don't* approve of them than to those who do. Beware of the marriage shift if your current romantic partner has low self-esteem.
Source: Swann, De La Ronde, & Hixon, 1994.

Narcissism and Relationships

A negative self-concept can evidently have an adverse impact on one's relationships, but an overly positive self-concept can be problematic, too. Narcissists possess highly inflated, unrealistic perceptions of their talents, desirability, and self-worth. Their self-perceptions are grandiose (Foster & Twenge, 2011), and they exhibit patterns of social cognition that have important implications for their relationships.

First, they're prone to strong self-serving biases (Stucke, 2003); if things go well, they want all the credit, but if things go wrong, they will accept none of the blame. They also have biased memories of others' reactions to them; they remember more acceptance and approval than they actually received (Rhodewalt & Eddings, 2002), but still tend to think that others don't treat them as well as they should (McCullough et al., 2003). Indeed, rejection from others is particularly hard for them to tolerate; their excessive pride leads them to overreact to imagined slights from others. Being full of themselves, they feel cruelly wronged when they judge that people are disrespectful or uncaring,

so they react more angrily and aggressively than others would (Brunell et al., 2011).

Furthermore, when narcissists enter close relationships, they are chronically less committed to their romantic partners than other people are. Their arrogant sense of entitlement leads them to stay on the prowl, looking for more desirable partners than the ones they have (Campbell & Foster, 2002). They work less hard to please their current partners and constantly think they deserve "better."

Narcissists obviously make rather poor partners, but it is sometimes surprisingly hard for all the rest of us to see that at first (Back et al., 2010). Early on, their self-assurance may be appealing, and it often takes time to realize how selfish and exploitative and touchy they really are. Thus, narcissism often takes the form of a "fatal attraction"; it may be attractive at first but deadly in the long run (Foster & Twenge, 2011), and it presents a challenge to us to be as astute in our judgments of potential partners as we can possibly be.

Overall, then, our self-concepts help direct our choices of intimate partners. Approval and acceptance from others is always pleasant, but in meaningful relationships over the long haul, people prefer reactions from others that confirm what they think of themselves. And that means that although most of us will be most content with spouses who uplift us, people with negative self-concepts will not; they feel better understood by, and closer to, partners who verify their low opinions of themselves (Letzring & Noftle, 2010).[3]

---

[3]Of course, self-concepts can change, and the ease with which they do depends on the certainty with which they are held (Chang-Schneider & Swann, 2010). The good news is that if you suspect you're a nincompoop but aren't really sure, positive feedback from an adoring lover may change your self-image as you enjoy, and come to believe, what your partner says (Stinson et al., 2010). The bad news is that if you're quite sure you're unworthy, you'll feel more at home around those who know you well enough to take you as you are—that is, those who *agree* that you're unworthy.

IMPRESSION MANAGEMENT

Others' impressions of us are obviously very important. And because they are, we often try to control the information that others receive about us. We sometimes try to make deliberate impressions on others, choosing our actions, our words, our apparel, our settings, and even our associates carefully to present a certain public image (Keating, 2006). On other occasions, when we're not consciously pursuing a particular impression, we often fall into habitual patterns of behavior that portray us in ways that have elicited desirable responses from others in the past (Lakin, 2006). So, whether or not we're thinking about it, we're often engaging in **impression management,** trying to influence the impressions of us that others form.

This is a significant idea for at least two reasons. First, nearly anything we do in the presence of others may be strategically regulated in the service of impression management. Women eat less on a date with an attractive man than they would have eaten had they been out with their girlfriends (Robillard & Jarry, 2007). Men take greater risks (and incur more sensational crashes) on their skateboards (Ronay & von Hippel, 2010), give more generously to charity (Iredale et al., 2008), and display flashier luxury goods[4] (Sundie et al., 2011) when they want to impress women. During sex, women cry out in exaggerated pleasure (Brewer & Hendrie, 2011), and both sexes will occasionally fake orgasms (about one-fourth of the men and two-thirds of the women in a Kansas sample had done so) (Muehlenhard & Shippee, 2010). Indeed, any public behavior may communicate meaningful information about us to others. The e-mail addresses we select (Back et al., 2008b), the Second Life avatars we build (Bélisle et al., 2008), and, of course, the Facebook profiles we construct (Back, Stopfer et al., 2010) all allow strangers to gauge some of our personality traits surprisingly well.

A second reason that impression management matters is that it is a pervasive influence on social life. Others' evaluations of us are eventful, and when we are in the presence of others, we are rarely unconcerned about what they may be thinking of us (Miller, 1996). By providing a means with which we can influence others' judgments, impression management increases our chances of accomplishing our interpersonal objectives. And there's rarely anything dishonest going on; impression management is seldom deceitful or duplicitous. Yes, people fake orgasms, and women tend to misrepresent their weight, and men their height, in their online profiles (Hitsch et al., 2010)—and I'm sure you know in what directions—but most impression management involves revealing, perhaps in a selective fashion, one's real attributes to others (Schlenker, 2003). By announcing some of their attitudes but not mentioning others, for example, people may appear to have something in common with almost anyone they meet; this simple tactic of impression management facilitates graceful and

---

[4]One does not buy a $440,000 Porsche Carrera GT with only two seats, a tiny trunk, and lousy gas mileage for transportation alone.

rewarding social interaction and does not involve untruthfulness at all. Because others reject frauds and cheats, people seldom pretend to be things they are not.

Strategies of Impression Management

Nevertheless, because most of us have diverse interests and talents, we can honestly attempt to create many distinct impressions, and we may seek different images in different situations. Indeed, people routinely use four different strategies of impression management (Jones & Pittman, 1982). We use **ingratiation** when we seek acceptance and liking from others; we do favors, pay compliments, mention areas of agreement, describe ourselves in desirable ways, and are generally charming to get others to like us. Ingratiation is a common form of impression management with romantic partners (Nezlek et al., 2007), and as long as such efforts are not transparently manipulative or obviously insincere (Marchand & Vonk, 2005), they usually do elicit favorable reactions from others (Proost et al., 2010).

On other occasions, when we wish our abilities to be recognized and respected by others, we may engage in **self-promotion,** recounting our accomplishments or strategically arranging public demonstrations of our skills. Self-promotion is a frequent strategy of impression management in a workplace (Nezlek et al., 2007), but even in professional settings, vigorous self-promotion can be risky for women because it makes them seem "unladylike" (Moss-Racusin & Rudman, 2010). Nevertheless, during a job interview, self-promotion makes a better impression than ingratiation does—and a combination of the two does even better (Proost et al., 2010).

Both ingratiation and self-promotion create socially desirable impressions, but other strategies create *un*desirable images. Through **intimidation,** people portray themselves as ruthless, dangerous, and menacing so that others will do their bidding. Such behavior is obnoxious and tends to drive others away, but if it's used only occasionally—or if the recipients are children or impoverished spouses with no place else to go—intimidation may get people what they want. Finally, using the strategy of **supplication,** people sometimes present themselves as inept or infirm to avoid obligations and to elicit help and support from others. People who claim that they're "just too tired" to do the dishes after a "hard day at work" are engaging in supplication. If ingratiation and self-promotion work for them, most people avoid using intimidation and supplication because most of us prefer to be liked and respected rather than feared or pitied. But almost everyone uses intimidation and supplication occasionally. If you've ever made a point of showing a partner that you were angry about something or sad about something else to get your way, you were using intimidation and supplication, respectively (Clark et al., 1996).

Impression Management in Close Relationships

Two specific features of impression management with intimate partners are worthy of mention. First, the motivation with which people manage their impressions differs, and these differences are consequential (Nezlek & Leary, 2002). People who are high in the trait of **self-monitoring** readily adjust their behavior to fit the varying norms of different situations. They're alert to social cues that suggest what they should do, and they are ready, willing, and able to tailor their behavior to fit in. By comparison, low self-monitors are both less attentive to social norms and less flexible; they have smaller repertoires of skills, so they behave more consistently from one situation to the next, making the same stable impressions even when they don't fit in. High self-monitors, then, are more changeable and energetic impression managers (Fuglestad & Snyder, 2009).

These different styles lead to different networks of friends. Because they more often switch images from one audience to the next, high self-monitors tend to have more friends than low self-monitors do, but they have less in common with each of them.[5] High self-monitors often surround themselves with "activity specialists," partners who are great companions for some particular pleasure—such as a "tennis buddy" or "ballet friend"—but with whom they are not compatible in other respects (Leone & Hawkins, 2006). High self-monitors strive to steer clear of any topics that would cause dispute, and the specialist friends allow them to really enjoy those particular activities—but if they threw a party and invited all those friends, very different people who have little in common with each other would show up. By comparison, low self-monitors must search harder for partners with whom they are more similar across the board. If low self-monitors had all their friends over, relatively few people would come, but they'd all be a lot alike.

These differences in style appear to be consequential as time goes by. When they first meet others, high self-monitors enjoy interactions of higher intimacy than low self-monitors do; they work to find common ground for a conversation and are good at small talk (Snyder & Simpson, 1984). Being active impression managers seems to help them to interact comfortably with a wide variety of people. On the other hand, they invest less of their time in each of their friends, so that they tend to have shorter, somewhat less committed relationships than low self-monitors do (Leone & Howkins, 2006). The interactive advantage enjoyed by high self-monitors when a relationship is just beginning may become a liability once the relationship is well established (Wright et al., 2007).

Thus, the greater attentiveness to social images evinced by high self-monitors influences the relationships they form. Would you rather be high or low on this trait? You can determine your own self-monitoring score using

---

[5]I should note that this and the following distinctions between high and low self-monitors are based on comparisons of the *highest* self-monitors, the 25 percent of us with the very highest scores, to the *lowest* self-monitors, the 25 percent of us with the lowest scores. Researchers sometimes do this to study the possible effects of a personality trait as plainly as possible, but you should recognize that half of us, those with scores ranging from somewhat below average to somewhat above, fall between the examples being described here.

the scale in Table 4.2. Just remember that only very high and very low scorers closely fit the portraits I've drawn here.

The second intriguing aspect of impression management in close relationships is that—although the impressions we make on our friends and lovers are much more influential than the images we create for acquaintances or strangers—we usually go to *less* trouble to maintain favorable images for our intimate partners than we do for others. We worry less about how we're coming across and try less hard to appear likeable and competent all the time (Leary et al., 1994). The longer people have known their partners, for instance, the less time they spend grooming themselves in the restroom during a dinner date (Daly et al., 1983). We pay less heed to the images we present to intimate partners than to the impressions we make on others, and there may be several reasons for this (Leary & Miller, 2000). For one thing, we know our friends and lovers like us, so there's less motivation to be charming to win their approval. Also, because they know us well, there's less we can do to have much effect on what they think. However, it's also likely that people simply get lazy. Being on one's best behavior requires concentration and effort. Polite behavior usually involves some form of self-restraint. We can relax around those who already know and love us, but that means that people are often much cruder with intimate partners than they are with anyone else they know (Miller, 1997b). People who are very decorous early in a relationship—who would never show up for breakfast without being showered and dressed—often become spouses who sit at the table in their underwear, unwashed, scratching and picking, and pilfering the last doughnut. This is ironic. Having behaved beautifully to win the love of a romantic partner, some of us never work at being so charming to that lover ever again. (And this may be a big problem in many relationships, as we'll see in chapter 6.)

SO, JUST HOW WELL DO WE KNOW OUR PARTNERS?

Let's add up the elements of social cognition we've encountered in this chapter. In a close relationship, partners often hold idealized but overconfident perceptions of each other, and when they act in accord with those judgments, they may elicit behavior from each other that fits their expectations but would not have otherwise occurred. Moreover, right or wrong, they are likely to interpret one another's actions in ways that fit their existing preconceptions. Combined with all this are the partners' efforts to adjust their behavior so that they make the impressions on each other that they want to make. Evidently, various processes are at work in intimate partnerships that cause us to see in our partners those attributes and motives that we expect or want (or that *they* want us to) see. How accurate, then, are our perceptions of our partners? How well do we know them?

The simple answer is, "not as well as we think we do" (Sillars, 1998). Of course, we have extensive knowledge about our partners (Gill & Swann, 2004). But as we saw in chapter 3, we routinely perceive them to be more like

TABLE 4.2. The Self-Monitoring Scale

Is each of the following statements true or false?

1. I find it hard to imitate the behavior of other people.
2. At parties or social gatherings, I do not attempt to say or do things that others will like.
3. I can only argue for ideas that I already believe.
4. I can make impromptu speeches even on topics about which I have almost no information.
5. I guess I put on a show to impress or entertain others.
6. I would probably make a good actor.
7. In a group I am rarely the center of attention.
8. In different situations and with different people I often act like very different persons.
9. I am not particularly good at making other people like me.
10. I'm not always the person I appear to be.
11. I would not change my opinions (or the way I do things) in order to please someone.
12. I have considered being an entertainer.
13. I have never been good at games like charades or improvisational acting.
14. I have trouble changing my behavior to suit different people and different situations.
15. At a party I let others keep the jokes and stories going.
16. I feel a bit awkward in public and do not show up quite as well as I should.
17. I can look anyone in the eye and tell a lie (if for a right end).
18. I may deceive people by being friendly when I really dislike them.

Give yourself a point for each of these statements that were *true* of you: 4, 5, 6, 8, 10, 12, 17, 18.
Then give yourself a point for each of these statements that were *false*: 1, 2, 3, 7, 9, 11, 13, 14, 15, 16.
What's your total score? If it's 13 or higher, you're a relatively high self-monitor. If it's 7 or lower, you're a relatively low self-monitor (Snyder, 1987). Scores between 7 and 13 are average.

Source: Snyder & Gangestad, 1986.

us than they really are. We believe that they agree with us more often than they really do, and we overestimate how similar their personality traits are to our own (Luo & Snider, 2009). As a result, we feel that we understand them, and they understand us, more than is actually the case (Pollmann & Finkenauer, 2009). Such misperceptions are not disadvantageous. Indeed, the more similarity and understanding we perceive in our partners, the more satisfying our relationships with them tend to be (Pollmann & Finkenauer, 2009). Still, we misunderstand our partners more than we realize. To a degree, our perceptions of our partners are fictions that portray our partners as people they are not.

Several factors determine just how accurate or inaccurate our judgments are. Interpersonal perception depends both on the people involved and on the situation they face.

Knowledge

The conclusion that we don't know our partners as well as we think we do isn't inconsistent with the fact that intimate partners know a great deal about each other. As their relationship develops and they spend more time together, two people do come to understand each other better (Brown et al., 2011). Married people perceive each other more accurately than dating couples or friends do, and acquaintances judge each other more accurately than strangers do (Letzring et al., 2006). Intimate partners interact often and care about each other—and, as we saw in chapter 3, usually have a lot in common—and all of these influences can contribute to accuracy (Connelly & Ones, 2010).

Motivation

However, our perceptions of others don't necessarily become more accurate as time goes by (Kenny et al., 2007). In fact, spouses who have been married for *shorter* lengths of time do better at inferring what their partners are thinking than spouses married longer do (Kilpatrick et al., 2002). Evidently, the interest and motivation with which we try to figure each other out help determine how insightful and accurate we will be (Thomas & Maio, 2008), and people who have recently moved in with each other (who are presumably highly motivated to understand each other [Clark & Wegener, 2008]) may understand each other as well as they ever will. But longer periods of very close contact, such as marriage, seem to gradually result in less, not more, accuracy as time goes by (Ickes, 2003).

In general, women spend more time thinking carefully about their relationships than men do (Acitelli, 2008). And remarkably, they may be especially astute during certain phases of their menstrual cycles: Women judge the strength and dominance of men more quickly and effortlessly when they are fertile than when they are not (Macrae et al., 2002). But are women generally better judges of others than men are? The answer is yes, but some of that has to do with men simply not trying as hard to understand others as women do (Hall & Mast, 2008). Finally, we all tend to understand beautiful people more than we do those who are plain, and that's because they *are* beautiful, and we're trying harder (Lorenzo et al., 2010). We know people better when we are motivated to do so.

Partner Legibility

Some of the traits people have are more visible than others—that is, they impel behavior that is observable and obvious—and the more evident a trait is, the

Do You Really Know What Others Think of You?

Okay, you know more about yourself than anyone else does. No one else, of course, is with you as much as you are. But other people are still likely to know some things about you that you *don't* know for two reasons. First, they have a different point of view. They can see what you're doing, and they're sometimes aware of behavior that escapes your notice (Vazire & Mehl, 2008). Have you ever been surprised by how you looked on a video? That's the perspective of you that others have all the time. Second, they're more objective. Whereas you and I are prone to self-serving biases, others evaluate us with more dispassion; they know better, for instance, just how physically attractive we are (Epley & Whitchurch, 2008).

You can more fully comprehend what others think of you if you recognize that they are generally unaware of your unspoken fears, good intentions, and other private experiences; they can judge only what you say and do (Chambers et al., 2008). As a result—and here comes some good news—others see us as less neurotic, more assertive, and more conscientious than we judge ourselves to be (Allik et al., 2010). They are less aware of our worries, occasional timidity, and unfulfilled plans than we are, so they don't hold our private moments of weakness against us the way we do. In general, we are reasonably well aware of the different impressions we make on different audiences such as parents, friends, and co-workers (Carlson & Furr, 2009). Still, to really understand what others think of you, you may actually have to ask.

more accurately it will be perceived. People who are sociable and extraverted, for instance, are likely to be accurately perceived as gregarious and affable, but high neuroticism is harder to detect (Vazire, 2010). Moreover, some people are generally easier to judge correctly than others are. One intriguing example of this was obtained when research participants watched videos of people on speed dates (Place et al., 2009). The observers could usually tell when men were interested in the women they had met, but women's interest was a little harder to judge (perhaps because more of the women were playing it cool). Nevertheless, some members of both sexes were quite transparent and easy to read, whereas others (about 20 percent of the group) consistently misled those who were watching. When people were hard to read, the observers routinely had no clue of what they were thinking.

Perceiver Ability

Some people may be hard to judge, but some judges are better than others. People who have good social skills tend to be adept at judging others (Hall et al., 2009), often because they're high in **emotional intelligence,** a set of abilities that describes a person's talents in *perceiving, using, understanding,* and *managing* emotions (Mayer et al., 2008). When people have emotional intelligence, they're adept at regulating their emotions, so they rarely overreact to frustrating events. They're also able to read others' feelings sensitively, and they enjoy more satisfying and more intimate interactions with others as a result (Mirgain & Cordova, 2007). Women tend to have higher emotional intelligence than men do (Brackett et al., 2005), and that's another reason they tend to be good at judging others.

Unsettling consequences may result from being a poor judge of others. When William Schweinle and William Ickes (2002) asked married men to watch videotapes of women discussing their divorces, they found (as you might expect) that some men read the women's thoughts and feelings better than others. The videos were highly charged and full of emotion, and the men had never met the women they were watching, but those who could accurately tell when the women were really angry or bitter tended to be satisfied with their own marriages. In contrast, other men considered the women to be more hostile than they really were; these men perceived criticism and rejection in the women's remarks that was not apparent to other perceivers. And creepily, those men were more likely to be wife beaters who abused their own wives (Schweinle et al., 2002). A thin-skinned tendency to perceive antagonism from female strangers that did not exist was correlated with mistreatment of one's own spouse.

Happily, training and practice can improve people's abilities to understand their partners. In one study, participants in a 10-hour empathy training program were able to understand their partners' thoughts and feelings more accurately 6 months later. Their partners were also more satisfied with their relationship (Long et al., 1999).

Threatening Perceptions

Intimate partners typically understand each other much better than they understand mere acquaintances, but they may not want to on those occasions when a partner's feelings or behavior is distressing or ominous. When accurate perceptions would be worrisome, intimate partners may actually be motivated to be *in*accurate in order to fend off doubts about their relationship (Ickes & Simpson, 2001). And that's a good thing because relationships suffer when people correctly perceive unwanted, threatening feelings in their partners (Simpson et al., 2003). Imagine this situation: You and your romantic partner are asked to examine and discuss several pictures of very attractive people your partner may be meeting later. Afterward, while watching a videotape of the two of you discussing the pictures, you try to discern exactly what your partner was thinking when he was inspecting the pictures of gorgeous women (or she was inspecting the pictures of handsome men) that could be potential rivals for you. How astute would you be? Would you really want to know that your partner found one of the pictures to be especially compelling and was really looking forward to meeting that person? Not if you're like most people. The more attractive (and thereby threatening) the photos were and the closer their relationship was, the *less* accurately dating partners perceived each other's thoughts and feelings in this situation (Simpson et al., 1995). Most people understood a partner's reactions to unattractive photos reasonably well, but they somehow remained relatively clueless about a partner's reactions to attractive pictures. They were inattentive to news they did not want to hear.

But not everyone successfully managed threatening perceptions in this manner. People with a preoccupied attachment style were actually *more* accurate in judging their partners when the partners inspected the attractive photos (Simpson et al., 1999). They were unsettled by their perceptions, however, and they evaluated their relationships less favorably as a result. Preoccupied people were like moths drawn to a flame; they were especially good at intuiting their partners' feelings in just those situations in which accuracy was disconcerting and costly. Such sensitivity may be one reason that such people are chronically anxious about their relationships. People with dismissing styles[6] do better when they're confronted with distressing information, because they divert their attention and simply ignore it (Edelstein & Gillath, 2008). This protects their feelings, but it does leave them rather clueless about what's going on (Fraley & Brumbaugh, 2007).

Perceiver Influence

Finally, we should remember that people are not passive judges of others. In a close relationship, they are engaged in continual interaction with their partners, behaving in accord with their expectations and reacting to the perceptions they construct. If they come to realize that their partners are not the people they wish they were, they may try to *change* their partners by encouraging some behaviors and discouraging others. In a sense, people are sometimes like sculptors who try to construct the partners they want from the raw material a real partner provides (Rusbult et al., 2009). If our partners seem dispirited, we may try to cheer them up. Or if they're too pompous and pretentious, we may try to bring them back to earth (De La Ronde & Swann, 1998). Because intimate partners are continually shaping and molding each other's behavior, perceptions that are initially inaccurate may become more correct as we induce our partners to become the people we want them to be.

Summary

With all these influences at work, our perceptions of our partners can range from outright fantasy to pinpoint correctness. We certainly know our partners

---

[6] Are you recognizing the terms *preoccupied* and *dismissing*? If not, go back to page 16 to refresh your memory.

better as a relationship develops, but motivation and attentiveness can come and go, and some people are easier to read than others. Some of us are more astute perceivers than others, too. In addition, even if you know your partner well, there may be occasions when *in*attention is profitable, helping you avoid doubt and distress. And partners influence each other, so perceptions can become either more or less accurate as time goes by. In general, then, we usually understand our partners less well than we think we do.

My important closing point is that our perceptions of our partners are clearly influential. Right or wrong, our judgments of our lovers and friends can either support or undermine our contentment in our relationships. Some of us look on the bright side, thinking well of our partners, using relationship-enhancing attributions, and expecting kindness and generosity—and that's what we get. Others of us, however, doubt our partners and expect the worst—and thereby make it more likely that our relationships will fail.

FOR YOUR CONSIDERATION

Martha looked forward to meeting Gale because those who knew her said that she was friendly, outgoing, and bright. But their paths happened to cross when Gale was suffering from a bad case of poison ivy; she was uncomfortable from the endless itching and drowsy from the allergy medicine, and altogether, she was having a really bad day. So, things did not go well when Martha said hello and introduced herself. Martha came away from their brief interaction thinking that Gale was really rather cold and unsociable.

After Gale recovered and was back in her usual spirits, she encountered Martha again and greeted her warmly and was surprised when Martha seemed distant and wary. What do you think the future holds for Martha and Gale? Why?

CHAPTER SUMMARY

Social cognition includes all of the processes of perception and thought with which we make sense of our social worlds.

First Impressions (and Beyond)

When we first meet others, we jump to conclusions because of stereotypes and *primacy effects*. *Confirmation biases* then affect our selection of subsequent data, and *overconfidence* leads us to put unwarranted faith in our judgments.

The Power of Perceptions

Partners' perceptions can be very consequential.

Idealizing Our Partners. Happy partners construct *positive illusions* that emphasize their partners' virtues and minimize their faults.

Attributional Processes. The explanations we generate for reasons that things happen are called *attributions*. Partners are affected by *actor/observer effects* and *self-serving* biases, and they tend to employ either *relationship-enhancing* or *distress-maintaining* patterns of attribution.

Memories. We edit and update our memories as time goes by. This process of *reconstructive memory* helps couples stay optimistic about their futures.

Relationship Beliefs. *Dysfunctional relationship beliefs* such as *destiny beliefs* are clearly disadvantageous. *Growth beliefs* are more realistic and profitable.

Expectations. Our expectations about others can become *self-fulfilling prophecies*, false predictions that make themselves come true.

Self-Perceptions. We seek reactions from others that are self-enhancing and complimentary *and* that are consistent with what we already think of ourselves—but *self-verification* leads people to seek intimate partners who support their existing self-concepts.

Impression Management

We try to influence the impressions of us that others form.

Strategies of Impression Management. Four different strategies of impression management—*ingratiation, self-promotion, intimidation*, and *supplication*—are commonplace.

Impression Management in Close Relationships. High self-monitors are less committed to their romantic partners, but all of us work less hard to present favorable images to our intimate partners than to others.

So, Just How Well Do We Know Our Partners?

We generally don't understand our partners as well as we think we do.

Knowledge. As a relationship develops and partners spend more time together, they typically do understand each other better.

Motivation. The interest and motivation with which people try to figure each other out help to determine how insightful and accurate they will be.

Partner Legibility. Some personality traits, such as extraversion, are more visible than others.

Perceiver Ability. Some judges are better than others, too. *Emotional intelligence* is important in this regard.

Threatening Perceptions. However, when accurate perceptions would be worrisome, intimate partners may actually be motivated to be inaccurate.

Perceiver Influence. Perceptions that are initially inaccurate may become more correct as we induce our partners to become the people we want them to be.

Summary. Right or wrong, our judgments matter.

CHAPTER 5

Communication

Nonverbal Communication ◆ Components of Nonverbal Communication ◆Nonverbal Sensitivity ◆ Verbal Communication ◆ Self-Disclosure ◆ Gender Differences in Verbal Communication ◆ Dysfunctional Communication and What to Do About It ◆ Miscommunication ◆ Saying What We Mean ◆ Active Listening ◆ Being Polite and Staying Cool ◆ The Power of Respect and Validation ◆ For Your Consideration ◆ Chapter Summary

Imagine that you and your romantic partner are seated alone in a comfortable room, discussing the topic of your last disagreement. Your conversation is more structured than most because before you say anything to your partner, you record a quick rating of what you intend to say next. You rate the intended impact of your message by pushing one of five buttons with labels ranging from *super negative* through *neutral* to *super positive*. Then, after you speak, your partner quickly rates his or her perception of your message in the same way before replying to you. This process continues as you take turns voicing your views and listening to what your partner says in return. You're engaging in a procedure called the *talk table* that allows researchers to get a record of both your private thoughts and your public actions. The notable point is that if you're currently unhappy with your relationship, you may not *intend* to annoy or belittle your lover, but you're likely to do so, anyway. Unhappy couples don't differ on average from happy, contented couples in what they are trying to say to each other, but the impact of their messages—what their partners think they hear—is more critical and disrespectful nonetheless (Gottman et al., 1976). And this is consequential because this single afternoon at the talk table predicts how happy the two of you will be later on; spouses whose communications are frustrating will be less happily married 5 years later (Markman, 1981).

Communication is incredibly important in intimate relationships. And it's more complex than we usually realize. Let's consider the simple model of communication shown in Figure 5.1. Communication begins with the sender's intentions, the message that the sender wishes to convey. The problem is that the sender's intentions are private and known only to him or her. For them to be communicated to the listener, they must be encoded into verbal and non-verbal actions that are public and observable. A variety of factors, such as the sender's mood or social skill, or noisy distractions in the surrounding environment, can influence or interfere with this process. Then, the receiver must

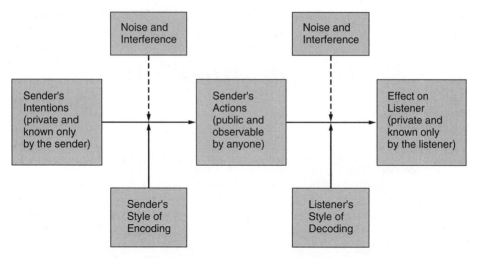

FIGURE 5.1. **A simple model of interpersonal communication.**
There is often a discrepancy—an *interpersonal gap*—between what the sender intends to say and what the listener thinks he or she hears.
Adapted from Gottman et al., 1976.

decode the speaker's actions, and interference can occur here as well (Albright et al., 2004). The final result is an effect on the receiver that is again private and known only to him or her.

The point here is that getting from one person's intentions to the impact of that person's message on a listener involves several steps at which error and misunderstanding may occur (Puccinelli, 2010). We usually assume that our messages have the impact that we intended, but we rarely *know* that they do. More often than we realize (Keysar & Henly, 2002), we face an **interpersonal gap** in which the sender's intentions differ from the effect on the receiver. Indeed, such gaps are actually *more* likely to occur in close relationships than they are among strangers (Savitsky et al., 2011). We don't expect our partners to misunderstand us, so we don't work as hard as we do with strangers to check that we're on the same page.

Interpersonal gaps are frustrating. And not only are they related to dissatisfaction, they can even prevent rewarding relationships from ever beginning! Consider what happens when a shy man has a chance to make his interest in dating someone known to her. Chatting after class, he may make a timid, innocent inquiry—"What are you doing this weekend?"—thinking that his romantic intentions are transparent and hoping for an enthusiastic reply. Unfortunately, he probably thinks that his amorous aims are more obvious to his potential partner than they really are (Cameron & Vorauer, 2008). If she fails to notice that he's hinting about a date and makes a bland, noncommittal response, he may perceive an explicit rejection of a clear-cut invitation that she never actually received. Wounded, he may then keep his distance, and she may never realize what has transpired.

This sort of thing actually happens (Vorauer et al., 2003). I don't want it to happen to you, however, so I'll do what I can in this chapter to help you close your own interpersonal gaps. But we'll start our survey of communication in relationships not with what people say in interaction but with what they *do*. Accompanying the spoken word in communication is a remarkable range of nonverbal actions that also carry many messages, whether you intend them or not.

NONVERBAL COMMUNICATION

Imagine that as part of a research study, you put on a cap that identifies you as a member of either an admired or disliked group, and you walk around town with it on, shopping, eating lunch, and applying for some jobs. You've put on the cap without looking at it, and you *don't know* what you're wearing. Would you be able to tell what sort of cap you have on by watching others' reactions to you? You might (Hebl et al., 2002). If you're wearing an obnoxious cap, your waitress may not be as warm and cheerful as usual. People you pass at the mall may glance at you and display a quick expression of distaste or disgust. Even if no one mentions your cap, others' behavior may clearly indicate that they don't like what they see. In fact, because you'd be curious and alert to how others responded, their sentiments might be unmistakably plain.

In such a situation, you'd probably notice the remarkable amount of information carried by nonverbal behavior, which includes all of the things people do in their interactions except for their spoken words and syntax. Indeed, nonverbal behavior can serve several functions in our transactions with others. Table 5.1 lists five such functions, and I'll emphasize three of them.

First, nonverbal behavior **provides information** about people's moods or meaning. If you playfully tease someone, for instance, your facial expression and the sound of your voice may be the only way listeners can tell that you don't intend to be antagonistic. This function is so important that we have had to invent emoticons, the imitation facial expressions people put in text messages, to show what we mean.

Nonverbal behavior also plays a vital part in **regulating interaction.** Nonverbal displays of interest often determine whether or not interaction ever begins, and, thereafter, subtle nonverbal cues allow people to take turns in a conversation seamlessly and gracefully.

Finally, by expressing intimacy and carrying signals of power and status, nonverbal behavior helps to **define** the **relationships** we share with others. People who are intimate with each other act differently toward one another than acquaintances do, and dominant, high-status people act differently than subordinates do. Without a word being spoken, observers may be able to tell who likes whom and who's the boss.

How are these functions carried out? The answer involves all of the diverse components of nonverbal communication, so we'll survey them next.

TABLE 5.1. Functions of Nonverbal Behavior in Relationships

Category	Description	Example
Providing information	A person's behavior allows others to make inferences about his or her intentions, feelings, traits, and meaning	A husband's facial expression leads his wife to judge that he is upset
Regulating interaction	Nonverbal behavior provides cues that regulate the efficient give-and-take of smooth conversations and other interactions	A woman looks at her partner continuously as the tone of her voice drops on her last word, and he starts speaking because he knows she's finished
Defining the nature of the relationship	The type of partnership two people share may be evident in their nonverbal behavior	Lovers stand closer to each other, touch more, and look at each other more than less intimate partners do
Interpersonal influence	Goal-oriented behavior designed to influence someone else	As a person requests a favor from his friend, he leans forward, touches him on the arm, and gazes intently
Impression management	Nonverbal behavior that is managed by a person or a couple to create or enhance a particular image	A couple may quarrel on the way to a party but then hold hands and pretend to be happy with each other once they arrive

Source: Data from Patterson, 2011.

Components of Nonverbal Communication

One clue to the enormous power of nonverbal communication is the number of different channels through which information can be transmitted. I'll describe six.

Facial Expression

People's facial expressions signal their moods and emotions in a manner you'll recognize anywhere you go (Matsumoto et al., 2009). Even if you don't speak the language in a foreign country, for example, you'll be able to tell if others are happy: If they are, the muscles in their cheeks will pull up the corners of their mouths, and the skin alongside their eyes will crinkle into folds. Obviously, they're *smiling,* and happiness, like several other emotions—sadness, fear, anger, disgust, and surprise—engenders a unique facial expression that's the same all over the world. In fact, the universality of these expressions suggests that they are hardwired into our species. People don't *learn* to smile when they're happy—they're born to do it. People who have been blind all their lives, for instance, display the same facial expressions all the rest of us do (Matsumoto & Willingham, 2009).

Compelling information is often available in facial expressions. Are you displaying a big smile in your Facebook profile photo, or do you look like a

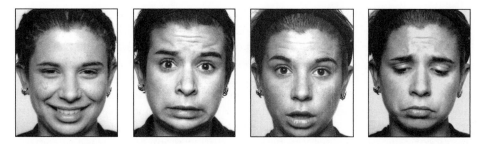

These are examples of the basic facial expressions of sadness, happiness, fear, and surprise (but not in that order!). You've never seen this woman before, but can you tell which emotion each photo depicts? I bet you can.
© *Paul Ekman*

sourpuss? The bigger the smiles college students posted during their first semester at school, the more satisfied they were with their social lives and their college careers when they were seniors four years later (Seder & Oishi, 2010). The broader the smiles people display in their college yearbooks, the less likely they are to be divorced later in life (Hertenstein et al., 2009). And even more impressively, the fuller and more genuine the smiles major league baseball players exhibited in their team photos in 1952, the longer their lives have been (Abel & Kruger, 2010)! Happy expressions are clearly correlated with success in life, and in some respects, a forecast of your future may be available to everyone you meet. We do a little better identifying emotions that are expressed by others from our own cultural groups than we do in recognizing the expressions of people from elsewhere in the world (Elfenbein & Ambady, 2003). Nevertheless, accurate recognition of others' emotions from their facial expressions is almost an automatic process; American college students can recognize happiness, sadness, anger, disgust, and surprise in three-quarters of a second or less (Tracy & Robins, 2008).

So, the universal meanings of facial expressions make them extremely informative—when they're authentic. Unfortunately, because facial expressions do figure so prominently in nonverbal communication, people sometimes try to deliberately manage them to disguise their true emotions. On occasion, this occurs due to **display rules,** cultural norms that dictate what emotions are appropriate in particular situations (Zaalberg et al., 2004). There are at least four ways we may try to modify our expressions of emotion to follow these rules. First, we may *intensify* our expressions, exaggerating them so that we appear to be experiencing stronger feelings than we really are. Even if you're underwhelmed by a gift you've just opened, for example, you should try to look pleased if the donor is present. Second, we sometimes *minimize* our expressions, trying to seem less emotional than we really are. Because Western culture assumes that "big boys don't cry," a man may stoically try not to seem too affected by a sad movie. Third, we may *neutralize* our expressions, trying to withhold our true feelings altogether. Good poker players try to do this so that they give no hint of what their cards may be. Finally, we can *mask* our real feelings by replacing them with an entirely different apparent emotion. A first runner-up in a beauty pageant who looks so thrilled when another contestant is named the winner is almost certainly masking her true feelings.

However, even when people try to control their expressions, the truth may leak out. First, feigned expressions often differ in subtle ways from authentic expressions. For instance, people can easily pull up the corners of their mouths when they want to fake a smile, but there are subtle differences in timing and movement between real and fake smiles that are often apparent to attentive viewers (Ambadar et al., 2009). Second, despite our efforts, authentic flashes of real emotion, or *microexpressions,* can be visible during momentary lapses of control. Even when you're consciously trying to control your expression, you may slip for an instant if you encounter an image of a severed hand (Porter & ten Brinke, 2008)!

Gazing Behavior

Obviously, facial expressions provide meaningful information about a partner's feelings. Gazing, the direction and amount of a person's looking behavior, is also influential (Wirth et al., 2010). For one thing, looking at someone communicates interest, and people with friendly expressions who catch our eye and keep looking seem more likable and attractive than those who glance at us and then look away (Mason et al., 2005). If you find someone looking your way in a singles bar and you don't want to talk to him or her, look away and don't look back.

Gazing also helps define the relationship two people share once interaction begins. Lovers really do spend more time looking at each other than friends do, and friends look more than acquaintances do (Kleinke, 1986). Moreover, when strangers spend time gazing into each other's eyes, they end up liking each other more than they would have if they'd spent the time together looking someplace else (Kellerman et al., 1989). A lot of looking can evidently communicate affection as well as simple interest.

But it can communicate dominance, too. In ordinary interaction, people usually look at their conversational partners more when they're listening (gazing at the speaker about 60 percent of the time, on average) than when they're speaking (looking at the listener about 40 percent of the time). However, powerful, high-status people tend to depart from these norms—they look more while speaking but less while listening than the average person does (Koch et al., 2010). Researchers summarize these patterns in a **visual dominance ratio** (VDR) that compares "look-speak" (the percentage of time a speaker gazes at a listener) to "look-listen." A high-power pattern of gazing turns the typical ratio of 40/60 on its head, producing a high VDR of 60/40 (Ellyson et al., 1992). Dominant partners in an interaction can insist, "Look at me when I'm talking to you!" but they often do not offer as much visual attention in return.

Body Movement

So far, I've been describing nonverbal communication only from the neck up, but the rest of the body is involved, too. Body movements routinely accompany and support our verbal communication, making it easier for us to convey what we mean—try describing the size of a fish you caught without using your hands (Holler et al., 2009)—but they can also replace spoken words entirely in the form of gestures that are widely understood. (A good example in North America, for better or worse, is a gesture in which one holds up one's hand with one's middle finger extended. The recipient of the gesture will probably know what it means.) The problem with gestures is that, unlike facial expressions, they vary widely from culture to culture (Pease & Pease, 2006). For instance, in the United States, touching your thumb to your index finger and extending the other fingers is a gesture that means "okay," or "good." However, in France it means "zero," in Japan it means "money," and in the Middle East it's an obscene insult (just like the American middle finger). The language of the face needs no interpreter, but that's not true of the language of gestures.

Less specific but still useful information can be conveyed by the posture or motion of the body (Hugill et al., 2010). For instance, the impressions observers get from brief (10-second) silent videotapes allow them to predict the teaching evaluations college professors will get from their students (Ambady & Rosenthal, 1993), and, even more remarkably, the sexual orientation of total strangers (check out the box on the next page) at levels noticeably better than chance. Only 30 seconds of observation allow strangers to make reasonably accurate judgments about our personality traits (Yeagley et al., 2007). One reason why body language is informative is that it's harder to control than facial expressions are; it's "leakier," which means that it's more likely to indicate what our true feelings are, even when we're trying to disguise them (Babad et al., 1989). U.S. customs inspectors, for example, use bodily signs of restlessness and anxiety, not facial expressions, to decide whether or not to search travelers' luggage for contraband (Kraut & Poe, 1980).

Body postures can also signal status. High-status people tend to adopt open, asymmetric postures in which the two halves of the body assume different positions (Carney et al., 2010). They take up a lot of space. In contrast, low-status people use closed, symmetric postures that are relatively compact. If a powerful boss is talking with a subordinate seated across from him or her, you can usually tell who's who just by watching them (Bente et al., 2010).

Touch

Physical contact with another person can also have various meanings. In many cultures, people may touch each other by shaking hands when they first meet, and—just as common sense suggests—there is useful information to be gained from the strength and vigor and fullness of grip with which someone shakes your hand. People with firm, full, long handshakes tend to be more extraverted and open to experience, and less neurotic, than people with wimpy handshakes are. Women with strong handshakes also tend to be more agreeable (Chaplin et al., 2000).

So, touch may be informative from the moment two people meet. Thereafter, different types of touches have distinctly different meanings. Positive, supportive feelings such as love (which, for instance, might lead you to stroke someone's arm) and sympathy (with you patting it) engender touches that are quite different from those that communicate disgust (pushing) or anger (hitting). The emotions communicated by touch are often so distinct, both the

Nonverbal Behavior and Sexual Orientation
Or, "Don't Ask, Don't Tell"? Who Has To Ask?

For 17 years, the U.S. Armed Forces maintained a "don't ask, don't tell" policy toward the sexual orientation of its personnel. Fearing that open same-sex sexuality would undermine the cohesion of its troops, the military asked its gays and lesbians not to advertise their orientations. Of course, the policy assumed that someone's sexual orientation wasn't already obvious—but often it is. Nonverbal channels of information allow attentive observers to assess the orientations of others very quickly with reasonable accuracy. A 10-second video of a person's body movements is all observers need to make correct judgments 72 percent of the time (Ambady et al., 1999).

What's visible in the videos? The patterns of a person's gestures and movement are key. Heterosexual men tend to swagger, swinging their shoulders when they walk, and heterosexual women tend to sway, moving their hips. People whose behavior includes the motions that are typical of the other sex are likely to be judged to be homosexual, and those perceptions are often correct (Johnson et al., 2007). Differences in posture and gazing are evident when people are just sitting and chatting, too (Knöfler & Imhof, 2007).

But the most remarkable result of these studies is the finding that people who get a glimpse of men's faces that lasts for only half a second can accurately judge whether they are gay or straight about 70 percent of the time (Rule & Ambady, 2008). We don't yet know exactly what it is about men's faces that informs such judgments, but one thing is clear: An attentive observer often has some idea of whether someone shares his or her sexual orientation before a single word is said.

recipient of the touch and bystanders watching it can tell what feelings are at work (Hertenstein et al., 2009).

Two people also tend to touch each other more as their relationship becomes more intimate (Emmers & Dindia, 1995), and that's a good thing. Loving touches are actually good for our health: Kissing your partner more often can reduce your cholesterol (Floyd et al., 2009), and getting 30 minutes of head and neck massage three times a week will reduce your blood pressure and your production of stress hormones (Holt-Lunstad et al., 2008). Touch can clearly convey closeness and affection, and it can have healing properties, too.

Interpersonal Distance

One aspect of touching that makes it momentous is that people have to be near each other for touching to occur. That means that the two partners are typically in a region of *interpersonal distance*—the physical space that separates two people—that is usually reserved for relatively intimate interactions. The **intimate zone** of interpersonal distance extends out from the front of our chests about a foot-and-a-half (Hall, 1966). (See Figure 5.2.) If two people are standing face-to-face to each other, their interaction is probably either quite loving or quite hostile. More interactions occur at greater distances in a **personal zone** that ranges from 1½ to 4 feet away from us. Within this range, friends are likely to interact at

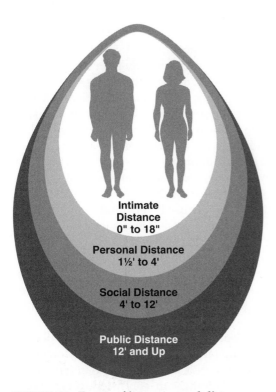

FIGURE 5.2. **Zones of interpersonal distance.**
There are four discrete regions of space in which different kinds of social interaction are likely to occur.

smaller distances and acquaintances at larger ones, so distancing behavior helps to define the relationships people share. Even further away, in a **social zone** (4 to 12 feet), interactions tend to be more businesslike. When you sit across a desk from an interviewer or a professor, you're in the social zone, and the distance seems appropriate; however, it would seem quite odd to stand 5 feet away from a good friend to hold a personal conversation. Beyond 12 feet, interactions tend to be quite formal. This is the **public zone,** which is used for structured interaction like that between an instructor and his or her students in a lecture class.

These distances describe the general patterns of interactions among North Americans, but they tend to be larger than those used by many other peoples of the world (Pease & Pease, 2006). French, Latin, and Arabic cultures prefer distances smaller than these. A person's sex and status also affect distancing behavior (Holland et al., 2004). Men tend to use somewhat larger distances than women do, and people usually stand further away from others of high status than from those of lower power and prestige. Whatever one's preferences, how-ever, spacing behavior is a subtle way to calibrate the desired intimacy of an interaction, and it may even be an indirect measure of the quality of a relation-ship: Spouses who are unhappy choose to maintain larger distances between each other than do spouses who are currently content (Crane et al., 1987).

Paralanguage

The final component of nonverbal communication isn't silent like the others can be. *Paralanguage* includes all the variations in a person's voice other than the actual words he or she uses, such as rhythm, pitch, loudness, and rate. Thus, paralanguage doesn't involve *what* people say, but *how* they say it. Good examples of distinctive paralanguage are the sounds we make—without using any words at all—that can tell people what we're feeling. If you wanted to show someone with just a brief sound that you were scared, or angry, or sad, could you do it? How about relieved, amused, or awed? Research participants are indeed able to reliably communicate these emotions and several more to listeners without using words (Simon-Thomas et al., 2009).

Paralanguage helps define relationships because lovers tend to talk to each other with different rhythms than friends use. Lovers tolerate longer delays in responding, are silent more often, and say less overall (Guerrero, 1997). People even speak differently to attractive strangers than to those who are less appealing; both men and women use a lower pitch when they leave voice messages for pretty, rather than plain, members of the other sex, and they sound more pleasant when they do so (Hughes et al., 2010). Can paralanguage help determine whether relationships ever start?

In fact, some voices are routinely more beguiling than others, and people with appealing voices tend to have alluring faces and bodies, too (Saxton et al., 2009). They also have sex at earlier ages and with more people than the rest of us do (Hughes et al., 2004). Even more intriguingly, if you listen to tapes of a variety of women counting from 1 to 10 at various times during their menstrual cycles, you'll hear that a woman's voice becomes more attractive just before she ovulates each month (Pipitone & Gallup, 2008). This is probably due to the effects of her changing hormones on her larynx, and it doesn't happen in women who are on the pill—but when nature is allowed to run its course, this is a fine example of the subtlety with which nonverbal channels communicate important information from one person to another.

Combining the Components

I've introduced the components of nonverbal communication as if they are independent, discrete sources of information, and, in one sense, they are: Each of them can have its own effects on interaction (Rashotte, 2002). Usually, however, they reinforce each other, working together to convey consistent information about a person's sentiments and intentions. When you're face-to-face with someone, all of these components are in play, and together, they often tell you what people really mean by what they say. Consider *sarcasm*, for instance, when people say one thing but mean another: Their true intent is conveyed not in their words but in their actions and paralanguage. Most of the time, our nonverbal behavior communicates the same message as our words, and we like people better when that's the case (Weisbuch et al., 2010). But when there *is* a discrepancy between people's words and actions, the truth behind their words usually lies in their nonverbal, not their verbal, communication (Vrij, 2006).

Our facial expressions and our paralanguage usually combine to make our feelings and meanings plain to attentive audiences.

Furthermore, all the channels may be involved in the nonconscious behavioral **mimicry** that occurs during a conversation when the participants adopt similar postures and mannerisms, display comparable expressions, and use similar paralanguage. If they're enjoying their interaction, people tend to synchronize their nonverbal behavior automatically without thinking about it;

Flirting

A great example of nonverbal communication—and the misunderstandings that can result from it—is the way people behave when they intentionally want to attract attention and to communicate their interest in others. If a woman wishes to be approached in a college bar, she's likely to look around the room, move to the music, and run her fingers through her hair (Cunningham & Barbee, 2008). But women don't like to be approached by men who haven't already caught their eye, so men need to get women to notice them. Taking up a lot of space, having an open posture, and touching other men (but not being touched in return) are all signs of high status that make a man stand out in a group. And men who behave this way—and who are frequently glancing around to see who's looking their way—are more likely to share a moment of eye contact with a woman that leads to some conversation (Renninger et al., 2004).

Then, if they begin to flirt, both men and women tend to smile more, move closer, gaze longer, and touch their partners more often than they do when they are less eager to stimulate others' interest (Moore, 2010). Their speech is more animated, involving more laughter and fewer silences, and their voices sound warmer. And coupled with these signals of interest and immediacy may be particular expressions such as a head cant, pouting mouth, and coy look that are fairly unique (Simpson et al., 1993). Together, these enticing actions clearly signal one's desire for continued interaction with a new partner.

Behavior that is merely flirtatious differs from behavior that is straightforwardly seductive. Actions that are intended to convey sexual interest involve even more eye contact, smiling, and touching, more intimate paralanguage, and smaller interpersonal distances than friendly flirtatiousness does (Koeppel et al., 1993). But the distinction is often lost on men, who tend to misread women's signals more than often than women misunderstand men's meanings. Men often see sexual overtones in the friendly behavior they receive from women, and women who intend their actions to be fun, frivolous, and festive (but nothing more) run a constant risk of being misunderstood. On the other hand, women who *are* sending sexual signals may be misunderstood, too, being thought to be merely friendly. Guys make both kinds of mistakes (Farris et al., 2008) because they're just not as good at reading others, on average, as women are (Brody & Hall, 2010). C'est la vie.

if one of them scratches his or her nose, the other is more likely to do so as well. When this occurs, the conversation tends to flow smoothly, and, more importantly, they tend to like each other even when they don't notice the mutual imitation taking place (Chartrand & van Baaren, 2009). Indeed, it seems to be rewarding to be met with nonverbal behavior from others that resembles our own. In one demonstration of this effect, research participants encountered a mechanical device that recorded the physical characteristics of their handshakes; then, when they supposedly greeted another person using the device, some of them received their own handshakes back instead of the real handshake from the new acquaintance. People liked their own handshakes more than those of someone else (Bailenson & Yee, 2007). In another study, participants watched a persuasive argument from an avatar in an IVE[1] that either used the recorded movements of a real person or simply mimicked the participant's own actions with a 4-second delay. People were not consciously aware of the mimicry, but they attributed more positive traits to the avatar and were more convinced by its argument when it duplicated their own actions than when it behaved like someone else (Bailenson & Yee, 2005). (Is this the future of high-tech advertising?) We are evidently charmed and more at ease when non-verbal mimicry takes place, and it can be surprisingly stressful to interact with someone who does not imitate us at all (Kouzakova et al., 2010).

The various components of nonverbal behavior also allow us to fine-tune the intimacy of our interactions to establish a comfortable level of closeness (Patterson, 2011). Imagine that you're seated next to an acquaintance on a two-person couch when the conversation takes a serious turn and your acquaintance mentions an intimate personal problem. If this development makes you uncomfortable—you've just received too much information—you can adjust the perceived intimacy of your interaction by nonverbally "backing off." You can turn away and lean back to get more distance. You can avert your gaze. And you can signal your discomfort through less animated paralanguage and a less pleasant facial expression, all without saying a word (Andersen et al., 2006). Nonverbal communication serves several important functions in interaction and is the source of useful subtlety in social life.

Nonverbal Sensitivity

Given all this, you might expect that it's advantageous for couples to do well at nonverbal communication, and you'd be right. The sensitivity and accuracy with which couples communicate nonverbally predict how happy their relationship will be. Husbands and wives who do poorly at nonverbal communication tend to be dissatisfied with their marriages, and, moreover, when such problems occur, it's usually the husband's fault (Noller, 2006).

What? How can research arrive at such a conclusion? Well, when nonverbal exchanges fail, there may be errors in encoding or decoding, or both (Puccinelli, 2010): The sender may enact a confusing message that is difficult to read (that's poor encoding), or the receiver may fail to correctly interpret a message that is clear to everyone else (and that's poor decoding). Women typically start with an advantage at both tasks because, if no deception is involved, women are both better encoders and more astute decoders than men are on average (Brody & Hall, 2010). (There's no difference in men's and women's abilities to detect deception, as we'll see in chapter 10.) Thus, the old stereotype about "women's intuition" actually has a basis in fact; more than men, women tend to attentively use subtle but real nonverbal cues to discern what's going on. Do women possess more skill at nonverbal communication, or are they just working harder at it? That's a good question, and I'll answer it shortly.

---

[1]What's an "IVE"? Look back at the box on p. 55. I told you that chapter 2 would come in handy!

Researchers can assess the quality of husbands' and wives' encoding and decoding by asking them to send specific nonverbal messages that are then decoded by the other spouse. The messages are statements that can have several different meanings, depending on how they are nonverbally enacted; for instance, the phrase, "I'm cold, aren't you?" could be either an affectionate invitation ("Come snuggle with me, you cute thing") or a spiteful complaint ("Turn up the damn heat, you cheapskate!"). In research on nonverbal sensitivity, a spouse is assigned a particular meaning to convey and is filmed sending the message. Then, impartial strangers are shown the film. If they can't figure out what the spouse is trying to communicate, the spouse's encoding is assumed to be faulty. On the other hand, if they *can* read the message but the other spouse *can't*, the partner's decoding is implicated.

In the first ingenious study of this sort, Patricia Noller (1980) found that husbands in unhappy marriages sent more confusing messages and made more decoding errors than happy husbands did. There were no such differences among the wives, so the poorer communication that Noller observed in the distressed marriages appeared to be the husbands' fault. Men in troubled marriages were misinterpreting communications from their wives that were clearly legible to total strangers. Even worse, such husbands were completely clueless about their mistakes; they assumed that they were doing a fine job communicating with their wives, and they were confident that they understood their wives and that their wives understood them (Noller & Venardos, 1986). The men were doing a poor job communicating and didn't know it, and that's why they seemed to be at fault.

On the other hand, to be fair, nonverbal marital miscommunication is not entirely due to husbands' shortcomings. In another study, Noller (1981) compared spouses' accuracy in decoding the other's messages to their accuracy in decoding communications from strangers. In unhappy marriages, *both* the husbands and wives understood strangers better than they understood each other. When they were dissatisfied, everyone was miscommunicating, despite being capable of adequate nonverbal communication with others.

This is a key point because, now that you're becoming a more sophisticated consumer of relationship science, you've probably already realized that a correlation between nonverbal miscommunication and relationship dissatisfaction is consistent with several possibilities. On the one hand, the partners' nonverbal skills may determine how satisfying their relationships are; poor skills may result in poor relationships, but good skills may promote pleasurable partnerships. On the other hand, the partners' satisfaction may determine how hard they work to communicate well; poor relationships may engender lazy (mis)communication, and good relationships may foster good communication.

Actually, both of these propositions are correct. Nonverbal insensitivity makes someone a less rewarding partner than he or she otherwise would be (Koerner & Fitzpatrick, 2002). But once partners grow dissatisfied for any reason, they tend to start tuning each other out, and that causes them to communicate less adeptly than they could if they really tried (Noller, 2006). In this fashion, nonverbal insensitivity and dissatisfaction can become a vicious cycle, with each exacerbating the other.

In any case, people's problems with communication may stem from either skill deficits or performance deficits, and the distinction is an important one. Some people simply aren't very talented at nonverbal communication, and their deficits are provocative (and a little eerie). For instance, men who beat their wives have more trouble than nonviolent men figuring out what their wives are feeling (Marshall & Holtzworth-Munroe, 2010). And abusive mothers have trouble identifying signs of distress in infants; they tend not to know when their babies are scared and unhappy (Kropp & Haynes, 1987). It's possible, then, that skill deficits give some people blind spots that make them less likely to realize just how much harm they are doing to others.

So, why is it that women do better at nonverbal communication than men do? Skill and motivation both seem to be involved: Women possess more talent, on average, and they apply themselves to the task, too (Ciarrochi et al., 2005). Men's performance improves when they're motivated to pay close attention and to judge others correctly, but they never do better than women (Hall & Mast, 2008), who naturally seem to judge others' emotions more quickly and accurately than men do (Hampson et al., 2006). Given the frustrating impact of nonverbal miscommunication, men's poorer performances can be a nuisance, so here's a tip: Watch someone's eyes. Women spend more time watching others' eyes than men do, and that appears to be one reason that they read others' expressions more accurately (Hall et al., 2010). And as this tip suggests, training and practice *can* improve one's skills (Blanch-Hartigan et al., 2011). The good news is that both men and women do better at nonverbal communication when they look and listen and put their minds to it, and we're usually more adept at reading our intimate partners' nonverbal cues than those of acquaintances or strangers (Zhang & Parmley, 2011). The bad news is that lazy inattention from either partner is likely to lead to more misunderstanding and less happiness and satisfaction than a couple would otherwise enjoy (Noller, 2006).

VERBAL COMMUNICATION

If nonverbal communication is so important, what about the things we actually say to each other? They are probably even more consequential, of course (Greene & Burleson, 2003). Verbal communication is a vital part of close relationships, and it is extensively involved in the development of intimacy in the first place (Derlega et al., 2008).

Self-Disclosure

Imagine that as part of a psychology experiment, you meet a stranger and engage in tasks that lead you to gradually reveal more and more personal information about yourself. For instance, you describe your relationship with your mother, an embarrassing moment, or a deep regret. The stranger does the same thing, and 45 minutes later, you know a lot of personal details about each other. What would happen? Would you like the stranger more than you would have if the two of you had just shared small talk for the same amount of time?

In most cases, the answer is definitely "yes." Experiences such as these usually generate immediate closeness between the participants. People who open up to each other, even when they're just following researchers' instructions, like each other more than do couples who do not reveal as much (Slatcher, 2010).

The process of revealing personal information to someone else is called **self-disclosure.** It is one of the defining characteristics of intimacy: Two people cannot be said to be intimate with each other if they do not share some personal, relatively confidential information with one another (Laurenceau et al., 2004).

How Self-Disclosure Develops

Of course, in real life, meaningful self-disclosure takes longer than 45 minutes. Most relationships begin with the exchange of superficial information—"small talk"—and only gradually move to more meaningful revelations. The manner in which this occurs is the subject of **social penetration theory,** which holds that relationships develop through systematic changes in communication (Altman & Taylor, 1973). People who have just met may feel free to talk with each other about only a few relatively impersonal topics: "Where are you from?" "What's your major?" But if this superficial conversation is rewarding, they're likely to move closer to each other by increasing two aspects of their communication:

1. Its *breadth:* the variety of topics they discuss, and
2. Its *depth:* the personal significance of the topics they discuss.

According to the theory, if we diagram all the things there are to know about someone, self-disclosure at the beginning of a new relationship is likely to take the form of a wedge that's both narrow (only a few different topics are being discussed) and shallow (only impersonal information is being revealed) (see Figure 5.3). As the relationship develops, however, the wedge should

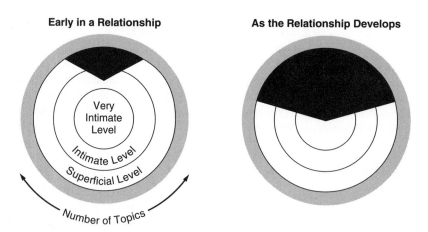

FIGURE 5.3. **Altman and Taylor's wedge of social penetration.**
If information about someone exists in several layers, self-disclosure increases in both breadth and depth as a relationship develops.

Are You a High "Opener"?

Some people are especially good at eliciting self-disclosure from others. Lynn Miller, John Berg, and Rick Archer (1983) developed the Opener Scale to assess this ability, and people who get high scores really do draw out more intimate information from others than do people who receive low scores on the scale. They do this through both verbal and non-verbal channels: High openers appear more attentive during conversation—gazing and nodding more, and looking interested—and they verbally express more interest in what others are saying (Purvis et al., 1984). They seem to be absorbed by what others have to say, so they tend to be very good interviewers (Shaffer et al., 1990).

Women tend to be better openers than men (Miller et al., 1983). The average score for women on the Opener Scale is 31, whereas 28 is typical for men. If your own score is 5 points higher than average, you're a fairly high opener, but if it's 5 points lower, your score is rather low. You can figure your score by rating yourself on each item using this scale:

0	1	2	3	4
Strongly disagree	Disagree	Neither agree nor disagree	Agree	Strongly agree

The Opener Scale

1. People frequently tell me about themselves.
2. I've been told that I'm a very good listener.
3. I'm very accepting of others.
4. People trust me with their secrets.
5. I easily get people to "open up."
6. People feel relaxed around me.
7. I enjoy listening to people.
8. I'm sympathetic to people's problems.
9. I encourage people to tell me how they are feeling.
10. I can keep people talking about themselves.

---

become broader (with more topics being discussed) and deeper (with more topics of personal significance being revealed).

In general, that is what happens (Derlega et al., 2008). In addition, early encounters between acquaintances usually involve obvious *reciprocity* in self-disclosure. New partners tend to match each other's level of openness, disclosing more as the other person does, and disclosing less if the other person's self-disclosure declines. Just how much people reveal about themselves, then, tends to depend on the specific partner and may vary considerably from relationship to relationship (Dindia, 2002). This also tends to be a gradual process, with new partners moving toward deeper topics by stages rather than all at once. Saying too much too soon can be risky; it violates others' expectations and often makes a poor impression (Buck & Plant, 2011). The best strategy is usually to be patient and to allow measured reciprocity to gradually increase the intimacy of your interactions.

However, an **interpersonal process model of intimacy** proposed by Harry Reis and Phillip Shaver (1988) argues that genuine intimacy is likely to develop between two people only when certain conditions have been met. When we open up to others, we want our disclosures to be received with apparent interest, sympathy, and respect. That is, we want *responsiveness* from others that indicates that they understand us and care about us. If they are suitably responsive, trust builds, disclosures deepen, and intimacy increases; alternatively, if they seem disinterested or uncaring, we back off and our disclosures decrease. So, for two people to become close, three things have to happen. First, they have to engage in meaningful self-disclosure. Authentic openness and honesty are generally good for relationships (Brunell et al., 2010). Then, they have to respond to each other's personal information with interest and empathy—and in heterosexual relationships, it's particularly valuable when men do this (Mitchell et al., 2008). Finally—and this is important—they each have to recognize that the other *is* being responsive. The judgment that one's partner is understanding and caring, which is known as *perceived partner responsiveness*, is a key part of the ongoing process by which intimacy develops (Laurenceau et al., 2005). If we don't perceive our partners to be caring, understanding, and respectful, we'll not tell them our secrets.

Secrets and Other Things We Don't Want to Talk About

Even when a relationship becomes quite intimate, we'll probably keep some things to ourselves. Social penetration is almost never total, and it probably shouldn't be because partners like and need some privacy, too (Petronio & Durham, 2008). No relationship is likely to be able to sustain total openness and intimacy over long periods of time (Derlega et al., 2008), and it may be a mistake to even try: Both intimate self-disclosure *and* selective secrecy contribute to marital satisfaction (Finkenauer, Kubacka et al., 2009). Some privacy is desirable even in a close, intimate relationship. (I'm reminded of a cover story in *Cosmopolitan* magazine that asked, if you've had an affair, "Should You Ever Tell?" Their answer, after much discussion, was "probably not.")

Of course, it's not always easy to keep a secret, especially in an intimate relationship. Doing so often requires hard work (Uysal et al., 2010), and it's risky, too: Relationships are undermined when people learn that their partners are concealing something (Finkenauer, Kerkhof et al., 2009). Why go to the trouble? There are several possible reasons. When they intentionally withhold information from others, "people generally long to protect themselves, protect their relationships, or protect others" (Afifi et al., 2007, p. 79). It's pretty straightforward, really: When people believe that keeping a secret is more trouble than it's worth, they usually reveal it to others after a while (Caughlin et al., 2005). On the other hand, if they worry that they or others may be harmed by an unwanted truth, they may strive to conceal it forever (Afifi et al., 2005).

Cautious Communication: Coming Out

You probably know someone who's openly gay or lesbian. LGBs (lesbians, gays, or bisexuals) are more likely to announce their sexual identities to friends and family, and to do so at earlier ages, than was the case a generation ago (Hunter, 2007). As one researcher wryly put it, "coming out has become a non-event, a 'big yawn'—everybody's doing it" (Savin-Williams, 2001, p. 201). Public acknowledgments of their identities are still important milestones for most LGBs, however, and it's an action they usually take thoughtfully and cautiously (if they do so at all).

Many gays and lesbians become aware of their attraction to the same sex years before they engage in sexual activity, when they're only 12 (on average). In the most typical sequence of events in such cases, they then realize that they are gay, lesbian, or bisexual around the age of 16; they have their first same-sex experience a year later, and they come out to someone for the first time just before they turn 18 (Floyd & Bakeman, 2006). These first disclosures usually go well, resulting in supportive, positive reactions because the confidant is typically a trusted friend (Savin-Williams, 2005). It's a year later on average, just before they turn 19, when they first tell a parent, usually their mothers (Floyd & Bakeman, 2006). This is often difficult, requiring no small amount of courage, and LGBs with a history of secure attachment to their parents are more likely to come out to them than insecure people are (Elizur & Minzer, 2001). A variety of parental reactions may then follow:

shock, denial, and anger are all common, and a small number of parents (4 percent) reject their sons or daughters, banning them from the family. Some parents are supportive, however, and most adjust with time (Savin-Williams, 2001).

A second common trajectory for coming out is notably different. In this pattern, same-sex attraction is noticed later (at the age of 16, on average), and the person has heterosexual experiences (at 19) before the first same-sex sexual experience (at 23). Self-identification as gay, lesbian, or bisexual follows in the mid-20s with disclosure to a friend, and then a parent—if a parent is told at all—following shortly thereafter (Floyd & Bakeman, 2006).

Thus, older LGBs take longer to realize who they are, so they are often independent adults (almost 26, on average) when they come out. By comparison, LGB teens usually live with a big secret for a couple of years before telling anyone, and it takes them 3 years to come out to a parent. Why so long? It's usually because they correctly recognize that their disclosure will be a turning point in their relationships with their families. And they rarely wish to injure anyone; instead, they seek to be honest and authentic rather than secretive and distant (Hunter, 2007). They disclose the truth to be closer to the ones they love, and the good news is that they usually succeed: It may take some time, but most parents come to accept a son's or daughter's same-sex orientation with either equanimity or encouragement (Savin-Williams, 2001).

There are also important issues that both partners may simply not want to talk about (Afifi, 2010). Explicitly or implicitly, partners may agree to steer clear of **taboo topics,** sensitive matters that, in the opinion of the partners, may threaten the quality of their relationship. Curiously, the most common taboo topic is the state of the relationship itself; in one survey, 68 percent of the respondents acknowledged that the current or future state of their romantic relationships was a subject that was better off not being mentioned (Baxter & Wilmot, 1985). (Other common taboos involved current relationships with *other* partners, avoided by 31 percent of the respondents, and past relationships [25 percent]. Discussion of past sexual experiences is also routinely avoided [Anderson et al., 2010].) People are often keenly interested in the likely future of their partnerships and are eager to learn their partners' expectations and intentions, but they don't ask. Instead, romantic partners may create *secret tests* of their lovers' fidelity and devotion (Baxter & Wilmot, 1984). They watch closely to see how their lovers respond to other attractive people (that's a "triangle test"); they contrive difficulties that the lover must overcome in order to demonstrate his or her devotion (an "endurance test"); and they find reasons to be apart to see how enthusiastically their lovers welcome their return (a "separation test"). This all seems like a lot of trouble when they could simply ask the partner what he or she is thinking—and they *do* often ask the partner's *friends*—but in many relationships, such matters seem too delicate to be discussed openly. Indeed, in many cases, it would cause the partners real stress to do so (Loving et al., 2009). Overall, the more taboo topics there are in a relationship, the less satisfied the partners are unless they believe that they're avoiding touchy topics to promote and protect their relationship (Dillow et al., 2009). Ducking discussions because of cowardice or incompetency erodes partners' satisfaction, but politely working together to maintain the partnership rarely has ill effects.

Self-Disclosure and Relationship Satisfaction

The bottom line is that self-disclosure that fits the situation breeds liking and contentment in close relationships. The more self-disclosure romantic couples share, for instance, the happier they tend to be (Sprecher & Hendrick, 2004). Indeed, happy lovers talk to each other differently than less intimate partners do. They're likely to have their own idiosyncratic codes and figures of speech that allow them to communicate in a manner that is not transparent to others. They use pet phrases and specialized vocabulary, or **idioms,** whose meaning is known only to them, and the more idioms they use, the happier they are (Dunleavy & Booth-Butterfield, 2009). The resulting interactions are so distinctive that strangers who listen to the conversations of couples in research studies can usually tell whether the speakers are close friends or just acquaintances (Planalp & Benson, 1992). The conversations of intimate partners are marked by more obvious knowledge of the other person, more personal self-disclosure, and greater relaxation than occurs between people who are not intimate.

Self-disclosure is linked to liking for several reasons (Collins & Miller, 1994). First, we tend to reveal more personal information to those we like. If we're attracted to others, we tend to be more open with them. However, we also tend to like others *because* we have self-disclosed to them. Everything else being equal, opening up to others causes us to like them more. Finally, and perhaps most importantly, it's rewarding to be entrusted with self-disclosures from others. People who engage in intimate disclosures are liked more by others than are those who say less about themselves (Sprecher et al., 2011). So, it feels good to

Attachment Styles and Communication

Attachment styles are evident in communicative behavior. Compared to avoidant people, those with secure styles generally exhibit warmer, more expressive nonverbal behavior involving more laughter, smiling, gazing, and touching; their greater comfort with intimacy and closeness is apparent in their actions (Tucker & Anders, 1998). Secure people also engage in more self-disclosure (Bradford et al., 2002), keep fewer secrets (Vrij et al., 2003), and express their emotions more honestly (Kafetsios, 2004) than insecure people do. Secure people are thus more open with their intimate partners than insecure people are, and that's one reason why their marriages tend to be more satisfying as the years go by (Cassidy & Shaver, 2010).

give and to receive self-disclosures, and this aspect of verbal communication is an essential building block of close relationships. Try it yourself for 45 minutes, and you'll probably make a new friend (Slatcher, 2010).

Finally, self-disclosure is not only good for our relationships, it's good for *us*. Compared to those who engage in more superficial small talk, people who have substantive, deep conversations and who make themselves known to others enjoy better health (Sloan, 2010) and more satisfaction with life (Mehl et al., 2010). And there's a particular sort of self-disclosure that you should absolutely, positively engage in more often: Tell those you love that you love them. Your honest expressions of fondness, regard, affection, and care are powerful rewards for those who want to be close to you (Floyd & Pauley, 2011), and it's not enough just to have such feelings; you have to *communicate* them in a way that makes them plain (Horan & Booth-Butterfield, 2010). But here's the real point of this paragraph: Affectionate communication is not just affirming and pleasing to your partner; it also can be remarkably beneficial to you. In lab studies, people who get randomly assigned to write love letters that express their affection for their partners experience improved neuroendocrine responses to stress (Floyd et al., 2007b) and, over time, lower cholesterol levels, heart rates, and blood pressures (Floyd et al., 2007a). Tell your partners of your affection for them. It'll be good for both of you.[2]

Gender Differences in Verbal Communication

People have made a lot of money writing books that describe men and women as different species that come from different planets and speak different languages. I've tried to combat that simple-minded way of thinking throughout this book because the sexes really are more similar than they are different. However, there are some gender differences in verbal communication that can influence our interactions. Men and women don't speak different languages, but they sometimes talk about different things.

---

[2] There's no need to tell them I put you up to it.

Topics of Conversation

If you read a transcript of a conversation between two friends, would you be able to tell if the participants were men or women? You might. Among themselves, women are more likely than men to discuss their feelings about their close relationships and other personal aspects of their lives. Feelings and people figure prominently in both the conversations and instant messages of women (Fox et al., 2007). In contrast, men tend to stick to more impersonal matters, discussing objects and actions such as cars and sports, gossiping about celebrities and politicians instead of friends, and seeking a few laughs instead of support and counsel (McHugh & Hambaugh, 2010). As a result, the conversations men have with each other tend to be less intimate and personal than the conversations women share (Reis, 1998).

However, when men and women interact with each other, these differences are less apparent than you might think. When young adults chatted with strangers online using written messages in Yahoo! Messenger, they were generally *un*able to correctly guess the sex of the person they were chatting with if the researchers didn't tell them. The sorts of things that distinguish men's and women's conversations (such as the latest sports results) rarely came up, so there was usually no way to determine with whom one was chatting (Williams & Mendelsohn, 2008). What differences there are in men's and women's discourse are clearly rather subtle.[3]

Styles of Conversation

Women are sometimes found to speak with less forcefulness than men do, being more indirect and seeming less certain (Mulac, 2006). It's a style of conversation in which one uses hedges to soften assertions and asks questions instead of making straightforward statements, as in this wry example: "Women are sort of more tentative than men, aren't they?" (Palomares, 2009, p. 539). However, as it turns out, women are more tentative than men only when they talk to men about masculine topics. And what's more, men are more tentative than women when they talk to women about feminine topics. *Both* sexes speak less forcefully when they're on the other's home turf, and there's no difference in men's and women's styles when they're discussing neutral topics with each other (Palomares, 2009). Women are, however, less profane (McHugh & Hambaugh, 2010).

There are also hackneyed stereotypes that suggest that women are more talkative than men, but that is not the case. Portable recordings of their interactions demonstrate that college women speak 16,215 words a day, on average, whereas men speak 15,559. It's a trivial difference (Mehl et al., 2007). What's more striking is that men speak up and say something less often than women do, but when they do get started, they talk longer, brooking no interruption (Leaper & Ayres, 2007). Women speak more often but produce fewer monologues.

So, despite some stereotypes to the contrary, there aren't sizable global differences in the way men and women talk. However, there *are* meaningful

---

[3] And seriously, isn't it a little ridiculous to suggest that men and women come from different planets and speak different languages when, if we don't already know who they are, we can't even tell them apart?

Texts, Status Updates, and Other Modern Forms of (Mis?)Communication

We send a lot of text and e-mail messages these days, and they offer us great convenience, global reach, and the opportunity for even more confusion in our communication with others. Texting, status updates, and other forms of computer-mediated communication (or CMC) differ in important ways from actually talking to someone. For one thing, the pace is slower, and we can take our time to consider what we want to say if we wish. Also, no "leaky" nonverbal behavior is involved, so we have more control over the messages we send. These qualities make CMC seem safer and more manageable to some people than actual conversation is, so that, for instance, shy people are more self-disclosing online than they are face-to-face (Brunet & Schmidt, 2008).

Text is a more pallid form of communication than talking, however, so we often go to some trouble to specify how a statement is meant to be read. Most of our e-mails (94 percent!) contain at least one phrase that should not be taken literally (Whalen et al., 2009), so we offer instructions such as emoticons that clarify our meaning. Hi, out there in textbook land, by the way: {*_*} The problem is that we usually think that we've resolved any doubt and that our messages are more exact and unambiguous than they really are. Because we know what we mean, we typically fail to appreciate how easily others can take our words differently (Kruger et al., 2005). Interpersonal gaps abound online.

Still, despite frequent misunderstandings, there's an astonishing amount of information about people available in CMC. For instance, strangers get some insight into our personalities from the e-mail addresses we choose (Back et al., 2008b), and if we use lots of exclamation points in our messages, they'll probably think we're female (McAndrew & De Jonge, 2011). But those stylistic characteristics pale by comparison to the wealth of personal details that many of us intentionally self-disclose on social networking sites. Almost everybody posts their birthdays, and most people post their hometowns—key bits of info that are hugely valuable to identity thieves—and of course, that just scratches the surface of the personal data people put out there. What's remarkable is that people are more self-disclosing on Facebook than they usually are in person (Christofides et al., 2010), and those who are seeking new relationships are particularly likely to post lots of personal details (Nosko et al., 2010). Established couples may even take private grievances public by squabbling on Facebook, posting acerbic comments back and forth that all their friends can see (Quenqua, 2010). People aren't entirely heedless of their privacy on Facebook, but they manage it less attentively online than they do in face-to-face communication.

Overall, though, the most important aspect of CMC for our relationships is the manner in which it provides us *access* to others. Web-based services have become so important in finding romantic partners that adults with Internet access at home are much more likely than others of the same sex, age, and education to even *have* a partner at all (Rosenfeld, 2010). Text-messaging also provides a private, rather continuous way to be in contact even when partners are miles (or continents) apart, conducting other activities, and that connection is often very comforting (Chen, 2011). Texting has become a familiar means of showing that one cares, and friends who share more texts generally grow closer over time (Valkenburg & Peter, 2009b).[5]

So, CMC certainly isn't perfect, and it can be disadvantageous if it begins to displace rich face-to-face interaction with others (DeAndrea et al., 2011). But most of us are clearly at home with our keypads, and CMC is here to stay. And that's the end of this box. Thanks for reading it. TTFN. LUMTP.

[5] But don't text in class. They may not mention it, but your professors hate it.

differences in language use from one person to the next, and the words we use are so informative that strangers can get accurate impressions of us by overhearing a few minutes of our conversation (Holleran et al., 2009). Our personalities are apparent in the words we use. For example, a careful analysis of the writings of almost 700 bloggers found that words such as *awful, worse, horrible,* and *annoying* were used more often by people who were high in neuroticism than by those who were less prone to fretfulness and worry. *Drinks* and *dancing* characterized extraverts, and *visiting, together, hug,* and other such friendly terms were related to agreeableness (Yarkoni, 2010).[4] Our vocabulary really does tell others who we are, and, notably, two people are likely to be more attracted to each other on a speed date if they use language the same way (Ireland et al., 2011).

Self-Disclosure

So far, we haven't encountered big differences in men's and women's verbal communication. But here's a difference that matters: In established relationships, women are more self-disclosing than men are, and in keeping with their higher scores on the "Opener" scale (see the box on page 157), they elicit more self-disclosure, too (Dindia, 2002). Indeed, men tend to offer their female partners more intimate self-disclosures than they provide their male partners (such as their best friends)—and the result is that interactions that include a woman tend to be more intimate and meaningful than are interactions that involve only men (Reis, 1998). Men open up to women, and women are open among themselves, but men disclose less to other men.

An important consequence of all this is that men often depend more on women for emotional warmth and intimacy than women do on them in return (Wheeler et al., 1983): Whereas women may have intimate, open, supportive connections with partners of both sexes, men are likely to share their most meaningful intimacy only with women. Consequently, a man may need a woman in his life to keep him from being lonely, but women don't usually need men in this way.

Instrumentality versus Expressivity

Importantly, however, this difference between men and women in self-disclosure is a *gender* difference that is more closely associated with people's

[4] If you don't quite recall what these traits are, take a look back at page 27.

gender roles than with their biological sex. Women engage in intimate verbal communication with trusted partners because they tend to be high in expressivity[6] and are comfortable talking about their feelings. This also comes naturally to men who are high in expressivity, as androgynous men are, and such men tend to have meaningful, intimate interactions with both sexes just as women do (Aubé et al., 1995). So, to refine the point I just made, it's really just traditional, macho men who have superficial conversations with their best friends and who need relationships with women to keep from being lonely. More than other men, macho guys shut out their male friends (Shaffer et al., 1996) and tend to be sad and lonely when they do not have a female romantic partner (Wheeler et al., 1983). In contrast, androgynous men (who are both assertive *and* warm) self-disclose readily to both sexes and enjoy meaningful interactions with all their friends; as a result, they tend not to be lonely, and as a bonus, they spend more time interacting with women than less expressive, traditional men do (Reis, 1986).

Given this, it's silly to think that men and women speak different languages and come from different planets. Many men *are* more taciturn than the average woman, but there are also men who are more open and self-disclosing than most women are. The typical intimacy of a person's interactions is tied to his or her level of expressivity, and once you take that into account, it doesn't much matter whether the person is a man or woman. Moreover, expressivity is a trait that ranges from low to high in both women and men, so it makes more sense to note individual differences in communicative style than to lump all men together and treat them as a group distinct from women.

Indeed, people also vary in how loquacious and effusive they are. Some of us put our thoughts and feelings into words quickly—we blurt out whatever we're thinking and thereby engage in animated, rapid-fire conversation—whereas others of us are slower, more deliberate, and more hesitant in verbalizing our feelings. The word is a bit goofy, but these differences in verbal style are said to be individual differences in **blirtatiousness** (Swann & Rentfrow, 2001). A talkative, highly blirtatious woman and a taciturn, close-mouthed man may get along fine when they meet (Swann et al., 2006)—he doesn't have to say much because she's happy to do all the talking—but they make a precarious match if they settle down together (Swann et al., 2003). She's likely to dominate the discussion of the conflicts that arise (as they always do; see chapter 11), and that pattern violates traditional expectations that make men the heads of their households. This doesn't bother progressive, androgynous men, but it does frustrate traditional guys, who tend to be dissatisfied in the long run when they are paired with assertive, talkative women (Angulo & Swann, 2007). Both members of a couple also make poor impressions on observers when the man is quiet and the woman is talkative during their conflict discussions (Sellers et al., 2007), so gender role stereotypes obviously influence what we take for granted in heterosexual interaction.

Indeed, men value instrumental communication skills such as the ability to give clear instructions and directions more than women do. And women value

---

[6]*Expressivity, instrumentality,* and *androgyny?* See pages 23–26.

expressive communication skills such as expressing affection and feelings more than men do. Still, both men and women consider expressive skills to be more important in close relationships than instrumental skills are (Burleson et al., 1996). They are sometimes caricatured as speaking different languages, but men and women agree that the ability to adequately communicate one's love, respect, and regard for one's partner is indispensable in close relationships (Floyd, 2006).

DYSFUNCTIONAL COMMUNICATION AND WHAT TO DO ABOUT IT

As we've seen, the more self-disclosing partners are, the more satisfied they tend to be (Sprecher & Hendrick, 2004). But not all our efforts to speak our minds and communicate with our partners have positive results. More often than we realize, an interpersonal gap causes misunderstanding in those who hear what we have to say. And the nature and consequences of miscommunication are very apparent in relationships in which the partners are distressed and dissatisfied. The verbal communications of unhappy partners often just perpetuate their discontent and make things worse instead of better.

Miscommunication

Indeed, we can gain valuable insights into what we shouldn't do when we talk with others by carefully comparing the communicative behaviors of happy lovers to those of unhappy partners. John Gottman and his colleagues at the University of Washington did this for over 30 years, and they observed several important patterns. First, unhappy people do a poor job of *saying what they mean* (Gottman, 1994b). When they have a complaint, they are rarely precise; instead, they're prone to **kitchen-sinking,** in which they tend to address several topics at once (so that everything but the "kitchen sink" gets dragged into the conversation). This usually causes their primary concern to get lost in the barrage of frustrations that are announced at the same time. If they're annoyed by overdrawn fees on a debit card, for instance, they may say, "It's not just your carelessness; it's those friends you hang out with, and your lousy attitude about helping out around the house." As a result, their conversations frequently drift **off-beam,** wandering from topic to topic so that the conversation never stays on one problem long enough to resolve it: "You never do what I ask. You're just as hard-headed as your mother, and you always take her side." Flitting from problem to problem on a long list of concerns makes it almost certain that none of them will get fixed.

Second, unhappy partners do a poor job of *hearing each other*. They rarely try to patiently double-check their understanding of their partners' messages. Instead, they jump to conclusions (often assuming the worst) and head off on tangents based on what they presume their partners really mean. One aspect of this is **mindreading,** which occurs when people assume that they understand their partners' thoughts, feelings, and opinions without asking. All intimate couples mindread to some extent, but distressed couples do so in critical and hostile ways; they tend to perceive unpleasant motives where neutral or positive ones actually exist: "You just said that to make me mad, to get back at me for yesterday." Unhappy partners also **interrupt** each other in negative ways more than contented couples do. Not all interruptions are obnoxious. People who interrupt their partners to express agreement or ask for clarification may actually be communicating happily and well. But people who interrupt to express disagreement or to change the topic are likely to leave their partners feeling disregarded and unappreciated (Daigen & Holmes, 2000).

Distressed couples also listen poorly by finding something wrong or unworkable with anything their partners say. This is **yes-butting,** and it communicates constant criticism of the others' points of view: "Yeah, we could try that, but it won't work because. . . ." Unhappy partners also engage in **cross-complaining** that fails to acknowledge others' concerns; instead of expressing interest in what their partners have to say, they just respond to a complaint with one of their own:

"I hate the way you let the dishes pile up in the sink."
"Well, I hate the way you leave your clothes lying around on the floor."

Finally, unhappy partners too often display *negative affect* when they talk with each other (Gottman & Levenson, 1992). They too often react to their partner's complaints with sarcastic disregard that is demeaning and scornful, and instead of mending their problems, they often make them worse. Damaging interactions like these typically begin with clumsy **criticism** that attacks a partner's personality or character instead of identifying a specific behavior that is causing concern. For instance, instead of delineating a particular frustration ("I get annoyed when you leave your wet towel on the floor"), a critic may inflame the interaction by making a global accusation of a character flaw ("You are such a slob!"). **Contempt** in the form of insults, mockery, or hostile humor is often involved as well. The partners' common response to such attacks is **defensiveness;** instead of treating the clumsy complaint as legitimate and reasonable, the partners seek to protect themselves from the unreasonable attack by making excuses or by cross-complaining, hurling counterattacks of their own. **Stonewalling** may follow as a partner "clams up" and reacts to the messy situation by withdrawing into a stony silence (Papp et al., 2009b). People may believe they're helping the situation by refusing to argue further, but their lack of responsiveness can be infuriating (Williams, 2007). Instead of demonstrating appropriate acknowledgment and concern for a partner's complaints, stonewalling typically communicates "disapproval, icy distance, and smugness" (Gottman, 1994b, p. 94). Ultimately, destructive **belligerence** may occur with one partner aggressively rejecting the other altogether ("So what? What are you gonna do about it?").

When communication routinely degenerates into these contentious patterns, the outlook for the relationship is grim (Gottman et al., 1998). Surly, churlish communication between spouses predicts discontent and distress down the road (Markman et al., 2010). In fact, videotapes of just the first 3 minutes of a marital conflict enable researchers to predict with 83 percent accuracy who will be divorced 6 years later (Carrère & Gottman, 1999). Couples whose marriages are doomed display noticeably more contempt, defensiveness, and belligerence than do those who will stay together. And among those who stay together, spouses who communicate well are happier and more content than those who suffer frequent misunderstanding (Markman et al., 2010).

The challenge, of course, is that it's not always easy to avoid these problems. When we're angry, resentful, or anxious, we may find ourselves cross-complaining, kitchen-sinking, and all the rest. How can we avoid these traps? Depending on the situation, we may need to send clearer, less inflammatory messages, listen better, or stay polite and calm, and often we need to do all three.

Saying What We Mean

Complaints that criticize a partner's personality or character disparage the partner and often make mountains out of molehills, portraying problems as huge, intractable dilemmas that cannot be easily solved. (Given some of the broad complaints we throw at our partners, it's no wonder that they sometimes get defensive.) It's much more sensible—and accurate—to identify as plainly and concretely as possible a specific behavior that annoyed us. This is **behavior description,** and it not only tells our partners what's on our minds but also focuses the conversation on discrete, manageable behaviors that, unlike personalities, can often be readily changed. A good behavior description specifies a particular event and does not involve generalities; thus, words such as *always* or *never* should never be used. This is *not* a good behavior description: "You're always interrupting me! You never let me finish!"

We should also use **I-statements** that specify our feelings. I-statements start with "I" and then describe a distinct emotional reaction. They force us to identify our feelings, which can be useful both to us and to our partners. They help us to "own" our feelings and to acknowledge them instead of keeping the entire focus on the partner. Thus, instead of saying, "You really piss me off," one should say, "I feel pretty angry right now."

This interaction would be going better if Mom had used a reasonable behavior description and Jeremy wasn't cross-complaining defensively. Do you see how both of them are communicating poorly?

Communicating Sympathy and Concern

Few of us know what to say when we encounter bereaved others who are suffering from the loss of a loved one. We want to express sympathy and support, but our words often seem inadequate to the task. However, grief, and others' reactions to it, have been studied by relationship researchers (Wortman & Boerner, 2007), and I can offer some advice about this important kind of communication. First, you *should* mention the person's loss (Okonski, 1996). The death of a beloved is a huge loss, something that the person will never forget (Carnelley et al., 2006). Assuming that the person's pain has ended or is no longer salient to him or her, even months later, is simply insensitive (Martin, 1997). Talking about the lost partner acknowledges the person's distress and communicates caring and concern. It may not be easy for you to do (Lewis & Manusov, 2009), but it's kind.

What should you say? Something simple. Try "I'm so sorry," or "I feel so sad for you" and then *stop*. Do not try to comfort the person with optimistic projections about the future. Do not imply that the loss is not the most tragic, awful thing that has ever happened. And do not offer advice about how the person can put his or her life back together. Such efforts may spring from good intentions, but each of them ultimately demeans the person's current suffering. Offer heartfelt sympathy and nothing more. Just nod your head and be a good listener and be nonjudgmental.

Thus, offering welcome comfort to others is more straightforward than you may have thought, as long as you avoid the pitfalls of saying too much. With this in mind, can you see what's wrong with the following dumb remarks? Each is a quote from someone who was probably trying—and failing—to be helpful (Martin, 1997; Wortman & Boerner, 2007):

"The sooner you let go, the better."

"Crying won't bring him back."

"He should have been wearing a seat belt."

"God needed her more than you did."

"You're young, you can have other children."

"You have many good years left."

A handy way to use both behavior descriptions and I-statements to communicate more clearly and accurately is to integrate them into **XYZ statements.** Such statements follow the form of "When you do **X** in situation **Y**" (that's a good behavior description), "I feel **Z**" (an I-statement). Listen to yourself next time you complain to your partner. Are you saying something like this:

"You're so inconsiderate! You never let me finish what I'm saying!"

Or, are you being precise and accurate and saying what you mean:

"When you interrupted me just now, I felt annoyed."

There's a big difference. One of those statements is likely to get a thoughtful, apologetic response from a loving partner, but the other probably won't.

Active Listening

We have two vital tasks when we're on the receiving end of others' messages. The first is to accurately understand what our partners are trying to say, and the second is to communicate that attention and comprehension to our partners so that they know we care about what they've said. Both tasks can be accomplished by **paraphrasing** a message, repeating it in our own words and giving the sender a chance to agree that that's what he or she actually meant. When people use paraphrasing, they don't assume that they understood their partners and issue an immediate reply. Instead, they take a moment to check their comprehension by rephrasing the message and repeating it back. This sounds awkward, but it is a terrific way to avoid arguments and conflict that would otherwise result from misunderstanding and mistakes. Whenever a conversation begins to get heated, paraphrasing can keep it from getting out of hand. Look what's wrong here:

WILMA: (sighing) I'm so glad your mother decided not to come visit us next week.
FRED: (irate) What's wrong with my mother? You've always been on her case, and I think you're an ungrateful witch!

Perhaps before Fred flew off the handle, some paraphrasing would have been helpful:

WILMA: (sighing) I'm so glad your mother decided not to come visit us next week.
FRED: (irate) Are you saying you don't like her to be here?
WILMA: (surprised) No, she's always welcome. I just have my paper due in my relationships class and I won't have much time then.
FRED: (mollified) Oh.

Another valuable listening skill is **perception checking,** which is the opposite of mindreading. In perception checking, people assess the accuracy of their inferences about a partner's feelings by asking the partner for clarification. This communicates one's attentiveness and interest, and it encourages the partner to be more open: "You seem pretty upset by what I said, is that right?"

Listeners who paraphrase and check their perceptions make an *active* effort to understand their partners, and that care and consideration are usually much appreciated. In terms of the interpersonal process model of intimacy, they are being *responsive*, and that's a good thing. Active listening like this is likely to help smooth the inevitable rough spots any relationship encounters. Indeed, people who practice these techniques typically report happier marriages than do those who simply assume that they understand what their partners mean by what they say (Markman et al., 1994).

Being Polite and Staying Cool

Still, even the most accurate sending and receiving may not do much good if our conversations are too often crabby and antagonistic. It's hard to remain mild and relaxed when we encounter contempt and belligerence from others, and people who deride or disdain their partners often get irascible, irritated reactions in return. Indeed, dissatisfied spouses spend more time than contented lovers do locked into patterns of *negative affect reciprocity* in which they're contemptuous of each other, with each being scornful of what the other has to say (Levenson et al., 1994). Happy couples behave this way, too—there are probably periods of acrimonious disregard in most relationships—but they break out of these ugly cycles more quickly than unhappy partners do (Burman et al., 1993).

In fact, defusing cycles of increasing cantankerousness when they begin may be very beneficial, but it may not be easy. Although XYZ statements and active listening skills can help prevent surly interactions altogether, Gottman and his colleagues argue that people rarely have the presence of mind to use them once they get angry (Gottman et al., 2000). It can be difficult or even "impossible to make 'I-statements' when you are in the 'hating-my-partner, wanting revenge, feeling-stung-and-needing-to-sting-back' state of mind" (Wile, 1995, p. 2).

Thus, being able to stay cool when you're provoked by a partner and being able to calm down when you begin to get angry are very valuable skills. You'll be better able to do this if you construe anger as just one way of thinking about a problem. Anger results from the perception that others are causing us illegitimate, unfair, avoidable grief. Use a different point of view to reduce or prevent anger altogether (Tice & Baumeister, 1993). Instead of thinking, "S/he

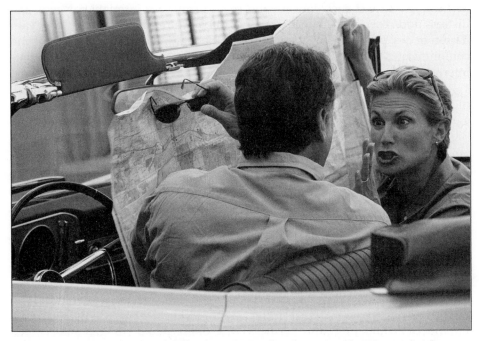

Unhappy partners often have difficulty saying what they mean, hearing each other, and staying polite and calm when disagreements arise.

has no right to say that to me!," it's more adaptive to think, "Hmm. Contrary statements from someone who loves me. I wonder why?"

Of course, it can be hard to maintain such a placid stream of thought when one is provoked. So, it's also a good idea to (try to) reduce the number of provocations you encounter by agreeing in advance to be polite to each other whenever possible (Gottman, 1994b). You may wish to schedule regular meetings at which you and your partner (politely) air your grievances; knowing that a problem will be addressed makes it easier to be pleasant to your partner the rest of the week (Markman et al., 1994). And under no circumstances should the two of you continue an interaction in which you're just hurling insults and sarcasm back and forth at each other. If you find yourself in such a pattern of negative affect reciprocity, take a temporary *time out* to stop the cycle. Ask for a short break—"Honey, I'm too angry to think straight. Let me take 10 minutes to calm down"—and then return to the issue when you're less aroused (Markman et al.). Go off by yourself and take no more than six long, slow, deep breaths per minute, and you will calm down, faster than you think (Tavris, 1989).

The Power of Respect and Validation

The key ingredients in all of these components of good communication—our conscious efforts to send clear, straightforward messages, to listen carefully and well, and to be polite and nonaggressive even when disagreements occur—are the indications we provide that we care about and respect our partners' points of view. We expect such concern and regard from our intimate partners, and distress and resentment build when we think we're disrespected. Thus, **validation** of our partners that acknowledges the legitimacy of their opinions and communicates respect for their positions is always a desirable goal in intimate interaction.

Validation does not require you to agree with someone. You can communicate appropriate respect and recognition of a partner's point of view without agreeing with it. Consider the following three responses to Barney's complaint:

	BARNEY: I hate it when you act that way.
Cross-complaining	BETTY: And I hate it when you get drunk with Fred.
Agreement	BETTY: Yeah, you're right. I'll stop.
Validation	BETTY: Yeah, I can see how you'd feel that way. You've got a point. But I'd like you to try to understand what I'm feeling, too.

Only the last response, which concedes the legitimacy of Barney's point of view but allows Betty her own feelings, invites an open, honest dialogue. We need not be inauthentic or nonassertive to respect our partners' opinions, even when we disagree with them.

Indeed, validating our partners will often make disagreement much more tolerable. All of the skills I have mentioned here support an atmosphere of responsive care and concern that can reduce the intensity and impact of disputes with our partners (Verhofstadt et al., 2005). You may even be able to set a troubled relationship on a more promising path by rehearsing these skills and pledging to be polite and respectful to one another when difficulties arise (Stanley et al., 2000).

FOR YOUR CONSIDERATION

James loved deer hunting season. He liked to sit shivering in a deer blind in the chill before dawn, sipping coffee, and waiting for what the day would bring. But his wife, Judy, always dreaded that time of year. James would be gone for several weekends in a row, and each time he returned he'd either be grumpy because he was empty-handed or he would have lots of venison—and extra work—for her to handle. The costs of his gas, permit, and lease were also substantial, and the expense kept them from enjoying an occasional weekend at that bed-and-breakfast at the lake she liked so much.

So, when Judy handed James a thermos of hot coffee and walked with him to the door at 4:30 in the morning on the first day of deer season, she was already feeling melancholy and lonely. She looked at him and tried to be cheerful, but her smile was forced and her expression downcast as she said in a plaintive tone, "Have a nice time, dear." James happily replied, "Okay, thanks, hon. See you Sunday night!" and was gone.

What do you think the future holds for James and Judy? Why?

CHAPTER SUMMARY

When a sender's intentions differ from the impact that a message has on the recipient, a couple faces an *interpersonal gap*.

Nonverbal Communication

Nonverbal communication serves vital functions, *providing information, regulating interaction,* and *defining the nature of the relationship* two people share.

Components of Nonverbal Communication. *Facial expression.* Facial expressions are good guides to others' moods, but cultural norms dictate what emotions are appropriate in particular situations.

Gazing behavior. The direction and amount of a person's looking is important in defining relationships and in regulating interaction.

Body movement. Gestures vary widely across cultures, but the posture and motion of the entire body are informative as well.

Touch. Different types of touch have distinctly different meanings.

Interpersonal distance. We use different zones of personal space—the *intimate, personal, social,* and *public* zones—for different kinds of interactions.

Paralanguage. Paralanguage involves all the variations in a person's voice, such as rhythm, rate, and loudness, other than the words he or she uses.

Combining the components. Mimicry occurs when people use similar nonverbal behavior without realizing it. Nonverbal actions allow us to fine-tune the intimacy of our interactions in subtle but real ways.

Nonverbal Sensitivity. Unhappy spouses, especially husbands, do a poor job at nonverbal communication.

Verbal Communication

Self-Disclosure. Intimacy involves sharing personal information about oneself to one's partner.

How self-disclosure develops. As a relationship develops, both the breadth and depth of self-disclosure increase. Intimacy develops when we perceive *responsiveness* in others that indicates that they understand us and care about us.

Secrets and other things we don't want to talk about. Couples avoid *taboo topics*, and some secrecy is routine even in intimate partnerships.

Self-disclosure and relationship satisfaction. Appropriate self-disclosure breeds liking and contentment, and in particular, expressions of affection are good for us.

Gender Differences in Verbal Communication. Women are more likely than men to discuss feelings and people, but men and women are equally talkative. However, macho men self-disclose relatively little to other men even when they are friends, and thus are likely to share their most meaningful intimacy only with women. A woman who is high in *blirtatiousness* is a precarious match for a taciturn man.

Dysfunctional Communication and What to Do About It

Miscommunication. Distressed couples have trouble saying what they mean, and they engage in destructive verbal behavior.

Saying What We Mean. Skillful senders use *XYZ statements* to focus on specific actions and make their feelings clear.

Active Listening. Good listeners use *paraphrasing* and *perception checking* to understand their partners.

Being Polite and Staying Cool. Happy couples also avoid extended periods of *negative affect reciprocity.*

The Power of Respect and Validation. Partners should communicate respect and recognition of the other's point of view even when they disagree.

CHAPTER 6

Interdependency

SOCIAL EXCHANGE ◆ Rewards and Costs ◆ What Do We Expect from Our Relationships? ◆ How Well Could We Do Elsewhere? ◆ Four Types of Relationships ◆ CL and CL$_{alt}$ as Time Goes By ◆ THE ECONOMIES OF RELATIONSHIPS ◆ Rewards and Costs Are Different ◆ Rewards and Costs as Time Goes By ◆ ARE WE REALLY THIS GREEDY? ◆ The Nature of Interdependency ◆ Exchange versus Communal Relationships ◆ Equitable Relationships ◆ Summing Up ◆ THE NATURE OF COMMITMENT ◆ The Consequences of Commitment ◆ FOR YOUR CONSIDERATION ◆ CHAPTER SUMMARY

If you've been in a relationship for a while, why are you *staying* in that relationship? Are you obligated to continue it for some reason? Are you simply waiting for something better to come along? Hopefully, your current relationships have been so rewarding that none of these questions will seem to apply. However, all of them provide the focus for this chapter, which will take an *economic* view of our dealings with others.

Our subject will be interdependency, our reliance on others and theirs on us for valuable interpersonal rewards. I'll examine why we stay in some relationships and leave others and ponder the nature of lasting relationships. I'll say nothing about love, which is the topic of another chapter. Instead, our focus will be the balance sheets with which we tally the profits and losses of our interactions with others. You may not yet have thought of yourself as an interpersonal accountant, but doing so provides powerful insights into the workings of close relationships.

SOCIAL EXCHANGE

Interdependency theories assume that people are like shoppers who are browsing at an interpersonal shopping mall. We're all looking for good buys. We seek interactions with others that provide maximum reward at minimum cost, and we stay only with those partners who provide sufficient profit (Rusbult et al., 2001). However, because everybody behaves this way, both partners in a relationship must be profiting to their satisfaction or the relationship is unlikely to continue.

From this perspective, social life entails the mutual exchange of desirable rewards with others, a process called **social exchange.** There are several different social exchange theories, but the ideas introduced by John Thibaut and Harold Kelley (1959; Kelley & Thibaut, 1978)—now known as *interdependence* *theory*—are most often used by relationship scientists, so I'll feature them here. Let's first consider the central elements of social exchange.

Rewards and Costs

The rewards of interactions are the gratifying experiences and commodities we obtain through our contact with others. They come in very different forms ranging from impersonal benefits, such as the directions you can get from strangers when you're lost, to personal intimacies, such as acceptance and support from someone you love. I'll use the term *reward* to refer to anything within an interaction that is desirable and welcome and that brings enjoyment or fulfillment to the recipient.

In contrast, *costs* are punishing, undesirable experiences. They can involve financial expenditures, such as buying dinner for your date, or actual injuries, such as split lips. However, some of the most important costs of intimate interaction are psychological burdens: uncertainty about where a relationship is headed, frustration over your partner's imperfections, and regret about all the things you don't get to do because you're in that relationship (Sedikides et al., 1994). All of the diverse consequences of interaction that are frustrating or distressing are costs.

We'll summarize the rewards and costs associated with a particular interaction with the term **outcome,** which describes the net profit or loss a person encounters, all things considered. Adding up all the rewards and costs involved,

$$\text{Outcomes} = \text{Rewards} - \text{Costs}$$

Obviously, if an interaction is more rewarding than punishing, a positive outcome results. But remember, the social exchange perspective asserts that people want the *best possible* outcomes. The simple fact that your interactions are profitable doesn't mean that they are good enough to keep you coming back to that partner. Indeed, one of the major insights of interdependence theory is its suggestion that whether your outcomes are positive or negative isn't nearly as important as how they compare to two criteria with which we evaluate the outcomes we receive. The first criterion involves our expectations, and the second involves our perceptions of how well we could manage without our current partner.

What Do We Expect from Our Relationships?

Interdependence theory assumes that each of us has an idiosyncratic **comparison level** (which I'll abbreviate as **CL**) that describes the value of the outcomes that we believe we deserve in our dealings with others. Our CLs are based on our past experiences. People who have a history of highly rewarding partnerships are likely to have high CLs, meaning that they expect and feel they deserve very good outcomes now. In contrast, people who have had troublesome relationships in the past are likely to expect less and to have lower CLs.

A person's comparison level represents his or her neutral point on a continuum that ranges all the way from abject misery to ecstatic delight. That makes our CLs the standards by which our *satisfaction* with a relationship is measured.

If the outcomes you receive exceed your CL, you're happy; you're getting more than the minimum payoff you expect from interaction with others. Just how happy you are depends on the extent to which your outcomes surpass your expectations; if your outcomes are considerably higher than your CL, you'll be very satisfied. On the other hand, if your outcomes fall below your CL, you're dissatisfied even if your outcomes are still pretty good and you're doing better than most people. This is a significant point: Even if you are still making a profit on your transactions with others, you may not be happy if the profit isn't big enough to meet your expectations. If you're a rich, spoiled celebrity, for instance, you may have an unusually high CL and be rather dissatisfied with a fabulous partner who would bedazzle the rest of us.

So, satisfaction in close relationships doesn't depend simply on how good our outcomes are in an absolute sense; instead, satisfaction derives from how our outcomes compare to our comparison levels, like this:

$$\text{Outcomes} - \text{CL} = \text{Satisfaction or Dissatisfaction}$$

How Well Could We Do Elsewhere?

However, another important assumption of interdependence theory is that satisfaction is not the only, or even the major, influence that determines how long relationships last. Whether or not we're happy, we use a second criterion, a **comparison level for alternatives** (or CL_{alt}), to determine whether we could be doing even better somewhere else. Your CL_{alt} describes the outcomes you'd receive by leaving your current relationship and moving to the best alternative partnership or situation you have available. And if you're a good accountant, you can see that our CL_{alt}s are also the lowest levels of outcome we will tolerate from our present partners. Here's why: If other relationships promise better profits than we currently receive, we're likely to leave our present partners and pursue those bigger payoffs. It wouldn't matter if we're currently satisfied with what we're getting; we'd still go because, according to interdependency theory, we always want the best deal we can get. Indeed, even if we are dissatisfied with our current relationships, we are unlikely to leave them unless a better alternative presents itself. This is a very important point, which helps explain why people stay in relationships that make them miserable: Even though they're unhappy where they are, they think they'd be worse off if they left. If they thought a better situation awaited them elsewhere, they'd go (Edwards et al., 2011). This idea—that our contentment with a relationship is not the major determinant of whether we stay in it or leave—is one of interdependence theory's most interesting insights.

Thus, our CL_{alt}s determine our *dependence* on our relationships. Whether or not we're satisfied, if we believe that we're already doing as well as we possibly can, we depend on our present partners and are unlikely to leave them (Ellis et al., 2002). Moreover, the greater the gap between our current outcomes and our poorer alternatives, the more dependent we are. If our current outcomes are only a little better than those that await us elsewhere, we don't need our current partners very much and may leave if our alternatives improve.

But would people really leave relationships in which they're already happy? Presumably, they would, if their CL_{alt}s are genuinely better than what they're getting now. To keep things simple when you consider this, think of a CL_{alt} as the global outcome, the net profit or loss, that a person believes will result from switching partners, all things considered (Kelley, 2002). If the whole process of ending a present partnership and moving to an alternative promises better outcomes, a person should move. It's just economic good sense.

A problem, of course, is that these are difficult calculations to make. There's a lot to consider. On the one hand, there are the new external attractions that can lure us away from our present partners. We need to assess the desirability and availability of alternative partners, and going it alone—being without a partner—is also an option to ponder. When other partners or simple solitude seem attractive, our CL_{alt}s go up. However, we will incur a variety of costs by leaving an existing relationship, and they can dramatically affect the net profit to be gained by moving elsewhere. For instance, social psychologist Caryl Rusbult demonstrated that one's **investments** in a present relationship, the things one would lose if the relationship were to end, are also important influences on one's decision to stay or go (e.g., Rusbult et al., 1994). The investments a person leaves behind can either be tangible goods, such as furniture and dishes you have to split with your ex, or intangible psychological benefits, such as love and respect from in-laws and friends (Goodfriend & Agnew, 2008). An unhappy spouse may refrain from filing for divorce, for example, not because she has no other options but because she doesn't want to accept the potential costs of confused children, disappointed parents, and befuddled friends. All of these would reduce the global desirability of leaving and, thus, reduce one's CL_{alt}.

Another complication is that a person's CL_{alt} is what he or she *thinks* it is, and a variety of factors can influence people's perceptions of their alternatives. Self-esteem, for one. When people don't like themselves, they doubt their desirability (Swann & Bosson, 2010) and underestimate their prospects with other partners. Learned helplessness can also be influential (Ciarrochi & Heaven, 2008). If people get stuck in a bad relationship for too long, they may lose hope and glumly underestimate their chances of doing better elsewhere. Access to information affects one's CL_{alt}, too. If you become a stay-at-home parent who doesn't work, you'll probably have much more limited information about potential alternatives than you would have if you went to work in a large city every day (Rusbult & Martz, 1995); as a result, you'll have a lower CL_{alt} than you would have if you got out and looked around.

Indeed, desirable alternatives will only enhance your CL_{alt} if you are aware of them, and if you're content with your current partners, you may not pay much attention to people who could be compelling rivals to your existing relationships. In fact, people who are satisfied with their existing relationships are relatively uninterested in looking around to see how they could be doing elsewhere. As a result, they think they have lower CL_{alt}s than do those who pay more attention to their alternatives (Miller, 2008). This may be important. College students who keep track of their options and monitor their alternatives with care switch romantic partners more often than do those who pay their alternatives less heed (Miller, 2008).

These results mean that although interdependence theory treats satisfaction and dependence as relatively independent influences on relationships, they are actually correlated. As an old cliché suggests, the grass may be greener in other relationships, but if you're happy with your current partner, you're less likely to notice. Still, there's wisdom in remembering that satisfaction with a relationship has only a limited role in a person's decision to stay in it or go. Consider the usual trajectory of a divorce: Spouses who divorce have usually been unhappy for quite some time before they decide to separate. What finally prompts them to act? Something changes: Their CL_{alt}s finally come to exceed their current outcomes (Albrecht & Kunz, 1980). Things may get so bad that their outcomes in the marriage slip below those that are available in alternative options that used to seem inadequate. Or the apparent costs of ending the marriage may decrease (which raises one's CL_{alt}): Because the spouses have been unhappy for so long, for instance, their kids, parents, and pastor may change their minds and support a divorce for the first time. Or the apparent rewards of leaving increase, perhaps because they have saved some money or found an alternative partner. (This also raises one's CL_{alt}.) The bottom line is that people don't divorce when they get unhappy; they divorce when, one way or the other, their prospects finally seem brighter elsewhere.

So, if we remember that CL_{alt} is a multifaceted judgment encompassing both the costs of leaving—such as lost investments—and the enticements offered by others, we get:

$$\text{Outcomes} - CL_{alt} = \text{Dependence or Independence}$$

In summary, the three key elements of social exchange are people's *outcomes, comparison levels* (CLs), and *comparison levels for alternatives* (CL_{alt}s). The net profits or losses people receive from interaction are their outcomes. When their outcomes exceed their expectations, or CLs, they are satisfied; however, if they are not doing as well as they expect (that is, when their outcomes are lower than their CLs), they are dissatisfied. In addition, when people's current outcomes are better than those they could get elsewhere (that is, when their outcomes exceed their CL_{alt}s), they depend on their current partners and are unlikely to leave. However, if their outcomes from their current partners get worse than those that can be readily obtained elsewhere (and their outcomes fall below their CL_{alt}s), they will be independent and will be likely to depart.

Four Types of Relationships

Let's see how these calculations combine to define the types of relationships people encounter. CLs, CL_{alt}s, and the outcomes people experience can all range from low to high along a continuum of outcome quality. Interdependence theory suggests that when we consider all three of these factors simultaneously, four different broad types of relationships result.

Consider what happens when people's outcomes exceed both their CLs and their CL_{alt}s. They're getting more from their partners than they expect *and* they believe they're doing better than they could anywhere else. So, they're happy and (as far as they're concerned) their relationships are stable. They're not going anywhere. This pleasant situation is depicted in Figure 6.1 in two different ways. In one case, a person's CL is higher than his or her CL_{alt} whereas in the other case the reverse is true. In these and all the other examples I'll explain, the specific amount of satisfaction (or dependence) a person feels depends on the extent to which CL (or CL_{alt}) differs from the person's current outcomes. However, in both graphs A_1 and A_2—and this is the point I wish to make—the person is in a happy, stable relationship. I showed you both graphs to demonstrate that, in terms of the simple classifications illustrated in Figure 6.1, it doesn't matter whether CL is higher than CL_{alt} or vice versa. Even if they're exactly the same, the same broad category will apply; if the person's current outcomes surpass both CL and CL_{alt}, that person will be content and unlikely to leave.

FIGURE 6.1. **Types of relationships in interdependence theory.**
These examples may look daunting at first glance, but a patient reading of the text will make them clear. A_1 and A_2 are different examples of the same broad type of relationship, and D_1 and D_2 are too. As you can see, for our purposes, when CL and CL_{alt} are both better than, or both worse than, one's current outcomes, it doesn't matter which of them is higher than the other; what matters is where each of them is relative to current outcomes.

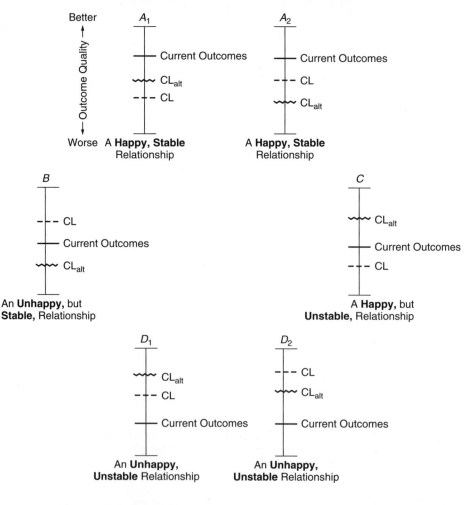

Power and (In)Dependence

Figure 6.1 portrays the situations that may face one member of a couple, but a relationship involves two people. How might their respective CL_{alt}s influence their interactions with each other? Let's assume that a romantic couple, Betty and Barney, receive similar outcomes from their relationship, and each depends on the other, but Barney's CL_{alt} is lower than Betty's (see Figure 6.2). That would mean that Barney needs Betty more than she needs him; if the relationship ended, he would lose more by moving to his next best option than she would. Because neither of them wants to leave their partnership, this might seem like a trivial matter, but, in fact, this disparity in dependence gives her more *power* than he has.

As we'll see in chapter 12, power is the ability to influence another person's behavior. A nuance of social exchange, the **principle of lesser interest,** suggests that the partner who depends less on a relationship has more power in that relationship (Waller & Hill, 1951). Or, the person with less to lose by ending a desired partnership gets to call the shots. In fact,

when it comes to winning arguments and getting one's way, the principle seems to be accurate; the more independent member of a romantic relationship is usually acknowledged by both partners to be the more dominant of the two (Berman & Bennett, 1982). So, for instance, if you want to get married more than your partner does, plan on doing more of the household chores (Erchull et al., 2010).

FIGURE 6.2. **Dependence and Power** In this situation, Betty and Barney depend on each other, and neither is likely to leave. Nevertheless, Betty's alternatives are better than Barney's, and that gives her more power in their relationship.

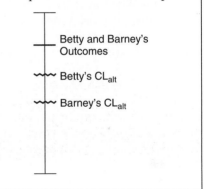

Contrast that situation with what happens when people's outcomes fall below their CLs but are still higher than their CL_{alt}s (in graph *B*). These folks are dissatisfied. They're getting less than they expect and feel they deserve, but they're still doing better than they think they can elsewhere. They're in an unhappy but stable relationship that they will not leave. Hopefully, you've never encountered such a situation yourself, but if you've ever had a lousy, low-paying job that you disliked but couldn't leave because it was the best job available at the time, you know what I'm talking about. That's the sort of fix these folks are in.

By comparison, if people's CL_{alt}s are higher than their outcomes but their CLs are lower, they're in a much more favorable situation (graph *C*, Figure 6.1). They're satisfied with their present partners but believe that they have even more attractive outcomes, all things considered, awaiting them somewhere else. Their current relationships are happy but unstable because they're not likely to stay where they are. In an analogous situation in the workplace, you'd face this situation if you liked your existing job but you got an even better offer from another employer. If you added it all up—including the friends you'd leave behind, the costs of relocating, and the uncertainties of your new position—and thought you'd be clearly better off by leaving—you would leave, wouldn't you?

Finally, people's outcomes may be lower than both their CLs and CL_{alt}s. Again, at this level of analysis, it wouldn't matter whether their CLs were lower than their CL_{alt}s (graph D_1) or vice versa (graph D_2); as long as their present outcomes were lower than both of them, they'd be in an unhappy and unstable relationship that probably wouldn't last much longer.

In real relationships, of course, a huge variety of configurations is possible as people's CLs, CL_{alt}s, and outcomes all range from excellent to poor. These four types of relationships are meant only to be general guides to diverse possibilities. CLs, CL_{alt}s, and outcomes may all change over time as well. In fact, changes in these variables lead to further interesting nuances of interdependence theory.

CL and CL_alt as Time Goes By

Imagine you find the perfect relationship. Your partner is loving, gorgeous, smart, rich, and generous, and is an award-winning chef, accomplished masseuse, and expert auto mechanic. He or she provides you outcomes that exceed your wildest dreams. When you get home each night, your partner has something exquisite for you to eat after you get your welcome-home massage and pedicure. Would you be satisfied? Of course you would. But what's likely to happen after you've enjoyed several straight months of this bliss?

You might get home one evening to find no massage and no supper because your partner has been delayed by traffic. "Hey," you might think, "where's my gourmet meal? Where's my backrub?" You've come to *expect* such marvelous treatment, which means your comparison level has risen. But if your CL goes up and your outcomes remain the same, satisfaction wanes. Once you get used to your perfect partner, you may find that you derive less pleasure from his or her pampering than you used to.

Indeed, interdependence theory predicts such a pattern. Because they are based on our experiences, our CLs tend to fluctuate along with the outcomes we receive. When we first encounter excellent outcomes, we're delighted, but our pleasure may slowly dwindle as we come to take such benefits for granted and our CLs rise. In this manner, rewarding relationships can gradually become less and less satisfying even though nothing (but our expectations) has changed.

Does this really happen in a good relationship? Well, perhaps. You certainly shouldn't expect the sort of happiness that would lead you to marry to continue indefinitely. A remarkable study that tracked more than 5,500 young adults in The Netherlands for 18 years (!) found that starting to date someone, choosing to cohabit, and getting married were all associated with noticeable increases in happiness. But the participants' delight faded over the years, and 14 years later they were no happier than they had been before they met their lovers (Soons et al., 2009). An even more amazing study in Germany kept in touch with over 30,000 people for 18 years; it also found that getting married made people happier, but only for a while (Lucas, 2007). Two years later, most of that delight had faded and the spouses were only as happy, on average, as they had been before they wed. Quite clearly, finding the love of your life doesn't make you happy forever.

Worse, since you were born, sociocultural influences may have caused our expectations to creep up and up. In the view of some observers, compared to our grandparents, we now expect our romances to be magical rather than merely pleasant, and deeply fulfilling instead of just fine, and it's hard to be happy when we expect so much (Amato et al., 2007). Indeed, on average, American marriages are less happy than they were 30 years ago, and our higher CLs may be partly responsible (Glenn, 1998).

Cultural changes have also increased our CL_{alt}s. Women's increased participation in the workforce has provided them both interesting coworkers and financial resources that make it easier for them to leave unhappy relationships (South et al., 2001). People are more mobile than ever before, changing residences and traveling at unprecedented rates (Putnam, 2000), so their options are more diverse. And legal, religious, and social barriers against divorce have gradually eroded (Berscheid & Lopes, 1997). No-fault divorce legislation that has made it easier for spouses to get divorces, for example, may be directly responsible for thousands of divorces that might not have otherwise occurred (Rodgers et al., 1999). Altogether, the costs of departing a marriage have declined even as many people have found more options and more partners available to them. We may even have entered an era of "permanent availability," in which people remain on the marriage market—continuing to size up the people they meet as potential future mates—even after they're married (Cherlin, 2009)! If you add up these influences and look back at Figure 6.1, maybe we shouldn't be surprised that the U.S. divorce rate has risen sharply since 1960; when CLs and CL_{alt}s are both high, people are more likely to find themselves in unhappy and unstable relationships.

THE ECONOMIES OF RELATIONSHIPS

As you can see, interdependence theory takes an unromantic view of close relationships. In describing some of its nuances, I even likened a happy, stable relationship to a desirable job with good benefits. But can the success or failure of close relationships really be reduced to nothing more than the profits or losses on an interaction spreadsheet? Are rewards and costs or the size of your "salary" everything that matters? The answer, of course, is "no." Too specific a focus on the rewards and costs of a couple's interactions can lead us to overlook important influences that can make or break a partnership. For instance, your ultimate success in an important relationship may someday depend on how well you adapt to external stresses that you cannot control (Randall & Bodenmann, 2009).

On the other hand, interdependence theory's businesslike emphasis on the outcomes people provide each other is enormously important. Counting up the rewards and costs of a relationship provides extraordinary information about its current state and likely future. And the picture of normal intimacy that emerges from studies of this sort is a bit surprising. The stereotype of intimate relations is that they are generous and loving, and, sure enough, couples who are nice to each other are more likely to stay together over time than are those who provide each other fewer rewards (e.g., Le et al., 2010). In one study, for instance, measures of generosity, affection, and self-disclosure administered at the very beginning of a dating relationship were quite accurate at predicting whether the couples would still be together 4 months later (Berg & McQuinn, 1986).

But costs are informative, too, and the surprise is that a lot of unpleasantness actually occurs in many relationships. On any given day, 44 percent of us are likely to be annoyed by a lover or friend (Averill, 1982). Each week, college students report an average of 8.7 aggravating hassles in their romantic relationships, a rate of more than one frustrating nuisance per day (Perlman, 1989). Most young adults complain that their lovers were overly critical, stubborn, selfish, *and* unreliable at least once during the past week (Perlman, 1989). Typical spouses report one or two unpleasant disagreements in their marriages each month (McGonagle et al., 1992). Long-term intimacy with another person apparently involves more irritation and exasperation than we may expect. Indeed, during their lives together, married people are likely to be meaner to each other than to anyone else they know (Miller, 1997b). This does *not* mean that close relationships are more punishing than rewarding overall; that's not true (in many cases) at all. However, on those (hopefully rare) occasions when intimates are at their worst, they're likely to be more tactless, impolite, sullen, selfish, and insensitive with each other than they would be with total strangers.

In fact, research has compared the manners in which people interact with their spouses and with total strangers on a problem-solving task (Vincent et al., 1975). When they were discussing issues with others they did not know well, people were polite and congenial; they withheld criticism, swallowed any disapproval, and suppressed signs of frustration. In contrast, with their spouses, people were much more obnoxious. They interrupted their lovers, disparaged their points of view, and openly disagreed. Intimacy and interdependence seemed to give people permission to be impolite instead of courteous and considerate.

Does this matter? You bet it does. Over time, irritating or moody behavior from a spouse puts a marriage at risk (Caughlin et al., 2000). Outright hostility is even worse (Renshaw et al., 2010). And even a few frustrations may be influential because negative behaviors in a close relationship seem to carry more psychological weight than similar amounts of positive behavior do. "Bad," it seems, "is stronger than good" (Baumeister et al., 2001).

Here's an example of what I mean. Imagine that you're walking down a sidewalk when a $20 bill blows into your path. There's no one else around, and it's obviously yours to keep. Does finding the money feel good? Of course it does. But now imagine that on another occasion you reach into a pocket where you put a $20 bill and find nothing but a hole. That's a disappointment. But which has the stronger effect on your mood, finding the new money or losing the money you already had? The answer is that losses usually affect us more than equivalent gains do; we like gains, but we really hate losses (Kahneman & Tversky, 1982).

Indeed, undesirable events in close relationships are more noticeable and influential than logically equivalent desirable events are (Baumeister et al., 2001). If you get one compliment and one criticism from your lover during an evening at home, for instance, they won't cancel each other out. The compliment will help soften the blow of the criticism, but the combination will leave you somewhat distressed. Bad is stronger than good.

In fact, to stay satisfied with a close relationship, we may need to maintain a rewards-to-costs ratio of at least 5-to-1. That figure comes from research by John Gottman and Robert Levenson (1992), who observed married couples who were revisiting the topic of their last argument. They carefully coded the partners' behavior during their discussion, giving each spouse a point for each attempt at warmth, collaboration, or compromise, and subtracting a point for each display of anger, defensiveness, criticism, or contempt. Some of the couples were able to disagree with each other in a manner that communicated respect and regard for each other, and the longer their conversations went on, the more positive their scores became. These couples, who were said to be at low risk of divorce by Gottman and Levenson, were maintaining a ratio of positive to negative exchanges of 5:1 or better. (See Figure 6.3.) However, other couples disagreed with sarcasm and disdain, and in those cases, the longer they talked, the worse their scores got. When the researchers compared the two groups at the time of the study, the low-risk couples were more satisfied with their marriages than the other couples were. No surprise there. More impressively, however, more than half (56 percent) of the high-risk couples were divorced or separated only 4 years later whereas just under a quarter (24 percent) of the low-risk couples had split up. A short discussion on a single afternoon clearly provided meaningful information about the chances that a marriage would last. And couples who did not maintain a substantial surfeit of positive exchanges faced twice the risk that their marriages would fail.

So, both rewards and costs are important influences on relationship satisfaction and stability, and there may need to be many more of the former than the latter if a relationship is to thrive. On the surface, this is a pretty obvious conclusion; we'd expect happy relationships to be more rewarding than punishing. In another study, for instance, 93 percent of the happily married couples reported making love more often than they argued, whereas none of the unhappily married couples did (Howard & Dawes, 1976). But if it's so obvious, why are there so many unhappy relationships? One possibility is that the partners disagree about the meaning and the value of the rewards they exchange (see the box on page 189). Some of the well-intentioned things that partners do for each other may not seem particularly thoughtful or affectionate to their partners. In addition, romantic partners simply don't notice all of the loving and affectionate behaviors their lovers provide; one study that tracked partners' perceptions for 4 weeks found that both men and women failed to notice about one-fourth of the positive behaviors that their partners said they performed (Gable et al., 2003). Husbands and wives with dismissing or fearful attachment styles are especially likely to miss some of the positive, loving things their spouses do for them (Carmichael et al., 2003). (This suggests the intriguing possibility that

FIGURE 6.3. **The arguments of couples at low and high risk of divorce.**
These are the actual charts of the conversations of two couples who had returned to the
topics of their last arguments. During their discussions, one couple remained (mostly)
polite and collaborative whereas the other was more disrespectful, sour, and sarcastic.
Which of these couples was much more likely to be separated or divorced
4 years later?[1]
(Pos-Neg = number of positive vs. negative exchanges.)
Gottman & Levenson, 1992.

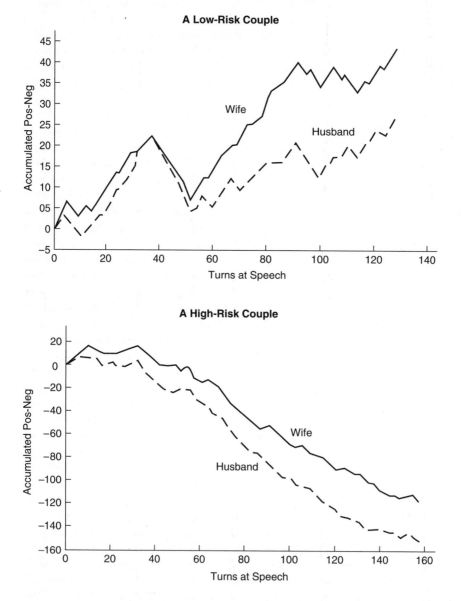

[1]Okay, I admit that's rather a dumb question. Isn't the answer obvious?

one reason such people are less comfortable with interdependent intimacy is that they don't fully realize how pleasant it can be!)

Rewards and Costs Are Different

Another more subtle answer is that rewards and costs have different, separate effects on our well-being in relationships, and this causes complexity. According to research by Shelly Gable (2008) and her colleagues, we try to do two things in our close relationships. First, we try to obtain rewards, and second, we try to avoid costs—and importantly, these are *not* the same things. In seeking rewards, we try to satisfy an appetite for desirable experiences that is known as an **approach motivation.** That is, we pursue pleasure and our motivation for doing something is to feel good, and when we draw near to—or *approach*—desired experiences, we feel positive emotions such as enthusiasm and excitement. Approach motivations for having sex, for instance, would be to feel close to our partners and to enjoy the physical experience (Cooper et al., 2008). Our desire to avoid costs is a different drive known as an **avoidance motivation.** That is, we also seek to elude or escape punishment and pain, so we strive to *avoid un*desired experiences and to reduce negative feelings such as anxiety and fear. Avoidance motivations for having sex would be to avoid rejection or to end a peevish partner's pouting.

The key point is that our approach and avoidance motives are not just two different sides of the same coin. They don't cancel each other out. Pleasure results from fulfilling our approach goals, and pain results from failing to fulfill our avoidance goals, but—and here's where this gets really interesting—pleasure and pain are different processes. They operate independently, involving different brain mechanisms and causing distinct emotions and behaviors (Cacioppo & Gardner, 1999). The provocative result is that pleasure and pain can coexist, or both may be absent, in any relationship. Moreover, because pleasure and pain are unrelated, safe and secure relationships in which nothing bad happens are not necessarily satisfying, and satisfying relationships are not always safe and secure.

Let's explore this idea more with a look at Figure 6.4, which shows the approach and avoidance dimensions arranged at right angles. Every relationship you have lies somewhere along both of those lines, and its current status is defined by how well you are fulfilling both your approach and avoidance goals. For instance, the vertical line is the approach dimension; relationships that are full of positive events are exciting and invigorating—so they would lie near the top of the line—whereas those that offer few positive outcomes are unfulfilling and stagnant (and they would land near the bottom). Importantly, dull relationships aren't actually painful, they're just not fun. The horizontal line is the avoidance dimension. Whether or not they're rewarding, some relationships are full of conflict and danger (which would put them on the left side of the line), whereas others are more placid (which is on the right); however, just because a partnership is safe and has no negatives doesn't necessarily mean it *is* fun. As Reis and Gable (2003, p. 142) assert, "the absence of conflict and criticism in a relationship need not imply the presence of joy and fulfillment, just as the presence of joy and fulfillment need not denote the absence of conflict and criticism."

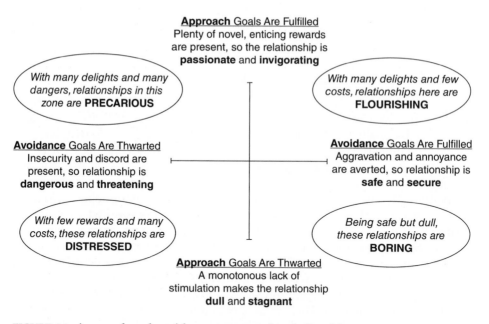

FIGURE 6.4. **Approach and avoidance processes in relationships.**
People seek rewards and want to avoid costs, but these are two different motivations that combine to influence our feelings in close relationships. When avoidance goals are fulfilled, people avoid costs but are not necessarily happy. When approach goals are fulfilled, people feel engaged and excited but may not feel safe and secure. Only when both motivations are fulfilled simultaneously are people wholly content.
Figure based on the insights of Reis & Gable, 2003, and Fincham & Beach, 2010.

So, why do we care, exactly? There are several reasons. First, in a really great relationship, we're able to fulfill both motivations at the same time. Such relationships are full of delights and aggravations are absent, and the partnership can be said to be *flourishing* (Fincham & Beach, 2010). (Take a good long look at Figure 6.4.) And clearly, in contrast, if neither motivation is being fulfilled so that costs are high and rewards are low, a relationship is *distressed*. But because our approach and avoidance motivations operate independently, one motivation may also be fulfilled while the other is not, and that allows some interesting possibilities. Consider a relationship that offers compelling attractions—so that it is passionate and exciting—but that is also replete with doubts and discord: There'd be a lot of drama, and the potent pleasures of the partnership would be infused with danger and uncertainty in a perilous and *precarious* mix. There'd be a lot to like, but one's costs would be too high, so the partners' feelings about the relationship might vacillate widely, depending on which motivation was salient to them at the time (Gable & Poore, 2008).

The interplay of the two motivations also presents a fourth possibility that's important enough to get its own paragraph. Consider what results when our avoidance goals are fulfilled and our costs and annoyances are very low—so there's really nothing to *dis*like about the relationship—but our approach motivation is unfulfilled, so there's not much to *like* about the relationship

"To Show You I Love You, I Washed Your Car"
Gender Differences in the Evaluation of Relationship Rewards

The various commodities and rewards people exchange in their relationships have no price tags, and partners sometimes disagree about what an exchange is worth. In a study by Wills et al., (1974), seven married couples kept track of their behavioral exchanges for 2 weeks. The rewards they exchanged either involved tasks and responsibilities (such as taking out the garbage) or emotion and affection (such as saying, "I love you"). When the spouses rated their pleasure with their partners' behavior, wives particularly appreciated their husbands' affectionate behavior, whereas husbands liked their wives' task-oriented help. The sexes apparently attached different values to such actions as doing the dishes and expressing warmth and love. The consequences of this sex difference were revealed when the husbands were asked to increase their affectionate behavior toward their wives. Most did, but they also engaged in more task-oriented helping, which suggests that they were confusing the two. One husband was no more affectionate than usual but was annoyed when he was asked why; he had washed his wife's car, and he thought that was a perfectly good way to communicate his affection for her. She didn't see it that way.

This study used a very small sample, so we shouldn't make too much of it. However, the results offer the useful lesson that although the language of social exchange sounds straightforward—rewards and costs, gains and losses—the reality is more complex. Exchanges with others involve a *psychological* arithmetic in which people's motives, beliefs, and emotions affect their perceptions of the outcomes they receive. Judgments of what favors are worth routinely differ for those who provide the favors and those who receive them (Zhang & Epley, 2009), and gender differences complicate things further. So, for example, when spouses are asked what they would change if they could, wives say they desire more emotion and affection from their husbands whereas the husbands say they want more sex (Heyman et al., 2009). What matters to me may not be quite the same as what matters to you, and those differing perceptions add complexity to our quest for mutually satisfying interaction.

either. The partnership would have few negatives, but it would lack novelty and stimulation; it would be dull, stale, and stagnant and, in a word, *boring*. Boredom is characterized by tedium, disinterest, and a lack of energy, and it occurs when nothing enticing, intriguing, or new is occurring in an intimate relationship (Harasymchuk & Fehr, 2010). There are no sparks, no excitement, no arousal, and no fun (Harasymchuk & Fehr, 2011). And, of course, this is not a good place to be: If husbands and wives are bored now, they're likely to be dissatisfied later. In the Early Years of Marriage Project,[2] spouses who thought that their marriages were becoming monotonous after a few years were less happy 9 years later than were spouses who weren't getting bored (Tsapelas et al., 2009). Boredom now is linked to dissatisfaction later. So, what do the

[2]See pages 44 and 403.

deleterious effects of boredom suggest we do to live happily ever after? Let me return to that in just a moment.

A second reason to note the roles of approach and avoidance motivations in our relationships is that the chronic strength of people's motive differ (Gable, 2006). Bad is generally stronger than good, for instance, but some people are very sensitive to negative events that wouldn't much ruffle others—and such people may feel especially threatened by disagreements or conflict with their partners. Indeed, a strong motive to avoid costs leads people to notice all of the annoying things their partners do whereas the motive to approach rewards leads them to focus on all the thoughtful and generous actions their partners take (Strachman & Gable, 2006). (Which point of view do you think makes people more content?) When they make small sacrifices to benefit their partners (such as going to a movie they don't much want to see), people with approach motives are pursuing greater intimacy with their partners; they feel good about their actions, and their relationships profit. In contrast, people with avoidance motives are trying to avoid conflict; they begrudge the sacrifice, and their relationships suffer (Impett et al., 2005). And as you might guess from these patterns, people who have high approach motivations are also generally less lonely and more content (Gable, 2006). They enter social situations eager to make new friends whereas people with high aversive motivations just want to avoid annoying, offending, or upsetting anybody. Evidently, there's more long-term profit in focusing on obtaining rewards, rather than cutting costs, in our close relationships (Impett et al., 2010b).

Finally, and perhaps most importantly, the independent operation of approach and avoidance motivations means that being happy may involve different strategies than those that are involved in not being unhappy. We want to avoid painful conflict and other costs, of course, but if we wish our relationships to prosper and to be fulfilling, we need to do more than simply avoid any unpleasantries. We need to combat boredom: We must strive to meet our partners' approach goals by providing them joyous, interesting, and exciting experiences (Strong & Aron, 2006).

This conclusion is also at the heart of a **self-expansion model** of human motivation that holds that we are attracted to partnerships that expand the range of our interests, skills, and experiences (Aron & Aron, 2000). Novel activities, the development of new talents, and the acquisition of new perspectives are all thought to be inherently gratifying (Nardone & Lewandowski, 2008), and that's why new loves are often so exhilarating: Newfound intimacy typically involves increases in knowledge and changes in mutuality that enhance and expand our self-concepts (Tucker & Aron, 1993).

But self-expansion usually slows once a new partner becomes familiar, and that's when many partnerships begin to feel more bland and ordinary than they initially seemed. The key to staying happy, according to the self-expansion model, is to combat boredom by creatively finding ways to continue your personal growth. Thus, as well as continually seeking out novel activities and challenges (Aron et al., 2000), consider the value of intentionally inventing new ways to play and have fun (Aune & Wong, 2002) and laugh together (Lee, 2008) during your daily routine (Graham, 2008). Monotony can make any relationship seem stale, but innovation and novelty may keep boredom at bay.

So, rewards and costs are different, and minimizing our costs isn't the same thing as increasing our rewards. And as our discussion of boredom suggests, relationships begin when a couple's interactions are rewarding, but that can change with time. Indeed, despite the partners' best intentions, many relationships gradually become less satisfying as time goes by. Let's take a closer look at how rewards and costs change as relationships develop.

Rewards and Costs as Time Goes By

Here's the situation: You've started dating a new person and things are going great. Your satisfaction is rising fast, and the two of you are quickly growing closer. Does continual bliss lie ahead? Probably not. After a period of initial excitement that is characterized by a rapid increase in satisfaction, most relationships—even those that are destined to succeed and prosper—hit a lull in which the partners' pleasure stalls for a time (see Figure 6.5). This can be disconcerting, but it shouldn't be surprising; according to a model of **relational turbulence** created by Leanne Knobloch and Denise Solomon (2004), we should *expect* a period of adjustment and turmoil as new partners become accustomed to their increasing interdependence. In particular, as the partners spend more and more time together, they disrupt each others' routines. Instead of waiting to be asked

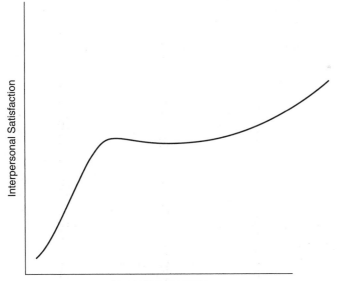

Level of Involvement

FIGURE 6.5. **Satisfaction in beginning relationships.**
After a rapid rise in satisfaction at the very beginning of their relationships, many couples encounter a lull as they adjust to their increasing interdependence. Successful relationships survive this period of re-evaluation and become even more satisfying, but at a more gradual rate.
Adapted from Eidelson, 1980.

out on a date, for instance, one of the partners may start *assuming* that they'll spend the weekend together, and that may interfere with the other's plans. The partners may also encounter some resistance from their friends as the new relationship absorbs more of their time and they see less of their old companions. Uncertainty and doubt can also accompany emerging commitment; both partners may wonder where the relationship is going and what the future holds, and the more uncertain they are, the more turbulent the situation is likely to be (Knobloch & Theiss, 2010). Altogether, the turbulence model suggests that an unsettled period of adjustment and reevaluation is likely to occur at moderate levels of intimacy in a developing relationship as the partners learn to coordinate their needs and accommodate each other.

The turbulence model is depicted in Figure 6.6. When intimacy levels are low in a beginning relationship, interdependence is minimal and there is negligible interference from one's partner and little doubt about the future of the partnership. However, as the partners draw closer, they need to adjust to increasing limitations to their autonomy, rising uncertainty, and, perhaps, mounting ambivalence from their friends, and this phase—the transition from

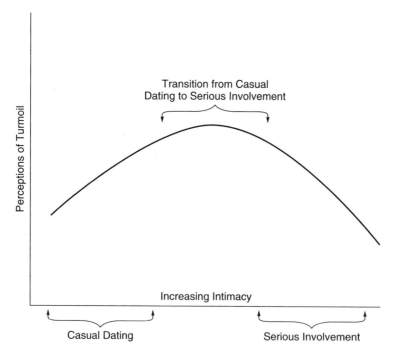

FIGURE 6.6. **The relational turbulence model.**
The amount of turmoil and turbulence in a new relationship increases as the partners spend more time together, and begin to interfere with each other's routines and to wonder where the relationship is headed. This turmoil reaches a peak when the couple decides to become more seriously involved, but it then declines as they adjust to their new interdependency.
Figure adapted from Knobloch & Donovan-Kicken, 2006.

casual dating to more serious involvement in the relationship—can be tumultuous (Solomon et al., 2010). If the relationship becomes more established and intimacy increases further, things settle down as doubts diminish, friends adjust, and the partners grow more adept at being interdependent. Successful relationships survive the turbulent transition to the partners' new status as a recognized couple, and a new but more gradual increase in satisfaction may occur as the relationship continues to develop. (Take another look at Figure 6.5.)

So, it's customary for increasing delight with a budding relationship to suddenly level off for a time as the partners adjust to their increasing interdependency. Are there predictable changes in satisfaction over longer stretches of time in established relationships? There are, and I've got good news and bad news for you. Let's begin with the bad news, which starts with Figure 6.7. Pictured there are the annual reports of marital satisfaction from 538 newlywed couples, many of whom were tracked for 10 years (if they stayed married that long). As you can see, the typical trajectory of marital bliss involved a gradual erosion of delight that resulted in people becoming less satisfied as the years rolled by (Kurdek, 1999). Even worse, recent studies that probed carefully for different trajectories of marital satisfaction over 4 (Lavner & Bradbury, 2010) and 20 years (Anderson et al., 2010) found that in a number of couples—about one in every six—the declines in contentment were much more severe. Some newlyweds find their dreams dashed rather quickly.

FIGURE 6.7. **The average trajectory of marital satisfaction.**
Some couples experience decreases in satisfaction that are steeper than this, but others don't experience any decline at all. In addition, on average, cohabiting gay and lesbian couples experience milder decreases in satisfaction than heterosexual couples do (Kurdek, 2008b).

Data from Kurdek, 1999.

The good news from the recent studies is that, despite the general trend pictured in Figure 6.7, a number of couples—about one in every five—don't experience any decline in their delight at all. Most marriages don't last as long as 25 years (Roberts, 2007), but some do, and clearly, it really is possible for some couples to live happily ever after.

What distinguished those who stayed happy from the majority who experienced a decline in their delight? There were several influences, and none of them will surprise a careful reader of our prior chapters. Spouses who stayed content tended to be low in neuroticism and high in self-esteem; they discussed touchy issues with affection and humor and without anger; and they encountered relatively few stressors such as economic hardship or ill health (Anderson et al., 2010; Lavner & Bradbury, 2010). Over time, then, the outcomes of their interactions were undoubtedly more positive than those of couples who were more fretful, insecure, surly, and beset with hassles and burdens—and interdependency theory argues that that's why they stayed more content.

It also turns out that happy couples keep their expectations in check so that their CLs don't get too high. Remember that it's hard to be satisfied when you expect things to be magnificent, and sure enough, on average, people who begin their marriages with the highest expectations of how special and wonderful wedlock will be are the least happy spouses a few years down the road. James McNulty and Ben Karney (2004) followed 82 newlywed couples across the first 4 years of their marriages and found that, over time, the happiest couples were those who had had the most realistic outlooks about what wedded life would be like. In contrast, spouses who had unrealistically positive expectations tended to be disappointed once the honeymoon was over. (In fact, more than one-fifth of the couples followed by McNulty and Karney were divorced after only 4 years.)

Indeed, I can offer several reasons why prudent and cautious expectations about the futures of your intimate relationships are more reasonable and sensible than romantic idealism is. First, we all know how to be polite and thoughtful, and we can behave that way when we want to, but it takes work. Once a courtship is over and a partner is won, for instance, people usually stop trying so hard to be consistently charming. The same people who would never fart noisily on a first date may become spouses who fart at will at the dinner table, perhaps dismissing their lack of propriety by saying, "Sorry, I couldn't help it." The point is that they *could* help it if they wanted to—they just didn't go to the trouble to do so (Miller, 2001).

Second, interdependency magnifies conflict and friction. We spend lots of time with our intimate partners and depend on them for unique, especially valuable rewards, and that means that they are certain to cause us more frustration—even inadvertently—than anyone else can. For instance, we're more affected by the moods (Caughlin et al., 2000) or work stress (Lavee & Ben-Ari, 2007) of intimate partners than by the similar difficulties of others. Frequent interaction also means that trivial annoyances may gradually cause real grief through sheer repetition in the same way that the light tapping of a slowly dripping faucet can drive you mad when you're trying to sleep at night (Cunningham et al., 2005).

Third, intimacy means that others know your secrets, foibles, and weaknesses. That gives them ammunition with which to wound and tease us when conflict occurs. But even when they have no wish to do us harm, their access to sensitive information practically guarantees that they will accidentally reveal some secret (Petronio, 2010), hurt our feelings (Kowalski, 2003), or embarrass us (Miller, 1996) sometime or other. They can unintentionally hurt us in ways others can't.

Fourth, even if people are usually aware of most of their incompatibilities and problems before they marry, there will almost always be some surprises ahead. These tend to be of two general types. First, there's learning the truth about things we thought we knew. Good examples of this are the *fatal attractions* I mentioned in chapter 3. You may know and even like the fact that your lover is fun-loving and spontaneous, but you may not appreciate how irresponsible, flighty, and unreliable that same behavior may seem after a few years of marriage when you have babies and a mortgage to contend with. Speaking of babies, the other type of unwelcome surprise is learning undesired things that you didn't know at all, and the real facts of parenthood are often good examples. If you don't have kids, you might assume that parenthood will be fun, your kids will be invariably adorable, and raising children will bring you and your partner closer together. The reality, however (as you know if you do have kids), is that "after the birth of a child the prognosis for the course of the marital relationship is unequivocally grim" (Stafford & Dainton, 1994, p. 270). I can safely say that parenthood is an extraordinary and often marvelous adventure, but it is unquestionably hard on the relationship between the parents. Children are endless work, and most parents experience a steep and unexpected decline in the time they spend having fun together (Claxton & Perry-Jenkins, 2008). When babies arrive, conflict increases, and satisfaction with the marriage (and love for one's partner) decrease (Doss et al., 2009), and this occurs around the world (Wendorf et al., 2011). If the parents don't expect such difficulties, they're going to be surprised.

Finally, all of this means that close relationships are often much different from the blissful, intimate idylls we want them to be, and the difference between what we expected and what we get can leave us feeling cheated and disappointed, sometimes unnecessarily so (Amato et al., 2007). To the extent that even great relationships involve hard work and sacrifice, people with misplaced, glorified expectations about relationships may end up disappointed in their outcomes even when they're doing better than everyone else.

So, through (a) **lack of effort;** because (b) **interdependency is a magnifying glass;** and through (c) **access to weaponry,** (d) **unwelcome surprises,** and (e) **unrealistic expectations,** people usually encounter unanticipated costs, even in good relationships (Miller, 1997b), and most spouses' satisfaction actually declines during the first years of marriage. These are all normal processes in close relationships, so it's naïve to think that you won't encounter them. More annoyances and nuisances lie ahead than you may have thought.

This may seem gloomy, but it isn't meant to be. Indeed, I don't want this analysis to seem pessimistic at all! To the contrary, knowledge is power, and

I suspect that being aware of the usual trajectory of marital satisfaction and thoroughly understanding these issues can help people avoid needless disappointment, and it may even help them to forestall or avoid a creeping decline in outcomes that would otherwise occur. If informed caution leads you to form reasonable expectations, you *should* be optimistic that your close relationships will succeed; a positive outlook that is rooted in good sense is likely to make lasting satisfaction more, rather than less, attainable (Churchill & Davis, 2010).

And importantly, if nothing else, this perspective reminds us of our constant responsibility to be as pleasant as possible to those whose company we value. We want great outcomes, but so do they, and even if they like us, they'll go elsewhere if we don't give them enough reward. This is a consequential idea, and it leads to some subtleties of the social exchange perspective that we have yet to consider.

ARE WE REALLY THIS GREEDY?

So far in this chapter, I have portrayed people as greedy hedonists who are concerned only with their own outcomes. That's not a complimentary portrayal, but it is useful because rewards and costs matter enormously in close relations. The research data support the basic precepts of interdependence theory quite well (Le et al., 2010). Nevertheless, our portrait so far is incomplete. There are good reasons that people will usually want their partners to prosper as well.

The Nature of Interdependency

Okay, you've got the idea: According to interdependence theory, people want maximum reward at minimum cost, and they want the best interpersonal deals they can get. Everybody behaves this way. But what happens when they get a good deal? Then they depend on their partners and don't want to leave them. That's significant because it means that they have an important stake in *keeping their partners happy,* so that their partners will continue providing those desired rewards. If you want to keep valued relationships going, it's to your advantage to ensure that your partners are just as dependent on you as you are on them, and a straightforward way to do that is to provide them high outcomes that make them want to stay (Murray et al., 2009).

Pursuing this strategy can influence the value of many transactions with a desired partner. Actions that would be costly if enacted with a stranger can actually be rewarding in a close relationship because they give pleasure to one's partner and increase the likelihood that one will receive valuable rewards in return (Kelley, 1979). Providing good outcomes to one's partner, even when it involves effort and sacrifice, can ultimately be self-serving if it causes a desirable relationship to continue. Indeed, even greedy people should be generous to others if it increases their own profits! As a writer to an advice column reported, "It is heaven to be with someone who enjoys making sure I'm taken care of in every way. And it makes me want to do everything I can to see that he's happy in return" (Mitchell & Sugar, 2007, p. A6).

So, interdependence theory suggests that in the quest for high outcomes, individuals will often be magnanimous to those on whom they depend because it is reasonable (and valuable) to do so. And if both partners in a relationship want it to continue, both of them should thoughtfully protect and maintain the other's well-being. If people need each other, it can be advantageous to be positively philanthropic to each other, increasing the partner's profits to keep him or her around. Thus, even if people are greedy, there is likely to be plenty of compassionate thoughtfulness and magnanimity in interdependent relationships.

Exchange versus Communal Relationships

Indeed, when people seek closeness with others, they are often rather generous, offering more to others than they seek in return (Beck & Clark, 2009). We seem to realize that rewarding interdependency is more likely to develop when we're *not* greedily pursuing instant profit. With this in mind, Margaret Clark and Judson Mills (1993) proposed a distinction between partnerships that are clearly governed by explicit norms of even exchange and other, more generous, relationships that are characterized by obvious concern for the partner's welfare. In **exchange relationships,** people do favors for others expecting to be repaid by receiving comparable benefits in return. If they accept a kindness from someone, people feel obligated to return a similar favor to even the scales. Thus, as Table 6.1 shows, people in exchange relationships don't like to be in one another's debt; they track each other's contributions to joint endeavors;

People (and cats) are usually generous to those on whom they depend.

B. Kliban (1935-1990), "If I Had Two Dead Rats", from the book Cat. Use by Permission Only. All Rights Reserved. © Judith K. Kliban

TABLE 6.1. **Differences between Exchange and Communal Relationships**

Situation	Exchange Relationships	Communal Relationships
When we do others a favor	We prefer those who pay us back immediately.	We prefer those who *don't* repay us immediately.
When others do us a favor	We prefer those who request immediate repayment.	We prefer those who do *not* request immediate repayment.
When we are working with others on a joint task	We seek to distinguish our contributions from those of others.	We don't make any clear distinction between others' work and our own.
When we help others	Our moods and self-evaluations change only slightly.	Our moods brighten and our self-evaluations improve.
When we don't help others	Our moods do not change.	Our moods get worse.
When we feel vulnerable or anxious	We are unwilling to tell others what we are feeling.	We are willing to tell others about our true feelings.
When we're married	We are less satisfied.	We are more satisfied.

Source: Beck & Clark, 2010b; Clark & Finkel, 2005; Clark et al., 2010.

they monitor the other person's needs only when they think there's a chance for personal gain; and they don't feel bad if they refuse to help the other person. As you might expect, exchange relationships are typified by superficial, often brief, relatively task-oriented encounters between strangers or acquaintances.

In contrast, in **communal relationships,** the partners feel a special concern for the other's well-being, and they provide favors and support to one another without expecting repayment (Beck & Clark, 2010b). As a result, people who seek a communal relationship avoid strict cost accounting, and they'd rather *not* have their kindnesses quickly repaid; they monitor their partners' needs even when they see no opportunity for personal gain; and they feel better about themselves when they help their partners. People often make small sacrifices on behalf of their partners in communal relationships, doing costly favors for each other, but they enjoy higher quality relationships as a result (Clark & Grote, 1998). Indeed, people like marriages to operate this way, and the more generosity and communal concern spouses display toward each other, the happier they are (Clark et al., 2010). Meaningful romantic attachments are usually communal relationships, but communal and exchange norms are about equally likely to apply to friendships, which may be of either type (Clark & Mills, 1993).

Indeed, the extent of our generosity in response to our partners' needs can vary from relationship to relationship, and Mills and Clark and their colleagues (Mills et al., 2004) have developed a short scale to measure *communal strength,* the motivation to be responsive to a particular partner's needs (see Table 6.2).

TABLE 6.2. A Measure of Communal Strength

You can compare the communal strength of your relationships with different partners by answering these questions more than once. For each relationship, fill in your partner's initials in the blank. Then answer each question by writing down your rating from the scale below:

0	1	2	3	4	5	6	7	8	9	10
not at all										extremely

1. How far would you be willing to go to visit ____?

2. How happy do you feel when doing something that helps ____?

3. How large a benefit would you be likely to give ____?

4. How large a cost would you incur to meet a need of ____?

5. How readily can you put the needs of ____ out of your thoughts?

6. How high a priority for you is meeting the needs of ____?

7. How reluctant would you be to sacrifice for ____?

8. How much would you be willing to give up to benefit ____?

9. How far would you go out of your way to do something for ____?

10. How easily could you accept not helping ____?

To determine your score, reverse the rating you gave to questions 5, 7, and 10. If your rating was 0, change it to 10; a 1 becomes a 9; 2 changes to 8; and so on. Then add up your ratings. Your sum is the strength of your communal motivation toward that particular partner.

Source: Mills et al., 2004.

As their feelings of communal strength increase, people *enjoy* making small sacrifices for their partners (Kogan et al., 2010), and their spouses are more satisfied with their marriages (Mills et al., 2004). Thoughtful concern for the well-being of one's partner is clearly connected to closeness and contentment in intimate partnerships.

But does the lack of apparent greed in communal relationships indicate that the principles of exchange we've been discussing do not apply there? Not at all. For one thing, tit-for-tat exchanges are probably also taking place in communal partnerships, but in a manner that involves more diverse rewards across a longer span of time (Clark, 1981). In more businesslike relationships, exchanges are expected to occur quickly, so that debts are rapidly repaid. They should also be comparable, so that you pay for what you get. In more intimate relationships, there's more versatility. What we do to meet a partner's needs may involve very different actions from what the partner did to meet our own needs. We can also wait longer to be repaid because we trust our partners and expect the relationship to continue. In this sense, both exchange and communal partnerships are "exchange" relationships in which people expect to receive benefits that fit those they provide, but the exchanges take different forms and are less obvious in communal relationships.

In addition, the exchange perspective may not seem to describe intimate relationships because, when they are healthy, the partners enjoy an "economy of surplus" and seem unconcerned with how well they're doing (Levinger, 1979). Both partners are prospering, and there seems to be little need to "sweat the small stuff" by explicitly quantifying their respective rewards and costs. People in happy and stable relationships, for instance, probably haven't been wondering "what has my partner done for me lately?" both because the partner has done plenty and because they're happy enough not to care. However, if their outcomes start falling and their heady profits evaporate, even intimate partners in (what were) communal relationships may begin paying close attention to the processes of exchange (Grote & Clark, 2001). Indeed, when dissatisfaction sets in, people in (what were) communal relationships often become very sensitive to minute injustices in the outcomes they receive (Jacobson et al., 1982). In a sense, they start "balancing their checkbooks" and "counting every penny."

So, a distinction between exchange and communal relationships isn't incompatible with interdependency theory at all. However, the workings of communal relationships do demonstrate how readily people provide benefits to those with whom they wish to develop close relationships and how quickly people begin to take others' welfare under consideration once interaction begins (Beck & Clark, 2009). Most people seem to recognize, as interdependency theory suggests, that if you want others to be nice to you, you've got to be nice to them.

Equitable Relationships

Another point of view argues that you not only have to be nice but also to be *fair*. **Equity** theorists extend the framework of social exchange to assert that people are most satisfied in relationships in which there is *proportional justice*, which means that each partner gains benefits from the relationship that are proportional to his or her contributions to it (Hatfield, 1983). A relationship is equitable when the ratio of your outcomes to your contributions is similar to that of your partner, or when

$$\frac{\text{Your outcomes}}{\text{Your contributions}} = \frac{\text{Your partner's outcomes}}{\text{Your partner's contributions}}$$

Note that equity does not require that two partners gain equal rewards from their interaction; in fact, if their contributions are different, equality would be inequitable. A relationship is fair, according to equity theory, only when a partner who is contributing more is receiving more as well.

Let's look at some examples. Here are three equitable relationships, with outcomes and contributions rated on a 0-to-100-point scale:

	Partner X		Partner Y
(a)	80/50	=	80/50
(b)	20/100	=	20/100
(c)	50/25	=	100/50

In relationships (a) and (b), both partners are receiving equal outcomes and making equal contributions, but the quality of outcomes is much higher for the partners in relationship (a) than for those in relationship (b). Equity theory emphasizes fairness, not the overall amount of rewards people receive, and because both (a) and (b) are fair, they should both be satisfying to the partners. (Do you think they would be? I'll return to this point later.) Relationship (c) is also equitable even though the partners do not make equal contributions or derive equal outcomes. Partner Y is working harder to maintain the relationship than partner X is, but both of them are receiving outcomes that are proportional to their contributions; each is getting two units of benefit for every unit he or she contributes, so Y's higher outcomes are fair.

In contrast, in inequitable relationships, the two ratios of outcomes to contributions are not equal. Consider these examples:

	Partner X		Partner Y
(d)	80/50	$\neq$	60/50
(e)	80/50	$\neq$	80/30

In relationship (d), the partners are working equally hard to maintain the relationship, but one of them is receiving better outcomes than the other. In (e), their outcomes are the same, but their contributions are different. In either case, the partners are likely to be distressed—even if they're getting good outcomes—because the relationship isn't fair. In such situations, one partner is **overbenefited,** receiving better outcomes than he or she deserves, and the other is **underbenefited,** receiving less than he or she should. Does that matter? Interdependence theory says it shouldn't, much, as long as both partners are prospering, but equity theory says it does.

The Distress of Inequity

One of the most interesting aspects of equity theory is its assertion that everybody is nervous in inequitable relationships. It's easy to see why underbenefited partners would be unhappy; they're being cheated and exploited, and they may feel angry and resentful. On the other hand, overbenefited partners are doing too well, and they may feel somewhat guilty (Guerrero et al., 2008). It's better to be over- than underbenefited, of course, but people are presumed to dislike unfairness, being motivated to change or escape it. So, equity theory proposes that the most satisfactory situation is an equitable division of outcomes; furthermore, the theory predicts that overbenefited people will be somewhat less content than those who have equitable relationships, and underbenefited people will be *much* less satisfied (Hatfield, 1983).

Ways to Restore Equity

If you're underbenefited, what can you do? First, you can try to restore *actual equity* by changing your (or your partner's) contributions or outcomes (Canary & Stafford, 2001). You can request better treatment so that your outcomes will improve—"it's your turn to cook dinner while I relax"—or you can reduce your contributions, hoping that your outcomes stay about the same. You could even sabotage your partner, reducing his or her outcomes so that they're no longer out of line (Hammock et al., 1989).

If these efforts fail, you can try to restore *psychological equity,* changing your perceptions of the relationship and convincing yourself it really is equitable after all. You could talk yourself into thinking that your partner is someone special who deserves the better deal. Or you could start doubting yourself and decide that you deserve your lousy outcomes.

Finally, as a last resort, you could *abandon the relationship* to seek fairness elsewhere. You could actually leave your partner, or perhaps just have an affair.

In any case, as all these examples suggest, equity theory argues that people are motivated to redress inequity when it occurs. That certainly makes sense if you're underbenefited. But would you really want to change things if you're overbenefited? Let's see what the data have to say.

How Much Is Enough? Being Treated Fairly versus Being Overbenefited

Several studies that have assessed the satisfaction of spouses and other romantic couples have obtained results that fit the predictions of equity theory very nicely (e.g., Sprecher, 1986; Stafford & Canary, 2006): Partners who were overbenefited were less relaxed and content than were those whose outcomes were equitable, and people who were underbenefited were less happy still. However, few of these studies assessed the participants' comparison levels or otherwise took note of just how good their outcomes were. (Remember, you can be overbenefited relative to how your partner is doing and still be getting crummy outcomes that could cause some dissatisfaction.) Other investigations that have tracked couples over time (often for several years) using a broader array of measures provide less support for the particulars of equity theory (e.g., Sprecher, 2001; Sprecher et al., 2010). Nobody likes being underbenefited—all studies agree on that—but being overbenefited is not always associated with reduced satisfaction. In fact, some people who are overbenefited like it just fine (Sprecher, 2001). Moreover, several studies that assessed the quality of partners' outcomes found that—just as interdependence theory asserts—the overall amount of reward that people receive is a better predictor of their satisfaction than is the level of equity they encounter (Cate et al., 1982; Cate et al., 1988). In these studies, it didn't matter what one's partner gave or got as long as one's own benefits were high enough, and the more rewards people said they received from a relationship, the better they felt about it.

There's complexity here. Some studies suggest that fairness is an important factor in the workings of intimate relationships, and some do not. One reason for these conflicting results may be that some people are more concerned with fairness in interpersonal relations than other people are. Across relationships, some people consistently value equity more than others do, and they, unlike other people, are more satisfied when equity exists than when it does not (Donaghue & Fallon, 2003). Curiously, however, such people tend to be less satisfied overall with their relationships than are people who are less concerned with equity (Buunk & Van Yperen, 1991). They may be paying too much attention to a careful accounting of their rewards and costs!

Nevertheless, no matter who we are, equity may be more important in some domains than in others. Two sensitive areas in which equity appears to be advisable are in the allocation of *household tasks* and *child care*. When these chores are divided equally, both spouses tend to be satisfied with their marriages: "When the burden of housework is shared, each spouse is likely to appreciate the other spouse's contribution, and there may be more leisure time for shared activities" (Amato et al., 2007, p. 166). In contrast, when one of the partners is doing most of the work, "bad feelings spill over and affect the quality of the marriage" (Amato et al., p. 166). Unfortunately, equitable allocation of these duties is often difficult for married women to obtain; even when they have similar job responsibilities outside the home, working wives tend to do about twice as many household chores as their husbands do (Davis et al., 2007). Cohabiting couples and gay and lesbian couples usually divide these tasks more fairly (Coltrane & Shih, 2010), so there may be something about marriage that leads men to do less around the house. Whenever it occurs, however, this inequity can produce considerable strain on the relationship (Claffey & Mickelson, 2009). Indeed, one general admonition offered by marriage researchers to modern couples is for men "to do more housework, child care, and affectional maintenance if they wish to have a happy wife" (Gottman & Carrère, 1994, p. 225). Equity in these conspicuous domains may be much more influential than similar fairness applied to other areas of a couple's interactions.

A third and perhaps most important reason why research results are mixed may be that equity is a salient issue when people are dissatisfied, but it's only a minor issue when people are content (Holmes & Levinger, 1994). When rewards are ample, equity may not matter. People who are prospering in their relationships may spend little time monitoring their exchanges and may casually dismiss any imbalances they do notice. (They might also tend to report that their partnerships are "fair" when researchers ask.) But if costs rise and rewards fall, people may begin tracking their exchanges much more carefully, displaying concern about who deserves to get what. And no matter what the truth is, people who are very dissatisfied are likely to perceive that they are being underbenefited by their partners (Grote & Clark, 2001). In this sense, then, inequity may not cause people to become dissatisfied; instead, being dissatisfied could lead people to think they're being treated unfairly.

Overall, the best conclusion appears to be that both the global quality of outcomes people receive *and* underbenefit, when it occurs, play important roles in predicting how satisfactory and enduring a relationship will be (Sprecher, 2001). Overbenefit doesn't seem to bother people much, and equity doesn't seem to improve a relationship if it is already highly rewarding. In contrast, the inequity that accompanies deprivation and exploitation—underbenefit—routinely causes distress (Kuijer et al., 2002), and selfishness is disliked wherever it's encountered (Allen & Leary, 2010). Still, the bottom line is that outcome level is probably a more important factor than inequity is; if our outcomes are poor and unsatisfactory, it isn't much consolation if they're fair, and if our outcomes are wonderful, inequity isn't a major concern.

Feminism Is Bad for Romance, Right?

Back in chapter 1, I reported that women married to traditional, masculine men are less content, on average, than are women with warmer, more expressive husbands. Now we've seen that unequal divisions of household labor breed resentment and distress. Both of these points suggest that (if you choose to marry), your chances for lasting marital bliss will be higher if you *don't* adhere to rigid, traditional expectations about what it means to be husband and wife (Amato et al., 2007). In fact, in the United States, women enjoy happier, healthier, and more stable romantic relationships when they are partnered with men who are feminists—that is, who believe in the equality of the sexes— than they do when their men are more traditional. They enjoy better sex, too (Rudman & Phelan, 2007).

Okay, women like their men to think of them as equals. But what about the guys? The old norms are clearly changing—a full 26 percent of wives who work now earn noticeably higher incomes than their husbands do (Jayson, 2009)—but a lot of people still think that women who believe in the equality of the sexes are likely to be homely, pushy, unromantic harpies who are lousy in bed (Rudman & Fairchild, 2007). However, to the contrary, female feminists are *less* hostile toward men than other women are (Anderson et al., 2009), and men who are partnered with feminist women enjoy more stable relationships and more sexual satisfaction than do men with traditional partners (Rudman & Phelan, 2007). Clearly, it's absurd to think that feminism is incompatible with romance. Thinking of one's lover as an equal partner may help create a relationship that is actually more rewarding and robust than a partnership that is based on the last century's old, outmoded expectations (Knudson-Martin & Mahoney, 2005).

Summing Up

So, what's the final answer? Is simple greed a good description of people's behavior in intimate relationships? The answer offered by relationship science is a qualified "yes." People are happiest when their rewards are high and their costs (and expectations) are low. But because we depend on others for the rewards we seek in intimate relationships, we have a stake in satisfying them, too. We readily protect the well-being of our intimate partners and rarely exploit them if we want those relationships to continue. Such behavior may be encouraged by selfish motives, but it is still thoughtful, generous, and often loving. So, even if it is ultimately greedy behavior, it's not undesirable or exploitative.

THE NATURE OF COMMITMENT

The good news is that happy dependence on an intimate partner leads to **commitment,** the intention to continue the relationship. People who both need their partners and who are currently content associate the concept of commitment with positive qualities such as sharing, supportiveness, honesty, faithfulness, and trust (Hampel & Vangelisti, 2008); they are affectionate, attentive, and

Attachment and Interdependency

The attachment dimension of avoidance of intimacy describes the comfort with which people accept intimate interdependency with others. So, as you might expect, avoidance figures prominently in several of the patterns we have encountered in this chapter. First, compared to those who are more secure, people who are high in avoidance are more attentive to their alternatives; they keep track of the other romantic options open to them (Miller, 2008) and they are more attracted to the newcomers they meet (Overall & Sibley, 2008). As a result, their CL_{alt}s tend to be higher than those of other people, and that leaves them less committed to their present partners (Miller, 2008). Avoidant people also value their independence and self-sufficiency, so their approach motivations are weaker; they are less highly motivated to pursue fulfillment from their partnerships with others than secure people are (Carnelley & Story, 2008). They are also less attracted to others who use communal norms; they prefer people who do *not* do favors for them without expecting something in return (Bartz & Lydon, 2008), and they think that others do favors for them out of obligation, not kindness (Beck & Clark, 2010a).

People who are anxious over abandonment fret that their partners may leave them, so they have strong avoidance motivations and nervously focus on averting conflict and other costly outcomes (Carnelley & Story, 2008). In addition, they tend to behave generously with new potential partners by using communal norms, but they get anxious when others behave communally toward them. The mere thought of closeness with a new partner makes them nervous (Bartz & Lydon, 2008).

In contrast, secure people are comfortable in communal situations, and they happily accept dependence from others by providing attentive support to their partners when it's needed (Simpson et al., 2002). And interestingly, the more accepting of our occasional neediness our partners are, the *less* needy we tend to be (Feeney, 2007). Adults seem to be like children in this regard; when they know safety and support are available if needed, they are more autonomous and self-reliant than they would be if support were less certain. Here's another reason, then, why secure people make desirable partners: Their relaxed acceptance of intimate interdependence makes it easier for their partners to stand on their own two feet.

---

respectful, and they happily plan to be together in the future (Weigel, 2008). (You can see why these people are staying put.) The bad news is that unhappy people can be committed to their relationships, too, not because they want to stay where they are but because they feel they *must*. For these people, commitment is probably experienced more as burdensome entrapment than as a positive feeling.

Different components of commitment are apparent in a handy commitment scale developed by Ximena Arriaga and Christopher Agnew (2001) that contains three themes. First, committed partners expect their relationship to continue. They also hold a long-term view, foreseeing a future that involves their partners. And finally, they are psychologically attached to each other so that

TABLE 6.3. Arriaga and Agnew's Commitment Scale

Answer each of the questions that follow using this scale:

1	2	3	4	5
not at all true	slightly true	moderately true	very true	extremely true

1. I feel very strongly linked to my partner—very attached to our relationship.
2. It pains me to see my partner suffer.
3. I am very affected when things are not going well in my relationship.
4. In all honesty, my family and friends are more important to me than this relationship.
5. I am oriented toward the long-term future of this relationship (e.g., I imagine being with my partner several years from now).
6. My partner and I joke about what things will be like when we are old.
7. I find it difficult to imagine myself with my partner in the distant future.
8. When I make plans about future events in my life, I think about the impact of my decisions on our relationship.
9. I intend to stay in this relationship.
10. I want to maintain our relationship.
11. I feel inclined to keep our relationship going.
12. My gut feeling is to continue in this relationship.

To determine your total commitment score, reverse the rating you used for questions 4 and 7. If you answered 1, change it to 5; 2 becomes 4; 4 becomes 2; and so on. Then add up your ratings. The higher your score, the greater your commitment.

Source: Arriaga & Agnew, 2001.

they are happier when their partners are happy, too. Each of these themes is represented by four questions on the commitment scale; take a look at Table 6.3 to see if you can tell which theme applies to each question.

This portrayal of commitment as a multifaceted decision is consistent with a well-known conceptualization of commitment developed by Caryl Rusbult and her colleagues known as the **investment model.** According to the investment model, commitment emerges from all of the elements of social exchange that are associated with people's CLs and CL_{alt}s (e.g., Rusbult et al., 2001). First, satisfaction increases commitment. People generally wish to continue the partnerships that make them happy. However, alternatives of high quality are also influential, and they *decrease* commitment. People who have enticing alternatives luring them away from their present partners are less likely to stay in their existing relationships. But people don't always pursue such alternatives even when they're available, if the costs of leaving their current relationships are too high. Thus, a third determinant of commitment is the size of one's investments in the existing relationship. High investments increase commitment regardless of the quality of one's alternatives and whether or not one is happy.

Altogether, then, the investment model suggests that people will wish to remain with their present partners when they're happy, or when there's no other desirable place for them to go, or when they won't leave because it would cost too much (see Figure 6.8). These influences are presumed to be equally important, and commitment emerges from the complex combination of all three. Thus, as people's circumstances change, relationships often survive periods in which one or both partners are dissatisfied, tempted by alluring alternatives, or free to walk out at any time. Episodes such as these may stress the relationship and weaken the partners' commitment, but the partnership may persist if the other components of commitment are holding it together.

In general, research results support the investment model quite well (Le & Agnew, 2003; Le et al., 2010). Satisfaction, the quality of one's alternatives, and the size of one's investments all tell us something useful about how committed a person is likely to be, and the model applies equally well to men and women, heterosexual and same-sex couples (Kurdek, 2008), and to Eastern (Lin & Rusbult, 1995), as well as Western, cultures. Moreover, the usefulness of the investment model provides general support for an exchange perspective on intimate relationships. The economic assessments involved in the investment model do a very good job of predicting how long relationships will last (Le et al., 2010), whether or not the partners will be faithful to each other (Drigotas et al., 1999), and even whether battered wives will try to escape their abusive husbands (Rusbult & Martz, 1995).

However, the investment model treats commitment as a unitary concept—that is, there's really only one kind of commitment—and other theorists argue that commitment not only springs from different sources, it comes in different forms (Rhoades et al., 2010). For instance, sociologist Michael Johnson (1999) asserts that there are actually three types of commitment. The first, **personal commitment,** occurs when people *want* to continue a relationship because they are attracted to their partners and the relationship is satisfying.

FIGURE 6.8. **The investment model of commitment.**
Satisfaction and investments are both positively related to commitment. The happier we are and the more we would lose by leaving, the greater our commitment to our present partners. However, high-quality alternatives undermine commitment; the more alluring our other options, the less committed we are.
From Rusbult et al., 1994.

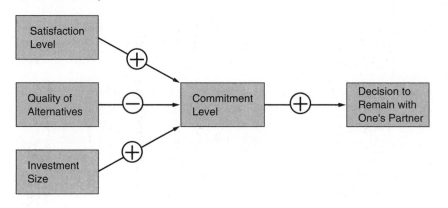

In contrast, the second type, **constraint commitment,** occurs when people feel they *have* to continue a relationship because it would be too costly for them to leave. In constraint commitment, people fear the social and financial consequences of ending their partnerships, and they continue them even when they wish they could depart. Finally, the third type of commitment, **moral commitment,** derives from a sense of moral obligation to one's partner or one's relationship. Here, people feel they *ought* to continue the relationship because it would be improper to end it and break their promises or vows. Spouses who are morally committed tend to believe in the sanctity of marriage and may feel a solemn social or religious responsibility to stay married no matter what.

Research using this scheme demonstrates that the three types of commitment do feel different to people, and there is value in distinguishing them in studies of relationships (Givertz et al., 2009; Ramirez, 2008). Personal commitment is often the strongest of the three, but constraint commitment and moral commitment can be influential, too (Cate et al., 2002). Even when people are unhappy and their personal commitment is low, for instance, they may stay in a partnership if constraint commitment is high because of financial or family pressures (Kurdek, 2006b). And when people embark on a long-distance romantic relationship, moral commitment does a better job of predicting whether or not the partnership will survive the period of separation than personal commitment does (Lydon et al., 1997). Evidently, moral commitment can keep a relationship going even when one's enthusiasm for the relationship wanes.

The Consequences of Commitment

Nevertheless, whatever its origins or nature, commitment substantially affects the relationships in which it occurs (Rusbult et al., 2001). The long-term orientation that characterizes commitment reduces the pain that would otherwise accompany rough spots in the relationship. When people feel that they're in a relationship for the long haul, they may be better able to tolerate episodes of high cost and low reward in much the same way that investors with a long-range outlook will hold on to shares of stock during periods of low earnings (Arriaga et al., 2007). In addition, commitment can lead people to think of themselves and their partners as a single entity, as "us" instead of "him" and "me" (Agnew et al., 2004). This may substantially reduce the costs of sacrifices that benefit the partner, as events that please one's partner produce indirect benefits for oneself as well.

Perhaps the most important consequence of commitment, however, is that it leads people to take action to protect and maintain a relationship even when it is costly for them to do so. Committed people engage in a variety of behavioral and cognitive maneuvers that both preserve and enhance the relationship and reinforce their commitment to it (Etcheverry & Le, 2005). We'll consider these *relationship maintenance mechanisms* in detail in chapter 14. However, to close this chapter, I'll briefly preview that material.

As one example, commitment promotes **accommodative behavior** in which people refrain from responding to provocation from their partners with similar ire of their own (Rusbult et al., 1998). Accommodating people tolerate destructive behavior from their partners without fighting back; they swallow insults, sarcasm, or selfishness without retaliating. By so doing, they avoid quarrels and altercations and help dispel, rather than perpetuate, their partners' bad moods. That's usually good for the relationship. Such behavior may involve considerable self-restraint, but it is not motivated by weakness; instead, accommodation often involves a conscious effort to protect the partnership from harm.

Committed people also display greater **willingness to sacrifice** their own self-interests for the good of the relationship (Impett & Gordon, 2008). They do things they wouldn't do if they were on their own, and they do not do things they would have liked to do in order to benefit their partners and their partnerships.

As a final example, commitment changes people's perceptions of their partnerships. Committed people exhibit **perceived superiority**—they think their relationships are better than those of other people (Buunk, 2001). In particular, they think that they enjoy more rewards and suffer fewer costs than other people encounter in their relationships (Broemer & Diehl, 2003).

People maintain their relationships with other mechanisms, but these three sufficiently illustrate the manner in which commitment motivates thoughts and actions that preserve partnerships. People seek maximum reward at minimum cost in their interactions with others, but dependency on a partner leads them to behave in ways that take the partner's well-being into account. As a result, committed partners often make sacrifices and accommodate their partners, doing things that are not in their immediate self-interest, to promote their relationships.

If people did these things indiscriminately, they would often be self-defeating. However, when they occur in interdependent relationships and when both partners behave this way, such actions provide powerful means of protecting and enhancing desired connections to others (Ramirez, 2008). In this manner, even if we are basically greedy at heart, we are often unselfish, considerate, and caring to those we befriend and love.

FOR YOUR CONSIDERATION

One of the things Gregg liked about Gail was that she was a great cook. When she would have him over to dinner, she would serve elaborate, delicious meals that were much more appealing than the fast food he often ate on his own. He liked to keep things tidy and neat, and he noticed that her apartment was always disheveled and cluttered, but he didn't much care because she was an exciting, desirable companion. However, once they were married, Gail cooked less often; they both worked, and she frequently called him before he came home to ask him to pick up take-out meals for dinner. He also became annoyed by her slovenly housekeeping. He did his fair share of housework, but a pile of unfolded laundry constantly occupied their living room couch, and they had to push it aside to sit together to watch television. She seemed not to notice just how scattered and disorganized her belongings were, and Gregg began to feel resentful.

What do you think the future holds for Gail and Gregg? Why?

CHAPTER SUMMARY

Social Exchange

Interdependence theory offers an economic view of relationships that suggests that people seek maximum reward at minimum cost.

Rewards and Costs. Rewards are gratifying and costs are punishing. The net profit or loss from an interaction is its *outcome.*

What Do We Expect from Our Relationships? People have *comparison levels* (CLs) that reflect their expectations for their interactions with others. When the outcomes they receive exceed their CLs, they're satisfied, but if their outcomes fall below their CLs, they're discontented.

How Well Could We Do Elsewhere? People also judge the outcomes available elsewhere using a *comparison level for alternatives* (CL_{alt}). When the outcomes they receive exceed their CL_{alt}s, they're dependent on their current partners.

Four Types of Relationships. Comparing people's CLs and CL_{alt}s with their outcomes yields four different relationship states: happy and stable; happy and unstable; unhappy and stable; and unhappy and unstable.

CL and CL_{alt} as Time Goes By. People adapt to the outcomes they receive, and relationships can become less satisfying as the partners' CLs rise. Cultural influences shape both our expectations and our CL_{alt}s.

The Economies of Relationships

Counting up the rewards and costs of a relationship provides extraordinary information about its current state and likely future.

Rewards and Costs Are Different. An *approach motivation* leads us to seek rewards, an *avoidance motivation* leads us to avoid costs, and the extent to which each is fulfilled defines different relationship states.

Rewards and Costs as Time Goes By. A *relational turbulence model* suggests that new relationships usually encounter a lull when partners adjust to their new status as an established couple. Thereafter, marital satisfaction usually decreases over the first years of marriage. This may be due to the partners' *lack of effort* and to the manner in which *interdependence magnifies small irritations,* and to other routine influences such as *unwelcome surprises* and *unrealistic expectations.* Insight may forestall or prevent these problems.

Are We Really This Greedy?

The Nature of Interdependency. Interdependent partners have a stake in keeping each other happy. As a result, generosity toward one's partner is often beneficial to oneself.

Exchange versus Communal Relationships. *Exchange relationships* are governed by a desire for immediate repayment of favors, whereas *communal relationships* involve selfless concern for another's needs.

Equitable Relationships. *Equity* occurs when both partners gain benefits from a relationship that are proportional to their contributions to it.
According to equity theory, people dislike inequity and are motivated to change or escape it. However, *overbenefit* is not always associated with reduced satisfaction with a relationship—but *underbenefit* is.

Summing Up. Both the quality of outcomes one receives and underbenefit, when it occurs, determine how happy and stable a relationship will be.

The Nature of Commitment

Commitment is the intention to continue a relationship. The *investment model* asserts that satisfaction, the quality of one's alternatives, and the size of one's investments influence commitment. However, there may be three kinds of commitment: *personal, constraint,* and *moral.*

The Consequences of Commitment. Committed people take action to protect and maintain their relationships, being accommodating, making sacrifices willingly, and considering their relationships to be better than most.

CHAPTER 7

Friendship

THE NATURE OF FRIENDSHIP ◆ Attributes of Friendships ◆ The Rules
of Friendship ◆ FRIENDSHIP ACROSS THE LIFE CYCLE ◆ Childhood
◆ Adolescence ◆ Young Adulthood ◆ Midlife ◆ Old Age ◆ DIFFERENCES
IN FRIENDSHIP ◆ Gender Differences in Same-Sex Friendships ◆ Individual
Differences in Friendship ◆ FRIENDSHIP DIFFICULTIES ◆ Shyness ◆ Loneliness
◆ FOR YOUR CONSIDERATION ◆ CHAPTER SUMMARY

I get by with a little help from my friends. *John Lennon*

Take a moment and think about your two best friends. Why are they such close companions? Why do you think of them as friends? You probably *like* but don't *love* them. (Or, at least, you're not "in love" with them, or you'd probably think of them as more than just "friends.") You've probably shared a lot of good times with them, and you feel comfortable around them; you know that they like you, too, and you feel that you can count on them to help you when you need it.

Indeed, the positive sentiments you feel toward your friends may actually be rather varied and complex. They annoy you sometimes, but you're fond of them, and because they're best friends, they know things about you that no one else may know. You like to do things with them, and you expect your relationship to continue indefinitely. In fact, if you look back at the features that define *intimacy* (way back on page 2), you may find that your connections to your best friends are quite intimate, indeed. You may have substantial knowledge of them, and you probably feel high levels of trust and commitment toward them; you may not experience as much caring, interdependence, and mutuality as you do with a romantic partner, but all three are present, nonetheless.

So, are friendships the same as but just less intimate than our romantic partnerships? Yes and no. Friendships are based on the same building blocks of intimacy as romances are, but the mix of components is usually different. Romances also have some ingredients that friendships typically lack, so their recipes do differ. But many of the elements of friendships and romances are quite similar, and this chapter will set the stage for our consideration of love (in chapter 8) by detailing what it means to *like* an intimate partner. Among other topics, I'll describe various features of friendship and question whether men and women can be "just friends."

THE NATURE OF FRIENDSHIP

Our friendships are indispensable sources of pleasure and support. One study of unmarried young adults found that over one-third of them (36 percent) considered a friendship to be their "closest, deepest, most involved, and most intimate" current relationship (Berscheid et al., 1989). A larger proportion (47 percent) identified a romantic relationship as their most important partnerships, but friendships were obviously significant connections to others. And they remain so, even after people marry. Another study that used an experience-sampling procedure[1] to track people's interactions found that they were generally having more fun when they were with friends than when they were alone or with family members, including their spouses. The best times occurred when both their spouses and their friends were present, but if it was one or the other, people derived more enjoyment and excitement from the presence of a friend than from the presence of a spouse (Larson & Bradney, 1988). Why? What's so great about friendship?

Attributes of Friendships

A variety of attributes come to mind when people think about a good friendship (Fuhrman et al., 2009; Hall, 2009). First, close friends feel *affection* for one another. They like, trust, and respect each other, and they value loyalty and authenticity, with both of them feeling free to be themselves without pretense. Second, a good friendship involves *communion*. The partners give and receive meaningful self-disclosures, emotional support, and practical assistance, and they observe a norm of equality, with both partners' preferences being valued. Finally, friends offer *companionship*. They share interests and activities, and consider each other to be sources of recreation and fun. At its best, friendship is clearly a close, rewarding relationship, which led Beverly Fehr (1996, p. 7) to define **friendship** as "a voluntary, personal relationship, typically providing intimacy and assistance, in which the two parties like one another and seek each other's company."

Differences between Friendship and Love

How, then, is friendship different from romantic attraction? As we'll see in chapter 8, love involves more complex feelings than liking does. Both liking and loving involve positive and warm evaluations of one's partner, but romantic love includes fascination with one's partner, sexual desire, and a greater desire for exclusiveness than friendship does (Giordano et al., 2006). Love relationships also involve more stringent standards of conduct; we're supposed to be more loyal to, and even more willing to help, our lovers than our friends (Fuhrman et al., 2009). The social norms that regulate friendship

---

[1]If a reminder about experience-sampling will be helpful, look back at page 59. (Chapter 2 continues to be useful, doesn't it?) In this study, participants wore pagers that prompted them to record what they were doing and who they were with every 2 hours during the day.

are less confining than those that govern romantic relationships, and friendships are easier to dissolve (Fehr, 1996). In addition, friendships are less likely to involve overt expressions of positive emotion, and friends, as a general rule, spend less of their free time together than romantic partners do.

These differences are not just due to the fact that so many of our friendships involve partners of the same sex. Friendships with members of the other sex are also less passionate and less committed than romances usually are (Fuhrman et al., 2009). So, friendships ordinarily entail fewer obligations and are less emotionally intense and less exclusive than romantic relationships. And unlike romantic relationships, friendships typically do not involve sexual intimacy (although some do; we'll consider "friends with benefits" later).

So, they are less passionate than romances, but rich friendships still contain all the other components that characterize rewarding intimacy with both friends and lovers. Let's consider several of those next.

Respect

When people respect others, they admire them and hold them in high esteem. The specific traits that seem to make a relationship partner worthy of respect include commendable moral qualities, consideration for others, acceptance of others, honesty, and willingness to listen to others (Frei & Shaver, 2002). We generally like those whom we respect, and the more we respect a friend or lover, the more satisfying our relationship with that person tends to be (Hendrick et al., 2010). Our closest friendships tend to be with others whom we respect (Guthrie et al., 2011).

Trust

We trust our partners when we are confident that they will behave benevolently toward us, selflessly taking our best interests into account (Rempel et al., 2001). Such confidence takes time to cultivate, but it is likely to develop when someone is alert to our wishes and reliably behaves unselfishly toward us (Simpson, 2007). Trust is invaluable in any close relationship because it makes interdependency more palatable; it allows people to be comfortable and relaxed in their friendships, and those who do not fully trust their partners tend to be guarded and cautious and less content (Rempel et al.). And the loss of trust has corrosive effects on any close relationship (Miller & Rempel, 2004); those who have been betrayed by a partner often find trust, and their satisfaction with their relationship, hard to recover (see chapter 10).

Capitalization

Good friends also tend to enhance, rather than diminish, our delight when we share good news or events with them. We don't always receive enthusiastic congratulations from others when we encounter good fortune; on occasion, we get bland best wishes, and sometimes others are simply uninterested. But good friends are usually pleased by our successes, and their excitement can increase our enjoyment of the event (Gable & Reis, 2010). So, in a pattern of interaction known as **capitalization,** we usually share good news with friends and receive enthusiastic, rewarding responses that are good for close relationships: We feel closer to those who excitedly enhance our happiness than to those who respond to our good fortune with apathy or indifference (Reis et al., 2010), and relationships in which capitalization routinely occurs are more satisfying and longer lasting than those in which it is infrequent (Gable et al., 2006).

Social Support

Successful capitalization enhances our enjoyment of positive events. We also rely on friends to help us through our difficulties, and there are several ways in which they can provide us help and encouragement. The aid, or *social support*, we receive from others can take four forms (Barry et al., 2009). We rely on our partners for *emotional support* in the form of affection, acceptance, and reassurance; *physical comfort* in the form of hugs and cuddling; *advice support* in the form of information and guidance; and *material support*, or tangible assistance in the form of money or goods. A partner who tries to reassure you when you're nervous about an upcoming exam is providing emotional support whereas a friend who loans you her car is providing material support. Don't take these distinctions too seriously, however, because these types of aid can and do overlap; because her generous concern would be touching, a friend who offers a loan of her car as soon as she learns that yours is in the shop could be said to be providing emotional as well as material support.

Social support can be of enormous value, and higher amounts of all four types of support are associated with higher relationship satisfaction and greater personal well-being as time goes by (Barry et al., 2009). Indeed, warm, attentive support from one's partners matters more than money when it comes to being happy; your income is likely to have less effect on your happiness than your level of social support does (North et al., 2008). Still, there are several complexities involved in the manner in which social support operates in close relationships. Consider these points:

- *Emotional support has real physiological effects.* People who have affectionate partners have chronically lower blood pressures, cholesterol levels, and stress hormone levels than do those who receive lesser amounts of encouragement and caring from others (Seeman et al., 2002). In lab procedures, they even experience less pain when they submerge their arms in ice-cold water (Brown et al., 2003). And when people are under stress, just thinking about a supportive friend tends to reduce their heart rates and blood pressures (Smith et al., 2004).
- *Effective social support also leads people to feel closer to those who provide it.* Sensitive, responsive support from others increases our happiness, self-esteem, and optimism about the future (Feeney, 2004), and all of these have beneficial effects on close relationships. In marriages, higher levels of support when the partners are newly married are associated with a lower likelihood of divorce 10 years later (Sullivan et al., 2010).
- But *some people are better providers of social support than others are.* For instance, attachment styles matter. Secure people, who readily accept interdependent

Friends Matter More Than We Think

You're aware of the pleasures to be found in a close friendship, but it's likely that your friends are influencing you even more than you realize. One way our friends often matter is in making or breaking our romantic relationships. They routinely help new romances get started by introducing us to potential new partners and running interference for us (Ackerman & Kenrick, 2009). And thereafter, they come to approve or disapprove of our ongoing romances, and their opinions count (Etcheverry et al., 2008). Our romances are imperiled when our friends disapprove of them: Even when they're (initially) satisfied with their relationships, young lovers are more likely to have broken up seven months later when their friends disapprove of their partnerships (Lehmiller & Agnew, 2007).

Our friends also have surprising influence on whether we're happy or sad (or fat or thin!). A remarkable 30-year study of the health of more than 12,000 people found that having happy friends makes it more likely that you'll be happy, too (Christakis & Fowler, 2009). Each friend we have who possesses good cheer increases the chance that we will also be happy by 15 percent. And our friends' friends also matter; each happy friend our friends have increases our chances of being happy by 10 percent even if we've never met that person! The norms supported and the experiences offered by our social networks are surprisingly potent, and they can work against, as well as for, us. For instance, if a friend gets heavy, the chance that you will also begin gaining too much weight goes up by 57 percent. Each *un*happy friend we have decreases the likelihood that we're happy by 7 percent. And loneliness is more contagious: We're 52 percent more likely to become lonely if a friend gets lonely first, and 25 percent more likely if a friend's friend becomes lonely (Cacioppo et al., 2009). We're typically more connected to others than we realize, and our friends usually matter more than we think.

intimacy with others, tend to provide effective support that reassures and bolsters the recipient, and they do so for altruistic, compassionate reasons (Davila & Kashy, 2009). In contrast, insecure people are more self-serving, tending to provide help out of obligation or for the promise of reward. Moreover, their support tends to be less effective, either because (in the case of avoidant people) they provide less help than secure people do or because (in the case of anxious people) their help is intrusive and controlling (Collins et al., 2006). People are generally more satisfied with the support they receive when their partners have secure, rather than insecure, attachment styles (Kane et al., 2007).

In addition, people tend to provide better support when they are attentive and empathic and thus are able to tell what their partners need (Verhofstadt et al., 2010). People too rarely ask straightforwardly for help when they need it (Bohns & Flynn, 2010), so those who are better able to read a particular partner's feelings tend to provide that partner more skillful support.

- Furthermore, *the best support fits our needs and preferences.* Not all social support is wholly beneficial to its recipients. Even when supportive friends are well-intentioned and altruistic, their support may be of the wrong type or be too plentiful (Brock & Lawrence, 2009); their efforts to help may threaten our self-esteem or be intrusive, and unwelcome indebtedness can occur if we accept such help (Gleason et al., 2008). So, social support sometimes comes with emotional costs, and for that reason, the best help may occasionally be **invisible support** that actually goes unnoticed by the recipient (Howland & Simpson, 2010). When cohabiting couples kept diaries of the support they gave and received during a stressful period in which one of them was preparing for a bar examination, the support that was most effective in reducing the test taker's anxiety was aid the partner provided that the test taker did not notice (Bolger et al., 2000). Sometimes, the best way to help a friend is to do so unobtrusively in a manner that does not add to his or her woes.

    When support *is* visible, it is more effective when it fits the recipient's current needs and goals (Brock & Lawrence, 2010). Another study with frantic law students preparing for a bar exam found that material support—for instance, a partner cooking dinner—was helpful, but emotional support simply made the examinees more anxious (Shrout et al., 2006). On the other hand, another investigation found that elderly people with impaired vision were annoyed by material support (probably because it made them feel more helpless) but heartened by emotional support (Reinhardt et al., 2006). Evidently, there's no sort of support that's suitable for all situations; the type of help and assistance a friend will appreciate will depend on his or her current needs, your capabilities, and the present state of your friendship (Iida et al., 2008). There are some consistent patterns—people with secure attachment styles generally like emotional support whereas those with dismissing styles prefer concrete advice and suggestions (Simpson et al., 2007)—but we need to be alert to personal preferences and the particular circumstances if we are to provide effective support.

- Regardless of what support is offered, one of the most important patterns in studies of social support is that *it's not what people do for us but what we* think *they do for us that matters* in the long run. The support we perceive is often only a rough match for the support we actually get (Lakey et al., 2002), and people become distressed when they believe that their partners are unsupportive whether or not their partners really are (Lakey et al., 2004). In fact, perceived support has more to do with our satisfaction with a partner than with the amount of aid he or she actually provides: When we're content with our friends and lovers, we perceive them to be supportive, but when we're dissatisfied, we perceive them to be neglectful and unhelpful (Kaul & Lakey, 2003). Our judgments aren't totally unrealistic; the more support our partners provide us, the more supportive we usually perceive them to be (Priem et al., 2009). Still, we're more likely to notice and appreciate their aid and assistance when we trust them and we're content with them, so that satisfaction may enhance perceived support at the same time that perceived support is increasing satisfaction (Collins et al., 2006). In general, then, our judgments of the aid we receive from others "are likely to possess both a kernel of truth and a shell of motivated elaboration" (Reis et al., 2004, p. 214).

- Finally, *our personal characteristics also affect our perceptions of social support* (Iida et al., 2008). People who doubt others' care and concern for them tend to take a biased, and undeservedly critical, view of others' efforts to aid them. In particular, people who have insecure attachment styles judge the social support they receive to be less considerate and less helpful than do those who hold more favorable, more confident views of themselves and their relationships (Collins & Feeney, 2010). Remarkably, even when their friends are being genuinely supportive, insecure people are likely to consider their partners' assistance and encouragement to be insufficient (Collins et al., 2010).

Overall, then, we rely on our friends and lovers for invaluable support, but the amount and quality of sustenance we (feel we) receive is affected by both our and our partners' characteristics. The social support we perceive is also greatly influenced by the quality of our relationships; in general, partners who make us happy seem more supportive than do those with whom we share less satisfying friendships. We're also more likely to *ask* for help when we need it from partners whom we trust and who are known to be responsive (Collins et al., 2010). On the whole, however, whether it is visible or invisible, the best support is assistance that indicates that our partners attentively understand and care about—and thus are *responsive*—to our needs (Maisel & Gable, 2009).

Responsiveness

Each of the characteristics of a good friendship we've just encountered—respect, trust, capitalization, and social support—leave us feeling valued, understood, or cared for, so they are all tied to a last component of rewarding intimacy that is probably the most important of them all (Reis, 2009): *responsiveness*, or attentive and supportive recognition of our needs and interests. Most of the time, our friends are interested in who we are and what we have to say. They pay attention to us, and thereby communicate that they value their partnerships with us. They are also usually warm and supportive, and they seem to understand and appreciate us. And these are all reasons *why* they're friends. The judgment that someone is attentive, respectful, caring, and supportive with respect to our needs and aspirations, which is known as **perceived partner responsiveness**, is powerfully rewarding,[2] and we are drawn to those who lead us to feel valued, validated, and understood.

Perceived partner responsiveness promotes intimacy (Maisel et al., 2008), encouraging self-disclosure, trust, and interdependency, and it is unquestionably good for relationships. Two people feel closer and more content with each other when they tune in and start looking out for each other's needs

---

[2]Indeed, perceived partner responsiveness is so influential, this is second time I've mentioned it. We encountered it as a key influence on self-disclosure back in chapter 5, on page 158.

Responsiveness in Action

One of the most successful relationship self-help books of all time is over 75 years old and still going strong. Dale Carnegie published *How to Win Friends and Influence People* in 1936, long before relationship scientists began studying the interactive effects of responsiveness. Carnegie firmly believed that the road to financial and interpersonal success lay in behaving toward others in a manner that made them feel important and appreciated. He suggested six straightforward ways to get others to like us, and the enduring popularity of his homespun advice helps demonstrate why responsiveness from a friend is so uplifting. Here are Carnegie's rules (1936, p. 110):

1. Become genuinely interested in other people.
2. Smile.
3. Remember that a man's name is to him the sweetest and most important sound in any language.
4. Be a good listener. Encourage others to talk about themselves.
5. Talk in terms of the other man's interest.
6. Make the other person feel important—and do it sincerely.

All of these actions help communicate the attention and support that constitute responsiveness, and modern research supports Carnegie's advice. To favorably impress the people you meet at a speed-dating event, for instance, offer them genuine smiles (Miles, 2009), and then focus on them, being warm, interested, and enthusiastic (Eastwick et al., 2010). It also helps to be Latin American. Latinos generally endorse a cultural norm of *simpático* that values friendly courtesy and congeniality, and sure enough, when they are left alone with a stranger in Texas, Mexican Americans talk more, look more, smile more, and enjoy the interaction more than American whites or blacks do. The people who meet them enjoy the interactions more, too (Holloway et al., 2009). Carnegie was on to something. People like to receive warm, attentive interest and support from others, and being responsive is a good way to make—and keep—friends.

(Canevello & Crocker, 2010). Moreover, when we generously attend to others, we tend to perceive that they are supportive and caring, too, and that also enhances our relationships (Lemay & Clark, 2008). And remarkably, being responsive to our partners is good for us as well as for them; students in freshmen dorms who strove to understand and support their roommates adjusted better to college life as time went by than did those who were less responsive (Canevello & Crocker, 2011). There's enormous value in the understanding, respect, and regard that's offered by a responsive partner, and it's clear that friends can supply us with potent interpersonal rewards.

The Rules of Friendship

Good friends can also be counted on to play by the rules. We don't often explicate our expectations about what it means to be a friend, but most of

TABLE 7.1. The Rules of Friendship

Don't nag
Keep confidences
Show emotional support
Volunteer help in time of need
Trust and confide in your partner
Share news of success with your partner
Don't be jealous of each other's relationships
Stand up for your partner in his/her absence
Seek to repay debts and favors and compliments
Strive to make him/her happy when you're together

Source: Argyle & Henderson, 1984.

us nevertheless have **rules for relationships** that are shared cultural beliefs about what behaviors friends should (or should not) perform. These standards of conduct help relationships operate more smoothly. We learn the rules during childhood, and one of the things we learn is that when the rules are broken, disapproval and turmoil result. For instance, in a seminal study, British researchers generated a large set of possible friendship rules and asked adults in Britain, Italy, Hong Kong, and Japan which of the rules they would endorse (Argyle & Henderson, 1984). Several rules for conducting friendships appeared to be universal, and they're listed in Table 7.1. As you can see, they involve trust, capitalization, and support as well as other desirable aspects of intimacy.

The rules are dictates about what we should and shouldn't do, but people don't always follow the rules of friendship. When they were asked to judge the proportion of people who honor a variety of different relationship rules, students at two San Francisco universities estimated that most rules are followed only 50 percent of the time (Gambrill et al., 1999). But that doesn't mean the rules are unimportant. The more closely we adhere to them, the closer and more satisfying our relationships are (Kline & Stafford, 2004). Moreover, in most cases when friendships fail, somebody hasn't been following the rules (Argyle & Henderson, 1984). Thus, whether or not we consciously think about them, there appear to be standards of behavior in friendships—the social rules of relationships—that can make or break our friendships.

FRIENDSHIP ACROSS THE LIFE CYCLE

Friendships vary with regard to the social contexts in which they are maintained (for instance, whether your friends are colleagues at work vs. neighbors at home), the degree of intimacy involved, and in the age and sex of the participants (Fehr, 1996). They also change in character as we grow and age. I'll examine some of those changes in this section.

Childhood

Preschool children have rudimentary friendships in which they have favorite playmates. Thereafter, the enormous changes that children encounter as they grow and mature are mirrored in their friendships, which gradually grow richer and more complex (Howes, 2011). One important change involves children's cognitive development; as they age, children are increasingly able to appreciate others' perspectives and to understand their wishes and points of view. Accompanying this increasing cognitive sophistication are changes in the interpersonal needs that are preeminent as children age. According to Duane Buhrmester and Wyndol Furman (1986), these key needs are *acceptance* in the early elementary years, *intimacy* in preadolescence, and *sexuality* during the teen years. The new needs are added on top of the old ones at each stage, so that older children have more needs to satisfy than younger children do. And the successful resolution of each stage requires the development of specific competencies that affect the way a child handles later stages; if those skills aren't acquired, problems occur.

For instance, when children enter elementary school, the companionship of, and *acceptance* by, other children is important; those who are not sufficiently accepted by their peers feel ostracized and excluded. Later, in preadolescence, children develop a need for *intimacy* that typically focuses on a friend who is similar to them in age and interests. This is when full-blown friendships that are characterized by extensive self-disclosure first emerge, and during this period, children develop the skills of perspective taking, empathy, and altruism that are the foundation for close adult relationships. Children who were not previously accepted by others may overcome their sense of isolation, but if they cannot, they may experience true loneliness for the first time. Thereafter, *sexuality* erupts, and the typical adolescent develops an interest in the other sex. Most adolescents initially have difficulty establishing relationships that will satisfy their new emerging needs, but most manage to form sensitive, caring, and open sexual relationships later on.

Overall, then, theorists generally agree that our relationships change as we grow older. The rich, sophisticated ways in which adults conduct their friendships are years in the making. And to some degree, success in childhood relationships paves the way for better adult outcomes. For instance, infants who are securely attached to their caregivers tend to be well liked when they start school; as a result, they form richer, more secure childhood friendships that leave them secure and comfortable with intimacy when they fall in love as young adults (Simpson et al., 2007). On the other hand, children who are rejected by their peers tend to encounter a variety of difficulties—such as dropping out of school, criminal arrests, and psychological maladjustment—more often than those who are well-liked (Bukowski & Cillessen, 1998). Peer rejection doesn't necessarily cause such problems, but it might: Interventions that teach social skills enhance children's acceptance by their peers, and that reduces their risk of later maladjustment (Waas & Graczyk, 1998).

Adolescence

There are other ways in which friendships change during the teen years. First, teens spend less and less time with their families and more and more time with their peers. An experience-sampling study in Chicago found that children in fifth grade spent 35 percent of their time with family members whereas seniors in high school were with their families only 14 percent of the time (Larson et al., 1996).

A second change is that adolescents increasingly turn to their friends for the satisfaction of important attachment needs (Fraley & Davis, 1997). Attachment theorists identify four components of attachment (Hazan & Zeifman, 1994): (a) *proximity seeking,* which involves approaching, staying near, or making contact with an attachment figure; (b) *separation protest,* in which people resist being separated from a partner and are distressed by separation from him or her; (c) *safe haven,* turning to an attachment figure as a source of comfort and support in times of stress; and (d) *secure base,* using a partner as a foundation for exploration of novel environments and other daring exploits. All of these components of attachment can be found in the relationships young children have with their parents, but, as they grow older, they gradually shift their primary attachments from their parents to their peers in a component-by-component fashion.

For instance, around the ages of 11 to 14, young adolescents often shift the location of their safe haven from their parents to their peers; if something upsets them, they'll seek out their friends before they approach their parents. Indeed, about a third of older teens identify a peer (who is usually a romantic partner rather than a friend), not a parent, as their primary attachment figure (Rosenthal & Kobak, 2010).

So, peers gradually replace parents in people's lives, but even young adults may still rely on their parents for some components of attachment. College students are most likely to seek proximity with their friends, and they tend to turn to friends as a safe haven, but they remain relatively unlikely to rely on friends as a secure base (Fraley & Davis, 1997). That's a role still often reserved for Mom or Dad. When people are moving to new locales, taking new jobs, and training for new professions, it's still comforting for most of them to know that they can return home for a visit, clean laundry, and free meals when they want to.

Young Adulthood

During their late teens and twenties, people enter young adulthood, a period in which a central task—according to Erik Erikson (1950), a historically prominent theorist—is the development of "intimacy versus isolation." It's at this age, Erikson believed, that we learn how to form enduring, committed intimate relationships.

For many readers of this book, the quest for intimacy is undertaken in a novel environment: a college some distance from home. Leaving home to go to school has probably influenced your friendships (Roberts & Dunbar, 2011), and you're not alone if you haven't seen much of your old high school friends

What's a Best Friend?

People usually have a lot of friendly acquaintances, a number of casual friends, a few close friends, and just one or two *best* friends with whom they share especially rich relationships. What's so special about a best friend? What distinguishes a best friend from all of the other people who are important to us?

The simple answer is that it's all a matter of degree (Fehr, 1996). Best friendships are more intimate than common friendships are, and all of the components of intimacy are involved. Consider *knowledge:* Best friends are usually our closest confidants. They often know secrets about us that are known to no one else, including our spouses! Consider *trust:* We typically expect a very high level of support from our best friends, so that a best friend is "someone who is there for you, no matter what" (Yager, 1997, p. 18). Consider

interdependence: When our best friends are nearby and available to us, we try to see more of them than our other friends; we interact with them more often and in a wider range of situations than we do with lesser buddies. And finally, consider *commitment:* We ordinarily expect that a best friend will be a friend forever. Because such a person "is *the* friend, before all others," best friendships routinely withstand "the tests of time and conflict, major changes such as moving, or status changes, such as marrying or having a child" (Yager, 1997, p. 18).

In general, then, best friendships are not distinctly different relationships of some unique type (Fehr, 1996). Instead, they are simply more intimate than other friendships—involving richer, more rewarding, and more personal connections to others—and that's why they are so prized.

lately. A year-long survey of a freshman class at the University of Denver found that the friendships the students had at home tended to erode and to be replaced by new relationships on campus as the year went by (Shaver et al., 1985). This didn't happen immediately, and the students' satisfaction with their social networks was lowest in the fall after they arrived at college. Almost all of the incoming students quickly found new companions, but many of these relationships were in flux; only a third of them were close friendships in the spring. The students were evidently shuffling and reshuffling their social networks, and those who were outgoing and self-disclosing had an easier time of it; socially skilled freshmen were more satisfied with their relationships than were those who were less adept. Nevertheless, by the end of the spring semester, most people were again content with their social networks. They had made new friends, but it had taken some time.

What happens after college? In one impressive study, 113 young adults kept diaries of their social interactions on two separate occasions, once when they were still in college and again 6 years after they had graduated (Reis et al., 1993). Overall, the participants saw less of their friends each week once they were out of school; in particular, the amount of time spent with same-sex friends and groups of three or more people declined. The total amount of time spent with friends or lovers of the other sex increased, but the number of those partners decreased, especially for men. Still, just as developmental theory suggests, the average intimacy levels of the participants' interactions increased during their twenties. After college, then, people tend to interact with fewer friends, but they have deeper, more interdependent relationships with the friends they have.

Midlife

What happens when people settle down with a romantic partner? The connection between people's friendships and their romances is very clear: When people have romantic partners, they spend less time with their families and friends. A pattern of **dyadic withdrawal** occurs; as people see more and more of a lover, they see less and less of their friends (Fehr, 1999). One study found that people spent an average of 2 hours each day with good friends when they were casually dating someone, but they saw their friends for less than 30 minutes per day once they became engaged (Milardo et al., 1983). Romantic couples do tend to have more contact with friends they have in common, but this doesn't offset declines in the total number of friends they have and the amount of time they spend with them.

The erosion of people's friendships doesn't stop once they get married. Friendships with members of the other sex are especially affected; people tend to see much less of friends who could be construed by a spouse to be potential romantic rivals (Werking, 1997). Still, even though they see less of their friends, spouses often have larger social networks than they did when they were single because they see a lot more of their in-laws (Milardo et al., 1983). (Make no mistake about this, and beware if you don't like your lover's family: You will see a lot more of them if you marry!)

Thus, people's social lives don't wither away completely when they commit themselves to a spouse and kids, but the focus of their socializing does shift from their personal friends to family and friends they share with their spouses. In fact, it appears to be hard on a marriage when a husband and wife have no friends in common. As you can see in Figure 7.1, couples have more marital problems when none of their personal friendships involve their spouses (Amato et al., 2007). Having some friends of one's own does no harm, but having only exclusive friendships seems to be risky.

Old Age

Ultimately, elderly people have smaller social networks and fewer friends than younger people do (Carstensen et al., 1999). They're not unsociable, they're just more selective: They have just as many close friends as they did when they were younger, but they spend less time with casual friends and other peripheral social partners (Fung et al., 2001).

A **socioemotional selectivity theory** argues that this change occurs because seniors have different interpersonal goals than younger people do (Löckenhoff & Carstensen, 2004). With a long life stretching out before them, young adults are presumed to pursue future-oriented goals aimed at acquiring information

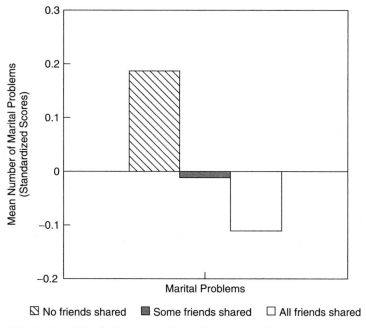

FIGURE 7.1. **Friendship networks and marital adjustment.**
Spouses encounter more frustrations and difficulties when they have no friends in common.
Source: Data from Amato et al., 2007.

that will be useful later in life. (That's presumably what you're doing now if you're in college.) With such ends in mind, young people seek relatively large social networks that include diverse social partners. However, when people age and their futures seem more and more finite, they presumably become oriented more toward the present than toward the future, and they emphasize emotional fulfillment to a greater extent (Fung & Carstensen, 2004). The idea is that as their time perspective shrinks, seniors aim for quality not quantity; they focus on a select group of satisfying friendships that are relatively free of conflict (Fingerman & Charles, 2010) and let more casual partnerships lapse. Indeed, the theory predicts that anyone who considers his or her future to be limited will also choose to spend more time with a small number of close friends instead of a wider variety of more casual buddies—and that's exactly what happens in younger adults whose time orientation is changed by contracting the human immunodeficiency virus that causes AIDS (Carstensen et al., 1999). In general, socioemotional selectivity theory seems to be a reasonable explanation for age-related changes in sociability.

Finally, let's note that the social support provided by friends may be especially important when we're older and somewhat less able. A 10-year longitudinal study of 2,812 seniors in Connecticut found that frequent interactions with friends reduced the risk that one would develop a disability (such as not

Can Pets Be Our Friends?

We've all heard that "a dog is a man's best friend." Really? Can a pet be a friend?

People certainly behave as if that's the case: The presence of a beloved pet can help someone manage stressful situations even better than a human friend can. In one study of this effect (Allen et al., 2002), people were asked to work a mental math problem for 5 minutes—rapidly counting backwards by threes from 7,654—when they were (a) alone, (b) with their spouses, or (c) with their pets but no one else. The presence of a pet was soothing; the difficult task caused only slight arousal when people were with their pets, but their heart rates and blood pressures went up substantially when they were alone, and their cardiovascular readings soared when their spouses were present. A human audience, even a loving partner, made the potentially embarrassing task more stressful, but a companion animal made it less taxing.

These results are intriguing, but they could be due to idiosyncrasies in the people who choose to have pets. So, in another test of this effect (Allen et al., 2001), businessmen who lived alone were *randomly assigned* either to adopt pets from an animal shelter or to continue to live alone. When they were then put under stress, the new pet owners displayed increases in blood pressure that were only half as large as those that occurred among those without pets. Moreover, the fewer friends the men had, the greater the benefits of owning a pet.

Obviously, a dog or a cat cannot supply the same responsiveness, respect, or trust that human friends can. But people often imagine that their pets have human traits and qualities (Epley et al., 2008), and they can feel that their relationships with their pets are just as close as their partnerships with other humans (Kurdek, 2008b). When they're distressed, pet owners are more likely to turn to their pets for solace than they are to seek out their parents, siblings, children, or (human) friends (Kurdek, 2009). And if they had to choose one or the other, one of every seven pet owners would discard their spouses rather than lose their pets (Italie, 2011)! So, given the pleasure and genuine support that pets provide, sure, as long as we use the term loosely, pets can be our friends.

being able to dress oneself or walk across a room) (Mendes de Leon et al., 1999). Moreover, if a disability did develop, close friendships were linked to a higher rate of recovery. Overall, elderly people who have good friends live longer, healthier lives than do those who are less connected to others (Sabin, 1993). Friendships are invaluable for as long as we live.

DIFFERENCES IN FRIENDSHIP

Friendships don't just differ across the life cycle; they also differ from person to person and from partner to partner. In this section of the chapter, we'll consider how the nature of friendships is intertwined with gender and other individual differences.

Gender Differences in Same-Sex Friendships

Consider these descriptions of two same-sex friendships:

Wilma and Betty are very close friends. They rely on each other for support and counsel, and if they experience any problems in their romantic relationships, they immediately call each other, asking for, and getting, all the advice and consolation they need. Wilma and Betty feel that they know everything about each other.

Fred and Barney are very close friends. Often, they stay up half the night playing cards or tinkering with Fred's beloved 1966 Chevy, which is constantly breaking down. They go everywhere together—to the bars, to ball games, and to work out. Barney and Fred feel they are the best of friends.

Do these two descriptions sound familiar? They might. A good deal of research shows that women's friendships are usually characterized by **emotional sharing** and self-disclosure, whereas men's friendships revolve around **shared activities,** companionship, and fun (Fehr, 1996; Marshall, 2010). It's an oversimplification, but a pithy phrase coined years ago by Wright (1982) is still serviceable today: Women's friendships are *"face-to-face,"* whereas men's are *"side-by-side."*[3]

This difference emerges from several specific patterns in same-sex friendships (Fehr, 1996):

- women spend more time talking to friends on the phone;
- men and women talk about different topics: Women are more likely to talk about relationships and personal issues, whereas men are more likely to talk about impersonal interests such as sports;
- women self-disclose more than men do;
- women provide their friends more emotional support than men do; and
- women express more feelings of affection in their friendships than men do.

Add all this up, and women's same-sex friendships tend to be closer and more intimate than men's are. The net result is that women typically have partners outside their romantic relationships to whom they can turn for sensitive, sympathetic understanding and support, but men often do not. For instance, ponder this provocative question (Rubin, 1986, p. 170): "Who would you turn to if you came home one night and your wife [or husband or lover] announced she [or he] was leaving you?" When research participants actually considered this question, nearly every woman readily named a same-sex friend, but only a few men did (Rubin, 1986). (In fact, most men could not come up with anyone to whom they could turn for solace if their lovers left them.)

Why are men's same-sex friendships less intimate than women's? Are men less capable of forming close friendships with each other, or are they just less

[3]This clever statement is oversimplified because it implies that women just talk and men just play, and of course that isn't true. Women share enjoyable activities with their friends about as often as men do (Fehr, 1996). However, men are more reluctant than women to share their feelings and fears with their friends, so emotional sharing does distinguish women's friendships from those of men, on average (Marshall, 2010).

Can Men and Women Be Close Friends?

Of course. They often are. Most people have had a close friendship with a member of the other sex, and such relationships are commonplace among college students. However, once they leave college, most people no longer maintain intimate cross-sex friendships (Marshall, 2010). Why? What's going on?

The first thing to note is that men and women become friends for the same reasons they grow close to their same-sex friends; the same responsiveness, trust, and social support are involved (Fuhrman et al., 2009). And because they are dealing with women instead of other men, men are often more open and expressive with their female friends than with their male companions (Fehr, 1996). Indeed, men who have higher levels of expressivity and women who have higher levels of instrumentality are more likely than their peers to have close friendships with the other sex (Lenton & Webber, 2006). As always, similarity attracts.

However, cross-sex friendships face hurdles that same-sex partnerships do not ordinarily encounter: determining whether the relationship is a friendship or a romance. Friendships are typically nonexclusive, nonsexual, equal partnerships, and people may find themselves in unfamiliar territory as they try to negotiate an intimate friendship with someone of the other sex (Werking, 1997). A big question is whether the partners—who, after all, are very close—will have sex. Men are more likely than women to think that sex would be a fine idea (Lehmiller et al., 2011), and they typically think their female friends are more interested in having sex than they really are (Koenig et al., 2007). In turn, women usually *under*estimate how much their male friends would like to sleep with them, so some misunderstanding often occurs: "Most women do not reciprocate their male friend's sexual yearnings, despite the fact that men sometimes delude themselves that their female friends do" (Buss, 2003, p. 262). As a result, "sexual tension" is often mentioned as the thing people dislike most about their cross-sex friendships (Marshall, 2010).

On the other hand, sexual titillation is sometimes one of the things people like *best* about their friendships with the other sex, and 60 percent of the young adults in one study reported that they had had sex with at least one friend whom they did not consider to be a romantic partner (Bisson & Levine, 2009). In most cases, the partners thought the sex had improved the relationship, bringing them closer together, without transforming their friendship into a romantic liaison. Thus, they became "friends with benefits" (Owen & Fincham, 2011).

Nevertheless, sex among friends is sometimes problematic; it can cause confusion and complicate the partnership, and most cross-sex friendships never become sexual (Halatsis & Christakis, 2009). Indeed, most of the time, people do not want to turn their cross-sex friendships into romances, and they actually strive to keep their partnerships platonic. There may be several reasons for this (Messman et al., 2000). Sometimes, people do not want to risk losing a rewarding relationship by changing it into something else. As one research participant reported (Werking, 1997, p. 102): "I really like her friendship. And if we became boyfriend-girlfriend, that might be fine. But then we might lose a friendship." In other cases, a sexual spark is missing and there is insufficient desire, and in still other instances, there are third parties involved (such as romantic partners) who would object.

Indeed, cross-sex friendships can be tricky when the people are married to others. Arguably, close friends who provide companionship and caring outside of one's marriage can reduce the emotional burden placed on one's spouse (Werking, 1997). However, a spouse may be threatened by one's close connection to a potential rival even when no sex is involved (as I'll make clear in chapter 10). As a result, married people are less likely than singles to have close cross-sex friendships, and that's a major reason that such relationships become less common after people finish their schooling.

willing? Usually, they are less willing; men seem to be fully capable of forming intimate friendships with other men when the circumstances support such closeness—but they generally choose not to do so because such intimacy is less socially acceptable among men than among women (Reis, 1998). And why is that? Cultural norms and gender roles appear to be the main culprits (Bank & Hansford, 2000). A traditional upbringing encourages men to be instrumental, but not expressive,[4] and (as we found in chapter 5), a person's expressivity predicts how self-disclosing he or she will be. Androgynous men tend to have closer friendships than traditional, sex-typed men do, but more men are sex-typed than androgynous. Also, in keeping with typical gender roles, we put pressure on men to display more *emotional constraint* than we put on women. Cultural norms lead men to be more reluctant than women to express their worries and emotions to others, and gender differences in the intimacy of friendship disappear in societies (such as the Middle East) where expressive male friendships are encouraged (Reis, 1998).

Thus, the lower intimacy of men's friendships probably isn't due to an inability to share meaningful, close attachments to other men. Instead, it's a choice that is supported by cultural pressures. Many men would probably have closer same-sex friendships if Western cultures did not discourage psychological intimacy with other men.

Individual Differences in Friendship

In addition to the effects of gender, there are several other differences from person to person that influence the friendships we form. One of these is **self-monitoring,** which we discussed in chapter 4. (Look back at pages 131–133.) High self-monitors tend to construct broad social networks of companions who are "activity specialists," pals with whom they share a particular pleasure, but not much else. As a result, high self-monitors tend to be somewhat less invested in their friendships than low self-monitors are; low self-monitors

---

[4]Would you like a quick reminder about the nature of instrumentality and expressivity? Look back at page 23 in chapter 1.

have fewer friends, but they tend to have more in common with each of them, and their friendships are more intimate, on average (Snyder & Simpson, 1987).

Another personal characteristic that influences our social networks is *sexual orientation*. In a convenience sample[5] of 1,415 people from across the United States, most heterosexual men and women did *not* have a close friend who was gay, lesbian, or bisexual, but most gays, lesbians, and bisexuals (or GLBs) *did* have friends who were straight (Galupo, 2009). Only about one in every six heterosexuals (knew that they) had GLB buddies, but about 80 percent of GLBs had close heterosexual friends. So, the friendship networks of straight people tend to be less diverse with regard to sexual orientation than those of GLBs. If heterosexuals are actually avoiding friendships with GLBs, they may be making a mistake: The friendships of gays, lesbians, and bisexuals with heterosexuals are just as close and rewarding, on average, as their friendships with other GLBs (Ueno et al., 2009), and the more contact heteros have with GLBs, the more they like them (Vonofakou et al., 2007).

Finally, some of us think of ourselves mostly as independent, autonomous agents, and the qualities that are foremost in our self-concepts are the traits that distinguish us from others. In contrast, others of us define ourselves to a greater extent in terms of our relationships to others; our self-concepts emphasize the roles we fill and the qualities we display in our intimate partnerships. An intriguing individual difference, an **interdependent self-construal,** describes the extent to which we think of ourselves as interdependent, rather than independent, beings. For those of us with a highly interdependent self-construal, relationships are central features in our self-concepts, and we "tend to think and behave so as to develop, enhance, and maintain harmonious and close relationships" with others (Cross & Morris, 2003, p. 513). An interdependent self-construal makes someone a desirable friend (Mann & Morry, 2011); compared to those who are more independent, interdependent people better understand others' opinions and values, and they strive to behave in ways that benefit others as well as themselves. Motivations supporting both independence and interdependence tend to be present in everyone, but Western cultures such as that of the United States tend to celebrate and emphasize independence and autonomy. So, highly interdependent self-construals are more common in other parts of the world (Cross et al., 2009).

FRIENDSHIP DIFFICULTIES

Now, in this last section of the chapter, let's examine some of the states and traits that interfere with rewarding friendships. We'll focus on two problems, *shyness* and *loneliness,* that are common but still painful. As we'll see, shy or lonely people usually want to develop close friendships, but they routinely behave in ways that make it difficult to do so.

These days, we may need every friend we've got. Extensive, face-to-face interviews with a nationally representative sample of Americans in 2004 found

---

[5]Chapter 2: the gift that keeps on giving. See p. 45.

Are Your Facebook "Friends" Really Your Friends?

Well, sure, some of the people you've friended on Facebook are confidants and companions who are clearly good friends. But if you're a typical user, you've *never met* 1 out of every 12 of the people on your list of "Friends" (LaFlam & Green, 2010), and you've accepted friend requests from people you actually dislike because you were too timid to tell them to go away and leave you alone. Your list also contains hundreds of "friends," so—of course—only a few of them meet our definition of *friendship* on page 213.

On the other hand, Facebook (or some other social networking site) is helping you stay in closer touch with your real friends (Carpenter et al., 2011), and it may be of particular benefit if you're shy. We all tend to be less inhibited online than we are face-to-face, and that's especially helpful to shy people, who engage in fuller self-disclosure online (Valkenburg & Peter, 2009a) and

spend even more time on Facebook than the rest of us do (Orr et al., 2009).

Still, interactions online are only small parts of our richest relationships. Offline intimacy is associated with *fewer* back-and-forth conversations on Facebook (Ivcevic et al., 2011); when two people are really close, they tend to conduct more of their interactions through other channels. And some people are finding the sheer amount of superficial interaction available on Facebook to be excessive (DeAndrea et al., 2011). Constant comments and updates from minor players in one's life can be distracting when one is trying to get some work done, so people are turning to programs such as "Anti-Social" to disable their own access to sites such as Facebook for specified lengths of time (della Cava, 2010). (Isn't it remarkable that such programs exist?) Evidently, large social networks filled with acquaintances can occasionally be too much of a good thing.

that intimate friendships are less common in the United States than they used to be (McPherson et al., 2006). The number of people who said they had no close confidant of any sort has soared from only 10 percent in 1985 (the last time these questions were asked) to 25 percent. One of every four adult Americans has no one to whom to turn for intimate counsel and support. Another 19 percent said they had only one confidant (who was often a spouse or a sibling), and, overall, the average number of intimate partners people had, including both close friends and lovers, plummeted from three (in 1985) to two. Many of us have dozens or hundreds of "friends" on Facebook, but only rarely are they companions who offer the rich rewards of meaningful intimacy. And once they leave school, only slightly more than half of all Americans (57 percent) have a close confidant to whom they are not related. Many Americans have none. Shyness and loneliness undoubtedly make things even worse.

Shyness

Have you ever felt anxious and inhibited around other people, worrying about their evaluations of you and feeling awkward in your conversations with them? Most of us have. Over 80 percent of us have experienced **shyness,** the syndrome

TABLE 7.2. The Shyness Scale

How shy are you? Rate how well each of the following statements describes you using this scale:

$$0 = \text{Extremely uncharacteristic of me}$$
$$1 = \text{Slightly characteristic of me}$$
$$2 = \text{Moderately characteristic of me}$$
$$3 = \text{Very characteristic of me}$$
$$4 = \text{Extremely characteristic of me}$$

___1.   I am socially somewhat awkward.

___2.   I don't find it hard to talk to strangers.

___3.   I feel tense when I'm with people I don't know well.

___4.   When conversing, I worry about saying something dumb.

___5.   I feel nervous when speaking to someone in authority.

___6.   I am often uncomfortable at parties and other social functions.

___7.   I feel inhibited in social situations.

___8.   I have trouble looking someone right in the eye.

___9.   I am more shy with members of the opposite sex.

The first thing you have to do to calculate your score is to reverse your answer to number 2. If you gave yourself a 0 on that item, change it to a 4; a 1 becomes a 3, a 3 becomes a 1, and a 4 should be changed to 0. (2 does not change.) Then add your ratings. The average score for both men and women is about 14.5, with a standard deviation of close to 6 points. Thus, if your score is 8 or lower, you're less shy than most people, but if your score is 20 or higher, you're more shy.

Source: Adapted from Cheek & Buss, 1981.

that combines social reticence and inhibited behavior with nervous discomfort in social settings (Miller, 2009). Take a look at Table 7.2; when people are shy, they fret about social disapproval and unhappily anticipate unfavorable judgments from others. They feel self-conscious and inept as well as uncomfortable or ineffective at making small talk (Arroyo & Harwood, 2011). As a result, they interact with others in an impoverished manner. If they don't avoid an interaction altogether, they behave in an inhibited, guarded fashion; they look at others less, smile less, speak less often, and converse less responsively (Ickes, 2009). Compared to people who are not shy, they manage everyday conversation poorly.

Shyness may beset almost anyone now and then. It's especially common when we're in unfamiliar settings, meeting attractive, high-status strangers for the first time, and it's less likely when we're on familiar turf interacting with old friends (Leary & Kowalski, 1995). However, some people are *chronically* shy, experiencing shyness frequently, and three characteristics distinguish them from people who are less shy. First, people who are routinely shy *fear negative evaluation* from others. The possibility that others might dislike them is rarely far from their minds, and the threat of derision or disdain from others is more frightening to them than it is to most people. They worry about social disapproval more than the rest of us do (Miller, 2009). Second, they tend to doubt themselves. *Poor self-regard* usually accompanies chronic shyness, and shy people tend to have low self-esteem. Finally, they feel less competent in their interactions with others, and sometimes with good reason: Overall, they have lower levels of *social skill* than do people who are not shy (Ickes, 2009).

This unwelcome combination of perceptions and behavior puts shy people between a rock and a hard place. They worry about what people are thinking of them and dread disapproval from others but don't feel capable of making favorable impressions that would avoid such disapproval. As a result, they adopt a cautious, relatively withdrawn style of interaction that deflects interest and enthusiasm from others (Oakman et al., 2003). For instance, if they find an attractive woman looking at them, shy men won't look back, smile, and say hello; instead, they'll look away and say nothing (Ickes, 2009). Rewarding conversations that would have ensued had the men been less shy sometimes do not occur at all.

The irony here is that by behaving in such a timid manner, people who are either temporarily or chronically shy often make the negative impressions on others that they were hoping to avoid in the first place. Instead of eliciting sympathy, their aloof, unrewarding behavior often seems dull or disinterested to others. Let's think this through. Imagine that you're at a dance, and some acquaintances are out on the floor moving to the music in a small mob. They call to you—"C'mon!"—urging you to join them, but because you're not a confident dancer and you don't want to look silly, you stay on the sidelines. You'd like to join them, but your concern over the evaluations you might receive is too strong, so you hang back and watch. The problem with your reticence, of course, is that instead of being sociable and encouraging everyone's happy enthusiasm, you're just standing there. Inside you may feel friendly, but from your behavior it's hard to tell. You're certainly not being playful, and to all appearances, you may seem awkward and a little dull. Indeed, it's probably safe to say that you're making a poorer impression on others standing on the sidelines than you would by joining the mob and dancing clumsily; nobody much cares how well you dance as long as you're lively and lighthearted, but people do notice when you're simply no fun.

In fact, shy behavior does not make a good impression on others, as Figure 7.2 shows. The timid, reserved, and hesitant behavior that characterizes shyness can seem aloof and unfriendly, and it is likely to be met by reactions from others that are less sociable and engaging than those elicited by more gregarious behavior (Bradshaw, 2006). Over time, shy people may be more likely to encounter neglect and rejection than understanding and empathy, and such outcomes may reinforce their shyness. Indeed, shy people make new friends much more slowly than do those who are not shy (Asendorpf & Wilpers, 1998). The friendships they do have are generally less satisfying and supportive, too, so they also tend to be lonelier than those who are not shy (Bradshaw, 2006). And these effects are consequential; when they marry, shy people experience more problems and are less content than are spouses who don't suffer from shyness (Baker & McNulty, 2010).

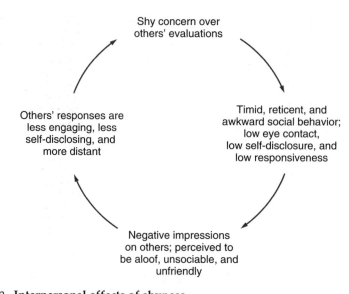

FIGURE 7.2. **Interpersonal effects of shyness.**
Shy behavior makes negative impressions on others, often creating the unfavorable evaluations that shy people fear. Poorer interactions result, fueling the shy person's fears, and the cycle continues.

Thus, shy behavior may make one's shyness even worse, and obviously, it's usually better to feel confident than shy in social life. On occasion, shyness can be useful; when people really are confronted with novel situations and don't know how to behave, brief bouts of shy caution may keep them from doing something inappropriate (Leary, 2010). More often, however, shy people run scared from the threat of social disapproval that hasn't occurred and never will, so their shyness is an unnecessary and counterproductive burden (Miller, 2009). Formal programs that help people overcome chronic shyness often teach them a more positive frame of mind, helping them manage their anxiety and apprehension about social evaluation. The programs also teach social skills, focusing on how to initiate conversations and how to be assertive. Both positive thinking and effective behavior are then rehearsed in role-playing assignments and other practice settings until the clients feel comfortable enough to try them on their own (Henderson & Zimbardo, 2010).

However, most shy people probably do not need formal training in interaction skills because they do just fine when they relax and quit worrying about how they're being judged. If you're troubled by shyness now, you may make better impressions on others if you actually care *less* about what they think. Evidence for this possibility comes from an intriguing study by Mark Leary (1986), who asked people to meet and greet a stranger in a noisy environment that was said to simulate a crowded singles bar. Leary created a multi-track tape of overlapping conversations, three different songs, radio static, and party noise (such as laughing and yelling)—it was definitely

TABLE 7.3. Doing Better with an Excuse for Failure

In Leary's (1986) study, when noise that was said to be impossibly "loud" gave shy people an excuse for their interactions to go badly, they behaved no differently than did people who were not shy. In contrast, "soft" noise that was not supposed to interfere with their conversations left them tense and anxious, even though the noise was played at exactly the same volume in both the "loud" and "soft" conditions.

	Change in Heart Rate (in beats per minute)	
	Noise Volume	
Participants' Chronic Shyness	"Soft"	"Loud"
Low	5.3	4.7
High	15.8	4.5

"noise"—and played it at a mildly obnoxious level as each couple conversed. Importantly, the tape was always played at the same volume, but some people were told that the noise was so loud that it would probably interfere with their conversation and make it hard for them to have a nice chat whereas others were told that the noise was soft enough that it wouldn't be a problem. Once these expectations were in place, people who were either shy or not shy were left alone with a stranger—a setting that is ordinarily threatening to shy people. Leary monitored the heart rates of his participants to track their anxiety and arousal, and Table 7.3 shows what he found. When the noise was "soft" and there wasn't a good excuse for their interactions to go poorly, shy people exhibited considerably more arousal and apprehension than normal people did; their heart rates increased three times as much, which is typical among those who are shy (Shimizu et al., 2011). Even worse, they looked obviously shy and uncomfortable to people who later watched videotapes of their conversations. On the other hand, when they had an excuse—the impossibly "loud" noise—that lowered everyone's expectations, they behaved as if they weren't shy at all. They exhibited a normal, moderate increase in heart rate as their interactions began and gave observers no clue that they were usually shy.

Interestingly, if they couldn't be blamed if their interactions went badly, the shy people in Leary's (1986) study stayed relatively relaxed and conducted their conversations without difficulty. In a sense, when they were given a non-threatening way to think about an upcoming interaction, their shyness disappeared. Their shyness, then, was not the result of some persistent lack of skill; it depended on the context in which interaction occurred. Similarly, shy people are much more relaxed when they interact with others relatively anonymously and at their own pace online (Shepherd & Edelmann, 2005). But add webcams to the mix, so shy people can see and be seen by their online partners, and their reticence returns; their self-disclosure drops and their shyness is again apparent (Brunet & Schmidt, 2007).

If their shyness comes and goes depending on whether others can see them, people (and this probably includes you if you feel shy) don't need additional training in basic social skills. What they do need is greater calm and self-confidence (Arroyo & Harwood, 2011), and although that may not be easy to come by, shy people should consider the alternative: They're not winning friends and influencing people by acting shy, so what do they have to lose by trusting themselves and expecting interactions to go well? If you're shy, instead of thinking about yourself the next time you make a new acquaintance, simply try to find out as much as you can about the other person.[6] Things will probably go better than you expect (Sasaki & Vorauer, 2010).

Loneliness

It's one thing to feel anxious and timid in social settings and another to feel dissatisfied, deprived, and distressed because you have no intimate friends. The unpleasant boredom, sadness, and desperation of *loneliness* occur when there is an unhappy discrepancy between the number and quality of partnerships we want and those we have (de Jong Gierveld et al., 2006). Loneliness isn't the same as being alone; we can often feel very content in complete solitude, at least for a while (Leary et al., 2003). Instead, loneliness occurs when we want more, or more satisfying, connections with others than we presently have (Mellor et al., 2008). Thus, if your relationships with others are all rather superficial, it's possible to be lonely even if you're surrounded by others and have lots of "friends" on Facebook.

Loneliness has different facets. Theorist Robert Weiss (1973) was the first to suggest that we can suffer either **social isolation,** being dissatisfied because we lack a social network of friends and acquaintances, or **emotional isolation,** being lonely because we lack a single intense relationship. Both elements of loneliness can be found on the UCLA Loneliness Scale, the measure most widely used in research on loneliness in adults (see Table 7.4). The scale has three themes (Hawkley et al., 2005). The first is *isolation* from others. Lonely people feel alone and less in contact with others than they want to be. They also feel less *close connection* to others than they wish to have. They perceive their relationships with others to be less meaningful and close than they want them to be. Finally, loneliness also results from experiencing too little *social connection* to people in general. Lonely people feel that they have insufficient ties to a network of friends and playmates, so they get too little pleasure and not enough social support from their interactions with others.

People suffer when they are poorly connected to others. Back in chapter 1, I suggested that humans have a *need to belong,* and loneliness is an example of what happens when the need goes unsatisfied. Compared to those with richer, more satisfying friendships, lonely people have chronically higher blood pressure and higher levels of stress hormones in their blood. They sleep more poorly and their immune systems don't work as well (Cacioppo & Hawkley, 2009).

---

[6]The box on page 219 has some tips on how to proceed.

TABLE 7.4. The UCLA Loneliness Scale (Version 3)

Instructions: The following statements describe how people sometimes feel. For each statement, please indicate how often you feel the way described by writing a number in the space provided. Here is an example:

How often do you feel happy?

If you never feel happy, you would respond "never"; if you always feel happy, you would respond "always."

NEVER	RARELY	SOMETIMES	ALWAYS
1	2	3	4

*1. How often do you feel that you are "in tune" with the people around you? ___

2. How often do you feel that you lack companionship? ___

3. How often do you feel that there is no one you can turn to? ___

4. How often do you feel alone? ___

*5. How often do you feel part of a group of friends? ___

*6. How often do you feel that you have a lot in common with the people around you? ___

7. How often do you feel that you are no longer close to anyone? ___

8. How often do you feel that your interests and ideas are not shared by those around you? ___

*9. How often do you feel outgoing and friendly? ___

*10. How often do you feel close to people? ___

11. How often do you feel left out? ___

12. How often do you feel that your relationships with others are not meaningful? ___

13. How often do you feel that no one really knows you well? ___

14. How often do you feel isolated from others? ___

*15. How often do you feel you can find companionship when you want it? ___

*16. How often do you feel that there are people who really understand you? ___

17. How often do you feel shy? ___

18. How often do you feel that people are around you but not with you? ___

*19. How often do you feel that there are people you can talk to? ___

*20. How often do you feel that there are people you can turn to? ___

Note that the word "lonely" does not appear on the scale. This is intentional. Men are less willing than women to admit that they're lonely, so none of the items uses the term. To determine your score, reverse the rating you provided on the items with an asterisk. If your answer was 1, change it to a 4; a 2 becomes a 3; 3 becomes 2, and 4 becomes 1. Then, add up your answers. Young men tend to be lonelier than women, and their average total is 42. The average for young women is 39 (Russell, 1996). The standard deviation of the scores for both sexes is 9.5. So, you're lonelier than most men if your score is 53 or higher, and you're lonelier than most women if your score is 49 or higher. You're less lonely than most men if your score is 31 or lower, and less lonely than most women if your score is 29 or lower. By the way, the average score for elderly people is 32. How do you compare to them?

Source: Russell, D.W. (1996).

And over time, the wear and tear of loneliness may have very noticeable effects on general well-being; a study of 3,000 elderly people in Iowa found that over a span of 4 years, 40 percent of those who were lonely were admitted to nursing homes, whereas only 10 percent of those who were not lonely were institutionalized (Cutrona et al., 1997). When it is prolonged, loneliness may have huge, deleterious effects on our health (Hawkley & Cacioppo, 2007).

The good news, however, is that loneliness is often a temporary state. A period of separation from one's social network can cause anyone distress, but it may be short lived, ending in reunion or the development of new friendships. The bad news is that some of the personal characteristics that are associated with loneliness are lasting traits that change only gradually—if at all—over time. For one thing, loneliness is heritable. That is, about half of the variation in loneliness from person to person (48 percent) is due to *genetic influences* that are inherited at birth (Boomsma et al., 2005). Some of us are literally born being more likely than others to experience bouts of loneliness in life. Indeed, people's *personalities* predict how lonely they will turn out to be; higher levels of extraversion, agreeableness, and conscientiousness are all linked to lower loneliness, whereas higher neuroticism increases the chances that we will be lonely (Cacioppo et al., 2006).

Loneliness also varies along with other attributes that are somewhat more changeable. *Insecure attachment* is one. Both dimensions of attachment—anxiety about abandonment and avoidance of intimacy—are related to loneliness, and the less anxious and less avoidant people are, the less lonely they tend to be (Wiseman et al., 2006). Self-esteem is another. Consistent with the sociometer model of self-esteem,[7] people who don't have satisfying, fulfilling connections to others tend not to like themselves very much: Lonely people tend to have *low self-esteem* (Cacioppo et al., 2006).

Moreover, men are lonelier than women are on average (Pinquart, 2003), but a lot depends on whether they are currently close to a female partner. Because women often have close friendships with other women, they usually enjoy plenty of intimacy in their lives even when they're not dating anyone. Men, on the other hand, share relatively superficial interactions with other men, and they tend to really open up only when they're with a woman. Thus, men seem to be dependent on women to avoid being lonely in a way that women are not dependent on them in return (as Table 7.5 shows).

It's actually more correct, however, to say that it's *macho* men who need women to keep from being lonely. One of the psychological ingredients that promotes meaningful, fulfilling interactions with others is *expressivity*,[8] and the qualities that make someone warm, sensitive, and kind appear to make it less likely that he or she will be lonely (Wheeler et al., 1983). Women tend to be high in expressivity, and that's probably a primary reason why they tend to be less lonely than men. But androgynous men are also high in expressivity, and unlike their more traditional macho brothers, they are

[7] Need a reminder about the sociometer model? Take a look back at page 28.

[8] You've probably got this one down, but it's on pages 23–25 if you want to review it.

TABLE 7.5. Loneliness in Men and Women with and without Romantic Partners

The table lists loneliness scores of young adults who do have romantic partners alongside the scores of those who do not. Women's loneliness does not depend much on whether or not they currently have a romantic partner, but men's loneliness does; men are much more lonely, on average, when they do not have an intimate relationship with a female partner.

	With a Romantic Partner	Without a Romantic Partner
Men	16.9	31.2
Women	20.2	24.3

Source: Data from Wheeler et al., 1983.

not more lonely than women are. So, the global difference between men and women in loneliness appears to be a gender difference rather than a sex difference. People who are low in expressivity (and that includes most men) tend toward loneliness when they are not paired with an expressive partner who brings intimacy into their lives, but many men (about a third of them) are just as expressive as most women (Bem, 1993), and they do not rely on women to keep from being lonely.

Finally, when people are lonely, they're not much fun. Their distress and desperation is evident in *negative attitudes toward others* (Tsai & Reis, 2009). Ironically, lonely people tend to mistrust and dislike the very people from whom they seek acceptance and regard. Perhaps as a result, their interactions are usually *drab and dull.* Lonely people are slow to respond to things that are said to them, they don't ask many questions, and they read rejection into innocent utterances from others, so they're not much fun to chat with (Edwards et al., 2001). In addition, they don't self-disclose much; their conversation is usually shallow and inconsequential, so it's hard for them to develop the intimacy they seek (Cacioppo & Hawkley, 2009).

Unfortunately, none of this escapes notice. The cynical outlook and dull, halfhearted manner of lonely people often elicit negative reactions from others, who typically feel that they don't know or like them very much (Tsai & Reis, 2009). Loneliness is thus similar to shyness in being potentially self-perpetuating, but it probably has more potent effects. Whereas shy behavior is essentially innocuous and aloof, lonely behavior is more corrosive and obnoxious. Shy people just keep their distance, but lonely people irritate and annoy us. On college campuses, lonely students have just as many interactions with their peers as anyone else, but they experience fewer positive outcomes such as support and affection and more negative outcomes such as conflict and distrust (Hawkley et al., 2005). Thus, even when they are surrounded by other

Can Ex-Lovers Just Be Friends?

Our social networks often change when we break up with a romantic partner, and we sometimes lose not only the partner but several shared friends. This is especially likely after a divorce, and the losses are usually greater for men. Everybody routinely experiences some loneliness when they divorce, but men ordinarily experience more social *and* emotional loneliness than women do (Dykstra & Fokkema, 2007). Does a breakup have to be absolute? Can ex-lovers just be friends?

Yes, they can. Modern couples are more likely to seek to sustain a friendship after a romance dies than your grandparents were (Allan, 2008), and some remain close for years. A study of almost 1,800 divorcees in the Netherlands found that about half of them were still in intermittent contact 10 years later—but of course, only some of those interactions were friendly

(Fischer et al., 2005). (Ex-spouses with children were much more likely than childless couples to stay in touch, but many of these relationships—almost 30 percent—were still antagonistic a full decade later.) When ex-lovers do remain friends, their partnerships are usually less satisfying than their other friendships because their intimate histories haunt them; they broke up because something wasn't working, and they continue to think that their ex-mates provide poorer emotional support than their other friends do (Schneider & Kenny, 2000).

These friendships also tend to fade when either partner begins a new romance. Nevertheless, while they last, friendships with ex-lovers thrive or falter for the same reasons other friendships do; only those who continue to provide each other valued rewards at low cost remain close friends (Busboom et al., 2002).

---

people, lonely people often behave in off-putting ways that can make their loneliness worse.

To add insult to injury, loneliness can also lead to depression (Cacioppo & Hawkley, 2009). Depression is a broader, more global state of dissatisfaction and distress than loneliness is—loneliness emerges from interpersonal troubles whereas depression stems from losses and setbacks of all sorts (Weeks et al., 1980)—but each can fuel the other, and being depressed makes it even harder to behave in effective ways that are inviting to others (Rehman et al., 2008). In addition to being gloomy and glum, depressed people engage in an obnoxious pattern of *excessive reassurance seeking*: They persistently probe for assurances that others like and accept them but doubt the sincerity of such declarations when they are received (Haeffel et al., 2007). Discontent and anxious, they continue to seek more convincing comfort and gradually wear out their partners' patience (Eberhart & Hammen, 2010).

None of this is pleasant. What are lonely people to do? If you're lonely now, the last few pages may seem pretty pessimistic, but all is certainly not lost. Some people are more likely than others to encounter loneliness, but the situations we encounter are clearly influential, too (Larose et al., 2002). Adverse

Lonely people tend to hold negative attitudes toward others, and that makes it harder for them to overcome their loneliness.

FOR BETTER OR FOR WORSE © 1989 Lynn Johnston Productions. Dist. by Universal Uclick. Reprinted with permission. All rights reserved.

circumstances can cause anyone to become lonely—but circumstances change, and it's important to remain hopeful. Loneliness need not last. Indeed, when young adults were hypnotized and asked to think of experiences involving friendship and belongingness, they were less shy, more sociable, happier, and less lonely than they were when they focused on feelings of loneliness (Cacioppo et al., 2006). One's outlook can make a tremendous difference.

In particular, college freshmen overcome loneliness more readily when they attribute their distress to unstable, short-lived influences rather than to lasting deficiencies in either themselves or others (Cutrona, 1982). Judging one's loneliness to be the result of temporary or changeable difficulties offers the optimistic possibility that things will improve, and hopefulness is more likely to cure loneliness than dour pessimism is (Newall et al., 2009). Furthermore, because loneliness emerges from the discrepancy between the partnerships we want and those we've got, lonely people should be careful not to set their sights too high. For instance, students who move away from home to go to school are *usually* lonely for a while; it comes with the (new, unfamiliar) territory (Weeks et al., 1980). But over the ensuing year, those who simply seek to make new friends usually succeed and become less lonely, whereas those who hunt for a compelling romance are usually disappointed and remain dejected (Cutrona, 1982).

To overcome loneliness then, we should seek new friendships, not romances, and to do that we need to be *friendly*. If you're lonely now, watch out for any sour, self-defeating attitudes (Masi et al., 2011). Are you beginning to think that people are generally selfish, shallow, and uncaring? That negative outlook is almost certainly making you less charming, and it may become a self-fulfilling prophecy: What you expect may be what you get. Indeed, if you take a more positive approach—focusing on others' good qualities, expecting them to be pleasant, and patiently recognizing that friendship takes time—you'll probably enjoy more rewarding interactions with others.

FOR YOUR CONSIDERATION

Don and Teddi became best friends when they went through graduate school together. They started their studies the same year and took the same classes, and they worked together on several projects outside of class. They learned that they were both conscientious and clever, and they came to respect and trust each other completely. Each learned the other's most intimate secrets. They also had great fun together. They were both nonconformists, and they shared a wry and offbeat sense of humor; they would frequently laugh at jokes that nobody else seemed to get. The night that Teddi finished her doctoral dissertation, they got drunk and almost had sex, but they were interrupted and the moment passed. And soon thereafter, they graduated and took jobs in different parts of the country; he moved to California and she went to Minnesota. Now, 6 years later, they have both married, and they see each other only every year or so at professional meetings.

What do you think the future holds for Don and Teddi's friendship? Why?

CHAPTER SUMMARY

The Nature of Friendship

Our friendships are indispensable sources of pleasure and support.

Attributes of Friendships. Close friendships are genuinely intimate relationships that involve affection, communion, and companionship, but they are usually less passionate and committed than romances are. They routinely involve:

- *Respect.* We usually admire our friends and hold them in high esteem.
- *Trust.* We are usually confident that our friends will behave benevolently toward us.
- *Capitalization.* Friends usually respond eagerly and energetically to our happy outcomes, sharing our delight and reinforcing our pleasure.
- *Social support.* This comes in various forms, including affection, advice, and material assistance. Some people are better providers of social support than others are, and the best support fits our needs and preferences. Invisible support that goes unnoticed by the recipient is sometimes very beneficial, but perceived support is very important; it's not what people do for us but what we *think* they do for us that matters in the long run.
- *Responsiveness.* Friends provide attentive and supportive recognition of our needs and interests, and *perceived partner responsiveness* is powerfully rewarding.

The Rules of Friendship. Friendships also have rules, which are shared beliefs among members of a culture about what behaviors friends should (or should not) perform.

Friendship across the Life Cycle

Childhood. As children grow and mature, their friendships gradually grow richer and more complex. The sophisticated ways in which adults conduct their friendships are years in the making.

Adolescence. During the teen years, adolescents increasingly turn to their friends for the satisfaction of important attachment needs.

Young Adulthood. After college, people tend to interact with fewer friends, but they have deeper relationships with the friends they have.

Midlife. *Dyadic withdrawal* occurs as people see more of a lover; they see less of their friends (but a lot more of their in-laws).

Old Age. *Socioemotional selectivity theory* suggests that seniors aim for quality, not quantity, in their friendships.

Differences in Friendship

Gender Differences in Same-Sex Friendships. Women's friendships are usually characterized by *emotional sharing* and self-disclosure, whereas men's friendships revolve around *shared activities*, companionship, and fun.

Individual Differences in Friendship. Low *self-monitors* have fewer friends than high self-monitors do, but their friendships are typically more intimate. *Interdependent self-construals* lead people to emphasize their relationships rather than their independence.

Friendship Difficulties

Shyness. Shy people fear social disapproval and behave timidly, often making the negative impressions that they were hoping to avoid. Many shy people interact comfortably with others when they are given an excuse for things to go poorly, so they need increased self-confidence instead of better social skills.

Loneliness. Dissatisfaction and distress occur when we want more, or more satisfying, connections with others, and both *social isolation* and *emotional isolation* may be involved. Loneliness results from genetic influences, insecure attachment, low self-esteem, and low expressivity. It is associated with negative attitudes and drab interactions that are unappealing to others. Hopeful attributions and reasonable expectations are helpful in overcoming loneliness.

CHAPTER 8

Love

A Brief History of Love ◆ Types of Love ◆ The Triangular Theory of Love ◆ Romantic, Passionate Love ◆ Companionate Love ◆ Compassionate Love ◆ Styles of Loving ◆ Individual and Cultural Differences in Love ◆ Culture ◆ Attachment Styles ◆ Age ◆ Men and Women ◆ Does Love Last? ◆ Why Doesn't Romantic Love Last? ◆ So, What Does the Future Hold? ◆ For Your Consideration ◆ Chapter Summary

Here's an interesting question: If someone had all the other qualities you desired in a spouse, would you marry that person if you were not in love with him or her? Most people reading this book would say "no." At the end of the twentieth century, huge majorities of American men and women considered romantic love to be necessary for marriage (Simpson et al., 1986). Along with all the other characteristics people want in a spouse—such as warmth, physical attractiveness, and dependability—young adults in Western cultures insist on romance and passion as a condition for marriage. What makes this remarkable is that it's such a new thing. Throughout history, the choice of a spouse has usually had little to do with romantic love (Ackerman, 1994); people married each other for political, economic, practical, and family reasons, but they did not marry because they were in love with each other. Even in North America, people began to feel that marriage requires love only a few decades ago. In 1967, 76 percent of women and 35 percent of men *would* have married an otherwise perfect partner whom they did not love (Kephart, 1967). These days, most people would refuse such a marriage.

In a sense, then, we have embarked on a bold experiment. Never before have people considered love to be an essential reason to marry (Coontz, 2005). People experience romantic passion all over the world, but there are still many places where it is not a precondition for marriage. North Americans use romance as a reason to marry to an unprecedented degree (Hatfield & Rapson, 2008). Is this a good idea? If there are various overlapping types of "love" and different types of lovers—and worse, if passion and romance decline over time—marriages based on love may often be prone to confusion and, perhaps, disappointment.

Consideration of these possibilities lies ahead. I'll start with a brief history of love and then ponder different varieties of love and different types of lovers. Then, I'll finish with a question of substantial interest: Does love last? (What do you think the answer is?)

A BRIEF HISTORY OF LOVE

Our modern belief that spouses should love one another is just one of many perspectives with which different cultures have viewed the experience of love (Hunt, 1959). Over the ages, attitudes toward love have varied on at least four dimensions:

- *Cultural value.* Is love a desirable or undesirable state?
- *Sexuality.* Should love be sexual or nonsexual?
- *Sexual orientation.* Should love involve heterosexual or same-sex partners?
- *Marital status.* Should we love our spouses, or is love reserved for others?

Different societies have drawn upon these dimensions to create some strikingly different patterns of what love is, or should be.

In ancient Greece, for instance, passionate attraction to another person was considered a form of madness that had nothing to do with marriage or family life. Instead, the Greeks admired platonic love, the nonsexual adoration of a beloved person that was epitomized by love between two men.

In ancient Egypt, people of royal blood often married their siblings, and in ancient Rome, "the purpose of marriage was to produce children, make favorable alliances, and establish a bloodline . . . it was hoped that husband and wife would be friends and get on amiably. Happiness was not part of the deal, nor was pleasure. Sex was for creating babies" (Ackerman, 1994, p. 37).

Heterosexual love took on more positive connotations in the concept of "courtly love" in the twelfth century. Courtly love required knights to seek love as a noble quest, diligently devoting themselves to an aristocratic lady love. It was very idealistic, very elegant, and—at least in theory—nonsexual. It was also explicitly adulterous. In courtly love, the male partner was expected to be unmarried and the female partner married to someone else! In the Middle Ages, marriage continued to have nothing to do with romance; in contrast, it was a deadly serious matter of politics and property. Indeed, passionate, erotic desire for someone was thought to be "dangerous, a trapdoor leading to hell, which was not even to be condoned between husband and wife" (Ackerman, 1994, p. 46).

Over the next 500 years, people came to believe that passionate love could be desirable and ennobling but that it was usually doomed. Either the lovers would be prevented from being with each other (often because they were married to other people), or death would overtake one or the other (or both) before their love could be fulfilled. It was not until the seventeenth and eighteenth centuries that Europeans, especially the English, began to believe that romantic passion could occasionally result in a happy ending. Still, the notion that one *ought* to feel passion and romance for one's husband or wife was not a widespread idea.

Even now, the assumption that romantic love should be linked to marriage is held only in some regions of the world. Nevertheless, you probably do think love and marriage go together. Why should your beliefs be different from those of most people throughout history? Why has the acceptance of and enthusiasm for marrying for love been most complete in North America (Hatfield & Rapson, 2008)? Probably because of America's individualism and economic prosperity (which allow most young adults to live away from home and choose their own marital partners) and its lack of a caste system or ruling class. The notion that individuals (instead of families) should choose marriage partners because of emotional attachments (not economic concerns) makes more sense to Americans than it does to many other peoples of the world. There are still many places where the idea that a young adult should leave home, fall in love, decide to marry, and then bring the beloved home to meet the family seems completely absurd (Buunk et al., 2010).

In any case, let's consider all the different views of love we just encountered:

- Love is doomed.
- Love is madness.
- Love is a noble quest.
- Love need not involve sex.
- Love and marriage go together.
- Love can be happy and fulfilling.
- Love has little to do with marriage.
- The best love occurs among people of the same sex.

Some of these distinctions simply reflect ordinary cultural and historical variations (Hatfield & Rapson, 2008). However, these different views may also reflect an important fact: There may be diverse forms of love. Let's ponder that possibility.

TYPES OF LOVE

Advice columnist Ann Landers was once contacted by a woman who was perplexed because her consuming passion for her lover fizzled soon after they were married. Ms. Landers suggested that what the woman had called "the love affair of the century" was "not love at all. It was one set of glands calling to another" (Landers, 1982, p. 2). There was a big distinction, Ms. Landers asserted, between horny infatuation and real love, which was deeper and richer than mere passion. Love was based in tolerance, care, and communication, Landers argued; it was "friendship that has caught fire" (p. 12).

Does that phrase characterize your experiences with romantic love? Is there a difference between romantic love and infatuation? According to a leading theory of love experiences, the answer to both questions is probably "yes."

The Triangular Theory of Love

Robert Sternberg (1987, 2006) proposed that three different building blocks combine to form different types of love. The first component of love is **intimacy.** It includes the feelings of warmth, understanding, trust, support, and sharing that often characterize loving relationships. The second component is **passion,** which is characterized by physical arousal and desire, excitement, and need. Passion often takes the form of sexual longing, but any strong emotional need that is satisfied by one's partner fits this category. The final ingredient of love is **commitment**, which includes feelings of permanence and stability as well as the decisions to devote oneself to a relationship and to work to maintain it. Commitment is mainly cognitive in nature, whereas intimacy is emotional and passion is a motive, or drive. The "heat" in loving relationships is assumed to come from passion, and the warmth from intimacy; in contrast, commitment reflects a decision that may not be emotional or temperamental at all.

In Sternberg's theory, each of these three components is said to be one side of a triangle that describes the love two people share. Each component can vary in intensity from low to high so that triangles of various sizes and shapes are possible. In fact, countless numbers of shapes can occur, so to keep things simple, we'll consider the relatively pure categories of love that result when one or more of the three ingredients is plentiful but the others are very low. As we proceed, you should remember that pure experiences that are this clearly defined may not be routine in real life.

Nonlove. If intimacy, passion, and commitment are all absent, love does not exist. Instead, you have a casual, superficial, uncommitted relationship between people who are probably just acquaintances, not friends.

Liking. Liking occurs when intimacy is high but passion and commitment are very low. Liking occurs in friendships with real closeness and warmth that do not arouse passion or the expectation that you will spend the rest of your life with that person. If a friend *does* arouse passion or is missed terribly when he or she is gone, the relationship has gone beyond liking and has become something else.

Infatuation. Strong passion in the absence of intimacy or commitment is infatuation, which is what people experience when they are aroused by others they barely know. Sternberg (1987) admits that he pined away for a girl in his 10th-grade biology class whom he never got up the courage to get to know. This, he now acknowledges, was nothing but passion. He was infatuated with her.

Empty love. Commitment without intimacy or passion is empty love. In Western cultures, this type of love may occur in burned-out relationships in which the warmth and passion have died, and the decision to stay is the only thing that remains. However, in other cultures in which marriages are arranged, empty love may be the first, rather than final, stage in the spouses' lives together.

None of the categories I've mentioned so far may seem much like love to you. That's probably because each is missing some important ingredient that we associate with being in love—and that is precisely Sternberg's point. Love is a multifaceted experience, and that becomes clear when we combine the three components of love to create more complex states.

Romantic love. When high intimacy and passion occur together, people experience romantic love. Thus, one way to think about romantic love is

"Love" can last a lifetime. But what kind of love do you think this couple shares?

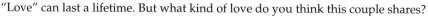

as a combination of liking and infatuation. People often become committed to their romances, but Sternberg argues that commitment is not a defining characteristic of romantic love. A summer love affair can be very romantic, for instance, even when both lovers know that it is going to end when the summer is over.

Companionate love. Intimacy and commitment combine to form love for a close companion, or companionate love. Here, closeness, communication, and sharing are coupled with substantial investment in the relationship as the partners work to maintain a deep, long-term friendship. This type of love is epitomized by a long, happy marriage in which the couple's youthful passion has gradually died down.

Fatuous love. Passion and commitment in the absence of intimacy create a foolish experience called *fatuous love*. ("Fatuous" means "stupid" and "lacking substance.") This type of love can occur in whirlwind courtships in which two partners marry quickly on the basis of overwhelming passion but don't know (or necessarily like) each other very well. In a sense, such lovers invest a lot in an infatuation—a risky business.

Consummate love. Finally, when intimacy, passion, and commitment are all present to a substantial degree, people experience "complete," or consummate, love. This is the type of love many people seek, but Sternberg (1987) suggests that it's a lot like losing weight: easy to do for a while, but hard to maintain over time.

Thus, according to the triangular theory of love, diverse experiences can underlie the simple expression, "I love you." (The different types of love are summarized in Table 8.1.) Another complication that makes love tricky is that the three components can change over time, so that people may encounter various types of love in a given relationship. Of the three, however, passion is assumed to be the most variable by far. It is also the least controllable, so that we may find our desire for others soaring and then evaporating rapidly in changes we cannot consciously control (Sternberg, 1987).

Is the theory right? Are these assertions accurate? Consider that, if the triangular theory's characterization of romantic love is correct, one of its major ingredients is a high level of passion that simply may not last. There's much to consider in wondering whether love lasts, however, so I'll put that off for a while. For now, I'll note that the three components of intimacy, passion, and commitment do all appear to be important aspects of loving relationships (Aron & Westbay, 1996); in particular, each of the three components makes a loving relationship more satisfying, and the most rewarding romances contain big servings of all three ingredients (Sternberg, 2006).

A Physiological Perspective

Studies of the physical foundations of love also suggest that passion and intimacy are distinct experiences. The regions of the brain that regulate our sexual desire for others appear to be different from those that manage our feelings of attachment and commitment to our lovers (Diamond, 2004). In some state-of-the-art studies of love, researchers are using fMRI technology to examine the activity in people's brains as they look at pictures of their lovers (as opposed to other people), and passion activates different areas of the brain than affection and commitment do, both in the United States (Aron et al., 2005) and in China (Xu et al., 2011). Thus, it really is possible to feel strong desire for those we do

TABLE 8.1. The Triangular Theory of Love: Types of Relationships

	Intimacy	Passion	Commitment
Nonlove	Low	Low	Low
Liking	High	Low	Low
Infatuation	Low	High	Low
Empty love	Low	Low	High
Romantic love	High	High	Low
Companionate love	High	Low	High
Fatuous love	Low	High	High
Consummate love	High	High	High

Source: Based on Sternberg, 2006.

not love and to feel little passion for those to whom we are happily attached (Diamond, 2004). (But you probably already knew that.)

Indeed, theorist Helen Fisher (2006) argues that it makes evolutionary sense for there to be three interrelated but distinct biological systems that control components of love experiences. First, there's *lust,* or the sex drive, which is regulated by the sex hormones. Lust drives successful reproduction by providing us the motivation to mate with others. Then there's *attraction,* which promotes the pursuit of a particular preferred romantic partner. Attraction drives pair-bonding by fueling romantic love, which is regulated by the levels of the neurotransmitters dopamine and (possibly) serotonin in specific regions of the brain that control feelings of reward (Aron et al., 2008). Increased levels of dopamine may be responsible for the excitement and exhilaration that occur when we fall in love, and reduced levels of serotonin may give us the energy to woo our beloveds indefatigably. This mix of neurotransmitters may be "why lovers feel euphoric, rejuvenated, optimistic, and energized, happy to sit up talking all night or making love for hours on end" (Ackerman, 1994, p. 165). Indeed, when people have just fallen in love, a look at their lovers makes pain not hurt as much. Romantic love also activates the areas of the brain that are affected by pain-relieving drugs, and sure enough, when they see their sweethearts, young lovers can shrug off pain (produced by a computer-controlled heating pad attached to a hand) that would be quite troubling under other circumstances (Younger et al., 2010). Finally, there's *attachment,* a term used here to describe the feelings of comfort, security, and connection to a long-term mate that keep a couple together long enough to protect and sustain their very young children. Attachment drives companionate love, which is regulated by the neuropeptide oxytocin. (More on that later.)

Thus, we may be equipped with three different physiological systems that evolved to facilitate some component of successful reproduction—and they support the triangular theory's proposition that the related experiences of passion, intimacy, and commitment can be rather independent of each other, separately ranging from weak to strong at any given time. On the other hand, intimacy, passion, and commitment are clearly interrelated in many loving relationships (Whitley, 1993). For instance, if men become sexually aroused by inspecting porn, they report more love for their romantic partners than they do when they're not turned on (Dermer & Pyszczynski, 1978).

As a result, as I warned you earlier, the clearly defined categories offered by the triangular theory may not seem so distinct in real life. People's actual experiences of love appear to be complex. For instance, a father's love for his son is likely to resemble his love for his own father, but the two feelings are also likely to differ in meaningful ways that the triangular theory does not readily explain. Different types of love probably overlap in a messier, more confusing way than the theory implies (Fehr, 2006).

Nevertheless, the theory offers a very useful framework for addressing different types of love, and whether or not it is entirely correct, it identifies two types of love that may be especially likely to occur in most romantic relationships over the long haul. Let's examine each of them more closely.

Romantic, Passionate Love

Has anyone ever told you, "I love you, but I'm not *in* love with you"? If so, it was probably bad news. As you probably knew, he or she was trying to say, "I like you, I care about you, I think you're a marvelous person with wonderful qualities and so forth, but I don't find you sexually desirable" (Myers & Berscheid, 1997, p. 360). Just as the triangular theory of love proposes, sexual attraction (or *passion*) appears to be one of the defining characteristics of romantic love (Regan, 2008). So, it's disappointing if a romantic partner implies, "I just want us to be friends."

The fact that romantic love involves passion is important. Passion involves activation and arousal, and remarkably, *any* form of strong arousal, good or bad, can influence our feelings of romantic love.

Arousal

A classic analysis of romantic love by Elaine Hatfield and Ellen Berscheid proposed that passionate attraction is rooted in two factors: (1) physiological arousal such as a fast heart beat that is coupled with (2) the belief that another person is the cause of your arousal (Berscheid & Walster, 1974). According to this two-factor perspective, romantic love is produced, or at least intensified, when feelings of arousal are associated with the presence of another attractive person.

Imagine this situation: You're in a park in North Vancouver, British Columbia, starting across a long, narrow bridge made of wooden planks that are suspended by wire, hanging hundreds of feet over a deep gorge. The bridge bounces and tilts and sways as you walk across it, and it has a low wire railing that comes up only to your waist. Far, far below is a rocky creek, and (because you're just like all the rest of us) you can't help but feel some nervous excitement (or perhaps outright fear) as you make your way across. But, then, right in the middle of the precarious bridge, you encounter an attractive person of the other sex who asks you to answer a few questions. You're shown a picture and asked to make up a story, and your interviewer thanks you warmly and invites you to call later if you have any questions. How attracted would you be to the person you met on the bridge?

This is just the question that was asked in a famous experiment by Dutton and Aron (1974), who sent attractive women to interview unaccompanied young men (between 19 and 35 years of age) either in the middle of the spooky suspension bridge or on another bridge that was stable and just a few feet off the ground in another part of the park. The stories that the men wrote were scored for sexual imagery, and Dutton and Aron found that the men on the swaying suspension bridge were thinking sexier thoughts than other men. In addition, those men were more likely to call the assistant later at her home. They were more attracted to her, and the arousal—or fear—caused by the dangerous bridge had evidently fueled their interest in her. Other men who encountered the same woman in a less dramatic place found her less compelling. On the precarious bridge, fear had apparently fueled attraction.

Or had it? Could nervous excitement caused by a shaky bridge really be mistaken, at least in part, for romantic attraction to a stranger? Well, try this

Is Romantic Love an Emotion?

I'll confess up front: The issue is still in doubt, so I don't have a definite answer to the question posed by the title of this box. Romantic love certainly involves fervent feelings and strong motives, but theorists in affective science typically reserve the term *emotion* for an organized response with particular characteristics. Many (but not all) researchers consider emotions to result from specific events that cause discrete physiological reactions and that elicit distinct patterns of expressive behavior and goal-oriented responses (Oatley et al., 2006). Emotions exist, theorists argue, because they promote effective, adaptive responses to important, recurring tasks (Keltner et al., 2006). Thus, if it is unequivocally an emotion, romantic love should have a concrete, useful function, and it should occur in response to particular stimuli, cause distinctive physical changes, be visible to others, and engender recognizable behavioral responses. (If you pause for a moment and consider these criteria, you may see why the issue is in doubt.)

In focusing our attention and energies on particular partners, romantic love promotes commitment that can increase our reproductive success (Gonzaga et al., 2008). It is also elicited by others who we think would make compelling mates. But it doesn't activate specific, delimited areas of the brain as many other emotions do; regions regulating reward switch on, but so do several other areas, so romantic love has more diffuse effects than other discrete emotions (Xu et al., 2011). People who are in love display enthusiastic interest in their partners, with lots of nodding, smiling, and close interpersonal distances (Gonzaga et al., 2006), but the extent to which these cues are definitive signals of love per se is arguable. And people find it more difficult to talk themselves into feeling in love than they do some other emotions. If you vividly envision the provocation that last made you angry, you can bring back some of your anger—but people have less success reigniting the preoccupied passion of romantic love on command (Aron, 2010). The existing evidence leads some observers to think that romantic love is more a mood with particular motives than a discrete emotion (Reis & Aron, 2008).

And why should you care, exactly? Well, consider that emotions are rather *brief* events (Oatley et al., 2006). Every other potent emotion you've ever experienced flared up quickly, burned brightly, and then faded away. Moods last longer, but they're more diffuse events that have more variable effects on our behavior; if romantic love is a mood, it may have different effects on different people.

So, exactly what sort of affective experience romantic love is remains undecided. But whatever it is, there's another question that now looms large: Other emotions, moods, and motives don't last forever, so does love last? Can our romantic, passionate attraction to a particular partner continue indefinitely? Keep this key question in the back of your mind as you continue reading, and we'll return to it at the end of the chapter.

procedure: You're a young man who runs in place for either 2 minutes or 15 seconds, so your pulse rate is high and you're breathing hard, or you're just a little more aroused than normal. Flushed with high or low arousal, you move to another room and inspect a video of a young woman whom you think you're about to meet. You and other men all see the same woman, but, through the wonders of makeup, she looks either quite attractive or rather unattractive. What do you think of her? When real research participants reported their reactions, it was clear that high arousal intensified the men's ordinary responses to the woman (White et al., 1981). The attractive version of the woman was always preferred to the unattractive version, of course, but as you can see in Table 8.2, the men liked the attractive model even more—and liked the unattractive model even less—when they were aroused than when they were calm. High arousal magnified the guys' responses, so that men who encountered an attractive woman when their pulses were racing thought that she was *really* hot.

Moreover, the effects of arousal on attraction do not depend on the type of arousal that is produced. In another procedure (White et al., 1981), men listened to one of three tapes:

- *Negatively arousing.* A description of the brutal mutilation and killing of a missionary while his family watched.
- *Positively arousing.* Selections from Steve Martin's comedy album, *A Wild and Crazy Guy.*[1]
- *Neutral.* A boring description of the circulatory system of a frog.

Thereafter, as before, the men viewed a video of an attractive or unattractive woman and provided their impressions of her. Arousal again fueled attraction, and it didn't matter what type of arousal it was. When the men had experienced either type of strong emotion—whether by laughing hard at the funny material or by being disgusted by the gory material—they were more attracted to the appealing woman and less attracted to the unappealing woman than they were when they had listened to the boring biology tape.

Taken together, these studies demonstrate that adrenaline fuels love. High arousal of various types, including simple exertion, and amusement, all seem to be able to enhance our feelings of romantic attraction to desirable potential

TABLE 8.2. Arousal and Attraction

	Attractiveness of the Woman	
Arousal of the Men	High	Low
Low	26.1	15.1
High	32.4	9.4

The higher the scores, the more desirable the men judged the woman to be. The physically attractive woman was always judged to be more desirable than the unattractive woman, but a faster heart beat accentuated this effect: When their pulses were racing, men thought that an attractive woman was more compelling and an unattractive woman was even less desirable.

Source: Data from White, Fishbein, & Rutstein, 1981.

[1] You've probably never heard this. You should.

partners. Consider the implications: Have you ever had a screaming argument with a lover and then found that it was especially sweet to "kiss and make up" a few minutes later? Might your anger have fueled your subsequent passion? Is that what being "in love" is like?

To some degree, it is. One useful measure of the passion component of romantic love is a Passionate Love Scale created by Elaine Hatfield and Susan Sprecher (1986). The short form of the scale is reprinted in Table 8.3; as you can see, the scale assesses fascination and preoccupation with, high desire for, and strong emotions about the object of one's love. Scores on the Passionate Love Scale increase as someone falls deeper and deeper into romantic love with someone else, only leveling off when the partners become engaged or start

TABLE 8.3. The Short Form of the Passionate Love Scale

This questionnaire asks you to describe how you feel when you are passionately in love. Please think of the person whom you love most passionately *right now*. Keep this person in mind as you complete this questionnaire.

Answer each item using this scale:

1	2	3	4	5	6	7	8	9
Not at all true				Moderately true				Definitely true

1. I would feel deep despair if _____ left me.
2. Sometimes I feel I can't control my thoughts; they are obsessively on _____.
3. I feel happy when I am doing something to make _____ happy.
4. I would rather be with _____ than anyone else.
5. I'd get jealous if I thought _____ was falling in love with someone else.
6. I yearn to know all about _____.
7. I want _____ physically, emotionally, mentally.
8. I have an endless appetite for affection from _____.
9. For me, _____ is the perfect romantic partner.
10. I sense my body responding when _____ touches me.
11. _____ always seems to be on my mind.
12. I want _____ to know me—my thoughts, my fears, and my hopes.
13. I eagerly look for signs indicating _____'s desire for me.
14. I possess a powerful attraction for _____.
15. I get extremely depressed when things don't go right in my relationship with _____.

Higher scores on the PLS indicate greater passionate love. Across all 15 items, the average rating per item—add up all your ratings and divide by 15—for both men and women is 7.15. If your average is 9 (the highest possible), you're experiencing more passionate love than most people, and if your average is 5.25 or lower, you're experiencing less.

Source: Hatfield & Sprecher, 1986.

living together. (Note that—as I mentioned earlier—American couples decide to marry or live together when their passion is at a peak.) The vision of romantic love that emerges from the Passionate Love Scale is one of need and desire— ecstasy when one is loved in return and agony when one is not—and these are clearly responses that burn brighter when one is aroused than when one is calm and relaxed.

So, one aspect of romantic love is the exhilaration and euphoria of high arousal, and various events that excite us may increase our feelings of love for our partners. Romance is more than just passion, however. It also involves our thoughts.

Thought

The two-factor theory of passionate love emphasizes the role of our thoughts and beliefs in accounting for arousal. Our judgments may also be linked to romance in other ways, with lovers thinking about each other in ways that differ from the ways they think about their friends. Some of these distinctions are apparent in the contents of a Love Scale and a Liking Scale created by Zick Rubin in 1973. Years before Hatfield and Sprecher created the Passionate Love Scale, Rubin created dozens of statements that reflected a wide range of interpersonal attitudes and asked people to use them to describe both a lover and a friend. The handful of items that epitomized people's romances ended up on a Love Scale that gives a partial indication of what lovers are thinking.

One theme in the items on the Love Scale is *intimacy,* just as the triangular theory of love defines it. Romance is characterized by openness, communication, and trust (see item 1 in Table 8.4). A second theme is needy *dependence* (see item 2 in Table 8.4). The dependence items describe ardent longing for one's partner that has much in common with the passion I've discussed. A last theme on the Love Scale, however, describes feelings that are not mentioned by the triangular theory: *caring.* Romantic lovers report concern for the welfare and well-being of their partners (see item 3). They want to take care of their partners and keep them happy.

TABLE 8.4. Rubin's (1973) Love and Liking Scales: Some Example Items

Rubin's Love Scale

1. I feel that I can confide in my partner about virtually anything.
2. If I could never be with my partner, I would be miserable.
3. I would do almost anything for my partner.

Rubin's Liking Scale

1. My partner is one of the most likable people I know.
2. My partner is the sort of person that I would like to be.
3. I think that my partner is unusually well-adjusted.

Thus, like other efforts to characterize love (e.g., Fehr, 2006), the Love Scale portrays romantic love as a multifaceted experience that involves both giving (i.e., caring) and taking (i.e., dependence). If you're in love with someone, it's probably partly selfish—you love your partner because of how that person makes you feel—and partly generous; you genuinely care for your partner and will work to satisfy and protect him or her. (In fact, compassionate concern for those we love may define yet another type of love, as we'll see on page 260.) In addition, these diverse sentiments are experienced with relative intensity and urgency: You'd do *anything* for your partner and be *miserable* without him or her.

Compare those thoughts and feelings to the sorts of things people say about their friends. As you can see in Table 8.4, the Liking Scale seems bland by comparison. People say they like their friends because their friends are nice, well-adjusted, likable people. But they love their lovers because they need them and would do anything the lover asks. There's a fervor to the thoughts that characterize romantic love that is lacking when we just like someone.

The specific judgments people make of their partners are important, too. As we saw in chapter 4, people tend to hold rosy views of their relationship partners, and their tendency to idealize and glorify their lovers is probably at a peak when they are most in love. In fact, the moment romance enters the picture, people start ignoring or reinterpreting undesirable information about potential partners. Imagine that you're a male college student who is asked to play the role of a restaurant owner who is evaluating the work of a woman who is pitching you an advertising campaign (Goodwin et al., 2002). You watch a video of her presentation, which is either coherent and clever or clumsy and inept. Would you be able to tell the difference between the competent and incompetent work? Of course you would. But what if you knew that you'd be going out on a date with the woman on Friday? Would the possibility of a romance influence your judgment? You may not think so, but when men really participated in a procedure like this, a romantic orientation had a big effect, as Figure 8.1 illustrates. The upcoming date obviously contaminated the men's judgment, magically transforming a lousy performance into one of much higher quality. Any distinction between good and bad work disappeared entirely when the possibility of romance was in play.

As these results suggest, in a real way, "love is blind": People underestimate or ignore their lovers' faults. They hold idealized images of their lovers that may differ in meaningful ways from the concrete realities they face. In fact, a major difference between love and friendship may be our imaginations—our lovers are fascinating, mysterious, and appealing in ways our friends are not (Aron et al., 2008).

Romantic love also makes it easier to put tempting alternatives to our present partners out of our minds. Here's another provocative procedure: Imagine yourself inspecting photos of attractive members of the other sex, picking the best-looking one of the bunch, and then writing essays on (a) why that person is attractive and (b) what a perfect first meeting with that person would be like. Clearly, the researchers have you pondering a compelling alternative to your

FIGURE 8.1. **Love is blind.**
When men expected to date a woman, they thought her lousy work was much better than it really was.
Source: Goodwin et al., 2002.

current romantic partner (Gonzaga et al., 2008). But the plot thickens; you're now asked to put the fantasy alternative out of mind and to stop thinking about him or her while you write another essay about (a) your love for your partner, (b) your sexual desire for your partner, or (c) just your current stream of thought. Can you do it? You can if you're mentally rehearsing your love for your partner. People were better able to distract themselves from the alternative—and they remembered less about the alternative's looks—when they envisioned their love for their partners than in the other two conditions. Evidently, love helps us focus our attention on one preferred partner to the exclusion of others. Rehearsing our romantic love for our partners even makes us less likely to notice other attractive people in the first place (Maner et al., 2008).

Finally, even our thoughts about ourselves can change when we fall in love. Arthur and Elaine Aron's *self-expansion model* suggests that love causes our self-concepts to expand and change as our partners bring us new experiences and new roles, and we gradually learn things about ourselves that we didn't know before (Aron & Aron, 2006). Indeed, a study that tracked young adults for 10 weeks while they fell in love found that their self-concepts become more diversified and their self-esteem went up, which were two reasons why falling in love was so delightful (Aron et al., 1995).

All of this is potent stuff. The arousal and cognition that characterize romantic, passionate love involve surging emotion, imagination and idealization, and occasional obsession (Aron et al., 2008). And it is the presence of this complex, hectic state that leads most North Americans to consider marriage. However, romantic passion may not be the reason they stay married in the years that follow. The longevity of a relationship may have more to do with companionate love.

Companionate Love

Because it does not depend on passion, companionate love is a more settled state than romantic love is. The triangular theory suggests that it is a combination of intimacy and commitment, but I can characterize it more fully as a "comfortable, affectionate, trusting love for a likable partner, based on a deep sense of friendship and involving companionship and the enjoyment of common activities, mutual interests, and shared laughter" (Grote & Frieze, 1994, p. 275). It takes the form of a rich, committed friendship with someone with whom our lives are intertwined.

Sounds pleasant, but isn't it a bit bland compared to the ecstasies of romantic passion? Perhaps so, but you may want to get used to it. When hundreds of couples who had been married at least 15 years were asked why their marriages had lasted, they *didn't* say that they'd do anything for their spouses or be miserable without them, like romantic lovers do (Lauer & Lauer, 1985). Instead, for both men and women, the two most frequent reasons were (a) "My spouse is my best friend," and (b) "I like my spouse as a person." Long-lasting, satisfying marriages seem to include a lot of companionate love.

A useful measure of companionate love is the Friendship-Based Love Scale created by Nancy Grote and Irene Frieze (1994). As you can see in Table 8.5, the feelings described by the scale are very different than those that accompany passionate love; friendship and companionship are much more in evidence on the Friendship-Based Love Scale than they are on measures of romantic love.

Of course, deep friendships also occur often in the context of romantic love. In one study, 44 percent of the young adults in premarital relationships reported that their romantic partners were also their closest friends (Hendrick & Hendrick, 1993). However, when they are a part of romantic love, friendships are combined (and sometimes confused) with sexual arousal and passion. The predominant importance of friendship in creating the experience is easier to detect in companionate love, when intimacy is paired with commitment, than in romantic love, when intimacy is paired with passion.

A Physiological Foundation

Companionate love also has a physiological foundation that differs from that of romantic love. The neuropeptide *oxytocin,* which promotes relaxation and reduces stress, seems to be involved (MacDonald & MacDonald, 2010). Oxytocin is released by mothers during childbirth and breastfeeding (and in fact, a synthetic form of oxytocin, pitocin, is used to induce labor), and the more oxytocin a young mother has in her blood, the more she'll cuddle and coo, look, and smile at her baby (Feldman et al., 2007). Among adults, a kiss

TABLE 8.5. The Friendship-Based Love Scale

Think about your closest current relationship, and then rate your agreement or disagreement with each of these questions on the following scale:

1	2	3	4	5
strongly disagree				strongly agree

1. I feel our love is based on a deep and abiding friendship.
2. I express my love for my partner through the enjoyment of common activities and mutual interests.
3. My love for my partner involves solid, deep affection.
4. An important factor in my love for my partner is that we laugh together.
5. My partner is one of the most likable people I know.
6. The companionship I share with my partner is an important part of my love for him or her.

The average total score for married men is 25.2, and the average total for married women is 26.4. Scores ranging between 21 and 30 are typical for men, and scores between 22 and 30 are routine for women. Scores on the scale are more highly correlated with relationship satisfaction and duration than scores on the Passionate Love Scale are.

Source: Adapted from Grote & Frieze, 1994.

from a lover stimulates the release of oxytocin (Hill et al., 2009), and a lot of it is produced during orgasm; oxytocin may be one of the causes of the relaxed lethargy that couples often experience after lovemaking (Floyd, 2006). Moreover, people who have higher levels of oxytocin in their blood tend to be warmer and kinder when they discuss touchy topics with their spouses (Gouin et al., 2010), and research participants who snort a spray of oxytocin start behaving more pleasantly during a disagreement with a lover (Ditzen et al., 2009). They also become more trusting toward strangers (Theodoridou et al., 2009). These patterns suggest that oxytocin promotes a soothing sense of well-being, and it may encourage enduring attachments to those who become associated with its presence in the bloodstream (Floyd, 2006). In short, the production of oxytocin may provide a biological basis for feelings of companionate love.

Still, even if dopamine is a key player in romantic love and oxytocin a central ingredient in companionate love, both agents are always present in the body in some amount, so we rarely encounter pure experiences of romantic and companionate love in which one is present and the other is not. Companionate lovers can and do experience passion, and romantic lovers can and do feel commitment. As we experience them, the distinctions between romantic and companionate love are much fuzzier than this discussion may have implied (Fehr, 2006). Nevertheless, if we're willing to tolerate some ambiguity, we can conclude that there appear to be at least two major types of love that frequently occur in American romance: a love that's full of passion that leads people to pair

---

A Type of Love You May Not Want to Experience
Unrequited Love

Have you ever loved someone who did not love you back? You probably have. Depending on the sample, 80 percent (Aron et al., 1998) to 90 percent of young adults (Baumeister et al., 1993) report that they have experienced unrequited love: romantic, passionate attraction to someone who did not return that love. It's a common experience that seems to be most frequent in one's late teens, between the ages of 16 and 20 (Hill et al., 1997). Still, it doesn't strike everybody; it happens to more men than women (Hill et al., 1997) and is more likely to befall people with a preoccupied attachment style than those with secure or avoidant styles (Aron et al., 1998).

Why do we experience such loves? Several factors may be involved. First, would-be lovers are very attracted to their unwilling targets, and they assume that relationships with them are worth working and waiting for. Second, they optimistically overestimate how much they are liked in return (Aron et al., 1998).

And third, perhaps most importantly, as painful as it is, unrequited love has its rewards. Along with their frustration, would-be lovers experience the real thrill, elation, and excitement of being in love (Baumeister et al., 1993).

It's actually worse to be the target of someone's undesired adoration. Sure, it's nice to be wanted, but those on the receiving end of unrequited love often find their pursuers' persistence to be intrusive and annoying, and they usually feel guilty when they turn their ardent pursuers down (Graupmann & Esber, 2005). They are usually nice, "well-meaning people who find themselves caught up in another person's emotional whirlwind and who themselves often suffer acutely as a result" (Baumeister & Wotman, 1992, p. 203). As distressing as it was to gradually realize that the objects of our affection would not become our steady partners, we may have made it harder on them when we fell into unrequited love.

---

off with each other, and a love that's full of friendship that underlies relationships that last. Over time, companionate love is typically stronger in enduring relationships than romantic, passionate love is, and it is more highly correlated with the satisfaction people enjoy (Fehr, 2001). I'll return to this point at the end of the chapter.

Compassionate Love

There's a third type of love that occurs in successful romances (Berscheid, 2010) that is not delineated by the triangular theory of love because the theory does not assert that considerate caring for other people is a specific component of love. Perhaps it should. An altruistic care and concern for the well-being of one's partner is a defining characteristic of **compassionate love**, a type of love that combines the trust and understanding of *intimacy* with compassion and *caring* that involves empathy, selflessness, and sacrifice on behalf of the beloved (Fehr & Sprecher, 2009b). (Now before we go any further, let's take

TABLE 8.6 Items from the Compassionate Love Scale

To what extent are these statements true about you?

1. I spend a lot of time concerned about the well-being of those people close to me.
2. If a person close to me needs help, I would do almost anything I could to help him or her.
3. I would rather suffer myself than see someone close to me suffer.

a moment and examine the label "compassionate" love. It sounds like a combination of romantic, passionate love [which obviously involves passion] and companionate love [which includes the word "companion"], but it is different from either one. Compassion involves empathy for others and the benevolent wish to aid those who are need help. Don't confuse companionate love with compassionate love.[2])

People who feel compassionate love tend to share the pain or joy that their loved ones experience, and they would rather suffer themselves than to allow someone close to them to be hurt. They are empathic and generous, and their care and concern for their loved ones are evident in a Compassionate Love Scale created by Susan Sprecher and Beverley Fehr (2005). (See Table 8.6.) As you might expect, compassionate lovers provide their partners more support than do those who are less compassionate, and they donate more money to disaster relief (Fehr & Sprecher, 2009a) and take more pleasure in helping others, too (Sprecher et al., 2007).

Compassionate love is highly correlated with experiences of romantic love and companionate love—they all have intimacy in common—but there are still differences among them that are worth noting. Whereas romantic love is "blind," compassionate love is rooted in more accurate understanding of our partners' strengths and weaknesses; we recognize their deficiencies, but we love them anyway (Neff & Karney, 2009). And the selfless concern that defines compassionate love may be invaluable in protecting and maintaining a relationship if the partners become infirm with age or if a "malevolent fate plunges one of the partners from 'better' to a permanent 'worse'" (Berscheid, 2010, p. 17). Is compassionate love necessary for continued satisfaction in long-term relationships? We don't yet know: Those studies have yet to be done. Nevertheless, along with passion and friendship, compassionate caring for one's partner may be another key ingredient in the very best experiences of love.

Styles of Loving

Another scheme for distinguishing different types of love experiences was offered by sociologist John Alan Lee (1988), who used Greek and Latin words

---

[2] And don't blame me for the similarity of the terms. It's not my fault.

TABLE 8.7. Styles of Loving

Eros	The erotic lover finds good looks compelling and seeks an intense, passionate relationship.
Ludus	The ludic lover considers love to be a game and likes to play the field.
Storge	The storgic lover prefers friendships that gradually grow into lasting commitments.
Mania	The manic lover is demanding, possessive, and excitable.
Agape	The agapic lover is altruistic and dutiful.
Pragma	The pragmatic lover is practical, careful, and logical in searching for a mate.

Source: Based on Lee, 1988.

to describe six styles of love that differ in the intensity of the loving experience, commitment to the beloved, desired characteristics of the beloved, and expectations about being loved in return. (See Table 8.7.) One style is **eros,** from which the word *erotic* comes. Eros has a strong physical component, and erotic lovers are likely to be heavily influenced by physical appearance and to believe in love at first sight.

A second style, **ludus** (pronounced "loo-dus"), treats love as an uncommitted game. Ludic lovers are often fickle and (try to) have several different partners at once. In contrast, a third style, **storge,** ("store-gay") leads people to de-emphasize strong emotion and to seek genuine friendships that gradually lead to real commitment.

A fourth style, **mania,** is demanding and possessive and full of vivid fantasy and obsession. A fifth style, **agape** ("ah-gaa-pay"), is giving, altruistic, and selfless, and treats love as a duty. Finally, the last style, **pragma,** is practical and pragmatic. Pragma leads people to dispassionately seek partners who will logically be a good match for them.

How useful are these distinctions? Instead of thinking of them as six additional types of love, it makes more sense to consider them as six themes in love experiences that overlap and are differentially related to the types of love we've considered so far. In particular, storge, mania, and pragma have little in common with romantic love, companionate love, or compassionate love; the obsession of mania and the cool, friendly practicality of storge and pragma differ noticeably from the loving intimacy at the heart of all three types of love (Graham, 2011). However, all of the components of love described by the triangular theory—that is, intimacy, passion, and commitment—are positively related to eros and agape (remember, love involves both giving *and* taking), and negatively related to ludus (which means that love is serious business) (Graham, 2011). So, some of the styles described by Lee (1988) are related to other widely studied types of love, but others of them are not. Susan and Clyde Hendrick have developed a Love Attitudes Scale to measure people's endorsement of the six styles, and they have found that men score higher on ludus than women do, whereas women are more storgic and pragmatic than men (Hendrick & Hendrick, 2006). Other researchers have detected a tendency for people to pair off with others who share similar attitudes toward love (Morrow et al., 1995). In general, then the love styles remind us of intriguing sources of individuality (such as practicality) that are sometimes overlooked.

INDIVIDUAL AND CULTURAL DIFFERENCES IN LOVE

Obviously, there are various different feelings people may be experiencing when they say, "I love you." To complicate things further, some people may be more likely than others to experience certain types of love. Several individual differences and cultural influences are linked to love, and I'll begin our consideration of them by considering whether love differs from one culture to the next.

Culture

If you're using fMRI, romantic love in China looks just like romantic love in the United States: The areas of the brain that are activated when people see photos of their romantic partners are generally the same in both cultures (Xu et al., 2011). This isn't surprising because romantic love appears to be a universal human experience that is found in all the peoples of the world (Hatfield et al., 2007). The distinction between romantic love and companionate love is also apparent in both Western and Eastern cultures (Shaver et al., 2001). Fundamentally, the various types of love seem to operate similarly in diverse cultures. Still, within these broad similarities lie some cultural nuances that make love a little different from place to place.

When they describe their experiences of falling in love, for instance, Americans emphasize the similarity and good looks of their partners more than Chinese people do, and the Chinese mention a desirable personality, others' opinions, and their own physical arousal more than Americans do (Riela et al., 2010). (Which group do you think is falling in love for the better reasons?) Then, when they're in love, married couples in the United States and China both feel a lot of compassionate caring and horny desire for their partners, but there are cultural differences, too. Romantic fantasies—thinking of love as a fairy tale, with expectations of living happily ever after—are more prominent in America, whereas acknowledgments that one's partner is baffling and incomprehensible and that love itself is a mixed blessing are more common in China (Jackson et al., 2006). (Again, which culture do you think has it right?) Finally, people in individualistic Western nations such as the United States are more likely than those in Eastern countries that emphasize interdependence to insist on love as a reason to marry (Levine et al., 1995). In particular, college students in China are more likely than those in the United States to be guided by their parents' wishes regarding whom they should marry (Zhang & Kline, 2009). Whereas marriage in China is often a family decision, young adults in America typically expect that their choice of a spouse will be entirely up to them. (Whom would your parents choose for you, if they could? See the box on the next page.)

Whom Do Your Parents Want You to Marry?

Arranged marriages in which one's spouse is chosen by one's family are still commonplace in Asia and the Middle East (Buunk & Solano, 2010), and they beg an interesting question: If it were (or is) up to them, who would (or do) your parents want you to marry? In general, your parents probably want the same qualities you do: They seek sons- and daughters-in-law with good economic prospects who are attractive, smart, stable, and kind. What's intriguing is that they probably have different *priorities* than you do, so that if they can't have it all—and who can?—they value some characteristics more than you do. Physical attractiveness doesn't matter as much to them as it does to you (Perilloux et al., 2011). You'll care more about whether your spouse smells nice and is the right height and a trim weight than your folks will, whereas they'll care more about your mate's race, social class, family background, and religion (Buunk & Solano, 2010). They also don't want you hooking up in casual sexual liaisons, especially if you're their daughter (Apostolou, 2009). Overall, then, parents think fundamental similarities and commitment are more vital than their offspring do, and that's true across cultures (Buunk & Solano, 2010). Might they have a point?

Attachment Styles

Because they are rather subtle, cultural influences on love are less consequential than some individual differences are. In particular, whatever one's culture, the attachment dimensions of anxiety over abandonment and avoidance of intimacy are enormously important because they are associated with all of the elements of love we've encountered: intimacy, passion, commitment, and caring.

- *Intimacy.* People with secure attachment styles generally have high regard for others, viewing them as trustworthy, dependable, and kind (Luke et al., 2004), and they tend to be more open with their partners, happily engaging in a lot of self-disclosure. Those who are insecure are more wary of others. In particular, people who are high in avoidance typically view others with suspicion, perceiving them to be dishonest and undependable (Collins & Allard, 2001). As a result, they tend to be close-mouthed, telling their partners relatively little about their feelings and desires (Feeney et al., 2000). In general, secure people enjoy greater intimacy with their partners than insecure people do (Mikulincer & Shaver, 2007).
- *Passion.* There's a lot of drama in the lives of preoccupied people, but much of it isn't pleasant. Their anxiety over abandonment often has them on edge, nervously experiencing apprehension rather than delight in their intimate interactions (Davis et al., 2004). Those who are avoidant of intimacy are more distant and detached, and their passion (such as it is) is more impersonal. So, you probably won't be surprised to find that the best, most fulfilling sex is enjoyed by people with secure attachment styles. Secure people have more frequent sex that involves more arousal, greater pleasure, more frequent orgasms, and greater satisfaction (Mikulincer & Shaver, 2007).

- *Commitment.* Secure people also tend to be more committed to their partnerships than insecure people are (Mikulincer & Shaver, 2007). This is also no surprise because day by day, secure people have more intimate, more positive, and more satisfying interactions with their lovers than insecure people do (Kafetsios & Nezlek, 2002).
- *Caring and caregiving.* Finally, when their partners are nervous and need support, insecure people are less effective caregivers, providing less reassurance than secure people do and leaving their partners less at ease (Simpson et al., 2002). In particular, people who are high in avoidance behave more negatively and sometimes get angry when they are asked to provide comfort and consolation to a needy partner (Campbell et al., 2001). Anxious people often offer a lot of help, but they tend to do so for selfish reasons, hoping to gain approval from their partners. Overall, compassionate love for one's partner is enhanced and increased by a secure attachment style and reduced by avoidance of intimacy (Sprecher & Fehr, 2011).

Thus, a secure style is positively related to all four of the building blocks that seem to create different love experiences, and sure enough, secure people experience more intense romantic, companionate, and compassionate love than insecure people do (Mikulincer & Shaver, 2005).

Importantly, however, all of us typically have several different partners, such as lovers, parents, and friends, who are important attachment figures at any one time, and we may be relatively secure in some of those relationships and somewhat insecure in others (Sibley & Overall, 2008). Lurking within the global orientations toward relationships that we label as attachment styles may be several different sets of feelings about specific partners, so that our attachment quality can vary from partner to partner (Overall et al., 2003). Those of us who are anxiously attached to our mothers, for instance, may nevertheless trust our romantic partners wholeheartedly. So, attachment varies from relationship to relationship, making attachment styles in loving partnerships rather complex (Sibley & Overall, 2008).

Still, the global attitudes I've described here are important. Varying levels of avoidance of intimacy and anxiety over abandonment characterize relationships all over the world (Schmitt, 2008). And they clearly set the stage for our dealings with others. Toddlers who are securely attached to their mothers tend to get along with others in elementary school and then to have close friendships in high school—and then, as a result of those successful friendships, they tend to have satisfying adult romances (Simpson et al., 2007). The potent, lasting influences of attachment styles demonstrate that not only are there different types of loves, there are different kinds of lovers.

Age

Another slowly changing personal characteristic that may affect love is one's age. As I suggested in chapter 2, age can be a tricky variable to study because it's usually confounded with experience and history. As people age, they may have (a) relationships of longer duration and (b) more relationships overall. So, if love does seem to change with age, it may be because age makes a difference or because of the length of people's relationships, the extent of their previous romantic experience, or some combination of all three.

Nevertheless, one thing seems clear about age: Most people mellow. When researchers compared spouses in their sixties to those in their forties, they found that the older couples interacted with more good cheer but less physical arousal. Their emotions were less intense, but more positive on the whole, even in marriages that were not particularly happy at the time (Levenson et al., 1994). Some of the burning, urgent, emotional intensity that leads young people to marry seems to dwindle with time to be replaced with a more genial and more mature outlook on love.

Men and Women

A potentially important individual difference that does not change with time is one's sex. On the whole, men and women are more similar than different when it comes to love (Canary & Emmers-Sommer, 1997). They experience the various types of love similarly, and there are few differences in the proportions of men and women who have each attachment style; men tend to be more dismissing than women are, but the difference is rather small (Schmitt, 2008). Women do experience more intense and more volatile emotions than men do, on average (Brody & Hall, 2008); nevertheless, there are rarely any differences between men and women on measures of romantic feelings such as the Love Scale (Rubin, 1973) and the Passionate Love Scale (Hatfield & Sprecher, 1986). Evidently, as we have seen before, it's just plain silly to think that men come from one planet and women come from another.

On the other hand, men tend to possess more romantic attitudes than women do; they're more likely than women to think that if you just love someone enough, nothing else matters (Sprecher & Metts, 1999). They're also more likely to believe that it's possible to experience "love at first sight," and they tend to fall in love faster than women do (Hatfield & Sprecher, 1986). Women are more cautious than men when it comes to love; they're more selective about *whom* they love, feeling passion more slowly and limiting their affection to partners of higher mate value (Kenrick et al., 1990). Men tend to be less discriminating, a fact that is reflected by their greater acceptance, on average, of casual sex (Schmitt, 2005b). (All of these patterns, I should remind you, are consistent with an evolutionary perspective, which predicts that women *should* be cautious about whom they love because their parental investments in any offspring are so much greater than men's [Buss, 2012]. In contrast, a sociocultural model attributes women's greater selectivity to their traditionally lower status in many societies; according to this perspective, careful selection of a high-status mate is one of the few means available to women to obtain resources that are more accessible to men [Wood & Eagly, 2007]. Which explanation do you find more convincing?)

Men also seem to put more stock in passion. Men and women agree that love should be affectionate and committed, but men also think it should be more passionate than women do (Fehr & Broughton, 2001). Indeed, of the three components of love, passion is most highly associated with men's satisfaction with their relationships, whereas commitment is the best predictor of satisfaction for women (Sternberg, 2006). This puts men in the position of relying on the component of love that, according to the triangular theory, is the least stable and reliable as time goes by.

DOES LOVE LAST?

So, how does the passage of time affect love? Does love last? This is a difficult question to answer conclusively because, as we've seen, there are different types of loves and idiosyncratic types of lovers. Your experiences with love through the years may differ from those of others. Nevertheless, the prototypical North American marriage occurs when people in their twenties who are flushed with romantic passion pledge to spend the rest of their lives together, probably expecting their passion to last. Will it? Despite the couples' good intentions, the best answer relationship science can provide is, probably not, at least not to the extent the partners expect.

The simple truth is that romantic love typically decreases after people marry (Sprecher & Regan, 1998). Scores on romantic and passionate love scales go down as the years go by (Tucker & Aron, 1993), and that's among couples who manage to stay married! After several years, husbands and wives are no longer claiming to the same degree that they'd do anything for each other or that they melt when they look into each other's eyes. Figure 8.2 provides an interesting example of this in a study conducted in India that compared couples who chose to marry for love—like most North Americans do—to couples whose marriages were arranged for them by their families (Gupta & Singh, 1982). Romantic couples who were still married after 10 years reported much lower scores on Rubin's (1973) Love Scale than did those who had been married only for a year or two. (Couples who divorced and were not married that long were not included in the data you see in Figure 8.2. What do you think their love scores would be?)

What's more, the decrease in a couple's romantic love may sometimes be quite rapid. After only two years of marriage, average spouses express affection for each other only half as often as they did when they were newlyweds (Huston & Chorost, 1994). Worldwide, divorces occur more frequently in the fourth year of marriage than at any other time (Fisher, 1995). Many, if not most, couples fail to maintain the urgent longing for each other that leads them to marry in the first place.

Why Doesn't Romantic Love Last?

In fact, if we consider it carefully, there may be several reasons why we should *expect* romantic love to decline over time (Walster & Walster, 1978).

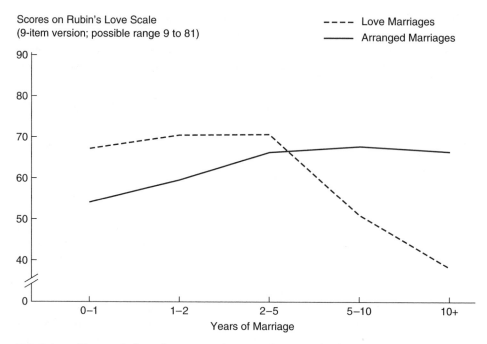

FIGURE 8.2. **Romantic love decreases after people marry for love.**
A study in India compared arranged marriages to those in which the spouses married because they were in love. Just as in the average American marriage, romantic love decreased substantially as the years went by after people married for love.
Source: Myers, D., 1993.

First, *fantasy* enhances romance. As I noted earlier, love is blind to some degree. Flushed with passion, lovers tend to idealize their partners and minimize or ignore information that should give them pause. Imagination, hope, and flights of fancy can make people who are quite different from us seem appealing, at least temporarily. The problem, of course, is that fantasy erodes with time and experience. To the extent that romance is enhanced by idealized glorification of one's partner, we should expect it to decline when people begin living together and reality slowly intrudes. "Ideals are easily tarnished, spells broken, sleights of hand exposed . . . romance fades over time because familiarity provides a more realistic, 'warts and all' view of the other; the harsh sunlight of the morning after dispels the enchantment of the moonlight" (Mitchell, 2002, p. 94).

In addition, sheer *novelty* adds excitement and energy to new loves. A first kiss is often much more thrilling than most of the thousands that follow, and when people are invigorated and fascinated by a new partner, they may be unable to appreciate how familiar and routine that same lover may seem 30 years later. Indeed, novelty causes sexual arousal in other species. For instance, if a male rat is caged with a female in estrus, he'll mate with her repeatedly until he appears to be sexually exhausted; however, if the first female is then replaced with another receptive female, the male will mount her with renewed interest and vigor. By continuing to replace an old partner with a new one, researchers can elicit two to three times as many ejaculations from the male as would have occurred with only the single female (Dewsbury, 1981). Researchers call this effect of novelty on arousal the *Coolidge effect*, referring to an old story that may or may not be true. Supposedly, President Calvin Coolidge and his wife were once touring a chicken farm when Mrs. Coolidge noticed a rooster covering one hen after another. Impressed with the bird's prowess, she asked the guide to mention the rooster to the president. When he heard about the rooster's stamina, Coolidge is said to have reflected a moment and then replied, "Please tell Mrs. Coolidge that there is more than one hen" (Walster & Walster, 1978).

Does novelty have similar effects on people? It might. Engaging in novel, arousing activities together gets romantic couples to feel more in love with each other (Strong & Aron, 2006). Furthermore, Roy Baumeister and Ellen Bratslavsky (1999) have suggested that romantic passion is directly related to changes in our relationships. When we're falling in love, our selves are expanding, everything is new and intimacy is increasing, and passion is likely to be very high. However, once a relationship is established, and novelty is lost, passion slowly subsides; the longer a relationship lasts, the less passionate it becomes (Ahmetoglu et al., 2010). This pattern is apparent in the results of a broad survey of U.S. sexuality that showed that an average couple's frequency of intercourse (one measure of their passion for each other) declines continually over the course of their marriage (Call et al., 1995). A similar pattern occurs in Germany, too (Klusmann, 2002). This decline is obviously confounded with age, as Figure 8.3 shows. However, people who remarry and change partners increase their frequency of sex, at least for a while, so aging does not seem to be wholly responsible for the decline of passion with time. Arguably, "romance thrives on novelty, mystery, and danger; it is dispersed by familiarity. Enduring romance is therefore a contradiction in terms" (Mitchell, 2002, p. 27).

Finally, as Figure 8.3 also implies, *arousal* fades as time goes by. As we've seen, there's no question that physical arousal—such as a rapid pulse rate and fast, shallow breathing—fuels passion. But it's impossible to stay keyed up forever! In the case of romantic love, the brain may simply not produce as much dopamine when a partner becomes familiar, so that even if your partner is as wonderful as ever, you're not as aroused. In any case, for whatever reason, the passion component of love is less lasting than either intimacy or commitment (Ahmetoglu et al., 2010), and that means that romantic love is less durable as well.

So, What Does the Future Hold?

Because three important influences on romantic passion—fantasy, novelty, and arousal—tend to dwindle over the years, romantic love decreases, too (Walster & Walster, 1978). Some couples *do* continue to feel lots of romantic love for each other, but even their feelings change somewhat over time. When they see photos of their beloved spouses, people who are still very much in love after

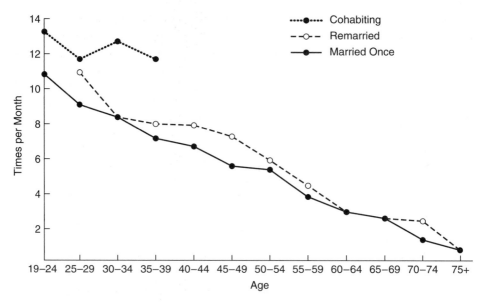

FIGURE 8.3. **Frequency of sexual intercourse by age.**
In general, most romantic relationships become less passionate as the years go by.
Source: Data from Call et al., 1995.

10 years of marriage still experience activation of the dopamine-rich reward centers in their brains, just as they did when they had just fallen in love—but other areas that are associated with monogamy and commitment in mammals become more active, too (Acevedo et al., 2011). The obsessive preoccupation with one's beloved that characterizes new love also tends to fade, even when desire and caring remain (Acevedo & Aron, 2009). The bottom line is that the burning love that gets people to marry tends not to stay the same, and that's one likely reason that the U.S. divorce rate is so high: A common complaint is that the "magic" has died (see chapter 13).

However, I really don't want this news to be depressing! To the contrary, I think it offers important advice about how long-term romances can succeed. Often, the love that encourages people to marry is not the love that keeps them together decades later. Passion declines, but intimacy and commitment both *increase* as we age (Ahmetoglu et al., 2010). Thus, companionate love is more stable than romantic love is (Sprecher & Regan, 1998). And, as we saw earlier, people who have been happily married for a long time typically express a lot of companionate love for their spouses (Lauer & Lauer, 1985). Such people are often genuinely happy, too: Although it does not rely on passion, companionate love is very satisfying to those who experience it (Hecht et al., 1994). And because intimacy and passion are correlated (Whitley, 1993), being good friends may help to keep your passion alive.

So, you should commit yourself only to a lover who is also a good friend. You can also purposefully and creatively strive to forestall any boredom that would undermine your contentment. Relationships become stagnant when they become repetitive and monotonous, and as we saw in chapter 6, boredom occurs not when bad things happen but when nothing interesting, exciting, or challenging occurs (Harasymchuk & Fehr, 2011). And because boredom is antithetical to love and satisfaction, it's very bad news (Tsapelas et al., 2009). When novelty is lost, create some more. Don't stop seeking out new and engaging ways to have fun together.

So, there's your game plan. Enjoy passion, but don't make it the foundation of the relationships that you hope will last. Nurture friendship with your lover. Try to stay fresh; grab every opportunity to enjoy novel adventures with your spouse (Strong & Aron, 2006). And don't be surprised or disappointed if your urgent desires gradually resolve into placid but deep affection for your beloved. That happy result is likely to make you a lucky lover.

FOR YOUR CONSIDERATION

Before David and Catherine met, neither of them had been in love, so they were both excited when their dating relationship gradually developed into a more intimate love affair. Each was the other's first lover, and they found sex to be both awkward and thrilling, and, within a few weeks, flushed with more romantic feelings than either of them had known, they decided to marry. But David soon became annoyed by Catherine's apparent desire to know everything about his day. She would call him every morning and afternoon when he was at work, just to "be in touch," and she would start to fret if he met clients over lunch or was out of the office running errands. For her part, Catherine was troubled by David's apparent reluctance to tell her what was on his mind. He prided himself on his self-sufficiency and didn't feel that it was necessary to tell her everything, and he began to feel crowded by her insistent probing.

What do you think the future holds for David and Catherine? Why?

CHAPTER SUMMARY

A Brief History of Love

Different societies have held very different perspectives on love, and only recently has love been associated with marriage.

Types of Love

The Triangular Theory of Love. *Intimacy, passion,* and *commitment* are thought to combine to produce eight different types of love.

Romantic, Passionate Love. Intimacy and passion, which increases when a person becomes aroused for any reason, combine to form romantic love. It is characterized by idealized evaluations of one's partner.

Companionate Love. Intimacy and commitment combine to form companionate love, a deep friendship with someone with whom one's life is intertwined. Happy spouses usually say that they are good friends.

Compassionate Love. Intimacy combines with selfless caring for the beloved to form compassionate love.

Styles of Loving. Six themes in love experiences that are differentially correlated with the various types of love have also been identified.

Individual and Cultural Differences in Love

Culture. Love is much the same around the world, but cultural nuances exist.

Attachment Styles. Secure people enjoy stronger experiences of romantic, companionate, and compassionate love than insecure people do.

Age. People mellow with age, experiencing less intense love as time goes by.

Men and Women. Men and women are more similar than different when it comes to love. However, women pick their lovers more carefully and fall in love less quickly than men do.

Does Love Last?

In general, romantic love decreases after people marry, sometimes quite rapidly.

Why Doesn't Romantic Love Last? Romance and passion involve *fantasy, novelty,* and *arousal,* and each fades with time.

So, What Does the Future Hold? Companionate love is very satisfying and is more stable than romantic love is. If lovers are good friends and work to battle boredom, they may improve their chances for a long, contented relationship.

CHAPTER 9

Sexuality

SEXUAL ATTITUDES ◆ Attitudes about Casual Sex ◆ Attitudes about Same-Sex Sexuality ◆ Cultural Differences in Sexual Attitudes ◆ SEXUAL BEHAVIOR ◆ Sex for the First Time ◆ Sex in Committed Relationships ◆ Infidelity ◆ Sexual Desire ◆ Safe, Sensible Sex ◆ SEXUAL SATISFACTION ◆ Sexual Communication ◆ Sexual Satisfaction and Relationship Satisfaction ◆ SEXUAL COERCION ◆ FOR YOUR CONSIDERATION ◆ CHAPTER SUMMARY

I have two questions for you. First, if a mischievous genie offered you a lifetime supply of compelling orgasms but required that you experience them alone and never again have sex with another person, would you accept the offer? Second, if you discovered on your honeymoon that your new spouse had been secretly taking a drug like Viagra to enhance his or her sexual response to you, would you be hurt?

Different people will undoubtedly answer these questions in different ways. Those who have not had sex with an intimate romantic partner for a long time may find compelling orgasms, even solitary ones, an attractive option. But I suspect that most people would be reluctant to give up a potential future of physical connections with a lover or lovers. Most of us would be disappointed were we no longer able to share sex with someone we love. And we want our lovers to find *us* compelling and to want us in return. So, it may be hurtful to learn that a partner's apparent desire for us is the result, at least in part, of some drug (Morgentaler, 2003).

As these questions may imply, there's a lot more to human sexuality than great orgasms. For some people, at least, sex need not always involve romantic intimacy, but for most people romantic intimacy involves sex. Our close romantic relationships often have a sexual component, and our sexual behavior and sexual satisfaction are often dependent on the nature, and health, of those relationships. As we'll see in this chapter, there's a close connection between sexuality and intimate relationships.

SEXUAL ATTITUDES

Attitudes about Casual Sex

Times have changed, and you're probably more accepting of premarital sexual intercourse[1] than your grandparents were. Forty years ago, most people disapproved of sex "before marriage," but these days, fewer than 25 percent of us think that premarital sex is "always or almost always wrong" (Wells & Twenge, 2005). The circumstances matter. Most of us still generally disapprove of sexual intercourse between people who aren't committed to each other (Willetts et al., 2004), so we hold a *permissiveness with affection standard* (Sprecher et al., 2006): We believe that sex between unmarried partners is acceptable as long as it occurs in the context of a committed, caring relationship. People are no longer expected to "save themselves for marriage" as our grandmothers were supposed to, but attachment and affection are still prerequisites for desirable sexual activity.

Do men and women differ in their sexual opinions? On average, they do: Men hold more permissive sexual values and attitudes, although the difference is shrinking over time, and how big it is depends on the particular attitude being measured (Petersen & Hyde, 2010). One of the larger sex differences is in attitudes toward casual premarital sex; men are more likely than women to think that sex without love is okay. This difference undoubtedly influences the things that men and women *regret* about their past sexual behavior: Whereas women are more likely than men to regret things they've done (such as having a one-night stand), men are more likely than women to regret things they *didn't* do (such as not having sex when someone was pursuing them). When it comes to casual sex, women tend to regret their actions, but men regret their *in*actions (Galperin et al., 2011).

A person's sex may be involved in other sexual attitudes, as well. Traditionally, women have been judged more harshly than men for being sexually experienced or permissive. Whereas men who have multiple sexual partners may be admired as "studs," women with the same number of partners may be dismissed as "sluts." This asymmetry is known as the *sexual double standard,* and years ago it was quite obvious, but it appears to be more subtle today (Crawford & Popp, 2003). These days, a woman who invites someone to have casual sex is evaluated *more* favorably by others than is a man who does the same thing; she is presumed to be warmer, less dangerous, and better in bed than he is (Conley, 2011). Moreover, men and women who are promiscuous are judged in the same way by others; both tend to be evaluated negatively (Marks & Fraley, 2005). However, a woman with a sexually transmitted infection is judged more harshly than a man is (G. Smith et al., 2008), and a woman who participates in a threesome is liked less than a man is (Jonason & Marks, 2009).[2]

---

[1] Not all people will marry, of course. But "premarital" is a more familiar, more convenient term than "unmarried" is.

[2] And no, it didn't matter if the three participants were two women and one man or two men and one woman; female participants were judged more negatively in both cases.

So, a strong sexual double standard no longer seems to exist, but a person's sex can still influence people's evaluations of his or her sexual experiences.

Attitudes about Same-Sex Sexuality

So far our discussion has focused on attitudes toward heterosexual sex. Attitudes about same-sex sexuality are decidedly more negative, with a large minority (43 percent) of adult Americans feeling that sexual relations between adults of the same sex are "morally wrong" (Saad, 2010). Same-sex sexuality engenders a lot of disregard. But the big news is that most Americans do *not* hold that view; they are clearly becoming more tolerant of same-sex couples as time goes by, and in 2010, for the first time ever, a majority of Americans (52 percent) considered gay and lesbian relations to be "morally acceptable" (Saad, 2010).

Interestingly, judgments of same-sex relationships have much to do with people's beliefs about *why* someone is gay or lesbian, as Figure 9.1 shows. By a very large margin, people consider homosexuality to be an acceptable lifestyle when they believe that sexual orientation results from biological influences that occur before we are born. On the other hand, by a substantial margin, people find homosexuality unacceptable if they believe that it is learned or chosen as a result of one's upbringing. Thus, it's important that for the last 30

FIGURE 9.1. **Tolerance of same-sex sexuality depends on one's beliefs about its origins.** Here are the results of a Gallup Poll conducted in the United States in May 2007. People were much more likely to be tolerant of same-sex sexuality—considering it to be an "acceptable alternative lifestyle"—if they believed that sexual orientation was something that people are born with. On the other hand, if they believed that people *choose* to be gay or lesbian as a result of their upbringing, they were intolerant of such behavior. *Source: Saad, 2007.*

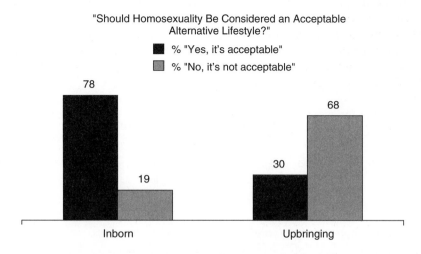

Respondents' Beliefs about the Origins of Sexual Orientation

years, the number of people who believe that one's sexuality is already set at birth has been gradually increasing, and the number of those who believe that people are taught to be gay or lesbian has declined (Saad, 2010). More people now believe that a same-sex orientation is born rather than made (and, for the record, they appear to be correct: Same-sex sexual behavior is clearly based, in part, in one's genes [Långström et al., 2010], and sizable majorities of gays and lesbians feel that they've had no choice whatsoever about their sexual orientations [Herek et al., 2010]. For more on this provocative issue, see the box on the next page).

A similar pattern underlies attitudes regarding the contentious topic of "gay marriage." A majority of Americans (53 percent) oppose formal marriages for same-sex couples (Jones, 2010), but their numbers are falling, and support for legal recognition of same-sex relationships is rising. In particular, a sizable majority of Americans now believe that same-sex couples should be allowed to enter into legally recognized civil unions (see Table 9.1). Social scientists are also going public with the conclusion that there is no empirical justification for denying gays and lesbians access to the legal benefits (involving, for instance, taxation, health insurance, pensions, and property rights) that heterosexual spouses enjoy (Myers & Scanzoni, 2005). Indeed, the American Psychological Association has resolved that because (a) same-sex relationships operate in much the same manner as heterosexual partnerships (Balsam et al., 2008), (b) sexual orientation has nothing to do with a person's ability to be a loving, nurturing parent (Biblarz & Stacey, 2010), and (c) marriage is good for people, including gays and lesbians (Riggle et al., 2010), it is ill-informed, unfair, and discriminatory to deny gays and lesbians legal recognition of their relationships. (The formal resolution stating the psychologists'

TABLE 9.1 Americans Now Approve of Civil Unions for Same-Sex Couples
Here are the results of four polls conducted jointly by the *Washington Post* and ABC News in recent years. Each of them surveyed a representative national sample of American adults. As you can see, not long ago, Americans were not in favor of formal, legal unions for same-sex couples—but they are now.

"Do you think gay and lesbian couples should or should not be allowed to form legally recognized civil unions, giving them the legal rights of married couples in areas such as health insurance, inheritance, and pension coverage?"

Date of Poll	"Should Be Allowed"	"Should **Not** Be Allowed"	No Opinion
September 7, 2003	40%	51%	9%
February 22, 2004	45%	48%	7%
November 1, 2007	55%	42%	3%
February 8, 2010	**66%**	**31%**	4%

Note: The margin of possible sampling error in each poll was ±3 percentage points.
Source: www.washingtonpost.com/wp-srv/politics/polls/postpoll_021010.html. Accessed August 20, 2011.

Can Same-Sex Sexuality Have Evolutionary Origins?

Sexual orientation has a genetic basis (Långström et al., 2010), but gays and lesbians tend not to have many children of their own. So, how does the evolutionary principle of sexual selection work to maintain a small but consistent proportion of gays and lesbians in a predominantly heterosexual population? There are several possibilities, and here are two, emerging from studies of gay men. First, gay men make great uncles; they devote themselves to their nieces and nephews more than other men do, and thereby help their siblings reproduce more successfully (Vasey & VanderLaan, 2010). Second, compared to other women, the sisters of gay men are more fecund—that is, more fertile—and they have more babies (Iemmola & Ciani, 2009). Thus, throughout history, gay men seldom may have fathered their own offspring, but their *sisters* had more children who received better care and protection, on average, than other children did. In difficult environments, it might have been even advantageous, on the whole, for same-sex orientations to run in one's family. It *is* possible, then, for same-sex sexuality to have evolutionary origins. The next time you hear sexual bigots claim that being gay or lesbian *can't* be natural because they don't have children, feel free to show them this box.

position is intriguing reading [and only four pages long]; it's available at http://www.apa.org/about/governance/council/policy/gay-marriage.pdf.)

So, attitudes about same-sex sexuality are changing, and they will probably slowly continue to become more positive. Gays and lesbians are more visible in public life than ever before—just check out the very popular TV shows, *Glee* and *Modern Family*—and the more contact people have with gays and lesbians, the more favorable their feelings toward them tend to be (Smith et al., 2009).

Cultural Differences in Sexual Attitudes

In general, then, sexual attitudes have become more permissive over time. And if you're an American witnessing these changes, you may be tempted to think of the United States as being more permissive than most countries. But you'd be wrong. In fact, the sexual attitudes of Americans look surprisingly conservative when compared to the opinions expressed by people in many other countries. Denmark has been registering gay and lesbian relationships as civil unions since 1989, Norway has been doing so since 1993, and Sweden since 1995 (Eskridge & Spedale, 2006), and full-fledged marriages became available to gays and lesbians in Argentina and Mexico City in 2010 (Warren, 2010). So, the United States certainly isn't leading the pack on that issue. Indeed, a large cross-cultural survey found that the United States held more conservative beliefs about premarital sex, extramarital sex, and same-sex relations than did

Australia, Germany, Great Britain, Israel, Russia, Spain, and Sweden (Widmer et al., 1998). Canada was more permissive than the United States, too, so countries that are close neighbors do not necessarily share the same sexual attitudes. Things may be changing, but Americans still hold relatively conservative sexual attitudes.

Within the United States, African Americans hold more permissive sexual attitudes than whites do, with Hispanic Americans and Asian Americans being more conservative, in that order (Fugère et al., 2008). However, African Americans hold more negative attitudes toward gays and lesbians than whites do (Vincent et al., 2009), and Republicans, religious fundamentalists, and older folks are more opposed to same-sex marriage than Democrats, nonreligious people, and young Americans are (Sherkat et al., 2011). Sexual attitudes are evidently shaped by a variety of historical, religious, political, and other societal influences: They clearly differ from country to country and from group to group.

SEXUAL BEHAVIOR

It's one thing to ask what people are thinking and another to find out what they're actually doing. Studies of sexual behavior are intriguing because they provide a context for our own actions. Do remember, however, as you read this next section, that broad descriptions of sexual behavior mask enormous variability in people's experiences. And behavior that is common is not necessarily healthier or more desirable than behavior that is less typical. We'll find that what is perhaps most important about sexual behavior in relationships is that it is desired by and satisfying for both partners.

Sex for the First Time

These days, almost all—95 percent—of us have intercourse before we get married (Finer, 2007). As you probably recall, typical Americans don't marry until their mid-to-late 20s, but the average age of first intercourse—the age at which half of us have had sex and half have not—is now 17 for both men and women. By the age of 20, rather few of us (only 15 percent) have not yet had sex (National Center for Health Statistics, 2007).

These are very different patterns than those your grandparents experienced—people in their generation usually waited 2 to 3 years longer to begin having sex (Wells & Twenge, 2005)—and there is both good news and bad news in the way we do things now. On the one hand, American teens are being more responsible than they used to be. Most adolescents use some form of birth control when they first have intercourse, and the teen birth rate is much lower now than it was 15 years ago (Hendrick, 2011). On the other hand, American teens are not being careful enough: More than one of every four female teenagers in the United States has a sexually transmitted infection! Most often, it's the human papillomavirus (HPV), the virus that causes genital warts, which is found in 18 percent of young women (Tanner, 2008).

Ignorance Isn't Bliss

Sex among unmarried teens is commonplace, and sexually transmitted infections are prevalent. In response to these patterns, there are now over 800 different programs being staged throughout the United States that seek to dissuade American teens from having sex (Kantor et al., 2008). These programs take various forms, but many of them provide no information whatsoever about how to prevent pregnancy and how to have safe sex. (Even worse, some of them teach *mis*information—such as "condoms don't work, and you'll get HIV if you have sex"—that has been repudiated by medical science [Lin & Santelli, 2008].) It's typical for U.S. sex education programs to promote abstinence by encouraging teens to make public promises to remain virgins. Such efforts may be well intended, but they don't work very well. Only one year after they make a virginity pledge, most teens (53 percent) deny having made one (Rosenbaum, 2006), and five years later, 82 percent claim that they never said any such thing (Rosenbaum, 2009). Worse, on average, graduates of abstinence programs are *not* less likely to have sex, but they *are* less likely to use contraception; most programs that preach abstinence do not get teens to delay having sex or to have fewer partners; they just discourage their pupils from having responsible, safe sex (Kirby, 2008; Rosenbaum, 2009).[3] Moreover, a fundamental rationale for abstinence education is factually incorrect: Sex that occurs in a steady relationship, which is the kind of sex most teens have, is *not* associated with adverse psychological

outcomes for teenagers, either when they begin having sex (Higgins et al., 2010) or over time (Else-Quest et al., 2005).

Thus, there are two points I'd like to make. First, knowledge is power. The better and more accurately informed teens are, the more sexually responsible and conscientious they tend to be (Kirby, 2008). The American teen birth rate is at an all-time low not because teens are remaining abstinent but because they are using condoms more than ever before when they do have sex (Hendrick, 2011). Education is beneficial; misinformation and ignorance are not.

Second, here's another example of the ethical imperative that underlies relationship science: When dispassionate, careful study of human partnerships can provide reliable knowledge that improves our chances for health and happiness, we *should* do those studies, even when they take us into sensitive territory. Some people still think that ignorance is bliss when it comes to human sexuality, but that's a point of view with which relationship scientists firmly disagree.

[3]Programs vary. An innovative program in Philadelphia that featured abstinence was able to get some kids to delay having sex for the first time by encouraging them to develop personal lists of goals and dreams that might be affected by having sex (Jemmott, 2010). Importantly, however, the program didn't preach abstinence or employ scare tactics like many others do, so it wasn't a typical abstinence program.

A sizable majority of teens have sex for the first time with someone who is a partner in a steady, emotionally important relationship, and they come to have intercourse following a gradual trajectory of increasingly intimate behavior in which kissing leads to petting, and intercourse ultimately follows (de Graaf et al., 2009). Relatively few people (21 percent) are merely acquaintances or casual friends of their first sexual partners (National Center for Health Statistics, 2004). Nevertheless, young women typically have mixed feelings when they first have sexual intercourse. Most of them are ambivalent about having sex, some are opposed, and only a third of them really want it to happen. Young men usually have a different view: Only a third of them are ambivalent, and most of them are eager for it to occur (National Center for Health Statistics, 2004).

Once a couple has sex, the context affects the consequences. When it follows explicit expressions of love and commitment from one's partner, first-time sex is usually experienced as a positive development that increases feelings of closeness (Higgins et al., 2010). When it occurs without such expressions, however, sex typically turns out to be an unwelcome development that results in uncertainty and regret (Metts, 2004). The relative power of the partners seems to matter because both sexes tend to experience more regret when their first intercourse is with someone several years older than they; sex occurs sooner and condoms are less likely to be used in such couples than among partners of similar ages (Mercer et al., 2006). Otherwise, men and women do not differ much in the specific things that cause them to regret a sexual experience—both sexes have pangs of remorse when they behave in a manner that is inconsistent with their morals, have drunken sex, or fail to use condoms (Oswalt et al., 2005).

Sex in Committed Relationships

So what motives lead people to choose to have sex? There are literally hundreds of different reasons. When students at the University of Texas at Austin were asked to "list all the reasons you can think of why you, or someone you have known, has engaged in sexual intercourse in the past," 237 distinct reasons were identified (Meston & Buss, 2007, p. 479). The most common reasons involved positive states: "attraction, pleasure, affection, love, romance, emotional closeness, arousal, the desire to please, adventure, excitement, experience, connection, celebration, curiosity, and opportunity" (Meston & Buss, p. 498). The infrequent reasons were more calculating and callous, involving the desires to do harm ("I was mad at my partner, so I had sex with someone else"), to gain some advantage ("I wanted to get a raise"), or to enhance one's social status ("I wanted to impress my friends"). Sexual motives evidently ranged from altruistic to vengeful and from intimate to impersonal.

Four themes seemed to underlie the sprawling list of specific reasons. One of them involved the *emotional* component of sex as a communication of love and commitment. Another involved the *physical* aspects of sex; it included both the physical pleasure to be gained from sex, and the physical attractiveness of a potential partner. Other reasons were more *pragmatic,* involving the wish to attain some goal or accomplish some objective that could range from making a baby to making someone jealous. Still other reasons were based in *insecurity,* involving the desire to boost one's self-esteem or to keep a partner from straying. Men and women endorsed emotional reasons with equal frequency, but men were more likely than women to have had sex for physical, pragmatic, and insecure reasons (Meston & Buss, 2007). These differences were often slight, but men nevertheless reported more varied, and more practical, reasons for having sex than women did. And clearly, although sex is often a loving act, it sometimes has no romantic aim.

The frequency with which people have sex is influenced by the nature—and duration—of their relationships. Young couples who are cohabiting have sex about three times per week, on average, whereas those who are married have sex about two times per week (Willetts et al., 2004). Couples in both kinds of relationships, however, have sex more often than those who are single (Smith, 2006), probably because singles are less likely to have consistent access to a sexual partner. Married people may sometimes envy the swinging life of singles, but they usually get more sex than singles do.

Another important factor associated with sexual frequency is a person's age. Look back at Figure 8.3 on page 270: Older people generally have sex much less frequently than younger people do. In 2009, most American men and women in their late twenties (86 percent) reported that they had had intercourse with someone in the past year. However, only about half of men (58 percent) and women (51 percent) in their fifties had done so, and a minority of men (43 percent) and women (22 percent) who were 70 or older had had vaginal sex (Herbenick et al., 2010b). Most elderly Americans have not had intercourse with anyone in the last 12 months. It's likely that physical changes associated with aging are influential in this regard (Call et al., 1995): Decreased hormone levels may reduce one's desire, and declines in physical health may erode one's vigor, so we shouldn't be surprised that sexual desire wanes somewhat over the years. In couples who have been together for a long time, however, there is another, more subtle possibility: The passion partners feel for one another may simmer down over the long haul as each becomes a familiar and routine sexual partner and the thrill of discovery and novelty is lost (Vohs & Baumeister, 2004). As I noted in chapter 8, this may be one reason that romantic love becomes less intense as relationships age, and the size of this effect (see Figure 8.3) leads me to offer this caution: If you're a young adult who's staying in a relationship (at least in part) because of great, hot sex, it's simply silly to expect that your passion, desire, and need for that partner will never change. Of course it will.

A final factor associated with sexual frequency is sexual orientation. When their relationships are young, gay men have more sex with their partners than lesbians or heterosexuals do. (See Figure 9.2, and keep this pattern in mind when I discuss sexual desire a few pages from now.) After 10 years together, everybody has sex less often, but the drop in frequency is greater for gays, and they end up having sex less frequently than heterosexual couples do. On the other hand, regardless of the duration of the relationship, lesbians

FIGURE 9.2. **Differences in sexual frequency by type and length of relationship.**
The figure displays the proportion of couples in each type of relationship who reported
having sex at least once a week. (There is no value provided for cohabiting relationships that lasted for more than 10 years because there were not enough couples in this
category to provide a reliable estimate.)
Source: Blumstein & Schwartz, 1983.

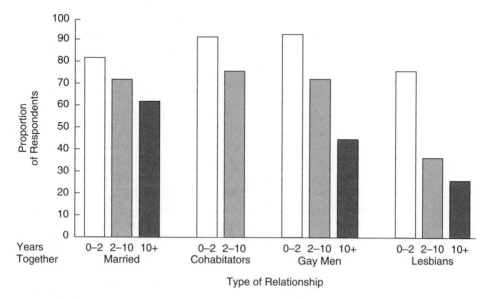

have sex less often than any other relationship group. When it's just up to
them, women have sex much less frequently than they do when there is a man
involved.

Infidelity

Most people around the world strongly disapprove of someone who is in a
committed relationship engaging in **extradyadic sex** (that is, having sex outside
the dyad, or couple, with someone other than one's partner) (Widmer et al.,
1998).[4] Thus, we might expect that sexual infidelity would be relatively rare.
But is it? A compilation of 47 different investigations involving more than
58,000 participants, most of them in the United States and most of them married, found that 21 percent of the women and 32 percent of the men had been
sexually unfaithful to their romantic partners at least once. Most husbands and
wives never have sex with other people after they marry, but about one out of
every five wives and one out of three husbands do (Tafoya & Spitzberg, 2007).

---

[4]The "sex" I'll be referring to in this section will be vaginal intercourse. Extradyadic behavior takes
a variety of forms ranging from erotic texting and cybersex to kissing, heavy petting, oral sex, and
intercourse (Luo et al., 2010), but people differ in their definitions of which of these are "cheating"
(Kruger et al., 2010). So that we'll all be on the same page, I'll focus on behavior that almost everybody considers to be unfaithful.

Men Report More Sexual Partners than Women Do. How?

The best, most comprehensive surveys of sex in the United States paint somewhat different pictures of the sexual behavior of men and women. In particular, the National Center for Health Statistics (2007) found that the average middle-aged American man has had seven sexual partners during his lifetime whereas the average woman has had only four. Men also report having sex more often than women do. Why don't these figures agree? One would think that each time a man has sex with a new partner, that partner does, too. So, why is this sex difference routinely found?

There are several possible reasons, and one is procedural. Despite their careful sampling techniques, surveys usually fail to include representative numbers of those particular women— prostitutes—who have sex with many men (if for no other reason than that they're not home at night when the surveys are usually conducted). When researchers make special efforts to include prostitutes in their samples, the average numbers of partners reported by men and women are more similar (Brewer et al., 2000).

Men and women also tend to define "sex" differently. If a heterosexual couple engages only in oral sex, for instance, he is more likely to say that they've had "sex" than she is (Gute et al., 2008). The sexes agree completely that vaginal intercourse is "sex," but men are more likely than women to count as "sex partners" lovers with whom intercourse did not occur.

However, the most important source of the discrepancy may be the tendency for men to exaggerate, and for women to minimize, the number of partners they've had. Men tend to *estimate* their number of partners, and they tend to give generous estimates, so that men who have had many partners almost always answer researchers' inquiries with round numbers, such as "30"; they almost never provide seemingly exact counts such as 26 or 27 (Brown & Sinclair, 1999). In contrast, women seem to count their partners more accurately and then subtract a partner or two from their announced totals (Wiederman, 2004). Self-reports like these are thus prone to biases that result both from impression management (Fisher, 2009) and reconstructive memory (Gillmore et al., 2010), topics we covered back in chapter 4, and they speak to some of the difficulties researchers face in studying intimate behavior.

One more point: When college students are asked how many sex partners they would like to have during the next year, the typical response from a majority of women is "one," and most men say "two" (Fenigstein & Preston, 2007). Only tiny minorities hope to have many partners. So, there is a sex difference of note here— men want to have more partners than women do—but very few people want to be promiscuous.

As you can see, men are more likely to cheat on their partners than women are. They hold more positive attitudes toward casual sex, and they often pursue extradyadic sex for the sake of sexual variety (whereas women are more likely to seek an emotional connection) (Blow & Hartnett, 2005). Indeed, these sex differences are particularly pronounced in the same-sex relationships of gay and lesbian couples, where male and female fidelity operate free of the influence of the other sex. Gay men have a lot more extradyadic sex than both lesbian women and heterosexual men do (Peplau et al., 2004).

Figure 9.3 depicts the results of a large survey of Americans back in the early 1980s that obtained data on spouses, cohabiting couples, and gay and lesbian couples (Blumstein & Schwartz, 1983), and it's obvious that gay men were more likely than anyone else to have had sex outside their primary relationships. In many cases, the gay men had such sex with the permission of their partners, who wanted the same freedom (Hoff & Beougher, 2010), and some observers have speculated that many heterosexual men would also behave this way if their female lovers would let them get away with it (Peplau, 2003)!

Certainly, however, not all men are promiscuous and not all women are chaste, and there is an influential individual difference that makes both men and women more likely to engage in extradyadic sex. For some of us, sex is connected to love and commitment: It's not especially rewarding to have sex with people we don't know well or don't care much about, and we have casual sex with acquaintances or strangers rarely, if at all. For others of us, however, sex has little to do with love and commitment; we think that "sex without love is OK," and we're content to have sex with people for whom we have no particular feelings. These different approaches to sex emerge from our **sociosexual orientations,** the traitlike collections of beliefs and behaviors that describe our feelings about sex (Simpson et al., 2004). Individual differences in *sociosexuality* were discovered by Jeff Simpson and Steve Gangestad (1991), who used the measure in the box on the next page to measure respondents' sociosexual

FIGURE 9.3. **Percentages of individuals reporting any instance(s) of extradyadic sex since the beginning of their relationships.**
Gay men clearly have more extradyadic sex than anyone else, but they may not be "cheating" on their partners. Note, too, that men and women who are cohabiting are more likely to have sex with other people than husbands and wives are. Marriage involves more thoroughgoing commitment than cohabiting does.
Source: Blumstein & Schwartz, 1983.

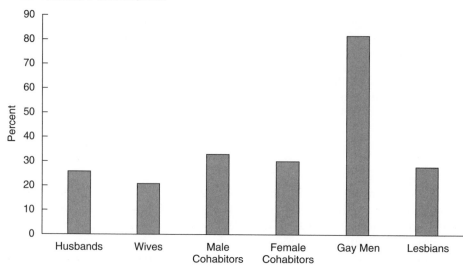

Measuring Sociosexuality

Sociosexuality describes the degree to which a person is comfortable having sex in the absence of any love or commitment. Jeff Simpson and Steve Gangestad (1991) developed this brief measure, the Sociosexual Orientation Inventory, to assess sociosexuality. Respondents are asked to answer these questions as honestly as possible:

1. With how many different partners have you had sex (sexual intercourse) within the past year?

    _____

2. How many different partners do you foresee yourself having sex with during the next five years? (Please give a *specific, realistic* estimate).

    _____

3. With how many different partners have you had sex on *one and only one* occasion? _____

4. How often do you fantasize about having sex with someone other than your current dating partner? (Circle one).

    1. never
    2. once every 2 or 3 months
    3. once a month
    4. once every 2 weeks
    5. once a week
    6. a few times each week
    7. nearly every day
    8. at least once a day

5. Sex without love is OK.

1	2	3	4	5	6	7	8	9

    I strongly   I strongly
    disagree   agree

6. I can imagine myself being comfortable and enjoying "casual" sex with different partners.

1	2	3	4	5	6	7	8	9

    I strongly   I strongly
    disagree   agree

7. I would have to be closely attached to someone (both emotionally and psychologically) before I could feel comfortable and fully enjoy having sex with him or her.

1	2	3	4	5	6	7	8	9

    I strongly   I strongly
    disagree   agree

Responses to the last item (# 7) are reverse scored, and a total score is computed by weighing the scores of some items more heavily than others. In general, higher numbers on each question (and for the total score) reflect an *unrestricted* sexual orientation, and lower numbers reflect a *restricted* orientation. Compared to those with a lower score, people with an unrestricted orientation "typically engage in sex earlier in their romantic relationships, are more likely to engage in sex with more than one partner at a time, and tend to be involved in sexual relationships characterized by less expressed investment, less commitment, and weaker affectional ties" (Simpson & Gangestad, 1991, p. 879). Sociosexuality is a good example of how characteristics of individuals have a powerful impact on the nature of sexual interactions.

orientations. People who were generally willing to have sex only in the context of a committed and affectionate relationship were said to have a "restricted" sociosexual orientation, whereas those who did not seek much closeness or commitment before pursuing sex were said to have "unrestricted" sociosexuality. As it turns out, people with unrestricted orientations tend to be dynamic, flirtatious people who are always on the prowl for new partners (Simpson et al., 2004). They're sociable and extraverted, and they drink a lot of alcohol (Clark, 2004). And around the world, men are more unrestricted on average than women are (Schmitt, 2005b).

It probably won't surprise you, then, to learn that sociosexuality is associated with the likelihood that people will have extradyadic sex. Over their lifetimes, compared to those with more restricted orientations, unrestricted people have more sexual partners and are more likely to cheat on their primary lovers (Ostovich & Sabini, 2004). David Seal and his colleagues (1994) shed light on this pattern in a clever study of heterosexual college students who were currently in dating relationships but who were asked to evaluate a computer dating video of an attractive member of the other sex. After viewing the tape, participants were told they could enter a drawing to win a free date with the person in the video, and they were invited to indicate how willing they would be—if they went on the date and had a good time—to engage in a series of physically intimate behaviors with the date. The researchers found that 36 percent of those who were unrestricted in their sociosexuality entered the drawing for the date whereas only 4 percent of those who were restricted did. (Remember, all the participants were currently involved in existing relationships!) Unrestricted individuals were also more interested in having sex with their new dates than restricted individuals were. Sociosexuality is clearly a meaningful characteristic that distinguishes those who are likely to cheat from those who are not.

It's intriguing, then, that when their faces are presented side-by-side, observers can generally distinguish people with unrestricted orientations (who tend to be on the prowl) from those with restricted orientations (who are more likely to be faithful) (Boothroyd et al., 2011). Unrestricted women tend to have facial features that are somewhat more masculine than those of other women—and remarkably, although their faces are more attractive, men consider them to be less desirable as long-term mates. They're lovely, but they seem less trustworthy than other women do (Campbell et al., 2009). Unrestricted men look more masculine, too, but women prefer the faces of restricted men for long-term mates (Boothroyd et al., 2008); they seem to sense that unrestricted men would make riskier husbands.

An evolutionary perspective has an interesting spin on all this. With their lower parental investment,[5] men can afford to engage in relatively casual sex, and, arguably, sexual selection[6] has historically favored men who mated with as many women as possible. But why would evolution encourage a woman to cheat? Given the potentially violent costs she might incur if her actions are discovered (Kaighobadi et al., 2008), what reproductive advantage would there be? One provocative answer is that she'd not be able to produce more children by having extradyadic sex, but she might be able to have *better* (that is,

---

[5]This key concept was introduced way back in chapter 1 on p. 33.
[6]Ditto. Chapter 1, p. 32.

healthier and more attractive) children. A **good genes hypothesis** suggests that some women—in particular, those with less desirable mates—can profit from a *dual mating* strategy in which they (a) pursue long-term partners who will contribute resources to protect and feed their offspring while (b) surreptitiously seeking good genes for their children from other men (Pillsworth & Haselton, 2006). By obtaining commitment and security from one man and having taller, stronger, healthier children with another, women could bear offspring who were especially likely to survive and thrive.

Some modern patterns of behavior are consistent with the good genes hypothesis. First, as we noted in chapter 3, women find sexy, symmetrical men—those who display visible markers of masculine fitness—to be especially compelling each month when they are fertile and can conceive a child (Thornhill & Gangestad, 2008). Second, children have more robust immune systems when their parents each give them different sets of genes of the type that regulate immune responses—and women whose partners have *similar* genes are more likely than those whose partners have *different* genes to have sex with other men, particularly when they're fertile (Garver-Apgar et al., 2006). If women were pursuing extradyadic sex simply for the sake of variety, it would be foolhardy to entertain other lovers during the few days they're fertile each month, but that's exactly what they do; women are more attracted to extradyadic mates when they're fertile than when they're not, and this tendency is more pronounced when their primary partners are relatively unattractive (Haselton & Larson, 2011).

If our ancient female ancestors behaved this way, they often would have had children who were healthier and more attractive than those who would have been fathered by the women's usual mates (and thus, their extradyadic sex would have offered some advantages). Does this sort of thing happen today? It does. A meta-analysis of 67 studies of paternity found that 2 percent of the world's children, on average, are being raised by men who don't know that someone else is the child's biological father (Anderson, 2006). Moreover, in the United States., about 1 out of every 400 pairs of fraternal twins involves simultaneous siblings who were fathered by two different men (Blickstein, 2005).

These results suggest that, historically, men have occasionally encountered situations involving **sperm competition,** which occurs when the sperm of two or more men occupy a woman's vagina at the same time (Shackelford & Goetz, 2007). Some researchers contend that in response to such situations, evolution has equipped men with a penis that is ideally shaped to scoop any semen from other men away from their partner's cervix (Gallup & Burch, 2006). Common sense might expect that a second lover would only push an earlier lover's ejaculate through the cervix and into the woman's uterus, but that's not what happens: Deep thrusts force any sperm that is already present behind the head of the penis, which then pulls the sperm out of the woman. Indeed, consistent with this notion, men with partners who put them at risk of sperm competition tend to have intercourse in a manner—involving a higher number of unusually deep thrusts over a longer period of time—that is particularly likely to displace any sperm that might be present (Goetz et al., 2005).

The Ins and Outs of Cybersex

There's a lot of real and imagined sexual activity taking place online these days. The Web offers a unique mix of characteristics that allow us to have rather personal contact with others cheaply and easily: *accessibility* to large numbers of people, *affordability* that makes a cyberdate inexpensive, and *anonymity* that lowers inhibitions and prevents our partners from following us home (Subotnik, 2007). The interactions that result often take place in "a sexual space midway between fantasy and action" (Ross, 2005, p. 342); they may fulfill our fantasies when we're only sitting at home typing, and they can feel very intimate even when we have very little, if any, factual information about our partners.

Is cybersex innocuous? Sex takes three broad forms online, and they have different implications for face-to-face relationships (Henline et al., 2007). First, people pursue porn. Most of us would not consider a partner's consumption of pornography to be a major transgression; only 11 percent of us would find it "unfaithful." But most porn portrays women in a demeaning manner—as horny sluts who are always ready to serve and please men—and there's a lot of gagging, slapping, and name-calling in porn (Bridges et al., 2010), so it may teach lessons that can have an adverse effect on close relationships. In particular, teens who consume a lot of porn tend to endorse casual, recreational attitudes toward sex and to think of women as sex objects, that is, devices to be used for men's pleasure (Brown & L'Engle, 2009; Peter & Valkenburg, 2007). And people who watch porn alone tend to be less interested in having actual sex with their partners (Albright, 2008) and less satisfied with their relationships overall (Maddox et al., 2011) than are people who watch porn *with* their partners—or not at all.

Visits to porn sites usually don't involve interactions with others online, but other forms of online sex do. Sometimes it's just sexy flirting and talking dirty, but an interaction becomes **cybersex** when it involves sexual chat for the purpose of sexual gratification (Daneback et al., 2005) with, as one example, the participants sharing explicit descriptions of sexual activities while they each masturbate. Cybersex is often shared anonymously by strangers who never meet (and who may not be who they say they are), but many of us, 45 percent, would find it to be a serious type of infidelity (Henline et al., 2007). Nevertheless, men and women are equally likely to engage in cybersex, and they do so at similar rates whether or not they are in committed face-to-face relationships (Daneback et al., 2005).

Even more consequential, however, may be the last form of online sex, which involves emotional involvement with someone at the other end of an Internet connection. People can and do form intimate connections with others they have never actually met, and such liaisons seem unfaithful to 39 percent of us. But because these partnerships are usually much more personal than the typical episode of cybersex—often involving deep self-disclosure—they are often more problematic for existing face-to-face relationships. People who become emotionally involved online are more likely to arrange a way to meet offline, and then real extradyadic sex sometimes occurs (Henline et al., 2007). Online sex can be a playful flight of fancy or a serious search for a new partner, and we sometimes don't know which until some damage has been done to our current relationships.

Thus, an evolutionary perspective argues that extradyadic sex can have reproductive benefits for some women, and that in response to such challenges, men have adapted. An entirely different perspective on infidelity focuses on the current quality of a couple's relationship. In general, as you'd expect, people are more likely to cheat when they're dissatisfied with their present partners and the quality of their alternatives is high (Tsapelas et al., 2011). Unhappy lovers who have tempting alternatives available to them are less likely to remain faithful. If they do cheat in such situations, women are more likely than men to break up with their old partners and begin a new long-term relationship with the new mate (Brand et al., 2007); thus, women are more likely to switch mates as a result of an affair. However, even when they are reasonably content in general, both men and women are are more likely to pursue extradyadic sex when the sex they have with their current partners is boring, monotonous, and too infrequent for their tastes (Krishnamurti & Loewenstein, 2008). Women are especially likely to be unfaithful when they want more sex than their partners do (but this doesn't happen all that often, as the next section shows).

Sexual Desire

Men's higher sociosexuality scores and more frequent infidelity may be results, in part, of another, broader difference between the sexes. On average, men have higher **sex drives** than women do. They experience more frequent and more intense sexual desires and are routinely more motivated to engage in sexual activity than women are (Vohs et al., 2004). One study of young adults found that men experienced episodes of sexual desire 37 times per week whereas women experienced only 9 (Regan & Atkins, 2006). Because you're being a thoughtful consumer of relationship science, you should remember that there are sizable individual differences among men and among women, and there are certainly many men who are chronically less horny than many women are. Nevertheless, a wide array of facts demonstrates that on average, and around the world (Lippa, 2009), men have higher sex drives than women do:

- Men masturbate more often. Almost half of all men who have a regular sexual partner still masturbate more than once a week, whereas only 16 percent of women who are in sexual relationships masturbate as frequently (Klusmann, 2002). In England, it's likely that 73 percent of the men between the ages of 16 and 44 have masturbated in the past month, but only 37 percent of the women have (Gerressu et al., 2008).
- Men want sex more often than women do, and they are more likely than women to feel dissatisfied with the amount of sex they get (Sprecher, 2002).
- In developing relationships, men typically want to begin having sex sooner than women do (Sprecher et al., 1995). As a result, women are usually the "gatekeepers" who decide when sex begins in a new relationship. On average, when he first wants to have sex, he has to wait, but when she wants to have sex, they do.
- Men fantasize about sex more often than women do (Leitenberg & Henning, 1995). Men think about sex 60 times per week; it crosses women's minds 15 times (Regan & Atkins, 2006).

- Men spend more money on sex, buying more sex toys and porn (Laumann et al., 1994). In particular, men sometimes pay to obtain sex—in one study in Australia, 23 percent of men had paid for sex at least once—but women almost never do (Pitts et al., 2004).
- Finally, as we've already seen, men are more accepting of casual sex, on average, than women are (Ostovich & Sabini, 2004). They'd like to have sex with more people, too (McBurney et al., 2005).

Add up these patterns, and the sex difference in sex drive may be no small matter. To a greater or lesser degree, each of these patterns may lead to misunderstanding or annoyance as heterosexual couples negotiate their sexual interactions. Some husbands may be chronically frustrated by getting less sex than they want at the same time that their wives are irritated by their frequent insistence for more. (I'm reminded, in this regard, of a clever bit in the movie *Annie Hall*, which beat *Star Wars* to win the Academy Award for Best Picture for 1977: On a split screen, both members of a romantic couple are visiting their therapists, who have asked how often they have sex; he laments, "Hardly ever, maybe three times a week," as she complains, "Constantly, I'd say three times a week.") The typical sex difference in sex drive means that some couples will encounter mismatches in sexual desire, and difficulty may result (Schwartz & Young, 2009). And the mismatch may get only worse with time; most women experience a drop in desire after they go through menopause (Birnbaum et al., 2007), so perhaps it shouldn't surprise us that a study of German 60-year-olds didn't find *any* couple in which she wanted as much sex as he did (Klusmann, 2006).

There may be further consequences of men wanting more sex than women do. As the gatekeepers who decide when sex occurs, women may find men willing to offer various concessions in exchange for sex (Kruger, 2008b). Men's greater interest in sex may put the principle of lesser interest[7] in action: Women's control over access to something that they have and that men want may give them power with which to influence their men. In some relationships, sex may be "a valued good for which there is a marketplace in which women act as sellers and men as buyers" (Baumeister & Vohs, 2004, p. 359).

This sounds pretty tacky, but partners need not be consciously aware of this pattern for it to affect their interactions. Instead, without ever thinking about it, people may just take it for granted that a woman who, over a period of time, accepts a series of gifts from a man—such as expensive dates and other desirable entertainments—should feel some obligation to offer sex in return (or else she should stop accepting the gifts). Advice columnists acknowledge this: "Women do not owe sexual favors for a free dinner, but when men bear the entire cost of dating, they believe the woman is interested in a romantic, eventually intimate relationship. They otherwise feel used and resent it" (Mitchell & Sugar, 2008, p. B2). A dark consequence of this pattern is that some men may feel justified in pressuring or coercing women to have sex when they feel that the women "owe it" to them (Basow & Minieri, 2011).

---

[7]Do you need to refresh your understanding of the principle of lesser interest? Look back at page 181.

Safe, Sensible Sex

There's a lot of casual sex going on, and only some of it is safe. Most college students—about three-fourths—have had **hookups,** or sexual interactions with nonromantic partners that usually last 1 night and that do not involve any expectation of a lasting relationship (Paul et al., 2008). Most hookups involve partners with whom one is well acquainted—much of the time, the partner is a friend—but a lot of hookups (37 percent) involve others who are either strangers or who are not well known (Grello et al., 2006). Some hookups just involve kissing and heavy petting, but about half of them include oral sex or intercourse (especially if people have been drinking), and when sex occurs, condoms are used only about half the time (Paul et al., 2008).

Sex is no safer in dating relationships—only half of the college students in one study used condoms consistently when they started having sex with a new romantic partner (Civic, 2000)—and off-campus, things may be even worse. A survey of 740 women (most of them in their 30s and 40s) who were seeking new partners on dating Web sites found that the women were generally very careful when they met a new guy face-to-face for the first time; they had long conversations, ran background checks, and negotiated boundaries before agreeing to a meeting, and then they met in a public place, carried pepper spray, or had

---

Love and Lust

Rob and Ashley are college students who have been dating for about 6 months. They spend a lot of time together, and they share the same tastes in music, video games, and movies. They feel strong sexual desires for one another, and they have sex three or four times a week. If you had to guess, how happy would you say Rob and Ashley are with each other? How much in love? And would you guess differently if you had been told that they *didn't* have much sexual desire for one another and had not had sex?

If you're like most people, your answer to the last question is "yes." Pamela Regan (1998) found that young adults judged couples to be more in love, more committed, happier, and more satisfied when they were hot for each other than was the case when they

felt little lust. The presence or absence of desire clearly influenced people's perceptions of a relationship, but, interestingly, whether or not the couple was actually having sex did not. Whether or not it was being fulfilled, lust led people to assume that love was at work. The connection ran the other way, too: Couples who were said to be in love were assumed to also desire each other sexually.

Regan's research demonstrated that people consider lust and love to go hand-in-hand. We want our romantic partners to feel sexual desire for us, and we want to feel it for them (Regan, 2004). And these results also suggest why any decline in passion as the years go by can be worrisome: If love and lust go together, partners may view declining lust as a sign of waning love.

a friend nearby. But all of that caution did not translate into safe sex. Perhaps because they already (believed that they) knew so much about each other, 30 percent of the women had sex with their new partners when they first met. And, overall, whenever it occurred, 77 percent of the women who met online partners did not use a condom when they first had sex (Padgett, 2007).

Thus, many people do not use condoms when they have sex with a new or temporary partner, and they forgo safe sex in an environment in which 1 of every 5 teen girls in the United States is infected with either HPV or genital herpes (Tanner, 2008). What is going on? Why is it that so many smart people are having so much unsafe sex? There are several reasons:

- *Underestimates of risk.* First, a lot of us are lousy at math. For instance, the chance that a woman will be infected with human immunodeficiency virus (or HIV, the virus that causes AIDS) in a single unprotected sexual encounter with an infected male is actually quite low, less than 1 percent. But of course, if you give a low-frequency event several chances to occur, the probability that it *will* occur at least once goes up. If a woman has unprotected sex with an infected man a few dozen times, it becomes very likely that she will become HIV positive; her chance of infection gets very high (Linville et al., 1993).

  In a similar manner, almost all of us underestimate the cumulative overall risk that a new partner who has been sexually active in the past is carrying a sexually transmitted infection, or STI (Knäuper et al., 2008), and that false sense of security deters condom use. Someone who has had several prior sexual partners is more likely to be infected than we think, even if the individual risk encountered with each of those partners was low. And we are particularly likely to underestimate a partner's risk when he or she is attractive; the better looking someone is, the lower the risk we perceive, and the less likely we are to use a condom if sex occurs (Knäuper et al., 2008).

  A particular bias known as the **illusion of unique invulnerability** can also influence our estimates of risk. Many of us believe that bad things are generally more likely to happen to others than to us, so we fail to take sensible precautions that would prevent foreseeable dangers (Burger & Burns, 1988). The irony here, of course, is that those who consider themselves relatively invulnerable to STIs are less likely to use condoms, and that makes them *more* likely to catch one. People even think they're unlikely to catch an STI *after* they've already got one. A representative national survey of young adults in the United States found that only 22 percent of those who tested positive for chlamydia, gonorrhea, or trichomoniasis had noticed any symptoms in the past year, so most people didn't know they were carrying a STI—and only 28 percent of those who *already had* one of these STIs believed that they were at risk of becoming infected (Wildsmith et al., 2010). There's a lot of biased—or simply ignorant—assessment of risk out there (O'Sullivan et al., 2010).

- *Faulty decision making.* People who intend to use condoms sometimes change their minds in the heat of the moment and then regret their decision afterward. What causes us to make poor decisions? *Sexual arousal,* for one. When college men are turned on, they see things differently than they do when they're not aroused: Diverse sexual behaviors (such as spanking, a threesome with another man, and sex with a 60-year-old woman) seem more appealing, morally questionable behavior (such as slipping a woman a drug to get sex) seems more acceptable, and condoms seem less desirable (Ariely & Loewenstein, 2006). Men, at least, really can get "carried away" when they get turned on.

Intoxication can also alter our decision making, particularly when we're sexually aroused (Ebel-Lam et al., 2009). When people get drunk, they're less likely to use condoms when they're having sex with someone for the first time, in part because intoxication leads them to ignore the potential consequences and to think that having sex is a great idea (Cooper, 2006). This is an example of a phenomenon known as **alcohol myopia,** which involves the reduction of people's abilities to think about and process all of the information available to them when they are intoxicated (Giancola et al., 2010). This limited capacity means that they are able to focus only on the most immediate and salient environmental cues. When they're drunk, people may not be able to think of anything but how attractive their partners are, and they completely forget their prior intentions to use the condoms they're carrying in a pocket or purse (MacDonald et al., 2000). Alcohol and arousal are evidently a recipe for high-risk sexual behavior.

- *Pluralistic ignorance.* One of the striking things about hookups is that they are not as popular as most people, including the participants, think they are. Both men and women do not enjoy hookups as much as they think other people do—big majorities of both men and women prefer dating someone to just hooking up (Bradshaw et al., 2010)—and, in particular, women tend to regret hookups that involve intercourse or oral sex (Fielder & Carey, 2010). Nevertheless, most young adults believe that *other* people generally approve of such behavior, and they therefore feel some social pressure to do the same (Hines et al., 2002).

  This is an example of **pluralistic ignorance,** which occurs when people wrongly believe that their feelings and beliefs are different from those of others. By misperceiving each other's true preferences, a group of people can end up following norms that everyone thinks are prevalent but that almost no one privately supports. Thus, college students may wisely want to have safe sex but fail to pursue it because they wrongly believe that it's unpopular. Our judgments of others' attitudes and actions influence our own sexual behavior, but those judgments are not always correct. Indeed, women think that men hold more negative attitudes toward condoms than they really do (Edwards & Barber, 2010). These days, men and women don't differ in their desires to use condoms (Hood & Shook, 2011).

- *Inequalities in power.* As we'll see in chapter 12, *power* is the ability to get a partner to do what you want. When two partners possess different levels of power, they are unlikely to use condoms if the more powerful partner opposes them (Woolf & Maisto, 2008). In general, the more powerful the woman is (Pulerwitz et al., 2000), and the more honest and forthright she is

(Impett et al., 2010), the more likely she and her partner are to use condoms when they have sex.

- *Abstinence education.* In order to convince teens that abstinence is the only way to go, some abstinence education programs teach their students that condoms don't work (which, of course, is nonsense) (Lin & Santelli, 2008). The undesired result is that when those teens have sex—and most of them do—they are less likely than other adolescents to use condoms (Rosenbaum, 2009).
- *Decreased intimacy and pleasure.* The most important deterrent of all, however, may be that people enjoy sex more, on average, when they don't use condoms than when they do. Both men and women find intercourse more pleasurable when condoms are not involved, with men being particularly likely to prefer unprotected sex (Randolph et al., 2007). People who don't use condoms consider their sex to be more intimate and emotionally satisfying (Smith et al., 2008), and, consequently, lots of people—30 percent of men and 41 percent of women—have had a partner try to talk them out of using a condom. Remarkably, people who have had intercourse with more than 10 different partners—and who therefore present a rather high cumulative risk of having a STI—are *more* likely than those who have had fewer partners to try to dissuade their new lovers from using condoms (Oncale & King, 2001).

Clearly, condom use is subject to diverse influences. Education can counteract some of the misunderstandings that deter condom use, but changing the perception that condoms are impersonal and unpleasant may be more difficult. So I have two suggestions. Condoms are less likely to "break the mood" when they're treated as a part of sexy foreplay (Scott-Sheldon & Johnson, 2006). Don't treat condoms as if they're a nuisance that interrupts your love-making; when it's time, help your partner put one on in a manner that creatively and deliberately enhances, rather than detracts from, your excitement and anticipation. I also suggest that these days it communicates more respect, care, and concern for each other when you *do* use a condom than when you do not. It's likely that a new partner who tries to talk you out of having safe sex does not value you or your relationship as much as one who is glad to respect your wishes (Otto-Salaj et al., 2010). And you certainly shouldn't be embarrassed to ask a new lover to use a condom. Most people will be glad you brought it up—and if your partner is reluctant to do what you want, you probably don't want to share yourself with that person anyway.

SEXUAL SATISFACTION

What people do in their sexual relationships is important, but how those actions make them *feel* is even more influential. It's good news, then, that when they are in good health, free of sexual problems, and have a steady partner, most people have happy sex lives (Heiman et al., 2011). When they had all three things going for them, for instance, only 6 percent of the women who participated in

How to Improve Your Sex Life:
Don't Believe Everything You Read (or Hear)

Sex is portrayed in various ways in the media, and not all of the lessons you can learn there are likely to benefit your relationships. In their efforts to appeal to the masses (few of whom, regrettably, will ever read this book), modern media reinforce stereotypes, play on fears, and show us a lot of casual, unprotected sex. For instance, condoms and other matters of sexual responsibility are rarely mentioned when sex shows up on television (Kunkel et al., 2007), and "reality" dating programs such as *The Bachelor* and *The Bachelorette* depict developing relationships as crass sexual competitions. Indeed, people who watch a lot of these shows tend to endorse the sexual double standard and to think that dating is a contest in which horny men care only about women's looks and pressure them for sex, blithely ignoring them when they pretend to be uninterested (Zurbriggen & Morgan, 2006). Magazines such as *Cosmopolitan* and *Cleo* suggest that a woman needs to develop mad skillz in bed if she expects a guy to remain committed to her. If she doesn't have plenty of tricks up her sleeve, she'll find it hard to keep a man. She has to tread lightly, though, because men are also said to be very sensitive about possible inadequacies and shortcomings (Farvid & Braun, 2006). And this last point is reinforced by endless streams of spam e-mail messages warning men that, if they don't increase their penis size, they will surely continue to disappoint their women.

Nonsense. The last time they had sex, most American teens (74 percent) used condoms (Fortenberry et al., 2010). There's a lot more safe sex in real life than on TV. And a survey of over 52,000 women on the Web found that a sizable majority of them were satisfied with the size of their partner's penis. Only 6 percent of the female respondents thought their partners were "small" (as opposed to "average" or "large"), and most of that group did wish that their partners were bigger. Still, overall, 84 percent of the women thought their men were just fine, 14 percent wished they were larger, and 2 percent wanted them to be smaller (Lever et al., 2006). Six out of every seven women have no wish for their men to be larger, and if that's a surprise, you've probably been reading the wrong magazines and visiting the wrong Web sites. Don't believe everything you read or hear about sex in close relationships.

a large study in Boston were dissatisfied with their overall sex lives (Lutfey et al., 2009). On the other hand, only about half of the Boston sample (51 percent) had had sex with anyone in the past month; many of them had had no available partner, and others simply hadn't been interested in having sex. And of those who had been sexually active, over a third (39 percent) had experienced frustrating problems with pain, a lack of desire, or difficulty reaching orgasm. Similar proportions of middle-aged and older men also experience problems with their sexual functioning (Klapper, 2010), so when all these influences are combined, a minority (43 percent) of Americans 45 and older are presently having satisfying sex (Crary, 2010).

That's disappointing. Is there anything we can do, if we're healthy, to attain more sexual satisfaction? Yes, probably, and a variety of investigations have offered some insights. Interestingly, in the United States, high levels of contentment are more common in people who have had only one lover in the past year than in those who have had two or more—and in general, people who are deeply committed to their partnerships and who value monogamy (and who remain faithful to one another) are likely to be satisfied with their sex lives (Waite & Joyner, 2001). It may be stimulating to have more than one lover, but most people seem to find more fulfillment in devoting themselves to one special mate. Indeed, U.S. men get more pleasure from sex with a steady relationship partner than they get from sex with anyone else (Herbenick et al., 2010a), and in Germany, Spain, Brazil, Japan, and the United States, the *fewer* sexual partners men have had during their lives, the more sexually satisfied they are now (Heiman et al., 2011).

The frequency with which people have sex is influential, too—at least for men. In one classic study, 89 percent of husbands and wives who had sex three times a week or more reported that they were content with their sex lives, whereas only 32 percent of spouses having sex just once a month felt the same sexual satisfaction (Blumstein & Schwartz, 1983). Of course, several things could be at work in a correlation like this, but two patterns are noteworthy. First, the frequency of sex matters more to men than to women (Heiman et al., 2011), and second, more frequent sex *does* increase the satisfaction newlywed men derive from their sex lives (McNulty & Fisher, 2008); over time, they're pleased when sex becomes more frequent and distressed if it slows.

But no matter how frequent they are, sexual interactions are most rewarding when they fulfill basic human needs for *autonomy, competence,* and *relatedness.* According to the tenets of Self-Determination Theory, we are happiest and healthiest when we routinely engage in activities that allow us to choose and control our own actions (that's *autonomy*), to feel confident and capable (that's *competence*), and to establish close connections to others (*relatedness*) (Deci & Ryan, 2000). Sex fits this framework, too (Smith, 2007): The best, most gratifying sexual interactions allow us to do the things we want, to do them well, and to feel loved and respected in the process.

That probably doesn't surprise you. What *is* notable is that a lot of people routinely have sex that is less satisfying than it could be because it doesn't fulfill those needs. In particular, people who subscribe to traditional gender roles tend to take it for granted that men should take the lead in directing sexual activity and that proper, feminine women should be submissive and subservient to their men; *he* makes the moves, and *she* does what he wants (Sanchez et al., 2006). The problem is that these expectations cast women into a passive role that undermines their autonomy in bed; they rarely choose the agenda and they rarely call the shots, so they often don't get what they want. And robbing women of their initiative and control decreases their sexual desire, reduces their arousal, and makes it harder for them to reach orgasm, so sex is a lot less fun for them (Kiefer & Sanchez, 2007). For their part, some men chafe at always having to be in control. Many men want to feel that they are compelling targets for their partners' desire, so it's exciting for them when, instead of being passive, women initiate sex and take the lead (Dworkin & O'Sullivan, 2005). Thus, the dictates of traditional gender roles seem to rob both men and women of some sexual freedom and abandon, so that their sexual interactions are less satisfying than they could be; couples who allow each other more autonomy and choice enjoy more gratifying sex (Sanchez et al., 2005).

The motivations that underlie our sexual interactions also seem to influence the satisfaction we derive from them (Stephenson et al., 2011). As we saw earlier (back on p. 281), people have sex for lots of different reasons, and one way to organize them is to employ the approach and avoidance dimensions I introduced in chapter 6.[8] We sometimes have sex to obtain (or "approach") positive outcomes such as increased intimacy or personal pleasure. For instance, if we seek to celebrate and enrich the intimacy of our relationships by having sex, we're pursuing positive outcomes. In contrast, when we have sex hoping to forestall or avoid unpleasant consequences, we are pursuing different goals. We may be seeking to prevent a partner's anger or to keep a partner from losing interest in us. Which type of motive do you think is more fulfilling? Sex diaries from students at UCLA revealed that sex was more satisfying, intimate, and fun when people engaged in sex for positive reasons. In contrast, when they had sex to avoid unwanted outcomes, they experienced more negative emotions and their relationships suffered; over time, partners who had sex for avoidance reasons were more likely to break up (Impett et al., 2005). People with strong approach motivations in bed also have more intense and longer lasting sexual desire for their partners (Impett et al., 2008). It's clear that those who have sex to express their love for their partners, to deepen their relationship, and to give and obtain physical pleasure eagerly pursue—and enjoy—sexual interactions more than do those who have sex for other reasons (Cooper et al., 2008).

Sexual Communication

Here's an influence on sexual satisfaction that's important enough to get its own subheading. A lot of people feel awkward talking about sex, so too often, they don't. Couples often have sex without ever discussing it at all: One of them might signal a desire for sex by moaning, intimate touching, and unbuttoning a shirt, while the other silently signals his or her consent simply by doing nothing to resist (Vannier & O'Sullivan, 2011). Is wordless sex a problem? It can be. It's wasteful if we never talk honestly, fearlessly, and openly with our partners about our sexual likes and dislikes, for one very big reason: Clear communication about sex is associated with greater satisfaction with sex (MacNeil & Byers, 2009). People who talk candidly about sex have more fulfilling sexual interactions with their partners than do those who just grunt and moan now and then.

---

[8]Do you need to refresh your memory about approach and avoidance motivations? Look back at pages 187–190.

The famous sex researchers William Masters and Virginia Johnson (1970) highlighted the importance of good sexual communication in a provocative study that compared the sexual experiences of heterosexuals and gays and lesbians. Masters and Johnson observed couples having sex and interviewed them extensively, and they concluded that the subjective quality of the sexual experience—including psychological involvement, responsiveness to the needs and desires of the partner, and enjoyment of each aspect of the sexual experience—was actually greater for gays and lesbians than it was for heterosexuals. Same-sex sex was better sex. One advantage of the sexual interactions shared by gays and lesbians was that both participants *were* of the same sex; knowing what they liked themselves, gays and lesbians could reasonably predict what their partners might like, too. However, Masters and Johnson argued that the primary foundation for more rewarding same-sex relations was good communication. Gays and lesbians talked more easily and openly about their sexual feelings than heterosexuals did. They would ask each other what was desired, provide feedback on what felt good, and generally guide their lovers on how to please them. In contrast, heterosexual couples exhibited a "persistent neglect" of open communication and a "potentially self-destructive lack of intellectual curiosity about the partner" (Masters & Johnson, p. 219).

The good news is that if heterosexuals honestly tell each other what they like and don't like and how each of them is doing, they're more likely to have superb sex, too (MacNeil & Byers, 2009). This sort of discussion is very intimate, and couples who engage in a lot of it not only enjoy more sexual satisfaction but also feel more contented overall in their relationships as well (Byers, 2005).

Better communication can also help us manage situations in which we do not want to have sex and our intentions are being misunderstood. You may have already learned the hard way that women and men sometimes interpret sexual situations differently, and frustration or antagonism can result. Men have stronger sexual desires than women do, and they're literally thinking about sex more often than women are, so they tend to read sexual interest into innocent behavior from women who have no sexual intentions (Haselton, 2003). This was first demonstrated in a classic study by Antonia Abbey (1982), who invited men and women to get acquainted with each other, chatting one-on-one, while another man and another woman observed their conversation. Both the men participating in the interactions and those watching them tended to interpret friendliness from the women as signs of sexual interest, even when the women doing the talking had no wish to be sexually provocative and the women looking on saw no such conduct. The men literally perceived signs of sexual flirtatiousness that were not intended and that probably did not exist.

This sort of thing isn't rare; most men (54 percent) have misperceived a woman's intentions at least once (Jacques-Tiura et al., 2007). Undoubtedly, some of those mistakes were relatively innocent, being rooted in cluelessness regarding nonverbal behavior that is more common in men than in women (Farris et al., 2008a). Moreover, men who reject traditional gender roles and who value equality between the sexes are unlikely to make these mistakes at all (Farris et al., 2008b). However, misjudgments of a woman's interest are

Attachment and Sexuality

People who are anxious about abandonment are needy, and people who want to avoid intimacy keep their distance, and both of these dimensions of attachment are closely tied to sexual behavior (Birnbaum, 2010). Perhaps because sex is often a very intimate act, avoidant people have less frequent sex with their romantic partners (Brassard et al., 2007), and more frequent sex with casual, short-term partners (Feeney & Noller, 2004), than secure people do. They tend not to have sex to foster closeness with, and to celebrate their intimacy with, their lovers (Birnbaum, 2007). On the contrary, in order to "get some space" and to maintain their freedom, men with a dismissing attachment style are more likely than secure men to cheat on their partners (Allen & Baucom, 2004).

By comparison, people who are high in attachment anxiety have more passionate, needier sex that springs from their desire to feel accepted by their partners (Davis et al., 2004). Passion is great, but it's tinged with desperation in anxious people; to avoid displeasing their partners, they are also less likely to

use condoms and to refuse to do things they don't want to do (Strachman & Impett, 2009). And with their endless appetites for reassurance, people who are high in anxiety also have more extramarital affairs than secure people do (Bogaert & Sadava, 2002).

Moreover, people with high levels of either anxiety or avoidance are less likely than secure people are to be honest and open in discussing their needs and desires with their partners (Davis et al., 2006). It shouldn't surprise us, then, that they're less satisfied with their sex lives—and their partners may be, too; people with avoidant spouses wish their sex was less detached and distant (Butzer & Campbell, 2008).

All things considered, the greatest sexual self-confidence, best communication, and most satisfaction with sex are enjoyed by people with secure attachment styles. Secure people are more playful and open to exploration in bed, and they more happily and readily commit themselves to faithful, monogamous intimacy (Mikulincer & Shaver, 2007). Great lovers tend to be secure lovers.

common—especially when everyone's been drinking—among macho men who consider sex to be an exploitative contest and who like to dominate women (Jacques-Tiura et al., 2007). These are the men who are most likely to engage in sexual coercion, and misperception of a woman's sexual interest is often the first step toward such unwelcome episodes (Farris et al., 2008b). Explicit, unambiguous communication is sometimes needed to set such men straight—and the best refusals are assertive, consistent, and persistent (Yagil et al., 2006). Don't be coy or playful when it's time to make your feelings known; plainly state your disinterest, and repeat as necessary.

Sexual Satisfaction and Relationship Satisfaction

Finally, let's note that sexual satisfaction does not occur in a vacuum; we are unlikely to be satisfied with our sex lives if we're *dis*satisfied with our relationships with our partners. Sexual satisfaction and relationship satisfaction go hand-in-hand. Whether they are married or cohabiting, heterosexual or not, couples who enjoy the most gratifying sexual interactions are generally quite satisfied with, and committed to, their relationships (Holmberg et al., 2010).

One reason that sexual satisfaction and relationship satisfaction are linked is that they are subject to similar influences. Similarity and stress are two examples. We like those who are like us, and spouses are more content when they share similar sexual histories. The larger the difference in the number of past sexual partners a husband and wife have had, the less happily married they are likely to be (Garcia & Markey, 2007). Furthermore, hassles and stress at work or at home affect both sexual satisfaction and relationship satisfaction in much the same way; people who are beset with frustration and difficulties tend to be discontented both in bed and in general (Bodenmann et al., 2010).

Most importantly, however, we tend to be more satisfied in intimate relationships in which there's good sex because fulfilling sex makes a partnership more gratifying, and love for a partner makes sex more rewarding in turn (Yucel & Gassanov, 2010). Pleasing sex with a partner reduces stress and improves one's mood in a way in which a solitary orgasm through masturbation does not. Then, that positive mood and a happy outlook increase the levels of physical affection and sexual activity that follow (Burleson et al., 2007). Sexual satisfaction thus increases relationship satisfaction, and vice versa.

What's more, this pattern persists throughout life. A study of elderly couples married for an average of 43 years found that, even though they had less of it than they used to, sex continued to be an influential component of their marital satisfaction (Hinchliff & Gott, 2004). Overall, then, studies of sexual satisfaction point out that sex isn't some kind of magical ingredient that automatically makes a relationship fulfilling. The best sex also seems to depend on:

- each person having his or her needs met by a partner who understands and respects one's specific sexual desires,
- valuing one's partner and being devoted to the relationship, and
- enjoying being with each other, in bed and out of it.

SEXUAL COERCION

These desirable ingredients are absent when one partner intentionally cajoles, induces, pressures, or even forces another to engage in sexual activities against his or her will. These actions can take various forms (DeGue & DiLillo, 2005). The *type of pressure* that is applied can range from (a) mildly coercive verbal persuasion (that may involve false promises, guilt induction, or threats to end the relationship); to (b) plying someone with alcohol or drugs to weaken his or her resistance; and on to (c) the threat of—or actual use of—physical force to compel someone's submission. The *unwanted sexual behavior* that results can range from touching and fondling to penetration and intercourse.

Take a look at Figure 9.4, which portrays these two dimensions. Together, they depict four different broad types of sexual violation. The boundaries

FIGURE 9.4. **Four broad types of sexual violation.**
Two different dimensions—the type of pressure that is applied and the unwanted behavior that results—combine to delineate four different broad types of sexual misconduct.
Source: Adapted from DeGue & DiLillo, 2005.

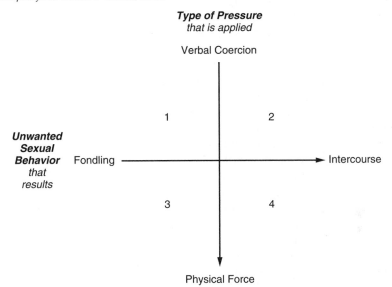

between them are not exact—they blend from one to the other depending on the specific circumstances—but they still make useful distinctions. The first category, in quadrant 1, includes interactions in which one person coaxes and cons another to submit to touching that he or she doesn't want. Because the violations that result are relatively less severe (and are not illegal), you may not consider them to be a form of sexual coercion; most college students take them for granted as a normal nuisance associated with dating (Oswald & Russell, 2006). Many of us still expect sex to be a competition in which men and women are adversaries— with women holding a prize that men seek to win through guile, persistence, and superior might—so interactions in which men ignore women's disinterest and "cop a feel" whenever possible may seem unremarkable (Krahé et al., 2007). However, because they are unwanted, these actions are not innocuous. They disrespect one's partner, and when they are directed at women, they are most likely to be enacted by men who quietly hold hostile attitudes toward women and who believe that all women would secretly like to be raped (Hoyt & Yeater, 2011). They also have a corrosive effect on relationships, being associated with both lower sexual satisfaction and relationship satisfaction (Katz & Myhr, 2008).

   In quadrant 2, verbal manipulation and/or intentional intoxication lead to penetration of the genitals. If a woman does not actively and strenuously protest this behavior, a lot of people will consider her to share the responsibility for the act (Cohn et al., 2008), so these behaviors are rarely prosecuted. Quadrants 3 and 4 involve various degrees of physical force (or a drug-induced stupor that leaves the victim unable to resist), and the behaviors there are more likely to seem patently illegal. Many legal jurisdictions would prosecute the actions in quadrant 4 as "forcible rape" if they became known.

Most men and women never direct any of these forms of sexual coercion toward the other sex (Spitzberg, 1999). Nevertheless, they are scarily common. Specific counts depend on the precise definitions employed, but one out of every six college women encounters coercion in some form every 2 months (Gidycz et al., 2008), and most women (56 percent) suffer such interactions during their college careers (Crown & Roberts, 2007). Overall, men use more physical force than women do—they are more likely to be the perpetrators than the victims in quadrants 3 and 4—but women are just as likely as men to verbally coerce reluctant partners to have unwanted intercourse; about 25 percent of both men and women have done so (Spitzberg, 1999).

These actions are certainly not compassionate and loving, and they're not even well-intentioned. The people who enact them tend to have belittling, unsympathetic, and surly attitudes toward the other sex (Hines, 2007). They do some damage, too: Women who have been forced or frightened into unwanted sex have poorer mental and physical health thereafter, especially if they are victimized more than once (de Visser et al., 2007).

So the prevalence of sexual coercion, whatever its form, is very distressing. What can be done to reduce its frequency? I have several suggestions. First, beware of potential partners who view sex as a contest. They are unlikely to have your best interests at heart. Second, beware of intoxication in either you or your partner; it makes people more likely to act inappropriately, and indeed, most episodes of sexual coercion involve alcohol or drugs (Hoyt & Yeater, 2011). Third, resolve to assertively resist unwanted advances; women who decide in advance to rebuff sexual misconduct are less likely to passively submit if such a situation develops (Gidycz et al., 2008). Fourth, reduce the need for such assertion by setting sexual boundaries with frank, direct discussion before you start an intimate interaction. (At a minimum, tell your partner, "If I say no, I'm gonna *mean* no.") Miscommunication and misunderstanding are often at work in interactions involving sexual coercion, and the distinction between right and wrong is clearer when the ground rules are laid out in advance (Winslett & Gross, 2008). Finally, consider the value of thinking of your lover as an equal partner whose preferences and pleasure are as important as your own. Not only is such respect and thoughtfulness incompatible with sexual coercion, if you and your lover both feel that way, you're likely to have great sex (Rudman & Phelan, 2007).

FOR YOUR CONSIDERATION

Chad was in love with Jennifer. He felt a lot of sexual desire for her, and he always enjoyed having sex with her, but he still felt something was missing. She was usually glad to have sex, and she seemed to enjoy it, too, but she rarely took any initiative and he typically did all the work. She usually just lay there, and he wanted her to be more active and take the lead now and then. He wished that she would be more inventive, and he wanted her to work him over occasionally. Nevertheless, he didn't say anything. Their sex was good, if not great, and he worried that any complaints would make things worse, not better, between them.

What do you think the future holds for Chad and Jennifer? Why?

CHAPTER SUMMARY

Sexual Attitudes

Attitudes about Casual Sex. People's attitudes about sex have become more permissive over time. Today, most people tolerate unmarried sex if the partners care for each other, but a *sexual double standard* may still lead us to judge women's sexuality more harshly than men's.

Attitudes about Same-Sex Sexuality. Americans do not consider homosexuality to be an acceptable lifestyle if they think sexual orientation is a choice. Nevertheless, there is no empirical basis for denying gays and lesbians the legal benefits of civil unions.

Cultural Differences in Sexual Attitudes. Sexual attitudes in the United States are relatively conservative compared to those of people in many other countries.

Sexual Behavior

Sex for the First Time. Almost all of us have sex before we marry, and the first time usually involves a steady close relationship. If the partners aren't close, some regret typically follows.

Sex in Committed Relationships. People have sex for diverse reasons, and their relationship status, age, and sexual orientation all influence the frequency with which sex occurs.

Infidelity. Men cheat more than women do, and they are more likely than women to have an unrestricted *sociosexual orientation*. The *good genes hypothesis* suggests that women cheat in order to have healthy offspring, and *sperm competition* may have evolved to counteract such behavior.

Sexual Desire. Men have higher *sex drives* than women do. This may lead to annoyance as heterosexual couples negotiate their sexual interactions.

Safe, Sensible Sex. Most college students have had *hookups*, sometimes having intercourse without condoms. Condom use is influenced by underestimates of risk, faulty decision making, pluralistic ignorance, inequalities of power, abstinence education, and concerns about intimacy and pleasure.

Sexual Satisfaction

Most people do not report high levels of sexual satisfaction. The best sex is motivated by approach goals and fulfills basic needs, but traditional gender roles tend to undermine women's choice and control in bed.

Sexual Communication. Direct and honest sexual communication is associated with greater sexual satisfaction. Because gays and lesbians discuss their preferences more openly than heterosexuals do, they enjoy better sex. Good communication may also avoid misperceptions of sexual intent.

Sexual Satisfaction and Relationship Satisfaction. Partners who are satisfied with their sex lives tend to be more satisfied with their relationships, with each appearing to make the other more likely.

Sexual Coercion

Various forms of pressure and behavioral outcomes describe four broad types of sexual violations. These are distressingly prevalent, but several strategies may make them less common.

CHAPTER 10

Stresses and Strains

PERCEIVED RELATIONAL VALUE ◆ HURT FEELINGS ◆
OSTRACISM ◆ JEALOUSY ◆ Two Types of Jealousy ◆ Who's Prone
to Jealousy? ◆ Who Gets Us Jealous? ◆ What Gets Us Jealous? ◆ Responses
to Jealousy ◆ Coping Constructively with Jealousy ◆ DECEPTION AND
LYING ◆ Lying in Close and Casual Relationships ◆ Lies and Liars ◆ So,
How Well Can We Detect a Partner's Deception? ◆ BETRAYAL ◆ Individual
Differences in Betrayal ◆ The Two Sides to Every Betrayal ◆ Coping with
Betrayal ◆ FORGIVENESS ◆ FOR YOUR CONSIDERATION ◆ CHAPTER SUMMARY

Let's take stock. In previous chapters, we have encountered adaptive and
maladaptive cognition, good and bad communication, and rewarding and
unrewarding social exchange. We've considered both beneficial and disadvantageous influences on close relationships. But that won't be true here. In this
chapter, we'll concentrate on various pitfalls, stumbling blocks, and hazards
that cause wear and tear in relationships. And importantly, the stresses and
strains I cover here—hurt feelings, ostracism, jealousy, lying, and betrayal—
are commonplace events that occur in most relationships somewhere along the
way. We've all had our feelings hurt (Vangelisti, 2009), and sooner or later,
almost everyone lies to their intimate partners (DePaulo et al., 2009). Even outright betrayals of one sort or another are surprisingly widespread and hard to
avoid (Baxter et al., 1997).

However, the fact that these incidents are commonplace doesn't mean they
are inconsequential. Negative events like these can be very influential. They
help explain why most of us report having had a very troublesome relationship
within the last 5 years (Levitt et al., 1996). And despite their idiosyncrasies, all
of these unhappy events may share a common theme (Leary, 2005): They suggest that we are not as well liked or well respected as we wish we were.

PERCEIVED RELATIONAL VALUE

Fueled by our need to belong,[1] most of us care deeply about what our intimate
partners think of us. We want them to want us. We want them to value our company and to consider their partnerships with us to be valuable and important.

[1]Need a reminder about the human need to belong? Look back at p. 4 in chapter 1.

We want our partners to evaluate their relationships with us positively, and sometimes, we want that relationship to be very meaningful and close. As a result, according to theorist Mark Leary (2010b), it's painful to perceive that our **relational value**—that is, the degree to which others consider their relationships with us to be valuable, important, or close—is lower than we would like it to be.

Over time, we're likely to encounter various degrees of acceptance and rejection in our dealings with others, and Leary (2001) has suggested that they can be arranged along the continuum described in Table 10.1. At the extreme of *maximal inclusion*, people seek our company and don't want to have a party unless we can come. They are somewhat less accepting, but still positively inclined toward us when they offer us *active inclusion:* They invite us to the party and are glad we can come. However, their acceptance is more passive when they don't invite us to the party but admit us if we show up, and they are *ambivalent*, neither accepting nor rejecting, when they genuinely don't care one way or the other whether we show up or not.

If we want others to like us and value their relationships with us, noncommittal ambivalence from them may be bad enough, but things can get worse. We encounter *passive exclusion* when others ignore us and wish we were elsewhere, and we suffer *active exclusion* when others go out of their way to avoid us altogether. However, the most complete rejection occurs when, in *maximal exclusion*, others order us to leave their parties when they find us there. In such instances, merely avoiding us won't do; they want us gone.

Our emotional reactions to such experiences depend on how much we want to be accepted by particular others, and just what their acceptance or rejection of us means. On occasion, people exclude us because they regard us positively, and such rejections are much less painful than are exclusions that result from our deficiencies or faults. Consider the game show *Survivor:* Contestants sometimes try to vote the most skilled, most able competitors off the island to increase their personal chances of winning the game. Being excluded because you're better than everyone else may not hurt much, but rejection that suggests that you're inept, insufficient, or inadequate usually does (Leary, 2005).

TABLE 10.1. Degrees of Acceptance and Rejection

Being accepted or rejected by others is not an all-or-nothing event. People can desire our company to greater or lesser degrees, and researchers use these labels to describe the different extents to which we may be included or excluded by others.

Maximal inclusion	Others seek us out and go out of their way to interact with us.
Active inclusion	Others welcome us but do not seek us out.
Passive inclusion	Others allow us to be included.
Ambivalence	Others do not care whether we are included or not.
Passive exclusion	Others ignore us but do not avoid us.
Active exclusion	Others avoid us, tolerating our presence only when necessary.
Maximal exclusion	Others banish us, sending us away, or abandon us.

Source: Adapted from Leary, 2001.

In addition, it's not much of a blow to be excluded from a party you didn't want to attend in the first place. Exclusion is much more painful when we want to be accepted by others than when we don't much care what they think of us. Indeed, it's also possible to be accepted and liked by others but be hurt because they don't like us as much as we want them to. This is what unrequited love is often like (Baumeister & Dhavale, 2001; see page 260). Those for whom we feel unrequited love may be fond of us in return, but if we want to be loved instead of merely liked, their mildness is painful.

All of these possibilities suggest that there is only a rough connection between the objective acceptance or rejection we receive from others and our *feelings* of acceptance or rejection that result, so we will focus on the *perception that others value their relationships with us less than we want them to* as a core ingredient of the stresses and strains that we will inspect in this chapter (Leary, 2010b). We feel hurt when our *perceived relational value* for others is lower than we want it to be.

HURT FEELINGS

In fact, the feelings of acceptance or rejection we experience in our dealings with others are related to their evaluations of us in a complex way: Maximal exclusion doesn't feel much worse than simple ambivalence does (Buckley et al., 2004). Take a careful look at Figure 10.1. The graph depicts people's reactions to evaluations from others that vary across a 10-point scale. Maximal exclusion is described by the worst possible evaluation, a 1, and maximal inclusion is described by the best possible evaluation, a 10; ambivalence, the point at which others don't care about us one way or the other, is the 5 at the mid-point of the scale. The graph demonstrates that once we find that others don't want us around, it hardly matters whether they dislike us a little or a lot: Our momentary judgments of our self-worth bottom out when people reject us to any extent (that is, when their evaluations range from 4 down to 1).

On the other hand, when it comes to acceptance, being completely adored doesn't improve our self-esteem beyond the boost we get from being very well-liked. Instead, we appear to be very sensitive to small differences in regard from others that range from ambivalence at the low end to active inclusion at the high end. As people like us more and more, we feel better and better about ourselves until their positive regard for us is fully ensured. This all makes sense from an evolutionary perspective (Leary, Haupt et al., 1998); carefully discerning degrees of acceptance that might allow access to resources and mates is more useful than monitoring the enmity of one's enemies. (After all, when it comes to reactions from potential mates, there are usually few practical differences between mild distaste and outright disgust!)

So, mild rejection from others usually feels just as bad as more extreme rejection does. But *decreases* in the *acceptance* we receive from others may have a greater impact, particularly when they occur in that range between ambivalence and active inclusion—that is, when people who liked us once appear to like us less now. Leary

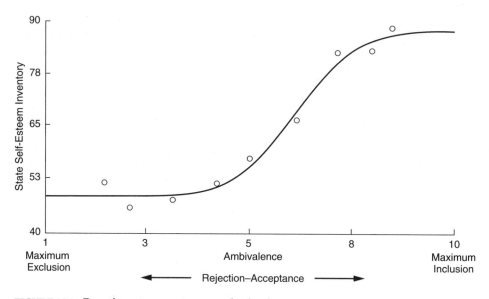

FIGURE 10.1. **Reactions to acceptance and rejection.**
This curve describes how our momentary feelings about ourselves map onto the treat-ment we receive from others. Self-esteem increases sharply as people move from being ambivalent about us to wanting us around, but any rejection at all causes our self-esteem to bottom out. When people prefer to ignore us, we feel nearly as bad about ourselves as we do when they order us to leave or throw us out.
Source: Data from Leary, Haupt et al., 1998.

and his colleagues demonstrated the potent impact of decreases in acceptance when they manipulated the evaluations that research participants received from new acquaintances (Buckley et al., 2004). As young adults talked about themselves to another person over an intercom system, they received intermittent approval ratings on a computer screen (see Figure 10.2); the ratings supposedly came from their conversation partner, but they were actually controlled by the experimenters, who provided one of four patterns of feedback. Some people received consistent acceptance, receiving only 5's and 6's, whereas others encountered constant rejec-tion, receiving only 2's and 3's. It's painful to be disliked by others, so of course, those who were accepted by the unseen acquaintance were happier and felt better about themselves than those who were rejected. But other people received evalu-ations that changed over time, starting poorly and getting better, or starting well and getting worse. In the latter case, over a span of 5 minutes, the research par-ticipants received successive ratings of 6, 5, 3, 3, and 2. Apparently, as the new acquaintance got to know them better, the less the acquaintance liked them.

The pattern of decreasing acceptance was particularly painful, causing more negative reactions than even constant rejection did (Buckley et al., 2004). Evidently, it's especially awful to experience drops in our perceived relational value—that is, **relational devaluation,** or apparent decreases in others' regard for us—and it causes a variety of unhappy emotions. When their partners

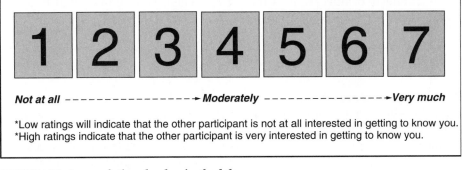

When told to begin, please start talking about yourself and do not stop until instructed to do so.

At one minute intervals, you will receive the other participant's answer to the question, "How much would you like to get to know the person who is speaking?," on the scale below.*

1 2 3 4 5 6 7

Not at all – – – – – – – – – – – – – – – –► *Moderately* – – – – – – – – – – – – – – –►*Very much*

*Low ratings will indicate that the other participant is not at all interested in getting to know you.
*High ratings indicate that the other participant is very interested in getting to know you.

FIGURE 10.2. **Low relational value in the lab.**
Imagine that as you describe yourself to someone in another room, one of these numbers lights up every 60 seconds, and you receive evaluations that start high but get worse and worse over time. After 5 minutes, the other person is giving you a "2" that indicates that he or she is quite uninterested in meeting you. How would you feel?
Source: Buckley et al., 2004.

turned against them, people felt sad, angry, and *hurt,* with the latter emotion being a particular sensation that is uniquely associated with losses of relational value (Leary & Leder, 2009). Hurt feelings have much in common with real pain; our physical responses are similar—several bodily systems respond to hurt feelings the same way they do to physical pain (DeWall, 2009)—and remarkably, the pain reliever acetaminophen reduces the pain of social rejection just as it does a headache:[2] After a week-and-a-half of daily doses of acetaminophen, college students had fewer hurt feelings at the end of the day than did other students who were taking a placebo (DeWall et al., 2010). Psychological wounds can cause real distress, and the sense of injury that characterizes hurt feelings—the feeling that relationship rules have been broken and that one has been damaged, shattered, cut, or stabbed—makes hurt feelings a distinct emotional experience (Feeney, 2005).

When relational devaluation occurs, some people experience more hurt than others do. As always, attachment styles are influential. People who have high levels of anxiety about abandonment experience more hurt in response to drops in perceived relational value than those with lower anxiety do (Besser & Priel, 2009). (As you can imagine, their nervous dread that others don't love them magnifies the hurt they feel.) And people who are high in avoidance of intimacy experience less pain when others withdraw; exclusion hurts less when you don't want to be close to others to begin with (Feeney, 2005). People's

---

[2]Acetaminophen, the active ingredient in the product known to Americans as Tylenol, is called *paracetamol* in most places outside North America.

levels of self-esteem matter, too: People with low self-esteem get their feelings hurt more easily than those with higher self-regard do (Ford & Collins, 2010).

In fact, self-esteem may be an important predictor of how people respond to potent experiences of rejection, such as ostracism. I can also detail the interpersonal effects of hurt feelings more fully when we examine what happens when people are ignored or given the "silent treatment."

OSTRACISM

A specific form of rejection that often occurs even in close relationships is **ostracism,** in which people are given the "cold shoulder" and ignored by those around them. When the silent treatment is intentional, ostracizers deliberately refrain from responding to others, sometimes pretending that their targets are not even present. Most of us have experienced ostracism; in one broad survey, 67 percent of Americans admitted that they had given an intimate partner the cold shoulder, and 75 percent reported that they had received such treatment from a loved one (Williams, 2001).

Why do people sometimes intentionally ignore their partners? Ostracizers usually justify their actions as an effective way to punish their partners, to avoid confrontation, or to calm down and cool off following a conflict, and they usually believe that the ostracism was beneficial in helping them achieve their goals (Sommer et al., 2001). But by its very nature, ostracism often leaves its targets wondering why they are being ignored (Williams, 2001). Only rarely is an explanation offered when a partner remains silent, and the victims of ostracism often have no idea why it is happening. They know only that they are being rejected, and they are more often angry, frustrated, and hurt than guilty and contrite. As a result, the targets of ostracism typically do not consider their partners' withdrawal to be a kind or effective way to behave, and they usually believe that the ostracism has damaged their relationships (Zadro et al., 2008).

Ostracism can be potent and painful because it threatens basic social needs (Williams, 2007). It's dehumanizing (Bastian & Haslam, 2010). In undermining our attachments to others, the silent treatment threatens our need to belong, damages our feelings of self-worth, and reduces our perceived control over our interactions. And our initial reactions to such threats usually involve numb disarray. Faced with interpersonal rejection, people's feelings become blunted (DeWall & Baumeister, 2006) and they start making dumb, self-defeating choices (Twenge, 2008). A "cold shoulder" even *feels* cold: When people feel excluded, they think the room is cooler and that warm food and drink are more desirable than they do when they have not been rejected (Zhong & Leonardelli, 2008). Time seems to pass more slowly, too; in one study in which they were asked to estimate how much time had passed during a 40-second interval, people who felt accepted by others offered an average (and quite accurate) estimate of 42 seconds, whereas those who felt rejected believed that 64 seconds had passed (Twenge et al., 2003). In general, it appears that rejection causes people to enter a lethargic state of mind in which rational planning and complex thought is reduced.

What happens next seems to depend on which of a person's needs are in the most peril (Williams, 2007). When belongingness is threatened, people who are being ostracized may work hard to regain their partners' regard, being compliant and doing what their tormentors want, especially when they think the relationship—and their relational value—can be repaired (Richman & Leary, 2009). However, they may also start looking for new, less punishing partners. After an experience with exclusion, people are often especially eager to make new, kinder friends (Maner et al., 2007).

More antagonistic reactions may occur when ostracism seems illegitimate and unjust and threatens people's feelings of control or self-worth (Warburton et al., 2006). When ostracized people get angry, they dismiss the opinions of those who are ignoring them as unfounded, unfair, and dim-witted, and they become more surly and aggressive (even toward innocent bystanders) than cowed and compliant (DeWall et al., 2009). In fact, instances of ostracism or romantic rejection precede most of the awful cases in which students take guns to school and shoot innocent classmates (Leary et al., 2006). Those who ostracize others are just as likely to frustrate and anger them as to shame or instruct them.

Researchers who study ostracism have developed a variety of ingenious procedures to create potent experiences of rejection in the lab. After short introductions to strangers, people have learned that no one wanted to work with them (Leary, 2005), and others have been ignored in face-to-face discussions or Internet chat rooms run by research assistants (Williams, 2001). But an inspired procedure created by Kipling Williams and his colleagues that involves a simple game of catch is especially nefarious (Williams & Zadro, 2005). If you encounter this procedure, you'll find yourself sitting for 5 minutes with two other people who begin playfully tossing and bouncing a racquetball back and forth. You've all just met, and you're all just passing time, waiting for an experimenter to return; so, the first minute of play, in which you frequently receive the ball, is pretty lighthearted. But then things change. Over the next 4 minutes, nobody tosses you the ball. The two other people gleefully toss the ball between themselves and completely ignore you, neither looking your way nor acknowledging any protest. It's as if you have ceased to exist.

Researchers have even conducted studies of ostracism online, and thousands of people around the world have now encountered a variation of the ball-tossing procedure on the Web (Williams & Jarvis, 2006). In this version, people believe that they are online with two other people represented by screen icons who are sending a Cyberball back and forth by clicking each other's icons. What happens next is all controlled by the computer program and there really aren't any other people involved, but as in real life, after a few warm-up throws, participants are partially or fully excluded from the "tossing" of the ball. What's striking is that this Internet ostracism is quite painful even when it is (apparently) dispensed by strangers one will never meet. In fact, even after people learn that their exclusion is controlled by the computer and that no real interpersonal evaluation is even remotely involved, they still get their feelings hurt when the computer program fails to toss them the ball (Zadro et al., 2004)! Ostracism even hurts when it is dispensed by groups we despise, such as the

Ku Klux Klan (Gonsalkorale & Williams, 2007). Our species seems to be quite sensitive to even the merest hint of social rejection.

So, ostracism is an obnoxious, unpleasant experience that is just as likely to engender hostility as compliance. And people with high self-esteem are relatively unlikely to put up with it. When they are ignored by others, people with high self-regard are more likely than those with lower self-esteem to end their relationships with their ostracizers and to seek new partners who will treat them better—and perhaps as a result, they get the silent treatment less often. In comparison, people with low self-esteem experience more ostracism, and they are more likely to carry a grudge and to ostracize others in return (Sommer & Rubin, 2005). Instead of leaving those who ostracize them, people with low self-regard are more likely to hang around but be spiteful.

In sum, then, we are likely to feel sadness, anger, and hurt when others ostracize us, and a core ingredient in such experiences seems to be the perception that those others do not value their relationships with us as much as we wish they did. Let's turn now to the special kind of threat to our relational value that occurs when we believe that a romantic rival is luring a beloved partner away.

JEALOUSY

A different kind of negative emotional experience results from the potential loss of a valued relationship to a real or imagined rival. **Jealousy** can involve a variety of feelings, ranging all the way from sad dejection to actual pride that one's partner is desirable to others, but the three feelings that define jealousy best are *hurt, anger,* and *fear* (Guerrero et al., 2005).[3]

Hurt follows from the perception that our partners do not value us enough to honor their commitments to our relationships, and fear and anxiety result from the dreadful prospect of abandonment and loss. But the unique element in jealousy is the romantic rival who threatens to lure a partner away: "To be jealous, one must have a relationship to lose and a rival to whom to lose it" (DeSteno & Salovey, 1994, p. 220). It's being cast aside for someone else that gets people angry, and that anger is usually directed both at the meddlesome rival and at the partner who is beginning to stray (Schützwohl, 2008b). Sometimes that anger turns violent; 13 percent of all the murders in the United States result from one spouse killing another, and when that occurs, jealousy is the most common motive (Buss, 2000).

Obviously, jealousy is an unhappy experience. But here's an interesting question: How would you feel if you *couldn't* make your lover jealous? Would you be disappointed if nothing you did gave your partner a jealous twinge? Most people probably would be, but whether or not that's a sensible point of

---

[3]Jealousy is sometimes confused with envy, but the two are quite different (Parrott & Smith, 1993). We envy someone when we wish we had what they have; envy is characterized by a humiliating longing for another person's possessions. In contrast, jealousy is the confused state of hurt, anger, and fear that results from the threat of losing what we already have, a relationship that we do not wish to give up.

view may depend on what type of jealousy we're talking about, why your partner is jealous, and what your partner does in response to his or her jealousy. Let's explore those issues.

Two Types of Jealousy

Reactive jealousy occurs when someone becomes aware of an actual threat to a valued relationship (Bringle & Buunk, 1991). The troubling threat may not be a current event; it may have occurred in the past, or it may be anticipated in the near future (if, for instance, your partner expresses the intention to date someone else), but reactive jealousy always occurs in response to a realistic danger. A variety of behaviors from one's partner can cause concern; just fantasizing about or flirting with someone else is considered "cheating" by most young adults in the United States (Kruger et al., 2010). Unfortunately, there may be a lot to be jealous about. In two surveys of over 800 American college students, lots of young adults reported having dated, kissed, fondled, or slept with someone while they were in a serious dating relationship with someone else (Brand et al., 2007). Half of the women and two-fifths of the men said they had kissed or fondled someone else, and a fifth of both men and women said they had had intercourse with a rival (most of them more than once).

In contrast, **suspicious jealousy** occurs when one's partner *hasn't* misbehaved and one's suspicions do not fit the facts at hand (Bringle & Buunk, 1991). Suspicious jealousy results in worried and mistrustful vigilance and snooping as the jealous partner seeks to confirm his or her suspicions, and it can range from a mildly overactive imagination to outright paranoia. In all cases, however, suspicious jealousy can be said to be unfounded; it results from situations that would not trouble a more secure and more trusting partner.

The distinction between the two types of jealousy is meaningful because almost everybody feels reactive jealousy when they realize that their partners have been unfaithful (Buss, 2000), but people vary a lot in their tendencies to feel suspicious jealousy in the absence of any provocation. Nevertheless, the distinction between the two isn't quite as sharp as it may seem. A jealous reaction to a partner's affair may linger on as suspicious jealousy years later because trust, once lost, is never fully regained. And people may differ in their judgments of what constitutes a real threat to their relationship (Guerrero, 1998). Knowledge that a partner is merely fantasizing about someone else may not trouble a secure partner who is not much prone to jealousy, but it may cause reactive jealousy in a partner who is insecure. So, the boundary between them can be vague, and as we explore individual differences in susceptibility to jealousy in our next section, I'll ask a generic question that refers to both types of jealousy.

Who's Prone to Jealousy?

On the whole, men and women do not differ in their jealous tendencies (Buunk, 1995), but there are individual differences in susceptibility to jealousy that lead

Suspicious jealousy does not fit the facts at hand.

some people to feel jealous more readily and more intensely than other people do. One obvious precursor of jealousy is *dependence* on a relationship (Rydell et al., 2004). When people feel that they need a particular partner because their alternatives are poor—that is, when people have a low CL_{alt}—any threat to their relationship is especially menacing. In contrast, people who have desirable alternatives tend to be less jealous because they have less to lose if the relationship ends (Hansen, 1985).

Jealousy also increases with feelings of *inadequacy* in a relationship (White, 1981). People who worry that they can't measure up to their partners' expectations or who fret that they're not what their lovers are looking for are less certain that their relationships will last, and they are more prone to jealousy than are people who feel certain they can keep their partners satisfied (Knobloch et al., 2001). Self-confidence in a relationship is undoubtedly affected by a person's global sense of self-worth, and people with high self-esteem do tend to be less prone to jealousy than those with low self-esteem (DeSteno et al., 2006). However, a person's perceptions of his or her adequacy as a partner in a specific relationship are especially important, and even people with generally high self-esteem can be prone to jealousy if they doubt their ability to fulfill a beloved partner.

One of the ingredients in such doubt is a discrepancy in the mate value each person brings to the relationship (Buss, 2000). If one partner is more desirable than the other, possessing (for example) more physical attractiveness, wealth, or talent, the less desirable partner is a less valuable mate, and that's a potential problem. The less desirable partner is likely to be aware that others could be a better match for his or her lover, and that may cause a sense of inadequacy that does not exist in other areas of his or her life (or with other partners). Here is another reason, then, why *matching* occurs with people pairing off with others of similar mate value (see chapter 3): Most of us want the most desirable partners we can get, but it can be threatening to realize that our partners could do better if they really wanted to.

In any case, consider the perilous situation that faces people who feel both dependent on and inadequate in their current relationships: They need their partners but worry that they're not good enough to keep them. It's no wonder that they react strongly to real or imagined signs that a romantic rival has entered the scene.

Of course, *attachment styles* influence jealousy, too. To some extent, people with a preoccupied style routinely find themselves in a similar fix: They greedily seek closeness with others, but they remain chronically worried that their partners don't love them enough in return. That's a recipe for jealousy, and sure enough, preoccupied people experience more jealousy than do those with the other three styles (Buunk, 1997). The folks who are least affected when a relationship is threatened are typically those with a dismissing style of attachment. Feeling self-sufficient and trying not to depend on others is apparently one way to stay relatively immune to jealousy (Guerrero, 1998).

Personality traits are also involved. People who are high in neuroticism, who tend to worry about a lot of things, are particularly prone to jealousy. On the other hand, agreeable people, who tend to be cooperative and trusting, are less likely than others to become jealous (Buunk & Dijkstra, 2006).

Finally, *traditional gender roles* also make jealousy more likely (Hansen, 1985). Macho men and feminine women experience more jealousy than androgynous people do, perhaps because the rules of traditional relationships tend to be quite strict. Their rigid expectations cause greater dismay if the partners break the rules by, for instance, forming a friendship with a co-worker of the other sex at work.

Who Gets Us Jealous?

We become jealous when our partners are interested in someone else, but not all rivals are created equal. It's particularly obnoxious when our friends start horning in on our romantic relationships; rivalry from a friend is more upsetting than is similar behavior from a stranger (Bleske & Shackelford, 2001). It's also especially painful when our partners start expressing renewed interest in their former lovers (Cann & Baucom, 2004). But no matter who they are, romantic rivals who have high mate value and who make us look bad by comparison are worrisome threats to our relationships, and they arouse more jealousy than do rivals who are milder competition.

And what kind of rivals are those? It depends on what our partners like. As you'll recall from chapter 3, women care more than men do about a mate's resources, so men are more jealous of other men who are self-confident, dominant, assertive, and rich than they are of rivals who are simply very handsome (Buunk & Dijkstra, 2006). On the other hand, a handsome rival is bad enough: Everybody likes lovely lovers (Eastwick & Finkel, 2008), so attractive competitors evoke more jealousy in both men and women than homely rivals do (Massar & Buunk, 2009). The good news is that our rivals are usually not as attractive to our partners as we think they are, so our fears are usually overblown—but the bad news is that we do make such mistakes, overestimating the desirability of our competition and thereby suffering more distress than is warranted (Hill, 2007).

What Gets Us Jealous?

Evolutionary psychology has popped up here and there in this book, and here's another place it's pertinent. In this case, an evolutionary perspective suggests that jealousy evolved to motivate behavior designed to protect our close relationships from the interference of others. Presumably, early humans who reacted strongly to interlopers—being vigilant to outside interference, fending off rivals, and working hard to satisfy and fulfill their current partners—maintained their relationships and reproduced more successfully than did those who were blasé about meddlesome rivals. This perspective thus suggests that because it offered reproductive advantages in the past, jealousy is now a natural, ingrained reaction that is hard to avoid (Buss, 2000). More provocatively, it also suggests that men and women should be especially sensitive to different sorts of infidelity in their romantic partners.

Remember (from chapter 1) that men face a reproductive problem that women do not have: *paternity uncertainty.* A woman always knows whether or not a particular child is hers, but unless he is completely confident that his mate hasn't had sex with other men, a man can't be certain (without using some advanced technology) that he is a child's father. And being cuckolded and raising another man's offspring is an evolutionary dead end; the human race did not descend from ancestors who raised other people's children and had none of their own! Indeed, the potential evolutionary costs of failing to detect a partner's infidelity are so great that natural selection may have favored men who were *too* suspicious of their partners' faithfulness over those who were not suspicious enough (Haselton & Buss, 2000). Unwarranted doubt about a partner's fidelity is divisive and painful, but it may not be as costly and dangerous to men in an evolutionary sense as being too trusting and failing to detect infidelity when it occurs. Thus, today men have more extramarital affairs than women do (Tafoya & Spitzberg, 2007), but it's men, not women, who are more accurate at detecting sexual infidelity in a cheating partner (Andrews et al., 2008). And vigilance is sometimes sensible; as we saw in chapter 9, about 2 percent of the world's children are being raised by men who do not know that the children were fathered by another man (Anderson, 2006).

For their part, women presumably enjoyed more success raising their children when they were sensitive to any signs that a man might withdraw the resources that were protecting and sheltering them and their children. Assuming that men were committed to them when the men in fact were not would have been risky for women, so sexual selection may have favored those who were usually skeptical of men's declarations of true love. Unfairly doubting a man's commitment may be obnoxious and self-defeating, but believing that a mate was devoted and committed when he was not may have been more costly still. In our ancestral past, women who frequently and naïvely mated with men who then abandoned them probably did not reproduce as successfully as did women who insisted on more proof that a man was there to stay. Thus, modern women are probably the "descendants of ancestral mothers who erred in the direction of being cautious," who tended to prudently underestimate the commitment of their men (Haselton & Buss, 2000, p. 83).

As a result of all this, an evolutionary perspective suggests that men should experience more jealousy at the thought of *sexual* infidelity in their mates, whereas women should react more to the threat of *emotional* infidelity, the possibility that their partners are falling in love with someone else. Either type of infidelity can provoke jealousy in either sex, of course, but they differ in their evolutionary implications. For a man, it's not a partner's love for someone else that's the bigger threat to his reproductive success—it's the *sex*; his children may still thrive if his mate loves another man, but he certainly does not want to raise the other man's children. For a woman, it's not a partner's intercourse with someone else that's more dangerous, it's the *love*; as long as he continues to provide needed resources, her children may still thrive even if he impregnates other women—but if he falls in love and moves out entirely, her kids' future may be imperiled.

This reasoning led David Buss and his colleagues (Buss et al., 1992, p. 252) to pose this compelling question to research participants:

Please think of a serious committed romantic relationship that you have had in the past, that you currently have, or that you would like to have. Imagine that you discover that the person with whom you've been seriously involved became interested in someone else. What would distress or upset you more (please pick only one):

    (A) Imagining your partner forming a deep emotional attachment to that person.

    (B) Imagining your partner enjoying passionate sexual intercourse with that other person.

Which one would you pick? Most of the men—60 percent—said the sex would upset them more, but only 17 percent of the women chose that option; instead, a sizable majority of the women—83 percent—reported that they would be more distressed by a partner's emotional attachment to a rival. Moreover, a follow-up study demonstrated that men and women differed in their physiological reactions to these choices (Buss et al., 1992). Men displayed more autonomic changes indicative of emotional arousal when they imagined a partner's sexual, rather than emotional, infidelity, but the reverse was true for women.

These results are consistent with an evolutionary perspective, but they have engendered controversy (Harris, 2005; Sagarin, 2005) with critics suggesting that they are less convincing than they seem. One straightforward complaint is methodological. The use of a "forced-choice" question in which research participants have to pick one option or the other can exaggerate a subtle and relatively minor difference between the sexes (DeSteno et al., 2002). If men find sexual infidelity only slightly more threatening than women do, a forced-choice question could yield the striking results Buss et al. (1992) obtained even if the actual difference in men's and women's outlooks was rather trivial. And in fact, when they are allowed to specify that they would find both types of infidelity equally upsetting, most people—both men and women—do (Lishner et al., 2008).

More subtly, the two types of infidelity may mean different things to women than they do to men (DeSteno & Salovey, 1996). Because men are more

Mate Poaching

The good news with regard to romantic rivalries is that huge majorities—99 percent!—of American college students say that they want to settle down with a mutually monogamous sexual partner at some point in their lives (Pedersen et al., 2002). Most of us expect to be faithful to one special person sometime down the road. However, the bad news is that *mate poaching,* behavior that is intended to attract someone who is already in a romantic relationship, is commonplace. Around the world, most men (54 percent) and quite a few women (34 percent) have tried to poach someone else's partner (Davies et al., 2007), and about four-fifths of them have succeeded at least once (Schmitt et al., 2004). Moreover, about 70 percent of us have encountered a poacher's efforts to lure us away from our partners (at least for one night), and most men (60 percent) and half of all women who have been pursued have succumbed to a poaching attempt (Schmitt et al., 2004).

What sort of person pursues someone else's mate? In general, mate poachers are horny, extraverted people who are low in agreeableness and conscientiousness and who approve of adulterous promiscuity (Schmitt & Buss, 2001); they also tend to be narcissistic and manipulative (Jonason et al., 2010) and to have avoidant attachment styles, so they are relatively disinterested in trusting intimacy with others (Schachner & Shaver, 2002). Instead, they're motivated to poach by the challenge and the ego boosts they experience when they're successful (Davies et al., 2010). None of this is very loving, and poachers sound like lousy long-term mates! Nevertheless, the more attractive they are, the more successful their poaching attempts tend to be (Schmitt et al., 2004), and their success

may lie in the fact that those who succumb to poaching attempts tend to resemble their pursuers; people who are lured away by poachers tend to be sexually attractive, horny, extraverted people who are open to experience and who do not much value sexual fidelity (Schmitt et al., 2004).

The poaching tactics used by men and women tend to differ. When they are trying to entice someone else's mate, women advertise their good looks and sexual availability, whereas men publicize their power and their willingness to provide their lovers desirable resources (Schmitt & Buss, 2001). The sexes also tend to adopt different approaches when they want to be poached and they wish to communicate to potential poachers that they are available. In such cases, women flaunt their beauty, promise access to sex, and complain about their current partners whereas men offer compliments and are overly generous to those whose attention they seek (Schmitt & Shackelford, 2003).

Presumably, people succumb to poaching when poachers offer benefits that are better than those available from their present partners (Greiling & Buss, 2000). In the long run, however, they may not be doing themselves a favor. Relationships that result from mate poaching inevitably begin with betrayal, and the partnerships that follow do not seem to be as satisfying and committed, on average, as those in which poaching does not occur. Poachers are untrustworthy, and to some degree, people get poached because they are looking around for something better, and everybody involved tends to *keep* looking around even after they start a new relationship. Having been unfaithful once, they tend to be unfaithful again (Foster et al., 2004).

accepting of casual sex, women may routinely assume that a man's sexual infidelity is just that: casual sex. His emotional infidelity, however, may mean that he's having sex with someone else *and* is in love with her, which would make emotional infidelity the more serious threat. For their part, men may assume that women often love someone without having sex, but usually love those with whom they *do* have sex, and that would make her sexual infidelity more momentous. In fact, men and women do generally hold such views (Whitty & Quigley, 2008). We tend to think that a cheating spouse is more likely to be emotionally attached to the illicit lover when the faithless spouse is a woman instead of a man (Sprecher et al., 1998). Thus, because we assume that sex and love are more closely connected for women than for men,[4] a choice between the two types of infidelity probably does mean different things for men than for women.

So, consider this: You've discovered that your partner has fallen in love with someone else *and* is having great sex with him or her. *Both* emotional and sexual infidelity have occurred. Which aspect of your partner's faithlessness, the sex or the love, bothers you more? This scenario answers the criticism that, individually, they mean different things to the different sexes, and in the United States, Korea, and Japan, more men than women chose sexual infidelity as the more hurtful insult (Buss et al., 1999). (In the United States, 61 percent of the men chose sexual infidelity as the more alarming threat, but only 13 percent of the women did.) In addition, the same sex difference is obtained when people rate their distress in response to the two infidelities instead of just picking the one that bothers them most (Edlund & Sagarin, 2009), and the pattern doesn't depend on how you ask the question. Indeed, men's greater concern with sexual infidelity occurs around the world; the extent to which people react jealously to sexual infidelity varies from culture to culture, but men routinely find it more distressing than women do (Frederick et al., 2008).

Various other research results are also consistent with the evolutionary perspective. The sex difference disappears when parents are asked to envision the infidelity of a daughter-in-law or son-in-law. Grandmothers face the same challenges to their reproductive success as grandfathers do, so an evolutionary perspective suggests that they should not differ in their reactions to infidelity from a child's partner. And indeed, when they imagine their sons or daughters having a cheating spouse, both mothers and fathers regard sexual infidelity to be more worrisome when it is committed by a daughter-in-law, and emotional infidelity to be more distressing when it is committed by a son-in-law (Shackelford et al., 2004). Siblings feel the same way about their sisters- and brothers-in-law (Michalski et al., 2007).

Moreover, men and women are differentially sensitive to the two types of threat. When the possibility exists, men are quicker to assume that sexual infidelity is occurring than women are, whereas women decide that emotional infidelity is occurring faster than men do (Schützwohl, 2005). After suspicions

---

[4] This assumption, you'll recall, is correct. On average, sex and love *are* more closely connected for women than for men. Look back at our discussion of sociosexuality on p. 285.

arise, men are more preoccupied by the threat of their mate's sexual infidelity whereas women fret more about their partner's emotional infidelity (Schütz-wohl, 2006). If they interrogate their partners, men are more likely than women to inquire about the sexual nature of the illicit relationship, whereas women are more likely than men to ask about its emotional nature (Kuhle et al., 2009). And if their suspicions are unfounded, men are more relieved to learn that sexual infidelity did not occur whereas women are more relieved to find that their part-ners are not in love with someone else (Schützwohl, 2008a).

Finally, the sex difference disappears, and men dread sexual infidelity only as much as women do when the cheating carries no risk of conceiving a child—that is, when their partners cheat with someone of the *same* sex in a gay or lesbian affair (Sagarin et al., 2003). Paternity uncertainty is irrelevant when a romantic rival is of the same sex as one's partner, and sure enough, men and women are equally threatened by the two types of infidelity in such situations. (And which kind of rival is worse? By a large margin, men consider a lover's affair with another man to be worse than one with a woman, but women think it would be equally awful for their men to cheat with either a woman or a man [Kruse et al., 2008]).

Our responses to the dreadful prospect of a partner's infidelity are com-plex, and men and women do *not* differ in their other reactions to a partner's faithlessness. All of us tend to get angry at the thought of a lover's sexual infi-delity, and we're hurt by the prospect of an emotional affair (Green & Sabini, 2006). Clearly, the most reasonable conclusion from all of these studies is that everybody hates both types of infidelity, and here, as in so many other cases, the sexes are more similar to each other than different. Still, to the extent that they differ at all, women are likely to perceive a partner's emotional attach-ment to a rival as more perilous than men do (e.g., Becker et al., 2004), just as an evolutionary perspective suggests. There are certainly other influences at work—for instance, as you can see in Figure 10.3, men with a dismissing attachment style are much more likely than other men to find emotional infi-delity a lesser threat (Levy & Kelly, 2010)—but it's clear that the threat of infi-delity is a salient, jealousy-provoking event for both men and women, and evolutionary psychology offers a fascinating, if arguable, explanation of our reactions to it.

Responses to Jealousy

People may react to the hurt, anger, and fear of jealousy in ways that have either beneficial or destructive effects on their relationships (Dindia & Timmerman, 2003). On occasion, jealous people lash out in ways that are unequivocally harm-ful, retaliating against their partners with violent behavior or verbal antag-onism, or with efforts to make them jealous in return (Guerrero et al., 2005). On other occasions, people respond in ways that may be intended to protect the relationship but that often undermine it further: spying on their partners, restricting their partners' freedom, or derogating or threatening their rivals. There are times, however, when people respond positively to jealousy by

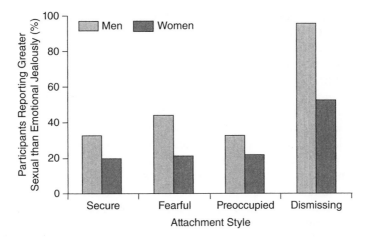

FIGURE 10.3. **Attachment style influences perceptions of sexual infidelity and emotional infidelity.**
Here's what young adults with different attachment styles said in New York City when they were asked the classic question from Buss et al. (1992) on page 318. Men were always more likely than women to choose sexual infidelity as the greater threat, but, nevertheless, most men and women found emotional infidelity to be more dreadful. Only those people with dismissing styles of attachment—those who were high in avoidance of intimacy but low in anxiety about abandonment—routinely thought that sexual infidelity was more distressing than emotional infidelity was.
Source: Levy & Kelly, 2010.

straightforwardly expressing their concerns and trying to work things out with their partners or by making themselves or their relationships more desirable (by, for instance, improving their appearance, sending the partner gifts, or doing more housework) (Guerrero & Andersen, 1998).

Attachment styles help determine what people will do. When they become jealous, people who are relatively comfortable with closeness—those with secure or preoccupied attachment styles—are more likely to express their concerns and to try to repair their relationships than are those with more avoidant styles (Guerrero, 1998). By comparison, people who are dismissing or fearful are more likely to avoid the issue or deny their distress by pretending nothing is wrong or by acting like they don't care.

Men and women often differ in their responses to jealousy, too, with consequences that can complicate heterosexual relationships. Imagine yourself in this situation: At a party, you leave your romantic partner sitting on a couch when you go to refill your drinks. While you're gone, your partner's old boyfriend or girlfriend happens by and sits for a moment, and they share a light kiss of greeting just as you return with the drinks. What would you do? When researchers showed people videotapes of a scenario like this and measured their intentions, men and women responded differently (Shettel-Neuber et al., 1978). Women said they would react to the rival's interference by seeking to *improve the relationship;* they intended to put on a show of indifference but compete with the rival by making themselves more attractive to their partners. In contrast, men said they would strive to *protect their egos;* they planned to get drunk, confront and threaten the rival, and pursue other women. Whereas women seemed to focus on preserving the existing relationship, men considered leaving it and salving their wounded pride with conquests of new partners.

Sex differences such as these have also been obtained in other studies (Miller & Maner, 2008), and one thing that makes them worrisome is that women are much more likely than men to *try* to get their partners jealous (White, 1980a). When they induce jealousy—usually by discussing or exaggerating their attraction to other men, sometimes by flirting with or dating them—they typically seek to test the relationship (to see how much he cares) or try to elicit more attention and commitment from their partners (Fleischmann et al., 2005). They evidently want their men to respond the way women do when they get jealous, with greater effort to protect and maintain the relationship. The problem, of course, is that that's not the way men typically react. Women who seek to improve their relationships by inducing jealousy in their men may succeed only in driving their partners away.

Coping Constructively with Jealousy

So, would you still be disappointed if you couldn't make your partner jealous? An unhappy mixture of hurt, anger, and fear occurs when your partner wants you but isn't sure he or she can keep you. It may be a natural thing for humans to feel, but it's often an ugly, awful feeling that results in terribly destructive behavior (Buss, 2000). Someday you may find yourself wishing that you could feel it less intensely and limit its effects. What can be done?

If you're prone to jealousy, consider spending less time on Facebook. There are lots of potentially threatening ambiguities on social network sites—flirty comments on your partner's wall, new friends on your lover's list who are unfamiliar to you, and new pictures of your partner in old relationships—that can cause unjustified jealousy, and the more time people spend on Facebook, the more jealousy they feel as a result (Muise et al., 2009). If you find yourself snooping a lot, and worrying needlessly as a result, you may want to step away from your screen (Hill, 2009).

When jealousy is justified and a rival is real, the experts suggest that we work on reducing the connection between the exclusivity of a relationship and our sense of self-worth (Salovey & Rodin, 1988). Finding that someone we love is attracted to a rival can be painful—but it doesn't mean that your partner is a horrible, worthless person, or that you are. We react irrationally when we act as though our self-worth totally depended on a particular relationship.

In fact, when they succeed in reducing unwanted jealousy, people tend to use two techniques that help them to maintain a sense of independence and self-worth (Salovey & Rodin, 1988). The first is *self-reliance,* which involves efforts to "stay cool" and to avoid feeling angry or embarrassed by refusing to dwell on the unfairness of the situation. The second is *self-bolstering,* boosting one's self-esteem by doing something nice for oneself and thinking about one's good qualities. Maintaining a sense of self-confidence about one's ability to act and to survive independently apparently helps keep jealousy at manageable levels.

When people are unable to do that on their own, formal therapy can help. Clinical approaches to the treatment of jealousy usually try to (a) reduce irrational, catastrophic thinking that exaggerates either the threat to the relationship or the harm that its loss would entail; (b) enhance the self-esteem of the jealous partner; (c) improve communication skills so the partners can clarify their expectations and agree on limits that prevent jealous misunderstandings; and (d) increase satisfaction and fairness in the relationship (Pines, 1998). Most of us don't need therapy to cope with jealousy. But it might help some of us if romantic relationships came with a warning label:

WARNING: It may be dangerous to your and your partner's health if you do not know beyond doubt that you are a valuable and worthwhile human being with or without your partner's love.

DECEPTION AND LYING

Other sources of stress and strain can certainly cause jealousy when they involve romantic rivals, but they involve rivals only now and then and occur much more often than jealousy does. Indeed, the hazards I'll consider next, lying and other forms of deception, occur so often in social life that they are commonplace (whether we realize it or not). As we'll see, deception of some sort or another occurs regularly even in intimate relationships that are based on openness and trust.

Deception is intentional behavior that creates an impression in the recipient that the deceiver knows to be untrue (Vrij et al., 2010). Outright lying in which people fabricate information and make statements that contradict the truth is the most straightforward example of deceptive behavior, but there are various other ways to convey misleading impressions without coming right out and saying things that are untrue (Buller & Burgoon, 1994). For instance, people may simply *conceal* information and not mention details that would communicate the truth, or they may *divert attention* from vital facts, abruptly changing topics to avoid the discussion of touchy subjects. On other occasions, they may mix truthful and deceptive information into *half-truths* that are misleading. I'll focus on lies because they have been studied much more extensively than other forms of deception, but we'll only be scratching the surface of the various ways intimate partners mislead each other.

Lying in Close and Casual Relationships

Research by Bella DePaulo and her colleagues (2009) has painted a remarkable portrait of lying in everyday life. College students who keep diaries of their interactions with others report telling two lies a day on average, lying to one out of every three people with whom they interact (DePaulo et al., 1996). Adults off campus tell fewer lies, about one per day, lying in one of every five interactions. Very few people, only 5 percent, report having told no lies at all in a given week. Most of these lies are casual, spontaneous events that are not considered to be serious by those who tell them, and most of them are successful; the liars are confident that their lies are accepted most (59 percent) of the time, and they feel that they've been caught lying only rarely (19 percent of the time). (On other occasions, they aren't sure of the result.)

In most interactions, the most common type of lie is one that benefits the liar, warding off embarrassment, guilt, or inconvenience, or seeking approval or material gain. In particular, when they are trying to appeal to a member of the other sex, men and women may tell lies that exaggerate their attractiveness. Men are more likely than women to misrepresent their ambition and income and to claim they are committed to a relationship when they are not. Women are more likely to promise but not provide sex, cry out in fake pleasure during sex (Brewer & Hendrie, 2011), and to fake orgasms (Muehlenhard & Shippee, 2009). Both sexes, then, tell selfish lies that are especially designed to appeal to the other sex (Haselton et al., 2005).

However, one-fourth of all lies are told to benefit others, protecting their feelings or advancing their interests, and when women interact with other women, such lies are as common as self-centered ones (DePaulo et al., 1996). People are especially likely to misrepresent the truth when brutal honesty would hurt the feelings of someone who is highly invested in the issue at hand. For instance, imagine that you really dislike a painting but are describing your feelings about it to an art student who may have painted it. Would you be totally honest? In just such a situation, no one was (DePaulo & Bell, 1996). People typically admitted that the painting wasn't one of their favorites, but they were much less critical than they had been in prior written evaluations of the piece.

Some lies are obviously undertaken to promote polite, friendly interaction with others. We often claim to agree with others when in fact we do not, and we often say that we are more pleased with events than we really are. Most lies in close relationships, where we expect our partners to be generous and honest, are benevolent, small lies like these (DePaulo & Kashy, 1998). People tell fewer self-serving, greedy lies—and fewer lies overall—to their lovers and friends than to acquaintances and strangers.

These patterns make lying sound rather innocuous in close relationships. However, people still tell a lot of lies to their intimate partners—in one study, 92 percent of the participants admitted that they had lied to their lovers (Cole, 2001)[5]—and when they do tell serious lies about topics that could destroy their reputations or relationships, they tell them more often to their closest partners than to anyone else (DePaulo et al., 2004). The biggest deceptions we undertake occur more often in our intimate relationships than anywhere else.

---

[5] And the other 8 percent may have been lying when they said they hadn't. That's ironic, isn't it?

In addition, lies can be consequential even when they go undetected. In general, people consider interactions in which they tell a lie for any reason to be less pleasant and less intimate than interactions in which they are totally honest, and lying to a close partner makes them particularly uncomfortable (DePaulo & Kashy, 1998). Despite its prevalence in social life, most of us judge lying harshly (Tyler et al., 2006), and people evidently know they're living dangerously when they lie to others. Moreover, lying in close relationships undermines the liar's trust in the partner who receives the lie (Sagarin et al., 1998). This is a phenomenon known as **deceiver's distrust:** When people lie to others, they often begin to perceive the recipients of the lies as less honest and trustworthy as a result. This seems to occur both because liars assume that other people are just like them, so they assume that others share their own deceitful motives, and because they feel better about themselves when they believe their faults are shared by others (Sagarin et al., 1998). In either case, lying can sully a relationship even when the liar is the only one who knows that any lying has taken place.

Liars are also likely to think that their lies are more harmless and inoffensive than the recipients do (Kaplar & Gordon, 2004). This is a common pattern when someone misbehaves in a partnership, and we'll see it again a few pages from now when I discuss betrayals: The recipient (or victim) of a partner's wrongdoing almost always considers it more informative and influential than the perpetrator does (Cameron et al., 2002). Thus, what liars consider to be a small fib may be considered to be a harmful and duplicitous deceit by others if the lie becomes known. But that begs the question, how often do liars get caught? As we'll see, the answer is, "it depends."

Lies and Liars

Some people do lie more than others do (Kashy & DePaulo, 1996). Those who are gregarious and sociable, and those who are more concerned with the impressions they make on others, tell more lies than do those who are less outgoing. In addition, people who have insecure attachment styles tell more lies than secure partners do (Gillath et al., 2010), and people who are low in conscientiousness lie a lot, too (Spain, 2011).

However, frequent liars are not necessarily more successful liars. High social skill makes people more convincing (Burgoon & Bacue, 2003), but a liar's performance also depends on the level of motivation (and guilt and fear) with which he or she enacts the lie. Lies are typically shorter and less detailed than truths are (Newman et al., 2003) unless the lie is important and the liar is highly motivated to get away with the lie; when liars care enough to send their very best, they create scripts that are more convincing than those authored by liars who are less highly motivated (DePaulo et al., 1983). However, when they deliver their lies, motivated liars do a poorer, more suspicious job than do those who have less to lose and who are more spontaneous and relaxed (Forrest & Feldman, 2000). People who really want to get away with a lie tend to be more obvious than they would be if they didn't care so much. In particular, people who are lying to make good impressions on attractive people of the other sex tend to be quite transparent both to the recipients of their lies and to anyone else who's watching (DePaulo et al., 1985)! People who are lying to unattractive targets, or to members of their own sex, are harder to detect.

What goes wrong when lies are detected? The liar's nonverbal behavior gives him or her away (DePaulo et al., 2003). When people are lying, they often speak hesitantly in a higher pitch and make more grammatical errors and slips of the tongue than they do when they're telling the truth (Vrij et al., 2001), and they blink less often (Leal & Vrij, 2008). Except for brief flashes ("microexpressions") of honesty when they're gaining control (Ekman & O'Sullivan, 1991), their facial expressions usually don't give them away; people know they're supposed to look sincere and to look others directly in the eye when they're trying to seem honest, and they are usually able to do so. But there tend to be discrepancies and mismatches between their tones of voice and their facial expressions, and inconsistencies in the things they say, that arouse suspicion (Porter & ten Brinke, 2010). None of these cues is certain evidence of lying all by itself; "there is no one cue that always indicates that a person is lying" (DePaulo, 1994, p. 85). Really, there is nothing that people do, "not a single verbal, non-verbal, or physiological cue [that is] uniquely related to deception" (Vrij, 2007, p. 324).

So, How Well Can We Detect a Partner's Deception?

The problem is that the specific reactions that indicate that a person is lying may be quite idiosyncratic. People differ in their mannerisms. Some of us speak hesitantly most of the time, whereas others are more verbally assertive; some people engage in frequent eye contact, whereas others rarely look us in the eye. Lying is usually apparent in changes in a person's ordinary demeanor, but to notice those changes, one may need some prior familiarity with the person's style (Vrij et al., 2010). People can learn to detect deception in others: When research participants get repeated opportunities to judge whether or not someone is lying—and are given continuing feedback about the accuracy of their judgments[6]—they do become better judges of that person's truthfulness. However, their improvement is limited to that particular person, and they're no better at detecting lying in anyone else (Zuckerman et al., 1984)!

Intimate partners have personal, idiosyncratic knowledge of each other that should allow them to be sensitive judges of each other's behavior. But they also *trust* each other (or their relationship probably isn't very intimate), and that leads them to exhibit a **truth bias** in which they assume that their partners are usually telling the truth (Burgoon & Levine, 2010). As a result, intimate partners often make very confident judgments of each other's veracity, but their confidence has nothing whatsoever to do with how accurate they are (DePaulo et al., 1997). This means that people are sometimes certain that their partners are telling the truth when their partners are actually lying.

---

[6]Researchers can provide this in a lab procedure, but it doesn't happen in real relationships. We don't often get exact and accurate feedback about our judgments of our lovers' truthfulness, do we? And no, watching episodes of the television show, *Lie to Me*, is not making you any better at detecting deception in others (Levine et al., 2010).

In fact, as relationships become intimate and trust increases, the partners' accuracy in detecting deception in each other doesn't improve, it declines (McCornack & Parks, 1990). Mere practice doesn't seem to be of much use where lie detection is concerned (Anderson et al., 2002). Indeed, experienced customs inspectors (Kraut & Poe, 1980), agents of the FBI, CIA, or National Security Agency, and psychiatrists (Ekman & O'Sullivan, 1991) all do no better than laypersons do at detecting lies told (or powder smuggled) by strangers. And that means they're not doing well at all. A sprawling meta-analysis of studies involving 24,483 research participants demonstrated that we correctly distinguish truths from lies 54 percent of the time (Bond & DePaulo, 2006)—but because we'd get 50 percent right just by flipping a coin, that's not very good.

Now, some people—including some Secret Service agents and some clinical psychologists—*can* catch liars readily (O'Sullivan, 2008). And if anyone routinely knows when *you're* lying, your intimate partners probably do. However, any belief that our partners are completely transparent to us is probably misplaced. People tend not to be very skilled lie detectors, and despite our considerable experience with our close friends and lovers, we usually do a poorer job of distinguishing their fact from fancy than we realize (DePaulo et al., 1997). In fact, not many lies in close relationships are detected at the time

---

Lying Online

The remarkable reach of the Web allows us to interact with lots of interesting people we would not otherwise meet, but it also allows those people to lie to us with relative impunity. With whom are we chatting when we send instant messages to a stranger online? It's often hard to say (McKenna, 2008). The information we receive from new acquaintances on the Web may result from some mixture of illusion, variable social skills, outright falsehoods, and truth (Orr, 2004). People's real personalities tend to be evident in their Facebook profiles (Back et al., 2010b), but there's a lot of exaggeration, too: Men are likely to lie about their financial status and height, women are likely to lie about their physical attractiveness and weight, and people of both sexes may even pretend to be the other sex online (O'Sullivan, 2008; Sprecher et al., 2008)!

Faced with occasional fictions and frauds, people tend to be cautiously suspicious when they interact online. We generally expect others to be less trustworthy, and if anything seems implausible, if people seem "too good to be true," most of us assume the worst. However, people we already know may actually be more honest with us online than they are over the phone or in person. When college students kept diaries of their communications with others for a week, they reported telling a lie in 37 percent of their phone calls and 27 percent of their face-to-face conversations, but in only 21 percent of their instant messages and 14 percent of their e-mails (Hancock et al., 2004). Conceivably, people lie more reluctantly whenever their remarks are written down and can be more easily checked later for accuracy. Thus, although they may sometimes tell huge lies to those who do not know them well, people tend to be more truthful online than when they're face-to-face.

they're told; if the truth comes out, it's usually later on, when information from others, physical evidence, and the occasional confession come into play (Burgoon & Levine, 2010).

Thus, people tell lots of lies, even in close relationships, and they get away with most of them. However, don't pat yourself on the back if you're currently deceiving a partner. Most people think that they're better at deceiving their partners than their partners are at deceiving them (Boon & McLeod, 2001), so your partner may be secretly proud about fooling you, too. And consider the big picture. People tell fewer lies in the relationships they find most rewarding, in part because lying violates shared expectations of honesty and trust. Keeping secrets isn't easy. And even if your lies go undetected, they may poison the atmosphere in your relationship, contributing to unwarranted suspicion and doubt. And you run the risk that if they are detected, your lies may seem to your partner to be a despicable example of our next topic: betrayal of an intimate partner.

BETRAYAL

People don't always do what we want or expect them to do. Some of the surprises our partners spring on us are pleasant ones (Afifi & Metts, 1998), but our partners occasionally do harmful things (or fail to do desirable things) that violate the expectations we hold for close confidants. Such acts are **betrayals,** disagreeable, hurtful actions by people we trusted and from whom we reasonably did not expect such treachery. Sexual and emotional infidelity and lying are common examples of betrayal, but any behavior that violates the norms of benevolence, loyalty, respect, and trustworthiness that support intimate relationships may be considered treasonous to some degree. People who reveal secrets about their partners, gossip about them behind their backs, tease in hurtful ways, break important promises, fail to support their partners, spend too much time elsewhere, or simply abandon a relationship are often thought to have betrayed their partners (Metts, 1994).

All of these actions involve painful drops in perceived relational value. When we are victimized by intimate partners, their betrayals demonstrate that they do not value their relationships with us as much as we had believed, or else, from our point of view, they would not have behaved as they did (Fitness & Warburton, 2009). The sad irony is that for losses of relational value of this sort to occur, we must have (or think we have) a desired relationship that is injured; thus, casual acquaintances cannot betray us as thoroughly and hurtfully as trusted intimates can (Jones & Burdette, 1994). We're not always hurt by the ones we love, but the ones we love *can* hurt us in ways that no one else can (Miller, 1997b).

In fact, when our feelings get hurt in everyday life, it's usually our close friends or romantic partners who cause us distress (Leary & Springer, 2001). Those partners are rarely being intentionally malicious—which is fortunate because it's very painful to believe that our partners intended to hurt us

(Vangelisti & Hampel, 2010)—but they often disappoint us anyway. Almost all of us have betrayed someone and have been betrayed by someone else in a close relationship at some time or another, and a betrayal has occurred in about half of the relationships we have now (Jones et al., 2001). Betrayal is a common event in close relationships.

Because caring and trust are integral aspects of intimacy, this may be surprising, but perhaps it shouldn't be. Most of us are close in some way to more than one person, and when people try to be loyal simultaneously to several different relationships, competing demands are inescapable. And when obligations overlap, occasional violations of the norms in a given relationship may be unavoidable (Baxter et al., 1997). If two of your close friends scheduled their weddings in different cities on the same day, for instance, you'd have to disappoint one of them, even without wanting to. Moreover, we occasionally face competing demands within a given relationship, finding ourselves unable to appropriately honor all of the responsibilities of a caring friend or lover. I once learned that the ex-wife of a good friend was now sleeping with my friend's best friend.[7] Honesty and openness required that I inform my friend of his other friend's—and, arguably, his ex-wife's—betrayal. However, caring and compassion suggested that he not be burdened with painful, embarrassing news he could do nothing about. It was a no-win situation. Seeking to protect my friend's feelings, I decided not to tell him about his other friend's betrayal—but a few months later, when he learned the truth, he was hurt and disappointed that I had kept such a secret from him. Perceived betrayals sometimes occur when people have the best intentions but simply cannot honor all of the overlapping and competing demands that intimacy and interdependency may make (Peetz & Kammrath, 2011).

Individual Differences in Betrayal

Nevertheless, some of us betray our partners more often than others do. Using the Interpersonal Betrayal Scale in Table 10.2, Warren Jones found that betrayal is more frequent among college students majoring in the social sciences, education, business, and the humanities than among those studying the physical sciences, engineering, and other technical fields (Jones & Burdette, 1994). Off-campus, betrayal is less frequent among those who are older, better educated, and religious. More importantly, those who report repeated betrayals of others tend to be unhappy and maladjusted. Betrayers tend to be resentful, vengeful, and suspicious people. They're prone to jealousy and cynicism, have a higher incidence of psychiatric problems, and are more likely than others to come from broken homes. Overall, betrayers do not trust others much, perhaps because they wrongly attribute to others the same motives they recognize in themselves (Couch & Jones, 1997).

---

[7] Here's an interesting question that's inspired by this example: Imagine that you discover your lover cheating on you with your best friend. Who, in your opinion, has committed the greater betrayal? Why?

TABLE 10.2. The Interpersonal Betrayal Scale

How often have you done each of these things? Respond to each item using this scale:

> 1 = I have never done this.
> 2 = I have done this once.
> 3 = I have done this a few times.
> 4 = I have done this several times.
> 5 = I have done this many times.

___ 1. Snubbing a friend when you are with a group you want to impress.

___ 2. Breaking a promise without good reason.

___ 3. Agreeing with people you really disagree with so that they will accept you.

___ 4. Pretending to like someone you detest.

___ 5. Gossiping about a friend behind his or her back.

___ 6. Making a promise to a friend with no intention of keeping it.

___ 7. Failing to stand up for what you believe in because you want to be accepted by the "in" crowd.

___ 8. Complaining to others about your friends or family members.

___ 9. Telling others information given to you in confidence.

___10. Lying to a friend.

___11. Making a promise to a family member with no intention of keeping it.

___12. Failing to stand up for a friend when he or she is being criticized or belittled by others.

___13. Taking family members for granted.

___14. Lying to your parents or spouse about your activities.

___15. Wishing that something bad would happen to someone you dislike.

Add up your answers to calculate your score. The average score for college men and women is 36. The average for adult men and women off campus is 35. However, in a sample of older people over age 65, the average score was 28. The standard deviation of the scores people get on the scale is 8 points, so if your own score is 44 or higher, your betrayal score is higher than average. On the other hand, if your score is 28 or lower, you betray others less often than most other people do.

Source: Jones & Burdette, 1994.

Men and women do not differ in their tendencies to betray others, but they do differ in the targets of their most frequent betrayals (Jones & Burdette, 1994). Men are more likely than women to betray their romantic partners and business associates, whereas women betray their friends and family members more often than men do. Whether one is at particular risk for betrayal from a man or woman seems to depend on the part one plays in his or her life.

The Two Sides to Every Betrayal

Those who betray their intimate partners usually underestimate the harm they do. As we saw in chapter 4, it's normal for people to be self-serving when they consider their actions, but when it comes to betrayal, this tendency leads people to excuse and minimize actions that their partners may find quite harmful (Cameronet al., 2002). Betrayers often consider their behavior to be inconsequential and innocuous, and they are quick to describe mitigating circumstances that vindicate their actions (Stillwell et al., 2008). However, their victims rarely share those views. Those who are betrayed routinely judge the transgression to be more severe than the betrayers do (Feeney & Hill, 2006).

These two different perspectives lead to disparate perceptions of the harm that is done. People who are betrayed almost never believe that such events have no effect on their relationships; 93 percent of the time, they feel that a betrayal damages the partnership, leading to lower satisfaction and lingering suspicion and doubt (Jones & Burdette, 1994). In contrast, the perpetrators acknowledge that their behavior was harmful only about half the time. They even think that the relationship has *improved* as a result of their transgression in one of every five cases. Such judgments are clearly ill-advised. We may feel better believing that our occasional betrayals are relatively benign, but it may be smarter to face the facts: Betrayals almost always have a negative, and sometimes lasting, effect on a relationship. Indeed, they are routinely the central complaint of spouses seeking therapy or a divorce (Amato & Previti, 2003).

Coping with Betrayal

Betrayal can be tough to take, and betrayals typically have adverse effects on the quality of a relationship. Still, when such events occur, some responses are more helpful than others. When they think back to past betrayals, college students report less anxiety and better coping when they say they tried to (a) face up to the betrayal instead of denying that it happened; (b) reinterpret the event in a positive light and use it as an impetus for personal growth; and (c) rely on their friends for support (Ferguson-Isaac et al., 1999). People seem to fare less well when they try to pretend it didn't happen, wallow in negative emotions such as bitterness and spite, and resort to drugs and alcohol to blot out the pain.

Victims of both sexes sometimes feel that they want to exact some form of painful revenge (Haden & Hojjat, 2006). When they are wronged, some people are more vengeful than others; they think that mistreatment from others should be repaid in kind, so that "if someone important to you does something negative to you, you should do something even more negative to them" (Eisenberger et al., 2004, p. 789). This seems to be a rather sour outlook, and, indeed, vengeful people tend to be high in neuroticism and low in agreeableness (McCullough et al., 2001). They ruminate about the wrongs they have encountered and are generally less happy with life than those who are less prone to vengeance; instead of moving on and getting past an event, they nurse a grudge and keep their wounds fresh (Carlsmith et al., 2008).

Thus, partners who have been betrayed sometimes take hurtful action. They withdraw, destroy old letters and gifts, pursue other relationships, and defame their partners to others (Yoshimura, 2007). None of this is good for a partnership,

A Practical Guide to Getting Away with It

Deception is corrosive and forgiveness is good for people, so I hesitate to offer advice about how to get away with betraying someone. Nevertheless, I'm here to present relationship science to you as objectively as possible, so here goes. Relationships are more adversely affected, and forgiveness is harder to obtain, if our partners catch us in an act of betrayal or learn of it from some third party than if we tell them of it ourselves when they ask (Afifi et al., 2001). (The least damaging mode of discovery, if our partners do learn of our betrayal, is for us to admit our wrongdoing without being asked [Essayli et al., 2010], but that's not the point of this box.)

So, admitting a wrong is better than being caught red-handed, but just what we say is important, too. When you're asked about a transgression you've committed, you shouldn't deny it outright, because your bold lie will compound your sins if (when?) the truth comes out. Instead, equivocate (Rycyna et al., 2009). Make your response as truthful as possible, and don't contradict the truth. A crafty strategy is to confess to a less serious offense; that often seems more trustworthy than claiming to be entirely innocent, and it avoids the consequences of admitting the more serious wrong (Sternglanz, 2004).

I'm *not* encouraging you either to betray or to deceive your partners. If you follow the guidelines presented here, you will be behaving disreputably. However, you will be in well-known company. When President Bill Clinton claimed, "I did not have sexual relations with that woman, Miss Lewinsky," he was equivocating; his statement was technically correct, if you take "sexual relations" to mean intercourse, but it side-stepped the fact that he did have sexual interactions with her. Still, it allowed many listeners to continue to think him entirely innocent, without him saying so, until more information became available. Even when his equivocation was discovered, some people did not think it much of a lie.

of course, so let's end our look at painful stresses and strains by focusing on the healing process that can help a relationship survive a partner's misbehavior.

FORGIVENESS

If a relationship is to continue to thrive after a painful incident of betrayal, forgiveness may be necessary (McCullough, 2008). Forgiveness is "a decision to give up your perceived or actual right to get even with, or hold in debt, someone who has wronged you" (Markman et al., 1994, p. 217). It's a process in which "harmful conduct is acknowledged" and "the harmed partner extends undeserved mercy" to the one who has misbehaved (Waldron & Kelley, 2008, p. 19). When you forgive someone, you discard the desire to retaliate, give up your grudge, and put aside any spite or disregard for your partner (Friesen & Fletcher, 2007); you don't condone—or forget—a partner's misbehavior, but you do communicate your "willingness to exit from a potential cycle of abuse and recrimination" (Fincham & Beach, 2002, p. 240), and that sets the stage for possible reconciliation and relationship repair.

It's not always easy to forgive someone, and it comes more readily to some people than to others. Attachment style matters: Anxiety about abandonment and avoidance of intimacy both make people less forgiving (Kachadourian et al., 2004). In particular, secure people are more forgiving because they engage in less angry rumination that keeps their partners' transgressions fresh in their minds (Burnette et al., 2007). Those who are high in agreeableness also forgive others relatively easily (Fehr et al., 2010), in part because they are better than other people at separating blame from anger; they can hold wrongdoers responsible for their misbehavior without getting angry and hostile toward them, and that is hard for less agreeable people to do (Meier & Robinson, 2004). Finally, neuroticism and narcissism impede forgiveness. Narcissists have a grandiose sense of entitlement that fosters vengefulness, not forgiveness (Exline et al., 2004), and neuroticism may lead people to maintain grudges for years (Maltby et al., 2008).

Still, no matter who we are, forgiveness comes more readily when some important ingredients exist. The first is a humble, sincere *apology.* Victims are more likely to forgive those who betray them when the offenders acknowledge their wrongs, accept responsibility for their actions, offer genuine atonement by expressing shame, regret, and remorse for their misbehavior, and promise better conduct in the future (Hannon et al., 2010; Tabak et al., 2011). Forgiveness is less likely to occur when excuses are given or when an apology seems insincere. If you have misbehaved and a relationship is suffering, you might do well to recognize that your behavior was harmful, and apologize—but only if you really mean it (Zechmeister et al., 2004).

A second component to forgiveness is *empathy* on the part of the victim (Fehr et al., 2010). People who can take their partners' perspectives and imagine why they behaved the way they did—and in particular, those who can admit that they're not perfect, either (Exline et al., 2008)—are much more likely to forgive them than are those in whom empathy is lacking.

Finally, forgiveness is less likely to occur when victims brood about their partners' transgressions and remain preoccupied with the damage done by their misbehavior (McCullough et al., 2007). We let go of anger and resentment when we forgive someone, but rumination about our hurt or our partners' flaws tends to keep our umbrage alive, and that makes forgiveness harder to attain (Ysseldyk et al., 2007).

Fortunately, forgiveness is more likely to occur in close, committed relationships than in those that are less committed (Guerrero & Bachman, 2010), because empathy occurs more easily and because the betrayers are more likely to apologize (Ferrara & Levine, 2009). Partners in (what were) satisfying relationships are also more likely to employ lenient, sympathetic attributions that explain the offenders' misconduct as benevolently as possible, and that, too, make forgiveness more feasible (Friesen et al., 2005).

And importantly, forgiveness can improve the relationships in which it occurs. Retribution rarely gets our partners to reform and behave better, but forgiveness can; when people are forgiven, they often become more repentant and even less likely to repeat the offense (Wallace et al., 2008). Forgiveness also fosters constructive, open communication that makes it more likely that a couple will solve their problems and be happier down the road (Perrier et al., 2008).

But perhaps even more significantly, people who are able to forgive their intimate partners usually enjoy more personal well-being—that is, more self-esteem, less hostility, less distress and tension, and more satisfaction with life—than do those from whom forgiveness is less forthcoming (Bono et al., 2008; Witvliet et al., 2008). Forgiveness reduces our hurt and pain, replacing anger with equanimity, and it moves us toward reconciliation with our partners (Williamson & Gonzales, 2007). Vengefulness does neither of these things, and it undermines, rather than strengthens relationships (Ysseldyk et al., 2007). There's no question that, within intimate relationships, forgiveness is more desirable and beneficial to those who wield it than is vengeance.

Forgiveness does have its limits. It won't transform a selfish scoundrel into a worthy partner, and no one is suggesting that you doggedly continue to forgive a faithless partner who repeatedly takes advantage of you. Forgiveness that is offered in the absence of genuine contrition may be perceived to be a license to offend again; after all, why should I behave better if I'm certain to be forgiven no matter what I do (Luchies et al., 2011b)? Forgiveness is advantageous when a partner misbehaves rarely and deserves to be forgiven, but it can actually be detrimental, eroding your self-respect (Luchies et al., 2010) and delaying any resolution to your problems (McNulty, 2010) when your partner is unrepentant.

So, forgiveness is good for us and our relationships—when our partners and our relationships are worthy of it. When in doubt, choose forgiveness. The stakes are higher in intimate partnerships. It's more painful when our partners misbehave, but there's more reason to work to repair any damage that is done. Intimacy does open the door to excruciating costs but it also offers the potential for invaluable, irreplaceable rewards.

FOR YOUR CONSIDERATION

When Ann returned from her business trip, she described her weekend as pretty dull and uneventful, so Paul was surprised when he found pictures on her digital camera of a raucous dinner at which she and some guys had obviously been drinking and carrying on. A picture of her sitting at a table beaming with pleasure as two good-looking men hugged her and kissed her cheeks really rattled him. Stung and unhappy, he became sullen and distant. He started giving her the cold shoulder and began to ponder how to "pay her back." Ann knew that she had been too flirtatious, but she was secretly titillated by one of the guys in the picture who was now e-mailing her with veiled suggestions about their next meeting. In addition, Ann wasn't sure what Paul knew or suspected, but she was beginning to resent his petulance.

What do you think the future holds for Ann and Paul? Why?

CHAPTER SUMMARY

Hazards are surprisingly common in close relationships.

Perceived Relational Value

We encounter various amounts of acceptance and rejection from others that inform us of our *relational value* to others. Our perception that they value their relationships with us less than we want them to is a core ingredient of the stresses and strains covered in this chapter.

Hurt Feelings

Drops in *perceived relational value* cause hurt feelings that leave us psychologically wounded and despondent.

Ostracism

People sometimes ignore their partners in order to achieve some goal, but the recipients of such ostracism usually resent it. People with high self-esteem tend not to put up with such treatment.

Jealousy

People experience the fear, anger, and hurt of *jealousy* when they face the potential loss of a valued relationship to a real or imagined rival.

Two Types of Jealousy. *Reactive jealousy* occurs when people get jealous in response to a real threat, whereas *suspicious jealousy* occurs when one's partner has not misbehaved and one's suspicions do not fit the facts at hand.

Who's Prone to Jealousy? Needing someone but worrying that you're not good enough to keep that person is a recipe for jealousy. Personality traits and attachment styles influence jealousy, too.

Who Gets Us Jealous? Rivals who are attractive to our partners are particularly threatening.

What Gets Us Jealous? Men are more likely than women to consider sexual infidelity to be more distressing than emotional infidelity. This finding has engendered criticism, but it has also been replicated around the world.

Responses to Jealousy. Attachment styles influence responses to jealousy, and men and women often differ in their responses, too.

Coping Constructively with Jealousy. People who succeed in reducing unwanted jealousy on their own often practice self-reliance and self-bolstering.

Deception and Lying

Deception is intentional behavior that creates an impression in the recipient that the deceiver knows to be untrue.

Lying in Close and Casual Relationships. There's a lot of lying in everyday life. Lies engender *deceiver's distrust,* which leads liars to perceive the recipients of their lies as untrustworthy.

Lies and Liars. No single cue always indicates that people are lying. Instead, discrepancies in their nonverbal behavior usually do.

So, How Well Can We Detect a Partner's Deception? Intimate partners have detailed knowledge of each other, but they also exhibit a *truth bias* that leads them to assume that their partners are being honest with them. Most lies are not detected at the time they're proffered.

Betrayal

Betrayals are hurtful actions by people we trusted and from whom we did not expect such misbehavior.

Individual Differences in Betrayal. Frequent betrayers tend to be unhappy and maladjusted people who are resentful, vengeful, and suspicious of others.

The Two Sides to Every Betrayal. Betrayers often consider their behavior to be inconsequential and innocuous, but their victims rarely share those views.

Coping with Betrayal. Victims who face up to a betrayal cope more constructively than do those who try to pretend it didn't happen. Victims of betrayal sometimes want revenge, but such people have a sour outlook.

Forgiveness

Forgiveness entails giving up the right to retaliate for others' wrongdoing. It occurs more readily when the betrayers apologize and the victims are empathic. Forgiveness usually improves the relationships in which it occurs when one's partner is repentant.

CHAPTER 11

Conflict

THE NATURE OF CONFLICT ◆ What Is Conflict? ◆ The Frequency of
Conflict ◆ THE COURSE OF CONFLICT ◆ Instigating Events ◆ Attributions ◆
Engagement and Escalation ◆ The Demand/Withdraw Pattern ◆
Negotiation and Accommodation ◆ Dealing with Conflict: Four Types
of Couples ◆ THE OUTCOMES OF CONFLICT ◆ Ending Conflict ◆ Can
Fighting Be Good for a Relationship? ◆ FOR YOUR CONSIDERATION ◆
CHAPTER SUMMARY

Do your friends and lovers always do everything you want, when you want
it? Of course not. It's hard to imagine an intimate relationship that does not
involve occasional friction and incompatibility in the desires, opinions, and
actions of the two partners. No matter how much two people care for each
other, no matter how well-suited they are to each other, dispute and disagreement will occur (Canary, 2003). And the more interdependent they are—the
more time they spend together and the wider the variety of activities and tasks
they try to coordinate—the more likely occasional conflict becomes (Miller,
1997b). Conflict is inevitable in close relationships.

It's also very influential. Over time, the manner in which two partners
manage their conflicts may either enhance or erode their love and regard for
each other. In this chapter, then, we'll examine the nature and sources of this
sometimes frustrating, sometimes fulfilling, but ultimately unavoidable aspect
of intimate relationships. We'll look at how conflicts unfold, how they escalate, and how people can respond to them more effectively. We'll also consider
whether conflict can be beneficial to relationships. (What do you think the
answer will be? Can conflict be advantageous?)

THE NATURE OF CONFLICT

What Is Conflict?

Interpersonal conflict occurs whenever one person's motives, goals, beliefs, opinions, or behavior interfere with, or are incompatible with, those of another. Conflict is born of dissimilarity, which may be passing in the form of moods, or lasting
in the form of beliefs and personality. Two people always differ in important
ways, but I'll employ a definition of conflict that involves active interference with

another's goals (Dal Cin et al., 2005): Conflict occurs when one's wishes or actions actually obstruct or impede those of someone else. When two partners are both able to do as they as they wish, no conflict exists. On the other hand, if one or both of them have to give up something that they want because of the other's influence, conflict occurs. Anger and hostility aren't necessary; we make some sacrifices to accommodate our partners generously and happily. And not all conflicts are overt; one partner is sometimes unaware of the difficulties he or she is causing the other (Fincham & Beach, 1999). It's enough that someone knowingly or unknowingly prevents another from getting or doing everything he or she wants.

Conflict is inescapable for two reasons. First, the moods and preferences of any two people will occasionally differ. Intermittent incompatibilities between two partners' goals and behaviors will inevitably arise. For instance, even if both members of a couple are extraverted, hard-partying social animals, one of them will occasionally be disappointed by the other's wish to leave a party before it's over; a case of the flu or an upcoming exam in a close relationships class will make one of them, but not the other, unwilling to stay late.

Second, conflict is unavoidable because there are certain tensions that are woven into the fabric of close relationships that will, sooner or later, always cause some strain. When they devote themselves to an intimate relationship, people often experience opposing motivations called **dialectics** that can never be entirely satisfied because they contradict each other (Baxter, 2004). Fulfilling one goal may endanger another, so partners must engage in a delicate balancing act that leaves them drawn in different directions at different times. And with each partner vacillating between the pursuit of these opposing goals, occasional conflict between their predominant individual motives is inescapable (Erbert, 2000).

For instance, one potent dialectic in close relationships is the continual tension between personal *autonomy and connection* to others. On one hand, people often want to be free to do what they want, so they value their independence and autonomy. On the other hand, they also seek warm, close connections to others that can make them dependent on particular partners. So, which do they pursue? Intimacy or freedom? Independence or belonging? It's reasonable to assume that most people want some of both, but embracing one of them can mean denying the other. So people's preferences may swing back and forth as they come to be more influenced by whichever motive has lately been less fulfilled. Maintaining an equilibrium between the two desires is a tricky balancing act (Kumashiro et al., 2008), and we can't simultaneously maintain high *in*dependence from a romantic partner and high *inter*dependence with him or her, so something's got to give. And conflict between the partners may occur as they strive to fulfill opposing motives at different rates and at different times.

Another powerful dialectic is the tension between *openness and closedness*. Intimacy involves self-disclosure, and intimate partners are expected to share their thoughts and feelings with one another. However, people also like their privacy, and there are some things that prudent partners want to keep to themselves (Petronio, 2010). On the one hand, there's candor and transparent authenticity, and on the other hand, there's discretion and restraint.

There's also friction between *stability and change.* People with pleasant partnerships will want to maintain and protect them, keeping things the way they are. But people also relish novelty and excitement (Strong & Aron, 2006). Too much stagnant predictability becomes mundane and monotonous (Harasymchuk & Fehr, 2011). So, people are attracted to both the familiar and the new, and occasional indecision and conflict may result.

Finally, there's dialectic tension between *integration* with *and separation* from one's social network. Would you rather go to that party with your friends or stay home and snuggle with your sweetheart tonight? Will you travel to your in-law's home for Thanksgiving again this year or stay home and begin your own family tradition? One's motive to stay involved with other people is sometimes at odds with the wish to devote oneself to a romantic partnership. For instance, people see less of their friends when they invest time and effort into a romantic relationship (Fehr, 1999), and finding a satisfying ratio of time spent with and time apart from other people can be difficult.

Altogether, these four dialectics—autonomy versus connection, openness versus closedness, stability versus change, and integration versus separation—accounted for more than one-third of the recent fights and arguments reported by married couples in one study (Erbert, 2000). And what's important is that these tensions typically continue to some degree throughout the entire life of a relationship (Baxter, 2004). The dilemmas posed by fluctuating, opposing motives in close relationships never end. Sooner or later, conflict occurs.

The Frequency of Conflict

How often do partners engage in conflict? Frequently, but the answer varies with the population studied and the way in which conflict is defined and assessed. Little children and their parents are often at odds; one study determined that some conflict occurred every 3.6 minutes in conversations between 4-year-olds and their mothers (Eisenberg, 1992)! Adolescents encounter an average of seven disagreements per day in their various relationships (Laursen & Collins, 1994), and dating couples report 2.3 conflicts per week when they keep diaries of their interactions (Lloyd, 1987). Spouses report seven memorable "differences of opinion" every 2 weeks (Papp et al., 2009a), and they experience one or two "unpleasant disagreements" each month (McGonagle et al., 1992). And, importantly, many conflicts are never addressed; in one investigation, Northwestern University students didn't mention to their partners 40 percent of the conflicts and irritations they identified in their dating relationships (Roloff & Cloven, 1990). Conflict not only is common in close relationships, it also probably occurs more often than we realize.

However, as you might expect, some people experience more conflict than other people do. Various influences are correlated with the amount of conflict we encounter:

Personality. People who are high in neuroticism are impulsive and irascible, and they have more unhappy disagreements with others than people of low neuroticism do (Heaven et al., 2006). In contrast, people high in agreeableness are good natured, cooperative, and generally easy to get along with, and they have fewer conflicts; if conflict does occur, they also react more constructively than people of low agreeableness do (Jensen-Campbell & Graziano, 2001).

Attachment style. People who are anxious about abandonment tend to fret that their partners may leave them, and—perhaps because they nervously expect the worst—they think that there is more conflict in their relationships than more secure partners do. In addition, when conflict does occur, they consider it to be more damaging to the relationship than their partners do (Campbell et al., 2005). Attachment anxiety apparently leads people to perceive danger and threat where it does not exist, and, ironically, their apprehension may gradually create the disputes and tension they fear (Baruch et al., 2010).

Stage of life. If you're a young adult, you may be experiencing more conflict with your partners than you used to. It's typical for people to develop lasting romances and to begin professional careers in their mid-20s, and, according to a longitudinal study of young adults in New York state, these life changes are routinely associated with increased conflict (Chen et al., 2006). As you can see in Figure 11.1, conflict with romantic partners increases steadily from our late teens to our mid-20s, but things settle down somewhat thereafter.

FIGURE 11.1. **Romantic conflict in young adulthood.**
The many changes accompanying passage into adulthood—which often include graduation from college and entry into new careers—are associated with increased conflict in our romantic relationships. But things settle down after a while.
Note. On the rating scale used by the researchers, a score of 0 indicated "no conflict," a score of 25 indicated "occasional mild disagreements," and 50 meant "some arguing and bickering with infrequent flare-ups."
Source: Data from Chen, Cohen, Kasen, Johnson, Ehrensaft, & Gordon, 2006.

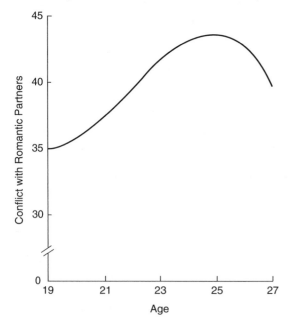

Relationships get even more placid in our elder years. Couples in their sixties usually have fewer disagreements about children and money and other touchy topics than middle-aged couples do (Levenson et al., 1993).

Similarity. Conflict emerges from incompatibility, so it's not surprising that the less similar dating partners are, the more conflict they experience (Surra & Longstreth, 1990). This pattern continues if people marry; spouses who share similar tastes and expectations encounter less conflict and enjoy happier marriages than do those who have less in common (Huston & Houts, 1998). Indeed, those who really believe that "opposites attract" are likely to learn some hard lessons if they start living with someone who is notably different from them. Dissimilarity fuels friction, not smooth sailing.

Alcohol. Finally, lest there be any doubt, alcohol does not make people more agreeable and courteous; instead, intoxication exacerbates conflict. An intriguing study of alcohol's effects invited men who were either sober or intoxicated to revisit a recent romantic conflict (MacDonald et al., 2000). Drunkenness made the men more sour and surly; in response to events of the same average intensity, intoxicated men were more hostile and blaming than sober men were. Adding alcohol to a frustrating disagreement is a bit like adding fuel to a fire.

THE COURSE OF CONFLICT

Instigating Events

So, what events cause conflict? A wide-ranging review of conflict studies by Donald Peterson (2002, p. 367) concluded that couples may disagree about almost any issue: "how to spend time together, how to manage money, how to deal with in-laws, frequency and mode of sexual intercourse, who did which chores, insufficient expressions of affect (not enough affection), exaggerated expressions of affect (moodiness, anger), personal habits, political views, religious beliefs, jealousies toward other men and women, relatives, and the couples' own children." You name it, and some couple somewhere is quarreling over it. After David Buss (1989) asked students at the University of Michigan to specify things that men do that upset women (and vice versa), he grouped their answers into 147 distinct sources of conflict. It's obvious that the interdependency that characterizes an intimate relationship provides "abundant opportunities for dispute" (Peterson, 2002, p. 367).

When spouses keep track of all of their disagreements over a span of 15 days, some topics recur more often than others (Papp et al., 2009a). As you can see in Table 11.1, those who are parents disagree more about how to manage, discipline, and care for their children—and when—than about anything else. (Remember that people who haven't read chapter 6 sometimes naïvely believe that having kids will make their marriages happier—but in fact, the reverse is true [Wendorf et al., 2011].) The division and performance of household chores and responsibilities are next on the list (remember, it's hard, but important, to divide them fairly [Amato et al., 2007]), and communication is

TABLE 11.1. Topics Discussed During Marital Conflict

Each night, husbands and wives made notes about any disagreements they had had that day. The topics they listed are presented in order of the frequency with which they were mentioned. Because a particular conflict could—and often did—touch on more than one topic, the frequencies exceed 100%.

Topic	Issues	Proportion of Conflicts
Children	Care for and discipline of the kids	38%
Chores	Allocation of and performance of household duties	25
Communication	Paying attention, listening, misunderstandings	22
Leisure	Choice of and time spent in recreation	20
Work	Time spent at work; co-workers	19
Money	Bills, purchases, spending, wages	19
Habits	Annoying behaviors	17
Relatives	Family, in-laws, stepchildren, ex-spouses	11
Commitment	The meaning of commitment; infidelity	9
Intimacy	Displays of affection; sex	8
Friends	Time spent and activities with friends	8
Personality	A partner's or one's own traits	7

Source: Data from Papp et al., 2009a.

third (involving problems with interpersonal gaps and perceived partner responsiveness). It's down in sixth place, but the most enduring, contentious, and sometimes surly disagreements revolve around money: who's earning and who's spending what, and what's being bought.

To make sense of this variety, Peterson (2002) classified the events that instigate conflicts into four common categories: criticism, illegitimate demands, rebuffs, and cumulative annoyances. **Criticism** involves verbal or nonverbal acts that are judged to communicate dissatisfaction with a partner's behavior, attitude, or trait (Cupach, 2007). It doesn't matter what the actor intends by his or her remark or behavior; what matters is that the target interprets the action as being unjustly critical. A mild suggestion about how to load the dishwasher to fit more stuff in may injure one's partner and engender conflict if the suggestion is judged to be needless criticism.

Illegitimate demands involve requests that seem unjust because they exceed the normal expectations that the partners hold for each other. Even when one partner is frantically completing a major project, for instance, the other may be upset by being asked to fix dinner *and* do the dishes three nights in a row.

Rebuffs involve situations in which "one person appeals to another for a desired reaction, and the other person fails to respond as expected" (Peterson, 2002, p. 371). Someone whose partner rolls over and goes to sleep after receiving an implicit invitation to have sex is likely to feel rebuffed.

Finally, **cumulative annoyances** are relatively trivial events that become irritating with repetition. Such events often take the form of *social allergies:* Through repeated exposure to small recurring nuisances, people may develop hypersensitive reactions of disgust and exasperation that seem out of proportion to any particular provocation. Women are especially likely to become annoyed with men's uncouth habits, such as belching at the dinner table, and men are likely to grow irritated with women's lack of consideration, such as being late for appointments and shopping too long (Cunningham et al., 2005).

Evolutionary psychology makes its own intriguing predictions about conflict in close relationships (Buss, 2012). From an evolutionary perspective, some conflict in heterosexual relationships flows naturally from differences in the partners' reproductive interests. Presumably, given their lower parental investment in any babies that may result, men can afford to be more interested in casual, uncommitted sex than women are; by comparison, women should be more prudent, offering access to sex only in return for meaningful commitment from a man. And in fact, the frustrations that men and women usually encounter early in a romantic relationship run right along these lines: "Women, far more than men, become angry and upset by those who want sex sooner, more frequently, and more persistently than they want. Men, far more than women, become angry and upset by those who delay sex or thwart their sexual advances" (Buss, 2000, p. 38). The question of whether to have sex is usually answered when people settle into established relationships, but the question of how often to have sex may persist for decades. Differences in sexual desire cause conflict for *most* couples, requiring negotiation, tradeoffs, and adjustment, and in most cases the difficulty never disappears completely (Elliott & Umberson, 2008). Individual differences in sexual tastes and drives can remain a source of distressing rebuffs as long as a relationship lasts.

I can also note that the sore points routinely encountered by gay and lesbian couples don't differ much from those that vex heterosexuals. Gay men are more likely than anyone else to disagree about the rules regarding extradyadic sex, but otherwise, gays and lesbians are just as likely as their straight brothers and sisters[1] to fuss about chores, communication, money, and all the rest of the topics in Table 11.1 (Solomon et al., 2005). When it comes to conflict, as with so many other aspects of intimacy, sexual orientation doesn't have much to do with how (or if) close relationships work.

Attributions

The differing perspectives that any two people bring to their interaction will often be another source of exasperating disagreement. *Actor-observer effects* guarantee that partners will have slightly different explanations for their actions than anyone else does, and *self-serving biases* lead them to judge their own actions more favorably than others do.[2] In particular, although people readily recognize self-serving attributions in others' judgments of events, they usually

---

[1] This can be taken literally. The married heterosexual participants in Solomon et al.'s (2005) study were siblings of the gay and lesbian participants. Clever procedure, wasn't it?

[2] If a reminder about these attributional patterns will come in handy, take a look back at pages 114–115 in chapter 4.

consider their own similarly biased perceptions to be impartial and fair (Pronin et al., 2002). Thus, two partners' attributions routinely differ, and this can create conflict in two different ways. First, frustrating misunderstandings can result if people fail to appreciate that their partners always have their own individual points of view. And second, if those differing views come to light, the partners may engage in **attributional conflict,** fighting over whose explanation is right and whose account is wrong (Orvis et al., 1976). Partners may agree entirely about what one of them did but simultaneously disagree completely about why that person did it. ("You left that there just to annoy me!" "No, I didn't. I went to answer the phone and forgot about it.") Attributional arguments are often hard to resolve because when people disagree with us, we tend to think they're biased, and that's exasperating (Kennedy & Pronin, 2008). Moreover, there may not be any single explanation for an event that is objectively and conclusively correct. People who may have behaved selfishly, for instance, will often have difficulty realizing that they were greedy, and they'll tend to be blind to the manner in which their own selfishness may elicit similar thoughtlessness in return. The interactions two partners share may be affected by so many subtle influences that reasonable people can, and often will, disagree about why things turn out the way they do.

Then, when any conflict occurs, the explanations with which intimate partners account for the frustrations they encounter have a huge influence on how distressed they feel and how angrily they respond. (See the box, "Mastering Our Anger," that begins on the next page.) If a partner's misbehavior is construed to be an unintentional accident, being attributed to external and unstable causes, the partner will seem relatively blameless, and strong emotion (and retribution) will be inappropriate. In contrast, if a partner's misdeeds are attributed to internal and stable sources, the misdeeds seem intentional and the partner seems malicious, selfish, indecent, or inept—and in such circumstances, one's inconvenience seems unjust, and one's anger fitting (Canary, 2003). It's no accident then, that happy couples are less likely than unhappy couples to regard their partners as selfishly motivated and as behaving unfairly with negative intent (Kluwer et al., 2009). Benevolent attributions paint a partner in a favorable light and make it seem likely that conflicts can be resolved, and that's one reason that such attributions promote continued satisfaction with a relationship (Fincham et al., 2000).

Specific responses to conflict are also shaped by our attributions for an event. When we judge that our partners can change an unwanted behavior—so that our efforts to resolve a conflict may pay off—we're more likely to announce our discontent and to constructively seek solutions than is the case when we believe that our partners cannot change (Kammrath & Dweck, 2006). People tend to just sit and stew when they think a problem is set in stone.

Engagement and Escalation

Indeed, once an instigating event occurs, partners must decide either to engage in conflict or to avoid the issue and let it drop. This decision is the first

Mastering Our Anger

A lot of people seem to believe that when they are cruelly provoked, their anger is something that just happens to them that is beyond their control. Even worse, popular notions suggest that once we get angry, it's dangerous to bottle it up; when we get "hot,"we have to "vent," or we'll suffer high blood pressure and continuing stress. However, there are two huge problems with such beliefs: First, they're wrong (Tice & Baumeister, 1993), and second, they promote behavior that may actually cause *higher* stress that lasts for longer periods of time (Olatunji et al., 2007).

Because it takes effort to control and manage angry emotion, people often "blow off steam" by directing furious, fuming behavior at their adversaries (or, occasionally, at innocent third parties). Releasing our ire is supposed to make us feel better, but that simple-minded notion ignores the interpersonal consequences of surly behavior. "When you 'let out' an emotion it usually lands on somebody else, and how you feel—relieved, angrier, depressed—is going to depend on what the other person does" (Tavris, 1989, p. 145). Sometimes, the targets of our wrath accept our anger, apologize, and strive to remediate their sins. But in close relationships, where people expect generous and tolerant treatment from each other, aggressive displays of anger often just get one's partners angry in return. And then there may be *two* irate people fussing and sniping at each other in a churlish interaction that perpetuates rather than reduces the anger in the air.

The bottom line is that "expressing anger *while you feel angry* nearly always makes you feel angrier" (Tavris, 1989, p. 223). People who lash out at their partners in the heat of anger often stay angry longer and suffer more cardiovascular stress than they would if they behaved more moderately. By comparison, those who gain control of their anger, calm down, and then voice their complaints in an assertive but less heated fashion are more likely to get understanding and cooperation from their partners; they are more likely to get what they want. The belief that it's a good idea to vent and blow off steam when you get angry may seem like common sense, but it's actually common *non*sense (Lohr et al., 2007).

So, how can we manage our anger? Because irritation and resentment are signs that something is wrong, we shouldn't ignore anger and pretend that it doesn't exist. But it's usually worthwhile to reduce the venom and fury we dump on our partners, and there are several ways to do this (Tice & Baumeister, 1993). First, we can *think differently.* Anger is inflamed by perceptions that our partners acted negligently or maliciously, so the attributions with which we explain some annoyance are key. When you feel anger coming on, consider why your partner may have behaved that way without wishing to injure or annoy you; rethinking the event may keep your indignation in check. Second, if you do get angry, *chill out.* Don't engage in infuriated interaction. Leave the room, take a walk, breathe slowly and deeply, and count to 10 (or 10,000). You will calm down, and you'll do so more quickly than you think if you breathe slowly, relax your muscles, and stop rehearsing the injustice in your mind. Finally, find *humor* where you can. It's impossible to feel jocular and angry at the same time, so anything that lightens your mood will decrease your anger (Yuan et al., 2010).

All of this is easier said than done, and some people will need to "practice, practice, and practice alternative responses" before they can reform their angry habits (Notarius et al., 1997, p. 245). The time to rehearse is when small annoyances occur, and it's very helpful when both partners are involved. And the good news is that destructive anger can be overcome; "if you each try to help the other person master a new way of dealing with anger, and do this repeatedly, you will find the old patterns giving way to change" (Notarius et al., 1997, p. 246).

choice point in Peterson's (2002) general model of conflict, which appears in Figure 11.2. (At first glance, you may find the figure a little daunting, but be patient; it cleverly illustrates several different manners in which conflict can unfold. Trace some of the paths and see.) *Avoidance* occurs only when both partners wish to evade the issue, and it presumably transpires either when the event is seen as insufficient to warrant active dispute or when the issue seems intractable and conflict will do no good (Zacchilli et al., 2009).

Otherwise, the issue is addressed and conflict is engaged. In some cases, the couple enters into *negotiation* and seeks to resolve the conflict through rational problem solving. However, in other cases, *escalation* occurs and the conflict heats up. Escalation often involves the dysfunctional forms of communication I described in chapter 5. Other issues may get dragged into the interaction, scornful disregard of the partner may be expressed, and belligerent demands and threats may be made. Angry fighting may ensue.

An analysis of intimate combat by Dan Canary (2003) made two points: First, partners sometimes say mean and nasty things to each other when they're fighting, and second, nasty remarks may be of two types. *Direct* tactics explicitly challenge one's partner; they're "in one's face." Direct tactics include (a) accusations that criticize the partner and attribute negative qualities to him or her; (b) hostile commands for compliance that sometimes involve threats of physical or emotional harm; (c) antagonistic questions; and (d) surly or sarcastic put-downs that communicate disgust or disapproval (including argumentative interruptions and shouting down one's partner). *Indirect* nasty tactics manage the conflict in a less straightforward manner; one's displeasure is veiled, and one's intentions are less explicit. Indirect tactics include (a) condescension or implied negativity that hints at animosity or arrogance; (b) dysphoric affect, such as melancholy, dejection, or whining; (c) attempts to change topics preemptively, and (d) evasive remarks that fail to acknowledge the partner or that fail to recognize the conflict. All of these behaviors are obnoxious to some degree, and they tend to inflame, rather than to resolve, conflict. Satisfied partners engage in these behaviors less often than discontented, disgruntled partners do, and married couples who routinely fight in such a manner are much more likely to divorce than are those who rarely act this way (Birditt et al., 2010).

Surly interaction has more damaging effects when it gets under your skin. Cantankerous conflict that involves the abrasive elements of contempt, defensiveness, stonewalling, or belligerence annoys, exasperates, or infuriates most

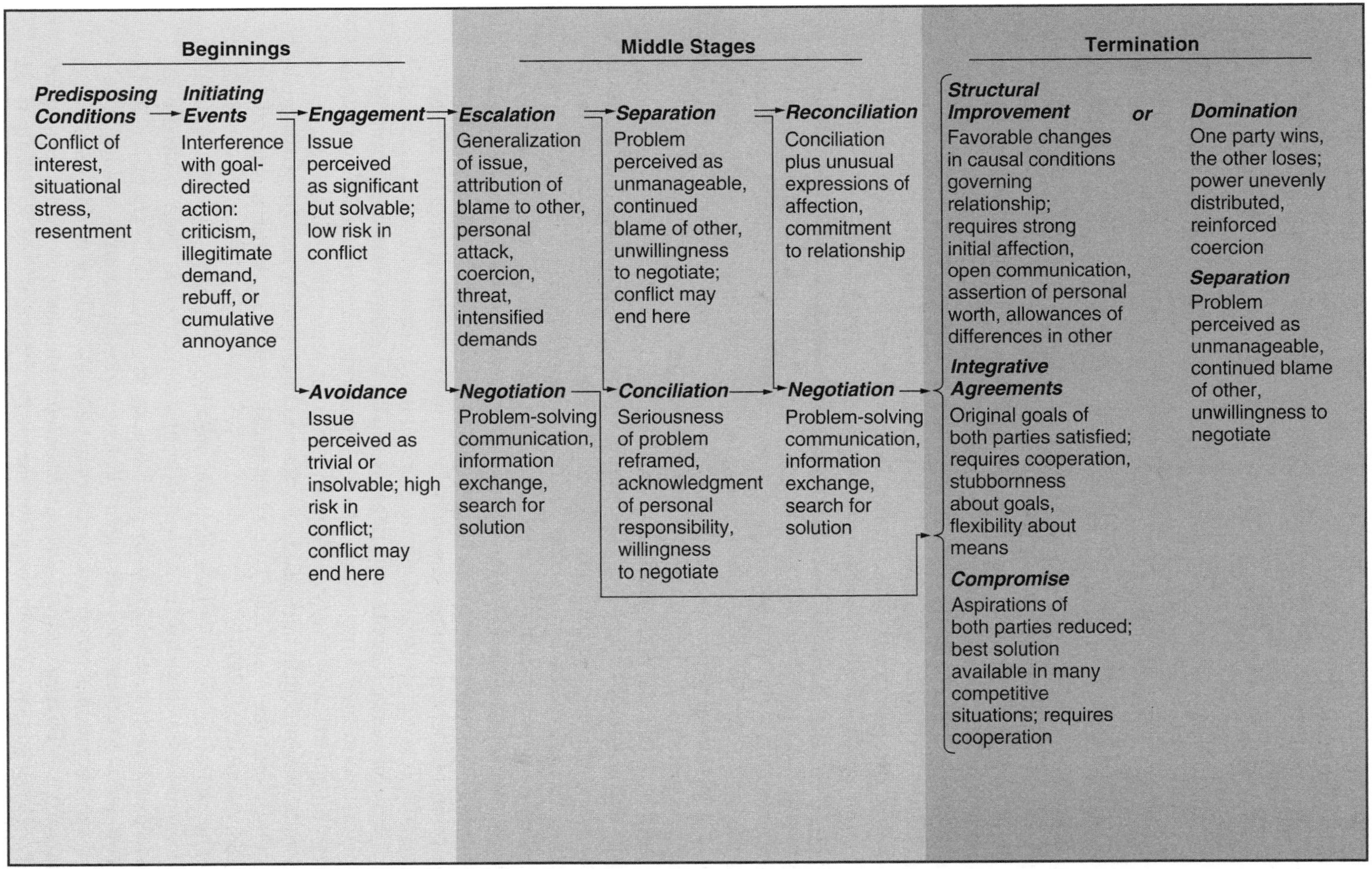

FIGURE 11.2. **The possible courses of conflict** from its beginnings, through its middle stages, to its termination. Arrows indicate the likely sequences, ending with *avoidance, separation,* or any of four other possible terminations of the conflict.
Source: Kelley, H., et al. (1993).

of us, and those emotional reactions engender physiological arousal and stress. Crabby, cranky interactions have real physical impact; they increase our heart rates and blood pressures, dump stress hormones into our bloodstreams, and depress our immune functions so that we are more susceptible to infection (Loving et al., 2006). When they are exposed to a cold virus under controlled conditions in a lab, people who have recently been experiencing chronic conflict at home are two-and-a-half times more likely to catch a cold and get sick (Cohen et al., 2003). Wounds even heal more slowly after hostile interactions with one's spouse (Gouin et al., 2010). Worse, these effects may accumulate over time; a study of more than 9,000 people in England over a span of 12 years found that those who encountered a lot of surly conflict in their close relationships were more likely to have heart attacks (De Vogli et al., 2007).

Ill-tempered petulance from one partner routinely gets the other (at least somewhat) angry, too. (Be *sure* not to skip the box on "Mastering Our Anger" three pages back.) But surly conflict turns especially fractious when the partners fall into a pattern of **negative affect reciprocity** in which the partners trade escalating provocations back and forth. This pattern is not often found in happy, well-adjusted couples (who do a better job of exiting the cycle when things start to heat up), but it is routinely exhibited by distressed, dissatisfied couples in deteriorating partnerships (Gottman et al., 1998): One person's testiness makes the other partner peevish, so he or she snaps back; the first person becomes more aggravated, and the second exhange is more noxious. Stronger words are shared, both partners fan the flames of the other's irritation, and both of them become increasingly angry and embittered as the interaction proceeds.

High emotion of this sort makes conflict particularly corrosive, so it's reassuring that some of us are less likely than others to become so upset (Smith et al., 2011). People with secure attachment styles experience milder physiological responses to conflict than insecure people do (Powers et al., 2006). Those who are high in avoidance of intimacy prefer to avoid discussion of sensitive issues, and they're more annoyed by sacrifices made on a partner's behalf (Mikulincer & Shaver, 2005), so they get more hostile and experience greater disruption of their immune systems when conflict occurs (Gouin et al., 2009). Those who are high in anxiety about abandonment get nervous during conflict, and they experience increases in heart rate and blood pressure that may lead to hypertension over time (Kim, 2006). Altogether, people with secure styles of attachment are less angry, cooler and calmer, and more collaborative and optimistic when conflict arises. They bounce back from conflict, putting dissension behind them and returning to a positive state of mind, more quickly, too (Salvatore et al., 2011).

The characteristics of one's partner are also influential. People typically experience less stress during an episode of conflict when their partners are securely attached than when their partners are insecure (Powers et al., 2006). We also tend to remain more at ease with lower blood pressures and lower levels of stress hormones when our partners have historically provided us effective social support (Heffner et al., 2004). Disagreements are evidently less worrisome when we know we can count on our partners for the help we really need.

Thus, conflicts that escalate too far or too often have physical as well as psychological effects. And these physiological reactions may be very influential; newlyweds who experience stronger surges of adrenalin when they discuss their conflicts are notably less likely to be happily married, or even married at all, 10 years later (Kiecolt-Glaser et al., 2003).

The Demand/Withdraw Pattern

Another unpleasant pattern of interaction that exacerbates conflict is the demand/withdraw pattern, in which "one member (the demander) criticizes, nags, and makes demands of the other, while the partner (the withdrawer) avoids confrontation, withdraws, and becomes defensive" (Eldridge & Christensen, 2002, p. 289). The pattern is objectionable in part because it is self-perpetuating. Frustrated by the withdrawer's retreat, the demander is likely to become more insistent that the issue be addressed; however, this increased pressure tends to make the withdrawer even more resistant and close-lipped, and the pattern continues. It's a dysfunctional way to manage conflict that leaves the demander feeling disregarded and misunderstood (Weger, 2005), and over time, it undermines a couple's satisfaction with their relationship (Baucom et al., 2010).

Men and women do not differ much in their other responses to conflict (Gayle et al., 2002), but there is a difference here: Around the world, women are the demanders and men the withdrawers more often than not (Christensen et al., 2006). Both men and women, in both heterosexual and same-sex couples, sometimes withdraw when their partners want to discuss and change the status quo (Baucom et al., 2010), but women are generally more likely than men to speak up and to initiate discussion of relationship problems (Denton & Burleson, 2007), and that puts them in the demander role more often. (Some of the evidence for that conclusion comes from sex differences on the Initiator Style Questionnaire. You can assess yourself with Table 11.2.)

Why do women demand and men withdraw? There are various possibilities. The pattern may emerge from the usual *gender differences* that distinguish men and women (Afifi & Joseph, 2009). Women are encouraged to be communal and expressive whereas men are encouraged to be independent and autonomous, and the demand/withdraw pattern may result from women seeking closeness and men defending their autonomy. Another explanation, the *social structure* hypothesis, argues that the demand/withdraw pattern results from pervasive differences in the power of men and women in society and marriage alike (Eldridge & Christensen, 2002). As we'll see in chapter 12, men tend to have more power in heterosexual relationships than women do, and if you're getting your way, you're likely to resist change.

In fact, both of these explanations are, in the main, correct. Researchers study such issues by asking couples to have two discussions, one in which the woman wants change and another in which the man wants change. When either men or women have an issue they want to discuss, they tend to demand, and when their partners raise a concern, both men and women sometimes withdraw. To some degree, then, the demand/withdraw pattern simply depends

TABLE 11.2. The Initiator Style Questionnaire

This research tool assesses one's inclination to give voice to complaints in a relationship with a particular partner. The higher your score, the more likely you are to initiate discussion of your concerns. Ponder your primary partnership, and consider how you typically respond to problems in your relationship (i.e., problems that are between you and your partner). Then rate each item on this scale:

1	2	3	4	5	6	7	8	9
Strongly Disagree							Strongly Agree	

1. When discussing a relationship problem, I usually try to keep the discussion going until we settle the issue.
2. I usually express my feelings about our relationship to my partner.
3. I usually keep my feelings about our relationship private and do not share them with my partner.
4. When I become aware of a problem in our relationship, I usually do not say anything about it.
5. I am the kind of person who generally feels comfortable discussing relationship problems.
6. When my partner wants to talk about a relationship problem, I am usually ready to do so as well.
7. I usually become silent or refuse to discuss a relationship problem further if my partner pressures or demands that I do so.
8. When my partner wants to talk about a relationship problem, I usually try to get out of the discussion.
9. When I become aware of a problem in our relationship, I usually try to start a discussion of that problem.
10. I am the kind of person who generally does not feel comfortable discussing relationship problems.

To determine your score, *reverse* the rating you gave items 3, 4, 7, 8, and 10. A rating of 1 should become a 9; a 3 becomes a 7, 5 stays the same, 6 becomes a 4, 8 becomes a 2, etc. Then add up your ratings. In a sample of married adults from North Carolina, typical scores for women ranged from 52 to 85, and ordinary scores for men ranged from 47 to 75. Above the usual range for your sex, you're more likely than most people to initiate discussion of your concerns, and below the range, you're less likely to do so.

Source: Denton & Burleson (2007). Reprinted by permission.

on who's pressing the issue (Caughlin & Scott, 2010). Women tend to press harder than men, however, and men withdraw more completely, so the data support both the gender differences and the social structure points of view (Baucom et al., 2010). Women press for desired change in a relationship more often than men do, men are more likely to withdraw, and imbalances of power affect who is and who isn't going to want to change the status quo (Holley & Levenson, 2010).

Negotiation and Accommodation

Not all conflicts turn heated or ugly, and those that do ultimately simmer down. And when loving partners are finally cool-headed, *negotiation* usually occurs. The partners announce their positions and work toward a solution in a sensible manner. In a best-case scenario, each is responsive to the other and each feels validated by the other's responses.[3]

Dan Canary's (2003) analysis of conflict tactics identified several ways in which partners can be nice to each other during their negotiations. Again, some of these are *direct*, openly addressing the issue, and another is *indirect*, skirting the issue but defusing ill feeling. Nice direct tactics include (a) showing a willingness to deal with the problem by accepting responsibility or by offering concessions or a compromise; (b) exhibiting support for the other's point of view through paraphrasing; (c) offering self-disclosure with "I-statements"; and (d) providing approval and affection. An indirect tactic is friendly, non-sarcastic humor that lightens the mood. Snarky, aggressive humor that teases or ridicules others isn't helpful, but witty good cheer that is respectful of others is very welcome in intimate conflict; it reduces angry emotion (Yuan et al., 2010), and when our partners use friendly humor in our discussions of conflict, we feel closer to them and are more satisfied with the solutions we reach (Campbell et al., 2008). Some problems are easier to solve than others, of course, but the use of kind tactics such as these during conflict helps to protect and maintain a relationship (Gottman et al., 1998).

Here's some more helpful advice for successful negotiation with a loved one. First, be optimistic. Expect that creative collaboration and your generous regard for each other will resolve (most of) your problem. Positive expectations will help you reach agreement (Liberman et al., 2010), whereas pessimism may just make things worse (DiPaola et al., 2010). Second, value your partner's outcomes as well as your own. Problems are solved more successfully when the partners take each other's perspectives, appreciate each other's points of view (Rizkalla et al., 2008), and are glad when the other gets (most of) what he or she wants (Gore & Cross, 2011). Promote a focus on the two of you as a couple instead of on each of you as separate individuals by always requesting that "*we*" do something instead of just telling your partner what to do; your partner will be less resistant to your suggestions when they're always about *us* instead of just about him or her (Mitnick et al., 2009). Finally, take an occasional short break from your discussion, especially if anyone begins to get annoyed or irritated (Sanford & Grace, 2011). Leave the room for a few minutes but keep thinking about your issue, and you may find your negotiation will go more smoothly when you return to it (Harinck et al., 2011).

Obviously, then, some responses to conflict are destructive, undermining a relationship, and others are constructive, helping to sustain it. Add this distinction to the difference between engaging a conflict and avoiding it that we

---

[3] For a refresher on *responsiveness* and *validation,* I invite you to look back at p. 218 in chapter 7 and p. 172 in chapter 5, respectively.

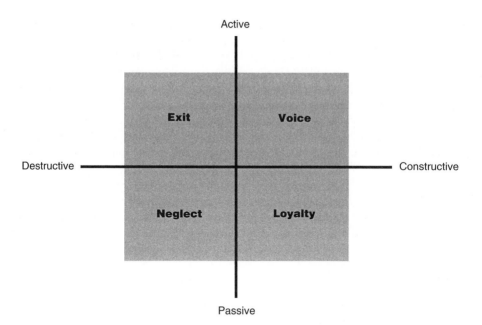

FIGURE 11.3. **A typology of responses to dissatisfaction in close relationships.**
Source: Adapted from Rusbult, 1987.

encountered earlier, and you've got four different types of reponses to conflict and dissatisfaction in a relationship that were identified by Caryl Rusbult (1987). Take a look at Figure 11.3; the four categories differ in being either *active* or *passive* and in being either *constructive* or *destructive:*

1. **Voice** is behaving in an active, constructive manner by trying to improve the situation by discussing matters with the partner, changing one's behavior in an effort to solve the problem, or obtaining advice from a friend or therapist.
2. **Loyalty** is behaving in a passive but constructive manner by optimistically waiting and hoping for conditions to improve.
3. **Exit** is behaving in an actively destructive manner by leaving the partner, threatening to end the relationship, or engaging in abusive acts such as yelling or hitting.
4. **Neglect** is behaving in a passive but destructive manner by avoiding discussion of critical issues and reducing interdependence with the partner. When one is neglectful, one stands aside and just lets things get worse.

If a relationship has been satisfying and their investments in it are high, people are more likely to employ the constructive responses of voice and loyalty than to neglect the relationship or exit from it (Rusbult et al., 1982). We typically seek to maintain relationships to which we are committed. And when that's the case, voice is more beneficial and productive than loyalty: Unlike voice, which communicates interest and concern and typically gets a positive, productive response from one's partner, loyalty usually just goes unnoticed and does no good (Overall et al., 2010b). Exit is even worse, of course, and it's more frequently employed when attractive alternative partners are available; people are more likely to bail out of a struggling relationship than to work to sustain it when tempting alternatives exist (Rusbult et al., 1982).

When both partners choose destructive responses to conflict, a relationship is at risk (Rusbult et al., 1986), so the ability to remain constructive in the face of a lover's temporary disregard, which I identified as **accommodation** back in chapter 6 (on page 209), is a valuable gift. When partners behave destructively, accommodation involves inhibiting the impulse to fight fire with fire and striving to react instead with calm forbearance. Couples with secure attachment styles do this more reliably than insecure couples do (Gaines & Henderson, 2002). I'll mention accommodation again in chapter 15; for now, I'll simply note that couples who are able to swallow occasional provocation from each other without responding in kind tend to be happier than are those who are less tolerant and who always bite back (Rusbult et al., 1998).

Dealing with Conflict: Four Types of Couples

Does the desirability of accommodation mean that you and your partner should avoid arguing with each other? Not at all. Even heated arguments can be constructive, and some couples who engage in forceful, robust arguments appear to have stable, satisfying marriages. Arguments support or erode a couple's satisfaction depending on the manner in which arguments are conducted.

Marriage researcher John Gottman (1993, 1994a, 1999) has studied conflict for years. In a typical procedure, he invites couples to discuss a continuing disagreement and then carefully inspects recordings of the resulting interactions. His results have led him to suggest that there are three discrete approaches to conflict that can lead to stable and enduring marriages. (Does one of them fit you well? Before you read further, I invite you to assess your own conflict type using the box on the next page. Really, stop here. Turn the page and check out the box.)

Volatile couples have frequent and passionate arguments. They plunge into fiery efforts to persuade and influence each other, and they often display high levels of negative affect, but they temper their anger with plenty of wit and evident fondness for each other.

Validators fight more politely. They tend to be calmer than volatile couples are, and they behave more like collaborators than like antagonists as they work through their problems. Their discussions may become heated, but they frequently validate each other by expressing empathy for, and understanding of, the other's point of view.

In contrast to volatiles and validators, **avoiders** rarely argue. They avoid confrontation, and if they do discuss their conflicts, they do so mildly and gingerly. As Gottman (1993, p. 10) reported:

> *The interviewer had a great deal of difficulty setting up the conflict discussion. . . . Once each person has stated his or her case, they tend to see the discussion as close to an end. They consider accepting these differences as a complete discussion. Once they understand their differences, they feel that*

Assessing Your Couple Conflict Type

Following are descriptions of how people in four different types of relationships handle conflict. Which type most closely describes how you and your partner deal with conflict in your relationship? For each description, indicate how often it applies to your conflicts to see which overall category fits you best:

A. In our relationship, conflicts may be fought on a grand scale, and that is okay, since our making up is even grander. We have volcanic arguments, but they are just a small part of a warm and loving relationship. Although we argue, we are still able to resolve our differences. In fact, our passion and zest for fighting actually leads to a better relationship with a lot of making up, laughing, and affection.

1 = Never
2 = Rarely
3 = Sometimes
4 = Often
5 = Very Often

B. In our relationship, when we are having conflict, we let each other know the other's opinions are valued and their emotions valid, even if we disagree with each other. Even when discussing a hot topic, we display a lot of self-control and are calm. When fighting we spend a lot of time validating each other as well as trying to persuade our partner or trying to find a compromise.

1 = Never
2 = Rarely
3 = Sometimes
4 = Often
5 = Very Often

C. In our relationship, conflict is minimized. We think it is better to "agree to disagree" rather than end up in discussions that will result in a deadlock. We don't think there is much to be gained from getting openly angry with each other. In fact, a lot of talking about disagreements seems to make matters worse. We feel that if you just relax about problems, they will have a way of working themselves out.

1 = Never
2 = Rarely
3 = Sometimes
4 = Often
5 = Very Often

D. We argue often and hotly. There are a lot of insults back and forth, name-calling, put-downs, and sarcasm. We don't really listen to what the other is saying, nor do we look at each other very much. One or the other of us can be quite detached and emotionally uninvolved, even though there may be brief episodes of attack and defensiveness. There are clearly more negatives than positives in our relationship.

1 = Never
2 = Rarely
3 = Sometimes
4 = Often
5 = Very Often

Source: Holman & Jarvis, 2000. Reprinted with permission. In terms of Gottman's couple types, scenario A reflects a volatile approach, B a validating approach, C an avoiding approach, and D a hostile approach.

*the common ground and values they share overwhelm these differences and
make them unimportant and easy to accept. Hence, there is very little give
and take and little attempt to persuade one another. The discussion has very
little emotion, either positive or negative. Often the proposed solutions to
issues are quite nonspecific.*

Rather than discuss a conflict with their partners, avoiders often just try to fix
it on their own or wait it out, hoping that the passage of time will solve the
problem.

Although they are very different, Gottman asserts that all three types of couples can last because they all maintain a high ratio of rewards to costs in their
approaches to conflict. Volatile couples exchange a lot of negative emotion, but
they balance the scales with even more affection and humor. Avoiders aren't
particularly effusive or amiable, but they don't have a lot of negative vibes to
overcome. As long as the positive, accepting components of their interactions
substantially outnumber the negative, quarrelsome ones—you may recall from
chapter 6 that an acceptable ratio is a minimum of 5 positive exchanges for every
1 negative—couples can fight loudly or not at all and do little damage to their
relationship.

In some couples, however, arguments are harmful, caustic events. For
Gottman, **hostiles** are couples who fail to maintain a 5-to-1 ratio of nice behavior to nasty conduct. Their discussions are sprinkled with too much criticism,
contempt, defensiveness, and withdrawal, and the longer they last, the more
oppressive they become. Some hostile couples actively address their disagreements but do so badly whereas others remain more detached and uninvolved
but snipe at each other in brief salvos of distaste. But whether or not they are
actively arguing, hostiles are simply meaner to each other than other couples
are, and that's why their conflicts are dangerous for their relationships.

Do the data support Gottman's assertions? A sizable survey of almost 2,000
married couples found that in 24 percent of them, at least one of the spouses
fought with a hostile style, and sure enough, those couples were less satisfied
and had more problems than anyone else (Busby & Holman, 2009). The most
common pattern, occurring in 25 percent of the marriages, was for both spouses
to have validating styles, and they were the most content of the bunch. In fact,
the calm, empathic, and respectful approach of validators was always advantageous; in another third of the couples, a validator was paired with someone
who was volatile or avoidant, and those couples were pretty happy, too. Couples in which both spouses were avoiders (2 percent of the sample) or volatile (5 percent) were rather rare, and that's probably a good thing: They were
less satisfied with their marriages than the couples in which (at least some)
validation occurred. So, Gottman's analysis is fairly sound. Heated arguments
do not necessarily do harm to intimate relationships, especially when they are
conducted with some empathy and respect. Real passion is not to be feared as
long as it's leavened with regard for one's partner. But under no circumstances
should you allow a conflict discussion to become sour, sarcastic, and surly.
Conflict *is* corrosive when it becomes venomous and acidic.

THE OUTCOMES OF CONFLICT

Ending Conflict

Eventually, conflicts end. Peterson (2002) described five ways in which conflicts can end, and I'll consider them in an order that ranges roughly from the most destructive and damaging to the most constructive and beneficial. (They're charted for you back in Figure 11.2.)

Separation occurs when one or both partners withdraw without resolving the conflict. Separation that ends a heated encounter may prevent irreparable harm to the relationship, and time apart may give combatants time to cool off and to think about their situation more constructively. It offers no solutions to a couple's problem, however, and may simply delay further discord.

Other conflicts end in conquest. In **domination,** one partner gets his or her way when the other capitulates. This happens routinely when one person is more powerful than the other, and the more powerful partner will typically be pleased with the outcome. Domination is aversive for the loser, however, and it may breed ill will and resentment (Zacchilli et al., 2009).

Compromise occurs when both parties reduce their aspirations so that a mutually acceptable alternative can be found. As Peterson suggested (2002, p. 380), the partners' "interests are diluted rather than reconciled"; neither partner gets everything he or she wants, but neither goes empty handed. This may be the best outcome available when one person's gain can come only at the expense of the other, but in other situations, better solutions are usually available.

Integrative agreements satisfy both partners' original goals and aspirations, usually through creativity and flexibility. They're not easy to reach and they typically take some work; partners may need to refine and prioritize their wishes, make selective concessions, and invent new ways of attaining their goals that do not impose upon their partners. Nevertheless, through determination, ingenuity, imagination, and generous cooperation, partners can often get the things they really want.

Finally, on occasion, the partners not only get what they want but also learn and grow and make desirable changes to their relationship. This pleasant outcome, **structural improvement,** isn't frequent, and when it occurs, it is usually the result of significant turmoil and upheaval. Partners may have encountered perilous stress and serious conflict to reach a point that leads them to rethink their habits and to muster both the courage and the will to change them. Still, structual improvement leaves a couple better off. As Peterson (2002, p. 382) wrote:

> Some change will take place in one or more of the causal conditions governing the relationship. Each person will know more about the other than before. Each person may attribute more highly valued qualities to the other than before. Having weathered the storm of previous conflict, each person may trust the other and their relationship more than before, and thus be willing to approach other previously avoided issues in a more hopeful and productive way. With these changes, the quality of the relationship will be improved over many situations and beyond the time of the immediate conflict with which the process began.

Can Fighting Be Good for a Relationship?

Is Peterson right? Can fighting sometimes yield beneficial results? Perhaps. As we near the end of this chapter, you may still feel that it would be better not to have quarrels, disagreements, and arguments in your intimate relationships. Some people certainly feel that way, believing that "disagreement is destructive" and that an argument is a sure sign that one's love is flawed (Eidelson & Epstein, 1982). But (as we noted back in chapter 4) that's a *dys*functional belief that is correlated with *dis*satisfaction, and relationship scientists generally take a different view. They recognize that the more unexpressed nuisances and irritants partners have, the less satisfied with their relationships they tend to be (Roloff & Cloven, 1990). Newlyweds who withdraw from conflict without resolving their disagreements tend to be less happy years later (Noller et al., 1994). And even more remarkably, middle-aged women who fail to speak up when something about their marriages is bothering them are four times more likely than their more vocal neighbors to *die* within the next 10 years (Eaker et al., 2007). Conflict is inevitable and it should not be ignored.

Indeed, the prevailing view among conflict researchers is that, for all the dilemmas it creates, conflict is an essential tool with which to promote intimacy. (Marriage expert John Gottman [1994b, p. 159] counseled, "The most important advice I can give to men who want their marriages to work is to try not to avoid conflict.") Conflict brings problematic issues and incompatibilities into the open, allowing solutions to be sought. Romantic illusions that idealize a relationship and minimize its flaws help us stay happy when the partnership is sound and its problems are minor—but they're treacherous when a relationship has major defects and they keep us from understanding the truth (McNulty, 2010). Indeed, recognizing real problems and being critical of them is the right thing to do when the problems are severe (McNulty & Russell, 2010). Handled well, conflict can defuse situations that would only fester and cause bigger problems later on. If you confront conflict head-on, there's no guarantee that your difficulties will be resolved and that contentment will follow (Fincham & Beach, 1999). Nevertheless, it is usually the deft and skillful management of conflict—not the absence of conflict—that allows relationships to grow and prosper (Fincham, 2003).

Of course, for many of us, this is easier said than done. We tend to bring the lessons we learned at home as teenagers with us into our adult romances (Whitton et al., 2008), and people clearly differ in the sensitivity and dexterity with which they manage conflict (Smith et al., 2008). In particular, boys who witness violent conflict between their parents tend to become men who handle conflict poorly, being more surly and sarcastic than their peers (Halford et al., 2000).

However, couples who are fighting badly do sometimes clean up their act. A study that followed couples as they became parents found that most of them maintained the same style of conflict over a span of 2 years; about half of them fought constructively, using plenty of validation and positive affect, and a quarter of them fought poorly, wallowing in antagonism and sour dissension for the full 24 months. Evidently, once you and your partner develop a style for managing conflict, it's likely to last. Still, about 20 percent of the young parents who had been fighting destructively *changed* their styles and became less cantankerous—and more satisfied with their relationships—over that span of time (Houts et al., 2008).

If you're fighting unpleasantly now, you can probably change, too, and I have some suggestions in this regard. First, for most of us, successful conflict management involves *self-control.* To the extent that you work at remaining optimistic, avoiding blaming attributions, and mastering your anger, you're more likely to be tolerant, flexible, and creative, and integrative agreements are more likely to be reached (Canary, 2003). Self-control may also be required for you to successfully execute this list of *don'ts* drawn from Gottman's (1994b) work:

- *Don't* withdraw when your partner raises a concern or complaint. Defensively avoiding a discussion of conflict is obnoxious and it doesn't fix anything. It's fair to ask that a difficult discussion be rescheduled for a more convenient time, but you should then feel obligated to honor that appointment.
- *Don't* go negative. Stifle your sarcasm, contain your contempt, and discard your disgust. Churlish, surly, and sour behavior has very corrosive effects on close relationships because (as you'll recall from chapter 6)[4] bad is stronger than good.
- *Don't* get caught in a loop of negative affect reciprocity. This is essential. Pay attention, and when you realize that you and your partner are hurling stronger and stronger insults and accusations back and forth, *stop.* Take a 10-minute break, gather yourself, calm down, and return to your discussion with an apology for the last disagreeable thing you said.

A very good way to steer clear of bad-tempered, ill-mannered interaction is to employ a technique that's taught by marriage therapists to help couples manage conflict constructively (Markman et al., 1994). The **speaker-listener technique** provides a structure for calm, clear communication about contentious issues that promotes the use of active listening skills and increases the chances that partners will understand and validate each other despite their disagreement. In particular, the speaker-listener technique is designed to interrupt the cycle of misperception that too often occurs when partners respond quickly to one another without checking their understanding of the other's intent.

To use the technique, the partners designate a small object as the *floor.* (See Table 11.3.) Whoever has the floor is the speaker. That partner's job is to concisely describe his or her feelings using "I-statements"; the listener's job is to listen without interrupting and then to paraphrase the speaker's message. When the speaker is satisfied that his or her feelings have been understood, the floor changes hands and the partners switch roles. This patient pattern of careful communication allows the partners to demonstrate their concern and respect for each other's feelings without falling into a noxious cycle of self-justification, mind reading, interruption, and defensiveness (Cornelius & Alessi, 2007).

[4]Page 184.

TABLE 11.3. The Speaker-Listener Technique

Want to stay cool when a discussion gets heated? Consider following these rules:

Rules for Both of You

1. *The Speaker has the floor.* Use a real object, such as a book or TV remote control, as the floor. Whoever holds the floor is the only person who gets to say anything until he or she is done.

2. *Share the floor.* When you're Speaker, don't go on and on. Keep each turn brief, and switch roles often as the floor changes hands.

3. *No problem solving.* The point of the technique is to delineate a disagreement, not to solve it. Collaborative brainstorming to solve the problem comes later.

Rules for the Speaker

4. *Speak for yourself. Don't try to be a mind reader.* Use "I" statements to describe your own thoughts, feelings, and concerns. Do not talk about your perceptions of your partner's motives or point of view.

5. *Stop and let the Listener paraphrase.* After a short time, stop and allow the Listener to paraphrase what you've just said. If he or she is not quite accurate, politely restate any points of confusion. The goal is to help the Listener really understand you.

Rules for the Listener

6. *Paraphrase what you hear.* Show the Speaker that you are listening by repeating back in your own words what you heard him or her say. The point is to make sure that you understood what was said.

7. *Focus on the Speaker's message. Don't rebut.* You should not offer your thoughts and opinions on the issue until you have the floor. Your job as Listener is to speak only in the service of understanding your partner.

Does this sound awkward? Perhaps, but it has its uses. As its creators suggest, the speaker-listener technique "isn't a normal way to communicate, but it is a relatively safe way to communicate on a difficult issue. Each person will get to talk, each will be heard, and both will show their commitment to discussing the problems constructively" (Markman et al., 1994, p. 67).

Note: Adapted from Markman et al., 1994.

If you strive to follow these suggestions, you'll probably manage conflict well. And when a conflict discussion is complete, you can grade your collaboration using a scorecard developed by George Bach and Peter Wyden (1983) known as the "Fight Effects Profile." (See Table 11.4.) If you have a "good" fight that has the positive effects listed in the table, your fight is likely to be good for your relationship.

I'm not underestimating how hard it is to fight fair and have a "good" fight. It requires self-discipline and genuine caring about one's partner. But the positive outcomes are usually worth the effort. From this perspective, instead of being a dreadful problem, conflict is a challenging opportunity—a chance to learn about one's partner and oneself, and a possibility for one's relationship to become more satisfying and more intimate. Strive to fight fairly, and consider using the Fight Effects Profile to grade your efforts the next time conflict puts your communication skills to the test.

TABLE 11.4. The Fight Effects Profile

Each fight is scored by each person from his or her point of view. In a good fight, both partners win. That is, both partners have considerably more positive outcomes than negative ones.

Category	Positive Outcome	Negative Outcome
Hurt	You feel less hurt, weak, or offended.	You feel more hurt, weak, or offended.
Information	You gain more information about your partner's feelings.	You learn nothing new.
Resolution	The issue is now more likely to be resolved.	Possibility of a solution is now less likely.
Control	You have gained more mutually acceptable influence over your partner's behavior.	You now have less mutually acceptable influence over your partner.
Fear	Fear of fighting and/or your partner is reduced.	Fear has increased.
Trust	You have more confidence that your partner will deal with you with good-will and with positive regard.	You have less confidence in your partner's goodwill.
Revenge	Vengeful intentions are not created by the fight.	Vengeful intentions are cre-ated stimulated by the fight.
Reconciliation	You make active efforts to undo any harm you have caused.	You do not attempt or encourage reconciliation.
Relational Evaluation	You feel you are more central to the other's concern and interest.	You feel you "count less" with your partner.
Self-Evaluation	You feel better about yourself: more confidence and more self-esteem.	You feel worse about yourself.
Cohesion-Affection	Closeness with and attraction to your partner have increased.	Closeness with and attraction to your partner have decreased.

Source: Adapted from Bach & Wyden, 1983.

FOR YOUR CONSIDERATION

John's wife, Tina, is a bit hot headed. When something bothers her, she wants to drop everything else and work on the problem, but she tends to do so with high emotion. She has a volatile temper; she gets angry easily, but she cools off just as fast. John is more placid, and he dislikes conflict. When he gets angry, he does so slowly, and he simmers rather than erupts. When there's something bothering him, he prefers to just go off by himself and engage in distracting entertainments instead of beginning a discussion that could turn into a fight.

Lately, Tina has become very frustrated because John is close lipped and unresponsive when she brings up a complaint. His reluctance to discuss her grievances is just making her annoyance and dissatisfaction worse. What do you think the future holds for Tina and John? Why?

CHAPTER SUMMARY

The Nature of Conflict

What Is Conflict? *Interpersonal conflict* occurs when people have to give up something that they want because of their partners' influence. Conflict is inescapable. There are tensions known as *dialectics* that are woven into the fabric of close relationships that will, sooner or later, always cause some strain.

The Frequency of Conflict. Conflict occurs often. Its frequency is associated with neuroticism and agreeableness, anxiety about abandonment, one's stage of life, incompatibility between partners, and the use of alcohol.

The Course of Conflict

Instigating Events. Four different categories of events cause most conflicts; these are *criticism, illegitimate demands, rebuffs,* and *cumulative annoyances.*

Attributions. Actor-observer effects and self-serving biases contribute to *attributional conflict* with partners fighting over whose explanation is right.

Engagement and Escalation. Once an instigating event occurs, partners must decide either to engage in conflict or to avoid the issue and let it drop. If escalation occurs and the conflict heats up, the nasty things that partners say to each other may be either direct or indirect. Surly interaction becomes especially fractious when the partners fall into a pattern of *negative affect reciprocity.*

The Demand/Withdraw Pattern. A frustrating demand/withdraw cycle occurs when one person approaches the other about a problem, and the partner responds by avoiding the issue or the person. Women tend to be the demanders and men the withdrawers more often than not.

Negotiation and Accommodation. Negotiation finally occurs when a couple works toward a solution in a sensible manner. *Voice, loyalty, exit,* and *neglect* are other responses to dissatisfaction in close relationships. *Accommodation* occurs when partners react with calm forbearance to the other's provocation.

Dealing with Conflict: Four Types of Couples. *Volatile* couples have frequent and passionate arguments. *Validators* have calmer, more relaxed discussions, and *avoiders* avoid confrontation. In contrast, the conflicts of *hostiles* are marked by negativity, and their marriages are more fragile than those of the other three groups.

The Outcomes of Conflict

Ending Conflict. There are five ways conflicts can end: *separation, domination, compromise, integrative agreement,* and *structural improvement.*

Can Fighting Be Good for a Relationship? Yes. Deft management of conflict allows relationships to grow and prosper. The *speaker-listener technique* provides a structure for calm, clear communication about touchy topics.

CHAPTER 12

Power and Violence

POWER AND INTERDEPENDENCE ◆ Sources of Power ◆ Types of
Resources ◆ Men, Women, and the Control of Resources ◆ The Process of
Power ◆ The Outcome of Power ◆ The Two Faces of Power ◆ VIOLENCE
IN RELATIONSHIPS ◆ The Prevalence of Violence ◆ Types of Couple
Violence ◆ Gender Differences in Intimate Violence ◆ Correlates
of Violence ◆ The Rationales of Violence ◆ Why Don't They All Leave?
◆ FOR YOUR CONSIDERATION ◆ CHAPTER SUMMARY

Who calls the shots in your relationship? Do you usually get your way? Or do you and your partner trade the lead with each of you getting some of what you want? Most people say that an ideal relationship would be an equal partnership, with both partners sharing the ability to make important decisions and to influence one another; at the turn of the century, for instance, 90 percent of young women and 87 percent of young men said they believed that dating partners should have "exactly equal say" in the relationship (Thornton & Young-DeMarco, 2001). In addition, people clearly prefer friendships in which the partners share similar amounts of power to friendships in which one of the partners is typically the boss (Veniegas & Peplau, 1997). This may not seem surprising; nevertheless, this preference for sharing power is an enormous departure from the traditional model endorsed by previous generations, in which men were the dominant partners in heterosexual relationships, making all the important decisions and calling all the shots. These days, few people explicitly announce that they want to emulate this old-fashioned model, but figuring out how to achieve equality in a relationship can be much more complicated than it sounds. How should decision making work in an egalitarian relationship? Should the partners make all decisions together? Or does each partner take responsibility for making exactly half the decisions? Does it matter which decisions are important and which ones aren't? Endorsing equality in a relationship is a simple matter, but making it a reality is a much greater challenge.

This chapter will explore the ways in which social power operates in intimate relationships. Social **power** is the ability to influence the behavior of others and to resist their influence on us (Huston, 2002). I'll identify some of the influences on power in relationships and consider the consequences of power for individuals and couples. Some of them, unfortunately, can be unpleasant.

POWER AND INTERDEPENDENCE

There are different ways to analyze social power, but the most widely adopted perspective is that of interdependency theory (Thibaut & Kelley, 1959), which we examined in chapter 6. In this chapter, I'll use interdependency ideas to describe the bases on which power is built, the processes by which power is wielded, and the outcomes that are produced by its use.

Sources of Power

From an interdependency perspective, power is based on the control of valuable resources. If I control access to something you want, you'll probably be motivated to comply with my wishes (within reason) so that I'll let you get it. I'll then have power over you; I'll be able to get you to do what *I* want, at least for a while. This is a simple idea, but (as you might expect) there are various subtleties involved in this view of social power.

First, the person who has power does not have to possess the desired resources; it is enough that he or she controls access to them. Imagine that you're shopping with a friend at a flea market and you discover the rare imported bootleg concert DVD that you've wanted for months, but that you keep losing to higher bidders on eBay. Better yet, it's cheap, but you don't have enough cash with you, and you need a loan from your friend to buy the elusive disc. Your friend doesn't have the object you desire, but his or her power in this situation will come from controlling your ability to get it. In a similar fashion, relationship partners can control our access to valuable interpersonal rewards—such as physical affection—and thereby have power over us.

Of course, one derives power from controlling a resource only if other people want it, and the greater their need or desire, the greater one's power. The example of the rare DVD is an illustration of this: If you have only a mild interest in the disc, a friend with the money to buy it has only a little power over you. But if you want the disc desperately, your friend has more power and will be able to ask for a sizable favor in return. Whenever we want something badly (be it a rare DVD or interpersonal intimacy) and believe we cannot get it elsewhere, the person who has what we want is able to exert control over us.

We encountered an example of one person's desire fueling another person's power back in the box on p. 181. The **principle of lesser interest** holds that in any partnership, the person who has less interest in continuing and maintaining the relationship has more power in that partnership (Waller & Hill, 1951). If your partner loves and needs you more than you love him or her, you'll get to do what you want more often than not. This sounds cold blooded, but it's true; in romantic relationships, the partner who is less committed to the relationship usually has more power (Lennon et al., 2011). I mentioned another example of this pattern in chapter 9 when I noted that men desire more sex, on average, than women do. Men's greater interest in sex gives women power; it's quite unromantic but rather enlightening to think of sex as a valuable resource that women can exchange for various benefits from men (Kruger, 2008b). This arrangement is explicit in the case of prostitution when women trade sex for money, but it often also operates in more subtle ways in many romantic relationships. It's not uncommon, for instance, for a woman to wait for a declaration of affection and emerging commitment from a man before allowing him access to sex.

Of course, if something we want is readily available elsewhere, we can just go there to get it, and the availability of alternative sources of desired resources is another critical factor in an interdependency perspective on power. If there is another friend at the flea market who can lend you the money you need, the first friend has less power over you. And if there are many people who would loan you the money, then you are not very dependent on any one of them, and not one of them has much power over you at all.

In the same fashion, the availability of alternatives influences the balance of power in an intimate relationship. Those with few alternatives to their existing partnerships (who therefore have low $CL_{alt}s$) will be more dependent on their relationships than will those with many other other potential partners (who thereby have high $CL_{alt}s$). And as we have just seen, being more dependent means having less power. If one partner has few alternatives and the other has many, there will be a larger imbalance of power than would be the case if they needed each other to similar degrees (Lennon et al., 2011).

In fact, differences in available alternatives may be one reason that men are typically more powerful than women in traditional marriages. When husbands work outside the home and their wives do not, they often have higher $CL_{alt}s$ for at least two important reasons. First, they may encounter larger numbers of other potential partners, and second, they're more likely to have the money to pursue them if they wish. In contrast, stay-at-home wives may not meet many other interesting men, and even if they do, they're likely to be economically dependent on their husbands, having little money of their own. Thus, the balance of power in a marriage sometimes changes when a wife enters the work force and gains new friends and money of her own (Fitch & Ruggles, 2000).

There are two more points to make about the interdependence perspective on power. First, interdependence theory recognizes two different broad types of power. On occasion, one can control a partner's outcomes no matter what the partner does; in such cases, one has a form of power known as **fate control:** One can autocratically determine what outcomes a partner receives, thereby controlling the other's fate. When she is his only option, a woman who refuses to have sex with her husband is exercising fate control; she can unilaterally determine whether or not sex occurs. A second, more subtle, type of power is **behavior control.** This occurs when, by changing one's own behavior, one encourages a partner to alter his or her actions in a desirable direction, too. If a woman offers to provide a special backrub if her partner cleans the garage, she's engaging in behavior control.

Of course, in almost all relationships, *both* partners have power over each other, and the last, and perhaps most essential, point of an interdependency perspective is that the interactions of two partners emerge from their mutual influence on one another. One partner's power over the other may be matched by the other's *counterpower* over the one, so that both partners are able to get each other to do what they want some of the time. For instance, a woman may have fate control over whether or not her husband has sex, but he probably has some behavior control over her in return; by cajoling her, pleasing her, or worse, threatening her, he may be able to get her to do what he wants. Two partners' abilities to influence one another may be diverse and variable, being strong in some situations and weak in others, but both of them will routinely have some control over what the other does.

Types of Resources

So, power is based on the resources we control—but what kinds of resources are involved? Table 12.1 lists six bases of power first identified by French and Raven (1959); this scheme has been applied to all kinds of interactions, including those that occur in intimate relationships. The first two types, **reward power** and **coercive power,** refer to a person's ability to bestow various rewards and punishments on someone else. The benefits and costs involved can be physical or material goods, such as a pleasant gift or a painful slap, or intangible, interpersonal gains and losses, such as reassuring approval or hurtful disdain (Raven, 2001). For example, if a husband craves a shoulder massage from his wife, she has reward power over him: She can rub his back or not, supplying or withholding a physical reward. But in return, he may have coercion power

TABLE 12.1. Resources that Grant One Power

Type of Power	Resource	Gets People to Do What You Want Them to Do Because
Reward power	Rewards	You can give them something they like or take away something they don't like.
Coercive power	Punishments	You can do something to them they don't like or take away something they do like.
Legitimate power	Authority or norms of equity, reciprocity, or social responsibility	They recognize your authority to tell them what to do.
Referent power	Respect and/or love	They identify with you, feeling attracted and wanting to remain close.
Expert power	Expertise	You have the broad understanding they desire.
Informational power	Information	You possess some specific knowledge they desire.

Source: Based on Raven, 2001.

over her: If he doesn't get his massage, he may sulk and be less affectionate, imposing intangible costs.

The capabilities to provide desired benefits or to impose aversive costs on our partners are very important and very influential, but there are other ways to influence people, too. **Legitimate power** exists when our partners believe that we have a reasonable right to tell them what to do, and they have an obligation to comply. In some cultures, for instance, a husband really is thought to be the boss, and a wife is supposed not only to love and honor him, but to *obey* him as well, doing whatever he asks. This form of legitimate power comes from being in a position of authority, but potent social norms can also impart legitimate power to requests that come from anyone (Raven, 2001). For instance, the norm of *reciprocity* encourages us to do unto others as they have done unto us, and if someone who has already done you a favor asks for some kindness in return, the norm obligates you to repay the good deed. *Equity* is also normative, and if your partner has done extra housework lately, an invitation to fold some laundry might be difficult to decline. Finally, a norm of *social responsibility* urges us to be generous to those who depend on us—to help those who cannot help themselves—and if your partner is sick in bed with the flu, a request for some juice may be hard to turn down. Any of these norms can impart power to a partner's desires, making them very influential, at least temporarily.

We have **referent power** over our partners when they adore us and wish to do what we want because they feel connected to us. Our wishes may change our partners' preferences about what they want to do when they love us and want to stay close to us. **Expert power** exists when our partners recognize our superior knowledge and experience and are influenced by us because we know more than they do. When a wife is a better cook than her husband, for instance, he'll often follow her advice and instructions without question when it's his turn to prepare dinner. Finally, we have **informational power** when we have specific pieces of information that influence our partners' behavior; our partners may do what we want if we offer to share a juicy bit of gossip with them.

Men, Women, and the Control of Resources

How are these resources used in your relationships? What goes on between you and your partner is largely up to both of you, but you may be influenced to a greater extent than you realize by the broad cultural patterns that surround you. Many of us applaud the notion of equal partnerships but still conduct relationships in which "there is an imbalance of power, with one person making more decisions, controlling more of the joint activities and resources, winning more arguments and, in general, being in a position of dominance" (Impett & Peplau, 2006, p. 283). And in most heterosexual relationships, the dominant partner is the man. Indeed, this won't be good news for most of you (but perhaps it really isn't news at all): "In no known societies do women dominate men. In all societies that accumulate wealth, men, on average, enjoy more power than women, on average, and this appears to have been true throughout human history" (Pratto & Walker, 2004, p. 242). Heterosexual couples who seek to share power equally are swimming upstream against long-standing tradition, and there are three reasons for this.

First, men and women generally face a disparity in *relative resources*. Men get paid more than women for the work they do (even when it's the same work): In the United States, women with full-time jobs presently earn only 80 percent as much as men do (Yen, 2010). Men are also far more likely to hold the reins of governmental, judicial, and corporate power; in 2011, for instance, only 16 percent of the members of the U.S. House of Representatives were women (they comprised 17 percent of the Senate), and, even worse, only 3 percent of the chief executive officers of America's 500 largest companies were women ("Women CEOs," 2010). Money and status confer reward power and legitimate power on those who possess them, and men often have more of both than women do. Indeed, it's much more common for wives to earn more than their husbands than it used to be, but in three of four American marriages, he still makes more money than she does (Fry & Cohn, 2010). And money is a source of power that can be used more flexibly than most other resources. Theorists describe some resources (such as money) as *universalistic* and others (such as love) as *particularistic* (Foa et al., 1993). Universalistic resources can be exchanged with almost anyone in a wide variety of situations, and whoever controls them has considerable freedom in deciding what to do with them (and with whom to do it). Particularistic resources are valuable in some situations but not in others, and they may confer power to their owner only with particular partners. A partner's love for you may give you referent power over him or her and no one else whereas a large pile of cash may provide you reward power over almost everyone you meet.

The second reason that equality is hard to attain is related to the first: *Social norms* support and maintain male dominance. Worldwide, most cultures are still governed by a norm of patriarchy that confers higher levels of expert and legitimate power on men than on women (Carli, 1999). Americans actually tend to think that women have skills that should make them more effective leaders than men; women are thought to be more honest, intelligent, compassionate, and creative and just as ambitious and hardworking as men ("Men or Women," 2008). But legitimate power still seems "unladylike" to some people, and when a woman seeks political office, the fact that she's seeking power undermines her appeal to voters—and of course, a man seeking office pays no such penalty (Okimoto & Brescoll, 2010). And if a woman does attain a position of leadership, she's likely to be evaluated more harshly than a man would be when she straightforwardly tells others what to do (Carli, 2001). Cultural norms still keep women in their place, so Americans tend to prefer that their surgeons, lawyers, and airline pilots be men rather than women (Morin & Cohn, 2008). Women are preferred as elementary school teachers.

Thus, cultural tradition suggests that it's ordinary and natural for men to make more money and to be in charge most of the time. And that underlies the third reason why equality is elusive: We're not sure what it looks like. Women usually get their way when it comes to decisions regarding household matters and the kids, and they get to pick the things the couple does on the weekend more often than men do (Morin & Cohn, 2008). So, women can rightly feel that they're influential at home. But just how much? Married Americans still report that wives buy most of the groceries, fix most of the meals, and wash most of the dishes; they also do most of the laundry and clean more of the house (Newport, 2008). Husbands do yard work and take care of the cars, but—and here's my point—that division of labor cannot possibly value wives' and husbands' time equally: The wives' duties are constant, and the husbands' are intermittent (Lachance-Grzela & Bouchard, 2010). Dinner gets eaten every night, but the cars' oil gets changed only every now and then. And when it comes to fundamental, central decisions regarding the relationship—such as "are we going to get married or just keep cohabiting?"—men usually get to call the shots (Sassler & Miller, 2011). Wives do control most household routines, but because their husbands are more likely to get their way when it really matters, the husbands are more powerful. This still tends to true, although to a lesser extent, even when women's disadvantage in relative resources is erased—that is, when they earn more than their husbands. For instance, wives with higher incomes do a smaller proportion of the household chores, but they still do most of them (Lachance-Grzela & Bouchard, 2010).

So, despite their expressed interests in equal partnerships, most heterosexual couples still tolerate substantial inequality (Askari et al., 2010)—and they may not realize just how one-sided their partnerships are. In a culture that takes male dominance for granted, genuine equality that honors both parties' interests equally is certainly unfamiliar, and it may even seem peculiar or excessive. But, if you're interested, Table 12.2 may help you judge your own partnerships more evenhandedly; it offers several considerations that may be eye-opening.

Finally, I'll also note that men often have a lot of coercive power due to their typically larger size and greater strength. But coercion is a clumsy, corrosive way to get what one wants. Fear and punishment are aversive, and they breed discontent. They also foster resistance, so partners who are coerced are actually *less* compromising than they would have been had gentler power been employed (Oriña et al., 2002). I'll return to this point later in the chapter when we examine violence in close relationships, but for now I'll simply point out that coercion is usually an inept, counterproductive way to influence an intimate partner.

The Process of Power

Power feels good. Powerful people are used to getting what they want, so they experience a lot of positive moods (Langner & Keltner, 2008) and high self-esteem (Wojciszke & Struzynska-Kujalowicz, 2007). They feel in control of things. In fact, compared to the rest of us, they tend to think that they can control events that are uncontrollable, such as the outcome of a roll of some dice (Fast et al., 2009). They also tend to act when there's something they want. They initiate negotiations instead of waiting for someone else to make the first move (Magee et al., 2007), and if there's just one cookie left on the plate, they'll take it without asking if anyone else wants it (Keltner et al., 2010). Indeed, they are relatively unlikely to realize that someone else was hoping to share the cookie because they're not

TABLE 12.2. Elements of Equality in Close Relationships

These are four dimensions with which to judge how close you're coming to true equality in your relationships. They are suggested for your consideration by Anne Rankin Mahoney, a sociologist, and Carmen Knudson-Martin, a marital and family therapist (2009).

Relative Status

Whose interests matter more?
Who defines what's important to the two of you?
How are low-status chores around the house handled?

Attention to the Other

Who is more likely to notice and attend to the feelings of his or her partner?
Who is more likely to notice and attend to the needs of his or her partner?
Do both of you give and receive care and concern?

Patterns of Accommodation

Whose accommodations are noticed and acknowledged, and whose are taken for granted?
Who arranges more of his or her daily activities around the other's life?

Well-Being

Who's better off psychologically and physically?
Does one person's well-being come at the expense of the other's good health?
Whose economic success is valued more?

very good at comprehending others' points of view. If you ask powerful people to quickly draw an "E" on their foreheads, they are much more likely than people of low power to draw the letter as if they were reading it, which makes it backward and illegible for anyone else—like this: Ǝ (Galinsky et al., 2006).

The self-importance of powerful people is also evident in their self-perceptions of their mate value.[1] When people feel powerful, they prefer partners who are more attractive than they'd pursue if they were less powerful (Brady et al., 2011). Furthermore, people who are randomly assigned to lead work groups in lab studies expect that their subordinates will find them sexually interesting, and if they approve of casual sex, they both judge their subordinates to be more sexually available and stage more flirtatious interactions with them than those of lesser power do (Kunstman & Maner, 2011). Those perceptions apparently persist in the workplace: Compared to mid-level managers, more powerful professionals are more adulterous, being 25 percent more likely to cheat on their current partners (Lammers et al., 2011). And they may not think they're misbehaving; powerful people judge others' moral transgressions more harshly than their own, so that, compared to less powerful people, they're more strict in condemning others' cheating while cheating more often themselves (Lammers et al., 2010).

[1] We first encountered *mate value* back on page 89.

By comparison, being powerless isn't so great. Those who find themselves in positions of low power suffer more depression, behave more cautiously, and timidly fear more punishment than powerful people do (Keltner et al., 2010). And, in keeping with these patterns, power differentials affect the behavior of people toward their intimate partners too. Let's inspect some of the ways in which power is expressed.

Conversation

The conversations two people share are likely to be influenced by the balance of power between them, and, for better or worse, women tend not to speak to men with the same implicit strength and power that they display toward other women. In particular, they allow themselves to be interrupted by men more often than they interrupt men in return.

In one of the first studies of this pattern, researchers surreptitiously recorded conversations of college students in public places (obtaining permission to analyze the recordings after the conversations were done) and then compared the conversations of same-sex dyads to those in which men and women conversed (Zimmerman & West, 1975). Women and men behaved similarly when they were talking to others of the same sex, but distinctive patterns emerged in interactions with the other sex. Men interrupted their female partners much more often than their female partners interrupted them (and they did most of the talking, too). That's important because people who get interrupted are judged to have lower status and to be less powerful than those who do the interrupting (Farley, 2008).

Now, fast-forward to this century and imagine that you and your lover have to decide how to spend a gift of $1,000. You each develop a personal list of your top five priorities and then get together to negotiate your options. If one of you frequently succeeds in interrupting the other, both of you are likely to judge him or her to be the more powerful partner (see Figure 12.1). And men still complete more of these interruptions than women do (Dunbar & Burgoon, 2005).

FIGURE 12.1. **Interruptions and Perceived Power.**
During discussions of personal priorities, the more often someone successfully interrupted his or her partner, the more powerful he or she was perceived to be. *Source: Dunbar & Burgoon, 2005.*

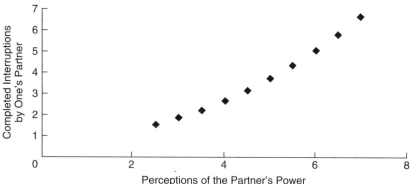

FIGURE 12.2. **Low- and high-power postures.**
People of high status and power assume postures that are asymmetric and that take up a lot of space. It's a safe bet that someone who assumes the posture on the right feels (or will soon feel) more powerful than someone who assumes the posture on the left. By the way, if you were told that one of these silhouettes is a man and the other is a woman, which would you say is which?
Source: Adapted from Frieze et al., 1978.

Nonverbal Behavior

Power is also communicated to others nonverbally, and powerful people use larger interpersonal distances, display more intense facial expressions, and assume postures that are less symmetrical and take up more space than those of people who are less powerful (Hall et al., 2005). Take a look at the two poses in Figure 12.2. They exemplify my postural point: The one on the right typifies someone of higher status. (That's obvious, isn't it?) Indeed, when people are posed in these positions by researchers, those who assume more space *feel* more powerful; moreover, male or female, their testosterone levels rise, and they take bolder risks in a gambling game (Carney et al., 2010). The pose on the right is clearly more powerful—and interestingly, it's more masculine, too. Men tend to take up more space with their postures than women do—one certainly ought not assume the pose on the right if one is wearing a dress—and they use distances and postures that are typical of high-status people more often than women do (Kalbfleisch & Herold, 2006).

Nonverbal Sensitivity

Remember, too, from chapter 5, that women are generally more accurate judges of others' emotions and meaning than men are. Women decode others' nonverbal communications more accurately than men do (Hall & Mast, 2008), and they are usually more aware of what others are feeling (Ciarrochi et al., 2005). This skill is a tremendous asset because the sensitivity and accuracy with

BORN LOSER® by Art and Chip Sansom

When a difference in status exists, it's usually up to the subordinate to understand what the boss is feeling rather than vice versa.
Reprinted by permission of United Media.

which a couple communicates nonverbally predicts how satisfied with each other they are likely to be (Noller, 2006).

On the other hand, a person's nonverbal sensitivity also has something to do with how powerful he or she is (Keltner et al., 2010). When two people differ in status, it's typically the job of the subordinate to keep track of what the boss is feeling, not the other way around. Powerful bosses don't have to care what their subordinates are feeling; underlings are supposed to do what a boss wants whether they like it or not. In contrast, subordinates can increase their own (limited) power when they carefully monitor their supervisors' moods; if they make requests when their bosses are in good moods (and stay out of sight when the bosses are cranky), they're more likely to get what they want.

Thus, in being adept users of nonverbal communication, women gain valuable information that can make them more pleasing partners and that can increase their influence over men. On the other hand, they also behave as subordinates do when they are dealing with people of higher status. Ironically, a useful and desirable talent may perpetuate a stereotypical pattern in which women sometimes behave as if they are the minions of men.

Styles of Power

Just what strategies, then, do men and women use in their efforts to influence each other? Toni Falbo and Anne Peplau (1980) addressed this question in a classic study that asked 50 lesbians, 50 gay men, 50 heterosexual women, and 50 heterosexual men to describe "how I get [my partner] to do what I want." Two themes characterized the participants' replies. First, they sometimes explicitly asked for what they wanted, straightforwardly announcing their wishes or making unambiguous requests. Their efforts to influence their partners were overt and *direct,* and their preferences were plain. On other occasions, however, people's actions were more *indirect*; they hinted at what they wanted or pouted when their wishes were unfulfilled, but they never came right out and said what they wanted. Importantly, the more satisfied people were with their relationships, the more likely they were

Influencing a Partner to Use a Condom

You'd think that it'd be taken for granted these days that people would expect to have safe sex when they begin having sex in a new relationship. Unfortunately, too often, one partner still needs to convince the other to use a condom. How do such negotiations proceed? The most common strategy is a direct one: People straightforwardly announce their wish to use a condom (Lam et al., 2004) and then back up the request with reward power, coercive power, or informational power (De Bro et al., 1994). Promised rewards often include the increased respect and closeness that compliance will bring, threatened costs include the discontent or withholding of sex that resistance will produce, and persuasive information often describes the risks that will be avoided by making the smart choice to employ a condom.

But people also make their wishes known through other more indirect means that do not involve explicit discussion (Lam et al., 2004). One effective tactic is to simply produce a condom and begin putting it on. Without saying a word, one can demonstrate that condom use is expected and appreciated. The reluctant partner may protest that such precautions aren't needed, but his or her objections probably won't last long if the proactive partner persists.

Indeed, when people *don't* want to use a condom, they usually don't mention their preference. Instead, they typically try to seduce their partners, getting them so turned on that sex proceeds without a pause for protection (De Bro et al., 1994). Thus, it may be useful, if you seek safe sex, to keep your wits about you and to remember that, with the force of supportive social norms behind you, your preference is likely to be more powerful than any defense your partner can deploy. Don't fall into the trap of thinking that your partner has more control over the situation than you do; that will make it harder for you to do the right thing and get what you want (Woolf & Maisto, 2008).

to use direct strategies. This could mean that when people have rewarding partnerships, they feel safe enough to be honest and forthright with their partners; on the other hand, it could also mean that people whose desires are expressed indirectly and ambiguously are less adept at getting what they want, and they're likely to be dissatisfied as a result. What's your guess? Does indirectness lead to dissatisfaction or follow from it? (Remember, it could be both.)

The second theme that distinguished different strategies described the extent to which people sought their goals through interaction with their partners (as opposed to doing what they wanted by themselves). Sometimes people reasoned or bargained with their partners in efforts to persuade them to provide some desired outcome; in such cases, people sought cooperation or collaboration from their partners, and their strategies were *bilateral*, involving both members of the couple. In contrast, on other occasions, people took independent *unilateral* action, doing what they wanted without involving their partners. Importantly, people who reported that they were more powerful than their partners said that they frequently used bilateral strategies whereas those who were less powerful were more likely to use unilateral strategies. Thus, people who were able to influence their partners successfully did just that, reasoning and negotiating with them to gain their compliance. In contrast, those possessing low power were less likely to seek their partners' cooperation; they just went off and did their own thing.

Falbo and Peplau (1980) found that, overall, gays and lesbians employed similar strategies, but there were differences in the strategies used by heterosexual men and women. On average, heterosexual men reported more extensive use of direct and bilateral styles whereas heterosexual women used more indirect and unilateral strategies. Thus, when they were dealing with their romantic partners, heterosexual men tended to use styles of influence that are characteristic of people who are satisfied and powerful whereas women adopted styles typically used by those who are powerless and discontent.

Wow. Do heterosexual men typically behave in a mature and assertive fashion in their romantic partnerships, asking for what they want and reasoning logically with their lovers while their partners pout and get moody without ever saying what they want? Well, yes, to a degree. That statement is obviously too sweeping, but in heterosexual relationships, men do tend to be more openly assertive than women. Moreover, this tends to be true from the moment a relationship begins. When they want to start a relationship, men use more direct strategies, such as asking a woman for a date, whereas women more often use indirect strategies, such as trying to seem friendly and waiting to be asked (Clark et al., 1999).

Importantly, however, this pattern isn't really a sex difference; it's a *gender* difference that's wrapped up with the sexes' relative resources.[2] Whether they are male or female, people who are high in instrumentality—who are, after all, assertive, self-confident people—tend to use direct, bilateral styles of power. By comparison, people who are low in instrumentality (and that includes most women) tend to use indirect, unilateral styles (Falbo, 1982).

Still, the strategies a person selects are influenced more by his or her *status* in a particular interaction than by his or her gender (Sagrestano et al., 2006). No matter who people are, they are unlikely to behave authoritatively and assertively in situations in which they have lower status than those they are trying to influence. Lynda Sagrestano (1992) demonstrated this when she asked men and women to respond to scenarios in which they were either experts with more knowledge than their partners or novices with lower expertise; both men and women used direct strategies of power when they were experts but indirect strategies when they were novices, and the sexes did not differ in the styles they selected. In addition, recall that there are no differences between the sexes in the ways that gays and lesbians try to influence their partners (Falbo & Peplau, 1980).

---

[2]Here's another opportunity to consider a difference between men and women with the sophistication I hoped to foster back in chapter 1. Sex differences are distinguished from gender differences on pages 22–23.

Add all this up, and it appears that the different styles of influence exhibited by heterosexual men and women in their romantic relationships are products of the routine differences in relative resources in those partnerships. Men and women do not differ in their power preferences in their same-sex partnerships, and women can be just as direct as men when that style pays off for them (Carothers & Allen, 1999), but men have traditionally held more power than women, both in and out of the home. This is changing. These days, each new generation of American women is higher in instrumentality than the one before (Twenge, 2009), and women are gaining more control over political and economic resources all the time. Both men and women are also becoming more egalitarian in their views of marriage (Bryant, 2003). Men probably have less automatic authority in their intimate relationships than they used to, and—here comes an important point—that may be a good thing: Disparities in power are linked to dissatisfaction in close relationships (Amato et al., 2007). People who have to hint and pout to get (some of) what they want tend to be less content than are those who can come right out and ask for what they desire.

The Outcome of Power

Altogether, then, most of us say we want to have equal partnerships with our lovers, but we're surrounded by a culture that takes male dominance for granted, and we often unwittingly perpetuate gender inequalities through our day-to-day interactions. The outcome of these influences in many cases is subtle asymmetry in partners' influence on one another, with a partnership seeming fair or even entirely equal when in reality he has more influence than she does. Here's an example. When spouses are interviewed about their political opinions, wives agree more with their husbands' answers, if the men answer the questions first, than husbands do when their wives go first—and this occurs even when the wives earn higher salaries and are more expert on the issues (Zipp et al., 2004). Male autonomy and assertion and female conformity and compliance seem so natural to many people that imbalances of power that fit this pattern can be hard to detect.

Nevertheless, the latest data on marital equality suggest that we should strive to create romantic partnerships in which both partners' wishes and preferences are given equal weight. Things have changed in the last quarter century. Spouses are much more likely to share decision-making than they used to be, and those who do enjoy marriages that are happier, less contentious, and less prone to divorce than those in which one of the partners calls most of the shots (Amato et al., 2007). Take a look at Figure 12.3. The results portrayed there combine the outcomes experienced by husbands and wives, and the sexes do fare somewhat differently when men relinquish their superior power: Women enjoy larger increases in happiness and more sizable declines in conflict, marital problems, and divorce proneness than men do. Notably, however, the changes are in the *same* direction for men; men are also (a little) happier and (somewhat) less prone to divorce, for instance, in equal partnerships. Everybody wins when power is shared, and nobody loses with, perhaps,

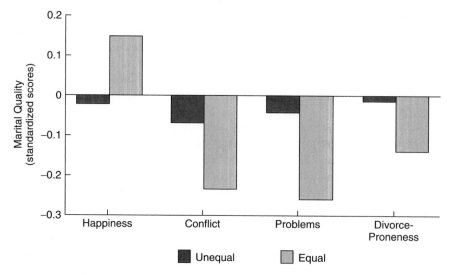

FIGURE 12.3. **Marital outcomes and the balance of power.**
Modern couples are happier, and they have less conflict, fewer problems, and are less
prone to divorce when they share their decision making equally. Much less advantageous outcomes occur when one of the partners calls most of the shots. Compared to
those with equalitarian marriages, couples are less happy, and they experience more
conflict, have more problems, and are more prone to divorce when one partner is more
powerful than the other.
Source: Data from Amato et al., 2007.

one exception: Men are also doing more housework than they used to, and they
don't like it much, but, of course, their female partners are pleased with this
development (Amato et al., 2007). The bottom line is that our modern relationships appear to be more stable and happier on the whole when both partners
matter to the same extent (Helms et al., 2010).

The Two Faces of Power

Our discussion thus far may have left you with the impression that power has
caustic effects on close relationships, but if that's the case, it's time to correct
that view. Imbalances of power can be problematic, but power itself is not
inherently undesirable at all. It does not always lead to the greedy exploitation
of one's partners. Indeed, when people adopt communal orientations[3] in
committed romantic relationships, they typically use their power for the benefit of their partners and their relationships, not for selfish ends (Gardner &
Seeley, 2001). When people care for each other and want to maintain a rewarding relationship, they become benevolent; they display concern for the welfare

---

[3]Need a refresher on the distinction between communal and exchange orientations? Take a look
back at p. 197 in chapter 6.

of their partners, and they use their influence to enhance the other's well-being as well as their own (Chen et al., 2001). Moreover, people with interdependent self-construals,[4] who emphasize interdependency with others, are routinely generous when they resolve disputes with others of lower power (Howard et al., 2007).

An old cliché asserts that "power corrupts," implying that people inevitably become greedy and selfish when they are able to get others to do what they want. But in interdependent, intimate relationships in which both partners want the desirable outcomes the other can provide, power need not be a corrosive, deleterious thing. Instead, committed, happy lovers often use their influence to benefit their partners and to enhance, rather than undermine, their mutual contentment.

There is also, however, a dark side to power. Some people, most of them men, actively seek to be the top dogs in their relationships, and they tend to be controlling, domineering people who have unhappy partners. Power is important to them, and when they are unable to get what they want through more legitimate influence, they may use violence in a sad but sometimes effective effort to exert control (Vescio et al., 2010). It is to this grimmest aspect of intimacy, the potential for intimate violence, to which we now turn.

VIOLENCE IN RELATIONSHIPS

We commit **violence** when we behave in a manner that is intended to do physical harm to others (Finkel & Eckhardt, 2012). The harm we intend may be quite minor or rather severe (Regan et al., 2006), a point that a leading research tool, the **Conflict Tactics Scale**, takes into consideration (Straus et al., 1996). With the scale, people describe their use of psychological and physical aggression against their romantic partners, responding to such items as "I insulted or swore at my partner," "I slapped my partner," and "I used a knife or gun on my partner." Violent actions range from those that do little harm, such as grabbing or pushing, to others that inflict atrocious injury, such as beatings and burnings (see Figure 12.4). And sadly, intimate violence of all types is more common than most people think.

The Prevalence of Violence

In the middle 1990s, the Centers for Disease Control and Prevention teamed up with the National Institute of Justice to conduct detailed phone interviews of 16,000 men and women in a National Violence Against Women Survey in the United States (Tjaden & Thoennes, 2000). The survey found that violence is as American as apple pie. Most of the women (52 percent) and even more men (66 percent) reported that they had been physically assaulted at some point in their lives, and 22 percent of the women and 7 percent of the men had

[4]Page 230 in Chapter 7.

FIGURE 12.4. **Comparative ratings of physical violence from items on the Conflict Tactics Scale**

Source: Data from Regan et al., 2006.

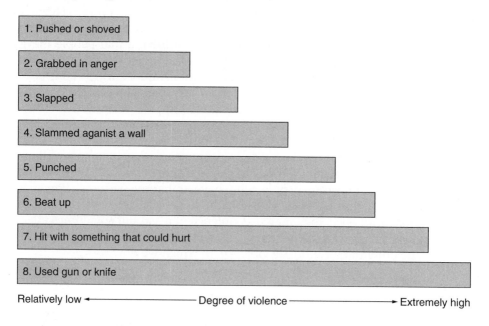

1. Pushed or shoved

2. Grabbed in anger

3. Slapped

4. Slammed aganist a wall

5. Punched

6. Beat up

7. Hit with something that could hurt

8. Used gun or knife

Relatively low ◄——————————— Degree of violence ——————————► Extremely high

experienced a violent assault by an intimate partner. The more men there were in a couple, the greater the likelihood that violence would occur; lesbian women encountered only about half as much violence as heterosexual women did, but gay men experienced twice as much violence as heterosexual men. The most common forms of violence were slapping or hitting, but on rare occasions, guns and knives were used.

Other wide-ranging American surveys have obtained similar results, indicating that some form of violence has occurred in almost one of every four couples (Whitaker et al., 2007). Studies that include acts of psychological aggression—such as screaming, ridicule, and threats directed at one's partner—find that such behavior occurs at one time or another in *most* relationships (Fergusson et al., 2005). However, as bad as it is, aggression of this sort seems less worrisome to most of us than physical violence does (Capezza & Arriaga, 2008), so I'll focus on violence here. And concern about intimate partner violence (or IPV) is warranted; in the United States, the Centers for Disease Control and Prevention (2011) estimate that IPV will cost nearly $9 billion in medical care, psychological services, and lost time from work this year.

Types of Couple Violence

It's one thing to describe the specific acts of violence that occur in close relationships, and another to explain why they occur. Michael Johnson (2008) has suggested that there are three major, distinct types of violence in romantic couples, and they spring from different sources. The most familiar type is **situational couple violence** (or SCV), which typically erupts from heated conflicts that get out of hand. It occurs when both partners are angry and is tied to specific arguments, so it is only occasional and is usually mild, being unlikely to escalate into serious, life-threatening forms of aggression. Often, it is also mutual, with both partners angrily and impulsively flying out of control.

A notably different kind of violence is **intimate terrorism** (or IT) in which one partner uses violence as a tool to control and oppress the other. The physical force and coercion that occurs in intimate terrorism may be just one tactic in a general pattern of threats, isolation, and economic subordination (see Figure 12.5 and the box on the next page), and when it is present in

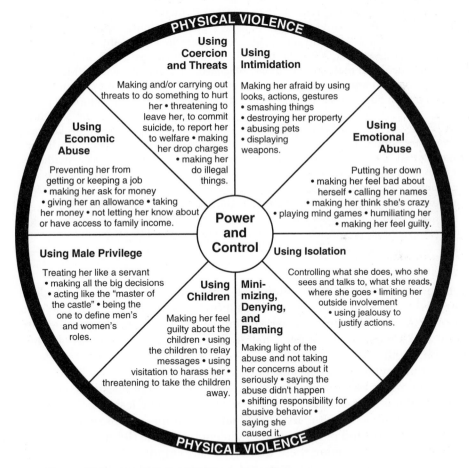

FIGURE 12.5. **The many facets of intimate terrorism.**
The variety of ways in which an intimate terrorist may attempt to influence a partner are portrayed as spokes in a wheel, and violence is the rim that unites them all. Women can be intimate terrorists, too, but the victim is portrayed as a woman here because eight out of nine intimate terrorists are men.
Source: Pence & Paymar, 1993.

Violence and Mate-Guarding

Evolutionary theorists suggest that there's value in doing what we can to induce our mates to be faithful to us. Everything else being equal, sexual selection favors those whose mates reproduce with them and no one else. It's a challenge to which many of us respond by striving to provide our partners with excellent rewards that would make it foolish and pointless for them to cheat on us. But that's hard to do if we're people of modest means and middling mate value (Miner et al., 2009), so some of us also engage in **mate-guarding;** we work to regulate and control our partners' access to potential rivals, and vice versa.

Some tactics of mate-guarding involve monopolization of a partner's time so that there's little opportunity to stray. Vigilance and surveillance—dropping by unexpectedly or calling at random—may also occur (Kaighobadi et al., 2010). But the point of this box is that, sadly, violence can also be used

to enforce a mate's fidelity (Buss & Duntley, 2006). The ability to do harm to one's partner is a form of coercive power, and jealous people sometimes use the threat of (more) physical punishment to control their partner's behavior.

In such relationships, violence is just one element in a web of control. For instance, men who threaten their partners into remaining faithful also tend to engage in verbal abuse, frequently insulting their partners' looks, intelligence, and general worth (McKibbin et al., 2007). In turn, those insults, the surveillance, and the threats are all positively correlated with actual violence inflicted on their mates (Shackelford et al., 2005) that becomes more likely when they worry—usually without good cause—that their mates have been unfaithful (Kaighobadi et al., 2009). Thus, we should be on our guard if a partner's possessiveness turns surly; violence may not be far behind.

a relationship, it occurs more often than situational couple violence. Indeed, compared to SCV, intimate terrorism is more likely to be one-sided, to escalate over time, and to involve serious injury to its target. It's also the form of IPV that's most likely to get a battered spouse to seek shelter elsewhere (Johnson, 2008).

The third type of couple violence is **violent resistance,** in which a partner forcibly fights back against intimate terrorism. Violent resistance occurs in some, but not all, cases of intimate terrorism, so it is the least common of the three. When IPV occurs, it is usually situational couple violence, occasionally intimate terrorism, and only sometimes violent resistance (Johnson, 2008).

The distinctions among these three types are important (Langhinrichsen-Rohling, 2010). For one thing, men and women are equally likely to engage in hotheaded, impulsive situational couple violence, but intimate terrorism is disproportionately authored by men. Women do engage in intimate terrorism, but much less often than men do (Johnson, 2008). (And as a result of this asymmetry, violent resistance is much more common in women than in men.) Does this mean that men are more violent toward their intimate partners than women are? That's actually a thorny question.

Gender Differences in Intimate Violence

Stereotypes may suggest that women engage in less intimate violence than men do, but if anything, it's the other way around; women are actually slightly more likely to engage in physical violence against their partners than men are (Archer, 2000). That sounds like a straightforward (if surprising) conclusion, but it has been the subject of considerable controversy and discussion among relationship scientists (e.g., Langhinrichsen-Rohling, 2010). For one thing, most studies of couple violence do not determine whether a person's actions were offensive or defensive in nature; if a man initiates a physical assault and his female partner fights back, each would have recently done some violence but under different circumstances (Allen et al., 2009).

Men and women also tend to exhibit violent behavior of different severity. Women are more likely to throw something, kick, bite, scratch, or punch their partners, whereas men are more likely to choke, strangle, or beat up theirs (Tanha et al., 2010). Thus, there's no question that men are more likely to do some damage; when couple violence occurs, most of the injuries (62 percent) are suffered by women (Archer, 2000). Men are also much more likely than women to rape or murder their partners (Tjaden & Thoennes, 2000). These brutal acts are often not assessed by studies of couple violence, but if they are included, men are clearly more aggressive than women (Buss & Duntley, 2006).

Sampling is also an issue. Surveys of young adults tend to detect more violence from women than from men—because there is, after all, a lot of it (Straus, 2008)—but studies focusing on distressed couples, such as those in marital therapy or those in court, usually find the husbands to be more violent than their wives (Johnson, 2008). Women are more likely to engage in indirect aggression—by trying to ruin someone's reputation by spreading rumors or gossip (Hess & Hagen, 2006), for example—but that isn't violence. Add all this up, and it appears that women can be just as violent as men, but they are less likely to cause injuries and less likely to use violence as a tool in an ongoing pattern of domination and influence. The sexes behave similarly in episodes of SCV, but a sizable majority of intimate terrorists—89 percent—are men (Johnson, 2008). And when they are victims of intimate terrorism, women typically face persistent violence that often does them harm. Why do men sometimes resort to physical force to hold sway over their female partners?

Correlates of Violence

Careful consideration of intimate partner violence recognizes the distinction between situational couple violence and intimate terrorism (Johnson, 2008). Most acts of violence in close relationships result from impetuous, impulsive failures of self-control (that's SCV), but some violence is part of a program of ruthless subjugation of one's partner (and that's IT). And importantly, SCV and IT seem to spring from somewhat different sources.

Situational Couple Violence

Both types of intimate partner violence are complex, emerging from various overlapping influences. A useful model of situational couple violence, the

I³ (or "I-cubed") **model** created by Eli Finkel and Christopher Eckhardt (2012), organizes influences on SCV into *instigating triggers* that cause one or both partners to be frustrated or on edge, *impelling influences* that make it more likely that the partners will experience violent impulses, and *inhibiting influences* that encourage the partners to refrain from acting on those impulses. When we've been angry, *most* of us have experienced violent impulses, but most of us didn't act on them (Finkel et al., 2009) and Finkel and Eckhardt's model suggests that we refrained from violence either because the impelling influences stimulating us to lash out were too weak or because the inhibiting forces dissuading us from physical action were too strong.

What sort of influences are these? Finkel (2008) suggested that both impelling and inhibitory influences could be distal, dispositional, relational, or situational. *Distal* influences include background factors such as cultural norms, economic conditions, and family experiences. *Dispositional* influences include personality traits and long-standing beliefs. *Relational* influences involve the current state of the couple's relationship, and *situational* influences include the immediate circumstances. These are all listed with some examples in Figure 12.6. The figure may seem intimidating at first, but don't fret; I'll walk you through it.

Instigating Triggers. The path to situational couple violence begins with instigating influences that cause one or both of the partners to become cantankerous or angry. Anything about a couple's interaction that causes frustration or aggravation can set the model in motion: Jealousy-evoking events, remembered or discovered betrayals, real or imagined rejection (Giordano et al., 2010), or any of the exasperating events that exacerbate conflict[5] will suffice. A particularly potent instigator, though, is verbal or physical abuse from one's partner: People are especially likely to become antagonistic when their partners curse or hit them first (Stith et al., 2004).

Impelling Influences. Then when someone's fired up, the impelling influences that are at work become important. Some of the influences that predispose one to violence are events from much earlier in life. For instance, people who witnessed violence between their parents (Milletich et al., 2010) and those who consumed a lot of aggressive media (such as violent movies and video games) over the years (Coyne et al., 2010) are more likely than others to engage in IPV. Other impelling influences are enduring personal characteristics. People with sour dispositions who are prone to anger (Dutton, 2010) or who are high in neuroticism (Hellmuth & McNulty, 2008) are also prone to intimate violence. So are men with traditional, sex-typed gender roles (Stith et al., 2004) and those with attitudes that condone a little force now and then as a normal way of doing things (Robertson & Murachver, 2009). (Thus, here's a bit of good news in this grim landscape: Some of the personal characteristics that predispose people to violence are *attitudes* that may be comparatively easy to change [Neighbors et al., 2010].) Still other impelling influences emerge from the partners' patterns

---

[5] Page 342 in chapter 11.

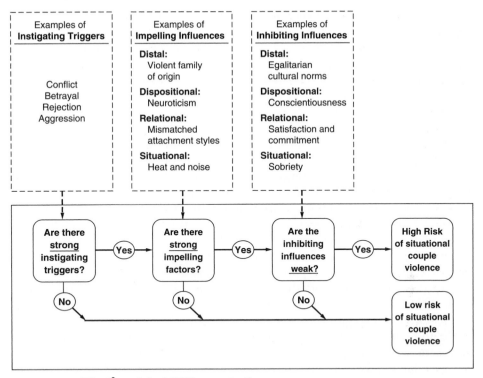

FIGURE 12.6. **The I³ model of SCV perpetration.**
If the answers to the three questions posed in the model are all "yes," situational
couple violence is likely to occur. If any of the answers is "no," violence is unlikely.
Examples of the influences that bear on each question are provided, but they are illus-
trative rather than exhaustive. Violence is the result of many sources, and the examples
provided were chosen because of their relevance to relationship science.
Source: Adapted from Finkel, 2008.

of interaction; for example, couples with poor communication skills (Simpson, Doss et al., 2007) or mismatched attachment styles (Doumas et al., 2008)
engage in more IPV than others do.[6] (The most troublesome mismatch pairs a

[6] The I³ model's distinction between distal, dispositional, relational, and situational influences is a
helpful way to organize the variety of influences that shape IPV, but don't take it too seriously. The
categories overlap, and to some degree, the placement of a particular influence in a specific category is arbitrary. For example, kids who grow up in violent homes are more likely than the rest of
us to have insecure attachment styles, and certain combinations of insecure styles in a marriage—
such as an anxious wife paired with an avoidant husband—are tricky (Godbout et al., 2009). So,
the distal influence of a violent childhood home produces a dispositional characteristic, attachment
insecurity, that becomes particularly problematic when it's combined with a partner's style in a
way that produces a trying relationship that's full of annoying vexations. All four types of influences are involved in this sequence of events, and there's no need for you to fuss too much about
what influences on IPV belong in which category. Instead, just note the wide variety of experiences
and traits that are associated with violence in intimate relationships. IPV has complex origins. It
results from multiple influences.

man who's high in avoidance of intimacy with a woman who is anxious about abandonment; they probably both push all of the other's buttons because both men and women are more violent in such couples.) And finally, the particular circumstances matter: Recent stress at work or school (Gormley & Lopez, 2010) or a hot, noisy, uncomfortable environment (Larrick et al., 2011) can also make one touchy.

Inhibiting Influences. All of the influences I've mentioned thus far are presumed to fuel one's violent impulses, but inhibiting influences counteract aggressive urges. Once again, these influences are of diverse types. Violence is less likely in cultures that promote gender equality (Archer, 2006), and conscientious people are less likely than others to aggress when they're angry (Jensen-Campbell et al., 2007), so both cultural and individual differences are involved. A particularly important personal characteristic is one's dispositional capacity for self-control. People who are generally able to control their impulses are less violent when they're provoked; in one study, teenagers in North Carolina who were low in self-control perpetrated seven-and-a-half *times* more violent acts against their dating partners than those who were high in self-control (Finkel et al., 2009).[7] In addition, couples with good problem-solving skills (Hellmuth & McNulty, 2008) and who are satisfied with their relationship (Fournier et al., 2011) are less likely to lash out, and sober people are more peaceable, too; lest there be any doubt, alcohol use does fuel IPV (Graham et al., 2011). The role of relationship commitment in SCV is also noteworthy: Commitment to one's partner makes violence less likely (Slotter et al., 2011), so spouses are less violent than cohabiting couples are (Brownridge, 2010). Otherwise, the various influences we've touched on here appear to operate similarly in both marriages and dating relationships (e.g., Gover et al., 2008).

Thus, the I[3] model holds that instigating triggers and impelling influences work together to create urges to be aggressive—but that people will nevertheless behave nonviolently when inhibiting influences are strong. However, if inhibiting influences are weak, violence may occur, and if inhibiting influences are *very* weak, relatively small provocations may be enough to elicit intimate violence. What's more, situational couple violence originates in circumstances that are shaped both by temporary passing influences and by dispositional and distal influences that are stable and lasting. Couples may have some bouts of SCV when tempers run high even when neither partner is particularly prone to violence.

But here's a key question: If IPV happens once, will it happen again? Regrettably, the smartest answer to that question is "yes." In a large national study in the United States, only 30 percent of those who had been violent in one romantic relationship were violent again within the next 5 years in a *different*, second relationship; most people who engaged in SCV—sometimes because they were fighting back after their partners threw the first punch—did not continue to be violent once they changed partners (Whitaker et al., 2010). On the other hand,

---

[7]Make a mental note about the value of *self-control*, will you? I'll have more to say about it in chapter 14.

once violence starts in a particular relationship, it tends to recur. In one study involving newlyweds, *76 percent* of the men who were physically aggressive when they were engaged perpetrated violence again in the first 30 months after the wedding—and much of their violence was severe (Lorber & O'Leary, 2004). Intimate violence is occasionally an isolated event—but more often it continues, at least sporadically, once it starts. This is especially true of the more chronic, even more dangerous form of IPV: intimate terrorism.

Intimate Terrorism

The I³ model also helps to explain intimate terrorism (Finkel & Eckhardt, 2012), but the mix of influences is different. Intimate terrorism seems to be rooted in influences that are more enduring than those that may trigger SCV, with people who terrorize their partners coming from two camps (Holtzworth-Munroe & Meehan, 2005). Some of them may resort to violence because they are rather clumsy and pathetic, and threats of harm are their wretched efforts to keep their partners from leaving. Others seem to be more malevolent; they are antisocial or narcissistic, and violence is just another tool with which to get what they want (Fowler & Westen, 2011).

Men who are intimate terrorists do not become brutal overnight. They have often witnessed violent conflict between their parents and have been sexually abused themselves (Afifi et al., 2009), growing up in homes that taught them traditional gender roles and rather hostile, misogynistic attitudes (Liebold & McConnell, 2004); they are much more likely than other men to think of women as adversaries to be used for one's satisfaction and pleasure. As a result, they engage in more surveillance and violence than most men even when a relationship has just begun (Williams & Frieze, 2005), and they may be generally aggressive, abusing their pets as well as their partners (Simmons & Lehmann, 2007). The signs that suggest that a man may be an abuser are often evident from the start.

This set of surly attitudes is often combined with feelings of inadequacy that make violence seem to be one of the terrorist's few resources of power (Bosson et al., 2009). Terrorists often feel intellectually inferior to their partners (Moore et al., 2008) and have low self-esteem (Cowan & Mills, 2004), often because they are plagued by poverty; violence is much more common in homes with low annual incomes than in homes that are affluent (Cunradi et al., 2002). Certainly, some spouse abusers are well-to-do people with plenty of self-respect who are just flat out mean; nevertheless, on average, intimate terrorists are not well off, and they appear to turn to coercive power because they control few other resources.

One of the most dreadful aspects of all this is the manner in which intimate aggression is transmitted from one generation to the next, with children who are raised in violent homes being more likely to be violent themselves (Gover et al., 2008). However, this cycle is not inevitable. Indeed, none of the contributing risk factors I've described here guarantee that violence will occur. Sons of the most violent American parents are 10 times more likely than the sons of nonviolent parents to beat their wives. Yet even in this extreme group, only 20 percent of those studied had committed severe acts of violence in the past 12 months; the other 80 percent had not recently engaged in any severe violence in their intimate relationships (Johnson, 2008). Thus, children from violent homes are more likely than others to misbehave, but many never do. Still, their increased risk for such behavior is disturbing; in the cycle of family violence, the evil that people do may, in fact, outlive them.

The Rationales of Violence

Overall, then, men who engage in intimate terrorism seem to subscribe to masculine codes that promote a man's authority over women, but many of them feel inadequate to the task; they "often feel, or fear, that they do not measure up to those codes. Attempting to shore up their masculine self-concept, they may try to control others, particularly those who are physically weaker than they are" (Wood, 2004, p. 558). Do such men even realize that they are being abusive, or do they consider their use of force to be customary treatment of women by men?

Julia Wood (2004) provided insight into the minds of such men when she interviewed 22 incarcerated men who had abused their female partners. All of the men felt that their behavior had been a legitimate response to the disrespect they had faced from their partners, and all mentioned their partners' provocation as the genesis of their abuse. They also felt that men were supposed to be dominant and superior to women and so were entitled to use violence to control and discipline them. On the other hand, most believed that they were not "real" wife abusers because they did not enjoy hurting women and they had limited their level of abuse, doing less harm than they could have. One man had stabbed his wife only once, and another had brutally beaten his wife but argued that he hadn't hit her as hard as he could. Perhaps as a result of these rationalizations, only about half of the men expressed regret and remorse about their actions. They understood that their actions were illegal, but they didn't necessarily believe that their actions were wrong.

What do women feel in response to such treatment? In a broad review of the intimate violence literature, Sally Lloyd and Beth Emery (2000) noted that women are ordinarily surprised when they encounter intimate aggression, and they often struggle to make sense of it. They are influenced by romantic norms that encourage them to "forgive and forget"and they labor under cultural norms that blame victims for their difficulties, so they "consistently ask themselves why they went out with the wrong kind of man, why they made him angry when they knew he had a violent temper, or why they were in the wrong place at the wrong time" (Lloyd & Emery, 2000, p. 508). As a result of these influences, women feel betrayed, but they sometimes also blame themselves for their partners' aggression and, due to shame, naïveté, or ignorance, they often remain silent about their plight.

Overall, intimate terrorism exacts a fearsome toll on its victims. Physical injuries are bad enough, but victims may also suffer negative psychological consequences ranging from lowered self-esteem and mistrust of men to depression and post-traumatic stress disorder (Mechanic et al., 2008). There are also

---

Stalking
Unwanted Intrusion

Another undesirable behavior that occurs in some relationships is intrusive pursuit of someone—often an ex-partner—who does not wish to be pursued. Legal definitions of *stalking* in most of the United States involve repeated, malicious following and harassing of an unwilling target that may include (depending on the state) unwanted phone calls, letters, and text messages, surveillance, and other invasions of privacy (Shannon, 2009).

All of the United States have laws against stalking, and with good reason: National surveys find that 7 percent of American women and 2 percent of men have been targets of a frightening, "somewhat dangerous" stalker (Basile et al., 2006). Other studies that focus more broadly on unwanted communications and other intrusions converge on the estimate that almost two-fifths of all women, and one-seventh of all men, have experienced unwelcome harassment from a persistent pursuer. Most of the victims of stalking (75 percent) are women, and their stalkers are usually male (Spitzberg et al., 2010).

Why do people pursue others who want nothing to do with them? There are several reasons because there are various kinds of stalkers; as Finch (2001) colorfully put it, stalkers may be bad, mad, or sad. They may be motivated by desires for revenge or jealous possessiveness and may wish either to intimidate or to exert control over their targets (Davis et al., 2011). Indeed, about half of all stalkers are people who pursue an ex-partner after the end of a romantic relationship, and they generally tend to be insecure, disagreeable, hostile men with low self-esteem who are very sensitive to rejection (Kamphuis et al., 2004). Alternatively, stalkers may be a little crazy (McEwan et al., 2009), being obsessed with someone who is a mere acquaintance or whom they don't even know; stalkers are complete strangers to their targets about one-fifth of the time. Or, finally, they may be lonely and possessed of poor social skills and may be seeking to form a relationship in an inept and hopeless way (Duntley & Buss, 2011). One-quarter of all stalkers are neighbors, co-workers, or other acquaintances such as teachers, bank tellers, or car mechanics, and they often wrongly believe that their victims are interested in them in return, even when they're told to "get lost" (Sinclair & Frieze, 2005).

Stalking is no trivial matter. Escape can be difficult, especially if modern technology is involved; in one case, a stalker hid a global positioning unit in a victim's car so he always knew where she was (Southworth et al., 2007). Faced with such harassment, victims often become anxious and fearful, and, even worse, some form of physical violence occurs in about one-third of all cases. The police are consulted half of the time (Spitzberg & Cupach, 2007). Thus, another dark cost of some relationships is that they don't fully end when one partner tries to exit them.

---

substantial social costs; battered women are often absent from work, and some become homeless when violence forces them to flee their homes. And at its most basic level, intimate violence makes a partnership much less desirable than it otherwise might be. The end of the relationship may follow (Lawrence & Bradbury, 2007).

Why Don't They All Leave?

Indeed, intimate violence causes many people to leave their partners. One study (Campbell et al., 1994) that followed battered women over two-and-a-half years found that at the end of that period,

> 43 percent of the participants had left their original partners, either remaining unattached (20 percent) or entering new, nonabusive relationships (23 percent),

> 23 percent remained with their partners but had successfully ended the violence for at least a year, and

> 33 percent were still in an abusive relationship, either as victims (25 percent) or as both victims and perpetrators of violence (8 percent).

Thus, in this sample, only one-third of the women stayed in an abusive partnership for an extended period. Perseverance and determination are often required to escape an abusive relationship, but most people do, one way or the other. But why don't all victims run from their persecutors?

There's a simple answer to that question. They don't leave because, despite the abuse, they don't think they'll be better off if they go (Edwards et al., 2011).[8] A decision to leave is complex. Some violent partners are sweet and loving part of the time, and intermittent violence may be one's only complaint about the relationship (Marshall et al., 2000). The costs of leaving may also seem too high; whatever investments one has made in the relationship will be lost, and one's alternatives may seem bleak (Rusbult & Martz, 1995). One's economic status is crucial in this regard; the financial expense of departing one's home may be too momentous to overcome if one is unemployed.

As if their economic dependence on the relationship and their psychological commitment to it were not enough, the fear of even greater violence may also prevent the victims of intimate terrorism from exiting the relationship. Some aggressive, controlling partners may react with extreme anger against their lovers if they try to leave (Tanha et al., 2010). The threat of such retaliation suggests that we should do all we can to assist and protect those who are trying to escape the coercive power of an abusive partner.

Finally, I need to acknowledge the unfortunate truth that some people don't leave because they don't want to go. Women who have high anxiety about abandonment are drawn to possessive, controlling men. A man's intrusive jealousy and surveillance reassures an anxious partner that he still cares, and, perversely, the more psychological abuse a woman has encountered in the past, the stronger her preference for abusive men (Zayas & Shoda, 2007). Moreover, such men prefer anxious women in return, probably because they're willing to tolerate their abuse. Thus, an arrangement in which a man is clearly controlling and dominant to a subservient partner, which would be intolerable to most of us, suits some couples. It's likely, however, that if the women

---

[8] This is an excellent example of the influence of our judgments of the outcomes awaiting us outside our current relationships, which we labeled as our *comparison level for alternatives* back in chapter 6. I invite you to look back at pages 177–179 for more discussion of these ideas.

involved in such relationships come to value themselves more, they will find their partners' harsh, inequitable behavior toward them to be less acceptable (Chang-Schneider & Swann, 2006). Power is all about getting what one wants, but violence should not be part of that equation.

FOR YOUR CONSIDERATION

During their first year of marriage, Britni and Jonathon fell into a pattern in which he kept track of their debit account and paid all their bills each month. She was still a senior in college and didn't have a job, but he was working and earning just enough money for them to live on each month if they were careful. He took pride in his prudent management of money, but both of them were glad when she graduated and got a great job that actually paid her a little more than Jonathon's did.

He was surprised, however, when she announced that she wanted to maintain her own checking and savings accounts. She suggested that they each put half of their earnings into a joint account that would pay the bills and then keep the rest of their money for their own use. He was hurt that she did not want to merge their monies and join financial forces, and he was annoyed when he realized that, if they each kept half their money, she would have a lot more money than he would after a few years. But she argued that she wanted to be allowed to do what she wanted with her extra earnings, spending or investing them as she saw fit, and she thought that separate accounts would actually avoid disagreements and conflict.

What do you think the future holds for Britni and Jonathon? Why?

CHAPTER SUMMARY

Power is the ability to influence the behavior of others and to resist their influence on us.

Power and Interdependence

Sources of Power. From an interdependency perspective, power is based on the control of valuable resources that are desired by others. The *principle of lesser interest* states that the partner who is less interested in continuing a relationship has more power in it.

There are two different broad types of power, *fate control* and *behavior control*. In almost all relationships, both partners have some power over each other with each being able to influence the other some of the time.

Types of Resources. There are six resources that provide people power. *Reward power* and *coercive power* refer to one's ability to bestow rewards and punishments, respectively, on someone else. *Legitimate power* exists when one partner has a reasonable right—by dint of authority, reciprocity, equity, or social responsibility—to tell the other what to do. A partner's love and affection provides the other *referent power*, knowledge and expertise creates *expert power*, and specific pieces of information lend one *informational power*.

Men, Women, and the Control of Resources. Men tend to control more resources than women do, in part because social norms maintain male dominance. The balance of power in close relationships is also affected by the universalistic or particularistic nature of the resources one controls.

The Process of Power. Powerful people interrupt others and tend to be unaware of others' feelings. The specific influence tactics people use may be direct or indirect and bilateral or unilateral.

The Outcome of Power. Spouses are much more likely to share decision making than they used to be, and those who do enjoy happier marriages than those who have marriages in which one partner is dominant.

The Two Faces of Power. When they are committed to a relationship, many people use power benevolently, generously enhancing their partners' well-being as well as their own. Unfortunately, this does not always occur.

Violence in Relationships

Violence is behavior that is intended to hurt someone else.

The Prevalence of Violence. Violence is as American as apple pie, occurring in one of every four couples in the United States.

Types of Couple Violence. There are three distinct types of violence in romantic couples: *situational couple violence, intimate terrorism,* and *violent resistance.* Men and women are equally likely to engage in situational couple violence, but a huge majority of those who employ intimate terrorism are men.

Gender Differences in Intimate Violence. Women are violent as often as men, but men are more likely to inflict injury.

Correlates of Violence. Situational couple violence springs from impelling and inhibiting influences that are distal, dispositional, relational, or situational. Intimate terrorism is committed by men who are hostile toward women and who are plagued by feelings of inadequacy.

The Rationales of Violence. Wife-abusing men feel superior to women and believe that their aggression is a legitimate response to their wives' disrespect. Women sometimes blame themselves for their abuse.

Why Don't They All Leave? Most victims of abuse leave their relationships, but they stay when they don't believe they'll be better off if they go. A few don't leave because they don't want to go.

CHAPTER 13

The Dissolution and Loss of Relationships

THE CHANGING RATE OF DIVORCE ◆ The Prevalence of Divorce ◆ Why Has the Divorce Rate Increased? ◆ THE PREDICTORS OF DIVORCE ◆ Levinger's Barrier Model ◆ Karney and Bradbury's Vulnerability-Stress-Adaptation Model ◆ Results from the PAIR Project ◆ Results from the Early Years of Marriage Project ◆ People's Personal Perceptions of Their Problems ◆ Specific Predictors of Divorce ◆ BREAKING UP ◆ Breaking Up with Premarital Partners ◆ Steps to Divorce ◆ THE AFTERMATH OF BREAKUPS ◆ Postdissolution Relationships ◆ Getting Over It ◆ Divorce Is Different ◆ The Children of Divorce ◆ FOR YOUR CONSIDERATION ◆ CHAPTER SUMMARY

Sometimes the stresses and strains two partners experience catch up with them. Perhaps their conflict is too constant and too intense. Perhaps their partnership is inequitable with one of them exploiting the other. Perhaps their passion has waned, and new attractions are distracting them. Or perhaps they are merely contented with each other, instead of delighted, so they are disappointed that the "magic" has died.

There are myriad reasons why relationships may fail, and the deterioration of any particular partnership may involve events and processes that are unique to a specific couple. On the other hand, there are also personal and cultural influences that can have generic, widespread effects on the stability of many intimate relationships, and relationship scientists have been identifying and studying them for years. In this chapter, we'll consider the correlates and consequences of the decline and fall of satisfaction and intimacy. I'll have a lot to say about divorce because a decision to end a marriage is often more deliberate and weighty, and the consequences more complicated, than those that emerge from less formal partnerships. There's also been much more research on divorce than on nonmarital breakups. Nevertheless, the dissolution of any intimate relationship—such as a cohabiting partnership, dating relationship, or friendship—can be momentous, so I'll examine how people adjust to the end of those partnerships, too. Let's start with a reminder that the cultural landscape we face today is quite different than the one our grandparents knew.

THE CHANGING RATE OF DIVORCE

The Prevalence of Divorce

As you recall, current divorce rates are much higher than they were when your grandparents married. In the United States, there are currently half as many divorces as marriages each year (Tejada-Vera & Sutton, 2010), so the chance that a recent marriage will ultimately end in separation or divorce still hovers around 50 percent. This is remarkable because it suggests that despite all the good intentions and warm feelings with which people marry, the chances that they will succeed in living out their lives together are about the same as the chance of getting "heads" when you flip a coin.

Indeed, a typical American marriage won't last nearly as long as people think it will. Only about two-thirds (64 percent) of married couples stay together for 10 years, and fewer than half reach their twenty-fifth wedding anniversary, so the average length of a marriage in the United States is just over 18 years (Goodwin et al., 2010). That figure counts all marriages, including those that end with the death of a spouse, but the leading cause of death of a marriage in its first 20 years is, of course, divorce. Lots of people don't turn 30 without having been divorced; the median age at which men encounter their (first) divorce is 31.8, and for women, it's 29.4 (Cohn, 2010).

Two other patterns that result, in part, from the high divorce rate are noteworthy. First, only about *half* (52 percent) of the adult U.S. population is presently married (Mather & Lavery, 2010). That's an all-time low. Second, 25 percent of American children—1 out of every 4 people under the age of 18—now live in single-parent homes, most of them run by their mothers (Wilcox & Marquardt, 2010). That rate is three times higher than it was in 1960.

Any way you look at it, divorce is now commonplace in America. Divorce rates have also increased in other countries over the last 50 years, but the United States has had the dubious distinction of being at the front of the pack. The divorce rate in the United States is higher than in all of Europe, Canada, or Japan (U.S. Census Bureau, 2011). Marriages are much less likely to end than other romantic relationships are—see the box on the next page—but they're also less likely to last than they used to be.

Why Has the Divorce Rate Increased?

There are no certain reasons why the second half of the twentieth century saw such a huge increase in U.S. rates of divorce. But there are several possibilities, and all of them may (or may not) be contributing influences.

One possibility is that we hold different, more demanding expectations for marriage than people used to. Our great-grandparents generally believed that if you wanted to live with a romantic partner, if you wanted to have children, and if you wanted to pay the bills and live well, you had to get married. Nowadays, however, cohabitation is widespread, there are lots of single parents, and most women have entered the workforce. As a result, marriage is no longer the practical necessity it used to be (Coleman et al., 2007). Instead, in the opinion

The Staying Power of Formal Commitment

Separation Rates in Different Types of Relationships

Study	Time Span	Spouses	Cohabs	Gays	Lesbians
Blumstein & Schwartz, 1983	1½ years	4%	14%	13%	18%
Kurdek, 2004	12 years	15%		19%	24%

			Civil Unions:	Yes	No
Balsam et al., 2008	3 years	3%		4%	9%

Note. All of these studies were conducted in the United States. Blumstein and Schwartz (1983) recruited a national sample (n = 2,082) through media publicity. Kurdek (2004) recruited newlyweds from Dayton, Ohio, and gays and lesbians through word of mouth and ads in gay magazines (n = 359). Balsam and her colleagues (2008) used records of civil unions in Vermont to find and contact newly joined gays and lesbians; they were asked to invite a married heterosexual sibling and a gay or lesbian friend who was not in a civil union to participate in the study with them. Altogether, the study tracked 798 people over three years. The figures for same-sex couples in the Balsam study include both gays and lesbians.

Here are the percentages of couples of various types who broke up during the course of three different studies. Each of these investigations has its strengths and weaknesses, but together they tell an interesting tale. Divorce is now commonplace, but across various spans of time married, heterosexuals are still less likely to break up than unmarried people are. It doesn't matter whether the unmarried couples are cohabiting heterosexuals or gays or lesbians—people who are just living together break up at about the same rate, which is more often than spouses do. Furthermore, when gays and lesbians enter into civil unions that legally recognize their relationship, they, too, are less likely to separate than are those who have not made a formal commitment to each other.

There are two take-home messages here. First, a marriage or civil union ups the ante on a relationship. They're harder to dissolve than less formal agreements are, and people who make such commitments are relatively likely to stand by them. Second, the romances of same-sex couples are just as stable as those of heterosexuals when they are afforded similar institutional support. We'll see more studies like this in the years to come, and they will probably demonstrate that when gays and lesbians are provided similar opportunities to establish fulfilling legal partnerships, their romances function just like those of heterosexuals. Should formal commitments of this sort for gays and lesbians be against the law? Why?

of some observers, people are more likely than ever before to pursue marriage as a path to personal fulfillment. Marriage is supposed to be play, not work; it's supposed to be exciting, not routine, and passionate, not warm (Amato, 2009). Thus, our expectations for marriage may be too high. A happy, warm, rewarding partnership may seem insufficient if it is measured against unrealistic expectations.

For instance, more than 40 years ago, Slater (1968, p. 99) warned that:

> Spouses are now asked to be lovers, friends, and mutual therapists in a society which is forcing the marriage bond to become the closest, deepest, most important and most enduring relationship of one's life. Paradoxically, then, it is increasingly likely to fall short of the emotional demands placed upon it and be dissolved.

We marry for love and passion and think that they won't change, and we expect our spouses to be soulmates who will never disappoint us. But these are lofty, perhaps impossibly high standards, and indeed, recent cultural history suggests that "no sooner had the ideal of the love match and lifelong intimacy taken hold than people began to demand the right to divorce" (Coontz, 2005, p. 8).

People may simply be expecting too much of marriage. The percentage of U.S. spouses who report that their marriages are "very happy" is lower now than it was 25 years ago (Wilcox & Marquardt, 2010), and the number of conflicts and problems that spouses report are higher (Amato et al., 2007). On the whole, the average perceived quality of U.S. marriages has declined since 1970.

But the broader culture has changed, too, and several societal influences may be affecting not only the expectations with which we begin our marriages but also the situations we encounter once we are wed. For instance, most women in the United States now work outside the home, and their entry into the workforce has had several effects. First, spouses report more conflict between work and family than they used to, and the more hours a wife works during the week, the lower the quality of her marriage tends to be (Amato et al., 2007). Car repairs, child care, and the scheduling and cooking of meals (to name just a few examples) are more problematic when both spouses are employed, and the amount of time spouses spend together tends to decline. Both spouses are also undoubtedly affected by their problems at work, so that decreases in job satisfaction are associated with increases in marital discord (Amato et al., 2007). Participation in the labor force also increases spouses' access to interesting, desirable, alternative partners, and divorce is more frequent when women work in occupations that surround them with men (McKinnish, 2007).

Furthermore, women earn more money than they used to, and, around the world, divorce rates are higher when women are financially independent of men (Barber, 2003). People who are able to support themselves have more freedom to choose divorce when a marriage deteriorates, and in the United States there is a straightforward, positive correlation between a woman's income and her odds of divorce: The more money she makes, the more likely it is that she will someday be divorced (Rogers, 2004). But don't think that your marriage will be more stable if you just do without money; poverty has even more effects on marital quality. In general, couples with money troubles who are experiencing financial strain are less content with their marriages than are those who are better off; in particular, couples with rather low incomes (under $25,000 per year) are twice as likely to divorce as are couples with higher incomes (over $50,000 per year) (Wilcox & Marquardt, 2010). Having money may make it easier to divorce, but being poor may cause stress that undermines a marriage, too.

Overall, then, women's increased participation in the labor force has plausibly increased conflict at home, made alluring, new romantic partners more available, and decreased wives' economic dependence on their husbands. Perhaps for all of these reasons, the trend is clear: As the proportion of American women employed outside the home increased during the twentieth century, so, too, did the divorce rate (Fitch & Ruggles, 2000).[1]

Our gender roles, the behaviors we expect from men and women, are changing, too. Women are gradually becoming more instrumental and being more assertive and self-reliant (Twenge, 2009), and the partners in many marriages are dividing household responsibilities more equitably (Amato et al. 2007). Over the last 25 years, less traditional gender roles and increases in the equality of family decision making have been associated with higher marital quality for both husbands and wives. However, the new division of household labor has had different effects on men than on women; husbands are less happy now that they're doing more household chores, but their wives are more content (see Figure 13.1).

By some accounts, Western culture is also becoming more individualistic, with people being less connected to the others around them than they used to be (Amato, 2009). Indeed, most of us are less tied to our communities than our grandparents were (Putnam, 2000). We're less likely to live near our extended families and less likely to know our neighbors; we participate in fewer clubs and social organizations, entertain at home less frequently, and move more often. As a result, we receive less social support and companionship from friends and acquaintances than our grandparents did (Oishi, 2010), and we rely on our spouses for more (Magdol & Bessel, 2003), and this may affect divorce rates in two different ways. First, as I've already noted, we ask more of our spouses than ever before. We expect them to fulfill a wider variety of interpersonal needs, and that increases the probability that they will disappoint us in some manner. In addition, people who are less connected to their communities are less affected by community norms that might discourage them from divorcing. And as it turns out, people who move often from place to place really are more prone to divorce than are those who stay in one place and put down roots (Magdol & Bessel, 2003).

Our shared perceptions of divorce are also less negative than they used to be. In many circles, a divorce used to be considered a shameful failure, and

---

[1] As I describe these various patterns, do remember, please, that all of these links between social changes and divorce rates are *correlations* that allow diverse possibilities to exist. A connection between women's working and divorce does not necessarily mean that employment undermines women's commitment to their marriages. To the contrary, women are more likely to seek employment when there is preexisting discord and strife in their marriages, so it is just as likely that marital dissatisfaction causes women to find work as it is that women's work causes marital dissatisfaction (Rogers, 1999). Keep an open mind as you consider the implications of societal change.

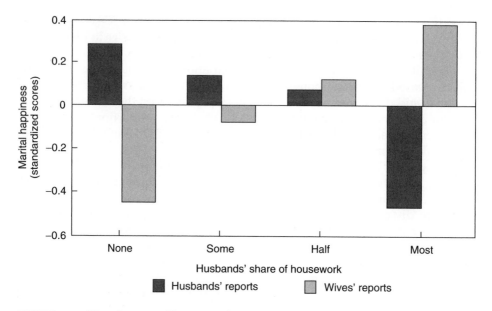

FIGURE 13.1. **Happiness and housework.**
The graph shows the average levels of marital happiness experienced by wives and husbands as the men do larger proportions of the household chores. Husbands grow less content, but their wives become more satisfied as the husbands do more housework. Two other facts are interesting: Somebody is always *really* unhappy when men do either most of the housework or none at all, and the only time both partners have above average happiness is when the housework is split 50–50. Is there news you can use here?
Source: Data from Amato et al., 2007.

the event itself was often a messy, lurid, embarrassing spectacle in which blame had to be assigned to someone. The advent of no-fault divorce laws in the United States during the 1970s made a divorce much easier to obtain; for the first time in most jurisdictions, once they had agreed on the division of property and child custody, spouses merely had to certify that they faced "irreconcilable differences," and their marriage was dissolved. No-fault laws helped make the procedure more socially acceptable (Rodgers et al., 1999). On average, we feel that a divorce is a more reasonable and more desirable response to a bad marriage than our parents did, and more favorable attitudes toward divorce appear to reduce the quality of our marriages as time goes by (Amato & Rogers, 1999). We may be less likely to work hard to rescue a faltering relationship when divorce seems an expedient alternative.

Most couples also cohabit before they marry these days, and as we saw in chapter 1, people who cohabit encounter an increased risk of divorce later on. Despite the widespread belief that cohabitation is a valuable trial run that allows people to avoid later problems, cohabitation is *positively* associated with the probability of divorce (Rhoades et al., 2009b). The good news is that couples who start living together after they become engaged to marry and

Divorce: Another Reason to Marry

Divorce is usually an unwelcome event, but it does serve valuable legal functions. In most jurisdictions, there are few laws that clearly govern what happens when a cohabiting couple splits up, and the division of their assets can be very messy indeed. In contrast, in a divorce that works well, a couple's property and debt are divided fairly, and formal rules for child custody, visitation, and support are arranged. The legal protection provided by a divorce is one of several reasons why many gays and lesbians are seeking the right to form formal matrimonial or civil unions in the United States (Henry, 2008).

"Gay marriage" is a contentious topic, but critics of the idea usually overlook the difficulties same-sex partners may face when they are denied access to a clean divorce. What do you think is fair when one member of a couple stays home to parent a child while the other gets rich working her way up the corporate ladder, and they finally decide to separate? In a case in California involving two lesbians, the woman who had been the stay-at-home mother found herself at a huge disadvantage when her partner wanted to keep most of the money she had earned (Leff, 2004). Only a few states have formal procedures that guide cases like this, and the pursuit of justice when relationships end is another reason why gays and lesbians want state legislatures to legitimize their intimate relationships.

who cohabit for a shorter, rather than longer, period of time do not divorce much more frequently than do those who marry without living together (Jose et al., 2010). Brief cohabitation that is limited to one's fiancé does not seem to put a subsequent marriage at much risk. On the other hand, people who cohabit before they become engaged (or who ever cohabit with more than one partner) are more likely to later divorce (Jose et al., 2010), probably because cohabitation changes their beliefs and expectations about marriage. Casual cohabitation seems to lead to (a) less respect for the institution of marriage, (b) less favorable expectations about the outcomes of marriage, and (c) increased willingness to divorce (Rhoades et al., 2009b), and all of these make divorce more likely.

Finally, as more parents divorce, more children witness family conflict and grow up in broken homes. Common sense may suggest that youngsters who suffer family disruption might be especially determined to avoid making the same mistakes, but, in reality, divorce is passed down from one generation to the next: Children who experience the divorce of their parents are more likely to be divorced themselves when they become adults (Bartell, 2006). Various processes may underlie this pattern. For one thing, children from divorced homes have less favorable views of marriage, and they report less trust in their partners when they begin their own romantic relationships; thus, compared to children from intact homes, they have less faith that their marriages will last (Cui & Fincham, 2010). Furthermore, to some degree, children learn how to behave in intimate relationships from the lessons provided by their parents, and those who remember a childhood home full of strife and discord tend to have more acrimonious marriages of poorer quality themselves (Riggio & Weiser, 2008). Thus, as divorce becomes more commonplace, more children become susceptible to divorce later on.

So, why has the divorce rate increased? There are reasons to believe that, compared to our grandparents' day

- We expect more out of marriage, holding it to higher standards.
- Working women have more financial freedom and better access to attractive alternatives, and they experience corrosive conflict between work and family.
- Creeping individualism and social mobility leave us less tied to, and less affected by, community norms that discourage divorce.
- New laws have made divorce more socially acceptable and easier to obtain.
- Casual cohabitation weakens commitment to marriage.
- Children of divorce are more likely to divorce when they become adults.

All of these possible influences are merely correlated with the increasing prevalence of divorce in the United States, so they all may be symptoms rather than causes of the societal changes that have promoted divorce. It's a rather long list of possibilities, however, and it provides another good example of the manner in which cultural influences shape intimate relationships. Arguably, the cultural climate supports lasting marriages less effectively than it did 40 or 50 years ago. But even with such changes, at least half of the marriages that begin this year will not end in divorce. (Not all of them will be happy, but at least they won't end in divorce.) What individual and relational characteristics predict who will and who will not ultimately separate? Let's turn to that next.

THE PREDICTORS OF DIVORCE

Whatever the cultural context, some marriages succeed and others fail, and as you'd expect, the differences between marital winners and losers have long been of interest to relationship scientists. Diverse models that explicate some of the sources of divorce have been proposed, and impressive longitudinal studies have now tracked some marriages for more than 25 years. In this section, we'll inspect both theories and research results that identify some of the predictors of divorce.

Levinger's Barrier Model

George Levinger (1976), a proponent of interdependency theory, used concepts like those I described in chapter 6 in a model that identified three types of factors that influence the breakup of relationships. The first of these is *attraction*. For Levinger, attraction is enhanced by the rewards a relationship offers (such as enjoyable companionship, sexual fulfillment, security, and social status), and it is diminished by its costs (such as irritating incompatibility and the invest-ment of time and energy). The second key influence on breakups is the *alter-natives* one possesses. The most obvious of these are other partners, but any alternative to a current relationship, such as being single or achieving occupa-tional success, may lure someone away from an existing partnership. Finally, there are the *barriers* around the relationship that make it hard to leave; these include the legal and social pressures to remain married, religious and moral constraints, and the financial costs of obtaining a divorce and maintaining two households.

A major contribution of Levinger's approach was to highlight the fact that unhappy partners who would like to break up may stay together because it would cost them too much to leave. He also persuasively argued that many barriers to divorce are psychological rather than material; distressed spouses may certainly stay married because they do not have enough money to divorce, but they may also stay together (even when they have sufficient resources to leave) because of the guilt or embarrassment they would feel—or cause others, especially their children (Poortman & Seltzer, 2007)—if they divorced.

Indeed, spouses report that there are several meaningful costs that would deter them from seeking a divorce (Previti & Amato, 2003). A survey of people married for 12 years demonstrated that the worry that their children would suffer, the threat of losing their children, religious norms, dependence on their spouses, and the fear of financial ruin were all perceived to be influen-tial barriers that discouraged divorce (Knoester & Booth, 2000). However, over that 12-year span, once other risk factors such as low education and parental divorce were taken into account, only two of those perceived barriers, depen-dence on one's spouse and religious beliefs, actually distinguished couples who divorced from those who did not. And if people had grown genuinely dissatisfied with their marriages, even those two barriers seemed insignificant: Once they wanted out of their marriages, there was no stopping them (Knoester & Booth, 2000).

Thus, people are usually aware of several obstacles that they would have to overcome in order to divorce, but once a marriage is on the rocks, those barriers do not seem momentous. Levinger's model helpfully reminds us of deterrents to divorce that run through people's minds, but it may not fully recognize how ineffective those deterrents may become once marital misery sets in.

Karney and Bradbury's Vulnerability-Stress-Adaptation Model

Benjamin Karney and Thomas Bradbury (1995) developed a general model of marital instability that highlights another three influences that can con-tribute to divorce. According to this view, some people enter marriage with *enduring vulnerabilities* that increase their risk of divorce. Such vulnerabilities might include adverse experiences in one's family of origin, poor education, maladaptive personality traits, bad social skills, or dysfunctional attitudes toward marriage. None of these characteristics makes divorce inevitable, but all of them can shape the circumstances a couple encounters, and all of them influence the *adaptive processes* with which people respond to stress. If a couple gets lucky and encounters only infrequent and mild difficulties, even those with poor coping and communication skills may live happily ever after.

However, almost every marriage must face occasional *stressful events* that require the partners to provide support to one another and to adjust to new circumstances. Some stressors (such as a period of unemployment or a major illness) befall some marriages and not others, whereas other stressors (such as pregnancy, childbirth, and parenting) are commonplace. Little frustrations that keep recurring can combine to be surprisingly stressful, too (Randall & Bodenmann, 2009). When stressful events occur, a couple must cope and adapt, but, depending on their vulnerabilities, some people are better able to do that than are others. Failure to cope successfully can make the stresses worse, and if poor coping causes marital quality to decline, a couple's coping may be further impaired (Neff & Karney, 2004). And ultimately, extended periods of dissatisfaction are presumed to lead to marital instability and divorce.

Take a look at Figure 13.2, and start tracing the paths from the top. Our past experiences and inborn traits equip all of us with strengths and weaknesses as relationship partners, and some of the weaknesses are "vulnerabilities" that undermine our abilities to cope effectively with stress and change (Stroud et al.,

FIGURE 13.2. **The vulnerability-stress-adaptation model of marriage.**
The model posits that partners bring vulnerabilities with them when they enter a marriage, and those vulnerabilities interact with both the stresses they encounter and their coping skills to determine how well their marriages function.
Source: Adapted from Karney & Badbury, 1995.

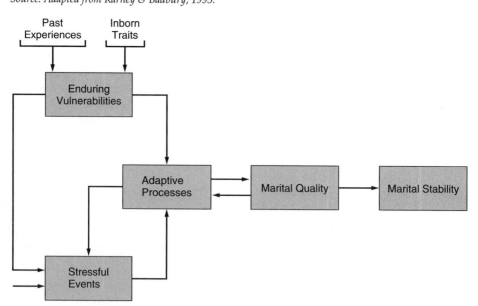

2010). Some vulnerabilities also make life more stressful—but no matter who we are, stress happens. In addition to the intermittent conflicts that occur at home, any frustrations and difficulties we experience individually at work or school can cause **stress spillover** in which we bring surly moods home and interact irascibly with our innocent partners (Repetti et al., 2009). Then, our coping skills and other "adaptive processes" determine whether our stress grows or is managed and reduced. And ultimately, each partner's ability to adapt successfully influences the quality of their marriage at the same time that marital quality is influencing the partners' abilities to adapt.

There are feedback loops and overlapping influences in the vulnerability-stress-adaptation model, and when it comes to stress, what doesn't kill us may make us stronger. Women with good communication skills who have already encountered moderate stress in their lives are likely to be more resilient and to adjust better to becoming mothers—a change that's always stressful—than other women who have similar skills but who haven't yet been tested by having to deal with stress (Broady & Neff, 2010). Successfully coping with our difficulties can improve our abilities to adapt to new nuisances. But the bottom line is that the quality of our marriages emerges from the interplay of who we are, the circumstances we encounter and the manner in which we respond to those circumstances, and, to some degree, these three important influences affect each other. It's possible for the roots of divorce to begin in childhood in an insecure attachment style or the lessons learned in a home filled with conflict, but if life treats us well or we work hard and well with our spouses to overcome life's difficulties (or perhaps just take a good college course on close relationships!), divorce need not occur.

Results from the PAIR Project

For decades, Ted Huston (2009) and his colleagues (Caughlin & Huston, 2006) have been tracking 168 couples who married in 1981. The project has focused on the manner in which spouses adapt to their lives together (or fail to do so) and is known as the Processes of Adaptation in Intimate Relationships (or PAIR) Project. There's enormous value in longitudinal studies like this, but their results can be a little sobering. Indeed, in the PAIR Project, after only 13 years, 35 percent of the couples had divorced and another 20 percent weren't happy; only 45 percent of the couples could be said to be happily married, and even they were less satisfied and less loving than they had been when they wed. And these, I should remind you, are typical results. Take a look back at Figure 6.7 on p. 193: Marital satisfaction routinely declines in most couples as time goes by.

Why? Huston and his colleagues examined three different explanations for why marriages go awry. One possibility is that spouses who are destined to be discontent begin their marriages being less in love and more at odds with each other than are those whose marriages ultimately succeed. This possibility, the *enduring dynamics* model, suggests that spouses bring to their marriages problems, incompatibilities, and enduring vulnerabilities that surface during their courtship; indeed, the partners are usually aware of these frustrations and shortcomings before they even wed (Jayson, 2009b). According to this model, then, marriages that are headed for divorce are weaker than others from the very beginning.

In contrast, a second possibility known as the *emergent distress* model suggests that the problematic behavior that ultimately destroys a couple begins after they marry. As time goes by, some couples fall into a rut of increasing conflict and negativity that did not exist when the marriage began. Thus, unlike the enduring dynamics model, the emergent distress perspective suggests that, when they begin, there is no discernible difference between marriages that will succeed and those that will fail; the difficulties that ruin some marriages usually develop later.

Finally, a third possibility is the *disillusionment* model. This approach suggests that couples typically begin their marriages with rosy, romanticized views of their relationship that are unrealistically positive. Then, as time goes by, and as the spouses stop working as hard to be adorable and charming to each other, reality slowly erodes these pleasant fictions. Romance may fade and some disappointment may occur in any marriage as people realize that their partnership is less wonderful than it originally seemed, but in some couples, "the ink is barely dry on the marriage license when doubts and disillusionment about marriage and the partner can begin to set in" (Kayser & Rao, 2006, p. 206).

The particulars of the three models are meaningful because each suggests a different way to improve marriages and to reduce the risk of divorce. According to the enduring dynamics model, rocky courtships lead to bad marriages, and premarital interventions that keep ambivalent couples from ever marrying should prevent many subsequent divorces. By comparison, the emergent distress model argues that couples need to guard against slow slides into disagreeableness and negativity, and interventions that encourage spouses to remain cheerful, generous, attentive, and kind should keep divorce from their door. And finally, the disillusionment model suggests that dispassionate and accurate perceptions of one's lover and one's relationship that preclude subsequent disappointment and disenchantment should also prevent divorce.

All of these are reasonable possibilities, but Huston and his colleagues found that only two of the three seemed to be at work in the marriages they followed. (Let's pause a moment. Which two models do you think were the winners?) First, consistent with the enduring dynamics model, the PAIR Project determined that, compared to couples who were still happy after several years, spouses who were unhappy had been less loving and affectionate and more ambivalent and negative toward each other when their marriages began. Couples who were destined to be distressed were less generous and less tender and more uncertain and more temperamental from the very start. Thus, any doubts or difficulties that people faced when they were engaged did not disappear once they were married. To the contrary, any indecision or incompatibilities were simply imported into their marital relationship, so that they remained less content over the years that followed.

So, the enduring dynamics model predicted how happy marriages would be. However, the best predictor of which couples would actually divorce was the disillusionment model. The drop in marital satisfaction during the first years of marriage was sharper and more pronounced in some couples than in others, and they were the spouses who were most at risk for divorce. They did not necessarily grow cantankerous or spiteful as the emergent distress model would expect; instead, they simply experienced the greatest change in their romantic feelings for each other. Their love faded more, and more rapidly, than did the romances of other couples.

In addition, a striking feature of the disillusionment that Huston and his colleagues observed was that many of the couples who were destined to divorce were *more* affectionate than most when their marriages began, and it took some time for their disappointment to develop. Couples whose marriages were short-lived—who were divorced within six (or fewer) years— usually began their marriages with less love and more ambivalence than did couples whose marriages would succeed. (Thus, you can see why, when disillusionment set in, they were divorced relatively quickly.) However, couples who ultimately divorced after longer periods—after seven or more years of marriage—were especially affectionate and romantic when their marriages began. They were more adoring than other couples, on average, and thus had further to fall (and, perhaps, were more surprised than most) when the usual drop in affectionate behavior following the honeymoon began. They ended up no less sentimental toward each other than other couples, but they experienced the biggest changes—that is, the steepest declines—in romantic behavior, and those changes predicted a delayed divorce.

Overall, then, at this stage of the PAIR Project, two conclusions seem sound. First, the size and speed of changes in romance best predict which couples will divorce, and second, the problems couples bring to their marriage determine how quickly a divorce will occur. Similar results have been obtained from other studies (e.g., Arriaga, 2001; Kurdek, 2002), so we can safely conclude that both the *level* of satisfaction a couple experiences and the *change* in that satisfaction over time are key players in relational outcomes. Importantly, couples that are doomed to divorce do not always turn surly and spiteful, but they do tend to lose the joy they once experienced (Gottman & Levenson, 2000).[2]

Results from the Early Years of Marriage Project

Another impressive longitudinal study, the Early Years of Marriage (EYM) Project directed by Terri Orbuch, has been following 174 white couples and

---

[2] I encourage you to take a moment to consider how this pattern maps onto people's approach and avoidance motivations, which we encountered on p. 187 back in chapter 6. Evidently, some marriages fail not because they are aversive and unpleasant but because they are not pleasant and delightful enough.

199 black couples in and around Detroit, Michigan, since they married in 1986 (Birditt et al., 2010). The EYM researchers have been particularly interested in the manner in which the social conditions that couples encounter may affect marital outcomes. And some sociological variables are important. In 2002, 16 years after the project began, 46 percent of the couples had already divorced, but the couples' race seemed to make a big difference: Just over a third (36 percent) of the white couples had divorced, but more than half (55 percent) of the black couples had dissolved their marriages.

Why were black couples more prone to divorce? There could be several reasons. On average, the black couples had cohabitated for a longer period and were more likely to have had children before getting married. They also had lower incomes and were more likely to come from broken homes, and all of these influences are positively correlated with one's risk of divorce (Wilcox & Marquardt, 2010). Overall, the EYM project is demonstrating, as other studies have (Wickrama et al., 2010), that the social context in which couples conduct their relationships may have substantial effects on the outcomes they encounter. Being poor can put any couple at risk for divorce no matter how much they respect and value marriage (Bryant et al., 2010).

People's Personal Perceptions of Their Problems

The various models and data we have encountered suggest that there are three general types of influences on our marital outcomes (Levinger & Levinger, 2003). At the broadest level are cultural norms and other variables that set the national stage for marriage. No-fault divorce laws and discrimination that affects economic opportunities are examples of the ways in which the *cultural context* may either support or undermine marital success.

More idiosyncratic are our *personal contexts,* the social networks of family and friends and the physical neighborhoods we inhabit. For instance, as I noted earlier, women who work with a wide variety of interesting male colleagues are more prone to divorce than are women who do not work outside their homes (McKinnish, 2007). Finally, there is a *relational context* that describes the intimate environment couples create through their own perceptions of, and interactions with, each other. The individual characteristics that lead us to react to our partners with either chronic good humor or pessimistic caution are some of the building blocks of the particular atmosphere that pervades a partnership.

I mention these three levels of analysis because people tend to focus on only one of them when they generate explanations for their marital problems. Yet another impressive longitudinal study, the Marital Instability Over the Life Course project conducted by Alan Booth and his colleagues, conducted phone interviews with a random sample of 1,078 Americans every few years from 1980 to 2000. When those who divorced were asked what caused their divorces, the most frequently reported reasons all involved some characteristic of their marital relationships, as Table 13.1 shows. Women complained of infidelity, substance use, or abuse more often than men, whereas men were more likely to

TABLE 13.1. "What Caused Your Divorce?"

Reason	% Total Cases	% Cases for Men	% Cases for Women
Infidelity	22	16	25
Incompatibility	19	19	19
Drinking or substance use	11	5	14
Grew apart	10	9	10
Personality problems	9	10	8
Communication difficulties	9	13	6
Physical or mental abuse	6	0	9
Love was lost	4	7	3
Don't know	3	9	0

The table values reflect the responses of 208 members of a random sample of spouses in the United States who were asked what had caused their divorces. Other causes such as financial problems or interference from family were mentioned on occasion, but the nine most frequent reasons are listed here.

Source: Adapted from Amato & Previti, 2003.

complain of poor communication or to announce that they did not know what had gone wrong. Ex-wives also had more complaints than ex-husbands did, on average, but very few accounts from either sex acknowledged the possible influences of the cultural or personal contexts in which they conducted their relationships.

Nevertheless, those broader contexts may have been important. The higher a couple's income had been, the less often abuse was mentioned as a cause of divorce and the more often personality clashes were mentioned. The more education the respondents had, the more often they complained of incompatibility with their ex-spouses. Thus, a couple's socioeconomic status (which includes education and income) helped to predict the problems they would encounter. The age at which they married mattered, too; people who married at younger ages were more likely to report that they had grown apart or that alcohol and drug use had been a problem.

When they grow discontent, people always complain about the particulars of their partnerships (Randall & Bodenmann, 2009). But broader influences may be important, too, as we'll see. The various factors that shape a couple's likelihood of divorce include not only the day-to-day interactions that may cause them pleasure or pain; the surrounding circumstances and culture can either promote or undermine their marriage, as well (Bryant et al., 2010).

Specific Predictors of Divorce

I have touched on a variety of variables that may put people at risk for divorce, and I'm about to list them and several more in the big table that begins on the next page. However, let me offer this caveat: Statements of general trends sometimes gloss over important qualifications. No one generalization will apply to every marriage, predictors may hold for some groups or stages of marriage but not others, and the apparent influence of a particular variable may reflect the other factors to which it was compared in a given study. For instance, some classic correlates of divorce (such as low income) may be more influential in young marriages than in older marriages that have already stood the test of time (Booth et al., 1986). To some degree, marriages that survive the initial effects of certain stressors may be less susceptible to their influences many years later. It may also be important to recognize that when several risks are combined, each may have stronger effects than it would have had by itself; being poor *and* poorly educated, for instance, can be much worse than facing either difficulty by itself (Rauer et al., 2008). Please keep these nuances in mind while inspecting Table 13.2, which presents a summary of key predictors of marital stability identified by modern research. The good news with regard to these complexities is that the effects of most of these influences probably haven't changed much for several decades (Amato, 2010). Most of them probably have similar effects on the satisfaction and stability gays and lesbians experience in their relationships, as well (Gottman et al., 2003).

TABLE 13.2   Predictors of Divorce: A Synthesis of the Literature

Predictor	Findings
Socioeconomic status	People with low-status occupations, less education, and lower incomes are more likely to divorce than are those with higher socioeconomic status. In particular, women with good educations are much less likely to divorce than women with poor educations (Wilcox & Marquardt, 2010).
Race	Due to their greater exposure to other risk factors such as low income, premarital birth, parental divorce, and cohabitation, black Americans are more likely to divorce than white Americans are (Orbuch & Brown, 2006).
Sex ratios	Around the world, divorce rates are higher when women outnumber men and the sex ratio is low (Barber, 2003).
Social mobility	People who move often from place to place are more prone to divorce than are those who stay in one place and put down roots (Magdol & Bessel, 2003).
No-fault legislation	Laws that make a divorce easier to obtain seem to improve our attitudes toward divorce and thereby make divorce more likely (Amato & Rogers, 1999).
Working women	Divorce rates increase when higher proportions of women enter the workforce (Fitch & Ruggles, 2000).
Age at marriage	People who marry as teenagers are more likely to divorce than are those who marry after age 25 (Glenn et al., 2010).
Prior marriage	Second marriages are more likely to end in divorce than first marriages are (Poortman & Lyngstad, 2007).
Parental divorce	Parents who divorce increase the chances that their children will divorce. However, as divorce becomes more commonplace, this effect is declining (Bartell, 2006).
Religion	Attendance at religious services is correlated with a lower risk of divorce, especially when both spouses attend regularly (Vaaler et al., 2009).
Teenage sex	First intercourse that is unwanted or that occurs before the age of 16 is associated with an increased risk of divorce (Paik, 2011).

Premarital cohabitation	Premarital cohabitation is associated with higher divorce rates, but the effect is slight if the couple is engaged to be married when cohabitation begins (Jose et al., 2010).
Premarital birth	Having a baby before marriage is associated with a higher risk of divorce for both the mother and the father (Heaton, 2002).
Children	Spouses who have no children are more likely to divorce, but the risk-reducing effect of children is most noticeable when the children are very young (Lyngstad & Jalovaara, 2010).
Stepchildren	Women who bring children with them into a second marriage are more likely to divorce, but that's not true of men; evidently, women may find it easier to be a stepparent than men do (Teachman, 2008).
Similarity	Spouses with lots in common are less likely to divorce (Clarkwest, 2007).
Personality attributes	The higher one's neuroticism, the more likely one is to divorce (Karney & Bradbury, 1995).
Attachment styles	People who are high in avoidance of intimacy are more likely to divorce (Ceglian & Gardner, 1999).
Genetics	A person who has an identical twin who gets divorced is about five times more likely to divorce than he or she would have been if the twin had not divorced, even if the two twins were separated at birth and have never met (Lykken, 2002).
Stress hormones	During their first year of marriage, couples who are destined to divorce have chronically higher amounts of the stress hormones epinephrine and norepinephrine in their blood than do couples who will not be divorced 10 years later (Kiecolt-Glaser et al., 2003).
Stressful life events	The occurrence of stressful life events (other than parenthood) increases the likelihood of divorce (Randall & Bodenmann, 2009).
Time together	Couples who share more time together are less likely to divorce (Poortman, 2005).
Alcohol and drug abuse	Drug dependency increases the likelihood of divorce (Amato & Previti, 2003).
Infidelity	Extradyadic sex increases the likelihood of divorce (Previti & Amato, 2004).
Attitudes toward marriage	People who are pessimistic about marriage are more likely to divorce (Segrin et al., 2005).
Marital interactions	Positive interactions predict stability, and negative interaction predicts divorce (Lavner & Bradbury, 2011). Couples that fail to maintain a 5-to-1 ratio of positive to negative behaviors are more likely to divorce (Gottman et al., 1998).
Sexual satisfaction	Greater satisfaction with one's sex life is associated with a lower likelihood of divorce (Karney & Bradbury, 1995).
Marital satisfaction	"Marital satisfaction has larger effects on marital stability than do most other variables" (Karney & Bradbury, 1995, p. 20). Individuals who are more satisfied with their marriages are less likely to divorce. Even so, satisfaction is far from being a perfect predictor of divorce.

BREAKING UP

I've spent some time describing who gets divorced, and now it's time to inspect *how* breakups happen. How do partners proceed when they want to dissolve their relationship? The first thing to note is that people do not lightly end relationships to which they were once committed. Most divorces, for instance, are characterized by multiple complaints that result in a long period of discontent, but there are also things that the partners like about each other; so, some ambivalence ordinarily occurs. Recall, too, from our discussion of interdependency theory in chapter 6, that people do not usually depart their partnerships just because they are dissatisfied. Although a long period of unhappiness and distress precedes most divorces, people typically initiate divorce only when they finally come to believe that they will be better off without their spouses (that is, only when their CL_{alt}s promise better outcomes than they are experiencing now). The decision to divorce results from complex calculations of distress and delight involving alternative, sometimes uncertain, possibilities.

Then, when that global decision is made, more choices await. Let's inspect what people do when they want to pull the plug on a failing partnership.

Breaking Up with Premarital Partners

The next time you want to end a romantic relationship, what do you think you'll do? Will you break the news to your partner straightforwardly, or will you simply start ignoring your partner's texts, change your status on Facebook, and start avoiding him or her? When she analyzed college students' accounts of their breakups, Leslie Baxter (1984) found that a major distinction between different trajectories of relationship dissolution involved the question of whether someone who wished to depart ever announced that intention to the partner who was to be left behind! In some instances, the effort to disengage was *direct*, or explicitly stated; however, in most cases, people used *indirect* strategies in which they tried to end the relationship without ever saying so.

A second key distinction, according to Baxter (1984), was whether one's effort to depart was *other-oriented*, trying to protect the partner's feelings, or *self-oriented*, being more selfish at the expense of the partner's feelings. On occasion, for instance, people announced their intention to end the relationship in a manner that allowed their partners a chance to respond and to save face; one direct, other-oriented strategy was to announce one's dissatisfaction but to talk things over and to negotiate, rather than demand, an end to the partnership. In contrast, when they were direct but more selfish, they sometimes simply announced that the relationship was over and ducked any further contact with their ex-partners.

A more indirect but rather selfish ploy was to behave badly, increasing the partner's costs so much that the partner decided to end the relationship. People were more considerate when they claimed that they wanted to be "just friends," but if they did so when they really wanted to end the relationship

---

The Rules of Relationships

Leslie Baxter (1986) once asked 64 male and 93 female college students in Oregon to write essays describing why they had ended a premarital romantic relationship. In all cases, the respondents had initiated the breakup, and their narratives (a term I explore further in the box on page 413) provided an intriguing look at the implicit standards with which they judged their relationships. Eight themes appeared in at least 10 percent of the essays, and they appear to be specific prescriptions that take the form of *relationship rules:* They describe standards that are expected of us and our relationships, and our partners may leave us if we consistently break them. Here they are, listed in order of the frequency with which they were mentioned:

- *Autonomy:* Allow your partner to have friends and interests outside your relationship; don't be too possessive. (Problems with possessiveness were mentioned 37 percent of the time.)
- *Similarity:* You and your partner should share similar attitudes, values, and interests; don't be too different. (Mentioned 30 percent of the time.)
- *Supportiveness:* Enhance your partner's self-worth and self-esteem;

don't be thoughtless or inconsiderate. (27 percent)
- *Openness:* Self-disclose, genuinely and authentically; don't be close-lipped. (22 percent)
- *Fidelity:* Be loyal and faithful to your partner; don't cheat. (17 percent)
- *Togetherness:* Share plenty of time together; don't take a night shift or move out of town. (16 percent)
- *Equity:* Be fair; don't exploit your partner. (12 percent)
- *Magic:* Be romantic; don't be ordinary. (10 percent)

Various other reasons were mentioned, but none as frequently as these. Men and women also differed somewhat in the frequency of their complaints; women were troubled by problems with autonomy, openness, and equity more often than men, whereas men complained about lost magic more often than women. As usual, women tended to be more pragmatic than men when they evaluated their relationships. But as we noted on page 405, both sexes typically focus on their relationship and ignore their personal and cultural contexts when they explain the failure of their partnerships.

---

altogether, this, too, was an indirect approach, with them misrepresenting their desire to depart.

Obviously, people made various moves when they wanted to end their relationships, and the differences between direct and indirect and other-oriented and self-oriented strategies were just two of the distinctions that Baxter (1984) observed. Other distinctions included:

- the *gradual* versus *sudden onset* of one's discontent. Only about a quarter of the time was there some critical incident that suddenly changed a partner's feelings about his or her relationship; more often, people gradually grew dissatisfied.
- an *individual* versus *shared desire* to end the partnership. Two-thirds of the time, only one partner wanted the relationship to end.

- the *rapid* versus *protracted* nature of one's *exit*. More often than not, people made several disguised efforts to end their relationships before they succeeded.
- the *presence* or *absence of repair attempts*. Most of the time, no formal effort to repair the relationship was made.

Add all this up, and the single most common manner in which premarital relationships ended involved gradual dissatisfaction that led one of the two partners to make repeated efforts to dissolve the relationship without ever announcing that intention and without engaging in any attempts to improve or repair the partnership. But even this most frequent pattern, which Baxter (1984) labeled **persevering indirectness,** occurred only one-third of the time, so a variety of other specific trajectories were commonplace, too.

Nevertheless, people generally agree about the typical elements, if not the specific strategies, of partners' efforts to end their relationships (Battaglia et al., 1998). Surveys of young adults find that the end of a close relationship routinely involves several familiar elements that are listed in Table 13.3. The

TABLE 13.3   A Typical Script for the End of a Close Relationship

The next time one of your relationships ends, you may find it following this general sequence of events. The mixed feelings that partners often experience when they contemplate a breakup are apparent in this generic script:

Step 1	One of the partners begins to lose interest in the relationship.
Step 2	The disinterested partner begins to notice other people.
Step 3	The disinterested partner withdraws and acts more distant.
Step 4	The partners try to work things out and resolve the problem.
Step 5	The partners spend less time together.
Step 6	Lack of interest resurfaces.
Step 7	Someone considers breaking up.
Step 8	They communicate their feelings in a "meeting of the minds."
Step 9	The partners again try to work things out.
Step 10	One or both partners again notice other people.
Step 11	They again spend less time together.
Step 12	They go out with other potential partners.
Step 13	They try to get back together.
Step 14	One or both again consider breaking up.
Step 15	They emotionally detach, with a sense of "moving on."
Step 16	They break up, and the relationship is dissolved.

Actual breakups are often very idiosyncratic, of course, but it's clear from this shared script that people generally expect the end of a close relationship to be characterized by ambivalence and twists and turns before the partnership finally ends.

Source: Data from Battaglia et al., 1998.

process usually begins when one partner grows bored with the relationship and begins noticing other people. That partner grows distant and less involved emotionally, but this often leads to an initial effort to restore the relationship and put things back the way they were. The partners spend less time together, however, and when a lack of interest resurfaces, thoughts of breaking up begin. Discussion of the relationship ensues, and the couple agrees to try again to work things out, but they continue to notice other people, and they become more withdrawn. They see others, but that engenders a short-lived desire to reunite that is followed by more contemplation of calling it quits. They prepare themselves psychologically and then break up.

Steps to Divorce

Obtaining a divorce is usually more complicated than breaking up with a pre-marital partner, but the ambivalence and vacillation that is evident in the typical sequence of events in Table 13.3 characterizes divorces, too. And marriages don't end overnight. Whereas someone's efforts to end a premarital romantic relationship can last several weeks, the process of ending a marriage can take several years. In one study of couples who stayed married for about a dozen years, the dissatisfied spouses typically spent the last five years of their marriages thinking about separating (Stewart et al., 1997)!

Over such a span of time, many idiosyncratic events may occur, but Steve Duck (Rollie & Duck, 2006) suggested that five general stages occur during the dissolution of most relationships. In an initial *personal phase*, a partner grows dissatisfied, often feeling frustration and disgruntlement. Then, in a subsequent *dyadic phase*, the unhappy partner reveals his or her discontent. Long periods of negotiation, confrontation, or attempts at accommodation may follow, and common feelings include shock, anger, hurt, and, sometimes, relief. But if the end of the relationship nears, a *social phase* begins. The partners publicize their distress, explaining their side of the story to family and friends and seeking support and understanding. As the relationship ends, a *grave-dressing phase* begins. Mourning decreases, and the partners begin to get over their loss by doing whatever cognitive work is required to put their past partnership behind them. Memories are revised and tidied up, and an acceptable story—a narrative—for the course of the relationship is created. Rationalization and reassessment are likely to occur. Finally, in a *resurrection phase*, the ex-partners re-enter social life as singles, often telling others that their experiences have changed them and that they're smarter and wiser now.

Within this general framework, the manner in which people dissolve their partnerships is likely to affect their feelings about each other afterward. In general, couples who do not identify and discuss the sources of their dissatisfaction have less positive feelings toward each other and are less likely to stay in touch than are those who do discuss their difficulties. Furthermore, for some couples, a breakup is just a transition to another form of a continuing relationship

Breaking up can be hard to do.

(Dailey et al., 2009). Various outcomes are possible when intimate relationships end. Let's turn to those next.

THE AFTERMATH OF BREAKUPS

When people are asked how much stress and change various events would cause in their lives, the death of a spouse and a divorce consistently show up at the top of the list (Miller & Rahe, 1997). The ends of our romantic partnerships are often momentous events—and although divorces are usually more complicated, the end of nonmarital romances can be powerfully affecting, too (Simon & Barrett, 2010). But when a couple breaks up, is that really the end of their relationship? Not necessarily.

Postdissolution Relationships

Most of the time, unmarried partners who decide to break up have less and less to do with each other as time goes by. Believing that what they had is unlikely to burn out completely, they may think that they will continue to be friends, but their commitment to each other gradually fades away entirely. This occurs in 60 percent of romances that end (Kellas et al., 2008). However, about a fifth of all couples (21 percent) find that they become *more* committed to each other (than they are when they decide to quit their romance) in the months following their breakup. Only rarely do couples rekindle their romances after calling it quits, but some partners do reconcile some of their differences, regain some trust, and ultimately become friends (Dailey et al., 2009).

Narratives: Our Stories of Our Pasts

Before you read this box, I encourage you to try a short exercise proposed by Weber and Harvey (1994, p. 294):

1. Think of a difficult or troublesome experience you have had in a close relationship.
2. What do you remember about this event? What happened? What did you do? How did you feel?
3. Why did this event occur in your relationship?
4. Have you ever told anyone about this experience and why it happened?

In answering these questions, you are creating a *narrative*, a story that is an "explanation of one's experience, such as in a personal relationship, emphasizing the characters and events that have marked its course" (Weber, 1992, p. 178). Narratives are awash with descriptions, expectations, feelings, interpretations of people's actions, and explanations of how events occurred, and they tend to bring order and a plot sequence to life's complex, messy events (Custer et al., 2008). Narratives of the ending of relationships may provide a history of the relationship's beginning, identification of a partner's flaws, understanding of the relationship's problems, reactions to the separation, and one's coping afterward. They are personal stories that spring from the narrator's perceptions, and they aren't necessarily "true." Indeed, depending on their past complaints, ex-partners routinely construct quite different accounts of a failed relationship (Harvey & Fine, 2006).

Narratives can serve several functions (Harvey & Fine, 2006). We often paint ourselves in a favorable light to justify our behaviors and to help maintain self-esteem. We can use narratives to influence the way others think of us, and in sharing them with others, we get a chance to express and work through our emotions. Formulating narratives helps us find meaning in what has happened in our lives, and people who keep journals that express their feelings usually cope better, enjoying better mental and physical health, than do those who do not introspect as deeply (Lepore & Greenberg, 2002). And the more complete our narratives are—the more coherence and detail we bring to the characters, feelings, sequence of events, and causes that constructed our relationships—the better our adjustment is likely to be (Kellas & Manusov, 2003). Thoughtful stories about what happened facilitate personal well-being, empathy for others, and a sense of growth (Lilgendahl & McAdams, 2011), so they are key elements in our recoveries from loss.

Otherwise, ex-lovers either experience no change in their connection to each other in the months after their breakup (usually because they've made a clean break and aren't communicating), or they experience a tumultuous series of ups and downs as they struggle to figure out where the other fits into their lives. This latter, turbulent pattern occurs 12 percent of the time (Kellas et al., 2008).

There are several points to make here. First, these various trajectories suggest that ex-lovers usually continue to be important parts of our lives, at least for a while. When a romance fizzles out, the partners often find them-selves involved with each other to some degree months later, whether they had intended to be or not. Whatever the partners' hopes, however, most of the pivotal events they encounter after a breakup are setbacks that undermine their commitment to a friendly postdissolution relationship (Kellas et al., 2008). They may have awkward, uncomfortable interactions, become jealous of the other's new love, or have their sexual advances rebuffed. Or they may finally find it easier to avoid each other, screening their calls or moving away. Certainly, ex-lovers do sometimes hook up, provide needed support, and find forgiveness after a breakup occurs, and, as I noted, some maintain a worthy friendship. Gays and lesbians, in particular, are more likely than heterosexuals to remain connected to ex-lovers after a romance ends (Harkless & Fowers, 2005). But in most cases, the task we face when a breakup occurs is ultimately to get on with our lives without our ex-partners. What's that adjustment like?

Getting Over It

Some relationships are richer than others, of course, and it's especially difficult to lose a partnership that's been characterized by high degrees of mutuality and self-expansion.[3] Our self-concepts have to change when we lose a relation-ship that has been a rewarding, central part of our self-definition (Slotter et al., 2010), and that can be a wrenching process. Strong emotions often occur. But they are usually not as intense as we think they will be, and they don't last for-ever. People do heal.

An intriguing experience-sampling study (Sbarra & Emery, 2005) obtained daily reports of the emotions experienced by young adults at the University of Virginia in the month after they ended a meaningful romantic relation-ship (that had been at least 4 months long). Participants carried beepers that prompted them to record their feelings at random times each day. Four emo-tional reactions were monitored (see Figure 13.3), and they demonstrated that, as you'd expect, breakups were painful. Compared to another group of students whose relationships were continuing, the ex-lovers were angry and sad, and their feelings of courage and strength (that is, "relief") were erod-ing. Two weeks later, as their romantic love for their ex-partners continued to recede, their anger was reduced and their sadness was ebbing, but their relief was lower, too. Their adjustment continued, however, and after another 2 weeks, they were no sadder than their peers and their relief had rebounded. A month into the process, they were noticeably less in love and their courage and strength were returning.

And importantly, all of this was less awful than they thought it would be. Every 2 weeks, another study asked young adults what they expected to feel if their current romances ended—and it then started tracking the actual responses of those whose relationships *did* end (Eastwick et al., 2008). In advance of a breakup, the participants correctly predicted the rate with which their distress would fade with time—they knew that time would heal their wounds—but

---

[3]These two concepts were introduced on pages 3 and 190, respectively.

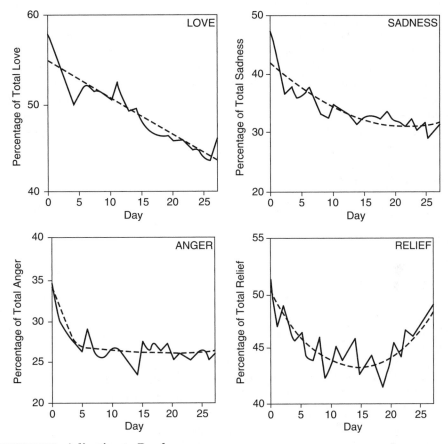

FIGURE 13.3. **Adjusting to Breakups.**
Young adults were sad and angry when they broke up with their romantic partners,
but those negative emotions became less intense with time. A month after the breakup,
they were more detached from their old relationships and bouncing back.
Source: Sbarra & Emery, 2005.

they overestimated the initial pain they would feel when the breakup occurred.
This sort of mistake is common. Our forecasts of our emotional responses to
events are often in error (Wilson & Gilbert, 2005). In this case, though, the
wrongful predictions offer some hopeful news: As awful as they often are, the
average breakup doesn't hurt as much as we think it will.

Of course, some breakups are worse than others. It's generally harder to
be rejected than to do the rejecting (Perilloux & Buss, 2008), especially if one
already has low self-esteem (Waller & MacDonald, 2010). In addition, anyone
who mopes and dwells on what they've lost and how lousy they feel during a breakup is likely to have a hard time; rumination prolongs our distress,
whereas reflection—seeking meaning in our experiences and looking to learn
from them—is associated with positive adjustment and recovery (Saffrey
& Ehrenberg, 2007). But people with insecure styles of attachment who are

anxious about abandonment are particularly likely to have trouble mentally letting go. They remain preoccupied with the ex-partner (and are especially upset at the thought of him or her with someone new), so they remain sadder longer than others do (Sbarra, 2006). (To get their minds off their ex-partners, they should start browsing dating sites to see who else is out there; anxious people detach more easily from a failed relationship when they set their sights on someone new [Spielmann et al., 2009].) People with secure attachment styles fare better after breakups. They brood less, so they're less likely to stay angry. They're also more likely to accept the finality of the relationship's end, so they start healing and recover from sadness sooner (Sbarra, 2006).

Divorce Is Different

The end of a marriage is usually much more complex. Estates must be divided, children provided for, and laws followed, and the event changes one's life, sometimes for better but often for worse.

Adjustment

Let's start with the good news. People are better off when they exit a miserable marriage, especially if they are leaving a hostile, abusive partner (Amato & Hohmann-Marriott, 2007). Spouses who are depressed and who have hit bottom when a marriage ends tend to feel better, rather than worse, after the divorce (Cohen et al., 2007). Making a change is desirable when a marriage is desolate and unsalvageable.

On the whole, however, divorces are difficult journeys that leave people less well off for years afterward. Figure 13.4 displays the results of a remarkable investigation, the German Socio-Economic Panel Study, which monitored the outcomes experienced by more than 30,000 people over a span of 18 years (Lucas, 2005). Several hundreds of them were divorced or widowed during the study, and both events were dreadful, causing big drops in people's satisfaction with their lives. This is evident in the figure, but there are three other patterns of note there, too. First, people who were destined to divorce were less happy years earlier; they even entered their marriages being less content. Second, their divorces typically halted a painful pattern of eroding contentment, and once they exited their distressed marriages, life started getting better. But third, years later, they still weren't as happy as they had been before the decline and fall of their marriages. Divorces are often monumental events in people's lives, and although time heals, it may not do so completely.

(While Figure 13.4 is fresh in our minds, let's also acknowledge the devastating losses suffered by people who are widowed. The magnitude of the loss is hard for outsiders to comprehend. *Twenty years* later, widows and widowers still hold imaginary conversations with their lost loves about once a month (Carnelley et al., 2006), and as you can see in the figure, their satisfaction with life is diminished for a very long time. Occasional bouts of grief still occur a decade later. So, like the loss of a child, this isn't a hurt that is ever forgotten, and generous, supportive friends will respect that. This is not a loss that people ever put behind them entirely.)

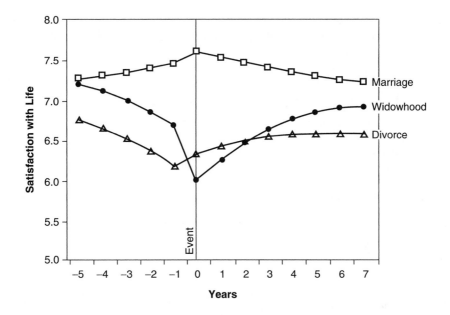

FIGURE 13.4. **Marriage, divorce, widowhood, and satisfaction with life.**
Here's what happened to thousands of people who got married, divorced, or were
widowed in Germany. Getting married did make people happier for a while, but a few
years later they were no happier than they had been before they wed. Being widowed
was dreadful, and despite substantial healing, it had lasting negative effects. And most
divorces ended a long period of declining happiness—but years later, divorced people
remained less happy than those whose marriages were intact.
Source: Lucas, 2007.

Back to divorce. Only two-thirds (68 percent) of those who get divorced
after their mid-20s ever remarry, but those who do have usually taken the
plunge for the second time within 4 years, on average (Goodwin et al., 2010).
Remarrying is often a turning point for divorced singles that is associated
with a boost in well-being (Blekesaune, 2008); indeed, if they stay unmarried,
divorced people are 55 percent more likely than their remarried peers to *die*
sometime during the next 40 years (Sbarra & Nietert, 2009). But whether or not
they remarry, over three-fourths of those who divorce will report, 6 years later,
that their divorce was a good thing (Hetherington, 2003).

So, outcomes vary. It can take years to adjust to the end of a marriage, but
most people gradually bounce back. However, others end up defeated by their
divorces, suffering distress and difficulty in their lives and their relationships
for years thereafter (Hetherington, 2003). And almost everyone finds that the
stresses don't end when the divorce is final; divorce changes one's social network and finances as well as one's intimate life.

Social Networks

People turn to their friends and family for support during a divorce, and the
time they spend with friends increases, especially in the first year (Hanson et al.,

Want to Protect the Planet? Don't Get Divorced

Here's another reason to feel lousy when you get divorced: Because you and your ex are no longer sharing the same living space—and you're certainly not taking showers together—you're consuming a lot more energy and other resources per person than you would have had you stayed together. Couples consume fewer resources per capita—lights, air conditioning, water for cooking and cleaning; you name it—than singles do. Careful estimates suggest that if all the divorced people in the United States used the same resources per person as those who stayed married, the country would save 73 billion kilowatt-hours of electricity, 627 billion gallons of water, and 38 million rooms of living space each year (Yu & Liu, 2007). Yow. Feel free, when you break up and move out, to get a roommate.

1998). However, people usually lose about half of the members of their social networks (such as some friends and most of the in-laws) when their marriages end, and in many cases, ex-spouses never make enough new friends to replace the ones they've lost (Terhell et al., 2004). So, people typically have smaller social networks for years following a divorce.

Moreover, not all of the remaining members of one's social network are likely to be supportive. About 50 percent of divorced people have interactions with their estranged spouses that are hostile or tense, and half of them also report that they have relatives who disapprove of their separation (Stewart et al., 1997). Not everyone who is close to a divorced person will offer desirable support.

Economic Resources

Women's finances usually deteriorate when they leave their marriages. National surveys in the United States find that their household incomes drop substantially, by about 27 percent, and this pattern has existed for decades (Sayer, 2006). Part of the reason is that only about 50 percent of fathers pay all the child support they are supposed to pay, and almost a quarter of them ignore custody payments altogether. In some cases, the fathers are too poor to meet their obligations, but even when there's money to be had, some ex-wives receive nothing unless support payments are automatically deducted from the father's paycheck (Meyer, 1999).

Men's economic well-being is less likely than women's to decline after divorce. Their household incomes tend to drop, too, but they're more likely than women to live by themselves after they divorce; the women are much more likely to have children in their households. So, if you count the number of mouths ex-spouses have to feed, men's per capita income goes *up* 34 percent in the year after they divorce whereas mothers' incomes drop 36 percent (Sayer, 2006). Men actually have more money to spend on their own needs and interests whereas women ordinarily have less. On average, then, a woman's standard of living decreases after she divorces, whereas a man's improves.

Relationships Between Ex-Spouses

When a couple has children, a divorce doesn't mean they're done dealing with each other (Braver et al., 2006). Parents usually have continued contact, and antagonism, ambivalence, nostalgia, or regrets may all shape their ongoing interactions. Emerging from these conflicting feelings appear to be four broad types of postmarital relationships (Ahrons, 1994): Fiery Foes, Angry Associates, Cooperative Colleagues, and Perfect Pals. For both Fiery Foes and Angry Associates, the spouses' animosity toward each other still defines their relationship. Despite their open disrespect for each other, Angry Associates have some capacity to work together in co-parenting their children, but Fiery Foes have very little; their bitterness keeps them at constant odds. Cooperative Colleagues aren't good friends, but they are civil and pleasant to each other and they are able to cooperate successfully in parenting tasks. Finally, Perfect Pals maintain "a strong friendship with mutual respect that did not get eroded by their decision to live separate lives" (Ahrons, p. 116). In a sample of divorced parents in the midwestern United States, half the ex-spouses had amicable relationships (38% Cooperative Colleagues, 12% Perfect Pals) and half had distressed relationships (25% Angry Associates and 25% Fiery Foes) a year after their divorces.

The Children of Divorce

The verdict is in. Decades of research involving hundreds of thousands of people converge on the conclusion that, compared to those whose parents stay married, children whose parents divorce exhibit lower levels of well-being both as adolescents and as young adults. Their psychological adjustment is poorer; they experience more depression and anxiety and less satisfaction with life. Their behavior is more problematic; they use more drugs, break more laws,

What do you think? Are these ex-spouses Fiery Foes, Angry Associates, or Cooperative Colleagues? (They don't appear to be Perfect Pals!)

make more unwanted babies, and get poorer grades. And, as we've already seen, their adult relationships are more fragile; the children of divorce are more likely than others to divorce themselves. These effects are usually not large, but they are reliable. That is, the global impact of a parental divorce is routinely negative but relatively modest (Amato, 2010).

Why are the children of divorce less well off? The outcomes I just noted are merely correlated with parental divorce, and there may be several reasons why these patterns exist. Spouses and families that experience a divorce may differ in several meaningful ways from those who don't, and a number of influences may be at work. For one thing, children of divorce *inherit* some of their greater risk for unstable marriages, so the stresses of their parents' divorce aren't entirely to blame (D'Onofrio et al., 2007). The same traits that make their parents poor partners—neuroticism or impulsivity, perhaps—may be passed on to the children when they're born, making the transmission of divorce from one generation to the next genetic instead of just experiential. Still, with due respect to the complexities involved, the divorce of one's parents often brings on several stresses that may also be very influential: the loss of a parent, parental stress, economic hardship, and family conflict (Lansford, 2009).

According to a **parental loss** view, children are presumed to benefit from having two parents who are devoted to their care, and children who lose a parent for any reason, including divorce, are likely to be less well off (Barber, 2000). Indeed, if a divorce does occur, children fare better when they spend time with both parents (Fabricius, 2003), and they do worse if one of their parents moves some distance away (Braver et al., 2003).

In contrast, a **parental stress** model holds that the quality, not the quantity, of the parenting a child receives is key, and any stressor (including divorce) that distracts or debilitates one's parents can have detrimental effects. According to this view, children's outcomes depend on how well a custodial parent adjusts to a divorce, and, consistent with this perspective, children of divorce usually start doing more poorly in school when their parents grow dissatisfied, long before they actually break up (Sun, 2001). Of course, one major stressor is **economic hardship,** and it may be the impoverished circumstances that sometimes follow divorce, not just the divorce per se, that adds to children's burdens. Any difficulties faced by the children are reduced if the custodial parent has sufficient resources to support them well (Sun & Li, 2002). (Indeed, you may be personally familiar with one of the unfortunate outcomes routinely faced by children of divorce: Compared to parents who stay married, those who divorce contribute less money toward their children's college educations [Turley & Desmond, 2011].)

All of these factors are influential, but the most potent influence of them all is **parental conflict** (Lansford, 2009). Acrimonious interactions between parents appear to be hard on children, and whether or not a divorce occurs, conflict in the home is associated with more anxiety (Riggio, 2004), poorer health (Miller & Chen, 2010), and more problematic behavior (Musick & Meier, 2010) in children. Take a look at Figure 13.5: As you might expect, children are happiest when they live in an intact family in which little conflict or discord occurs, and

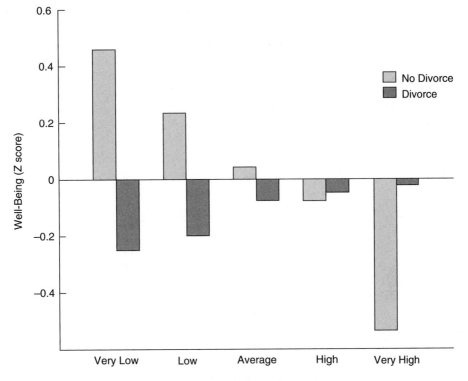

FIGURE 13.5. **Parents' marital discord, divorce, and children's psychological well-being.**
The figure compares the outcomes of children whose parents divorced to those of children who stayed in intact homes and takes note of family discord and conflict. When divorce occurred in low-conflict families, children fared poorly, but they were even worse off when there was a lot of discord at home and the parents did not divorce. Spouses who ponder "staying together for the sake of the children" should consider whether they can provide their children a peaceable home.
Source: Amato, 2003.

their well-being is much lower when divorce occurs in a low-conflict home. But if they live amidst constant conflict, children are worse off when the parents *don't* divorce; when a divorce breaks up an angry, embattled household, there's almost no decrease in the children's well-being at all (Amato, 2003). Thus, the question of whether unhappy spouses should "stay together for the sake of the children" seems to depend on whether they can be civil toward each other; children suffer when a peaceable marriage is disrupted, but they are better off going through a divorce if their homes are full of conflict (Musick & Meier, 2010).

There are two more points to make. First, there's no question that children are less affected by divorce if they are able to maintain high-quality relationships with their parents thereafter. Whatever their sources, the poorer outcomes often experienced by children of divorce are greatly reduced when the children continue to have meaningful, loving contact with their parents and grandparents (Henderson et al., 2009). When parents cooperate to become attentive, devoted co-parents, their children grow up having better relationships with them and with the rest of their extended families (Ahrons, 2007). Second, many of the poorer outcomes experienced by children of divorce gradually fade with time (Sun & Li, 2002). People are resilient, and children heal if they are provided sufficient love and support (Harvey & Fine, 2004). Divorcing or remarrying parents may find it helpful to remember that their children will probably be just fine if they enjoy freedom from poverty and receive loving, reliable, consistent parenting that is free of parental conflict.

FOR YOUR CONSIDERATION

Connie and Bobby married during their senior year in high school when she became pregnant with their first child. They didn't have much money, and the baby demanded a lot of attention, so neither of them went to college, and after a few years and another child, it appeared that neither of them would. Bobby now works as a long-haul trucker, so he is gone for several days at a time. Connie is a cashier at a grocery store, and she is increasingly disgruntled. She has always felt that she deserved more than the modest life she leads, and she has started viewing Bobby with hidden disrespect. He is a cheerful, friendly man who is very warm to his children, but he lacks ambition, and Connie is beginning to think that he'll never "move up in the world." So, she feels very flattered by the flirtatious regional manager of the grocery store chain who asks her out for drinks and dinner when Bobby is on the road. She fantasizes about how much more exciting her life would be if she were married to the manager, and she has decided to sleep with him to see what that's like.

In your opinion, what should Connie do? What does the future hold for Connie and Bobby? Why?

CHAPTER SUMMARY

The Changing Rate of Divorce

The Prevalence of Divorce. Divorce became much more common during the twentieth century, particularly in the United States.

Why Has the Divorce Rate Increased? High expectations for marriage, women working, changing gender roles, creeping individualism, no-fault divorce legislation, and premarital cohabitation may all have played a part. Children are also more likely to come from broken homes.

The Predictors of Divorce

Levinger's Barrier Model. When attraction and barriers are low but alternative attractions are high, divorce is likely.

Karney and Bradbury's Vulnerability-Stress-Adaptation Model. Enduring *personal vulnerabilities, stressful events,* and the *adaptive processes* with which people cope with their difficulties combine to influence marital quality.

Results from the PAIR Project. *Enduring dynamics* predict how happy marriages will be, but *disillusionment* best predicts which couples will actually divorce.

Results from the Early Years of Marriage Project. The social context in which couples conduct their relationships is important.

People's Personal Perceptions of Their Problems. Divorced spouses identify infidelity, incompatibility, and drug use as the three most common reasons why they sought a divorce.

Specific Predictors of Divorce. A variety of societal, demographic, relational, and personal influences are related to an increased risk of divorce.

Breaking Up

Breaking Up with Premarital Partners. *Persevering indirectness* is the most common strategy for breaking up.

Steps to Divorce. When spouses divorce, they often go through personal, dyadic, social, and grave-dressing phases that are followed by a resurrection phase.

The Aftermath of Breakups

Postdissolution Relationships. Some couples continue a friendship after a romantic breakup, but most partnerships fade away completely.

Getting Over It. Strong emotions often occur, but they're usually not as intense as we expect, and they don't last forever.

Divorce Is Different. Divorces are often monumental events, and the consequences can last for years.

The Children of Divorce. Children of divorce exhibit reduced well-being, but they can prosper if their parents stay involved with them and are civil to each other. Children fare better if surly, hostile parents do divorce than if they do not.

CHAPTER 14

Maintaining and Repairing Relationships

MAINTAINING AND ENHANCING RELATIONSHIPS ◆ Staying Committed ◆
Staying Content ◆ REPAIRING RELATIONSHIPS ◆ Do It Yourself ◆
Preventive Maintenance ◆ Marital Therapy ◆ IN CONCLUSION ◆
FOR YOUR CONSIDERATION ◆ CHAPTER SUMMARY

This is our last chapter, and we're getting near the end of this book. So, it's time to take stock. What do you know now that you didn't know before we started? Only you know for sure, but here are some possibilities:

- The styles of behavior that are often expected of men—the styles that encourage them to be assertive and self-reliant but that do not encourage them to be warm and tender—do not train them to be very desirable partners in long-term intimate relationships.
- People with low self-esteem sometimes sabotage their own relationships by making mountains out of molehills and perceiving rejection where none exists.
- Proximity, familiarity, and convenience are influential in determining whether or not rewarding relationships ever begin. There may be lots of people with whom we could have wonderful relationships that we'll simply never meet.
- Looks matter, and if you're not physically attractive, a lot of people will pass you by instead of wanting to get to know you.
- We don't know or understand our romantic partners as well as we think we do; a lot of misperception persists even in successful relationships.
- People try hard to make good impressions on us when we're getting to know them, but they put less effort into being polite, decorous, and delightful once we like or love them.
- Men generally do not do as well at nonverbal communication as women do, and deficiencies in nonverbal communication are correlated with dissatisfaction in close relationships.
- More often than we realize, our partners do not receive the messages we intend to send when we talk with them.
- Bad is stronger than good, and the occasional sour or critical interactions we have with our partners are more influential than the nice things we do for them.

- Over the long haul, intimate relationships are much more costly than we usually expect them to be.
- Romantic, passionate love is one of the primary reasons we choose to marry, but it tends to decline over time.
- About one-third of us are not comfortable and relaxed with interdependent intimacy; we either worry that our partners don't love us enough, or we are ill at ease when they get too close.
- Men tend to want more sex than women do, and frustration often results.
- Sooner or later, it's likely that our partners will betray us in some manner that causes us hurt and pain.
- Conflict is unavoidable.
- Marriages are less happy, on average, than they used to be, and divorce is more common.

Yikes. That's quite a list. And it's just a sampling of the unfortunate facts we've encountered; several other influences, such as the personality traits of neuroticism and narcissism or the states of jealousy or loneliness create difficulties in close relationships, too.

Altogether, these patterns may paint a gloomy picture, and, indeed, the surprisingly low success rates of modern marriages suggest that many partnerships are not as wonderful as we hope they will be. On the other hand, there are also a lot of optimistic facts among the topics we have considered. Here are a few:

- A lot of men, about one-third of them, are just as warm and tender and sensitive and kind as women routinely are. And those that aren't can probably learn to be warmer and more expressive than they are now.
- Happy lovers perceive their partners and explain their behavior in generous ways that give the partners the benefit of any doubt and portray them as kind and caring even when they occasionally misbehave.
- Most people seek and are comfortable in an interdependent and intimate relationship with a romantic partner.

Relationships are complex, and they are usually more costly than we expect them to be. But now that you've read this book, you shouldn't be as pessimistic as this comic strip character is.

Reprinted by permission of TMS Reprints.

Jeff Macnelly's Shoe

- In happy relationships, when passion decreases, it is replaced by a deep, affectionate friendship that is rich, warm, and satisfying to those who experience it.
- Authentic forgiveness benefits both the recipient and the giver, and it is easiest to attain in those close, satisfying relationships that are most worth saving.
- Perhaps most importantly, almost all of us can be more thoughtful, more charming, and more rewarding romantic partners if we try to be. Men do better at nonverbal communication when they are motivated to get it right. We can reduce or eliminate verbal misunderstandings when we take the time to check the accuracy of our interpretations. And with attentive effort, we can be more polite, less selfish, more considerate, and less critical toward our partners than we would otherwise be.

There are lots of reasons to hope that, with wisdom and work, we can live happily ever after. Indeed, I don't think there's any question that "knowledge is power": With better understanding of close relationships, we are better equipped to prevent some problems and to readily overcome others. And the best news of all may be that when we're committed to our partnerships, we engage in a variety of actions that help to protect and maintain the satisfaction we enjoy. Furthermore, if they occur, many problems can be repaired, and many wounds can be healed. When we encounter disappointments in our relationships, we are often able to fully surmount our difficulties if we wish.

In this concluding chapter, then, we'll survey both the mechanisms with which partners perpetuate their satisfaction and the interventions with which faltering contentment can be restored. Despite the hurdles that must be overcome, many relationships not only survive, they thrive.

MAINTAINING AND ENHANCING RELATIONSHIPS

I introduced the idea that people often behave in various ways that protect and maintain desirable relationships back in chapter 6 (on pages 208–209). **Relationship maintenance mechanisms,** the strategic actions people take to sustain their partnerships, have been studied by researchers from two different scholarly camps. Social psychologists schooled in Caryl Rusbult's *investment model*[1] have identified several behaviors that follow from commitment to a relationship, and communication scholars have noted other actions that distinguish happy partners from those who are less content. Let's examine both sets of findings.

Staying Committed

People who are committed to a partnership, who want and expect it to continue, think and behave differently than less committed partners do. They perceive themselves, their partners, and their relationship in ways that help to sustain the partnership, and they act in ways that avoid or defuse conflict and that enrich the relationship.

---

[1] I suspect a look back at page 207 will come in handy.

Cognitive Maintenance Mechanisms

People's perspectives change in several important ways when they are committed to their relationships. First, they think of themselves not as separate individuals but as part of a greater whole that includes them *and* their partners. They perceive greater overlap between their partners' lives and their own, and they use more plural pronouns, with *we, us,* and *ours* replacing *I, me,* and *mine* (Agnew et al., 1998). This change in self-definition is referred to as **cognitive interdependence,** and it probably makes some of the other maintenance mechanisms I mention in this chapter more likely to occur (Fitzsimons & Kay, 2004).

Second, committed partners think of each other with **positive illusions,** idealizing each other and perceiving their relationship in the best possible light (Conley et al., 2009; Luo et al., 2010). A partner's faults are judged to be relatively trivial, the relationship's deficiencies are considered to be relatively unimportant, and a partner's misbehavior is dismissed as an unintentional or temporary aberration (Neff & Karney, 2003). A characteristic that makes these positive illusions interesting is that people are often well aware of the specific obnoxious and thoughtless things their partners sometimes do, but by misremembering them and explaining them away, they are able to maintain global evaluations of their partners that are more positive than the sum of their parts (Karney et al., 2001). And as long as they are not too unrealistic, these rose-colored perceptions help protect people's happiness by taking the sting out of a partner's occasional missteps.

A specific type of positive illusion can be said to be a third cognitive maintenance mechanism. Committed partners tend to think that their relationships are better than most, and the happier they are, the more exceptional they consider their relationships to be (Reis et al., 2011). This **perceived superiority** makes one's partnership seem even more special (Buunk & Ybema, 2003) and really does make a relationship more likely to last (Rusbult et al., 2000).

Satisfied partners are also less likely to be on the prowl, looking for other lovers. Attractive rivals can distract our partners and lure them away from us only when our partners know they exist, but contented lovers display an **inattention to alternatives** that leaves them relatively uninterested and unaware of how well they could be doing in alternative relationships (Miller, 2008). People who are not very committed to their current partnerships monitor their other options with more inquisitiveness and eagerness than do those who are more content with what they've already got; given the chance in a lab procedure, for instance, they linger longer and more carefully inspect photos of attractive members of the other sex (Miller, 1997a). Uncommitted lovers continue to shop around for better partners, and that puts their current relationships at risk: Young adults who are alert to their other options at the beginning of a college semester are less likely to still be with the same romantic partner when the semester is done (Miller & Simeon, 2011). In contrast, committed lovers are relatively heedless of how well they could be doing in other relationships—they're not paying much attention to such possibilities—and that helps to protect and maintain their current partnerships.

Finally, when committed partners do notice attractive rivals to their relationships, they judge them to be less desirable alternatives than others think them to be. Commitment leads people to disparage those who could lure them away from their existing relationships (Lydon et al., 2003), and this **derogation of tempting alternatives** allows people to feel that other potential partners are less attractive than the ones they already have. One of the things that makes this perceptual bias interesting is that it is strongest when the alternatives are most tempting and thereby pose the greatest threat to one's relationship. For instance, committed partners do not derogate images of attractive members of the other sex when they are said to be professional models in another city far away, but they do find them less attractive when they are said to be fellow students on one's own campus (Simpson et al., 1990). What's more, whereas single men find women who are not on birth control pills to be more attractive when the women are fertile than when they are not each month, committed men judge a potential alternative to be *less* attractive when she is fertile than when she is not (Miller & Maner, 2010). To protect their relationships, happy lovers tend to underestimate the desirability of other potential partners.

Behavioral Maintenance Mechanisms

As you can see, the cognitive things people do to maintain their relationships generally involve subtle changes in perception or judgment of others, their relationships, and themselves. Other maintenance mechanisms involve changes in the things people do.

For one thing, committed people are often willing to make various personal sacrifices, such as doing things they would prefer not to do, or not doing things that they would like to do in order to promote the well-being of their partners or their relationships (Impett & Gordon, 2008). This **willingness to sacrifice** often involves trivial costs such as seeing a movie that doesn't interest you because your partner wants to go, but it can also involve substantial costs in which people endure rather long periods of deprivation in order to preserve or enrich their partnerships. If you're already married, for instance, your spouse may be having to go to a lot of trouble to help you go to school; but, if he or she is committed to your future together, that's a price that your spouse may be willing to pay.

Relationships are also likely to prosper when our partners behave toward us in ways that encourage us to gradually become the people that we want to be. When our partners encourage us to be all that we can be—supporting the development of skills we want to learn, endorsing our acceptance of promising new roles and responsibilities, and promoting the self-growth we seek—both our relationships and our personal well-being are enhanced (Overall et al., 2010a). This is the **Michelangelo phenomenon,** named for the famous sculptor who created uplifting works of art from ordinary blocks of stone (Rusbult et al., 2009). People have rarely finished growing and changing when their partnerships begin, and they remain more committed to a relationship when their partners are attentive and responsive to their needs and desires and help them become who they wish to be (Finkel et al., 2010).

Committed lovers also tend to swallow minor mistreatment from their partners without biting back. This is **accommodation,** the willingness to control the impulse to respond in kind to a partner's provocation and to instead respond constructively (Rusbult et al., 1998). Accommodation occurs when people tolerate a partner's bad mood, pointless criticism, thoughtlessness, and other nuisances with placidity and poise. It does not involve martyrdom; to the contrary, as long as a partner's offenses are only occasional or temporary, accommodation provides an effective means of avoiding useless conflict that might merely perpetuate an aversive interaction. And when both partners are inclined to "stay cool" instead of "fighting fire with fire," they tend to have a happy relationship (Rusbult et al., 2001).

I should note, however, that accommodation takes work. It requires us to bite our tongues and hold our tempers, so it involves active self-restraint—and in fact, **self-control** (the ability to manage one's impulses, control one's thoughts, persevere in pursuit of desired goals, and curb unwanted behavior) is generally good for our relationships. Self-control enables us to refrain from lashing out in response to provocation, so people high in self-control rarely, if ever, engage in intimate partner violence (Finkel et al., 2009). Forgiveness requires us to stop nursing a grudge, so self-control makes forgiveness more likely, too (Jenkins et al., 2011). And we use self-control to withstand temptation, so it aids our efforts to resist the lure of attractive alternatives; when they're already in relationships, people say it's easier for them to remain faithful—and they actually are less flirtatious toward new acquaintances—the more self-control they have (Pronk et al., 2011).

In fact, people differ in their dispositional levels of self-control (that is, their usual abilities to regulate their impulses) and, if you have any sense, you'll seek a partner with ample ability to persevere and refrain, as needed. That's because the more self-control two partners possess—that is, the greater the sum of their combined abilities to make good decisions and to do the right thing—the smoother and more satisfying their relationship will routinely be (Vohs et al., 2011). No matter who we are, though, self-control is reduced when we are stressed, distracted, or fatigued (Buck & Neff, 2011), so people are less accommodating, less forgiving, and more tempted by alternatives when they are temporarily spent (Luchies et al., 2011a). We tend to be at our worst when we are tired and taxed. It's good news, then, that feeling connected to family and friends bolsters self-control; acceptance by a loving partner enhances our abilities to behave in ways that protect our relationships (Blackhart et al., 2011).[2]

Self-control can be difficult, but there's another behavioral maintenance mechanism that is easier to enact: **play.** Couples are usually content when they find ways to engage in novel, challenging, exciting, and pleasant activi-

---

[2]Here's another benefit of self-control in close relationships: It shows that we care. We rarely improve our relationships by trying to change our partners—that usually just annoys them—but our efforts do pay off when we try to change *ourselves*. Our partners are typically pleased when they realize that we are striving to behave better—for instance, trying to communicate more clearly and to manage conflict more reasonably—and they're more satisfied when we successfully exert some self-control (Hira & Overall, 2011). Think of the benefits to be gained when *both* partners do this.

The Most Obvious Box in the Book:
Don't Cheat

Obviously, if you want to protect and maintain a valued relationship, you shouldn't subject it to potentially lethal stress and strain. So, don't cheat on your partner. Most of us (62 percent) think that if we found out that our spouses were having affairs, we'd leave and get a divorce (Jones, 2008)—and sure enough, infidelity *is* the leading reason marriages end (Amato & Previti, 2003). For most of us, faithlessness is an awful betrayal that ruins trust and damages a relationship more than other problems do; if they seek therapy, for instance, spouses who are grappling with infidelity are noticeably more distressed and depressed than other therapy couples typically are (Atkins et al., 2010). Nevertheless, therapy usually helps. On average, infidelity couples are much improved—being much less unhappy—after they complete a program of marital therapy like those coming up in a few pages (Atkins et al., 2010).

Thus, here are two bits of good advice. First, if you discover that your partner in (what had been) a worthy relationship has been unfaithful, try not to act in haste. Calm counsel can assist you in understanding what happened and in reaching an informed, profitable decision about how best to put your pain behind you (Snyder et al., 2007). You may find that the relationship is reparable, so "couples should never throw away a marriage in the midst of a crisis of infidelity; you never know when you're going to need it later" (Pittman & Wagers, 2005, p. 1419). Second, do your part to protect your partnership by steering clear of temptation. Seek a social network that will support your faithfulness instead of undermining your monogamy, and handle attractive alternatives (including co-workers, Facebook confidants, and, especially, former lovers) with caution (Glass & Staeheli, 2003).

---

ties together (Strong & Aron, 2006). In short, those who play together tend to stay together. In formal studies of this simple truth, couples have been tied together on one side at the wrists and ankles and invited to crawl through an obstacle course while pushing a foam cylinder with their heads (Aron et al., 2000). Prizes could be won if they completed the course quickly enough, so the task was exciting, goofy fun. Compared to couples who engaged in a more mundane activity, those that played like this felt that their relationships were of higher quality when the day was done. And sure enough, out in the real world, spouses who get up and go out to hike, bike, dance, or to attend concerts, lectures, and shows feel that their marriages are of higher quality than do those who just stay home and watch television (Strong & Aron, 2006). Finding time to play in inventive and creative ways is beneficial in close relationships.

Finally, those who are committed to a partnership are more likely to offer **forgiveness** after a partner's betrayal (Guerrero & Bachman, 2010). Forgiveness quickens the healing of both the relationship and the partner who was wronged—it is less stressful to forgive an intimate partner than to nurse a grudge—so forgiveness promotes good health both in relationships and in those who give it (Bono et al., 2008).

Staying Content

A second collection of maintenance activities has been identified by communication scholars Dan Canary and Laura Stafford (2001), who distilled hundreds of reports (including 500 term papers from college students) describing what people did to maintain their relationships into the manageable number of categories that appear in Table 14.1. As you can see, contented partners try to foster *positivity*, being polite, staying cheerful, and remaining upbeat; they encourage *openness* and self-disclosure, sharing their own thoughts and feelings and inviting their partners to do the same; they provide *assurances* that announce their love, commitment, and regard for each other; they share a *social network*, having friends in common and spending time with their partner's family; and they *share tasks* around the home in an equitable fashion, handling their fair share of household responsibilities (Weigel, 2008). There are some topics that contented partners choose to avoid, but they also seek to provide *support* to one another, to maintain good *humor*, and to spend sufficient time together, and they apologize when they are wrong.

Similar activities are used to maintain close friendships (Oswald et al., 2004), and that should be no surprise. If you take a look (way back on p. 2) at the components of intimacy in chapter 1, you'll see that most of the maintenance mechanisms identified by Canary and Stafford promote and encourage intimacy between friends and lovers. Knowledge, caring, interdependence,

TABLE 14.1. Canary and Stafford's Relational Maintenance Strategies

Strategy	Examples: "I . . ."
Positivity	Try to be cheerful and to act nice
	Attempt to make our interactions enjoyable
Openness	Encourage him to disclose thoughts and feelings to me
	Seek to discuss the quality of our relationship
Assurances	Stress my commitment to her
	Imply that our relationship has a future
Sharing a Social Network	Focus on common friends and affiliations
	Show that I am willing to do things with his friends and family
Sharing Tasks	Help equally with tasks that need to be done
	Do my fair share of the work we have to do
Sharing Activities	Share time with her
	Share specific routine activities with him
Support	Seek advice
	Comfort her in time of need
Conflict Management	Apologize when I am wrong
	Am patient and forgiving with him
Avoidance	Avoid discussing certain topics
	Respect each other's privacy and her need to be alone
Humor	Call him by a funny nickname
	Tease her

Source: Stafford, 2003.

A Prescription for Contentment:
1. Appreciate your partner. 2. Express your gratitude.
3. Repeat.

People adapt to pleasant circumstances, and if you're lucky (and wise and diligent) enough to have a great relationship, there's a danger that you'll come to take it for granted. (In the language of interdependency theory, your comparison level will creep upward.) But if you grow lazily accustomed to your good fortune, you won't be as delighted with it as you should be. That would be wasteful, so I have a specific prescription for how you can savor your satisfaction, maintain your relationship, and feel better about life all at the same time.

Tune in. Feel obligated to take notice of the thoughtful acts of affection, benevolence, and generosity your partner provides you. Then, each week, share with your partner a list of the three kindnesses, large or small, you enjoyed the most.

Happy people are naturally adept at noticing their blessings (Wood et al., 2010), but any of us can learn to pay better attention to them, and it's likely that our moods and subjective well-being will improve when we do. Indeed, people who start "gratitude journals" in

which they keep track of their joys and good fortune become genuinely happier (Lyubomirsky, 2007).

Then, when we express our gratitude to our partners, we provide them powerfully rewarding acknowledgment and affection (Gordon et al., 2011). Our evident appreciation reduces the costs of the favors they do us so that their small sacrifices are easier for us to bear—and the result is that they take more pleasure in continuing their efforts on our behalf (Lambert et al., 2010).

In our journey through this book, we've found that bad is stronger than good, and that couples are less affectionate toward each other as time goes by. But we know that now, so we're equipped to avoid the creeping disillusionment that erodes too many partnerships. Your assignment is clear: Take conscious note of the good things in your relationship, celebrate them, and communicate your recognition and appreciation of them to your partner. Both of you will be happier if you appreciate your partner, express your gratitude, and repeat (Algoe, 2011).

mutuality, trust, and commitment are all likely to be enhanced by maintenance strategies that involve openness, assurances of one's love and commitment, reliable support, and plenty of shared friends and activities. The actions people take to stay happy in close relationships seem to involve the creation and preservation of rewarding intimacy with their partners.

Furthermore, these various actions seem to work. Partners who routinely do the things listed in Table 14.1 enjoy greater fondness for each other and greater commitment to their relationships than do those who work less hard to maintain their partnerships (Stafford, 2003)—and this is especially true when *both* partners behave this way (Oswald & Clark, 2006). Don't fret if you find the long list of activities in Table 14.1 a little daunting; three of them are more important than the others, and they're easy to remember. Of the bunch, the best predictors of how happy a marriage will be are positivity, assurances, and sharing tasks (Canary et al., 2002). Spouses who do their fair share of housework, who are typically in good spirits, and who regularly express their love and regard for their partners are especially likely to be happily wed.

I do have a cautionary note, however: Kindnesses done for a partner on Valentine's Day are unlikely to still be keeping him or her satisfied on the Fourth of July. Canary and his colleagues (2002) found that the beneficial effects of these maintenance mechanisms were short lived: If these desirable activities stopped, contentment soon began to decline. The clear implication is that in order to maintain happy relationships, we have to *keep at it*. And here's where *self-control* is pertinent again (Kammrath & Peetz, 2011); over the long haul, we need to continue to strive to be routinely cheerful, loving, and fair. Those of us who take occasional breaks from being generous, jovial, and affectionate toward our partners do so at our peril.

REPAIRING RELATIONSHIPS

The maintenance mechanisms that protect and preserve relationships have something in common with taking good care of your car. If you shopped wisely and made a good buy, you're likely to be a happy driver if you conscientiously engage in a consistent program of thoughtful maintenance, regularly changing the oil, adding antifreeze, and generally taking care of business. Still, sooner or later, despite your efforts, things may break, and a repair rather than a tune-up will be in order. If the repair is simple, you may want to do it yourself, but there may also be occasions in which you'll need professional help. Happily, when relationships break, as with cars, help is available.

Do It Yourself

One way to solve the problems we encounter in our relationships is to fix them ourselves. Our perceptions of our own behavior tend to be contaminated by self-serving biases, and it's often hard for us to recognize how we are contributing to the relational difficulties we face. Third-party observers can usually be more dispassionate and fair in their perceptions of our relationships than we can. Nevertheless, if you want to do it yourself, there's plenty of advice available. Television shows, magazines, self-help books, and podcasts are full of suggestions that may help you improve your relationships. And consumers of this material often feel that the advice has been helpful; people who read self-help books, for instance, usually feel that the books were beneficial to them (Ellis, 1993).

There are often problems, however, with the popular advice the media provide. For one thing, the backgrounds of people who freely give advice are sometimes as bogus as the advice itself; there are well-known authors who boast of their "Ph.D." degrees who either did not graduate from an accredited university or did not study a helping profession or behavioral science in graduate school. According to Wikipedia, John Gray, the best-selling author of *Men Are from Mars, Women Are from Venus* (1992), received his Ph.D. from Columbia Pacific University, a distance-learning place of which you have never heard (because it was shut down by the state of California). Dr. Laura Schlessinger, best-selling author of *The Proper Care and Feeding of Marriage* (2007), has a Ph.D. in physiology, not psychology. In addition, some advisers do not base their counsel on sound research; instead, they give voice to their personal opinions, which are sometimes at odds with the facts. Too often, people spend good money on crackpot theories that are contradicted by relationship science (Donahue, 2007).

On other occasions, advisers imply that change is simple and easy to achieve, thus encouraging people to be overly optimistic about their abilities to resolve their difficulties on their own. And because such advice is given to general audiences, it isn't tailored to the specific situations individuals face. Relevant, explicit directions on what to do are often lacking, and even if the guidelines provided are fairly clear, there may be no objective observer who can monitor the partners' compliance with the instructions or provide corrective feedback on implementing them.

The biggest problem of all, though, is that lay advice may be simply wrong, and its popularity often has nothing to do with its accuracy. Back in chapter 1, I asserted that relationship scientists disagree strongly with the simpleminded notion that men come from Mars and women come from Venus; now that you've read this book, what do you think?

Here's another example. A book entitled, *The Rules: Time-Tested Secrets for Capturing the Heart of Mr. Right,* was a number 1 "nonfiction" best seller a while back. According to its authors (Fein & Schneider, 1995), *The Rules* described "a simple way of acting around men that can help any woman win the heart of the man of her dreams" (p. 5). If readers followed the advice provided, "he will not just marry you, but feel crazy about you forever! What we're promising you is 'happily ever after'" (p. 6). Sounds great, doesn't it? Unfortunately, the rules were wrong. In order to enhance their desirability, readers were advised to stay aloof and mysterious and to avoid seeming too eager to develop a new relationship. As the authors admitted, "in plain language, we're talking about playing hard to get" (p. 6). But playing hard-to-get doesn't work, and relationship science has known that for 40 years. Men are not particularly attracted to women who artificially delay the progress of a developing relationship; what's attractive to a man is a desirable woman who plays hard-to-get for everyone *but him* (Walster et al., 1973). Specifically, *The Rules* instructed women to avoid seeing a man more than twice a week, to avoid much self-disclosure early on, and to avoid telling him what they did when they were apart, and these and other rules are *negatively* correlated with men's commitment to a new partner (Agnew & Gephart, 2000). On the whole, women who followed *The Rules* probably had more trouble attracting and keeping men than did other women. That's not very useful advice. (Indeed, one of the authors filed for divorce a few years after the book came out.)

Of course, not all popular advice is flawed, and some of it is very credible. Some self-help books, for instance, are written by reputable, well-respected scientists (e.g., Gottman, 2011; Orbuch, 2009). And on the positive side, such help is inexpensive. Readers of self-help books can refer to them many times, going back to absorb material at their own pace. Credible books may also be acceptable to people who are too embarrassed to seek formal therapy, and they can provide readers a positive attitude and general encouragement that facilitates their efforts to address their problems.

Along those lines, let me acknowledge that I'm glad you read *this* book. It's not designed as a self-help book, but I hope that the information I gathered here has been useful to you. I believe that there is enormous value in the scientific study of close relationships, and I hope that I've provided you material that will help you understand your own relationships with more sophistication. I bet that there's a lot here that you can apply to your own circumstances to enjoy even richer, more rewarding partnerships.

Preventive Maintenance

There are also occasions, when you're taking care of your car, when the smart thing to do is to invest in major maintenance *before* anything goes wrong. After a few years, for instance, you should replace your timing belt; it's a part inside a gasoline engine that, at best, will leave you stranded, or, at worse, will destroy your engine if it breaks. It's an expensive change to make, and when your engine is running fine, it's easy to put off. But there's no question that it's a wise choice.

Similarly, couples who are engaged to be married usually feel that they're sailing along just fine, and there's no need to prepare for the new phase of their relationship that wedlock will bring. However, some preventive maintenance may be valuable then, too. Before problems begin, fine-tuning a couple's expectations and communication skills may pay big dividends.

Premarital counseling is available in various forms ranging from informal visits with a pastor, priest, or rabbi to structured training under the guidance of psychologists or marriage and family therapists. (Halford [2011] provides a review of these programs.) Computer-based instruction that people access at home is also available (Braithwaite & Fincham, 2009). To keep things simple here, I'll touch on the PREP program, which is one of the best-known relationship skills courses.

The Prevention and Relationship Enhancement Program, or PREP, typically involves about 12 hours of training spread across five sessions (Markman et al., 1994). Meetings focus on several topics that may be familiar by now to readers of this book:

- *The power of commitment to change partners' outlooks and behavior.* Couples are encouraged to take a long-range view of the future they are striving to create together.
- *The importance of having fun together.* Couples are urged to make a point of playing together on a regular basis.

- *The value of open communication about sex.* Couples are advised to express their desires clearly and openly and to try something new every now and then.
- *The consequences of inappropriate expectations.* Couples are encouraged to be aware of their expectations, to be reasonable in what they expect, and to communicate their expectations clearly.

Participants are also taught the *speaker-listener technique,* which I described back on pages 358–359.

Does the PREP program work? In general, the answer seems to be yes. The average person who participates in a premarital prevention program like PREP is better off afterward than 79 percent of those who do not participate, at least for a while (Hawkins et al., 2008). For the first 3 or 4 years of their marriages, newlyweds who receive marriage and relationship training are more content than are those who do not receive such training (Blanchard et al., 2009). However, most of the participants in such training have been middle-class whites who were highly motivated to make their marriages work, and the long-term effects of the training are still uncertain (Hawkins et al., 2008). Nevertheless, it appears that some premarital preventive maintenance facilitates a few years of smooth sailing when marriages begin.

Marital Therapy

Once real problems emerge, more intensive interventions may be needed. Professional helpers may use a variety of therapeutic approaches, and three different broad types of therapies appear to be helpful for most people most of the time. As we'll see, they differ with regard to (a) their focus on problematic behavior, thoughts, or feelings; (b) their focus on individual vulnerabilities or the couple's interaction as the source of dysfunction; and (c) their emphasis on past events or present difficulties as the source of distress (Baucom et al., 2006). Therapy that involves both members of a couple is most common, but people in troubled relationships often profit from individual therapy even when their partners refuse to seek help with them.

Behavioral Approaches

Most of the time, unhappy spouses aren't very nice to each other, and a classic intervention, **behavioral couple therapy** (or BCT), encourages them to be more pleasant and rewarding partners. BCT focuses on the couple's present interactions and seeks to replace any negative and punishing behavior with more gracious and generous actions. Couples are taught communication skills that help them express affection and manage conflict coolly, and they are specifically encouraged to do things that benefit and please their partners.

Desirable behavior is elicited in several ways. Therapists may schedule "love days" (Weiss et al., 1973) in which one partner deliberately sets out to do favors and kindnesses that are requested by the other. Alternatively, the couple may enter into agreements to reward positive behavior from their partners with desirable behavior of their own. In one such agreement, a *quid pro quo contract*,[3] behavior change from one partner is directly linked to behavior change by the other (Jacobson & Margolin, 1979). For instance, she may agree to do the laundry every Sunday if he cleans the bathroom on Saturday, and he'll clean the bathroom if she did the laundry on the previous Sunday. This sort of contract fails to increase positive exchanges if either partner falters, so *good faith contracts*, parallel agreements in which behavior change is rewarded with special privileges, are also used (Weiss et al., 1974). In a good faith contract, he may agree to clean the bathroom every Saturday, and when he does, he gets to choose the activity for that evening; she may agree to do the laundry every Sunday, and when she does, he assumes all the responsibility for bathing the children and putting them to bed that night.

Getting partners to behave more generously is important, but it doesn't always change the grudging disregard that distressed couples often feel for each other by the time they seek therapy. For that reason, a descendant of BCT focuses on partners' cognitions and judgments of their relationship as well as their conduct (Epstein & Baucom, 2002). In addition to encouraging desirable behavior, **cognitive-behavioral couple therapy** (or CBCT) seeks to change various aspects of the ways partners think about and appraise their partnership. The therapy addresses spouses' *selective attention*, their tendency to notice some things and to ignore others, and tries to instill more reasonable *expectancies*, more forgiving *attributions*, and more adaptive *relationship beliefs* in each partner. Participants are taught to track and test their thoughts, actively considering various attributions for any negative behavior, recognizing and challenging unrealistic beliefs, and generating lists of the pros and cons of the expectations they hold. CBCT acknowledges that people often import into their marriages problematic habits of thinking that they have learned in past relationships, but it still focuses mainly on current patterns in a couple's interaction; the idea is that, no matter where maladaptive cognition came from, a couple will be more content when they are able to perceive and judge each other fairly, kindly, and reasonably.

An even more recent descendant of BCT is **integrative behavioral couple therapy** (IBCT), an approach that seeks both to encourage more desirable behavior and to teach the partners to tolerantly accept the incompatibilities that they cannot change (Christensen et al., 2010). IBCT teaches the communication skills and employs the behavior modification techniques of BCT, but it also assumes that even when two partners behave desirably and well, some frustrating incompatibilities will always remain; for that reason, an important goal of therapy is to teach spouses adaptive emotional reactions to the nuisances they will inevitably face. Acceptance of one's own and one's partner's imperfections is promoted through three techniques (Wheeler & Christensen, 2002). With *empathic joining*, spouses are taught to express their pain and vulnerabilities without any blame or resentment that will make their partners defensive; the point is to engender empathy by helping each spouse understand the other's feelings. Spouses are also taught to view their problems with *unified detachment*, an intellectual perspective that defuses emotion and helps the couple understand their

---

[3] *Quid pro quo* is Latin that means "something for something."

TABLE 14.2. Core Features of Marital Therapies

Therapeutic Approach	Primary Focus on		
	Behavior, Cognitions, or Emotions	Individual or Couple	Present or Past
Behavioral Couple Therapy	Behavior	Couple	Present
Cognitive-Behavioral Couple Therapy	Cognitions	Both	Present
Integrative Behavioral Couple Therapy	Emotions	Both	Present
Emotionally Focused Therapy	Emotions	Both	Present
Insight-Oriented Couple Therapy	Emotions & Cognitions	Individual	Past

Source: Adapted from Baucom et al., 2006.

problematic patterns of interaction with cool dispassion. The couple is invited to describe the events that cause frustration and to identify the triggers that set them in motion while avoiding the negative emotion that usually results from such events. Finally, in *tolerance building,* spouses are taught to become less sensitive and to react less intensely when problematic behavior occurs; negative patterns of interaction are rehearsed and analyzed in therapy sessions, and the partners are actually encouraged to give up their efforts to change everything they dislike in each other. The focus of IBCT is on the couple's present patterns of interaction, whatever their origins, and it seeks collaborative change in both their interactive behavior and their individual emotional reactions to it.

Thus, the three behavioral approaches share a focus on the partners' actions toward each other, but they differ in their additional elements. BCT seeks to change spouses' behavior, whereas CBCT seeks to change their behavior and their cognitions, and IBCT seeks to change their behavior and their emotions. (See Table 14.2.) Each approach may appeal to some couples more than others, but, importantly, they all work (Baucom et al., 2006). Between 60 and 70 percent of the couples who seriously undertake any of these therapies achieve notable reductions in their dissatisfaction and distress that lasts for years (Christensen et al., 2010).

Emotionally Focused Therapy

Another relatively recent innovation, emotionally focused couple therapy (or EFCT), is derived from attachment theory (Johnson, 2009). Throughout this book, we've seen that people who are securely attached to their partners are more content and comfortable in intimate relationships, and EFCT strives to improve relationships by increasing the partners' attachment security. Like the behavioral approaches, EFCT seeks to reestablish desirable patterns of interaction between spouses, but its primary focus is on the emotions the partners experience as they seek to fulfill their attachment needs. People are thought to need emotional security, and they seek it from their spouses, but frustration and distress can result when one spouse seeks reassurance and acceptance ineffectively and the other spouse responds in a negative manner. In one common pattern, a partner who wants more attention and affection will pursue it in a way that seems critical and blaming to the other, who then responds by retreating to an even greater distance. No one is soothed and no one is happy, and the cycle of obnoxious pursuit and withdrawal may intensify.

EFCT tries to identify such maladaptive cycles of emotional communication and to replace them with restructured interactions that allow the partners to feel safe, loved, and securely connected to one another. Three stages are involved (Johnson, 2004). In the first, problematic patterns of communication or conflict are identified, and the couple is encouraged to think of themselves as collaborators united in a fight against a common foe; the therapist also helps the spouses explore the unmet needs for acceptance and security that fuel their conflict. In the second stage, the partners begin to establish constructive new patterns of interaction that acknowledge the other's needs and that provide more reassurance and comfort. Finally, in the third stage, the partners rehearse and reinforce their responsiveness to each other, and they rely on their newfound security to fearlessly seek new solutions to old problems. The entire process covers nine steps, which are listed in Table 14.3, during 10 to 20 sessions of treatment.

TABLE 14.3.   Specific Steps in Emotionally Focused Couple Therapy

With the help of a therapist, couples who complete EFCT will encounter each of the following phases of treatment:

Stage One: Assessment of the Problem

Step 1:   Partners describe their problems, often describing a recent fight in detail.

Step 2:   Partners identify the emotional fears and needs that underlie their arguments.

Step 3:   Partners put their emotions into words so that the other understands.

Step 4:   Partners realize that they're both hurting and that neither of them is individually to blame.

Stage Two: Promoting New Styles of Interaction That Foster Bonding

Step 5:   Partners identify and admit their deepest feelings, including their needs for reassurance, acceptance, and comfort.

Step 6:   Partners acknowledge and begin to accept the other's feelings; they also explore their own new responses to what they have learned.

Step 7:   Partners begin new patterns of interaction based on openness and understanding; they once again become allies rather than adversaries.

Stage Three: Rehearsal and Maintenance of Desirable New Styles of Interaction

Step 8:   Partners collaboratively invent new solutions to old problems.

Step 9:   Partners thoughtfully rehearse and consolidate their new, more accepting behavior toward each other.

Source: Adapted from Johnson, 2004.

The focus of therapy is a couple's present interaction, but the partners are encouraged to consider how their individual needs contribute to their joint outcomes, so both individual and interactive sources of dysfunction are examined. And EFCT is quite effective with couples who are moderately distressed; about 70 percent of them overcome their dissatisfaction by the time treatment is complete (Johnson, 2004).

Insight-Oriented Therapy

A final family of therapies has descended from the psychodynamic traditions of Sigmund Freud, who assumed that people often carried unconscious injuries and scars from their past relationships that could, without their knowledge, complicate and contaminate their present partnerships. (See the box on the next page.) Various interventions seek to promote partners' insights into such problematic "baggage" (e.g., Scharff & de Varela, 2005), but a prototypical example of this approach is Douglas Snyder's (2002) insight-oriented couple therapy (IOCT). IOCT emphasizes individual vulnerabilities to a greater extent than the other therapies I have mentioned (see Table 14.2); it strives to help people comprehend how the personal habits and assumptions they developed in other relationships may be creating difficulty with their present partners. Thus, it also examines past events to a fuller extent than other therapies do; IOCT assumes that the origins of marital dissatisfaction often lie in difficulties the spouses encountered in prior relationships.

A primary tool of IOCT is *affective reconstruction*, the process through which a spouse re-imagines and revisits past relationships in an effort to identify the themes and coping styles that characterized conflicts with past partners (Snyder & Schneider, 2002). A person is guided through close inspection of his or her relational history, and careful attention is given to the patterns of any interpersonal injuries. The therapist then helps the client understand the connections that may exist between the themes of the person's past relationships and his or her present problems.

The insight that emerges from affective reconstruction helps the partners adopt more benign judgments of the other's behavior. Each spouse becomes more aware of his or her vulnerabilities, and the joint expression of fears and needs builds empathy between the partners. The therapist is also likely to portray both spouses as doing the best that they can, given their personal histories, so that blaming and acrimony are reduced. Then, because (as we've seen before) knowledge is power, the spouses slowly construct new, more rewarding patterns of interaction that avoid the pitfalls of the past.

All of this typically takes 15 to 20 sessions with a therapist. Like the emotionally focused and behavioral approaches to therapy, IOCT appears to help most couples, and in at least one study (Snyder et al., 1991), it had substantial staying power, leaving spouses better adjusted 4 years later than BCT did.

Common Features of Marital Therapy

There are several other varieties of marital therapy available in the marketplace (see Harway, 2005), but I focused on just the behavioral approaches,

Central Tenets of Insight-Oriented Therapy

Most marital therapists who use a psycho-dynamic orientation stress three fundamental propositions:

1. In the ways they choose a mate and behave toward their partners, people are frequently influenced by hidden tensions and unresolved needs of which they are unaware.

2. Many of these unconscious conflicts stem from events that took place either in one's family of origin or in prior romantic relationships.

3. The major therapeutic goal is for the clients to gain insight into their unconscious conflicts—to understand why they feel and act the way they do—so that they have the freedom to choose to feel and act differently.

EFCT, and IOCT because careful studies suggest that they work for most couples (Baucom et al., 2006). Most people who seriously participate in any of these therapies are likely to be better off afterward, and (as a rough average) about two-thirds of them will no longer be dissatisfied with their marriages (Snyder et al., 2006). There are no guarantees, and success in therapy is likely to depend on the sincerity of one's investment in, and the amount of effort one devotes to, the process. But *marital therapy helps* most couples. If you ever wish to repair a faltering intimate relationship, help is available.

So, which of these therapies is for you? Over the years, this question has aroused a lot of competition and occasional argument among professional helpers, but I have a very simple answer: Pick the therapy—and the therapist—that appeal to you the most. This is not an idle suggestion. The best therapy for you is very likely to be the one that sounded most interesting as you read these last few pages, and there are three reasons why.

First, despite their different labels and different emphases, the therapies I have introduced all share some common features, and that may be why they all work (Wampold, 2007). Each provides a reasonable explanation of why a couple has been experiencing difficulty, and each provides a hopeful new perspective on how such difficulties can be overcome. Toward that end, each provides a means of changing patterns of interaction that have been causing distress, and each increases a couple's repertoire of more effective, more desirable behavior. They pursue these ends with different rationales, but all of these therapies equip couples with more constructive and more satisfying ways of relating to each other. So, these various approaches all share some core elements that make them more similar than they may superficially seem.

Second, given this, the *therapist* you select may be just as important as the therapy you choose. Marital therapy is much more likely to be successful when both members of the couple respect and trust their therapist (Summers & Barber, 2003), so you should seek an accomplished therapist who seems credible and persuasive to you. A professional helper who espouses a therapeutic approach you find plausible is likely to seem more skilled and knowledgeable than is one who uses an approach you find less compelling.

Finally, a therapeutic approach that interests you may be more likely to offer hope that real change is possible, and such optimism can be very influential (Snyder et al., 2006). Positive expectations make therapy more effective. Compared to those who are pessimistic about the outcome of therapy, spouses who believe that benefits will result from their efforts are likely to work harder and to maintain higher spirits, and both increase the chances that the therapy will succeed.

Along those lines, let me remind you of the dangers in believing, as some people do, that "great relationships just happen" and "partners cannot change." We encountered these and other dysfunctional relationship beliefs back in chapter 4, and I hope that the disadvantages of such beliefs now seem even clearer. People who hold such views are less likely to seek therapy when problems arise in their marriages, and if they do enter therapy, they tend to do so halfheartedly. As a result, their situations are less likely to improve. You can lead a horse to water, but you can't make him drink.

Indeed, that old cliché suggests one last thing that all these marital therapies have in common: They are all underutilized. Most people who divorce do so without ever consulting a marital therapist, and the minority who do usually wait to seek help until their problems are severe (Doss et al., 2004). This is particularly true of men; they're slower to recognize that problems exist, less likely to believe that therapy will help, and slower to seek therapy when it's warranted than women are (Doss et al., 2003). Given the effectiveness of marital therapy, this is regrettable. I hope that, now that you know that you'll probably get your money's worth, you'll not delay in contacting a therapist if the need arises.

Indeed, time usually counts. The sooner marital problems are addressed, the easier they are to solve. The greater a couple's distress, the harder it is to reverse (Snyder et al., 2006). Why wait? Consider the possibilities: Therapy doesn't always work, and there is always the chance, once a couple's problems are understood, that a therapist will recommend dissolving the marriage. But if that's the case, a great deal of distressing uncertainty and pain may be avoided. Alternatively, if a relationship is salvageable and therapy can be helpful, a couple can reduce their discomfort and return to profitable partnership sooner when therapy is sought promptly. Either way, there's little point in waiting to address the inevitable difficulties intimate partners will face.

IN CONCLUSION

Overall, then, just like cars, relationships can get preventive maintenance that can keep them from breaking down, and they can often be fixed when they do falter. I think that this is a clever analogy (which is why I used it), but I need to point out that there's one way in which it is quite misleading: Sooner or later, no matter how you take care of them, cars wear out and must be replaced, and that's not necessarily true of intimate relationships at all. Sure, there are some people who regularly trade in their lovers, like their cars, for newer, flashier models (Campbell & Foster, 2002), but most of you out there hope that you will ultimately construct an intimate relationship with a particular partner that you will find fulfilling for the rest of your life.

And you may. I hope that, having studied the modern science of close relationships, you are now better equipped to create, understand, and manage successful, happy, rewarding relationships that last. I hope that, by shopping wisely and then making attentive and thoughtful investments in the care and feeding of your partnerships, you are able to develop and maintain relationships that remain gratifying to you forever. After all, some people do. When 100 couples who had been contentedly married for 45 years were asked to explain their success (Lauer et al., 1990), they replied that:

- They valued marriage and considered it a long-term commitment.
- A sense of humor was a big help.
- They were similar enough that they agreed about most things.
- They genuinely liked their spouses and enjoyed spending time with them.

I hope that you're able to do the same.

FOR YOUR CONSIDERATION

When she reached the end of this book, Carolyn decided to talk with her husband about her increasing discontent with him and their marriage. He had been considerate and charming when they were engaged, but she had come to feel that he had stopped trying to please her, and she felt lonely and hurt. She felt that she was constantly changing to accommodate his wishes but that he was doing little to satisfy her in return. He never asked her how her day had been. It was a little thing, but it nettled her, and it was just one example of his self-absorption and apparent lack of care. However, when she suggested that they seek therapy, he resolutely refused. So, she decided to go by herself; she went to the website of the American Association for Marriage and Family Therapy at www.aamft.org, found a therapist, and made an individual appointment.

What do you think the future holds for Carolyn and her husband? Why?

CHAPTER SUMMARY

With better understanding of close relationships, people are better equipped to prevent some problems and to overcome others.

Maintaining and Enhancing Relationships

Relationship maintenance mechanisms are strategic actions people take to sustain their partnerships.

Staying Committed. People who want a relationship to continue think and behave differently than less committed partners do. Cognitive maintenance mechanisms include *cognitive interdependence, positive illusions, perceived superiority, inattention to alternatives,* and *derogation of alternatives.*

Behavioral maintenance mechanisms include *willingness to sacrifice,* the *Michelangelo phenomenon, accommodation, self-control, play,* and *forgiveness.*

Staying Content. Communication scholars have identified several more activities that seem to help partners stay content. These include *positivity, openness, assurances,* a shared *social network,* the *sharing* of *tasks,* good *humor,* and the provision of *support* to one another.

Partners who routinely engage in these activities are happier than are those who work less hard to maintain their relationships. However, people need to *keep doing them* in order for them to be beneficial.

Repairing Relationships

Regular maintenance helps keep relationships in good condition, but they may still break down and need repair.

Do It Yourself. There's plenty of advice available but some of it is faulty. However, some self-help information is provided by reputable scientists, and it may be very beneficial to its consumers.

Preventive Maintenance. Premarital counseling comes in various forms. One example, the Prevention and Relationship Enhancement Program, results in increased satisfaction during the first years of marriage.

Marital Therapy. Professional helpers may use several different therapies. *Behavioral couple therapy* seeks to establish less punishing and more pleasant patterns of interaction between partners. *Cognitive-behavioral couple therapy* focuses on maladaptive cognitions. *Integrative behavioral couple therapy* tries to teach troubled spouses to accept the incompatibilities that they cannot change. *Emotionally focused couple therapy* seeks to make partners more secure. *Insight-oriented couple therapy* seeks to free spouses from the emotional baggage they carry from prior relationships.

All of these therapeutic approaches share certain core features. Couples who trust their therapists and enter therapy with positive expectations are likely to derive real benefit from any of them.

In Conclusion

My hope is that, having studied the modern science of close relationships, you are better equipped to create, understand, and manage successful, happy, rewarding relationships that last. I wish you the very best in the interpersonal journey that awaits you.

References

Abbey, A. (1982). Sex differences in attributions for friendly behavior: Do males misperceive females' friendliness? *Journal of Personality and Social Psychology, 42,* 830–838.

Abel, E. L., & Kruger, M. L. (2010). Smile intensity in photographs predicts longevity. *Psychological Science, 21,* 542–544.

Acevedo, B. P., & Aron, A. (2009). Does a long-term relationship kill romantic love? *Review of General Psychology, 13,* 59–65.

Acevedo, B. P., Aron, A., Fisher, H. E., & Brown L. L. (2011). Neural correlates of long-term intense romantic love. *Social Cognitive and Affective Neuroscience.* doi: 10.1093/scan/nsq092

Acitelli, L. K. (2008). Knowing when to shut up: Do relationship reflections help or hurt relationship satisfaction? In J. P. Forgas & J. Fitness (Eds.), *Social relationships: Cognitive, affective, and motivational processes* (pp. 115–129). New York: Psychology Press.

Acitelli, L. K., Wickham, R. E., Brunson, J., & Nguyen, M. (2011, January). *When couples read stories about other couples' relationships.* Poster presented at the meeting of the Society for Personality and Social Psychology, San Antonio, TX.

Ackerman, D. (1994). *A natural history of love.* New York: Random House.

Ackerman, J. M., & Kenrick, D. T. (2009). Cooperative courtship: Helping friends raise and raze relationship barriers. *Personality and Social Psychology Bulletin, 35,* 1285–1300.

Afifi, T., Caughlin, J., & Afifi, W. (2007). The dark side (and light side) of avoidance and secrets. In B. H. Spitzberg & W. R. Cupach (Eds.), *The dark side of interpersonal communication* (2nd ed., pp. 61–92). Mahwah, NJ: Erlbaum.

Afifi, T. D., & Joseph, A. (2009). The standards for openness hypothesis: A gendered explanation for why avoidance is so dissatisfying. In T. D. Afifi & W. A. Afifi (Eds.), *Uncertainty, information management, and disclosure decisions: Theories and applications* (pp. 341–362). New York: Routledge.

Afifi, T. D., Olson, L. N., & Armstrong, C. (2005). The chilling effect and family secrets: Examining the role of self-protection, other protection, and communication efficacy. *Human Communication Research, 31,* 564–598.

Afifi, T. O., MacMillan, H., Cox, B. J., Asmundson, G. J. G., Stein, M. B., & Sareen, J. (2009). Mental health correlates of intimate partner violence in marital relationships in a nationally representative sample of males and females. *Journal of Interpersonal Violence, 24,* 1398–1417.

Afifi, W. (2010). Uncertainty and information management in interpersonal contexts. In S. Smith & S. Wilson (Eds.), *New directions in interpersonal communication research* (pp. 94–114). Thousand Oaks, CA: Sage.

Afifi, W. A., & Metts, S. (1998). Characteristics and consequences of expectation violations in close relationships. *Journal of Social and Personal Relationships, 15,* 365–392.

Afifi, W. S., Falato, W. L., & Weiner, J. L. (2001). Identity concerns following a severe relational transgression: The role of discovery method for the relational outcomes of infidelity. *Journal of Social and Personal Relationships, 18,* 291–308.

Agnew, C. R., & Gephart, J. M. (2000). Testing *The Rules* of commitment enhancement: Separating fact from fiction. *Representative Research in Social Psychology, 24,* 41–47.

Agnew, C. R., Loving, T. J., Le, B., & Goodfriend, W. (2004). Thinking close: Measuring relational closeness as perceived self-other inclusion. In D. J. Mashek & A. Aron (Eds.), *Handbook of closeness and intimacy* (pp. 103–115). Mahwah, NJ: Erlbaum.

Agnew, C. R., Van Lange, P. A. M., Rusbult, C. E., & Langston, C. A. (1998). Cognitive interdependence: Commitment and the mental representation of close relationships. *Journal of Personality and Social Psychology, 74,* 939–954.

Ahmetoglu, G., Swami, V., & Chamorro-Premuzic, T. (2010). The relationship between dimensions of love, personality, and relationship length. *Archives of Sexual Behavior, 39,* 1181–1190.

Ahrons, C. (1994). *The good divorce.* New York: HarperCollins.

Ahrons, C. R. (2007). Family ties after divorce: Long-term implications for children. *Family Process, 46,* 53–65.

Ainsworth, M. D. S., Blehar, M. C., Waters, E., & Wall, S. (1978). *Patterns of attachment: A psychological study of the strange situation.* Hillsdale, NJ: Erlbaum.

Albrecht, S. L., & Kunz, P. R. (1980). The decision to divorce: A social exchange perspective. *Journal of Divorce, 3,* 319–337.

Albright, J. M. (2008). Sex in America online: An exploration of sex, marital status, and sexual identity in Internet sex seeking and its impacts. *Journal of Sex Research, 45,* 175–186.

Albright, L., Cohen, A. I., Malloy, T. E., Christ, T., & Bromgard, G. (2004). Judgments of communicative intent in conversation. *Journal of Experimental Social Psychology, 40,* 290–302.

Algoe, S. (2011, January). *Gratitude fuels upward spirals of mutually-responsive behavior.* Paper presented at the meeting of the Society for Personality and Social Psychology, San Antonio, TX.

Ali, L. (2007, November 5). Knocking yourself up. *Newsweek,* p. 53.

Ali, L., & Miller, L. (2004, July 12). The secret lives of wives. *Newsweek,* p. 46–54.

Allan, G. (2008). Flexibility, friendship, and family. *Personal Relationships, 15,* 1–16.

Allen, A. B., & Leary, M. R. (2010). Reactions to others' selfish actions in the absence of tangible consequences. *Basic and Applied Social Psychology, 32,* 26–34.

Allen, C. T., Swan, S. C., & Raghavan, C. (2009). Gender symmetry, sexism, and intimate partner violence. *Journal of Interpersonal Violence, 24,* 1816–1834.

Allen, E. S., & Baucom, D. H. (2004). Adult attachment and patterns of extradyadic involvement. *Family Process, 43,* 467–488.

Allen, K., Blascovich, J., & Mendes, W. B. (2002). Cardiovascular reactivity in the presence of pets, friends, and spouses: The truth about cats and dogs. *Psychosomatic Medicine, 64,* 727–739.

Allen, K., Shykoff, B. E., & Izzo, J. L., Jr. (2001). Pet ownership, but not ACE inhibitor therapy, blunts home blood pressure responses to mental stress. *Hypertension, 38,* 815–820.

Allik, J., Realo, A., Mõttus, R., Borkenau, P., Kuppens, P., & Hrebíčková, M. (2010). How people see others is different from how people see themselves: A replicable pattern across cultures. *Journal of Personality and Social Psychology, 99,* 870–882.

Altman, I., & Taylor, D. A. (1973). *Social penetration: The development of interpersonal relationships.* New York: Holt, Rinehart & Winston.

Amato, P. R. (2003). Reconciling divergent persepectives: Judith Wallerstein, quantitative family research, and children of divorce. *Family Relations, 52,* 332–339.

Amato, P. R. (2009). Institutional, companionate, and individualistic marriage: A social psychological perspective on marital change. In H. Peters & C. Dush (Eds.), *Marriage and family: Perspectives and complexities* (pp. 75–90). New York: Columbia University Press.

Amato, P. R. (2010). Research on divorce: Continuing trends and new developments. *Journal of Marriage and Family, 72,* 650–666.

Amato, P. R., Booth, A., Johnson, D. R., & Rogers, S. J. (2007). *Alone together: How marriage in America is changing.* Cambridge, MA: Harvard University Press.

Amato, P. R., & Hohmann-Marriott, B. (2007). A comparison of high- and low-distress marriages that end in divorce. *Journal of Marriage and Family, 69,* 621–638.

Amato, P. R., & Previti, D. (2003). People's reasons for divorcing: Gender, social class, the life course, and adjustment. *Journal of Family Issues, 24,* 602–626.

Amato, P. R., & Rogers, S. J. (1999). Do attitudes toward divorce affect marital quality? *Journal of Family Issues, 20,* 69–86.

Ambadar, Z., Cohn, J. F., & Reed, L. I. (2009). All smiles are not created equal: Morphology and timing of smiles perceived as amused, polite, and embarrassed/nervous. *Journal of Nonverbal Behavior, 33,* 17–34.

Ambady, N., Hallahan, M., & Conner, B. (1999). Accuracy of judgments of sexual orientation from thin slices of behavior. *Journal of Personality and Social Psychology, 77,* 538–547.

Ambady, N., & Rosenthal, R. (1993). Half a minute: Predicting teacher evaluations from thin slices of nonverbal behavior and physical attractiveness. *Journal of Personality and Social Psychology, 64,* 431–441.

American Society of Plastic Surgeons. (2011). *2010 cosmetic surgery gender distribution.* Retrieved from: http://www.plasticsurgery.org/News-and-Resources/Statistics.html/2010-women-cosmetic-surgery-minally-invasive-statistics.pdf

Ames, D. R., Kammrath, L. K., Suppes, A., & Bolger, N. (2010). Not so fast: The (not-quite-complete) dissociation between accuracy and confidence in thin-slice impressions. *Personality and Social Psychology Bulletin, 36,* 264–277.

Andersen, P. A., Guerrero, L. K., & Jones, S. M. (2006). Nonverbal behavior in intimate interactions and intimate relationships. In V. Manusov & M. L. Patterson (Eds.), *The Sage handbook of nonverbal communication* (pp. 259–277). Thousand Oaks, CA: Sage.

Anderson, D. E., DePaulo, B. M., & Ansfield, M. E. (2002). The development of deception detection skill: A longitudinal study of same-sex friends. *Personality and Social Psychology Bulletin, 28,* 536–545.

Anderson, J. R., Van Ryzin, M. J., & Doherty, W. J. (2010). Developmental trajectories of marital happiness in continuously married individuals: A group-based modeling approach. *Journal of Family Psychology, 24,* 587–596.

Anderson, K. G. (2006). How well does paternity confidence match actual paternity? Evidence from worldwide nonpaternity rates. *Current Anthropology, 47,* 513–520.

Anderson, K. J., Kanner, M., & Elsayegh, N. (2009). Are feminists man haters? Feminists' and non-feminists' attitudes toward men. *Psychology of Women Quarterly, 33,* 216–224.

Anderson, M., Kunkel, A., & Dennis, M. R. (2010). "Let's (not) talk about that": Bridging the past sexual experiences taboo to build healthy romantic relationships. *Journal of Sex Research, 47,* 1–11.

Anderson, S. L., Adams, G., & Plaut, V. C. (2008). The cultural grounding of personal relationship: The importance of attractiveness in everyday life. *Journal of Personality and Social Psychology, 95,* 352–368.

Andrews, P. W., Gangestad, S. W., Miller, G. F., Haselton, M. G., Thornhill, R., & Neale, M. C. (2008). Sex differences in detecting sexual infidelity: Results of a maximum likelihood method for analyzing the sensitivity of sex differences to underreporting. *Human Nature, 19,* 347–373.

Angulo, S. K., & Swann, W. B., Jr. (2007, January). *The sexist roots of the precarious couple effect: Violating traditional gender roles can undermine communication patterns in couples.* Poster presented at the meeting of the Society for Personality and Social Psychology, Memphis, TN.

Apostolou, M. (2009). Parent-offspring conflict over mating: The case of short-term mating strategies. *Personality and Individual Differences, 47,* 895–899.

Archer, J. (2000). Sex differences in aggression between heterosexual partners: A meta-analytic review. *Psychological Bulletin, 126,* 651–680.

Archer, J. (2006). Cross-cultural differences in physical aggression between partners: A social-role analysis. *Personality and Social Psychology Review, 10,* 133–153.

Argyle, M., & Henderson, M. (1984). The rules of friendship. *Journal of Social and Personal Relationships, 1,* 211–237.

Ariely, D., & Loewenstein, G. (2006). The heat of the moment: The effect of sexual arousal on sexual decision making. *Journal of Behavioral Decision Making, 19,* 87–98.

Aron, A. (2010). Behavior, the brain, and the social psychology of close relationships. In C. R. Agnew, D. E. Carlston, W. G. Graziano, & J. R. Kelly (Eds.), *Then a miracle occurs: Focusing on behavior in social psychological theory and research* (pp. 283–298). New York: Oxford University Press.

Aron, A., & Aron, E. N. (2000). Self-expansion motivation and including other in the self. In W. Ickes & S. Duck (Eds.), *The social psychology of personal relationships* (pp. 109–128). Chichester, England: Wiley.

Aron, A., & Aron, E. N. (2006). Romantic relationships from the perspective of the self-expansion model and attachment theory: Partially overlapping circles. In M. Mikulincer & G. S. Goodman (Eds.), *Dynamics of romantic love: Attachment, caregiving, and sex* (pp. 359–382). New York: Guilford Press.

Aron, A., Aron, E. N., & Allen, J. (1998). Motivations for unreciprocated love. *Personality and Social Psychology Bulletin, 24,* 787–796.

Aron, A., Fisher, H., Mashek, D. J., Strong, G., Li, H., & Brown, L. L. (2005). Reward, motivation, and emotion systems associated with early-stage intense romantic love. *Journal of Neurophysiology, 94,* 327–337.

Aron, A., Fisher, H. E., Strong, G., Acevedo, B., Riela, S., & Tsapelas, I. (2008). Falling in love. In S. Sprecher, A. Wenzel, & J. Harvey (Eds.), *Handbook of relationship initiation* (pp. 315–336). New York: Psychology Press.

Aron, A., Mashek, D. J., & Aron, E. N. (2004). Closeness as including the other in the self. In D. J. Mashek & A. Aron (Eds.), *Handbook of closeness and intimacy* (pp. 27–41). Mahwah, NJ: Erlbaum.

Aron, A., Norman, C. C., Aron, E. N., McKenna, C., & Heyman, R. E. (2000). Couples' shared participation in novel and arousing activities and experienced relationship quality. *Journal of Personality and Social Psychology, 78,* 273–284.

Aron, A., Paris, M., & Aron, E. N. (1995). Falling in love: Prospective studies of self-concept change. *Journal of Personality and Social Psychology, 69,* 1102–1112.

Aron, A., Steele, J. L., Kashdan, T. B., & Perez, M. (2006). When similars do not attract: Tests of a prediction from the self-expansion model. *Personal Relationships, 13,* 387–396.

Aron, A., & Westbay, L. (1996). Dimensions of the prototype of love. *Journal of Personality and Social Psychology, 70,* 535–551.

Aronson, E., & Cope, V. (1968). My enemy's enemy is my friend. *Journal of Personality and Social Psychology, 8,* 8–12.

Arriaga, X. B. (2001). The ups and downs of dating: Fluctuations in satisfaction in newly formed romantic relationships. *Journal of Personality and Social Psychology, 80,* 754–765.

Arriaga, X. B., & Agnew, C. R. (2001). Being committed: Affective, cognitive, and conative components of relationship commitment. *Personality and Social Psychology Bulletin, 27,* 1190–1203.

Arriaga, X. B., & Rusbult, C. E. (1998). Standing in my partner's shoes: Partner perspective taking and reactions to accommodative dilemmas. *Personality and Social Psychology Bulletin, 24,* 927–948.

Arriaga, X. B., Slaughterbeck, E. S., Capezza, N. M., & Hmurovic, J. L. (2007). From bad to worse: Relationship commitment and vulnerability to partner imperfections. *Personal Relationships, 14,* 389–409.

Arroyo, A., & Harwood, J. (2011). Communication competence mediates the link between shyness and relationship quality. *Personality and Individual Differences, 50,* 264–267.

Asch, S. E. (1946). Forming impressions of personality. *Journal of Abnormal and Social Psychology, 41,* 258–290.

Asendorpf, J. B., & Wilpers, S. (1998). Personality effects on social relationships. *Journal of Personality and Social Psychology, 74,* 1531–1544.

Ash, J., & Gallup, G. G., Jr. (2008). Brain size, intelligence, and paleoclimatic variation. In G. Geher & G. Miller (Eds.), *Mating intelligence: Sex, relationships, and the mind's reproductive system* (pp. 313–335). New York: Erlbaum.

Askari, S. F., Miriam, L., Erchull, M. J., Staebell, S. E., & Axelson, S. J. (2010). Men want equality, but women don't expect it: Young adults' expectations for participation in household and child care chores. *Psychology of Women Quarterly, 34,* 243–252.

Assad, K. K., Donnellan, M. B., & Conger, R. D. (2007). Optimism: An enduring resource for romantic relationships. *Journal of Personality and Social Psychology, 93,* 285–297.

Atkins, D. C., Marín, R. A., Lo, T. T. Y., Klann, N., & Hahlweg, K. (2010). Outcomes of couples with infidelity in a community-based sample of couple therapy. *Journal of Family Psychology, 24,* 212–216.

Aubé, J., Norcliffe, H., Craig, J., & Koestner, R. (1995). Gender characteristics and adjustment-related outcomes: Questioning the masculinity model. *Personality and Social Psychology Bulletin, 21,* 284–295.

Aune, K. S., & Wong, N. C. H. (2002). Antecedents and consequences of adult play in romantic relationships. *Personal Relationships, 9,* 279–286.

Averill, J. R. (1982). *Anger and aggression: An essay on emotion.* New York: Springer.

Babad, E., Bernieri, F., & Rosenthal, R. (1989). Nonverbal communication and leakage in the behavior of biased and unbiased teachers. *Journal of Personality and Social Psychology, 56,* 89–94.

Bach, G. R., & Wyden, P. (1983). *The intimate enemy: How to fight fair in love and marriage.* New York: Avon Books.

Bachman, J. G., Johnston, L. D., & O'Malley, P. M. (2001). *Monitoring the future: Questionnaire responses from the nation's high school seniors, 2000.* Ann Arbor, MI: Institute for Social Research.

Back, M. D., Schmukle, S. C., & Egloff, B. (2008a). Becoming friends by chance. *Psychological Science, 19,* 439–440.

Back, M. D., Schmukle, S. C., & Egloff, B. (2008b). How extraverted is honey.bunny77@hotmail.de? Inferring personality from e-mail addresses. *Journal of Research in Personality, 42,* 1116–1122.

Back, M. D., Schmukle, S. C., & Egloff, B. (2010). Why are narcissists so charming at first sight? Decoding the narcissism–popularity link at zero acquaintance. *Journal of Personality and Social Psychology, 98,* 132–145.

Back, M. D., Stopfer, J. M., Vazire, S., Gaddis, S., Schmukle, S. C., Egloff, B., & Gosling, S. D. (2010). Facebook profiles reflect actual personality, not self-idealization. *Psychological Science, 21,* 372–374.

Bailenson, J. N., & Yee, N. (2005). Digital chameleons: Automatic assimilation of nonverbal gestures in immersive virtual environments. *Psychological Science, 16,* 814–819.

Bailenson, J. N., & Yee, N. (2007). Virtual interpersonal touch and digital chameleons. *Journal of Nonverbal Behavior, 31,* 225–242.

Baker, L. R., & McNulty, J. K. (2010). Shyness and marriage: Does shyness shape even established relationships? *Personality and Social Psychology Bulletin, 36,* 665–676.

Baker, L. R., & Oswald, D. L. (2010). Shyness and online social networking services. *Journal of Social and Personal Relationships, 27,* 873–889.

Baldinger, A. (2008, July 29). Stop! in the name of travel costs. *Houston Chronicle,* p. E4.

Baldwin, M. W., & Keelan, J. P. R. (1999). Interpersonal expectations as a function of self-esteem and sex. *Journal of Social and Personal Relationships, 16,* 822–833.

Balsam, K. F., Beauchaine, T. P., Rothblum, E. D., & Solomon, S. E. (2008). Three-year follow-up of same-sex couples who had civil unions in Vermont, same-sex couples not in civil unions, and heterosexual married couples. *Developmental Psychology, 44,* 102–116.

Bank, B. J., & Hansford, S. L. (2000). Gender and friendship: Why are men's best same-sex friendships less intimate and supportive? *Personal Relationships, 7,* 63–78.

Bar, M., Neta, M., & Linz, H. (2006). Very first impressions. *Emotion, 6,* 269–278.

Barber, N. (2000). *Why parents matter: Parental investment and child outcomes.* Westport, CT: Bergin and Garvey.

Barber, N. (2003). Divorce and reduced economic and emotional interdependence: A cross-national study. *Journal of Divorce and Remarriage, 39,* 113–124.

Barry, R. A., Bunde, M., Brock, R. L., & Lawrence, E. (2009). Validity and utility of a multidimensional model of received support in intimate relationships. *Journal of Family Psychology, 23,* 48–57.

Bartell, D. S. (2006). Influence of parental divorce on romantic relationships in young adulthood: A cognitive-developmental perspective. In M. A. Fine & J. H. Harvey (Eds.), *Handbook of divorce and relationship dissolution* (pp. 339–360). Mahwah, NJ: Erlbaum.

Bartholomew, K. (1990). Avoidance of intimacy: An attachment perspective. *Journal of Social and Personal Relationships, 7,* 147–178.

Bartholomew, K., & Horowitz, L. M. (1991). Attachment styles among young adults: A test of a four-category model. *Journal of Personality and Social Psychology, 61,* 226–244.

Bartz, J. A., & Lydon, J. E. (2008). Relationship-specific attachment, risk regulation, and communal norm adherence in close relationships. *Journal of Experimental Social Psychology, 44,* 655–663.

Baruch, A. T., Pietromonaco, P. R., & Powers, S. I. (2010, January). *Attachment style as a predictor of newlyweds' reactions to conflict.* Poster presented at the meeting of the Society for Personality and Social Psychology, Las Vegas, NV.

Basile, K. C., Swahn, M. H., Chen, J., & Saltzman, L. E. (2006). Stalking in the United States: Recent national prevalence estimates. *American Journal of Preventive Medicine, 31,* 172–175.

Basow, S. A., & Minieri, A. (2011). "You owe me": Effects of date cost, who pays, participant gender, and rape myth beliefs on perceptions of rape. *Journal of Interpersonal Violence, 26,* 479–497.

Bastian, B., & Haslam, N. (2010). Excluded from humanity: The dehumanizing effects of social ostracism. *Journal of Experimental Social Psychology, 46,* 107–113.

Battaglia, D. M., Richard, F. D., Datteri, D. L., & Lord, C. G. (1998). Breaking up is (relatively) easy to do: A script for the dissolution of close relationships. *Journal of Social and Personal Relationships, 15,* 829–845.

Baucom, B. R., McFarland, P. T., & Christensen, A. (2010). Gender, topic, and time in observed demand-withdraw interaction in cross- and same-sex couples. *Journal of Family Psychology, 24,* 233–242.

Baucom, D. H., Epstein, N., & Stanton, S. (2006). The treatment of relationship distress: Theoretical perspectives and empirical findings. In A. Vangelisti & D. Perlman (Eds.), *The Cambridge handbook of personal relationships* (pp. 745–769). New York: Cambridge University Press.

Baumeister, R. F., & Bratslavsky, E. (1999). Passion, intimacy, and time: Passionate love as a function of change in intimacy. *Personality and Social Psychology Review, 3,* 49–67.

Baumeister, R. F., Bratslavsky, E., Finkenauer, C., & Vohs, K. D. (2001). Bad is stronger than good. *Review of General Psychology, 5,* 323–370.

Baumeister, R. F., & Dhavale, D. (2001). Two sides of romantic rejection. In M. R. Leary (Ed.), *Interpersonal rejection* (pp. 55–71). New York: Oxford University Press.

Baumeister, R. F., & Leary, M. R. (1995). The need to belong: Desire for interpersonal attachments as a fundamental human motivation. *Psychological Bulletin, 117,* 497–529.

Baumeister, R. F., & Vohs, K. D. (2004). Sexual economics: Sex as a female resource for social exchange in heterosexual interactions. *Personality and Social Psychology Review, 8,* 339–363.

Baumeister, R. F., & Wotman, S. R. (1992). *Breaking hearts: The two sides of unrequited love.* New York: Guilford Press.

Baumeister, R. F., Wotman, S. R., & Stillwell, A. M. (1993). Unrequited love: On heartbreak, anger, guilt, scriptlessness, and humiliation. *Journal of Personality and Social Psychology, 64,* 377–394.

Baxter, L. A. (1984). Trajectories of relationship disengagement. *Journal of Social and Personal Relationships, 1,* 29–48.

Baxter, L. A. (1986). Gender differences in the heterosexual relationship rules embedded in break-up accounts. *Journal of Social and Personal Relationships, 3,* 289–306.

Baxter, L. A. (2004). Relationships as dialogues. *Personal Relationships, 11,* 1–22.

Baxter, L. A., Mazanec, M., Nicholson, J., Pittman, G., Smith, K., & West, L. (1997). Everyday loyalties and betrayals in personal relationships. *Journal of Social and Personal Relationships, 14,* 655–678.

Baxter, L. A., & West, L. (2003). Couple perceptions of their similarities and differences: A dialectical perspective. *Journal of Social and Personal Relationships, 20,* 491–514.

Baxter, L. A., & Wilmot, W. W. (1984). "Secret tests": Social strategies for acquiring information about the state of the relationship. *Human Communication Research, 11,* 171–201.

Baxter, L. A., & Wilmot, W. W. (1985). Taboo topics in close relationships. *Journal of Social and Personal Relationships, 2,* 253–269.

Beach, S. R. H., Whitaker, D. J., Jones, D. J., & Tesser, A. (2001). When does performance feedback prompt complementarity in romantic relationships? *Personal Relationships, 8,* 231–248.

Beck, L. A., & Clark, M. S. (2009). Offering more support than we seek. *Journal of Experimental Social Psychology, 45,* 267–270.

Beck, L. A., & Clark, M. S. (2010a). Looking a gift horse in the mouth as a defense against increasing intimacy. *Journal of Experimental Social Psychology, 46,* 676–679.

Beck, L. A., & Clark, M. S. (2010b). What constitutes a healthy communal marriage and why relationship stage matters. *Journal of Family Theory & Review, 2,* 299–315.

Becker, D. V., Sagarin, B. J., Guadagno, R. E., Millevoi, A., & Nicastle, L. D. (2004). When the sexes need not differ: Emotional responses to the sexual and emotional aspects of infidelity. *Personal Relationships, 11,* 529–538.

Becker, O. A., & Lois, D. (2010). Selection, alignment, and their interplay: Origins of lifestyle homogamy in couple relationships. *Journal of Marriage and Family, 72,* 1234–1248.

Bellavia, G., & Murray, S. (2003). Did I do that? Self-esteem-related differences in reactions to romantic partners' moods. *Personal Relationships, 10,* 77–95.

Bélisle, J., Bodur, H. O., & Nantel, J. (2008, February). *Perception in virtual worlds: Personality impressions based on avatars in the virtual world Second Life.* Poster presented at the meeting of the Society for Personality and Social Psychology, Albuquerque, NM.

Bem, S. L. (1993). *The lenses of gender: Transforming the debate on sexual inequality.* New Haven, CT: Yale University Press.

Ben-Ari, A., & Lavee, Y. (2007). Dyadic closeness in marriage: From the inside story to a conceptual model. *Journal of Social and Personal Relationships, 24,* 627–644.

Bente, G., Leuschner, H., Al Issa, A., & Blascovich, J. J. (2010). The others: Universals and cultural specificities in the perception of status and dominance from nonverbal behavior. *Consciousness and Cognition, 19,* 762–777.

Berant, E., Mikulincer, M., & Shaver, P. R. (2008). Mothers' attachment style, their mental health, and their children's emotional vulnerabilities: A 7-year study of children with congenital heart disease. *Journal of Personality, 76,* 31–65.

Berdahl, J. L. (2007). The sexual harassment of uppity women. *Journal of Applied Psychology, 92,* 425–437.

Berenson, K. R., & Andersen, S. M. (2006). Childhood physical and emotional abuse by a parent: Transference effects in adult interpersonal relations. *Personality and Social Psychology Bulletin, 32,* 1509–1522.

Berg, J. H., & McQuinn, R. D. (1986). Attraction and exchange in continuing and noncontinuing dating relationships. *Journal of Personality and Social Psychology, 50,* 942–952.

Berkman, L. F., & Glass, T. A. (2000). Social integration, social networks, social support and health. In L. F. Berkman & I. Kawachi (Eds.), *Social epidemiology* (pp. 137–174). New York: Oxford University Press.

Berman, J. S., & Bennett, J. B. (1982, August). *Love and power: Testing Waller's principle of least interest.* Paper presented at the meeting of the American Psychological Association, Washington, DC.

Bernstein, W. M., Stephenson, B. O., Snyder, M. L., & Wicklund, R. A. (1983). Causal ambiguity and heterosexual affiliation. *Journal of Experimental Social Psychology, 19,* 78–92.

Berscheid, E. (2010). Love in the fourth dimension. *Annual Review of Psychology, 61,* 1–25.

Berscheid, E., & Lopes, J. (1997). A temporal model of relationship satisfaction and stability. In R. J. Sternberg & M. Hojjat (Eds.), *Satisfaction in close relationships* (pp. 129–159). New York: Guilford Press.

Berscheid, E., Snyder, M., & Omoto, A. M. (1989). Issues in studying close relationships: Conceptualizing and measuring closeness. In C. Hendrick (Ed.), *Review of personality and social psychology: Vol. 10. Close relationships* (pp. 63–91). Newbury Park, CA: Sage.

Berscheid, E., Snyder, M., & Omoto, A. M. (2004). Measuring closeness: The Relationship Closeness Inventory (RCI) revisited. In D. J. Mashek & A. Aron (Eds.), *Handbook of closeness and intimacy* (pp. 81–101). Mahwah, NJ: Erlbaum.

Berscheid, E., & Walster, E. (1974). A little bit about love. In T. Huston (Ed.), *Foundations of interpersonal attraction* (pp. 355–381). New York: Academic Press.

Besser, A., & Priel, B. (2009). Emotional responses to a romantic partner's imaginary rejection: The roles of attachment anxiety, covert narcissism, and self-evaluation. *Journal of Personality, 77,* 287–325.

Biblarz, T. J., & Stacey, J. (2010). How does the gender of parents matter? *Journal of Marriage and Family, 72,* 3–22.

Biesanz, J. C., Neuberg, S. L., Smith, D. M., Asher, T., & Judice, T. N. (2001). When accuracy-motivated perceivers fail: Limited attentional resources and the reemerging self-fulfilling prophecy. *Personality and Social Psychology Bulletin, 27,* 621–629.

Birditt, K. S., Brown, E., Orbuch, T. L., & McIlvane, J. M. (2010). Marital conflict behaviors and implications for divorce over 16 years. *Journal of Marriage and Family, 72,* 1188–1204.

Birnbaum, G. E. (2007). Attachment orientations, sexual functioning, and relationship satisfaction in a community sample of women. *Journal of Social and Personal Relationships, 24,* 21–35.

Birnbaum, G. E. (2010). Bound to interact: The divergent goals and complex interplay of attachment and sex within romantic relationships. *Journal of Social and Personal Relationships, 27,* 245–252.

Birnbaum, G. E., Cohen, O., & Wertheimer, V. (2007). Is it all about intimacy? Age, menopausal status, and women's sexuality. *Personal Relationships, 14,* 167–185.

Birnie, C. J., & Lydon, J. E. (2011, January). *Intimacy, attachment, and well-being in heterosexual romantic relationships over time.* Poster presented at the meeting of the Society for Personality and Social Psychology, San Antonio, TX.

Bisson, M. A., & Levine, T. R. (2009). Negotiating a friends with benefits relationship. *Archives of Sexual Behavior, 38,* 66–73.

Blackhart, G. C., Nelson, B. C., Winter, A., & Rockney, A. (2011). Self-control in relation to feelings of belonging and acceptance. *Self and Identity, 10,* 152–165.

Blanchard, V. L., Hawkins, A. J., Baldwin, S. A., & Fawcett, E. B. (2009). Investigating the effects of marriage and relationship education on couples' communication skills: A meta-analytic study. *Journal of Family Psychology, 23,* 203–214.

Blanch-Hartigan, D., Andrzejewski, S. A., Hill, K. M., Wittenbraker, C. H., & Yu, X. (2011, January). *The effectiveness of training to improve interpersonal sensitivity: A meta-analysis.* Poster presented at the meeting of the Society for Personality and Social Psychology, San Antonio, TX.

Blascovich, J., & McCall, C. (2010). Attitudes in virtual reality. In J. P. Forgas, J. Cooper, & W. D. Crano (Eds.), *The psychology of attitudes and attitude change* (pp. 283–297). New York: Psychology Press.

Blekesaune, M. (2008). Partnership transitions and mental distress: Investigating temporal order. *Journal of Marriage and Family, 70,* 879–890.

Bleske, A. L., & Shackelford, T. K. (2001). Poaching, promiscuity, and deceit: Combating mating rivalry in same-sex friendships. *Personal Relationships, 8,* 407–424.

Blickstein, I. (2005). Superfecundation and superfetation. In I. Blickstein & L. G. Keith (Eds.), *Multiple pregnancy: Epidemiology, gestation, and perinatal outcome* (2nd ed., pp. 102–107). London: Taylor and Francis.

Blow, A. J., & Hartnett, K. (2005). Infidelity in committed relationships II: A substantive review. *Journal of Marital & Family Therapy, 31,* 217–233.

Blumstein, P., & Schwartz, P. (1983). *American couples: Money, work, sex.* New York: William Morrow.

Bodenmann, G., Atkins, D. C., Schär, M., & Poffet, V. (2010). The association between daily stress and sexual activity. *Journal of Family Psychology, 24,* 271–279.

Bogaert, A. F., & Sadava, S. (2002). Adult attachment and sexual behavior. *Personal Relationships, 9,* 191–204.

Bohns, V. K., & Flynn, F. J. (2010). "Why didn't you just ask?": Underestimating the discomfort of help-seeking. *Journal of Experimental Social Psychology, 46,* 402–409.

Bolger, N., Zuckerman, A., & Kessler, R. C. (2000). Invisible support and adjustment to stress. *Journal of Personality and Social Psychology, 79,* 953–961.

Bond, C. F., Jr., & DePaulo, B. M. (2006). Accuracy of deception judgments. *Personality and Social Psychology Review, 10,* 214–234.

Bono, G., McCullough, M. E., & Root, L. M. (2008). Forgiveness, feeling connected to others, and well-being: Two longitudinal studies. *Personality and Social Psychology Bulletin, 34,* 182–195.

Boomsma, D. I., Willemsen, G., Dolan, C. V., Hawkley, L. C., & Cacioppo, J. T. (2005). Genetic and environmental contributions to loneliness in adults: The Netherlands twin register study. *Behavior Genetics, 35,* 745–752.

Boon, S. D., & McLeod, B. A. (2001). Deception in romantic relationships: Subjective estimates of success at deceiving and attitudes toward deception. *Journal of Social and Personal Relationships, 18,* 463–476.

Booth, A., Johnson, D. R., White, L. K., & Edwards, J. N. (1986). Divorce and marital instability over the life course. *Journal of Family Issues, 7,* 421–442.

Boothroyd, L. G., Cross, C. P., Gray, A. W., Coombes, C., & Gregson-Curtis, K. (2011). Perceiving the facial correlates of sociosexuality: Further evidence. *Personality and Individual Differences, 50,* 422–425.

Boothroyd, L. G., Jones, B. C., Burt, D. M., DeBruine, L. M., & Perrett, D. I. (2008). Facial correlates of sociosexuality. *Evolution and Human Behavior, 29,* 211–218.

Boothroyd, L. G., Jones, B. C., Burt, D. M., & Perrett, D. I. (2007). Partner characteristics associated with masculinity, health, and maturity in male faces. *Personality and Individual Differences, 43,* 1161–1173.

Bornstein, R. F. (1989). Exposure and affect: Overview and meta-analysis of research. *Psychological Bulletin, 106,* 265–289.

Bosson, J. K., Johnson, A. B., Niederhoffer, K., & Swann, W. B., Jr. (2006). Interpersonal chemistry through negativity: Bonding by sharing negative attitudes about others. *Personal Relationships, 13,* 135–150.

Bosson, J. K., Vandello, J. A., Burnaford, R. M., Weaver, J. R., & Wasti, S. A. (2009). Precarious manhood and displays of physical aggression. *Personality and Social Psychology Bulletin, 35,* 623–634.

Bowlby, J. (1969). *Attachment and loss: Vol. 1. Attachment.* New York: Basic Books.

Boyes, A. D., & Fletcher, G. J. O. (2007). Metaperceptions of bias in intimate relationships. *Journal of Personality and Social Psychology, 92,* 286–306.

Boynton, M. (2008, February). *What Rapunzel and Lady Godiva have in common: Using hair length as a cue for sexual availability.* Poster presented at the meeting of the Society for Personality and Social Psychology, Albuquerque, NM.

Brackett, M. A., Warner, R. M., & Bosco, J. S. (2005). Emotional intelligence and relationship quality among couples. *Personal Relationships, 12,* 197–212.

Bradbury, T. N. (2002). Invited program overview: Research on relationships as a prelude to action. *Journal of Social and Personal Relationships, 19,* 571–599.

Bradford, S. A., Feeney, J. A., & Campbell, L. (2002). Links between attachment orientations and dispositional and diary-based measures of disclosure in dating couples: A study of actor and partner effects. *Personal Relationships, 9,* 491–506.

Bradshaw, C., Kahn, A. S., & Saville, B. K. (2010). To hook up or date: Which gender benefits? *Sex Roles, 62,* 661–669.

Bradshaw, S. D. (2006). Shyness and difficult relationships: Formation is just the beginning. In D. C. Kirkpatrick, S. Duck, & M. K. Foley (Eds.), *Relating difficulty: The processes of constructing and managing difficult interaction* (pp. 15–41). Mahwah, NJ: Erlbaum.

Brady, S. E., Lord, C. G., & Hill, S. E. (2011, January). *Evaluating others based on attractiveness: Power enhances preference for physically attractive partners.* Poster presented at the meeting of the Society for Personality and Social Psychology, San Antonio, TX.

Braithwaite, S. R., & Fincham, F. D. (2009). A randomized clinical trial of a computer based preventive intervention: Replication and extension of ePREP. *Journal of Family Psychology, 23,* 32–38.

Brand, R. J., Markey, C. M., Mills, A., & Hodges, S. D. (2007). Sex differences in self-reported infidelity and its correlates. *Sex Roles, 57,* 101–109.

Brase, G. L., & Guy, E. C. (2004). The demographics of mate value and self-esteem. *Personality and Individual Differences, 36,* 471–484.

Brassard, A., Shaver, P. R., & Lussier, Y. (2007). Attachment, sexual experience, and sexual pressure in romantic relationships: A dyadic approach. *Personal Relationships, 14,* 475–493.

Braver, S. L., Ellman, I. M., & Fabricius, W. V. (2003). Relocation of children after divorce and children's best interests: New evidence and legal considerations. *Journal of Family Psychology, 17,* 206–219.

Braver, S. L., Shapiro, J. R., & Goodman, M. R. (2006). Consequences of divorce for parents. In M. A. Fine & J. H. Harvey (Eds.), *Handbook of divorce and relationship dissolution* (pp. 313–337). Mahwah, NJ: Erlbaum.

Brehm, S. S., & Brehm, J. W. (1981). *Psychological reactance: A theory of freedom and control.* New York: Academic Press.

Brennan, K. A., Clark, C. L., & Shaver, P. R. (1998). Self-report measurement of adult attachment: An integrative overview. In J. A. Simpson & W. S. Rholes (Eds.), *Attachment theory and close relationships* (pp. 46–76). New York: Guilford Press.

Brewer, D. D., Potterat, J. J., Garrett, S. B., Muth, S. Q., Roberts, J. M., Kasprzyk, D., Montano, D. E., & Darrow, W. W. (2000). Prostitution and the sex discrepancy in reported number of sexual partners. *Proceedings of the National Academy of Science, 97,* 12385–12388.

Brewer, G., & Archer, J. (2007). What do people infer from facial attractiveness? *Journal of Evolutionary Psychology, 5*, 39–49.

Brewer, G., & Hendrie, C. A. (2011). Evidence to suggest that copulatory vocalizations in women are not a reflexive consequence of orgasm. *Archives of Sexual Behavior, 40*, 559–564.

Bridges, A. J., Wosnitzer, R., Scharrer, E., Sun, C., & Liberman, R. (2010). Aggression and sexual behavior in best-selling pornography videos: A content analysis update. *Violence Against Women, 16*, 1065–1085.

Bringle, R. G., & Buunk, B. P. (1991). Extradyadic relationships and sexual jealousy. In K. McKinney & S. Sprecher (Eds.), *Sexuality in close relationships* (pp. 135–153). Hillsdale, NJ: Erlbaum.

Broady, E. F., & Neff, L. A. (2010, January). *Boosting marital immunity: Stress inoculation effects in early marriage.* Poster presented at the meeting of the Society for Personality and Social Psychology, Las Vegas, NV.

Brock, R. L., & Lawrence, E. (2009). Too much of a good thing: Underprovision versus overprovision of partner support. *Journal of Family Psychology, 23*, 181–192.

Brock, R. L., & Lawrence, E. (2010). Support adequacy in marriage: Observing the platinum rule. In K. Sullivan & J. Davila (Eds.), *Support processes in intimate relationships* (pp. 3–25). New York: Oxford University Press.

Brody, L. R., & Hall, J. A. (2008). Gender and emotion in context. In M. Lewis, J. M. Haviland-Jones, & L. Feldman Barrett (Eds.), *Handbook of emotions* (3rd ed., pp. 395–408). New York: Guilford Press.

Brody, L. R., & Hall, J. A. (2010). Gender, emotion, and socialization. In J. Chrisler & D. McCreary (Eds.), *Handbook of gender research in psycholog* (Vol. 1, pp. 429–454). New York: Springer.

Broemer, P., & Diehl, M. (2003). What you think is what you get: Comparative evaluations of close relationships. *Personality and Social Psychology Bulletin, 29*, 1560–1569.

Brown, J., Bernieri, F., & Reyna, N. (2011, January). *Perceiving others from zero-acquaintance to ten weeks: A developmental study.* Poster presented at the meeting of the Society for Personality and Social Psychology, San Antonio, TX.

Brown, J. D., & L'Engle, K. L. (2009). X-rated: Sexual attitudes and behaviors associated with U.S. early adolescents' exposure to sexually explicit media. *Communication Research, 36*, 129–151.

Brown, J. L., Sheffield, D., Leary, M. R., & Robinson, M. E. (2003). Social support and experimental pain. *Psychosomatic Medicine, 65*, 276–283.

Brown, J. L., & Vanable, P. A. (2009). The effects of assessment mode and privacy level on self-reports of risky sexual behaviors and substance use among young women. *Journal of Applied Social Psychology, 39*, 2756–2778.

Brown, N. R., & Sinclair, R. C. (1999). Estimating number of lifetime sexual partners: Men and women do it differently. *Journal of Sex Research, 36*, 292–297.

Brownridge, D. A. (2010). Does the situational couple violence-intimate terrorism typology explain cohabitors' high risk of intimate partner violence? *Journal of Interpersonal Violence, 25*, 1264–1283.

Brumbaugh, C. C., & Fraley, R. C. (2007). Transference of attachment patterns: How important relationships influence feelings toward novel people. *Personal Relationships, 14*, 513–530.

Brunell, A. B., Davis, M., Rhodes, J., & DePaoli, J. (2011, January). *Narcissism and interpersonal transgressions.* Poster presented at the meeting of the Society for Personality and Social Psychology, San Antonio, TX.

Brunell, A. B., Kernis, M. H., Goldman, B. M., Heppner, W., Davis, P., Cascio, E. V., & Webster, G. D. (2010). Dispositional authenticity and romantic relationship functioning. *Personality and Individual Differences, 48*, 900–905.

Brunet, P. M., & Schmidt, L. A. (2007). Is shyness context specific? Relation between shyness and online self-disclosure with and without a live webcam in young adults. *Journal of Research in Personality, 41*, 938–945.

Brunet, P. M., & Schmidt, L. A. (2008). Are shy adults really bolder online? It depends on the context. *CyberPsychology & Behavior, 11*, 707–709.

Bryant, A. N. (2003). Changes in attitudes toward women's roles: Predicting gender-role traditionalism among college students. *Sex Roles, 48*, 131–142.

Bryant, C. M., Wickrama, K. A. S., Bolland, J., Bryant, B. M., Cutrona, C. E., & Stanik, C. E. (2010). Race matters, even in marriage: Identifying factors linked to marital outcomes for African Americans. *Journal of Family Theory & Review, 2,* 157–174.

Buck, A. A., & Neff, L. A. (2011, January). *Stress spillover in early marriage: The role of self-regulatory depletion.* Poster presented at the meeting of the Society for Personality and Social Psychology, San Antonio, TX.

Buck, D. M., & Plant, E. A. (2011). Interorientation interactions and impressions: Does the timing of disclosure of sexual orientation matter? *Journal of Experimental Social Psychology, 47,* 333–342.

Buckley, K. E., Winkel, R. E., & Leary, M. R. (2004). Reactions to acceptance and rejection: Effects of level and sequence of relational evaluation. *Journal of Experimental Social Psychology, 40,* 14–28.

Buhrmester, D., & Furman, W. (1986). The changing functions of friends in childhood: A neoSullivanian perspective. In V. J. Derlega & B. A. Winstead (Eds.), *Friendship and social interaction* (pp. 41–62). New York: Springer-Verlag.

Bukowski, W. M., & Cillessen, A. H. (Eds.). (1998). *Sociometry then and now: Building on six decades of measuring children's experiences with the peer group.* San Francisco: Jossey-Bass.

Buller, D. B., & Burgoon, J. K. (1994). Deception: Strategic and nonstrategic communication. In J. A. Daly & J. M. Wiemann (Eds.), *Strategic interpersonal communication* (pp. 191–223). Hillsdale, NJ: Erlbaum.

Burger, J. M., & Burns, L. (1988). The illusion of unique invulnerability and use of effective contraception. *Personality and Social Psychology Bulletin, 14,* 264–270.

Burgoon, J. K., & Bacue, A. E. (2003). Nonverbal communication skills. In J. O. Greene & B. R. Burleson (Eds.), *Handbook of communication and social interaction skills* (pp. 179–219). Mahwah, NJ: Erlbaum.

Burgoon, J. K., & Levine, T. R. (2010). Advances in deception detection. In S. Smith & S. Wilson (Eds.), *New directions in interpersonal communication research* (pp. 201–220). Thousand Oaks, CA: Sage.

Burleson, B. R., Kunkel, A. W., Samter, W., & Werking, K. J. (1996). Men's and women's evaluations of communication skills in personal relationships: When sex differences make a difference—and when they don't. *Journal of Social and Personal Relationships, 13,* 201–224.

Burleson, M. H., Trevathan, W. R., & Todd, M. (2007). In the mood for love or vice versa? Exploring the relations among sexual activity, physical affection, affect, and stress in the daily lives of mid-aged women. *Archives of Sexual Behavior, 36,* 357–368.

Burman, B., Margolin, G., & John, R. S. (1993). America's angriest home videos: Behavioral contingencies observed in home reenactments of marital conflict. *Journal of Consulting and Clinical Psychology, 61,* 28–39.

Burnette, J. L., Taylor, K. W., Worthington, E. L., & Forsyth, D. R. (2007). Attachment and trait forgivingness: The mediating role of angry rumination. *Personality and Individual Differences, 42,* 1585–1596.

Burns, G. L., & Farina, A. (1992). The role of physical attractiveness in adjustment. *Genetic, Social, and General Psychology Monographs, 118,* 157–194.

Burriss, R. P., Rowland, H. M., & Little, A. C. (2009). Facial scarring enhances men's attractiveness for short-term relationships. *Personality and Individual Differences, 46,* 213–217.

Burton, L. M., Bonilla-Silva, E., Ray, V., Buckelew, R., & Freeman, E. H. (2010). Critical race theories, colorism, and the decade's research on families of color. *Journal of Marriage and Family, 72,* 440–459.

Busboom, A. L., Collins, D. M., Givertz, M. D., & Levin, L. A. (2002). Can we still be friends? Resources and barriers to friendship quality after romantic relationship dissolution. *Personal Relationships, 9,* 215–223.

Busby, D. M., & Holman, T. B. (2009). Perceived match or mismatch on the Gottman conflict styles: Associations with relationship outcome variables. *Family Process, 48,* 531–545.

Buss, D. M. (1989). Sex differences in human mate preferences: Evolutionary hypotheses tested in 37 cultures. *Behavioral and Brain Sciences, 12,* 1–14.

Buss, D. M. (2000). *The dangerous passion: Why jealousy is as necessary as love and sex.* New York: Free Press.

Buss, D. M. (2003). *The evolution of desire: Strategies of human mating* (rev. ed.). New York: Basic Books.

Buss, D. M. (2012). *Evolutionary psychology: The new science of the mind* (4th ed.). Boston, MA: Pearson.

Buss, D. M., & Duntley, J. D. (2006). The evolution of aggression. In M. Schaller, J. A. Simpson, & D. T. Kenrick (Eds.), *Evolution and social psychology* (pp. 263–285). New York: Psychology Press.

Buss, D. M., Larsen, R. J., Westen, D., & Semmelroth, J. (1992). Sex differences in jealousy: Evolution, physiology, and psychology. *Psychological Science, 3,* 251–255.

Buss, D. M., & Schmitt, D. P. (1993). Sexual strategies theory: An evolutionary perspective on human mating. *Psychological Review, 100,* 204–232.

Buss, D. M., & Shackelford, T. K. (2008). Attractive women want it all: Good genes, economic investment, parenting proclivities, and emotional commitment. *Evolutionary Psychology, 6,* 134–146.

Buss, D. M., Shackelford, T. K., Kirkpatrick, L. A., Choe, J. C., Lim, H. K., Hasegawa, M., Hasegawa, T., & Bennett, K. (1999). Jealousy and the nature of beliefs about infidelity: Tests of competing hypotheses about sex differences in the United States, Korea, and Japan. *Personal Relationships, 6,* 125–150.

Buss, D. M., Shackelford, T. K., Kirkpatrick, L. A., & Larsen, R. J. (2001). A half century of mate preferences: The cultural evolution of values. *Journal of Marriage and the Family, 63,* 491–503.

Butzer, B., & Campbell, L. (2008). Adult attachment, sexual satisfaction, and relationship satisfaction: A study of married couples. *Personal Relationships, 15,* 141–154.

Buunk, A. P., Park, J. H., & Duncan, L. A. (2010). Cultural variation in parental influence on mate choice. *Cross-Cultural Research, 44,* 23–40.

Buunk, A. P., & Solano, A. C. (2010). Conflicting preferences of parents and offspring over criteria for a mate: A study in Argentina. *Journal of Family Psychology, 24,* 391–399.

Buunk, B. (1987). Conditions that promote breakups as a consequence of extra-dyadic involvements. *Journal of Social and Clinical Psychology, 5,* 271–284.

Buunk, B. P. (1995). Sex, self-esteem, dependency and extradyadic sexual experience as related to jealousy responses. *Journal of Social and Personal Relationships, 12,* 147–153.

Buunk, B. P. (1997). Personality, birth order and attachment styles as related to various types of jealousy. *Personality and Individual Differences, 23,* 997–1006.

Buunk, B. P. (2001). Perceived superiority of one's own relationship and perceived prevalence of happy and unhappy relationships. *British Journal of Social Psychology, 40,* 565–574.

Buunk, B. P., & Dijkstra, P. (2006). Temptation and threat: Extradyadic relations and jealousy. In A. L. Vangelisti & D. Perlman (Eds.), *The Cambridge handbook of personal relationships* (pp. 533–555). New York: Cambridge University Press.

Buunk, B. P., Dijkstra, P., Fetchenhauer, D., & Kenrick, D. T. (2002). Age and gender differences in mate selection criteria for various involvement levels. *Personal Relationships, 9,* 271–278.

Buunk, B. P., & VanYperen, N. W. (1991). Referential comparisons, relational comparisons, and exchange orientation: Their relation to marital satisfaction. *Personality and Social Psychology Bulletin, 17,* 709–717.

Buunk, B. P., & Ybema, J. F. (2003). Feeling bad, but satisfied: The effects of upward and downward comparison upon mood and marital satisfaction. *British Journal of Social Psychology, 42,* 613–628.

Byers, E. S. (2005). Relationship satisfaction and sexual satisfaction: A longitudinal study of individuals in long-term relationships. *Journal of Sex Research, 42,* 113–118.

Byrne, D., Ervin, C. E., & Lamberth, J. (1970). Continuity between the experimental study of attraction and real-life computer dating. *Journal of Personality and Social Psychology, 16,* 157–165.

Byrne, D., & Nelson, D. (1965). Attraction as a linear function of proportion of positive reinforcements. *Journal of Personality and Social Psychology, 1,* 659–663.

Cacioppo, J. T., & Gardner, W. L. (1999). Emotions. *Annual Review of Psychology, 50,* 191–214.

Cacioppo, J. T., Fowler, J. H., & Christakis, N. A. (2009). Alone in the crowd: The structure and spread of loneliness in a large social network. *Journal of Personality and Social Psychology, 97,* 977–991.

Cacioppo, J. T., & Hawkley, L. C. (2009). Loneliness. In M. R. Leary & R. H. Hoyle (Eds.), *Handbook of individual differences in social behavior* (pp. 227–240). New York: Guilford Press.

Cacioppo, J. T., Hawkley, L. C., Ernst, J. M., Burleson, M., Berntson, G. G., Nouriani, B., & Spiegel, D. (2006). Loneliness within a nomological net: An evolutionary perspective. *Journal of Research in Personality, 40,* 1054–1085.

Call, V., Sprecher, S., & Schwartz, P. (1995). The incidence and frequency of marital sex in a national sample. *Journal of Marriage and the Family, 57,* 639–652.

Cameron, J. J., Ross, M., & Holmes, J. G. (2002). Loving the one you hurt: Positive effects of recounting a transgression against an intimate partner. *Journal of Experimental Social Psychology, 38,* 307–314.

Cameron, J. J., Stinson, D. A., Gaetz, R., & Balchen, S. (2010). Acceptance is in the eye of the beholder: Self-esteem and motivated perceptions of acceptance from the opposite sex. *Journal of Personality and Social Psychology, 99,* 513–529.

Cameron, J. J., & Vorauer, J. D. (2008). Feeling transparent: On metaperceptions and miscommunications. *Social and Personality Psychology Compass 2,* 1093–1108.

Campbell, A. (2010). Oxytocin and human social behavior. *Personality and Social Psychology Review, 14,* 281–295.

Campbell, J., Miller, P., Cardwell, M., & Belknap, R. A. (1994). Relationship status of battered women over time. *Journal of Family Violence, 9,* 99–111.

Campbell, L., Cronk, L., Simpson, J. A., Milroy, A., Wilson, C. L., & Dunham, B. (2009). The association between men's ratings of women as desirable long-term mates and individual differences in women's sexual attitudes and behaviors. *Personality and Individual Differences, 46,* 509–513.

Campbell, L., Martin, R. A., & Ward, J. R. (2008). An observational study of humor use while resolving conflict in dating couples. *Personal Relationships, 15,* 41–55.

Campbell, L., Simpson, J. A., Boldry, J., & Kashy, D. A. (2005). Perceptions of conflict and support in romantic relationships: The role of attachment anxiety. *Journal of Personality and Social Psychology, 88,* 510–531.

Campbell, L., Simpson, J. A., Kashy, D. A., & Rholes, W. S. (2001). Attachment orientations, dependence, and behavior in a stressful situation: An application of the actor-partner interdependence model. *Journal of Social and Personal Relationships, 18,* 821–843.

Campbell, W. K., & Foster, C. A. (2002). Narcissism and commitment in romantic relationships: An investment model analysis. *Personality and Social Psychology Bulletin, 28,* 484–495.

Canary, D. J. (2003). Managing interpersonal conflict: A model of events related to strategic choices. In J. O. Greene & B. R. Burleson (Eds.), *Handbook of commmunication and social interaction skills* (pp. 515–549). Mahwah, NJ: Erlbaum.

Canary, D. J., & Emmers-Sommer, T. M. (1997). *Sex and gender differences in personal relationships.* New York: Guilford Press.

Canary, D. J., & Stafford, L. (2001). Equity in the preservation of personal relationships. In J. H. Harvey & A. E. Wenzel (Eds.), *Close romantic relationships: Maintenance and enhancement* (pp. 133–151). Mahwah, NJ: Erlbaum.

Canary, D. J., Stafford, L., & Semic, B. A. (2002). A panel study of the associations between maintenance strategies and relational characteristics. *Journal of Marriage and the Family, 64,* 395–406.

Canevello, A., & Crocker, J. (2010). Creating good relationships: Responsiveness, relationship quality, and interpersonal goals. *Journal of Personality and Social Psychology, 99,* 78–106.

Canevello, A., & Crocker, J. (2011, January). *Responding to you benefits me: How being responsive promotes own optimal functioning.* Paper presented at the meeting of the Society for Personality and Social Psychology, San Antonio, TX.

Cann, A., & Baucom, T. R. (2004). Former partners and new rivals as threats to a relationship: Infidelity type, gender, and commitment as factors related to distress and forgiveness. *Personal Relationships, 11,* 305–318.

Capezza, N. M., & Arriaga, X. B. (2008). You can degrade but you can't hit: Differences in perceptions of psychological versus physical aggression. *Journal of Social and Personal Relationships, 25,* 225–245.

Carey, B. (2010, May 23). Families' lives, taped, analyzed and archived. *Houston Chronicle,* p. A10.

Carli, L. L. (1999). Gender, interpersonal power, and social influence. *Journal of Social Issues, 55,* 81–98.

Carli, L. L. (2001). Gender and social influence. *Journal of Social Issues, 57,* 725–741.

Carlsmith, K. M., Wilson, T. D., & Gilbert, D. T. (2008). The paradoxical consequences of revenge. *Journal of Personality and Social Psychology, 95,* 1316–1324.

Carlson, E. N., & Furr, R. M. (2009). Evidence of differential meta-accuracy: People understand the different impressions they make. *Psychological Science, 20,* 1033–1039.

Carmichael, C. L., Gable, S. L., & Reis, H. T. (2003, February). *Who sees what in close relationships? Attachment and sensitivity to daily relationship behaviors using a quasi-signal detection paradigm.* Paper presented at the meeting of the Society for Personality and Social Psychology, Los Angeles, CA.

Carmichael, C. L., Tsai, F., Smith, S. M., Caprariello, P. A., & Reis, H. T. (2007). The self and intimate relationships. In C. Sedikides & S. J. Spencer (Eds.), *The self* (pp. 285–309). New York: Psychology Press.

Carnegie, D. (1936). *How to win friends and influence people.* New York: Pocket Books.

Carnelley, K., & Story, A. (2008, February). *Adult attachment and appetitive and aversive goals.* Poster presented at the meeting of the Society for Personality and Social Psychology, Albuquerque, NM.

Carnelley, K. B., Wortman, C. B., Bolger, N., & Burke, C. T. (2006). The time course of grief reactions to spousal loss: Evidence from a national probability sample. *Journal of Personality and Social Psychology, 91,* 476–492.

Carney, D. R., Colvin, C. R., & Hall, J. A. (2007). A thin slice perspective on the accuracy of first impressions. *Journal of Research in Personality, 41,* 1054–1072.

Carney, D. R., Cuddy, A. J. C., & Yap, A. J. (2010). Power posing: Brief nonverbal displays affect neuroendocrine levels and risk tolerance. *Psychological Science, 21,* 1363–1368.

Carothers, B. J., & Allen, J. B. (1999). Relationships of employment status, gender roles, insult, and gender with use of influence tactics. *Sex Roles, 41,* 375–386.

Carpenter, J., LaFlam, J., & Green, M. (2011, January). *Status updates vs. private messages: The effects of Facebook communication on relationship closeness.* Poster presented at the meeting of the Society for Personality and Social Psychology, San Antonio, TX.

Carrère, S., & Gottman, J. M. (1999). Predicting divorce among newlyweds from the first three minutes of a marital conflict discussion. *Family Process, 38,* 293–301.

Carstensen, L. L., Isaacowitz, D. M., & Charles, S. T. (1999). Taking time seriously: A theory of socioemotional selectivity. *American Psychologist, 54,* 165–181.

Carton, J. S., Kessler, E. A., & Pape, C. L. (1999). Nonverbal decoding skills and relationship well-being in adults. *Journal of Nonverbal Behavior, 23,* 91–100.

Carver, C. S., & Scheier, M. F. (2009). Optimism. In M. R. Leary & R. H. Hoyle (Eds.), *Handbook of individual differences in social behavior* (pp. 330–342). New York: Guilford Press.

Cassidy, J., & Shaver, P. R. (Eds.). (2010). *Handbook of attachment* (2nd ed.). New York: Guilford Press.

Castro, F. N., & de Araújo Lopes, F. (2010). Romantic preferences in Brazilian undergraduate students: From the short term to the long term. *Journal of Sex Research, 47,* 1–7.

Cate, R. M., Levin, L. A., & Richmond, L. S. (2002). Premarital relationship stability: A review of recent research. *Journal of Social and Personal Relationships, 19,* 261–284.

Cate, R. M., Lloyd, S. A., Henton, J. M., & Larson, J. (1982). Fairness and reward level as predictors of relationship satisfaction. *Social Psychology Quarterly, 45,* 177–181.

Cate, R. M., Lloyd, S. A., & Long, E. (1988). The role of rewards and fairness in developing premarital relationships. *Journal of Marriage and the Family, 50,* 443–452.

Caughlin, J. P., Afifi, W. A., Carpenter-Theune, K. E., & Miller, L. E. (2005). Reasons for, and consequences of, revealing personal secrets in close relationships: A longitudinal study. *Personal Relationships, 12,* 43–59.

Caughlin, J. P., & Huston, T. L. (2006). The affective structure of marriage. In A. L. Vangelisti & D. Perlman (Eds.), *The Cambridge handbook of personal relationships* (pp. 131–155). New York: Cambridge University Press.

Caughlin, J. P., Huston, T. L., & Houts, R. M. (2000). How does personality matter in marriage? An examination of trait anxiety, interpersonal negativity, and marital satisfaction. *Journal of Personality and Social Psychology, 78,* 326–336.

Caughlin, J. P., & Scott, A. M. (2010). Toward a communication theory of the demand/withdraw pattern of interaction in interpersonal relationships. In S. Smith & S. Wilson (Eds.), *New directions in interpersonal communication research* (pp. 180–200). Thousand Oaks, CA: Sage.

Ceglian, C. P., & Gardner, S. (1999). Attachment style: A risk for multiple marriages? *Journal of Divorce & Remarriage, 31,* 125–139.

Centers for Disease Control and Prevention. (2011). *Understanding intimate partner violence.* Washington, DC: National Center for Injury Prevention and Control. Retrieved from http://www.cdc.gov/violenceprevention/pdf/IPV_factsheet-a.pdf

Chambers, J. R., Epley, N., Savitsky, K., & Windschitl, P. D. (2008). Knowing too much: Using private knowledge to predict how one is viewed by others. *Psychological Science, 19,* 542–548.

Chang-Schneider, C., & Swann, W. B., Jr. (2006, January). *Who abuses and who gets abused? Selection and perpetuation of unhealthy relationships.* Poster presented at the meeting of the Society for Personality and Social Psychology, Palm Springs, CA.

Chang-Schneider, C., & Swann, W. B., Jr. (2010). The role of uncertainty in self-evaluative processes: Another look at the cognitive-affective crossfire. In R. M. Arkin, K. C. Oleson, & P. J. Carroll (Eds.), *Handbook of the uncertain self* (pp. 216–231). New York: Psychology Press.

Chaplin, W. F., Phillips, J. B., Brown, J. D., Clanton, N. R., & Stein, J. L. (2000). Handshaking, gender, personality, and first impressions. *Journal of Personality and Social Psychology, 79,* 110–117.

Chartrand, T. L., Dalton, A. N., & Fitzsimons, G. J. (2007). Nonconscious relationship reactance: When significant others prime opposing goals. *Journal of Experimental Social Psychology, 43,* 719–726.

Chartrand, T.L., & van Baaren, R. (2009). Human mimicry. *Advances in Experimental Social Psychology, 41,* 219–274.

Cheek, J. M., & Buss, A. H. (1981). Shyness and sociability. *Journal of Personality and Social Psychology, 41,* 330–339.

Chen, G. M. (2011). Tweet this: A uses and gratifications perspective on how active Twitter use gratifies a need to connect with others. *Computers in Human Behavior, 27,* 755–762.

Chen, H., Cohen, P., Kasen, S., Johnson, J. G., Ehrensaft, M., & Gordon, K. (2006). Predicting conflict within romantic relationships during the transition to adulthood. *Personal Relationships, 13,* 411–427.

Chen, H., Luo, S., Yue, G., Xu, D., & Zhaoyang, R. (2009). Do birds of a feather flock together in China? *Personal Relationships, 16,* 167–186.

Chen, S., Fitzsimons, G. M., & Andersen, S. M. (2007). Automaticity in close relationships. In J. A. Bargh (Ed.), *Social psychology and the unconscious: The automaticity of higher mental processes* (pp. 133–172). New York: Psychology Press.

Chen, S., Lee-Chai, A. Y., & Bargh, J. A. (2001). Relationship orientation as a moderator of the effects of social power. *Journal of Personality and Social Psychology, 80,* 173–187.

Cheng, C. (2005). Processes underlying gender-role flexibility: Do androgynous individuals know more or know how to cope? *Journal of Personality, 73,* 645–673.

Cheng, C. M., Ferguson, M. J., & Chartrand, T. L. (2003, May). *Automatic evaluation of physical attractiveness: What is beautiful is automatically good.* Paper presented at the meeting of the American Psychological Society, Atlanta, GA.

Cherlin, A. J. (2009). *The marriage-go-round: The state of marriage and the family in America today.* New York: Knopf.

Cherlin, A. J. (2010). Demographic trends in the United States: A review of research in the 2000s. *Journal of Marriage and Family, 72,* 403–419.

Choi, N., Fuqua, D. R., & Newman, J. L. (2007). Hierarchical confirmatory factor analysis of the Bem Sex Role Inventory. *Educational and Psychological Measurement, 67,* 818–832.

Chopik, W. J., Edelstein, R. S., & Fraley R. C. (2011, January). *Adult attachment across the lifespan: Gender and relationship status moderate age-related differences in attachment orientations.* Poster presented at the meeting of the Society for Personality and Social Psychology, San Antonio, TX.

Christakis, N. A., & Fowler, J. H. (2009). *Connected: The surprising power of our social networks and how they shape our lives.* New York: Little, Brown.

Christensen, A., Baucom, B., Atkins, D. C., & Yi, J. (2010). Marital status and satisfaction five years following a randomized clinical trial comparing traditional versus integrative behavioral couple therapy. *Journal of Consulting and Clinical Psychology, 78,* 225–235.

Christensen, A., Eldridge, K., Catta-Preta, A. B., Lim, V. R., & Santagata, R. (2006). Cross-cultural consistency of the demand/withdraw interaction pattern in couples. *Journal of Marriage and Family, 68,* 1029–1044.

Christofides, E., Muise, A., & Desmarais, S. (2010, January). *The effect of personality factors in predicting information disclosure online.* Poster presented at the meeting of the Society for Personality and Social Psychology, Las Vegas, NV.

Churchill, A. C., & Davis, C. G. (2010). Realistic orientation and the transition to motherhood. *Journal of Social and Clinical Psychology, 29,* 39–67.

Ciarrochi, J., & Heaven, P. C. L. (2008). Learned social hopelessness: The role of explanatory style in predicting social support during adolescence. *Journal of Child Psychology and Psychiatry, 49,* 1279–1286.

Ciarrochi, J., Hynes, K., & Crittenden, N. (2005). Can men do better if they try harder: Sex and motivational effects on emotional awareness. *Cognition and Emotion, 19,* 133–141.

Civic, D. (2000). College students' reasons for nonuse of condoms within dating relationships. *Journal of Sex & Marital Therapy, 26,* 95–105.

Claffey, S. T., & Mickelson, K. D. (2009). Division of household labor and distress: The role of perceived fairness for employed mothers. *Sex Roles, 60,* 819–831.

Clark, A. P. (2004). Self-perceived attractiveness and masculinization predict women's sociosexuality. *Evolution and Human Behavior, 25,* 113–124.

Clark, C. L., Shaver, P. R., & Abrahams, M. F. (1999). Strategic behaviors in romantic relationship initiation. *Personality and Social Psychology Bulletin, 25,* 707–720.

Clark, J. K., & Wegener, D. T. (2008). Unpacking outcome dependency: Differentiating effects of dependency and outcome desirability on the processing of goal-relevant information. *Journal of Experimental Social Psychology, 44,* 586–599.

Clark, M. S. (1981). Noncomparability of benefits given and received: A cue to the existence of friendship. *Social Psychology Quarterly, 44,* 375–381.

Clark, M. S., & Finkel, E. J. (2005). Willingness to express emotion: The impact of relationship type, communal orientation, and their interaction. *Personal Relationships, 12,* 169–180.

Clark, M. S., & Grote, N. K. (1998). Why aren't indices of relationship costs always negatively related to indices of relationship quality? *Personality and Social Psychology Review, 2,* 2–17.

Clark, M. S., Lemay, E. P., Jr., Graham, S. M., Pataki, S. P., & Finkel, E. J. (2010). Ways of giving benefits in marriage: Norm use, relationship satisfaction, and attachment-related variability. *Psychological Science, 21,* 944–951.

Clark, M. S., & Mills, J. (1993). The difference between communal and exchange relationships: What it is and is not. *Personality and Social Psychology Bulletin, 15,* 684–691.

Clark, M. S., Pataki, S. P., & Carver, V. H. (1996). Some thoughts and findings on self-presentation of emotions in relationships. In G. J. O. Fletcher & J. Fitness (Eds.), *Knowledge structures in close relationships: A social psychological approach* (pp. 247–274). Mahwah, NJ: Erlbaum.

Clark, R. D., III, & Hatfield, E. (1989). Gender differences in receptivity to sexual offers. *Journal of Psychology and Human Sexuality, 2,* 39–55.

Clark, R. D., III, & Hatfield, E. (2003). Love in the afternoon. *Psychological Inquiry, 14,* 227–231.

Clarkwest, A. (2007). Spousal dissimilarity, race, and marital dissolution. *Journal of Marriage and Family, 69,* 639–653.

Claxton, A., & Perry-Jenkins, M. (2008). No fun anymore: Leisure and marital quality across the transition to parenthood. *Journal of Marriage and Family, 70,* 28–43.

Cleveland, H. H., Udry, J. R., & Chantala, K. (2001). Environmental and genetic influences on sex-typed behaviors and attitudes of male and female adolescents. *Personality and Social Psychology Bulletin, 27,* 1587–1598.

Clore, G. L., & Byrne, D. (1974). A reinforcement-affect model of attraction. In T. L. Huston (Ed.), *Foundations of interpersonal attraction* (pp. 143–170). New York: Academic Press.

Coan, J. A., Schaefer, H. S., & Davidson, R. J. (2006). Lending a hand: Social regulation of the neural response to threat. *Psychological Science, 17,* 1032–1039.

Cohen, S. (2004). Social relationships and health. *American Psychologist, 59,* 673–684.

Cohen, S., Doyle, W. J., Turner, R., Alper, C. M., & Skoner, D. P. (2003). Sociability and susceptibility to the common cold. *Psychological Science, 14,* 389–395.

Cohen, S., Klein, D. N., & O'Leary, D. (2007). The role of separation/divorce in relapse into and recovery from major depression. *Journal of Social and Personal Relationships, 24,* 855–873.

Cohn, D. (2010, June 4). At long last, divorce. *Pew Research Center.* Retrieved from http://pewresearch.org/pubs/1617/long-duration-marriage-end-divorce-gore

Cohn E. S., Goforth, E. C., & Brown, T. M. (2008, February). *In the eye of the beholder: Do behavior, reputation, and individual differences affect victim and perpetrator responsibility for acquaintance rape?* Poster presented at the meeting of the Society for Personality and Social Psychology, Albuquerque, NM.

Cole, T. (2001). Lying to the one you love: The use of deception in romantic relationships. *Journal of Social and Personal Relationships, 18,* 107–129.

Coleman, M., Ganong, L. H., & Wazzinik, K. (2007). *Family life in 20th century America.* Westport, CT: Greenwood Press.

Collins, N. L., & Allard, L. M. (2001). Cognitive representations of attachment: The content and function of working models. In G. J. O. Fletcher & M. S. Clark (Eds.), *Blackwell handbook of social psychology: Interpersonal processes* (pp. 60–85). Malden, MA: Blackwell.

Collins, N. L., & Feeney, B. C. (2004). Working models of attachment shape perceptions of social support: Evidence from experimental and observational studies. *Journal of Personality and Social Psychology, 87,* 363–383.

Collins, N. L., & Feeney, B. C. (2010). An attachment theoretical perspective on social support dynamics in couples: Normative processes and individual differences. In K. Sullivan & J. Davila (Eds.), *Support processes in intimate relationships* (pp. 89–120). New York: Oxford University Press.

Collins, N. L., Ford, M. B., Guichard, A. C., Kane, H. S., & Feeney, B. C. (2010). Responding to need in intimate relationships: Social support and caregiving processes in couples. In M. Mikulincer & P. R. Shaver (Eds.), *Prosocial motives, emotions, and behavior: The better angels of our nature* (pp. 367–389). Washington, DC: American Psychological Association.

Collins, N. L., Guichard, A. C., Ford, M. B., & Feeney, B. C. (2006). Responding to need in intimate relationships: Normative processes and individual differences. In M. Mikulincer & G. S. Goodman (Eds.), *Dynamics of romantic love: Attachment, caregiving, and sex* (pp. 149–189). New York: Guilford Press.

Collins, N. L., & Miller, L. C. (1994). Self-disclosure and liking: A meta-analytic review. *Psychological Bulletin, 116,* 457–475.

Coltrane, S., & Shih, K. Y. (2010). Gender and the division of labor. In J. Chrisler & D. McCreary (Eds.), *Handbook of gender research in psychology* (Vol. 2, pp. 401–422). New York: Springer.

Confer, J. C., Easton, J. A., Fleischman, D. S., Goetz, C. D., Lewis, D. M. G., Perilloux, C., & Buss, D. M. (2010). Evolutionary psychology: Controversies, questions, prospects, and limitations. *American Psychologist, 65,* 110–126.

Conley, T. D. (2011). Perceived proposer personality characteristics and gender differences in acceptance of casual sex offers. *Journal of Personality and Social Psychology, 100,* 309–329.

Conley, T. D., Roesch, S. C., Peplau, L. A., & Gold, M. S. (2009). A test of positive illusions versus shared reality models of relationship satisfaction among gay, lesbian, and heterosexual couples. *Journal of Applied Social Psychology, 39,* 1417–1431.

Connelly, B. S., & Ones, D. S. (2010). An other perspective on personality: Meta-analytic integration of observers' accuracy and predictive validity. *Psychological Bulletin, 136,* 1092–1122.

Coontz, S. (2005). *Marriage, a history: From obedience to intimacy or how love conquered marriage.* New York: Viking.

Cooper, M. L. (2006). Does drinking promote risky sexual behavior? A complex answer to a simple question. *Current Directions in Psychological Science, 15,* 19–23.

Cooper, M. L., Talley, A. E., Sheldon, M. S., Levitt, A., & Barber, L. L. (2008). A dyadic perspective on approach and avoidance motives for sexual behavior. In A. J. Elliot (Ed.), *Handbook of approach and avoidance motivation* (pp. 615–631). New York: Psychology Press.

Cooper, M., O'Donnell, D., Caryl, P. G., Morrison, R., & Bale, C. (2007). Chat-up lines as male displays: Effects of content, sex, and personality. *Personality and Individual Differences, 43,* 1075–1085.

Cooper, M. L., & Sheldon, M. S. (2002). Seventy years of research on personality and close relationships: Substantive and methodological trends over time. *Journal of Personality, 70,* 783–812.

Cornelius, T. L., & Alessi, G. (2007). Behavioral and physiological components of communication training: Does the topic affect the outcome? *Journal of Marriage and Family, 69,* 608–620.

Couch, L. L., & Jones, W. H. (1997). Conceptualizing levels of trust. *Journal of Research in Personality, 31,* 319–336.

Cowan, G., & Mills, R. D. (2004). Personal inadequacy and intimacy predictors of men's hostility toward women. *Sex Roles, 51,* 67–78.

Coyne, J. C., Rohrbaugh, M. J., Shoham, V., Sonnega, J. S., Nicklas, J. M., & Cranford, J. A. (2001). Prognostic importance of marital quality for survival of congestive heart failure. *American Journal of Cardiology, 88,* 526–529.

Coyne, S. M., Nelson, D. A., Graham-Kevan, N., Keister, E., & Grant, D. M. (2010). Mean on the screen: Psychopathy, relationship aggression, and aggression in the media. *Personality and Individual Differences, 48,* 288–293.

Crane, R. D., Dollahite, D. C., Griffin, W., & Taylor, V. L. (1987). Diagnosing relationships with spatial distance: An empirical test of a clinical principle. *Journal of Marital and Family Therapy, 13,* 307–310.

Crary, D. (2010, May 7). More older Americans open to nonmarital sex. *Houston Chronicle,* p. A6.

Crawford, M., & Popp, D. (2003). Sexual double standards: A review and methodological critique of two decades of research. *Journal of Sex Research, 40,* 13–26.

Crocker, J., & Luhtanen, R. K. (2003). Level of self-esteem and contingencies of self-worth: Unique effects on academic, social, and financial problems in college students. *Personality and Social Psychology Bulletin, 29,* 701–712.

Cross, S. E., Hardin, E. E., & Swing, B. G. (2009). Independent, relational, and collective-interdependent self construals. In M. R. Leary & R. H. Hoyle (Eds.), *Handbook of individual differences in social behavior* (pp. 512–526). New York: Guilford Press.

Cross, S. E., & Morris, M. L. (2003). Getting to know you: The relational self-construal, relational cognition, and well-being. *Personality and Social Psychology Bulletin, 29,* 512–523.

Crown, L., & Roberts, L. J. (2007). Against their will: Young women's nonagentic sexual experiences. *Journal of Social and Personal Relationships, 24,* 385–405.

Cui, M., Conger, R. D., Bryant, C. M., & Elder, G. H. (2002). Parental behavior and the quality of adolescent friendships: A social contextual perspective. *Journal of Marriage and the Family, 64,* 676–689.

Cui, M., & Fincham, F. D. (2010). The differential effects of parental divorce and marital conflict on young adult romantic relationships. *Personal Relationships, 17,* 331–343.

Cunningham, M. R. (1989). Reactions to heterosexual opening gambits: Female selectivity and male responsiveness. *Personality and Social Psychology Bulletin, 15,* 27–41.

Cunningham, M. R., & Barbee, A. P. (2008). Prelude to a kiss: Nonverbal flirting, opening gambits, and other communication dynamics in the initiation of romantic relationships. In S. Sprecher, A. Wenzel, & J. Harvey (Eds.), *Handbook of relationship initiation* (pp. 97–120). New York: Psychology Press.

Cunningham, M. R., Barbee, A. P., & Philhower, C. L. (2002). Dimensions of facial physical attractiveness: The intersection of biology and culture. In G. Rhodes & L. A. Zebrowitz (Eds.), *Facial attractiveness: Evolutionary, cognitive and social perspectives* (pp. 193–238). Westport, CT: Ablex.

Cunningham, M. R., Roberts, A. R., Barbee, A. P., Druen, P. B., & Wu, C. (1995). "Their ideas of beauty are, on the whole, the same as ours": Consistency and variability in the cross-cultural perception of female physical attractiveness. *Journal of Personality and Social Psychology, 68,* 261–279.

Cunningham, M. R., Shamblen, S. R., Barbee, A. P., & Ault, L. K. (2005). Social allergies in romantic relationships: Behavioral repetition, emotional sensitization, and dissatisfaction in dating couples. *Personal Relationships, 12,* 273–295.

Cunradi, C. B., Caetano, R., & Schafer, J. (2002). Socioeconomic predictors of intimate partner violence among White, Black, and Hispanic couples in the United States. *Journal of Family Violence, 17,* 377–389.

Cupach, W. R. (2007). "You're bugging me!": Complaints and criticism from a partner. In B. Spitzberg & W. Cupach (Eds.), *The dark side of interpersonal communication* (2nd ed., pp. 143–168). Mahwah, NJ: Erlbaum.

Cupach, W. R., & Spitzberg, B. H. (Eds.). (2011). *The dark side of close relationships II*. New York: Routledge.

Cuperman, R., & Ickes, W. (2009). Big five predictors of behavior and perceptions in initial dyadic interactions: Personality similarity helps extraverts and introverts, but hurts "disagreeables." *Journal of Personality and Social Psychology, 97*, 667–684.

Curtis, R. C., & Miller, K. (1986). Believing another likes or dislikes you: Behaviors making the beliefs come true. *Journal of Personality and Social Psychology, 51*, 284–290.

Custer, L., Holmberg, D., Blair, K., & Orbuch, T. L. (2008). "So how did you two meet?" Narratives of relationship initiation. In S. Sprecher, A. Wenzel, & J. Harvey (Eds.), *Handbook of relationship initiation* (pp. 453–470). New York: Psychology Press.

Cutrona, C. E. (1982). Transition to college: Loneliness and the process of social adjustment. In L. A. Peplau & D. Perlman (Eds.), *Loneliness: A sourcebook of current theory, research, and therapy* (pp. 291–309). New York: Wiley Interscience.

Cutrona, C. E., Russell, D. W., de la Mora, A., & Wallace, R. B. (1997). Loneliness and nursing home admissions among rural older adults. *Psychology and Aging, 12*, 574–589.

D'Onofrio, B. M., Turkheimer, E., Harden, K. P., Slutske, W. S., Heath, A. C., Madden, P. A. F., & Martin, N. G. (2007). A genetically informed study of the intergenerational transmission of marital instability. *Journal of Marriage and Family, 69*, 793–809.

Daigen, V., & Holmes, J. G. (2000). Don't interrupt! A good rule for marriage? *Personal Relationships, 7*, 185–201.

Dailey, R. M., Rossetto, K. R., Pfiester, A., & Surra, C. A. (2009). A qualitative analysis of on-again/off-again romantic relationships: "It's up and down, and all around." *Journal of Social and Personal Relationships, 26*, 443–466.

Dal Cin, S., Holmes, J. G., & Young, S. B. (2005, January). *Goal compatibility and relationship outcomes: It's the little things that matter.* Paper presented at the meeting of the Society for Personality and Social Psychology, New Orleans, LA.

Daly, J. A., Hogg, E., Sacks, D., Smith, M., & Zimring, L. (1983). Sex and relationship affect social self-grooming. *Journal of Nonverbal Behavior, 7*, 183–189.

Daneback, K., Cooper, A., & Månsson, S. (2005). An Internet study of cybersex participants. *Archives of Sexual Behavior, 34*, 321–328.

Darley, J. M., & Gross, P. H. (1983). A hypothesis-confirming bias in labeling effects. *Journal of Personality and Social Psychology, 44*, 20–33.

Davies, A. P. C., Shackelford, T. K., & Hass, R. G. (2007). When a "poach" is not a poach: Redefining human mate poaching and re-estimating its frequency. *Archives of Sexual Behavior, 36*, 702–716.

Davies, A. P. C., Shackelford, T. K., & Hass, R. G. (2010). Sex differences in perceptions of benefits and costs of mate poaching. *Personality and Individual Differences, 49*, 441–445.

Davila, J. & Cobb, R. J. (2004). Predictors of change in attachment security during adulthood. In W. S. Rholes & J. A. Simpson (Eds.), *Adult attachment: Theory, research, and clinical implications* (pp. 133–156). New York: Guilford Press.

Davila, J., & Kashy, D. A. (2009). Secure base processes in couples: Daily associations between support experiences and attachment security. *Journal of Family Psychology, 23*, 76–88.

Davis, D., Shaver, P. R., & Vernon, M. L. (2004). Attachment style and subjective motivations for sex. *Personality and Social Psychology Bulletin, 30*, 1076–1090.

Davis, D., Shaver, P. R., Widaman, K. F., Vernon, M. L., Follette, W. C., & Beitz, K. (2006). "I can't get no satisfaction": Insecure attachment, inhibited sexual communication, and sexual dissatisfaction. *Personal Relationships, 13*, 465–483.

Davis, K. E., Swan, S. C., & Gambone, L. J. (2011). Why doesn't he just leave me alone? Persistent pursuit: A critical review of theories and evidence. *Sex Roles.* DOI: 10.1007/s11199-010-9882-3

Davis, S. N., Greenstein, T. N., & Marks, J. P. G. (2007). Effects of union type on division of household labor. *Journal of Family Issues, 28*, 1246–1272.

DeAndrea, D. C., Tong, S. T., & Walther, J. B. (2011). Dark sides of computer-mediated interaction. In W. Cupach & B. Spitzberg (Eds.), *The dark side of close relationships II* (pp. 95–118). New York: Routledge.

De Bro, S. C., Campbell, S. M., & Peplau, L. A. (1994). Influencing a partner to use a condom: A college student perspective. *Psychology of Women Quarterly, 18,* 165–182.

Deci, E. L., & Ryan, R. M. (2000). The 'what' and 'why' of goal pursuits: Human needs and the self-determination of behavior. *Psychological Inquiry, 11,* 227–268.

de Graaf, H., Vanwesenbeeck, I., Meijer, S., Woertman, L., & Meeus, W. (2009). Sexual trajectories during adolescence: Relation to demographic characteristics and sexual risk. *Archives of Sexual Behavior, 38,* 276–282.

DeGue, S., & DiLillo, D. (2005). "You would if you loved me": Toward an improved conceptual and etiological understanding of nonphysical male sexual coercion. *Aggression and Violent Behavior, 10,* 513–532.

de Jong Gierveld, J., van Tilburg, T., & Dykstra, P. A. (2006). Loneliness and social isolation. In A. L. Vangelisti & D. Perlman (Eds.), *The Cambridge handbook of personal relationships* (pp. 485–499). New York: Cambridge University Press.

De La Ronde, C., & Swann, W. B., Jr. (1998). Partner verification: Restoring shattered images of our intimates. *Journal of Personality and Social Psychology, 75,* 374–382.

della Cava, M. R. (2010, February 10). 'Friends' no more? *USA Today,* pp. 1A–2A.

Della Sala, S. (Ed.). (2010). *Forgetting.* New York: Psychology Press.

Denissen, J. J. A., Penke, L., Schmitt, D. P., & van Aken, M. A. G. (2008). Self-esteem reactions to social interactions: Evidence for sociometer mechanisms across days, people, and nations. *Journal of Personality and Social Psychology, 95,* 181–196.

Denrell, J. (2005). Why most people disapprove of me: Experience sampling in impression formation. *Psychological Review, 112,* 951–978.

Denton, W. H., & Burleson, B. R. (2007). The Initiator Style Questionnaire: A scale to assess initiator tendency in couples. *Personal Relationships, 14,* 245–268.

DePaulo, B. M. (1994). Spotting lies: Can humans learn to do better? *Current Directions in Psychological Science, 3,* 83–86

DePaulo, B. (2006). *Singled out: How singles are stereotyped, stigmatized, and ignored, and still live happily ever after.* New York: St. Martin's Press.

DePaulo, B. (2011). Living single: Lightening up those dark, dopey myths. In W. Cupach & B. Spitzberg (Eds.), *The dark side of close relationships II* (pp. 409–438). New York: Routledge.

DePaulo, B. M., Ansfield, M. E., Kirkendol, S. E., & Boden, J. M. (2004). Serious lies. *Basic and Applied Social Psychology, 26,* 147–167.

DePaulo, B. M., & Bell, K. L. (1996). Truth and investment: Lies are told to those who care. *Journal of Personality and Social Psychology, 71,* 703–716.

DePaulo, B. M., Charlton, K., Cooper, H., Lindsay, J. J., & Muhlenbruck, L. (1997). The accuracy–confidence correlation in the detection of deception. *Personality and Social Psychology Review, 1,* 346–357.

DePaulo, B. M., & Kashy, D. A. (1998). Everyday lies in close and casual relationships. *Journal of Personality and Social Psychology, 74,* 63–79.

DePaulo, B. M., Kashy, D. A., Kirkendol, S. E., Wyer, M. M., & Epstein, J. A. (1996). Lying in everyday life. *Journal of Personality and Social Psychology, 70,* 979–995.

DePaulo, B. M., Lanier, K., & Davis, T. (1983). Detecting the deceit of the motivated liar. *Journal of Personality and Social Psychology, 45,* 1096–1103.

DePaulo, B. M., Lindsay, J. J., Malone, B. E., Muhlenbruck, L., Charlton, K., & Cooper, H. (2003). Cues to deception. *Psychological Bulletin, 129,* 74–112.

DePaulo, B. M., Morris, W. L., & Sternglanz, R. W. (2009). When the truth hurts: Deception in the name of kindness. In A. L. Vangelisti (Ed.), *Feeling hurt in close relationships* (pp. 167–190). New York: Cambridge University Press.

DePaulo, B. M., Stone, J. I., & Lassiter, G. D. (1985). Telling ingratiating lies: Effects of target sex and target attractiveness on verbal and nonverbal deceptive success. *Journal of Personality and Social Psychology, 48,* 1191–1203.

Derlega, V. J., Winstead, B. A., & Greene, K. (2008). Self-disclosure and starting a close relationship. In S. Sprecher, A. Wenzel, & J. Harvey (Eds.), *Handbook of relationship initiation* (pp. 153–174). New York: Psychology Press.

Dermer, M., & Pyszczynski, T. A. (1978). Effects of erotica upon men's loving and liking responses for women they love. *Journal of Personality and Social Psychology, 36,* 1302–1309.

DeSteno, D., Bartlett, M. Y., Braverman, J., & Salovey, P. (2002). Sex differences in jealousy: Evolutionary mechanism or artifact of measurement? *Journal of Personality and Social Psychology, 83,* 1103–1116.

DeSteno, D. A., & Salovey, P. (1994). Jealousy in close relationships: Multiple perspectives on the green-eyed monster. In A. L. Weber & J. H. Harvey (Eds.), *Perspectives on close relationships* (pp. 217–242). Boston: Allyn & Bacon.

DeSteno, D. A., & Salovey, P. (1996). Evolutionary origins of sex differences in jealousy? Questioning the "fitness" of the model. *Psychological Science, 7,* 367–372.

DeSteno, D., Valdesolo, P., & Bartlett, M. Y. (2006). Jealousy and the threatened self: Getting to the heart of the green-eyed monster. *Journal of Personality and Social Psychology, 91,* 626–641.

Devine, P. G., & Monteith, M. J. (1999). Automaticity and control in stereotyping. In S. Chaiken & Y. Trope (Eds.), *Dual-process theories in social psychology* (pp. 339–360). New York: Guilford Press.

de Visser, R. O., Rissel, C. E., Richters, J., & Smith, A. M. A. (2007). The impact of sexual coercion on psychological, physical, and sexual well-being in a representative sample of Australian women. *Archives of Sexual Behavior, 36,* 676–686.

De Vogli, R., Chandola, T., & Marmot, M. G. (2007). Negative aspects of close relationships and heart disease. *Archives of Internal Medicine, 167,* 1951–1957.

DeWall, C. N. (2009). The pain of exclusion: Using insights from neuroscience to understand emotional and behavioral responses to social exclusion. In M. J. Harris (Ed.), *Bullying, rejection, and peer victimization: A social cognitive neuroscience perspective* (pp. 201–224). New York: Springer.

DeWall, C. N., & Baumeister, R. F. (2006). Alone but feeling no pain: Effects of social exclusion on physical pain tolerance and pain threshold, affective forecasting, and interpersonal empathy. *Journal of Personality and Social Psychology, 91,* 1–15.

DeWall, C. N., MacDonald, G., Webster, G. D., Masten, C. L., Baumeister, R. F., Powell, C.,... Eisenberger, N. I. (2010). Acetaminophen reduces social pain: Behavioral and neural evidence. *Psychological Science, 21,* 931–937.

DeWall, C. N., Twenge, J. M., Gitter, S. A., & Baumeister, R. F. (2009). It's the thought that counts: The role of hostile cognition in shaping aggressive responses to social exclusion. *Journal of Personality and Social Psychology, 96,* 45–59.

Dewsbury, D. A. (1981). Effects of novelty on copulatory behavior: The Coolidge effect and related phenomena. *Psychological Bulletin, 89,* 464–482.

Diamond, L. M. (2004). Emerging perspectives on distinctions between romantic love and sexual desire. *Current Directions in Psychological Science, 13,* 116–119.

Diamond, L. M. (2006). The intimate same-sex relationships of sexual minorities. In A. Vangelisti & D. Perlman (Eds.), *The Cambridge handbook of personal relationships* (pp. 293–312). New York: Cambridge University Press.

Diamond, L. M., & Fagundes, C. P. (2010). Psychobiological research on attachment. *Journal of Social and Personal Relationships, 27,* 218–225.

Diener, E., Gohm, C. L., Suh, E., & Oishi, S. (2000). Similarity of the relations between marital status and subjective well-being across cultures. *Journal of Cross-Cultural Psychology, 31,* 419–436.

Dillow, M. R., Dunleavy, K. N., & Weber, K. D. (2009). The impact of relational characteristics and reasons for topic avoidance on relational closeness. *Communication Quarterly, 57,* 205–223.

Dindia, K. (2002). Self-disclosure research: Knowledge through meta-analysis. In M. Allen, & R. W. Preiss et al. (Eds.), *Interpersonal communication research: Advances through meta-analysis* (pp. 169–185). Mahwah, NJ: Erlbaum.

Dindia, K. (2006). Men are from North Dakota, women are from South Dakota. In K. Dindia & D. J. Canary (Eds.), *Sex differences and similarities in communication* (pp. 3–20). Mahwah, NJ: Erlbaum.

Dindia, K., & Timmerman, L. (2003). Accomplishing romantic relationships. In J. O. Greene & B. R. Burleson (Eds.), *Handbook of communication and social interaction skills* (pp. 685–721). Mahwah, NJ: Erlbaum.

Dinero, R. E., Conger, R. D., Shaver, P. R., Widaman, K. F., & Larsen-Rife, D. (2008). Influence of family of origin and adult romantic partners on romantic attachment security. *Journal of Family Psychology, 22,* 622–632.

Dion, K. K., Berscheid, E., & Walster, E. (1972). What is beautiful is good. *Journal of Personality and Social Psychology, 24,* 285–290.

DiPaola, B. M., Roloff, M. E., & Peters, K. M. (2010). College students' expectations of conflict intensity: A self-fulfilling prophecy. *Communication Quarterly, 58,* 59–76.

Ditzen, B., Schaer, M., Gabriel, B., Bodenmann, G., Ehlert, U., & Heinrichs, M. (2009). Intranasal oxytocin increases positive communication and reduces cortisol levels during couple conflict. *Biological Psychiatry, 65,* 728–731.

Dixson, B. J., Dixson, A. F., Bishop, P. J., & Parish, A. (2010). Human physique and sexual attractiveness in men and women: A New Zealand–U.S. comparative study. *Archives of Sexual Behavior, 39,* 798–806.

Dixson, B. J., Grimshaw, G. M., Linklater, W. L., & Dixson, A. F. (2011). Eye-tracking of men's preferences for waist-to-hip ratio and breast size of women. *Archives of Sexual Behavior, 40,* 43–50.

Donaghue, N., & Fallon, B. J. (2003). Gender-role self-stereotyping and the relationship between equity and satisfaction in close relationships. *Sex Roles, 48,* 217–230.

Donahue, D. (2007, January 18). Self-help for body and soul. *USA Today,* p. 5D.

Donnellan, M. B., Conger, R. D., & Bryant, C. M. (2004). The Big Five and enduring marriages. *Journal of Research in Personality, 38,* 481–504.

Dooley, T. (2010, March 1). This is not your parents' marriage. *Houston Chronicle,* pp. D1–D2.

Doss, B. D., Atkins, D. C., & Christensen, A. (2003). Who's dragging their feet? Husbands and wives seeking marital therapy. *Journal of Marital & Family Therapy, 29,* 165–177.

Doss, B. D., Rhoades, G. K., Stanley, S. M., & Markman, H. J. (2009). The effect of the transition to parenthood on relationship quality: An 8-year prospective study. *Journal of Personality and Social Psychology, 96,* 601–619.

Doss, B. D., Simpson, L. E., & Christensen, A. (2004). Why do couples seek marital therapy? *Professional Psychology: Research and Practice, 35,* 608–614.

Doumas, D. M., Pearson, C. L., Elgin, J. E., & McKinley, L. L. (2008). Adult attachment as a risk factor for intimate partner violence: The "mispairing" of partners' attachment styles. *Journal of Interpersonal Violence, 23,* 616–634.

Downs, A. C., & Lyons, P. M. (1991). Natural observations of the links between attractiveness and initial legal judgments. *Personality and Social Psychology Bulletin, 17,* 541–547.

Drigotas, S. M., Rusbult, C. E., Wieselquist, J., & Whitton, S. W. (1999). Close partner as sculptor of the ideal self: Behavioral affirmation and the Michelangelo phenomenon. *Journal of Personality and Social Psychology, 77,* 293–323.

Driscoll, R., Davis, K. W., & Lipetz, M. E. (1972). Parental interference and romantic love. *Journal of Personality and Social Psychology, 24,* 1–10.

Dunbar, N. E., & Burgoon, J. K. (2005). Perceptions of power and interactional dominance in interpersonal relationships. *Journal of Social and Personal Relationships, 22,* 207–233.

Dunleavy, K. N., & Booth-Butterfield, M. (2009). Idiomatic communication in the stages of coming together and falling apart. *Communication Quarterly, 57,* 416–432.

Dunn, M. J., Brinton, S., & Clark, L. (2010). Universal sex differences in online advertisers' age preferences: Comparing data from 14 cultures and 2 religious groups. *Evolution and Human Behavior, 31,* 383–393.

Duntley, J. D., & Buss, D. M. (2011). The evolution of stalking. *Sex Roles.* DOI: 10.1007/s11199-010-9832-0

Dush, C. M. K., & Amato, P. R. (2005). Consequences of relationship status and quality for subjective well-being. *Journal of Social and Personal Relationships, 22,* 607–627.

Dutton, D. G. (2010). Anger in intimate relationships. In M. Potegal, G. Stemmier, & C. Spielberger (Eds.), *International handbook of anger: Constituent and concomitant biological, psychological, and social processes* (pp. 535–544). New York: Springer.

Dutton, D. G., & Aron, A. P. (1974). Some evidence for heightened sexual attraction under conditions of high anxiety. *Journal of Personality and Social Psychology, 30,* 510–517.

Dweck, S., & Ivey, M. (1998). *Baby, all those curves and me with no brakes: Over 500 new no-fail pickup lines for men and women.* New York: Hyperion.

Dworkin, S. L., & O'Sullivan, L. (2005). Actual versus desired initiation patterns among a sample of college men: Tapping disjunctures within traditional male sexual scripts. *Journal of Sex Research, 42,* 150–158.

Dykstra, P. A., & Fokkema, T. (2007). Social and emotional loneliness among divorced and married men and women: Comparing the deficit and cognitive perspectives. *Basic and Applied Social Psychology, 29,* 1–12.

Eagly, A. H., & Diekman, A. B. (2003). The malleability of sex differences in response to changing social roles. In L. G. Aspinwall & U. M. Staudinger (Eds.), *A psychology of human strengths: Fundamental questions and future directions for a positive psychology* (pp. 103–115). Washington, DC: American Psychological Association.

Eaker, E. D., Sullivan, L. M., Kelly-Hayes, M., D'Agostino, R. B., Sr., & Benjamin, E. J. (2007). Marital status, marital strain, and risk of coronary heart disease or total mortality: The Framingham Offspring Study. *Psychosomatic Medicine, 69,* 509–513.

Eastwick, P. W. (2009). Beyond the Pleistocene: Using phylogeny and constraint to inform the evolutionary psychology of human mating. *Psychological Bulletin, 135,* 794–821.

Eastwick, P. W., & Finkel, E. J. (2008). Sex differences in mate preferences revisited: Do people know what they initially desire in a romantic partner? *Journal of Personality and Social Psychology, 94,* 245–264.

Eastwick, P. W., Finkel, E. J., Krishnamurti, T., & Loewenstein, G. (2008). Mispredicting distress following romantic breakup: Revealing the time course of the affective forecasting error. *Journal of Experimental Social Psychology, 44,* 800–807.

Eastwick, P. W., Finkel, E. J., Mochon, D., & Ariely, D. (2007). Selective versus unselective romantic desire. *Psychological Science, 18,* 317–319.

Eastwick, P. W., Richeson, J. A., Son, D., & Finkel, E. J. (2009). Is love colorblind? Political orientation and interracial romantic desire. *Personality and Social Psychology Bulletin, 35,* 1258–1268.

Eastwick. P. W., Saigal, S. D., & Finkel, E. J. (2010). Smooth operating: A structural analysis of social behavior (SASB) perspective on initial romantic encounters. *Social Psychological and Personality Science, 1,* 344–352.

Ebbesen, E. B., Kjos, G. L., & Konecni, V. J. (1976). Spatial ecology: Its effects on the choice of friends and enemies. *Journal of Experimental Social Psychology, 12,* 505–518.

Ebel-Lam, A. P., MacDonald, T. K., Zanna, M. P., & Fong, G. T. (2009). An experimental investigation of the interactive effects of alcohol and sexual arousal on intentions to have unprotected sex. *Basic and Applied Social Psychology, 31,* 226–233.

Eberhart, N. K., & Hammen, C. L. (2006). Interpersonal predictors of onset of depression during the transition to adulthood. *Personal Relationships, 13,* 195–206.

Eberhart, N. K., & Hammen, C. L. (2010). Interpersonal style, stress, and depression: An examination of transactional and diathesis-stress models. *Journal of Social and Clinical Psychology, 29,* 23–38.

Edelstein, R. S., & Gillath, O. (2008). Avoiding interference: Adult attachment and emotional processing biases. *Personality and Social Psychology Bulletin, 34,* 171–181.

Edlund, J. E., & Sagarin, B. J. (2009). Sex differences in jealousy: Misinterpretation of nonsignificant results as refuting the theory. *Personal Relationships, 16,* 67–78.

Edlund, J. E., & Sagarin, B. J. (2010). Mate value and mate preferences: An investigation into decisions made with and without constraints. *Personality and Individual Differences, 49,* 835–839.

Edwards, G. L., & Barber, B. L. (2010). Women may underestimate their partners' desires to use condoms: Possible implications for behaviour. *Journal of Sex Research, 47,* 59–65.

Edwards, K. M., Gidycz, C. A., & Murphy, M. J. (2011). College women's stay/leave decisions in abusive dating relationships: A prospective analysis of an expanded investment model. *Journal of Interpersonal Violence, 26,* 1446–1462.

Edwards, R., Bello, R., Brandau-Brown, F., & Hollems, D. (2001). The effects of loneliness and verbal aggressiveness on message interpretation. *Southern Communication Journal, 66,* 139–150.

Eidelson, R. J. (1980). Interpersonal satisfaction and level of involvement: A curvilinear relationship. *Journal of Personality and Social Psychology, 39,* 460–470.

Eidelson, R. J., & Epstein, N. (1982). Cognition and relationship maladjustment: Development of a measure of dysfunctional relationship beliefs. *Journal of Consulting and Clinical Psychology, 50,* 715–720.

Eisenberg, A. R. (1992). Conflicts between mothers and their young children. *Merrill-Palmer Quarterly, 38,* 21–43.

Eisenberger, R., Lynch, P., Aselage, J., & Rohdieck, S. (2004). Who takes the most revenge? Individual differences in negative reciprocity norm endorsement. *Personality and Social Psychology Bulletin, 30,* 787–799.

Ekman, P., & O'Sullivan, M. (1991). Who can catch a liar? *American Psychologist, 46,* 913–920.

Eldridge, K. A., & Christensen, A. (2002). Demand-withdraw communication during couple conflict: A review and analysis. In P. Noller & J. A. Feeney (Eds.), *Understanding marriage: Developments in the study of couple interaction* (pp. 289–322). Cambridge, England: Cambridge University Press.

Elfenbein, H. A., & Ambady, N. (2003). Universals and cultural differences in recognizing emotions. *Current Directions in Psychological Science, 12,* 159–164.

Elizur, Y., & Mintzer, A. (2001). A framework for the formation of gay male identity: Processes associated with adult attachment style and support from family and friends. *Archives of Sexual Behavior, 30,* 143–167.

Elliot, A. J., & Niesta, D. (2008). Romantic red: Red enhances men's attraction to women. *Journal of Personality and Social Psychology, 95,* 1150–1164.

Elliot, A. J., Kayser, D. N., Greitemeyer, T., Lichtenfeld, S., Gramzow, R. H., Maier, M. A., & Liu, H. (2010). Red, rank, and romance in women viewing men. *Journal of Experimental Psychology: General, 139,* 399–417.

Elliott, S., & Umberson, D. (2008). The performance of desire: Gender and sexual negotiation in long-term marriages. *Journal of Marriage and Family, 70,* 391–406.

Ellis, A. (1993). The advantages and disadvantages of self-help therapy materials. *Professional Psychology: Research & Practice, 24,* 335–339.

Ellis, B. J., Simpson, J. A., & Campbell, L. (2002). Trait-specific dependence in romantic relationships. *Journal of Personality, 70,* 611–659.

Ellyson, S. L., Dovidio, J. F., & Brown, C. E. (1992). The look of power: Gender differences and similarities in visual dominance behavior. In C. Ridgeway (Ed.), *Gender and interaction: The role of microstructures in inequality* (pp. 50–80). New York: Springer-Verlag.

Else-Quest, N. M., Hyde, J. S., & DeLamater, J. D. (2005). Context counts: Long-term sequelae of premarital intercourse or abstinence. *Journal of Sex Research, 42,* 102–112.

Elwert, F., & Christakis, N. A. (2008). The effect of widowhood on mortality by the causes of death of both spouses. *American Journal of Public Health, 98,* 2092–2098.

Emmers, T. M., & Dindia, K. (1995). The effect of relational stage and intimacy on touch: An extension of Guerrero and Andersen. *Personal Relationships, 2,* 225–236.

Enke, A. (2011, January). *The effectiveness of female date-initiation tactics.* Poster presented at the meeting of the Society for Personality and Social Psychology, San Antonio, TX.

Epley, N., Akalis, S., Waytz, A., & Cacioppo, J. T. (2008). Creating social connection through inferential reproduction: Loneliness and perceived agency in gadgets, gods, and greyhounds. *Psychological Science, 19,* 114–120.

Epley, N., & Whitchurch, E. (2008). Mirror, mirror on the wall: Enhancement in self-recognition. *Personality and Social Psychology Bulletin, 34,* 1159–1170.

Epstein, N., & Baucom, D. H. (2002). *Enhanced cognitive-behavioral therapy for couples: A contextual approach.* Washington, DC: American Psychological Association.

Erbert, L. A. (2000). Conflict and dialectics: Perceptions of dialectical contradictions in marital conflict. *Journal of Social and Personal Relationships, 17,* 638–659.

Erchull, M. J., Liss, M., Axelson, S. J., Staebell, S. E., & Askari, S. F. (2010). Well…she wants it more: Perceptions of social norms about desires for marriage and children and anticipated chore participation. *Psychology of Women Quarterly, 34,* 253–260.

Erikson, E. (1950). *Childhood and society.* New York: Norton.

Eskridge, W. N., Jr., & Spedale, D. R. (2006). *Gay marriage: For better or worse? What we've learned from the evidence.* New York: Oxford University Press.

Essayli, J. H., Darby, R. S., Harris, C. R., & Larsen, B. (2010, January). *Infidelity, confessions, and relationship dissolution.* Poster presented at the meeting of the Society for Personality and Social Psychology, Las Vegas, NV.

Etcheverry, P. E., & Agnew, C. R. (2004). Subjective norms and the prediction of romantic relationship state and fate. *Personal Relationships, 11,* 409–428.

Etcheverry, P. E., & Le, B. (2005). Thinking about commitment: Accessibility of commitment and prediction of relationship persistence, accommodation, and willingness to sacrifice. *Personal Relationships, 12,* 103–123.

Etcheverry, P. E., Le, B., & Charania, M. R. (2008). Perceived versus reported social referent approval and romantic relationship commitment and persistence. *Personal Relationships, 15,* 281–295.

Exline, J. J., Baumeister, R. F., Bushman, B. J., Campbell, W. K., & Finkel, E. J. (2004). Too proud to let go: Narcissistic entitlement as a barrier to forgiveness. *Journal of Personality and Social Psychology, 87,* 894–912.

Exline, J. J., Baumeister, R. F., Zell, A. L., Kraft, A. J., & Witvliet, C. V. O. (2008). Not so innocent: Does seeing one's own capability for wrongdoing predict forgiveness? *Journal of Personality and Social Psychology, 94,* 495–515.

Fabricius, W. V. (2003). Listening to children of divorce: New findings that diverge from Wallerstein, Lewis, and Blakeslee. *Family Relations, 52,* 385–396.

Falbo, T. (1982). PAQ types and power strategies used in intimate relationships. *Psychology of Women Quarterly, 6,* 399–405.

Falbo, T., & Peplau, L. A. (1980). Power strategies in intimate relationships. *Journal of Personality and Social Psychology, 38,* 618–628.

Farley, S. D. (2008). Attaining status at the expense of likeability: Pilfering power through conversational interruption. *Journal of Nonverbal Behavior, 32,* 241–260.

Farris, C., Treat, T. A., Viken, R. J., & McFall, R. M. (2008a). Perceptual mechanisms that characterize gender differences in decoding women's sexual intent. *Psychological Science, 19,* 348–354.

Farris, C., Treat, T. A., Viken, R. J., & McFall, R. M. (2008b). Sexual coercion and the misperception of sexual intent. *Clinical Psychology Review, 28,* 48–66.

Farvid, P., & Braun, V. (2006). 'Most of us guys are raring to go anytime, anyplace, anywhere': Male and female sexuality in *Cleo* and *Cosmo. Sex Roles, 55,* 295–310.

Fast, N. J., Gruenfeld, D. H., Sivanathan, N., & Galinsky, A. D. (2009). Illusory control: A generative force behind power's far-reaching effects. *Psychological Science, 20,* 502–508.

Feeney, B. C. (2004). A secure base: Responsive support of goal strivings and exploration in adult intimate relationships. *Journal of Personality and Social Psychology, 87,* 631–648.

Feeney, B. C. (2007). The Dependency Paradox in close relationships: Accepting dependence promotes independence. *Journal of Personality and Social Psychology, 92,* 268–285.

Feeney, B. C., & Cassidy, J. (2003). Reconstructive memory related to adolescent-parent conflict interactions: The influence of attachment-related representations on immediate perceptions and changes in perceptions over time. *Journal of Personality and Social Psychology, 85,* 945–955.

Feeney, J. A. (1999). Adult attachment, emotional control, and marital satisfaction. *Personal Relationships, 6,* 169–185.

Feeney, J. A. (2002). Attachment, marital interaction, and relationship satisfaction: A diary study. *Personal Relationships, 9,* 39–55.

Feeney, J. A. (2005). Hurt feelings in couple relationships: Exploring the role of attachment and perceptions of personal injury. *Personal Relationships, 12,* 253–271.

Feeney, J. A., & Hill, A. (2006). Victim-perpetrator differences in reports of hurtful events. *Journal of Social and Personal Relationships, 23,* 587–608.

Feeney, J. A., & Noller, P. (2004). Attachment and sexuality in close relationships. In J. H. Harvey, A. Wenzel, & S. Sprecher (Eds.), *The handbook of sexuality in close relationships* (pp. 183–201). Mahwah, NJ: Erlbaum.

Feeney, J. A., Noller, P., & Roberts, N. (2000). Attachment and close relationships. In C. Hendrick & S. S. Hendrick (Eds.), *Close relationships: A sourcebook* (pp. 185–201). Thousand Oaks, CA: Sage.

Fehr, B. (1996). *Friendship processes.* Thousand Oaks, CA: Sage.

Fehr, B. (1999). Stability and commitment in friendships. In J. M. Adams & W. H. Jones (Eds.), *Handbook of interpersonal commitment and relationship stability* (pp. 259–280). Dordrecht, Netherlands: Kluwer.

Fehr, B. (2001). The status of theory and research on love and commitment. In G. Fletcher & M. Clark (Eds.), *Blackwell handbook of social psychology: Interpersonal processes* (pp. 331–356). Malden, MA: Blackwell.

Fehr, B. (2006). A prototype approach to studying love. In R. J. Sternberg & K. Weis (Eds.), *The new psychology of love* (pp. 225–246). New Haven, CT: Yale University Press.

Fehr, B. (2008). Friendship formation. In S. Sprecher, A. Wenzel, & J. Harvey (Eds.), *Handbook of relationship initiation* (pp. 29–54). New York: Psychology Press.

Fehr, B., & Broughton, R. (2001). Gender and personality differences in conceptions of love: An interpersonal theory analysis. *Personal Relationships, 8,* 115–136.

Fehr, B., & Sprecher, S. (2009a). Compassionate love: Conceptual, measurement, and relational issues. In B. Fehr, S. Sprecher, & L. Underwood (Eds.), *The science of compassionate love: Theory: research, and applications* (pp. 27–52). Chichester, England: Wiley-Blackwell.

Fehr, B., & Sprecher, S. (2009b). Prototype analysis of the concept of compassionate love. *Personal Relationships, 16,* 343–364.

Fehr, R., Gelfand, M. J., & Nag, M. (2010). The road to forgiveness: A meta-analytic synthesis of its situational and dispositional correlates. *Psychological Bulletin, 136,* 894–914.

Fein, E., & Schneider, S. (1995). *The rules: Time-tested secrets for capturing the heart of Mr. Right.* New York: Warner Books.

Feingold, A. (1992). Good-looking people are not what we think. *Psychological Bulletin, 111,* 304–341.

Feldman, R., Weller, A., Zagoory-Sharon, O., & Levine, A. (2007). Evidence for a neuroendrocinological foundation of human affiliation: Plasma oxytocin levels across pregnancy and postpartum period predict mother-infant bonding. *Psychological Science, 18,* 965–970.

Felmlee, D. H. (2001). From appealing to appalling: Disenchantment with a romantic partner. *Sociological Perspectives, 44,* 263–280.

Felmlee, D., Orzechowicz, D., & Fortes, C. (2010). Fairy tales: Attraction and stereotypes in same-gender relationships. *Sex Roles, 62,* 226–240.

Fenigstein, A., & Preston, M. (2007). The desired number of sexual partners as a function of gender, sexual risks, and the meaning of "ideal." *Journal of Sex Research, 44,* 89–95.

Ferguson-Isaac, C., Ralston, T. K., & Couch, L. L. (1999, June). *Testing assumptions about coping with interpersonal betrayal.* Paper presented at the meeting of the International Network on Personal Relationships, Louisville, KY.

Fergusson, D. M., Horwood, L. J., & Ridder, E. M. (2005). Partner violence and mental health outcomes in a New Zealand birth cohort. *Journal of Marriage and Family, 67,* 1103–1119.

Ferrara, M. H., & Levine, T. R. (2009). Can't live with them or can't live without them? The effects of betrayal on relational outcomes in college dating relationships. *Communication Quarterly, 57,* 187–204.

Festinger, L., Schachter, S., & Back, K. W. (1950). *Social pressures in informal groups: A study of human factors in housing.* New York: Harper & Brothers.

Fielder, R. L., & Carey, M. P. (2010). Predictors and consequences of sexual "hookups" among college students: A short-term prospective study. *Archives of Sexual Behavior, 39,* 1105–1119.

Figueredo, A. J., Sefcek, J. A., & Jones, D. N. (2006). The ideal romantic partner personality. *Personality and Individual Differences, 41,* 431–441.

Finch, E. (2001). *The criminalization of stalking: Constructing the problem and evaluating the solution.* London: Cavendish.

Fincham, F. D. (2001). Attributions in close relationships: From Balkanization to integration. In G. J. O. Fletcher & M. S. Clark (Eds.), *Blackwell handbook of social psychology: Interpersonal processes* (pp. 3–31). Malden, MA: Blackwell.

Fincham, F. D. (2003). Marital conflict: Correlates, structure, and context. *Current Directions in Psychological Science, 12,* 23–27.

Fincham, F. D., & Beach, S. R. H. (1999). Conflict in marriage: Implications for working with couples. *Annual Review of Psychology, 50,* 47–77.

Fincham, F. D., & Beach, S. R. H. (2002). Forgiveness in marriage: Implications for psychological aggression and constructive communication. *Personal Relationships, 9*, 239–251.

Fincham, F. D., & Beach, S. R. H. (2010). Of memes and marriage: Toward a positive relationship science. *Journal of Family Theory & Review, 2*, 4–24.

Fincham, F. D., Harold, G. T., & Gano-Phillips, S. (2000). The longitudinal association between attributions and marital satisfaction: Direction of effects and role of efficacy expectations. *Journal of Family Psychology, 14*, 267–285.

Finer, L. B. (2007). Trends in premarital sex in the United States, 1954–2003. *Public Health Reports, 122*, 73–78.

Fingerman, K. L. (2009). Consequential strangers and peripheral ties: The importance of unimportant relationships. *Journal of Family Theory & Review, 1*, 69–86.

Fingerman, K. L., & Charles, S. T. (2010). It takes two to tango: Why older people have the best relationships. *Current Directions in Psychological Science, 19*, 172–176.

Fink, B., Grammer, K., & Thornhill, R. (2001). Human (*Homo sapiens*) facial attractiveness in relation to skin texture and color. *Journal of Comparative Psychology, 115*, 92–99.

Fink, B., Neave, N., Manning, J. T., & Grammer, K. (2006). Facial symmetry and judgments of attractiveness, health and personality. *Personality and Individual Differences, 41*, 491–499.

Finkel, E. J. (2008). Intimate partner violence perpetration: Insights from the science of self-regulation. In J. P. Forgas & J. Fitness (Eds.), *Social relationships: Cognitive, affective and motivational processes* (pp. 271–288). New York: Psychology Press.

Finkel, E. J., DeWall, C. N., Slotter, E. B., Oaten, M., & Foshee, V. A. (2009). Self-regulatory failure and intimate partner violence perpetration. *Journal of Personality and Social Psychology, 97*, 483–499.

Finkel, E. J., & Eckhardt, C. I. (2012). Intimate partner violence. In J. Simpson & L. Campbell (Eds.), *The Oxford handbook of close relationships*. New York: Oxford University Press.

Finkel, E. J., Kumashiro, M., Rusbult, C. E., & Reis, H. T. (2010, July). *When and how do romantic partners promote versus impede the pursuit of individuals' important personal goals?* Paper presented at the International Association for Relationship Research Conference, Herzliya, Israel.

Finkel, E. J., Slotter, E. B., DeWall, C. N., Oaten, M., & Foshee, V. A. (2009). Self-regulatory failure and intimate partner violence perpetration. *Journal of Personality and Social Psychology, 97*, 483–499.

Finkenauer, C., Kerkhof, P., Righetti, F., & Branje, S. (2009). Living together apart: Perceived concealment as a signal of exclusion in marital relationships. *Personality and Social Psychology Bulletin, 35*, 1410–1422.

Finkenauer, C., Kubacka, K. E., Engels, R. C. M. E., & Kerkhof, P. (2009). Secrecy in close relationships: Investigating its intrapersonal and interpersonal effects. In T. D. Afifi & W. A. Afifi (Eds.), *Uncertainty, information management, and disclosure decisions: Theories and applications* (pp. 300–319). New York: Routledge.

Firestone, R. W., & Catlett, J. (1999). *Fear of intimacy.* Washington, DC: American Psychological Association.

Fischer, T. F. C., de Graff, P. M., & Kalmijn, M. (2005). Friendly and antagonistic contact between former spouses after divorce: Patterns and determinants. *Journal of Family Issues, 26*, 1131–1163.

Fisher, H. (1995). The nature and evolution of romantic love. In W. Jankowiak (Ed.), *Romantic passion: A universal experience?* (pp. 23–41). New York: Columbia University Press.

Fisher, H. (2006). The drive to love: The neural mechanism for mate selection. In R. J. Sternberg & K. Weis (Eds.), *The new psychology of love* (pp. 87–115). New Haven, CT: Yale University Press.

Fisher, H. (2008, November). *Similar brain responses in those in love for many years or just several months.* Paper presented at the meeting of the Society for Neuroscience, Washington, DC.

Fisher, T. D. (2009). The impact of socially conveyed norms on the reporting of sexual behavior and attitudes by men and women. *Journal of Experimental Social Psychology, 45*, 567–572.

Fiske, S. T. (2004). Developing a program of research. In C. Sansone, C. C. Morf, & A. T. Panter (Eds.), *The Sage handbook of methods in social psychology* (pp. 71–90). Thousand Oaks, CA: Sage.

Fitch, C. A., & Ruggles, S. (2000). Historical trends in marriage formation: The United States 1850–1990. In L. J. Waite (Ed.), *The ties that bind: Perspectives on marriage and cohabitation* (pp. 59–88). New York: Aldine de Gruyter.

Fitness, J., & Warburton, W. (2009). Thinking the unthinkable: Cognitive appraisals and hurt feelings. In A. Vangelisti (Ed.), *Feeling hurt in close relationships* (pp. 34–49). New York: Cambridge University Press.

Fitzsimons, G. M., & Finkel, E. J. (2010). Interpersonal influences on self-regulation. *Current Directions in Psychological Science, 19*, 101–105.

Fitzsimons, G. M., & Kay, A. C. (2004). Language and interpersonal cognition: Causal effects of variations in pronoun usage on perceptions of closeness. *Personality and Social Psychology Bulletin, 30*, 547–557.

Fleischmann, A. A., Spitzberg, B. H., Andersen, P. A., & Roesch, S. C. (2005). Tickling the monster: Jealousy induction in relationships. *Journal of Social and Personal Relationships, 22*, 49–73.

Fletcher, G. J. O., Simpson, J. A., & Thomas, G. (2000). Ideals, perceptions, and evaluations in early relationship development. *Journal of Personality and Social Psychology, 80*, 933–940.

Fletcher, G. J. O., Tither, J. M., O'Loughlin, C., Friesen, M., & Overall, N. (2004). Warm and homely or cold and beautiful? Sex differences in trading off traits in mate selection. *Personality and Social Psychology Bulletin, 30*, 659–672.

Flinn, M., & Alexander, R. (2007). Runaway social selection in human evolution. In S. W. Gangestad & J. A. Simpson (Ed.), *The evolution of mind: Fundamental questions and controversies* (pp. 249–255). New York: Guilford Press.

Floyd, F. J., & Bakeman, R. (2006). Coming-out across the life course: Implications of age and historical context. *Archives of Sexual Behavior, 35*, 287–297.

Floyd, K. (2006). *Communicating affection: Interpersonal behavior and social context.* New York: Cambridge University Press.

Floyd, K., Boren, J. P., Hannawa, A. F., Hesse, C., McEwan, B., & Veksler, A. E. (2009). Kissing in marital and cohabiting relationships: Effects of blood lipids, stress, and relationship satisfaction. *Western Journal of Communication, 73*, 113–133.

Floyd, K., Mikkelson, A. C., Hesse, C., & Pauley, P. M. (2007). Affectionate writing reduces total cholesterol: Two randomized, controlled trials. *Human Communication Research, 33*, 119–142.

Floyd, K., Mikkelson, A. C., Tafoya, M. A., et al. (2007). Human affection exchange: XIII. Affectionate communication accelerates neuroendocrine stress recovery. *Health Communication, 22*, 123–132.

Floyd, K., & Pauley, P. M. (2011). Affectionate communication is good, except when it isn't: On the dark side of expressing affection. In W. Cupach & B. Spitzberg (Eds.), *The dark side of close relationships II* (pp. 145–173). New York: Routledge.

Foa, U. G., Converse, J., Törnblom, K. Y., & Foa, E. B. (Eds.). (1993). *Resource theory: Explorations and applications.* San Diego: Academic Press.

Ford, M. B., & Collins, N. L. (2010). Self-esteem moderates neuroendocrine and psychological responses to interpersonal rejection. *Journal of Personality and Social Psychology, 98*, 405–419.

Forrest, J. A., & Feldman, R. S. (2000). Detecting deception and judge's involvement: Lower task involvement leads to better lie detection. *Personality and Social Psychology Bulletin, 26*, 118–125.

Forsyth, D. R., & Schlenker, B. R. (1977). Attributional egocentrism following performance of a competitive task. *Journal of Social Psychology, 102*, 215–222.

Fortenberry, J. D., Schick, V., Herbenick, D., Sanders, S. A., Dodge, B., & Reece, M. (2010). Sexual behaviors and condom use at last vaginal intercourse: A national sample of adolescents ages 14 to 17 years. *Journal of Sexual Medicine, 7* (Suppl. 5), 305–314.

Foster, J. D., Shrira, I., & Campbell, W. K. (2004, February). *Subsequent relationships of the mate poached.* Paper presented at the meeting of the Society for Personality and Social Psychology, Austin, TX.

Foster, J. D., & Twenge, J. M. (2011). Narcissism and relationships: From light to dark. In W. Cupach & B. Spitzberg (Eds.), *The dark side of close relationships II* (pp. 381–407). New York: Routledge.

Fournier, B., Brassard, A., & Shaver, P. R. (2011). Adult attachment and male aggression in couple relationships: The demand-withdraw communication pattern and relationship satisfaction as mediators. *Journal of Interpersonal Violence, 26*, 1982–2003.

Fowler, K. A., & Westen, D. (2011). Subtyping male perpetrators of intimate partner violence. *Journal of Interpersonal Violence, 26*, 607–639.

Fox, A. B., Bukatko, D., Hallahan, M., & Crawford, M. (2007). The medium makes a difference: Gender similarities and differences in instant messaging. *Journal of Language and Social Psychology, 26*, 389–397.

Fraley, R. C. (2002). Attachment stability from infancy to adulthood: Meta-analysis and dynamic modeling of developmental mechanisms. *Personality and Social Psychology Review, 6*, 123–151.

Fraley, R. C., & Brumbaugh, C. C. (2007). Adult attachment and preemptive defenses: Converging evidence on the role of defensive exclusion at the level of encoding. *Journal of Personality, 75*, 1033–1050.

Fraley, R. C., & Davis, K. E. (1997). Attachment formation and transfer in young adults' close friendships and romantic relationships. *Personal Relationships, 4*, 131–144.

Fraley, R. C., & Waller, N. G. (1998). Adult attachment patterns: A test of the typological model. In J. A. Simpson & W. S. Rholes (Eds.), *Attachment theory and close relationships* (pp. 77–114). New York: Guilford Press.

Franiuk, R., Cohen, D., & Pomerantz, E. M. (2002). Implicit theories of relationships: Implications for relationship satisfaction and longevity. *Personal Relationships, 9*, 345–367.

Franiuk, R., Pomerantz, E. M., & Cohen, D. (2004). The causal role of theories of relationships: Consequences for satisfaction and cognitive strategies. *Personality and Social Psychology Bulletin, 30*, 1494–1507.

Frederick, D. A., & Haselton, M. G. (2007). Why is muscularity sexy? Tests of the fitness indicator hypothesis. *Personality and Social Psychology Bulletin, 33*, 1167–1183.

Frederick, D., Haselton, M., & Filossof, Y. (2008, February). *Love, lust, and loyalty: Sex differences in responses to and reasons for infidelity among 65,029 online participants.* Poster presented at the meeting of the Society for Personality and Social Psychology, Albuquerque, NM.

Frederick, D., & IBP Project Members. (2011, January). *The International Body Project: Preferences for male muscularity and body fat across 10 world regions.* Poster presented at the meeting of the Society for Personality and Social Psychology, San Antonio, TX.

Freeman, J. B., Johnson, K. L., Ambady, N., & Rule, N. O. (2010). Sexual orientation perception involves gendered facial cues. *Personality and Social Psychology Bulletin, 36*, 1318–1331.

Frei, J. R., & Shaver, P. R. (2002). Respect in close relationships: Prototype definition, self-report assessment, and initial correlates. *Personal Relationships, 9*, 121–139.

French, J. R. P., Jr., & Raven, B. H. (1959). The bases of social power. In D. Cartwright (Ed.), *Studies in social power* (pp. 150–167). Ann Arbor: University of Michigan Press.

Friesen, M. D., & Fletcher, G. J. O. (2007). Exploring the lay representation of forgiveness: Convergent and discriminant validity. *Personal Relationships, 14*, 209–223.

Friesen, M. D., Fletcher, G. J. O., & Overall, N. C. (2005). A dyadic assessment of forgiveness in intimate relationships. *Personal Relationships, 12*, 61–77.

Frieze, I. H., Olson, J. E., & Russell, J. (1991). Attractiveness and income for men and women in management. *Journal of Applied Social Psychology, 21*, 1039–1057.

Frieze, I. H., Parsons, J. E., Johnson, P. B., Ruble, D. N., & Zellman, G. L. (1978). *Women and sex roles: A social psychological perspective.* New York: Norton.

Fry, R., & Cohn, D. (2010, January 19). New economics of marriage: The rise of wives. *Pew Research Center.* Retrieved from http://pewresearch.org/pubs/1466/economics-marriage-rise-of-wives

Frye, N. E., & Karney, B. R. (2004). Revision in memories of relationship development: Do biases persist over time? *Personal Relationships, 11*, 79–97.

Fugère, M. A., Escoto, C., Cousins, A. J., Riggs, M. L., & Haerich, P. (2008). Sexual attitudes and double standards: A literature review focusing on participant gender and ethnic background. *Sexuality & Culture, 12*, 169–182.

Fuglestad, P. T., & Snyder, M. (2009). Self-monitoring. In M. R. Leary & R. H. Hoyle (Eds.), *Handbook of individual differences in social behavior* (pp. 574–591). New York: Guilford Press.

Fung, H. H., & Carstensen, L. F. (2004). Motivational changes in response to blocked goals and foreshortened time: Testing alternatives to Socioemotional Selectivity Theory. *Psychology and Aging, 19*, 68–78.

Fung, H. H., Carstensen, L. F., & Lang, F. R. (2001). Age-related patterns in social networks among European-Americans and African-Americans: Implications for socioemotional selectivity across the life span. *International Journal of Aging and Human Development, 52,* 185–206.

Furnham, A., Petrides, K. V., Constantinides, A. (2005). The effects of body mass index and waist-to-hip ratio on ratings of female attractiveness, fecundity, and health. *Personality and Individual Differences, 38,* 1823–1834.

Furnham, A., Swami, V., & Shah, K. (2006). Body weight, waist-to-hip ratio and breast size correlates of ratings of attractiveness and health. *Personality and Individual Differences, 41,* 443–454.

Fuhrman, R. W., Flannagan, D., & Matamoros, M. (2009). Behavior expectations in cross-sex friendships, same-sex friendships, and romantic relationships. *Personal Relationships, 16,* 575–596.

Gable, S. L. (2006). Approach and avoidance social motives and goals. *Journal of Personality, 74,* 175–222.

Gable, S. L. (2008). Approach and avoidance motivation in close relationships. In J. P. Forgas & J. Fitness (Eds.), *Social relationships: Cognitive, affective and motivational processes* (pp. 219–234). New York: Psychology Press.

Gable, S. L., Gonzaga, G. C., & Strachman, A. (2006). Will you be there for me when things go right? Supportive responses to positive event disclosures. *Journal of Personality and Social Psychology, 91,* 904–917.

Gable, S. L., & Poore, J. (2008). Which thoughts count? Algorithms for evaluating satisfaction in relationships. *Psychological Science, 19,* 1030–1036.

Gable, S. L., & Reis, H. T. (2010). Good news! Capitalizing on positive events in an interpersonal context. *Advances in Experimental Social Psychology, 42,* 195–257.

Gable, S. L., Reis, H. T., & Downey, G. (2003). He said, she said: A quasi-signal detection analysis of daily interactions between close relationship partners. *Psychological Science, 14,* 100–105.

Gagné, F. M., & Lydon, J. E. (2003). Identification and the commitment shift: Accounting for gender differences in relationship illusions. *Personality and Social Psychology Bulletin, 29,* 907–919.

Gagné, F. M., & Lydon, J. E. (2004). Bias and accuracy in close relationships: An integrative review. *Personality and Social Psychology Review, 8,* 322–338.

Gaines, S. O., Jr., & Henderson, M. C. (2002). Impact of attachment style on responses to accommodative dilemmas among same-sex couples. *Personal Relationships, 9,* 89–93.

Galinsky, A. D., Magee, J. C., Inesi, M. E., & Gruenfeld, D. H. (2006). Power and perspectives not taken. *Psychological Science, 17,* 1068–1074.

Gallup, G. G., Jr., & Burch, R. L. (2006). The semen-displacement hypothesis: Semen hydraulics and the intra-pair copulation proclivity model of female infidelity. In S. M. Platek & T. K. Shackelford (Eds.), *Female infidelity and paternal uncertainty: Evolutionary perspectives on male anti-cuckoldry tactics* (pp. 129–140). New York: Cambridge University Press.

Galperin, A., Haselton, M. G., Poore, J., von Hippel, W., Buss, D. M., & Gonzaga, G. (2011, January). *Sex differences in sexual regret.* Poster presented at the meeting of the Society for Personality and Social Psychology, San Antonio, TX.

Galupo, M. P. (2009). Cross-category friendship patterns: Comparison of heterosexual and sexual minority adults. *Journal of Social and Personal Relationships, 26,* 811–831.

Gambrill, E., Florian, V., & Thomas, K. (1999). *Rules people use in making and keeping friends.* Unpublished manuscript, University of California, Berkeley.

Gangestad, S. W., & Buss, D. M. (1993). Pathogen prevalence and human mate preference. *Ethology and Sociobiology, 14,* 89–96.

Gangestad, S. W., & Simpson, J. A. (2000). The evolution of human mating: Trade-offs and strategic pluralism. *Behavioral and Brain Sciences, 23,* 573–644.

Gangestad, S. W., Thornhill, R., & Garver-Apgar, C. E. (2010a). Fertility in the cycle predicts women's interest in sexual opportunism. *Evolution and Human Behavior, 31,* 400–411.

Gangestad, S. W., Thornhill, R., & Garver-Apgar, C. E. (2010b). Men's facial masculinity predicts changes in their female partners' sexual interests across the ovulatory cycle, whereas men's intelligence does not. *Evolution and Human Behavior, 31,* 412–424.

Garcia, L. T., & Markey, C. (2007). Matching in sexual experience for married, cohabiting, and dating couples. *Journal of Sex Research, 44,* 250–255.

Gardner, W. L., & Seeley, E. A. (2001). Confucius, 'jen,' and the benevolent use of power: The interdependent self as a psychological contract preventing exploitation. In A. Y. Lee-Chai &

J. A. Bargh (Eds.), *The use and abuse of power: Multiple perspectives on the causes of corruption* (pp. 263–280). Philadelphia: Psychology Press.

Garver-Apgar, C. E., Gangestad, S. W., Thornhill, R., Miller, R. D., & Olp, J. J. (2006). Major histocompatibility complex alleles, sexual responsivity, and unfaithfulness in romantic couples. *Psychological Science, 17,* 830–835.

Gatzeva, M., & Paik, A. (2011). Emotional and physical satisfaction in noncohabitating, cohabiting, and marital relationships: The importance of jealous conflict. *Journal of Sex Research, 48,* 29–42.

Gaunt, R. (2006). Couple similarity and marital satisfaction: Are similar spouses happier? *Journal of Personality, 74,* 1401–1420.

Gayle, B. M., Preiss, R. W., & Allen, M. (2002). A meta-analytic interpretation of intimate and nonintimate interpersonal conflict. In M. Allen, R. W. Preiss, B. M. Gayle, & N. A. Burrell (Eds.), *Interpersonal communication research: Advances through meta-analysis* (pp. 345–368). Mahwah, NJ: Erlbaum.

Geary, D. C. (2010). *Male, female: The evolution of human sex differences* (2nd ed.). Washington, DC: American Psychological Association.

Geary, D. C. (2000). Evolution and proximate expression of human paternal investment. *Psychological Bulletin, 126,* 55–77.

Gerressu, M., Mercer, C. H., Graham, C. A., Wellings, K., & Johnson, A. M. (2008). Prevalence of masturbation and associated factors in a British national probability survey. *Archives of Sexual Behavior, 37,* 266–278.

Giancola, P. R., Josephs, R. A., Parrott, D. J., & Duke, A. A. (2010). Alcohol myopia revisited: Clarifying aggression and other acts of disinhibition through a distorted lens. *Perspectives on Psychological Science, 5,* 265–278.

Gibson-Davis, C. M. (2009). Money, marriage, and children: Testing the financial expectations and family formation theory. *Journal of Marriage and Family, 71,* 146–160.

Gidycz, C. A., Van Wynsberghe, A., & Edwards, K. M. (2008). Prediction of women's utilization of resistance strategies in a sexual assault situation: A prospective study. *Journal of Interpersonal Violence, 23,* 571–588.

Gildersleeve, K., Larson, C., Pillsworth, E., & Haselton, M. (2011, January). *Can men detect ovulation? Evidence that men prefer women's high-fertility body odor.* Poster presented at the meeting of the Society for Personality and Social Psychology, San Antonio, TX.

Gill, M. J., & Swann, W. B., Jr. (2004). On what it means to know someone: A matter of pragmatics. *Journal of Personality and Social Psychology, 86,* 405–418.

Gillath, O., Sesko, A. K., Shaver, P. R., & Chun, D. S. (2010). Attachment, authenticity, and honesty: Dispositional and experimentally induced security can reduce self- and other-deception. *Journal of Personality and Social Psychology, 98,* 841–855.

Gillmore, M. R., Leigh, B. C., Hoppe, M. J., & Morrison, D. M. (2010). Comparison of daily and retrospective reports of vaginal sex in heterosexual men and women. *Journal of Sex Research, 47,* 279–284.

Gillum, J. (2009, February 26). Number of households with kids hits new low. *USA Today,* p. 4D.

Giordano, P. C., Manning, W. D., & Longmore, M. A. (2006). Adolescent romantic relationships: An emerging portrait of their nature and developmental significance. In A. C. Crouter & A. Booth (Eds.), *Romance and sex in emerging adulthood: Risks and opportunities* (pp. 127–150). Mahwah, NJ: Erlbaum.

Giordano, P. C., Soto, D. A., Manning, W. D., & Longmore, M. A. (2010). The characteristics of romantic relationships associated with teen dating violence. *Social Science Research, 39,* 863–874.

Givertz, M., Segrin, C., & Hanzal, A. (2009). The association between satisfaction and commitment differs across marital couple types. *Communication Research, 36,* 561–584.

Gladue, B. A., & Delaney, H. J. (1990). Gender differences in perception of attractiveness of men and women in bars. *Personality and Social Psychology Bulletin, 16,* 378–391.

Glass, S. P., & Staeheli, J. C. (2003). *Not 'just friends': Protect your relationship from infidelity and heal the trauma of betrayal.* New York: Free Press.

Glasser, C. L., Robnett, B., & Feliciano, C. (2009). Internet daters' body type preferences: Race-ethnic and gender differences. *Sex Roles, 61,* 14–33.

Gleason, M. E. J., Iida, M., Shrout, P. E., & Bolger, N. (2008). Receiving support as a mixed blessing: Evidence for dual effects of support on psychological outcomes. *Journal of Personality and Social Psychology, 94,* 824–838.

Glenn, N. D. (1998). The course of marital success and failure in five American 10-year marriage cohorts. *Journal of Marriage and the Family, 60,* 569–576.

Glenn, N. D., Uecker, J. E., & Love, R. W. B., Jr. (2010). Later first marriage and marital success. *Social Science Research, 39,* 787–800.

Godbout, N., Dutton, D. G., Lussier, Y., & Sabourin, S. (2009). Early exposure to violence, domestic violence, attachment representations, and marital adjustment. *Personal Relationships, 16,* 365–384.

Goel, S., Mason, W., & Watts, D. J. (2010). Real and perceived attitude agreement in social networks. *Journal of Personality and Social Psychology, 99,* 611–621.

Goetz, A. T., Shackelford, T. K., Weekes-Shackelford, V. A., Euler, H. A., Hoier, S., Schmitt, D. P., & LaMunyon, C. W. (2005). Mate retention, semen displacement, and human sperm competition: A preliminary investigation of tactics to prevent and correct female infidelity. *Personality and Individual Differences, 38,* 749–763.

Gonsalkorale, K., & Williams, K. D. (2007). The KKK won't let me play: Ostracism even by a despised outgroup hurts. *European Journal of Social Psychology, 37,* 1176–1186.

Gonzaga, G. C., Carter, S., & Buckwalter, J. G. (2010). Assortative mating, convergence, and satisfaction in married couples. *Personal Relationships, 17,* 634–644.

Gonzaga, G. C., Haselton, M. G., Smurda, J., Davies, M. S., & Poore, J. C. (2008). Love, desire, and the suppression of thoughts of romantic alternatives. *Evolution and Human Behavior, 29,* 119–126.

Gonzaga, G. C., Keltner, D., & Ward, D. (2008). Power in mixed-sex stranger interactions. *Cognition & Emotion, 22,* 1555–1568.

Gonzaga, G. C., Turner, R. A., Keltner, D., Campos, B., & Altemus, M. (2006). Romantic love and sexual desire in close relationships. *Emotion, 6,* 163–179.

Gonzales, J. E., & Luévano, V. X. (2011, January). *Forget the little black dress: Fertility, women's use of red, sexual desire, and men's mating-effort.* Poster presented at the meeting of the Society for Personality and Social Psychology, San Antonio, TX.

Gonzales, M. A., Gilbert, R. L., & Murphy, N. A. (2010, August). *Sexual satisfaction and sexual feelings in 3D virtual relationships.* Poster presented at the meeting of the American Psychological Association, San Diego, CA.

Goodfriend, W., & Agnew, C. R. (2008). Sunken costs and desired plans: Examining different types of investments in close relationships. *Personality and Social Psychology Bulletin, 34,* 1639–1652.

Goodwin, P. Y., Mosher, W. D., & Chandra, A. (2010). Marriage and cohabitation in the United States: A statistical portrait based on Cycle 6 (2002) of the National Survey of Family Growth. *Vital and Health Statistics, 23*(28). Retrieved from http://www.cdc.gov/nchs/data/series/sr_23/sr23_028.pdf

Goodwin, R., & Gaines, S. O., Jr. (2004). Relationship beliefs and relationship quality across cultures: Country as a moderator of dysfunctional beliefs and relationship quality in three former Communist societies. *Personal Relationships, 11,* 267–279.

Goodwin, S. A., Fiske, S. T., Rosen, L. D., & Rosenthal, A. M. (2002). The eye of the beholder: Romantic goals and impression biases. *Journal of Experimental Social Psychology, 38,* 232–241.

Gordon, C. L., Arnette, R. A. M., & Smith, R. E. (2011). Have you thanked your spouse today? Felt and expressed gratitude among married couples. *Personality and Individual Differences, 50,* 339–343.

Gore, J. S., & Cross, S. E. (2011). Conflicts of interest: Relational self-construal and decision making in interpersonal contexts. *Self and Identity, 10,* 185–202.

Gormley, B., & Lopez, F. G. (2010). Psychological abuse perpetration in college dating relationships: Contributions of gender, stress, and adult attachment orientations. *Journal of Interpersonal Violence, 25,* 204–218.

Gosling, S. D., Sandy, C. J., John, O. P., & Potter, J. (2010). Wired but not weird: The promise of the Internet in reaching more diverse samples. *Behavioral and Brain Sciences, 33,* 94–95.

Gottman, J. M. (1993). The roles of conflict engagement, escalation, and avoidance in marital interaction: A longitudinal view of five types of couples. *Journal of Consulting and Clinical Psychology, 61,* 6–15.

Gottman, J. M. (1994a). *What predicts divorce? The relationship between marital processes and marital outcomes.* Hillsdale, NJ: Erlbaum.

Gottman, J. M. (1994b). *Why marriages succeed or fail.* New York: Simon & Schuster.

Gottman, J. M. (1999). *The marriage clinic: A scientifically-based marital therapy.* New York: Norton.

Gottman, J. M. (2011). *The science of trust: Emotional attunement for couples.* New York: Norton.

Gottman, J. M., & Carrère, S. (1994). Why can't men and women get along? Developmental roots and marital inequities. In D. J. Canary & L. Stafford (Eds.), *Communication and relational maintenance* (pp. 203–229). San Diego: Academic Press.

Gottman, J. M., Carrère, S., Swanson, C., & Coan, J. A. (2000). Reply to 'From basic research to interventions.' *Journal of Marriage and the Family, 62,* 265–273.

Gottman, J. M., Coan, J., Carrère, S., & Swanson, C. (1998). Predicting marital happiness and stability from newlywed interactions. *Journal of Marriage and the Family, 60,* 5–22.

Gottman, J. M., & Levenson, R. W. (1992). Marital processes predictive of later dissolution: Behavior, physiology, and health. *Journal of Personality and Social Psychology, 63,* 221–233.

Gottman, J. M., & Levenson, R. W. (2000). The timing of divorce: Predicting when a couple will divorce over a 14–year period. *Journal of Marriage and the Family, 62,* 737–745.

Gottman, J. M., Levenson, R. W., Gross, J., Frederickson, B. L., McCoy, K., Rosenthal, L., Ruef, A., & Yoshimoto, D. (2003). Correlates of gay and lesbian couples' relationship satisfaction and relationship dissolution. *Journal of Homosexuality, 45,* 23–43.

Gottman, J. M., Notarius, C., Gonso, J., & Markman, H. (1976). *A couple's guide to communication.* Champaign, IL: Research Press.

Gouin, J., Carter, S. C., Pournajafi-Nazarloo, H., Glaser, R., Malarkey, W. B., Loving, T. J., Stowell, J., & Kiecolt-Glaser, J. K. (2010). Marital behavior, oxytocin, vasopressin, and wound healing. *Psychoneuroendicrinology, 35,* 1082–1090.

Gouin, J., Glaser, R., Loving, T. J., Malarkey, W. B., Stowell, J., Houts, C., & Kiecolt-Glaser, J. K. (2009). Attachment avoidance predicts inflammatory responses to marital conflict. *Brain, Behavior, and Immunity, 23,* 898–904.

Gover, A. R., Kaukinen, C., & Fox, K. A. (2008). The relationship between violence in the family of origin and dating violence among college students. *Journal of Interpersonal Violence, 23,* 1667–1693.

Graham, J. M. (2008). Self-expansion and flow in couples' momentary experiences: An experience sampling study. *Journal of Personality and Social Psychology, 95,* 679–694.

Graham, J. M. (2011). Measuring love in romantic relationships: A meta-analysis. *Journal of Social and Personal Relationships,* DOI: 10.1177/0265407510389126

Graham, K., Bernards, S., Wilsnack, S. C., & Gmel, G. (2011). Alcohol may not cause partner violence but it seems to make it worse: A cross-national comparison of the relationship between alcohol and severity of partner violence. *Journal of Interpersonal Violence, 26,* 1503–1523.

Graupmann, V., & Erber, R. (2005, January). *So unhappy together: Maintaining unwanted relationships.* Poster presented at the meeting of the Society for Personality and Social Psychology, New Orleans, LA.

Gray, J. (1992). *Men are from Mars, women are from Venus.* New York: HarperCollins.

Graziano, W. G., & Bruce, J. W. (2008). Attraction and the initiation of relationships: A review of the empirical literature. In S. Sprecher, A. Wenzel, & J. Harvey (Eds.), *Handbook of relationship initiation* (pp. 269–295). New York: Psychology Press.

Green, B. L., & Kenrick, D. T. (1994). The attractiveness of gender-typed traits at different relationship levels: Androgynous characteristics may be desirable after all. *Personality and Social Psychology Bulletin, 20,* 244–253.

Green, M. C., & Sabini, J. (2006). Gender, socioeconomic status, age, and jealousy: Emotional responses to infidelity in a national sample. *Emotion, 6,* 330–334.

Greene, J. O., & Burleson, B. R. (Eds.). (2003). *Handbook of communication and social interaction skills.* Mahwah, NJ: Erlbaum.

Greiling, H., & Buss, D. M. (2000). Women's sexual strategies: The hidden dimension of extra-pair mating. *Personality and Individual Differences, 28*, 929–963.

Greitemeyer, T. (2010). Effects of reciprocity on attraction: The role of partner's physical attractiveness. *Personal Relationships, 17*, 317–330.

Grello, C. M., Welsh, D. P., & Harper, M. S. (2006). No strings attached: The nature of casual sex in college students. *Journal of Sex Research, 43*, 255–267.

Griffitt, W., & Veitch, R. (1974). Preacquaintance attitude similarity and attraction revisited: Ten days in a fall-out shelter. *Sociometry, 37*, 163–173.

Grote, N. K., & Clark, M. S. (2001). Perceiving unfairness in the family: Cause or consequence of marital distress? *Journal of Personality and Social Psychology, 80*, 281–293.

Grote, N. K., & Frieze, I. H. (1994). The measurement of friendship-based love in intimate relationships. *Personal Relationships, 1*, 275–300.

Grote, N. K., & Frieze, I. H. (1998). "Remembrance of things past": Perceptions of marital love from its beginnings to the present. *Journal of Social and Personal Relationships, 15*, 91–109.

Guéguen, N. (2009). Menstrual cycle phases and female receptivity to a courtship solicitation: An evaluation in a nightclub. *Evolution and Human Behavior, 30*, 351–355.

Guerrero, L. K. (1997). Nonverbal involvement across interactions with same-sex friends, opposite-sex friends and romantic partners: Consistency or change. *Journal of Social and Personal Relationships, 14*, 31–58.

Guerrero, L. K. (1998). Attachment-style differences in the experience and expression of romantic jealousy. *Personal Relationships, 5*, 273–291.

Guerrero, L. K., & Andersen, P. A. (1998). Jealousy experience and expression in romantic relationships. In P. A. Andersen & L. K. Guerrero (Eds.), *Handbook of communication and emotion* (pp. 155–188). San Diego: Academic Press.

Guerrero, L. K., & Bachman, G. F. (2010). Forgiveness and forgiving communication in dating relationships: An expectancy-investment explanation. *Journal of Social and Personal Relationships, 27*, 801–823.

Guerrero, L. K., La Valley, A. G., & Farinelli, L. (2008). The experience and expression of anger, guilt, and sadness in marriage: An equity theory explanation. *Journal of Social and Personal Relationships, 25*, 699–724.

Guerrero, L. K., Trost, M. R., & Yoshimura, S. M. (2005). Romantic jealousy: Emotions and communicative responses. *Personal Relationships, 12*, 233–252.

Gupta, U., & Singh, P. (1982). Exploratory study of love and liking and type of marriages. *Indian Journal of Applied Psychology, 19*, 92–97.

Gustavsson, L., Johnsson, J. I., & Uller, T. (2008). Mixed support for sexual selection theories of mate preferences in the Swedish population. *Evolutionary Psychology, 6*, 575–585.

Gute, G., Eshbaugh, E. M., & Wiersma, J. (2008). Sex for you, but not for me: Discontinuity in undergraduate emerging adults' definitions of "having sex." *Journal of Sex Research, 45*, 329–337.

Guthrie, M. F., Hendrick, C., & Hendrick, S. S. (2011, January). *Respect in friendships associated with level of friendship, gender, and romantic relationships.* Poster presented at the meeting of the Society for Personality and Social Psychology, San Antonio, TX.

Guttentag, M., & Secord, P. F. (1983). *Too many women? The sex ratio question.* Beverly Hills, CA: Sage.

Haden, S. C., & Hojjat, M. (2006). Aggressive responses to betrayal: Type of relationship, victim's sex, and nature of aggression. *Journal of Social and Personal Relationships, 23*, 101–116.

Haeffel, G. J., Voelz, Z. R., & Joiner, T. E., Jr. (2007). Vulnerability to depressive symptoms: Clarifying the role of excessive reassurance seeking and perceived social support in an interpersonal model of depression. *Cognition & Emotion, 21*, 681–688.

Halatsis, P., & Christakis, N. (2009). The challenge of sexual attraction within heterosexuals' cross-sex friendship. *Journal of Social and Personal Relationships, 26*, 919–937.

Hald, G. M., & Høgh-Olesen, H. (2010). Receptivity to sexual invitations from strangers of the opposite gender. *Evolution and Human Behavior, 31*, 453–458.

Halford, W. K. (2011). *Marriage and relationship education: What works and how to provide it.* New York: Guilford Press.

Halford, W. K., Sanders, M. R., & Behrens, B. C. (2000). Repeating the errors of our parents? Family-of-origin spouse violence and observed conflict management in engaged couples. *Family Process, 39,* 219–235.

Hall, E. T. (1966). *The hidden dimension.* Garden City, NY: Doubleday.

Hall, J. (2009, November). *Sex differences in friendship expectations: A meta-analysis.* Paper presented at the meeting of the International Association for Relationship Research, Lawrence, KS.

Hall, J. A., Andrzejewski, S. A., & Yopchick, J. E. (2009). Psychosocial correlates of interpersonal sensitivity: A meta-analysis. *Journal of Nonverbal Behavior, 33,* 149–180.

Hall, J. A., Coats, E. J., & LeBeau, L. S. (2005). Nonverbal behavior and the vertical dimension of social relations: A meta-analysis. *Psychological Bulletin, 131,* 898–924.

Hall, J. A., & Mast, M. S. (2008). Are women always more interpersonally sensitive than men? Impact of goals and content domain. *Personality and Social Psychology Bulletin, 34,* 144–155.

Hall, J. A., Park, N., Song, H., & Cody, M. J. (2010). Strategic misrepresentation in online dating: The effects of gender, self-monitoring, and personality traits. *Journal of Social and Personal Relationships, 27,* 117–135.

Hall, J. K., Hutton, S. B., & Morgan, M. J. (2010). Sex differences in scanning faces: Does attention to the eyes explain female superiority in facial expression recognition? *Cognition & Emotion, 24,* 629–637.

Hamermesh, D. S., & Parker, A. M. (2005). Beauty in the classroom: Instructors' pulchritude and putative pedagogical productivity. *Economics of Education Review, 24,* 369–376.

Hammock, G., Rosen, S., Richardson, D., & Bernstein, S. (1989). Aggression as equity restoration. *Journal of Research in Personality, 23,* 398–409.

Hampel, A. D., & Vangelisti, A. L. (2008). Commitment expectations in romantic relationships: Application of a prototype interaction-pattern model. *Personal Relationships, 15,* 81–102.

Hampson, E., van Anders, S. M., & Mullin, L. I. (2006). A female advantage in the recognition of emotional facial expressions: Test of an evolutionary hypothesis. *Evolution and Human Behavior, 27,* 401–416.

Hancock, J. T., Thom-Santelli, J., & Ritchie, T. (2004). Deception and design: The impact of communication technology on lying behavior. *Proceedings of the Conference on Computer Human Interaction, 6,* 130–136.

Hannon, P. A., Rusbult, C. E., Finkel, E. J., & Kamashiro, M. (2010). In the wake of betrayal: Amends, forgiveness, and the resolution of betrayal. *Personal Relationships, 17,* 253–278.

Hansen, G. L. (1985). Perceived threats and marital jealousy. *Social Psychology Quarterly, 48,* 262–268.

Hanson, T. L., McLanahan, S. S., & Thomson, E. (1998). Windows on divorce: Before and after. *Social Science Research, 27,* 329–349.

Harasymchuk, C., & Fehr, B. (2010). A script analysis of relational boredom: Causes, feelings, and coping strategies. *Journal of Social and Clinical Psychology, 29,* 988–1019.

Harasymchuk, C., & Fehr, B. (2011, January). *Relational boredom: Verification of a prototype structure using explicit and implicit measures.* Poster presented at the meeting of the Society for Personality and Social Psychology, San Antonio, TX.

Hardie, J. H., & Lucas, A. (2010). Economic factors and relationship quality among young couples: Comparing cohabitation and marriage. *Journal of Marriage and Family, 72,* 1141–1154.

Harinck, F., & De Dreu, C. K. W. (2011). When does taking a break help in negotiations? The influence of breaks and social motivation on negotiation processes and outcomes. *Negotiation and Conflict Management Research, 4,* 33–46.

Harkless, L. E., & Fowers, B. J. (2005). Similarities and differences in relational boundaries among heterosexuals, gay men, and lesbians. *Psychology of Women Quarterly, 29,* 167–176.

Harknett, K. (2008). Mate availability and unmarried parent relationships. *Demography, 45,* 555–571.

Harris, C. R. (2005). Male and female jealousy, still more similar than different: Reply to Sagarin (2005). *Personality and Social Psychology Review, 9,* 76–86.

Harris, M. J., & Garris, C. P. (2008). You never get a second chance to make a first impression: Behavioral consequences of first impressions. In N. Ambady & J. Skowronski (Eds.), *First impressions* (pp. 147–168). New York: Guilford.

Harvey, J. H., & Fine, M. A. (2004). *Children of divorce: Stories of loss and growth.* Mahwah, NJ: Erlbaum.

Harvey, J. H., & Fine, M. A. (2006). Social construction of accounts in the process of relationship termination. In M. A. Fine & J. H. Harvey (Eds.), *Handbook of divorce and relationship dissolution* (pp. 189–199). Mahwah, NJ: Erlbaum.

Harway, M. (2005). *Handbook of couples therapy.* New York: Wiley.

Haselton, M. G. (2003). The sexual overperception bias: Evidence of a systematic bias in men from a survey of naturally occurring events. *Journal of Research in Personality, 37,* 34–47.

Haselton, M. G., & Buss, D. M. (2000). Error Management Theory: A new perspective on biases in cross-sex mind reading. *Journal of Personality and Social Psychology, 78,* 81–91.

Haselton, M. G., Buss, D. M., Oubiad, V., & Angleitner, A. (2005). Sex, lies, and strategic interference: The psychology of deception between the sexes. *Personality and Social Psychology Bulletin, 31,* 3–23.

Haselton, M. G., & Gangestad, S. W. (2006). Conditional expression of women's desires and men's mate guarding across the ovulatory cycle. *Hormones and Behavior, 49,* 509–518.

Haselton, M. G., & Larson, C. M. (2011, January). *The evolution of women's mating psychology: Conflicts between adaptations facilitating pair-bonds and adaptations threatening them.* Paper presented at the meeting of the Society for Personality and Social Psychology, San Antonio, TX.

Hatfield, E. (1983). Equity theory and research: An overview. In H. H. Blumberg, A. P. Hare, V. Kent, & M. Davies (Eds.), *Small groups and social interaction* (Vol. 2, pp. 401–412). Chichester, England: Wiley.

Hatfield, E., & Rapson, R. L. (2008). Passionate love and sexual desire: Multidisciplinary perspectives. In J. P. Forgas & J. Fitness (Eds.), *Social relationships: Cognitive, affective and motivational processes* (pp. 21–37). New York: Psychology Press.

Hatfield, E., Rapson, R. L., & Martel, L. D. (2007). Passionate love and sexual desire. In S. Kitayama & D. Cohen (Eds.), *Handbook of cultural psychology* (pp. 760–779). New York: Guilford Press.

Hatfield, E., & Sprecher, S. (1986). Measuring passionate love in intimate relationships. *Journal of Adolescence, 9,* 383–410.

Haub, C. (2010). Births outside marriage now common in many countries in Europe. *Population Research Bureau.* Retrieved from http://www.prb.org/Articles/2010/birthsoutsidemarriage .aspx

Hawkins, A. J., Blanchard, V. L., Baldwin, S. A., & Fawcett, E. B. (2008). Does marriage and relationship education work? A meta-analytic study. *Journal of Consulting and Clinical Psychology, 76,* 723–734.

Hawkley, L. C., Browne, M. W., & Cacioppo, J. T. (2005). How can I connect with thee? Let me count the ways. *Psychological Science, 16,* 798–803.

Hawkley, L. C., & Cacioppo, J. T. (2007). Aging and loneliness: Downhill quickly? *Current Directions in Psychological Science, 16,* 187–191.

Hazan, C., & Shaver, P. (1987). Romantic love conceptualized as an attachment process. *Journal of Personality and Social Psychology, 52,* 511–524.

Hazan, C., & Zeifman, D. (1994). Sex and the psychological tether. In K. Bartholomew & D. Perlman (Eds.), *Attachment processes in adulthood* (pp. 151–178). London: Jessica Kingsley.

Heaton, T. B. (2002). Factors contributing to increasing marital stability in the U.S. *Journal of Family Issues, 23,* 392–409.

Heaven, P. C. L., Smith, L., Prabhakar, S. M., Abraham, J., & Mete, M. E. (2006). Personality and conflict communication patterns in cohabiting couples. *Journal of Research in Personality, 40,* 829–840.

Hebl, M. R., Foster, J. B., Mannix, L. M., & Dovidio, J. F. (2002). Formal and interpersonal discrimination: A field study of bias toward homosexual applicants. *Personality and Social Psychology Bulletin, 28,* 815–825.

Hecht, M. L., Marston, P. J., & Larkey, L. K. (1994). Love ways and relationship quality in heterosexual relationships. *Journal of Social and Personal Relationships, 11,* 25–43.

Heffner, K. L., Kiecolt-Glaser, J. K., Loving, T. J., Glaser, R., & Malarkey, W. B. (2004). Spousal support satisfaction as a modifier of physiological responses to marital conflict in younger and older couples. *Journal of Behavioral Medicine, 27,* 233–254.

Heider, F. (1958). *The psychology of interpersonal relations.* New York: Wiley.

Heilman, M. E., & Wallen, A. S. (2010). Wimpy and undeserving of respect: Penalties for men's gender-inconsistent success. *Journal of Experimental Social Psychology, 46,* 664–667.

Heiman, J. R., Long, J. S., Smith, S. N., Fisher, W. A., Sand, M. S., & Rosen, R. C. (2011). Sexual satisfaction and relationship happiness in midlife and older couples in five countries. *Archives of Sexual Behavior, 40,* 741–753.

Hellmuth, J. C., & McNulty, J. K. (2008). Neuroticism, marital violence, and the moderating role of stress and behavioral skills. *Journal of Personality and Social Psychology, 95,* 166–180.

Helms, H. M., Proulx, C. M., Klute, M. M., McHale, S. M., & Crouter, A. C. (2006). Spouses' gender-typed attributes and their links with marital quality: A pattern analytic approach. *Journal of Social and Personal Relationships, 23,* 843–864.

Helms, H. M., Walls, J. K., Crouter, A. C., & McHale, S. M. (2010). Provider role attitudes, marital satisfaction, role overload, and housework: A dyadic approach. *Journal of Family Psychology, 24,* 568–577.

Henderson, C. E., Hayslip, B., Jr., Sanders, L. M., & Louden, L. (2009). Grandmother-grandchild relationship quality predicts psychological adjustment among youth from divorced families. *Journal of Family Issues, 30,* 1245–1264.

Henderson, L., & Zimbardo, P. (2010). Shyness, social anxiety, and social anxiety disorder. In S. Hofmann & P. DiBartolo (Eds.), *Social anxiety: Clinical, developmental, and social perspectives* (pp. 65–93). New York: Academic Press.

Hendrick, B. (2011, February 2). Teen birth rate is declining. *WebMD Health News.* Retrieved from http://www.webmd.com/parenting/news/20110202/teen-birth-rate-is-declining

Hendrick, C., & Hendrick, S. S. (2006). Styles of romantic love. In R. J. Sternberg & K. Weis (Eds.), *The new psychology of love* (pp. 149–170). New Haven: Yale University Press.

Hendrick, S. S., Dicke, A., & Hendrick, C. (1998). The Relationship Assessment Scale. *Journal of Social and Personal Relationships, 15,* 137–142.

Hendrick, S. S., & Hendrick, C. (1993). Lovers as friends. *Journal of Social and Personal Relationships, 10,* 459–466.

Hendrick, S. S., Hendrick, C., & Logue, E. M. (2010). Respect and the family. *Journal of Family Theory & Review, 2,* 126–136.

Henline, B. H., Lamke, L. K., & Howard, M. D. (2007). Exploring perceptions of online infidelity. *Personal Relationships, 14,* 113–128.

Henrich, J., Heine, S. J., & Norenzayan, A. (2010). The weirdest people in the world? *Behavioral and Brain Sciences, 33,* 61–135.

Henry, R. (2008, April 16). Married gay couples find divorce doesn't come easy. *Houston Chronicle,* p. A6.

Herbenick, D., Reece, M., Schick, V., Sanders, S. A., Dodge, B., & Fortenberry, J. D. (2010a). An event-level analysis of the sexual characteristics and composition among adults ages 18 to 59: Results from a national probability sample in the United States. *Journal of Sexual Medicine, 7* (Suppl. 5), 346–361.

Herbenick, D., Reece, M., Schick, V., Sanders, S. A., Dodge, B., & Fortenberry, J. D. (2010b). Sexual behavior in the United States: Results from a national probability sample of men and women ages 14–94. *Journal of Sexual Medicine, 7* (Suppl. 5), 255–265.

Herbst, K. C., Gaertner, L., & Insko, C. A. (2003). My head says yes but my heart says no: Cognitive and affective attraction as a function of similarity to the ideal self. *Journal of Personality and Social Psychology, 84,* 1206–1219.

Herek, G. M., Norton, A. T., Allen, T. J., & Sims, C. L. (2010). Demographic, psychological, and social characteristics of self-identified lesbian, gay, and bisexual adults in a U.S. probability sample. *Sexuality Research and Social Policy, 7,* 176–200.

Hertenstein, M. J., Hansel, C. A., Butts, A. M., & Hile, S. N. (2009). Smile intensity in photographs predicts divorce later in life. *Motivation and Emotion, 33,* 99–105.

Hertenstein, M. J., Holmes, R., McCullough, M., & Keltner, D. (2009). The communication of emotion via touch. *Emotion, 9,* 566–573.

Herz, R. S., & Inzlicht, M. (2002). Sex differences in response to physical and social factors involved in human mate selection. *Evolution and Human Behavior, 23,* 359–364.

Hess, N. H., & Hagen, E. H. (2006). Sex differences in indirect aggression: Psychological evidence from young adults. *Evolution and Human Behavior, 27,* 231–245.

Hetherington, E. M. (2003). Intimate pathways: Changing patterns in close personal relationships across time. *Family Relations, 52,* 318–331.

Heyman, R. E., Hunt-Martorano, A. N., Malik, J., & Smith-Slep, A. M. (2009). Desired change in couples: Gender differences and effects on communication. *Journal of Family Psychology, 23,* 474–484.

Higgins, J. A., Trussell, J., Moore, N. B., & Davidson, J. K. (2010). Virginity lost, satisfaction gained? Physiological and psychological sexual satisfaction at heterosexual debut. *Journal of Sex Research, 47,* 384–394.

Hill, C. A., Blakemore, J. E. O., & Drumm, P. (1997). Mutual and unrequited love in adolescence and young adulthood. *Personal Relationships, 4,* 15–23.

Hill, M. (2009, August 14). Facebook spurs cyber-jealousy. *Bryan-College Station Eagle,* p. A12.

Hill, S. E. (2007). Overestimation bias in mate competition. *Evolution and Human Behavior, 28,* 118–123.

Hill, W. L., Wilson, C., & Lebovitz, E. (2009, February). *Kissing chemicals: Hormonal changes in response to kissing.* Paper presented at the meeting of the American Association for the Advancement of Science, Chicago, IL.

Hinchliff, S., & Gott, M. (2004). Intimacy, commitment, and adaptation: Sexual relationships within long-term marriages. *Journal of Social and Personal Relationships, 21,* 595–609.

Hines, D. A. (2007). Predictors of sexual coercion against women and men: A multilevel, multinational study of university students. *Archives of Sexual Behavior, 36,* 403–422.

Hines, D., Saris, R. N., & Throckmorton-Belzer, L. (2002). Pluralistic ignorance and health risk behaviors: Do college students misperceive social approval for risky behavior on campus and in media? *Journal of Applied Social Psychology, 32,* 2621–2640.

Hinsz, V. B., Matz, D. C., & Patience, R. A. (2001). Does women's hair signal reproductive potential? *Journal of Experimental Social Psychology, 37,* 166–172.

Hira, S. N., & Overall, N. C. (2011). Improving intimate relationships: Targeting the partner versus changing the self. *Journal of Social and Personal Relationships, 28,* 610–633

Hitsch, G. J., Hortaçsu, A., & Ariely, D. (2010). What makes you click? Mate preferences in online dating. *Quantitative Marketing and Economics, 8,* 393–427.

Hoff, C. C., & Beougher, S. C. (2010). Sexual agreements among gay male couples. *Archives of Sexual Behavior, 39,* 774–787.

Hohmann-Marriott, B. E. (2006). Shared beliefs and the union stability of married and cohabiting couples. *Journal of Marriage and Family, 68,* 1015–1028.

Holland, R. W., Roeder, U. R., van Baaren, R. B., Brandt, A. C., & Hannover, B. (2004). Don't stand so close to me: The effects of self-construal on interpersonal closeness. *Psychological Science, 15,* 237–242.

Holler, J., Shovelton, H., & Beattie, G. (2009). Do iconic hand gestures really contribute to the communication of semantic information in a face-to-face context? *Journal of Nonverbal Behavior, 33,* 73–88.

Holleran, S. E., Mehl, M. R., & Levitt, S. (2009). Eavesdropping on social life: The accuracy of stranger ratings of daily behavior from thin slices of natural conversations. *Journal of Research in Personality, 43,* 660–672.

Holley, S. R., Sturm, V. E., & Levenson, R. W. (2010). Exploring the basis for gender differences in the demand-withdraw pattern. *Journal of Homosexuality, 57,* 666–684.

Holloway, R. A., Waldrip, A. M., & Ickes, W. (2009). Evidence that a *simpático* self-schema accounts for differences in the self-concepts and social behavior of Latinos versus whites (and blacks). *Journal of Personality and Social Psychology, 96,*1012–1028.

Holman, T. B., Galbraith, R. C., Timmons, N. M., Steed, A., & Tobler, S. B. (2009). Threats to parental and romantic attachment figures' availability and adult attachment insecurity. *Journal of Family Issues, 30,* 413–429.

Holman, T. B., & Jarvis, M. O. (2003). Hostile, volatile, avoiding, and validating couple-conflict types: An investigation of Gottman's couple-conflict types. *Personal Relationships, 10,* 267–282.

Holmberg, D., Blair, K. L., & Phillips, M. (2010). Women's sexual satisfaction as a predictor of well-being in same-sex versus mixed-sex relationships. *Journal of Sex Research, 47,* 1–11.

Holmes, J. G. (2002). Interpersonal expectations as the building blocks of social cognition: An interdependence theory perspective. *Personal Relationships, 9,* 1–26.

Holmes, J. G. (2004). The benefits of abstract functional analysis in theory construction: The case of interdependence theory. *Personality and Social Psychology Review, 8,* 146–155.

Holmes, J. G., & Levinger, G. (1994). Paradoxical effects of closeness in relationships on perceptions of justice: An interdependence-theory perspective. In M. J. Lerner & G. Mikula (Eds.), *Entitlement and the affectional bond: Justice in close relationships* (pp. 149–173). New York: Plenum.

Holmes, J. G., & Wood, J. V. (2009). Interpersonal situations as affordances: The example of self-esteem. *Journal of Research in Personality, 43,* 250.

Holt-Lunstad, J., Birmingham, W. A., & Light, K. C. (2008). Influence of a "warm touch" support enhancement intervention among married couples on ambulatory blood pressure, oxytocin, alpha amylase, and cortisol. *Psychosomatic Medicine, 70,* 976–985.

Holtzworth-Munroe, A., & Meehan, J. C. (2005). Partner violence and men: A focus on the male perpetrator. In W. M. Pinsof & J. Lebow (Eds.), *Family psychology: The art of the science* (pp. 167–190). New York: Oxford University Press.

Honeycutt, J. M. (1996). How "helpful" are self–help relational books? Common sense or counterintuitive information. *Personal Relationship Issues, 3,* 1–3.

Hood, K. B., & Shook, N. J. (2011, January). *Attitudes, perceptions, and gender: Differences among college students' attitudes toward condom use.* Poster presented at the meeting of the Society for Personality and Social Psychology, San Antonio, TX.

Horan, S. M., & Booth-Butterfield, M. (2010). Investing in affection: An investigation of affection exchange theory and relational qualities. *Communication Quarterly, 58,* 394–413.

Houts, R. M., Barnett-Walker, K. C., Paley, B., & Cox, M. J. (2008). Patterns of couple interaction during the transition to parenthood. *Personal Relationships, 15,* 103–122.

Howard, E. S., Gardner, W. L., & Thompson, L. (2007). The role of the self-concept and the social context in determining the behavior of power holders: Self-construal in intergroup versus dyadic dispute resolution negotiations. *Journal of Personality and Social Psychology, 93,* 614–631.

Howard, J. W., & Dawes, R. M. (1976). Linear prediction of marital happiness. *Personality and Social Psychology Bulletin, 2,* 478–480.

Howes, C. (2011). Friendship in early childhood. In K. Rubin, W. Bukowski, & B. Laursen (Eds.), *Handbook of peer interactions, relationships, and groups* (pp. 180–194). New York: Guilford Press.

Howland, M., & Simpson, J. A. (2010). Getting in under the radar: A dyadic view of invisible support. *Psychological Science, 21,* 1878–1885.

Hoyt, T., & Yeater, E. A. (2011). Individual and situational influences on men's responses to dating and social situations. *Journal of Interpersonal Violence, 26,* 1723–1740.

Hsueh, A. C., Morrison, K. R., & Doss, B. D. (2009). Qualitative reports of problems in cohabitating relationships: Comparisons to married and dating relationships. *Journal of Family Psychology, 23,* 236–246.

Hughes, S. M., Dispenza, F., & Gallup, G. G., Jr. (2004). Ratings of voice attractiveness predict sexual behavior and body configuration. *Evolution and Human Behavior, 25,* 295–304.

Hughes, S. M., Farley, S. D., & Rhodes, B. C. (2010). Vocal and physiological changes in response to the physical attractiveness of conversational partners. *Journal of Nonverbal Behavior, 34,* 155–167.

Hughes, S. M., & Gallup, G. G., Jr. (2003). Sex differences in morphological predictors of sexual behavior: Shoulder to hip and waist to hip ratios. *Evolution and Human Behavior, 24,* 173–178.

Hugill, N., Fink, B., & Neave, N. (2010). The role of human body movements in mate selection. *Evolutionary Psychology, 8,* 66–89.

Hunt, M. M. (1959). *The natural history of love.* New York: Knopf.

Hunter, S. (2007). *Coming out and disclosures: LGBT persons across the life span.* New York: Haworth Press.

Huston, T. L. (2002). Power. In H. H. Kelley, E. Berscheid, A. Christensen et al. (Eds.), *Close relationships* (pp. 265–314). Clinton Corners, NY: Percheron Press.

Huston, T. L. (2009). What's love got to do with it? Why some marriages succeed and others fail. *Personal Relationships, 16,* 301–327.

Huston, T. L., & Chorost, A. F. (1994). Behavioral buffers on the effect of negativity on marital satisfaction: A longitudinal study. *Personal Relationships, 1,* 223–239.

Huston, T. L., & Houts, R. M. (1998). The psychological infrastructure of courtship and marriage: The role of personality and compatibility in romantic relationships. In T. N. Bradbury (Ed.), *The developmental course of marital dysfunction* (pp. 114–151). New York: Cambridge University Press.

Hyde, J. S. (2007). New directions in the study of gender similarities and differences. *Current Directions in Psychological Science, 16,* 259–263.

Ickes, W. (1985). Sex-role influences on compatibility in relationships. In W. Ickes (Ed.), *Compatible and incompatible relationships* (pp. 187–208). New York: Springer-Verlag.

Ickes, W. (2000). Methods of studying close relationships. In W. Ickes & S. Duck (Eds.), *The social psychology of personal relationships* (pp. 159–180). Chichester, England: Wiley.

Ickes, W. (2003). *Everyday mind reading: Understanding what other people think and feel.* Amherst, NY: Prometheus Books.

Ickes, W. (2009). *Strangers in a strange lab: How personality shapes our initial encounters with others.* New York: Oxford University Press.

Ickes, W., & Barnes, R. D. (1978). Boys and girls together—and alienated: On enacting stereotyped sex roles in mixed-sex dyads. *Journal of Personality and Social Psychology, 36,* 669–683.

Ickes, W., & Simpson, J. A. (2001). Motivational aspects of empathic accuracy. In G. J. O. Fletcher & M. S. Clark (Eds.), *Blackwell handbook of social psychology: Interpersonal processes* (pp. 229–249). Malden. MA: Blackwell.

Iemmola, F., & Ciani, A. C. (2009). New evidence of genetic factors influencing sexual orientation in men: Female fecundity increase in the maternal line. *Archives of Sexual Behavior, 38,* 393–399.

Igarashi, T., Takai, J., & Yoshida, T. (2005). Gender differences in social network development via mobile phone text messages: A longitudinal study. *Journal of Social and Personal Relationships, 22,* 691–713.

Iida, M., Seidman, G., Shrout, P. E., Fujita, K., & Bolger, N. (2008). Modeling support provision in intimate relationships. *Journal of Personality and Social Psychology, 94,* 460–478.

Impett, E. A., Breines, J. G., & Strachman, A. (2010a). Keeping it real: Young adult women's authenticity in relationships and daily condom use. *Personal Relationships, 17,* 573–584.

Impett, E. A., Gable, S. L., & Peplau, L. A. (2005). Giving up and giving in: The costs and benefits of daily sacrifice in intimate relationships. *Journal of Personality and Social Psychology, 89,* 327–344.

Impett, E. A., & Gordon, A. M. (2008). For the good of others: Toward a positive psychology of sacrifice. In S. Lopez (Ed.), *Positive psychology: Exploring the best in people* (Vol. 2, pp. 79–100). Westport, CT: Praeger.

Impett, E. A., Gordon, A. M., Kogan, A., Oveis, C., Gable, S. L., & Keltner, D. (2010b). Moving toward more perfect unions: Daily and long-term consequences of approach and avoidance goals in romantic relationships. *Journal of Personality and Social Psychology, 99,* 948–963.

Impett, E. A., & Peplau, L. A. (2006). "His" and "her" relationships? A review of the empirical evidence. In A. L. Vangelisti & D. Perlman (Eds.), *The Cambridge handbook of personal relationships* (pp. 273–291). New York: Cambridge University Press.

Impett, E. A., Peplau, L. A., & Gable, S. L. (2005). Approach and avoidance sexual motives: Implications for personal and interpersonal well-being. *Personal Relationships, 12,* 465–482.

Impett, E. A., Strachman, A., Finkel, E. J., & Gable, S. L. (2008). Maintaining sexual desire in intimate relationships: The importance of approach goals. *Journal of Personality and Social Psychology, 94,* 808–823.

Iredale, W., Van Vugt, M., & Dunbar, R. (2008). Showing off in humans: Male generosity as a mating signal. *Evolutionary Psychology, 6,* 386–392.

Ireland, M. E., Slatcher, R. B., Eastwick, P. W., Scissors, L. E., Finkel, E. J., & Pennebaker, J. W. (2011). Language style matching predicts relationship initiation and stability. *Psychological Science, 22,* 39–44.

Italie, L. (2011, January 26). Pups or paramours? 14 percent prefer pets. *Houston Chronicle,* p. A6.

Ivcevic, Z., & Ambady, N. (2011, January). *Face to (Face)book: Comparing online and offline social behavior.* Poster presented at the meeting of the Society for Personality and Social Psychology, San Antonio, TX.

Iyengar, S. S. (2007, October). *The effects of gender and race on mate selection: Evidence from a speed-dating experiment.* Paper presented at the meeting of the Society for Experimental Social Psychology, Chicago, IL.

Jackson, J. J., Wood, D., Bogg, T., Walton, K. E., Harms, P. D., & Roberts, B. W. (2010). What do conscientious people do? Development and validation of the Behavioral Indicators of Conscientiousness (BIC). *Journal of Research in Personality, 44,* 501–511.

Jackson, T., Chen, H., Guo, C., & Gao, X. (2006). Stories we love by: Conceptions of love among couples from the People's Republic of China and the United States. *Journal of Cross-Cultural Psychology, 37,* 446–464.

Jacobson, N. S., Follette, W. C., & McDonald, D. W. (1982). Reactivity to positive and negative behavior in distressed and nondistressed married couples. *Journal of Consulting and Clinical Psychology, 50,* 706–714.

Jacobson, N. S., & Margolin, G. (1979). *Marital therapy: Strategies based on social learning and behavior exchange principles.* New York: Brunner/Mazel.

Jacques-Tiura, A. J., Abbey, A., & Parkhill, M. R., & Zawacki, T. (2007). Why do some men misperceive women's sexual intentions more frequently than others do? An application of the Confluence Model. *Personality and Social Psychology Bulletin, 33,* 1467–1480.

Jasieńska, G., Lipson, S. F., Ellison, P. T., Thune, I., & Ziomkiewicz, A. (2006). Symmetrical women have higher potential fertility. *Evolution and Human Behavior, 27,* 390–400.

Jasieńska, G., Ziomkiewicz, A., Ellison, P. T., Lipson, S. F., & Thune, I. (2004). Large breasts and narrow waists indicate high reproductive potential in women. *Proceedings of the Royal Society of London B, 271,* 1213–1217.

Jayson, S. (2009a, March 26). Gender roles see a "conflict" shift. *Houston Chronicle,* pp. 9B–10B.

Jayson, S. (2009b, December 1). With this nagging doubt, I thee wed. *USA Today,* p. 1A.

Jayson, S. (2010, November 18). We're just not that into marriage. *USA Today,* p. 1A.

Jemmott, J. B. (2010). Efficacy of a theory-based abstinence-only intervention over 24 months: A randomized controlled trial with young adolescents. *Archives of Pediatrics & Adolescent Medicine, 164,* 152–159.

Jenkins, N., Sinclair, E., Myerberg, L., & Burnette, J. L. (2011, January). *Forgiveness as a mechanism of self-regulation: An ego-depletion model.* Poster presented at the meeting of the Society for Personality and Social Psychology, San Antonio, TX.

Jensen-Campbell, L. A., & Graziano, W. G. (2001). Agreeableness as a moderator of interpersonal conflict. *Journal of Personality, 69,* 323–362.

Jensen-Campbell, L. A., Graziano, W. G., & West, S. G. (1995). Dominance, prosocial orientation, and female preferences: Do nice guys really finish last? *Journal of Personality and Social Psychology, 68,* 427–440.

Jensen-Campbell, L. A., Knack, J. M., Waldrip, A. M., & Campbell, S. D. (2007). Do Big Five personality traits associated with self-control influence the regulation of anger and aggression? *Journal of Research in Personality, 41,* 403–424.

Jöchle, W. (1973). Coitus-induced ovulation. *Contraception, 7,* 523–564.

Johnson, K. L., Gill, S., Reichman, V., & Tassinary, L. G. (2007). Swagger, sway, and sexuality: Judging sexual orientation from body motion and morphology. *Journal of Personality and Social Psychology, 93,* 321–334.

Johnson, M. P. (1999). Personal, moral, and structural commitment to relationships: Experiences of choice and constraint. In J. M. Adams & W. H. Jones (Eds.), *Handbook of interpersonal commitment and relationship stability* (pp. 73–87). New York: Kluwer Academic/Plenum.

Johnson, M. P. (2008). *A typology of domestic violence: Intimate terrorism, violent resistance, and situational couple violence.* Boston: Northeastern University Press.

Johnson, S. M. (2004). *Creating connection: The practice of emotionally focused couple therapy* (2nd ed.). New York: Brunner-Routledge.

Johnson, S. M. (2009). Attachment theory and emotionally focused therapy for individuals and couples: Perfect partners. In J. H. Obegi, & E. Berant (Eds.), *Attachment theory and research in clinical work with adults* (pp. 410–433). New York: Guilford Press.

Johnson, W., McGue, M., Krueger, R. F., & Bouchard, T. J., Jr. (2004). Marriage and personality: A genetic analysis. *Journal of Personality and Social Psychology, 86,* 285–294.

Jokela, M. (2009). Physical attractiveness and reproductive success in humans: Evidence from the late 20th century United States. *Evolution and Human Behavior, 30,* 342–350.

Jonason, P. K., & Fisher, T. D. (2009). The power of prestige: Why young men report having more sex partners than young women. *Sex Roles, 60,* 151–159.

Jonason, P. K., Li, N. P., & Buss, D. M. (2010). The costs and benefits of the Dark Triad: Implications for mate poaching and mate retention tactics. *Personality and Individual Differences, 48,* 373–378.

Jonason, P. K., & Marks, M. J. (2009). Common vs. uncommon sexual acts: Evidence for the sexual double standard. *Sex Roles, 60,* 357–365.

Jones, D. (1995). Sexual selection, physical attractiveness, and facial neotony: Cross-cultural evidence and implications. *Current Anthropology, 36,* 723–748.

Jones, E. E., & Pittman, T. (1982). Toward a general theory of strategic self-presentation. In J. Suls (Ed.), *Psychological perspectives on the self* (pp. 231–262). Hillsdale, NJ: Erlbaum.

Jones, J. M. (2008, March 25). Most Americans not willing to forgive unfaithful spouse. *Gallup Poll News Service.* Retrieved from http://www.gallup.com/poll/105682/Most-Americans-Willing-Forgive-Unfaithful-Spouse.aspx

Jones, J. M. (2010, May 24). American's opposition to gay marriage eases slightly. *Gallup Poll News Service.* Retrieved from http://www.gallup.com/poll/128291/Americans-Opposition-Gay-Marriage-Eases-Slightly.aspx

Jones, J. T., & Cunningham, J. D. (1996). Attachment styles and other predictors of relationship satisfaction in dating couples. *Personal Relationships, 3,* 387–399.

Jones, J. T., Pelham, B. W., Carvallo, M., & Mirenberg, M. C. (2004). How do I love thee? Let me count the Js: Implicit egotism and interpersonal attraction. *Journal of Personality and Social Psychology, 87,* 665–683.

Jones, W. H., & Burdette, M. P. (1994). Betrayal in relationships. In A. L. Weber & J. H. Harvey (Eds.), *Perspectives on close relationships* (pp. 243–262). Boston: Allyn & Bacon.

Jones, W. H., Crouch, L. L., & Scott, S. (1997). Trust and betrayal: The psychology of trust violations. In R. Hogan, J. Johnson, & S. R. Briggs (Eds.), *Handbook of personality psychology* (pp. 466–482). New York: Academic Press.

Jones, W. H., Moore, D. S., Schratter, A., & Negel, L. A. (2001). Interpersonal transgressions and betrayals. In R. M. Kowalski (Ed.), *Behaving badly: Aversive behaviors in interpersonal relationships* (pp. 233–256). Washington DC: American Psychological Association.

Jose, A., O'Leary, K. D., & Moyer, A. (2010). Does premarital cohabitation predict subsequent marital stability and marital quality? A meta-analysis. *Journal of Marriage and Family, 72,* 105–116.

Judge, T. A., & Cable, D. M. (2004). The effect of physical height on workplace success and income: Preliminary test of a theoretical model. *Journal of Applied Psychology, 89,* 428–441.

Judge, T. A., Hurst, C., & Simon, L. S. (2009). Does it pay to be smart, attractive, or confident (or all three)? Relationships among general mental ability, physical attractiveness, core self-evaluations, and income. *Journal of Applied Psychology, 94,* 742–755.

Kachadourian, L. K., Fincham, F., & Davila, J. (2004). The tendency to forgive in dating and married couples: The role of attachment and relationship satisfaction. *Personal Relationships, 11,* 373–393.

Kafetsios, K. (2004). Attachment and emotional intelligence abilities across the life course. *Personality and Individual Differences, 37,* 129–145.

Kafetsios, K., & Nezlek, J. B. (2002). Attachment styles in everyday social interaction. *European Journal of Social Psychology, 32,* 719–735.

Kahneman, D., & Tversky, A. (1982). The psychology of preferences. *Scientific American, 246,* 160–173.

Kaighobadi, F., Shackelford, T. K., & Buss, D. M. (2010). Spousal mate retention in the newlywed year and three years later. *Personality and Individual Differences, 48,* 414–418.

Kaighobadi, F., Shackelford, T. K., Popp, D., Moyer, R. M., Bates, V. M., & Liddle, J. R. (2009). Perceived risk of female infidelity moderates the relationship between men's personality and partner-directed violence. *Journal of Research in Personality, 43,* 1033–1039.

Kaighobadi, F., Starratt, V. G., Shackelford, T. K., & Popp, D. (2008). Male mate retention mediates the relationship between female sexual infidelity and female-directed violence. *Personality and Individual Differences, 44,* 1422–1431.

Kalbfleisch, P. J., & Herold, A. L. (2006). Sex, power, and communication. In K. Dindia & D. J. Canary (Eds.), *Sex differences and similarities in communication* (2nd ed., pp. 299–313). Mahwah, NJ: Erlbaum.

Kammrath, L. K., Ames, D. R., & Scholer, A. A. (2007). Keeping up impressions: Inferential rules for impression change across the Big Five. *Journal of Experimental Social Psychology, 43,* 450–457.

Kammrath, L. K., & Dweck, C. (2006). Voicing conflict: Preferred conflict strategies among incremental and entity theorists. *Personality and Social Psychology Bulletin, 32,* 1497–1508.

Kammrath, L. K., & Peetz, J. (2011). The limits of love: Predicting immediate versus sustained caring behaviors in close relationships. *Journal of Experimental Social Psychology, 47*, 411–417.

Kamphuis, J. H., Emmelkamp, P. M. G., & de Vries, V. (2004). Informant personality descriptions of postintimate stalkers using the Five Factor Profile. *Journal of Personality Assessment, 82*, 169–178.

Kanazawa, S. (2010). Evolutionary psychology and intelligence research. *American Psychologist, 65*, 279–289.

Kane, H. S., Jaremka, L. M., Guichard, A. C., Ford, M. B., Collins, N. L., & Feeney, B. C. (2007). Feeling supported and feeling satisfied: How one partner's attachment style predicts the other partner's relationship experiences. *Journal of Social and Personal Relationships, 24*, 535–555.

Kane, H., McCall, C., Collins, N., & Blascovich, J. (2009, February). *Understanding the effects of social support from a significant other in an immersive virtual environment.* Paper presented at the meeting of the Society for Personality and Social Psychology, Tampa, FL.

Kantor, L. M., Santelli, J. S., Teitler, J., & Balmer, R. (2008). Abstinence-only policies and programs: An overview. *Sexuality Research & Social Policy, 5*, 6–17.

Kaplan, R. M., & Kronick, R. G. (2006). Marital status and longevity in the United States population. *Journal of Epidemiology & Community Health, 60*, 760–765.

Kaplar, M. E., & Gordon, A. K. (2004). The enigma of altruistic lying: Perspective differences in what motivates and justifies lie telling within romantic relationships. *Personal Relationships, 11*, 489–507.

Karney, B. R., & Bradbury, T. N. (1995). The longitudinal course of marital quality and stability: A review of theory, methods, and research. *Psychological Bulletin, 118*, 3–34.

Karney, B. R., & Bradbury, T. N. (2000). Attributions in marriage: State or trait? A growth curve analysis. *Journal of Personality and Social Psychology, 78*, 295–309.

Karney, B. R., & Bradbury, T. N. (2005). Contextual influences on marriage: Implications for policy and intervention. *Current Directions in Psychological Science, 14*, 171–174.

Karney, B. R., Davila, J., Cohan, C. L., Sullivan, K. T., Johnson, M. D., & Bradbury, T. N. (1995). An empirical investigation of sampling strategies in marital research. *Journal of Marriage and the Family, 57*, 909–920.

Karney, B. R., & Frye, N. E. (2002). "But we've been getting better lately": Comparing prospective and retrospective views of relationship development. *Journal of Personality and Social Psychology, 82*, 222–238.

Karney, B. R., McNulty, J. K., & Frye, N. E. (2001). A social-cognitive perspective on the maintenance and deterioration of relationship satisfaction. In J. H. Harvey & A. E. Wenzel (Eds.), *Close romantic relationships: Maintenance and enhancement* (p 195–214). Mahwah, NJ: Erlbaum.

Karremans, J. C., Frankenhuis, W. E., & Arons, S. (2010). Blind men prefer a low waist-to-hip ratio. *Evolution and Human Behavior, 31*, 182–186.

Kashy, D. A., Campbell, L., & Harris, D. W. (2006). Advances in data analytic approaches for relationships research: The broad utility of hierarchical linear modeling. In A. L. Vangelisti & D. Perlman (Eds.), *The Cambridge handbook of personal relationships* (pp. 73–89). New York: Cambridge University Press.

Kashy, D. A., & DePaulo, B. M. (1996). Who lies? *Journal of Personality and Social Psychology, 70*, 1037–1051.

Katz, J., & Myhr, L. (2008). Perceived conflict patterns and relationship quality associated with verbal sexual coercion by male dating partners. *Journal of Interpersonal Violence, 23*, 798–814.

Kaul, M., & Lakey, B. (2003). Where is the support in perceived support? The role of generic relationship satisfaction and enacted support in perceived support's relation to low distress. *Journal of Social and Clinical Psychology, 22*, 59–78.

Kavanagh, P. S., Robins, S. C., & Ellis, B. J. (2010). The mating sociometer: A regulatory mechanism for mating aspirations. *Journal of Personality and Social Psychology, 99*, 120–132.

Kayser, K., & Rao, S. S. (2006). Process of disaffection in relationship breakdown. In M. A. Fine & J. H. Harvey (Eds.), *Handbook of divorce and relationship dissolution* (pp. 201–221). Mahwah, NJ: Erlbaum.

Keating, C. F. (2006). Why and how the silent self speaks volumes: Functional approaches to nonverbal impression management. In V. Manusov & M. L. Patterson (Eds.), *The Sage handbook of nonverbal communication* (pp. 321–339). Thousand Oaks, CA: Sage.

Kellas, J. K., Bean, D., Cunningham, C., & Cheng, K. Y. (2008). The ex-files: Trajectories, turning points, and adjustment in the development of post-dissolutional relationships. *Journal of Social and Personal Relationships, 25,* 23–50.

Kellas, J. K., & Manusov, V. (2003). What's in a story? The relationship between narrative completeness and adjustment to relationship dissolution. *Journal of Social and Personal Relationships, 20,* 285–307.

Kellerman, J., Lewis, J., & Laird, J. D. (1989). Looking and loving: The effects of mutual gaze on feelings of love. *Journal of Research in Personality, 23,* 145–161.

Kelley, H. H. (1979). *Personal relationships: Their structures and processes.* Hillsdale, NJ: Erlbaum.

Kelley, H. H. (2002). Love and commitment. In H. H. Kelley, E. Berscheid, A. Christensen et al. (Eds.), *Close relationships* (pp. 265–314). Clinton Corners, NY: Percheron Press.

Kelley, H. H., & Thibaut, J. W. (1978). *Interpersonal relations: A theory of interdependence.* New York: Wiley.

Kelly, E. L., & Conley, J. J. (1987). Personality and compatibility: A prospective analysis of marital stability and marital satisfaction. *Journal of Personality and Social Psychology, 52,* 27–40.

Keltner, D., Gruenfeld, D., Galinsky, A., & Kraus, M. W. (2010). Paradoxes of power: Dynamics of the acquisition, experience, and social regulation of social power. In A. Guinote & T. Vescio (Eds.), *The social psychology of power* (pp. 177–208). New York: Guilford Press.

Keltner, D., Haidt, J., & Shiota, M. N. (2006). Social functionalism and the evolution of emotions. In M. Schaller, J. A. Simpson, & D. T. Kenrick (Eds.), *Evolution and social psychology* (pp. 115–142). New York: Psychology Press.

Kennedy, K. A., & Pronin, E. (2008). When disagreement gets ugly: Perceptions of bias and the escalation of conflict. *Personality and Social Psychology Bulletin, 34,* 833–848.

Kenny, D. A., & Ledermann, T. (2010). Detecting, measuring, and testing dyadic patterns in the actor-partner interdependence model. *Journal of Family Psychology, 24,* 359–366.

Kenny, D. A., West, T. V., Cillessen, A. H. N., Cole, J. D., Dodge, K. A., Hubbard, J. A., & Schwartz, D. (2007). Accuracy in judgments of aggressiveness. *Personality and Social Psychology Bulletin, 33,* 1225–1236.

Kenrick, D. T., Griskevicius, V., Neuberg, S. L., & Schaller, M. (2010). Renovating the pyramid of needs: Contemporary extensions built upon ancient foundations. *Perspectives on Psychological Science, 5,* 292–314.

Kenrick, D. T., Sadalla, E. K., Groth, G., & Trost, M. R. (1990). Evolution, traits, and the stages of human courtship: Qualifying the parental investment model. *Journal of Personality, 58,* 97–116.

Kephart, W. (1967). Some correlates of romantic love. *Journal of Marriage and the Family, 29,* 470–479.

Keysar, B., & Henly, A. S. (2002). Speakers' overestimation of their effectiveness. *Psychological Science, 13,* 207–212.

Kiecolt-Glaser, J. K., Bane, C., Glaser, R., & Malarkey, W. B. (2003). Love, marriage, and divorce: Newlyweds' stress hormones foreshadow relationship changes. *Journal of Consulting and Clinical Psychology, 71,* 176–188.

Kiefer, A. K., & Sanchez, D. T. (2007). Scripting sexual passivity: A gender role perspective. *Personal Relationships, 14,* 269–290.

Kilpatrick, S. D., Bissonnette, V. L., & Rusbult, C. E. (2002). Empathic accuracy and accommodative behavior among newly married couples. *Personal Relationships, 9,* 369–393.

Kim, H. K., & McKenry, P. C. (2002). The relationship between marriage and psychological well-being: A longitudinal analysis. *Journal of Family Issues, 23,* 885–911.

Kim, Y. (2006). Gender, attachment, and relationship duration on cardiovascular reactivity to stress in a laboratory study of dating couples. *Personal Relationships, 13,* 103–114.

Kimmel, A. J. (2004). Ethical issues in social psychology research. In C. Sansone, C. C. Morf, & A. T. Panter (Eds.), *The Sage handbook of methods in social psychology* (pp. 45–70). Thousand Oaks, CA: Sage.

King, R. B., & Bratter, J. L. (2007). A path toward interracial marriage: Women's first partners and husbands across racial lines. *Sociological Quarterly, 48,* 343–369.

Kirby, D. B. (2008). The impact of abstinence and comprehensive sex and STD/HIV education programs on adolescent sexual behavior. *Sexuality Research & Social Policy, 5,* 18–27.

Kite, M. E., Deaux, K., & Haines, E. L. (2008). Gender stereotypes. In F. L. Denmark & M. A. Paludi (Eds.), *Psychology of women: A handbook of issues and theories* (2nd ed., pp. 205–236). Westport, CT: Praeger.

Klapper, B. (2010, November 23). Poll: Boomers bemoan sex life. *Bryan-College Station Eagle*, p. A5.

Kleinke, C. L. (1986). Gaze and eye contact: A research review. *Psychological Bulletin, 100*, 78–100.

Kleinke, C. L., & Dean, G. O. (1990). Evaluation of men and women receiving positive and negative responses with various acquaintance strategies. *Journal of Social Behavior and Personality, 5*, 369–377.

Kline, S. L., & Stafford, L. (2004). A comparison of interaction rules and interaction frequency in relationship to marital quality. *Communication Reports, 17*, 11–26.

Klohnen, E. C., & Luo, S. (2003). Interpersonal attraction and personality: What is attractive—Self similarity, ideal similarity, complementarity, or attachment security? *Journal of Personality and Social Psychology, 85*, 709–722.

Klusmann, D. (2002). Sexual motivation and the duration of partnership. *Archives of Sexual Behavior, 31*, 275–287.

Klusmann, D. (2006). Sperm competition and female procurement of male resources. *Human Nature, 17*, 283–300.

Kluwer, E. S., Tumewu, M., & van den Bos, K. (2009). Men's and women's reactions to fair and unfair treatment in relationship conflict. *Personal Relationships, 16*, 455–474.

Knapp-Kline, K., Pennington, L. M., Freeman, B., Boyd, C. H., & Burkey, M. (2005, May). *The Rapunzel effect: Health and length of hair on perceptions of attractiveness.* Poster presented at the meeting of the Association for Psychological Science, New Orleans, LA.

Knäuper, B., Kornik, R., Atkinson, K., Guberman, C., & Aydin, C. (2005). Motivation influences the underestimation of cumulative risk. *Personality and Social Psychology Bulletin, 31*, 1511–1523.

Knee, C. R. (1998). Implicit theories of relationships: Assessment and prediction of romantic relationship initiation, coping, and longevity. *Journal of Personality and Social Psychology, 74*, 360–370.

Knee, C. R., & Bush, A. L. (2008). Relationship beliefs and their role in romantic relationship initiation. In S. Sprecher, A. Wenzel, & J. Harvey (Eds.), *Handbook of relationship initiation* (pp. 471–485). New York: Psychology Press.

Knee, C. R., Nanayakkara, A., Vietor, N. A., Neighbors, C., & Patrick, H. (2001). Implicit theories of relationships: Who cares if romantic partners are less than ideal? *Personality and Social Psychology Bulletin, 27*, 808–819.

Knee, C. R., Patrick, H., & Lonsbary, C. (2003). Implicit theories of relationships: Orientations toward evaluation and cultivation. *Personality and Social Psychology Review, 7*, 41–55.

Knee, C. R., Patrick, H., Vietor, N. A., & Neighbors, C. (2004). Implicit theories of relationships: Moderators of the link between conflict and commitment. *Personality and Social Psychology Bulletin, 30*, 617–628.

Knobloch, L. K., & Donovan-Kicken, E. (2006). Perceived involvement of network members in courtships: A test of the relational turbulence model. *Personal Relationships, 13*, 281–302.

Knobloch, L. K., & Solomon, D. H. (2004). Interference and facilitation from partners in the development of interdependence within romantic relationships. *Personal Relationships, 11*, 115–130.

Knobloch, L. K., Solomon, D. H., & Cruz, M. G. (2001). The role of relationship development and attachment in the experience of romantic jealousy. *Personal Relationships, 8*, 205–224.

Knobloch, L. K., & Theiss, J. A. (2010). An actor-partner interdependence model of relational turbulence: Cognitions and emotions. *Journal of Social and Personal Relationships, 27*, 595–619.

Knoester, C., & Booth, A. (2000). Barriers to divorce: When are they effective? When are they not? *Journal of Family Issues, 21*, 78–99.

Knöfler, T., & Imhof, M. (2007). Does sexual orientation have an impact on nonverbal behavior in interpersonal communication? *Journal of Nonverbal Behavior, 31*, 189–204.

Knudson-Martin, C., & Mahoney, A. R. (2005). Moving beyond gender: Processes that create relationship equality. *Journal of Marital & Family Therapy, 31*, 235–258.

Koball, H. L., Moiduddin, E., Henderson, J., Goesling, B., & Besculides, M. (2010). What do we know about the link between marriage and health? *Journal of Family Issues, 31*, 1019–1040.

Koch, E. J., & Shepperd, J. A. (2008). Testing competence and acceptance explanations of self-esteem. *Self and Identity, 7,* 54–74.

Koch, S. C., Baehne, C. G., Kruse, L., Zimmerman, F., & Zumbach, J. (2010). Visual dominance and visual egalitarianism: Individual and group-level influences of sex and status in group inter-actions. *Journal of Nonverbal Behavior, 34,* 137–153.

Koenig, B. L., Kirkpatrick, L. A., & Ketelaar, T. (2007). Misperception of sexual and romantic inter-ests in opposite-sex friendships: Four hypotheses. *Personal Relationships, 14,* 411–429.

Koeppel, L. B., Montagne-Miller, Y., O'Hair, D., & Cody, M. J. (1993). Friendly? Flirting? Wrong? In P. J. Kalbfleisch (Ed.), *Interpersonal communication: Evolving interpersonal relationships* (pp. 13–32). Hillsdale, NJ: Erlbaum.

Koerner, A. F., & Fitzpatrick, M. A. (2002). Nonverbal communication and marital adjustment and satisfaction: The role of decoding relationship relevant and relationship irrelevant affect. *Communication Monographs, 69,* 33–51.

Kogan, A., Impett, E. A., Oveis, C., Hui, B., Gordon, A. M., & Keltner, D. (2010). When giving feels good: The intrinsic benefits of sacrifice in romantic relationships for the communally moti-vated. *Psychological Science, 21,* 1918–1924.

Kouzakova, M., van Baaren, R., & van Knippenberg, A. (2010). Lack of behavioral imitation in human interactions enhances salivary cortisol levels. *Hormones and Behavior, 57,* 421–426.

Kowalski, R. M. (2003). *Complaining, teasing, and other annoying behaviors.* New Haven, CT: Yale University Press.

Krahé, B., Bieneck, S., & Scheinberger-Olwig, R. (2007). The role of sexual scripts in sexual aggres-sion and victimization. *Archives of Sexual Behavior, 36,* 687–701.

Kraus, M. W., & Chen, S. (2010). Facial-feature resemblance elicits the transference effect. *Psycho-logical Science, 21,* 518–522.

Kraut, R. E., & Poe, D. B. (1980). Behavioral roots of person perception: The deception judgments of customs inspectors and laymen. *Journal of Personality and Social Psychology, 39,* 784–798.

Krishnamurti, T., & Loewenstein, G. (2008, February). *How good does infidelity feel: A survey of desire and satisfaction with primary and secondary partners.* Poster presented at the meeting of the Soci-ety for Personality and Social Psychology, Alburquerque, NM.

Kropp, J. P., & Haynes, O. M. (1987). Abusive and nonabusive mothers' ability to identify general and specific emotion signals of infants. *Child Development, 58,* 187–190.

Kruger, D. J. (2008a). Male financial consumption is associated with higher mating intentions and mating success. *Evolutionary Psychology, 6,* 603–612.

Kruger, D. J. (2008b). Young adults attempt exchanges in reproductively relevant currencies. *Evolu-tionary Psychology, 6,* 204–212.

Kruger, D. J., Fisher, M. L., Strout, S. L., & Fitzgerald, C. (2010, May). *Was that cheating? Perceptions vary by type of behavior and reproductive strategy.* Poster presented at the meeting of the Associa-tion for Psychological Science, Boston, MA.

Kruger, D. J., & Fitzgerald, C. J. (2011). Reproductive strategies and relationship preferences associ-ated with prestigious and dominant men. *Personality and Individual Differences, 50,* 365–369.

Kruger, D. J., Fitzgerald, C. J., & Peterson, T. (2010). Female scarcity reduces women's marital ages and increases variance in men's marital ages. *Evolutionary Psychology, 8,* 420–431.

Kruger, J., Epley, N., Parker, J., & Ng, Z. (2005). Egocentrism over e-mail: Can we communicate as well as we think? *Journal of Personality and Social Psychology, 89,* 925–936.

Kruger, J., & Gilovich, T. (1999). "Naïve cynicism" in everyday theories of responsibility assess-ment: On biased assumption of bias. *Journal of Personality and Social Psychology, 76,* 743–753.

Kruger, J., & Gilovich, T. (2004). Actions, intentions, and self-assessment: The road to self-enhancement is paved with good intentions. *Personality and Social Psychology Bulletin, 30,* 328–339.

Kruse, S. A., Okdie, B. M., Hull, C. A., Sagarin, B. J., & Guadagno, R. E. (2008, February). *Mate selec-tion and attitudes toward infidelity: A new twist.* Poster presented at the meeting of the Society for Personality and Social Psychology, Albuquerque, NM.

Kuhle, B. X., Smedley, K. D., & Schmitt, D. P. (2009). Sex differences in the motivation and mitiga-tion of jealousy-induced interrogations. *Personality and Individual Differences, 46,* 499–502.

Kuijer, R. G., Buunk, B. P., Ybema, J. F., & Wobbes, T. (2002). The relation between perceived inequity, marital satisfaction and emotions among couples facing cancer. *British Journal of Social Psychology, 41*, 39–56.

Kumashiro, M., Rusbult, C. E., & Finkel, E. J. (2008). Navigating personal and relational concerns: The quest for equilibrium. *Journal of Personality and Social Psychology, 95*, 94–110.

Kunkel, D., Eyal, K., Donnerstein, E., Farrar, K. M, Biely, E., & Rideout, V. (2007). Sexual socialization messages on entertainment television: Comparing content trends 1997–2002. *Media Psychology, 9*, 595–622.

Kunstman, J. W., & Maner, J. K. (2011). Sexual overperception: Power, mating motives, and biases in social judgment. *Journal of Personality and Social Psychology, 100*, 282–294.

Kurdek, L. A. (1999). The nature and predictors of the trajectory of change in marital quality for husbands and wives over the first 10 years of marriage. *Developmental Psychology, 35*, 1283–1296.

Kurdek, L. A. (2002). Predicting the timing of separation and marital satisfaction: An eight-year prospective longitudinal study. *Journal of Marriage and the Family, 64*, 163–179.

Kurdek, L. A. (2004). Are gay and lesbian cohabiting couples *really* different from heterosexual married couples? *Journal of Marriage and Family, 66*, 880–900.

Kurdek, L. A. (2005). What do we know about gay and lesbian couples? *Current Directions in Psychological Science, 14*, 251–254.

Kurdek, L. A. (2006a). Differences between partners from heterosexual, gay, and lesbian cohabiting couples. *Journal of Marriage and Family, 68*, 509–528.

Kurdek, L. A. (2006b). The nature and correlates of deterrents to leaving a relationship. *Personal Relationships, 13*, 521–535.

Kurdek, L. A. (2008). A general model of relationship commitment: Evidence from same-sex partners. *Personal Relationships, 15*, 391–405.

Kurdek, L. A. (2008a). Change in relationship quality for partners from lesbian, gay male, and heterosexual couples. *Journal of Family Psychology, 22*, 701–711.

Kurdek, L. A. (2008b). Pet dogs as attachment figures. *Journal of Social and Personal Relationships, 25*, 247–266.

Kurdek, L. A. (2009). Pet dogs as attachment figures for adult owners. *Journal of Family Psychology, 23*, 439–446.

Kurdek, L. A., & Schmitt, J. P. (1986). Interaction of sex role self-concept with relationship quality and relationship beliefs in married, heterosexual cohabiting, gay, and lesbian couples. *Journal of Personality and Social Psychology, 51*, 365–370.

Kurzban, R., & Weeden, J. (2005). HurryDate: Mate preferences in action. *Evolution and Human Behavior, 26*, 227–244.

Kwang, T., & Swann, W. B., Jr. (2010). Do people embrace praise even when they feel unworthy? A review of critical tests of self-enhancement versus self-verification. *Personality and Social Psychology Review, 14*, 263–280.

Lachance-Grzela, M., & Bouchard, G. (2010). Why do women do the lion's share of housework? A decade of research. *Sex Roles, 63*, 767–780.

Lackenbauer, S. D., Campbell, L., Rubin, H., Fletcher, G. J. O., & Troister, T. (2010). The unique and combined benefits of accuracy and positive bias in relationships. *Personal Relationships, 17*, 475–493.

LaFlam, J., & Green, M. C. (2010, January). *Norms: How people use Facebook to share and connect with others.* Poster presented at the meeting of the Society for Personality and Social Psychology, Las Vegas, NV.

Lakey, B., Adams, K., Neely, L., Rhodes, G., Lutz, C. J., & Sielky, K. (2002). Perceived support and low emotional distress: The role of enacted support, dyad similarity and provider personality. *Personality and Social Psychology Bulletin, 28*, 1546–1555.

Lakey, B., Drew, J. B., Anan, R. M., Sirl, K., & Butler, C. (2004). Negative interpretations of interpersonal situations and the relation between low perceived support and psychological distress among divorced adults. *Journal of Applied Social Psychology, 34*, 1030–1047.

Lakin, J. L. (2006). Automatic cognitive processes and nonverbal communication. In V. Manusov & M. L. Patterson (Eds.), *The Sage handbook of nonverbal communication* (pp. 59–77). Thousand Oaks, CA: Sage.

Lam, A. G., Mak, A., & Lindsay, P. D. (2004). What really works? An exploratory study of condom negotiation strategies. *AIDS Education & Prevention, 16*, 160–171.

Lambert, N. M., Clark, M. S., Durtschi, J., Fincham, F. D., & Graham, S. M. (2010). Benefits of expressing gratitude: Expressing gratitude to a partner changes one's view of the relationship. *Psychological Science, 21*, 574–580.

Lammers, J., Stapel, D. A., & Galinsky, A. D. (2010). Power increases hypocrisy: Moralizing in reasoning, immorality in behavior. *Psychological Science, 21*, 737–744.

Lammers, J., Stoker, J. I., Stapel, D. A., & Jordan, J. (2011, January). *Licentious leaders: Power increases adultery.* Poster presented at the meeting of the Society for Personality and Social Psychology, San Antonio, TX.

Landers, A. (1982). *Love or sex . . . and how to tell the difference.* Chicago: Field Enterprises.

Langhinrichsen-Rohling, J. (2010). Controversies involving gender and intimate partner violence in the United States. *Sex Roles, 62*, 179–193.

Langner, C. A., & Keltner, D. (2008). Social power and emotional experience: Actor and partner effects within dyadic interactions. *Journal of Experimental Social Psychology, 44*, 848–856.

Långström, N., Rahman, Q., Carlström, E., & Lichtenstein, P. (2010). Genetic and environmental effects on same-sex sexual behavior: A population study of twins in Sweden. *Archives of Sexual Behavior, 39*, 75–80.

Lansford, J. E. (2009). Parental divorce and children's adjustment. *Perspectives on Psychological Science, 4*, 140–152.

Larose, S., Guay, F., & Boivin M. (2002). Attachment, social support, and loneliness in young adulthood: A test of two models. *Personality and Social Psychology Bulletin, 28*, 684–693.

Larrick, R. P., Timmerman, T. A., Carton, A. M., & Abrevaya, J. (2011). Temper, temperature, and temptation: Heat-related retaliation in baseball. *Psychological Science, 22*, 423–428.

Larson, R. W., & Bradney, N. (1988). Precious moments with family members and friends. In R. M. Milardo (Ed.), *Families and social networks* (pp. 107–126). Thousand Oaks, CA: Sage.

Larson, R., Richards, M. H., Moneta, G., Holmbeck, G., & Duckett, E. (1996). Changes in adolescents' daily interactions with their families from ages 10 to 18: Disengagement and transformation. *Developmental Psychology, 32*, 744–754.

Lassek, W. D., & Gaulin, S. J. C. (2008). Waist–hip ratio and cognitive ability: Is gluteofemoral fat a privileged store of neurodevelopmental resources? *Evolution and Human Behavior, 29*, 26–34.

Lassek, W. D., & Gaulin, S. J. C. (2009). Costs and benefits of fat-free muscle mass in men: Relationship to mating success, dietary requirements, and native immunity. *Evolution and Human Behavior, 30*, 322–328.

Lauer, J., & Lauer, R. (1985, June). Marriages made to last. *Psychology Today*, pp. 22–26.

Lauer, R. H., Lauer, J. C., & Kerr, S. T. (1990). The long-term marriage: Perceptions of stability and satisfaction. *International Journal of Aging and Human Development, 31*, 189–195.

Laumann, E. O., Gagnon, J. H., Michael, R. T., & Michaels, S. (1994). *The social organization of sexuality: Sexual practices in the United States.* Chicago: University of Chicago Press.

Laurenceau, J., Barrett, L. F., & Rovine, M. J. (2005). The interpersonal process model of intimacy in marriage: A daily-diary and multilevel modeling approach. *Journal of Family Psychology, 19*, 314–323.

Laurenceau, J., Rivera, L. M., Schaffer, A. R., & Pietromonaco, P. R. (2004). Intimacy as an interpersonal process: Current status and future directions. In D. J. Mashek & A. Aron (Eds.), *Handbook of closeness and intimacy* (pp. 81–101). Mahwah, NJ: Erlbaum.

Laursen, B., & Collins, W. A. (1994). Interpersonal conflict during adolescence. *Psychological Bulletin, 115*, 197–209.

Lavee, Y., & Ben-Ari, A. (2007). Relationship of dyadic closeness with work-related stress: A daily diary study. *Journal of Marriage and Family, 69*, 1021–1035.

Lavner, J. A., & Bradbury, T. N. (2010). Patterns of change in marital satisfaction over the newlywed years. *Journal of Marriage and Family, 72*, 1171–1187.

Lavner, J. A., & Bradbury, T. N. (2011, January). *Pathways and antecedents to divorce in newlywed couples: Findings from a ten-year study.* Paper presented at the meeting of the Society for Personality and Social Psychology, San Antonio, TX.

Lawrence, E., & Bradbury, T. N. (2007). Trajectories of change in physical aggression and marital satisfaction. *Journal of Family Psychology, 21,* 236–247.

Le, B., & Agnew, C. R. (2003). Commitment and its theorized determinants: A meta-analysis of the investment model. *Personal Relationships, 10,* 37–57.

Le, B., Dove, N. L., Agnew, C. R., Korn, M. S., & Mutso, A. A. (2010). Predicting nonmarital romantic relationship dissolution: A meta-analytic synthesis. *Personal Relationships, 17,* 377–390.

Leal, S., & Vrij, A. (2008). Blinking during and after lying. *Journal of Nonverbal Behavior, 32,* 187–194.

Leaper, C., & Ayres, M. M. (2007). A meta-analytic review of gender variations in adults' language use: Talkativeness, affiliative speech, and assertive speech. *Personality and Social Psychology Review, 11,* 328–363.

Leary, M. R. (1986). The impact of interactional impediments on social anxiety and self-presentation. *Journal of Experimental Social Psychology, 22,* 122–135.

Leary, M. R. (2001). Toward a conceptualization of interpersonal rejection. In M. R. Leary (Ed.), *Interpersonal rejection* (pp. 3–20). New York: Oxford University Press.

Leary, M. R. (2005). Varieties of interpersonal rejection. In K. D. Williams, J. P. Forgas, & W. von Hippel (Eds.), *The social outcast: Ostracism, social exclusion, rejection, and bullying* (pp. 35–51). New York: Psychology Press.

Leary, M. R. (2010a). Affiliation, acceptance, and belonging: The pursuit of interpersonal connection. In S. Fiske, D. Gilbert, & G. Lindzey (Eds.), *Handbook of social psychology* (5th ed., Vol. 2, pp. 864–897). Hoboken, NJ: Wiley.

Leary, M. R. (2010b). Social anxiety as an early warning system: A refinement and extension of the self-presentation theory of social anxiety. In S. Hofmann & P. DiBartolo (Eds.), *Social anxiety: Clinical, developmental, and social perspectives* (pp. 472–489). New York: Academic Press.

Leary, M. R. (2011). *Introduction to behavioral research methods* (6th ed.). New York: Pearson.

Leary, M. R., & Baumeister, R. F. (2000). The nature and function of self-esteem: Sociometer theory. In M. Zanna (Ed.), *Advances in experimental social psychology* (Vol. 32, pp. 1–62). San Diego: Academic Press.

Leary, M. R., Haupt, A. L., Strausser, K. S., & Chokel, J. T. (1998). Calibrating the sociometer: The relationship between interpersonal appraisals and state self-esteem. *Journal of Personality and Social Psychology, 74,* 1290–1299.

Leary, M. R., Herbst, K. C., & McCrary, F. (2003). Finding pleasure in solitary activities: Desire for aloneness or disinterest in social contact? *Personality and Individual Differences, 35,* 59–68.

Leary, M. R., & Kowalski, R. M. (1995). *Social anxiety.* New York: Guilford Press.

Leary, M. R., & Leder, S. (2009). The nature of hurt feelings: Emotional experience and cognitive appraisals. In A. Vangelisti (Ed.), *Feeling hurt in close relationships* (pp. 15–33). New York: Cambridge University Press.

Leary, M. R., & Miller, R. S. (1986). *Social psychology and dysfunctional behavior: Origins, diagnosis, and treatment.* New York: Guilford Press.

Leary, M. R., & Miller, R. S. (2000). Self-presentational perspectives on personal relationships. In W. Ickes & S. Duck (Eds.), *The social psychology of personal relationships* (pp. 129–155). Chichester, England: Wiley.

Leary, M. R., Nezlek, J. B., Downs, D. L., Radford-Davenport, J., Martin, J., & McMullen, A. (1994). Self-presentation in everyday interactions. *Journal of Personality and Social Psychology, 67,* 664–673.

Leary, M. R., & Springer, C. A. (2001). Hurt feelings: The neglected emotion. In R. M. Kowalski (Ed.), *Behaving badly: Aversive behaviors in interpersonal relationships* (pp. 151–175). Washington DC: American Psychological Association.

Leary, M. R., Twenge, J. M., & Quinlivan, E. (2006). Interpersonal rejection as a determinant of anger and aggression. *Personality and Social Psychology Review, 10,* 111–132.

Lee, E. (2008, February). *The benefit of shared laughter in relationships.* Poster presented at the meeting of the Society for Personality and Social Psychology, Albuquerque, NM.

Lee, J. A. (1988). Love-styles. In R. J. Sternberg & M. L. Barnes (Eds.), *The psychology of love* (pp. 38–67). New Haven, CT: Yale University Press.

Lee, L., Loewenstein, G., Ariely, D., Hong, J., & Young, J. (2008). If I'm not hot, are you hot or not? *Psychological Science, 19,* 669–677.

Leff, L. (2004, May 23). Divorce "most important" benefit of gay marriage. *The Bryan-College Station Eagle*, p. B6.

Lehmiller, J. J., & Agnew, C. R. (2007). Perceived marginalization and the prediction of romantic relationship stability. *Journal of Marriage and Family, 69*, 1036–1049.

Lehmiller, J. J., VanderDrift, L. E., & Kelly, J. R. (2011). Sex differences in approaching friends with benefits relationships. *Journal of Sex Research, 48, 275–284.*

Lehnart, J., Neyer, F. J., & Eccles, J. (2010). Long-term effects of social investment: The case of partnering in young adulthood. *Journal of Personality, 78,* 639–670.

Leitenberg, H., & Henning, K. (1995). Sexual fantasy. *Psychological Bulletin, 117,* 469–496.

Lemay, E. P., Jr., & Clark, M. S. (2008). How the head liberates the heart: Projection of communal responsiveness guides relationship promotion. *Journal of Personality and Social Psychology, 94,* 647–671.

Lemay, E. P., Jr., Clark, M. S., & Greenberg, A. (2010). What is beautiful is good because what is beautiful is desired: Physical attractiveness stereotyping as projection of interpersonal goals. *Personality and Social Psychology Bulletin, 36,* 339–353.

Lennon, C. A., Stewart, A. L., Harman, J. J., & Keneski, E. (2011, January). *Extending Rusbult's model: The role of power in relationships.* Poster presented at the meeting of the Society for Personality and Social Psychology, San Antonio, TX.

Lenton, A. P., & Francesconi, M. (2010). How humans cognitively manage an abundance of mate options. *Psychological Science, 21,* 528–533.

Lenton, A., & Webber, L. (2006). Cross-sex friendships: Who has more? *Sex Roles, 54,* 809–820.

Leone, C., & Hawkins, L. B. (2006). Self-monitoring and close relationships. *Journal of Personality, 74,* 739–778.

Lepore, S. J., & Greenberg, M. A. (2002). Mending broken hearts: Effects of expressive writing on mood, cognitive processing, social adjustment and health following a relationship breakup. *Psychology and Health, 17,* 547–560.

Leslie, L. A., Huston, T. L., & Johnson, M. P. (1986). Parental reactions to dating relationships: Do they make a difference? *Journal of Marriage and the Family, 48,* 57–66.

Letzring, T. D., & Noftle, E. E. (2010). Predicting relationship quality from self-verification of broad personality traits among romantic couples. *Journal of Research in Personality, 44,* 353–362.

Letzring, T. D., Wells, S. M., & Funder, D. C. (2006). Information quantity and quality affect the realistic accuracy of personality judgment. *Journal of Personality and Social Psychology, 91,* 111–123.

Levenson, R. W., Carstensen, L. L., & Gottman, J. M. (1993). Long-term marriage: Age, gender, and satisfaction. *Psychology and Aging, 8,* 301–313.

Levenson, R. W., Carstensen, L. L., & Gottman, J. M. (1994). Influence of age and gender on affect, physiology, and their interrelations: A study of long-term marriages. *Journal of Personality and Social Psychology, 67,* 56–68.

Lever, J., Frederick, D. A., & Peplau, L. A. (2006). Does size matter? Men's and women's views on penis size across the lifespan. *Psychology of Men and Masculinity, 7,* 129–143.

Levine, R., Sato, S., Hashimoto, T., & Verma, J. (1995). Love and marriage in eleven cultures. *Journal of Cross-Cultural Psychology, 26,* 554–571.

Levine, T. R., Serota, K. B., & Shulman, H. C. (2010). The impact of *Lie to Me* on viewers' actual ability to detect deception. *Communication Research, 37,* 847–856.

Levinger, G. (1976). A social psychological perspective on marital dissolution. *Journal of Social Issues, 32,* 21–47.

Levinger, G. (1979). A social exchange view on the dissolution of pair relationships. In R. L. Burgess & T. L. Huston (Eds.), *Social exchange in developing relationships* (pp. 169–193). New York: Academic Press.

Levinger, G., & Levinger, A. C. (2003). Winds of time and place: How context has affected a 50-year marriage. *Personal Relationships, 10,* 285–306.

Levitt, M. J., Silver, M. E., & Franco, N. (1996). Troublesome relationships: A part of human experience. *Journal of Social and Personal Relationships, 13,* 523–536.

Levy, K. N., & Kelly, K. M. (2010). Sex differences in jealousy: A contribution from attachment theory. *Psychological Science, 21,* 168–173.

Lewin, T. (2010, January 24). Researchers shocked at kids' online time. *Houston Chronicle*, p. G8.

Lewis, K., Kaufman, J., Gonzalez, M., Wimmer, A., & Christakis, N. (2008). Tastes, ties, and time: A new social network dataset using Facebook.com. *Social Networks, 30,* 330–342.

Lewis, T., & Manusov, V. (2009). Listening to another's distress in everyday relationships. *Communication Quarterly, 57,* 282–301.

Li, N. P. (2008). Intelligent priorities: Adaptive long- and short-term mate preferences. In G. Geher & G. Miller (Eds.), *Mating intelligence: Sex, relationships, and the mind's reproductive system* (pp. 105–119). New York: Erlbaum.

Li, N. P., Bailey, J. M., Kenrick, D. T., & Linsenmeier, J. A. W. (2002). The necessities and luxuries of mate preferences: Testing the tradeoffs. *Journal of Personality and Social Psychology, 82,* 947–955.

Li, N. P., Valentine, K. A., & Patel, L. (2011). Mate preferences in the US and Singapore: A cross-cultural test of the mate preference priority model. *Personality and Individual Differences, 50,* 291–294.

Liberman, V., Anderson, N. R., & Ross, L. (2010). Achieving difficult agreements: Effects of positive expectations on negotiation processes and outcomes. *Journal of Experimental Social Psychology, 46,* 494–504.

Liebold, J. M., & McConnell, A. R. (2004). Women, sex, hostility, power, and suspicion: Sexually aggressive men's cognitive associations. *Journal of Experimental Social Psychology, 40,* 256–263.

Lilgendahl, J. P., & McAdams, D. P. (2011). Constructing stories of self-growth: How individual differences in patterns of autobiographical reasoning relate to well-being in midlife. *Journal of Personality, 79,* 391–428.

Lin, A. J., & Santelli, J. S. (2008). The accuracy of condom information in three selected abstinence-only education curricula. *Sexuality Research & Social Policy, 5,* 56–70.

Lin, Y. W., & Rusbult, C. E. (1995). Commitment to dating relationships and cross-sex friendships in America and China. *Journal of Social and Personal Relationships, 12,* 7–26.

Linville, P., Fischhoff, B., & Fischer, G. (1993). AIDS risk perceptions and decision bias. In J. B Pryor & G. D. Reeder (Eds.), *The social psychology of HIV infection* (pp. 1–38). Hillsdale, NJ: Erlbaum.

Lippa, R. A. (2005). Sexual orientation and personality. *Annual Review of Sex Research, 16,* 119–153.

Lippa, R. A. (2007). The preferred traits of mates in a cross-national study of heterosexual and homosexual men and women: An examination of biological and cultural influences. *Archives of Sexual Behavior, 36,* 193–208.

Lippa, R. A. (2009). Sex differences in sex drive, sociosexuality, and height across 53 nations: Testing evolutionary and social structural theories. *Archives of Sexual Behavior, 38,* 631–651.

Lippa, R., & Hershberger, S. (1999). Genetic and environmental influences on individual differences in masculinity, femininity, and gender diagnosticity: Analyzing data from a classic twin study. *Journal of Personality, 67,* 127–155.

Lishner, D. A., Nguyen, S., Stocks, E. L., & Zillmer, E. J. (2008). Are sexual and emotional infidelity equally upsetting to men and women? Making sense of forced-choice responses. *Evolutionary Psychology, 6,* 667–675.

Little, A. C., Burt, D. M., & Perrett, D. I. (2006). Assortative mating for perceived facial personality traits. *Personality and Individual Differences, 40,* 973–984.

Little, A. C., Penton-Voak, I. S., Burt, D. M., & Perrett, D. I. (2002). Evolution and individual differences in the perception of attractiveness: How cyclic hormonal changes and self-perceived attractiveness influence female preferences for male faces. In G. Rhodes & L. A. Zebrowitz (Eds.), *Facial attractiveness: Evolutionary, cognitive, and social perspectives* (pp. 59-90). Westport, CT: Ablex Publishing.

Lloyd, S. A. (1987). Conflict in premarital relationships: Differential perceptions of males and females. *Family Relations, 36,* 290–294.

Lloyd, S. A., & Emery, B. C. (2000). The context and dynamics of intimate aggression against women. *Journal of Social and Personal Relationships, 17,* 503–521.

Löckenhoff, C. E., & Carstensen, L. F. (2004). Socioemotional Selectivity Theory, aging, and health: The increasingly delicate balance between regulating emotions and making tough choices. *Journal of Personality, 72,* 1395–1424.

Lohr, J. M., Olatunji, B. O., Baumeister, R. F., & Bushman, B. J. (2007). The psychology of anger venting and empirically supported alternatives that do not harm. *Scientific Review of Mental Health Practice, 5,* 53–64.

Long, E. C. J., Angera, J. J., Carter, S. J., Nakamoto, M., & Kalso, M. (1999). Understanding the one you love: A longitudinal assessment of an empathy training program for couples in romantic relationships. *Family Relations, 48,* 235–242.

Lorber, M. F., & O'Leary, K. D. (2004). Predictors of the persistence of male aggression in early marriage. *Journal of Family Violence, 19,* 329–338.

Lorenzo, G. L., Biesanz, J. C., & Human, L. J. (2010). What is beautiful is good and more accurately understood: Physical attractiveness and accuracy in first impressions of personality. *Psychological Science, 21,* 1777–1782.

Loving, T. J. (2006). Predicting dating relationship fate with insiders' and outsiders' perspectives: Who and what is asked matters. *Personal Relationships, 13,* 349–362.

Loving, T. J., Gleason, M. E. J., & Pope, M. T. (2009). Transition novelty moderates daters' cortisol responses when talking about marriage. *Personal Relationships, 16,* 187–203.

Lucas, R. E. (2005). Time does not heal all wounds: A longitudinal study of reaction and adaptation to divorce. *Psychological Science, 16,* 945–950.

Lucas, R. E. (2007). Adaptation and the set-point model of subjective well-being. *Current Directions in Psychological Science, 16,* 75–79.

Luchies, L. B., Finkel, E. J., Davis, J. L., Green, J. D., & Coy, A. E. (2011b, January). *Is high expected forgiveness a license to transgress? Comparing actual behavior to forecasted behavior.* Poster presented at the meeting of the Society for Personality and Social Psychology, San Antonio, TX.

Luchies, L. B, Finkel, E. J., & Fitzsimons, G. M. (2011a). The effects of self-regulatory strength, content, and strategies on close relationships. *Journal of Personality, DOI: 10.1111/j.1467-6494.2010.00701.x*

Luchies, L. B., Finkel, E. J., McNulty, J. K., & Kumashiro, M. (2010). The doormat effect: When forgiving erodes self-respect and self-concept clarity. *Journal of Personality and Social Psychology, 98,* 734–749.

Luke, M. A., Maio, G. R., & Carnelley, K. B. (2004). Attachment models of the self and others: Relations with self-esteem, humanity-esteem, and parental treatment. *Personal Relationships, 11,* 281–303.

Lutz-Zois, C. J., Bradley, A. C., Mihalik, J. L., & Moorman-Eavers, E. R. (2006). Perceived similarity and relationship success among dating couples: An idiographic approach. *Journal of Social and Personal Relationships, 23,* 865–880.

Luo, S. (2009). Partner selection and relationship satisfaction in early dating couples: The role of couple similarity. *Personality and Individual Differences, 47,* 133–138.

Luo, S., Cartun, M. A., & Snider, A. G. (2010). Assessing extradyadic behavior: A review, a new measure, and two new models. *Personality and Individual Differences, 49,* 155–163.

Luo, S., & Snider, A. G. (2009). Accuracy and biases in newlyweds' perceptions of each other: Not mutually exclusive but mutually beneficial. *Psychological Science, 20,* 1332–1339.

Luo, S., & Zhang, G. (2009). What leads to romantic attraction: Similarity, reciprocity, security, or beauty? Evidence from a speed-dating study. *Journal of Personality, 77,* 933–964.

Luo, S., Zhang, G., Watson, D., & Snider, A. G. (2010). Using cross-sectional couple data to disentangle the causality between positive partner perceptions and marital satisfaction. *Journal of Research in Personality, 44,* 665–668.

Lutfey, K. E., Link, C. L., Rosen, R. C., Wiegel, M., & McKinlay, J. B. (2009). Prevalence and correlates of sexual activity and function in women: Results from the Boston Area Community Health (BACH) survey. *Archives of Sexual Behavior, 38,* 514–527.

Luxen, M. F., & Buunk, B. P. (2006). Human intelligence, fluctuating asymmetry and the peacock's tail: General intelligence (g) as an honest signal of fitness. *Personality and Individual Differences, 41,* 897–902.

Lydon, J. E., Fitzsimons, G. M., & Naidoo, L. (2003). Devaluation versus enhancement of attractive alternatives: A critical test using the calibration paradigm. *Personality and Social Psychology Bulletin, 29,* 349–359.

Lydon, J., Pierce, T., & O'Regan, S. (1997). Coping with moral commitment to long-distance dating relationships. *Journal of Personality and Social Psychology, 73,* 104–113.

Lykins, A. D., Meana, M., & Kambe, G. (2006). Detection of differential viewing patterns to erotic and non-erotic stimuli using eye-tracking methodology. *Archives of Sexual Behavior, 35,* 569–575.

Lykken, D. T. (2002). How relationships begin and end: A genetic perspective. In A. L. Vangelisti, H. T. Reis, & M. A. Fitzpatrick (Eds.), *Stability and change in relationships* (pp. 83–102). Cambridge, England: Cambridge University Press.

Lyngstad, T. H., & Jalovaara, M. (2010). A review of the antecedents of union dissolution. *Demographic Research, 23,* 257–292.

Lynn, M. (2009). Determinants and consequences of female attractiveness and sexiness: Realistic tests with restaurant waitresses. *Archives of Sexual Behavior, 38,* 737–745.

Lyubomirsky, S. (2007). *The how of happiness: A scientific approach to getting the life you want.* New York: Penguin Press.

MacDonald, G., Zanna, M. P., & Holmes, J. G. (2000). An experimental test of the role of alcohol in relationship conflict. *Journal of Experimental Social Psychology, 36,* 182–193.

MacDonald, K., & MacDonald, T. M. (2010). The peptide that binds: A systematic review of oxytocin and its prosocial effects in humans. *Harvard Review of Psychiatry, 18,* 1–21.

MacDonald, T. K., MacDonald, G., Zanna, M. P., & Fong, G. (2000). Alcohol, sexual arousal, and intentions to use condoms in young men: Applying alcohol myopia theory to risky sexual behavior. *Health Psychology, 19,* 290–298.

MacDonald, T. K., & Ross, M. (1999). Assessing the accuracy of predictions about dating relationships: How and why do lovers' predictions differ from those made by observers? *Personality and Social Psychology Bulletin, 25,* 1417–1429.

MacNeil, S., & Byers, E. S. (2009). Role of sexual self-disclosure in the sexual satisfaction of long-term heterosexual couples. *Journal of Sex Research, 46,* 3–14.

Macrae, C. N., Alnwick, K. A., Milne, A. B., & Schloerscheidt, A. M. (2002). Person perception across the menstrual cycle: Hormonal influences on social-cognitive functioning. *Psychological Science, 13,* 532–536.

Madden, M. (2010). Four or more: The new demographic. *Pew Research Center.* Retrieved from http://www.pewinternet.org/Presentations/2010/Jun/Four-or-More--The-New-Demographic .aspx

Maddox, A. M., Rhoades, G. K., & Markman, H. J. (2011). Viewing sexually-explicit materials alone or together: Associations with relationship quality. *Archives of Sexual Behavior, 40,* 441–448.

Madey, S. F., Simo, M., Dillworth, D., Kemper, D., Toczynski, A., & Perella, A. (1996). They do get more attractive at closing time, but only when you are not in a relationship. *Basic and Applied Social Psychology, 18,* 387–393.

Magee, J. C., Galinsky, A. D., & Gruenfeld, D. H. (2007). Power, propensity to negotiate, and moving first in competitive interactions. *Personality and Social Psychology Bulletin, 33,* 200–212.

Magdol, L., & Bessel, D. R. (2003). Social capital, social currency, and portable assets: The impact of residential mobility on exchanges of social support. *Personal Relationships, 10,* 149–169.

Mahoney, A. R., & Knudson-Martin, C. (2009). Gender equality in intimate relationships. In C. Knudson-Martin & A. Mahoney (Eds.), *Couples, gender, and power: Creating change in intimate relationships* (pp. 3–16). New York: Springer.

Maisel, N. C., & Gable, S. L. (2009). The paradox of received social support: The importance of responsiveness. *Psychological Science, 20,* 928–932.

Maisel, N. C., Gable, S. L., & Strachman, A. (2008). Responsive behaviors in good times and in bad. *Personal Relationships, 15,* 317–338.

Major, B., Carrington, P. I., & Carnevale, P. J. D. (1984). Physical attractiveness and self-esteem: Attributions for praise from an other-sex evaluator. *Personality and Social Psychology Bulletin, 10,* 43–50.

Malle, B. F. (2006). The actor-observer asymmetry in attribution: A (surprising) meta-analysis. *Psychological Bulletin, 132,* 895–919.

Malouff, J. M., Thorsteinsson, E. B., Schutte, N. S., Bhullar, N., & Rooke, S. E. (2010). The five-factor model of personality and relationship satisfaction of intimate partners: A meta-analysis. *Journal of Research in Personality, 44,* 124–127.

Maltby, J., Wood, A. M., Day, L., Kon, T. W. H., Colley, A., & Linley, P. A. (2008). Personality predictors of levels of forgiveness two and a half years after the transgression. *Journal of Research in Personality, 42,* 1088–1094.

Maner, J. K., DeWall, N., Baumeister, R. F., & Schaller, M. (2007). Does social exclusion motivate interpersonal reconnection? Resolving the "porcupine problem." *Journal of Personality and Social Psychology, 92,* 42–55.

Maner, J. K., Rouby, D. A., & Gonzaga, G. C. (2008). Automatic inattention to attractive alternatives: The evolved psychology of relationship maintenance. *Evolution and Human Behavior, 29,* 343–349.

Mann, S., & Morry, M. M. (2011, January). *Why are some friendships more satisfying than others? Relational-interdependent self-construal and friendship preferences.* Poster presented at the meeting of the Society for Personality and Social Psychology, San Antonio, TX.

Marchand, M. A. G., & Vonk, R. (2005). The process of becoming suspicious of ulterior motives. *Social Cognition, 23,* 242–256.

Marcus, D. K., & Miller, R. S. (2003). Sex differences in judgments of physical attractiveness: A social relations analysis. *Personality and Social Psychology Bulletin, 29,* 325–335.

Markey, P. M., Funder, D. C., & Ozer, D. J. (2003). Complementarity of interpersonal behaviors in dyadic interactions. *Personality and Social Psychology Bulletin, 29,* 1082–1090.

Markey, P. M., & Kurtz, J. E. (2006). Increasing acquaintanceship and complementarity of behavioral styles and personality traits among college roommates. *Personality and Social Psychology Bulletin, 32,* 907–916.

Markey, P. M., Lowmaster, S., & Eichler, W. (2010). A real-time assessment of interpersonal complementarity. *Personal Relationships, 17,* 13–25.

Markey, P. M., & Markey, C. N. (2007). Romantic ideals, romantic obtainment, and relationship experiences: The complementarity of interpersonal traits among romantic partners. *Journal of Social and Personal Relationships, 24,* 517–533.

Markman, H. J. (1981). Prediction of marital distress: A 5-year follow-up. *Journal of Consulting and Clinical Psychology, 49,* 760–762.

Markman, H. J., Rhoades, G. K., Stanley, S. M., Ragan, E. P., & Whitton, S. W. (2010). The premarital communication roots of marital distress and divorce: The first five years of marriage. *Journal of Family Psychology, 24,* 289–298.

Markman, H., Stanley, S., & Blumberg, S. L. (1994). *Fighting for your marriage: Positive steps for preventing divorce and preserving a lasting love.* San Francisco: Jossey-Bass.

Marks, M. J., & Fraley, R. C. (2005). The sexual double standard: Fact or fiction? *Sex Roles, 52,* 175–186.

Marshall, A. D., & Holtzworth-Munroe, A. (2010). Recognition of wives' emotional expressions: A mechanism in the relationship between psychopathology and intimate partner violence perpetration. *Journal of Family Psychology, 24,* 21–30.

Marshall, L. L., Weston, R., & Honeycutt, T. C. (2000). Does men's positivity moderate or mediate the effect of their abuse on women's relationship quality? *Journal of Social and Personal Relationships, 17,* 660–675.

Marshall, T. C. (2010). Gender, peer relations, and intimate romantic relationships. In J. Chrisler & D. McCreary (Eds.), *Handbook of gender research in psychology* (Vol. 2, pp. 281–310). New York: Springer.

Marston, P. J., Hecht, M. L., Manke, M. L., McDaniel, S., & Reeder, H. (1998). The subjective experience of intimacy, passion, and commitment in heterosexual loving relationships. *Personal Relationships, 5,* 15–30.

Martin, J. (1997, October 21). Bereaved may face insensitivity. *Houston Chronicle,* p. 10F.

Martins, Y., Preti, G., Crabtree, C. R., Runyan, T., Vainius, A. A., & Wysocki, C. J. (2005). Preference for human body odors is influenced by gender and sexual orientation. *Psychological Science, 16,* 694–701.

Masi, C. M., Chen, H., Hawkley, L. C., & Cacioppo, J. T. (2011). A meta-analysis of interventions to reduce loneliness. *Personality and Social Psychology Review, 15,* 219–266.

Mason, M. F., Tatkow, E. P., & Macrae, C. N. (2005). The look of love: Gaze shifts and person perception. *Psychological Science, 16,* 236–239.

Massar, K., & Buunk, A. P. (2009). Rivals in the mind's eye: Jealous responses after subliminal exposure to body shapes. *Personality and Individual Differences, 46,* 129–134.

Master, S. L., Eisenberger, N. I., Taylor, S. E., Naliboff, B. D., Shirinyan, D., & Lieberman, M. D. (2009). A picture's worth: Partner photographs reduce experimentally induced pain. *Psychological Science, 20,* 1316–1318.

Masters, W. H., & Johnson, V. F. (1970). *Human sexual inadequacy.* Boston: Little, Brown.

Mather, M., & Lavery, D. (2010). In U.S., proportion married at lowest recorded levels. *Population Reference Bureau.* Retrieved from http://www.prb.org/Articles/2010/usmarriagedecline .aspx

Mathes, E. W., & Kozak, G. (2008). The exchange of physical attractiveness for resource potential and commitment. *Journal of Evolutionary Psychology, 6,* 43–56.

Matsumoto, D., Olide, A., Schug, J., Willingham, B., & Callan, M. (2009). Cross-cultural judgments of spontaneous facial expressions of emotion. *Journal of Nonverbal Behavior, 33,* 213–238.

Matsumoto, D., & Willingham, B. (2009). Spontaneous facial expressions of emotion of congenitally and noncongenitally blind individuals. *Journal of Personality and Social Psychology, 96,* 1–10.

Mayer, J. D., Roberts, R. D., & Barsade, S. G. (2008). Human abilities: Emotional intelligence. *Annual Review of Psychology, 59,* 507–536.

McAndrew, F. T., & de Jonge, C. R. (2011). Electronic person perception: What do we infer about people from the style of their e-mail messages? *Social Psychological and Personality Science, 2,* 403–407.

McBurney, D. H., Zapp, D. J., & Streeter, S. A. (2005). Preferred number of sexual partners: Tails of distributions and tales of mating systems. *Evolution and Human Behavior, 26,* 271–278.

McCarthy, E. (2009, January 11). Romantic comedies toxic to love life. *Houston Chronicle,* p. E7.

McClure, M. J., Lydon, J. E., Baccus, J., Baldwin, M. W., & Foley, J. E. (2008, February). *Failures in the interpersonal presentation of the anxiously attached.* Paper presented at the meeting of the Society for Personality and Social Psychology, Albuquerque, MN.

McClure, M. J., Lydon, J. E., Baccus, J. R., & Baldwin, M. W. (2010). A signal detection analysis of chronic attachment anxiety at speed dating: Being unpopular is only the first part of the problem. *Personality and Social Psychology Bulletin, 36,* 1024–1036.

McCornack, S. A, & Parks, M. R. (1990). What women know that men don't: Sex differences in determining the truth behind deceptive messages. *Journal of Social and Personal Relationships, 7,* 107–118.

McCrae, R. R., & Costa, P. T., Jr. (1997). Personality trait structure as a human universal. *American Psychologist, 52,* 509–516.

McCrae, R. R., & Costa, P. T., Jr. (2010). The Five-Factor Theory of personality. In O. P. John, R. W. Robins, & L. A. Pervin (Eds.), *Handbook of personality: Theory and research* (3rd ed., pp. 159–181). New York: Guilford.

McCullough, M. E. (2008). *Beyond revenge: The evolution of the forgiveness instinct.* New York: Jossey-Bass.

McCullough, M. E., Bellah, C. G., Kilpatrick, S. D., & Johnson, J. L. (2001). Vengefulness: Relationships with forgiveness, rumination, well-being, and the Big Five. *Personality and Social Psychology Bulletin, 27,* 601–610.

McCullough, M. E., Bono, G., & Root, L. M. (2007). Rumination, emotion, and forgiveness: Three longitudinal studies. *Journal of Personality and Social Psychology, 92,* 490–505.

McCullough, M. E., Emmons, R. A., Kilpatrick, S. D., & Mooney, C. N. (2003). Narcissists as "victims": The role of narcissism in the perception of transgressions. *Personality and Social Psychology Bulletin, 29,* 885–893.

McEwan, T. E., Mullen, P. E., & MacKenzie, R. (2009). A study of the predictors of persistence in stalking situations. *Law and Human Behavior, 33,* 149–158.

McFarland, C., & Ross, M. (1987). The relation between current impression and memories of self and dating partners. *Personality and Social Psychology Bulletin, 13,* 228–238.

McGonagle, K. A., Kessler, R. C., & Schilling, E. A. (1992). The frequency and determinants of marital disagreements in a community sample. *Journal of Social and Personal Relationships, 9,* 507–524.

McHugh, M. C., & Hambaugh, J. (2010). She said, he said: Gender, language, and power. In J. Chrisler & D. McCreary (Eds.), *Handbook of gender research in psychology* (Vol. 1, pp. 379–410). New York: Springer.

McKenna, K. Y. A. (2008). MySpace or your place: Relationship initiation and development in the wired and wireless world. In S. Sprecher, A. Wenzel, & J. Harvey (Eds.), *Handbook of relationship initiation* (pp. 235–247). New York: Psychology Press.

McKibbin, W. F., Goetz, A. T., Shackelford, T. K., Schipper, L. D., Starratt, V. G., & Stewart-Williams, S. (2007). Why do men insult their intimate partners? *Personality and Individual Differences, 43,* 231–241.

McKinnish, T. G. (2007). Sexually integrated workplaces and divorce: Another form of on-the-job search. *Journal of Human Resources, 42,* 331–352.

McNulty, J. K. (2010). When positive processes hurt relationships. *Current Directions in Psychological Science, 19,* 167–171.

McNulty, J. K., & Fisher, T. D. (2008). Gender differences in response to sexual expectancies and changes in sexual frequency: A short-term longitudinal study of sexual satisfaction in newly married couples. *Archives of Sexual Behavior, 37,* 229–240.

McNulty, J. K., & Karney, B. R. (2002). Expectancy confirmation in appraisals of marital interactions. *Personality and Social Psychology Bulletin, 28,* 764–775.

McNulty, J. K., & Karney, B. R. (2004). Positive expectations in the early years of marriage: Should couples expect the best or brace for the worst? *Journal of Personality and Social Psychology, 86,* 729–743.

McNulty, J. K., Neff, L. A., & Karney, B. R. (2008). Beyond initial attraction: Physical attractiveness in newlywed marriage. *Journal of Family Psychology, 22,* 135–143.

McNulty, J. K., & Russell, V. M. (2010). When "negative" behaviors are positive: A contextual analysis of the long-term effects of problem-solving behaviors on changes in relationship satisfaction. *Journal of Personality and Social Psychology, 98,* 587–604.

McPherson, M., Smith-Lovin, L., & Brashears, M. E. (2006). Social isolation in America: Changes in core discussion networks over two decades. *American Sociological Review, 71,* 353–375.

Mealey, L., Bridgstock, R., & Townsend, G. C. (1999). Symmetry and perceived facial attractiveness: A monozygotic co-twin comparison. *Journal of Personality and Social Psychology, 76,* 151–158.

Mechanic, M. B., Weaver, T. L., & Resick, P. A. (2008). Mental health consequences of intimate partner abuse: A multidimensional assessment of four different forms of abuse. *Violence Against Women, 14,* 634–654.

Mehl, M. R., & Robbins, M. L. (2011). Naturalistic observation sampling: The Electronically Activated Recorder (EAR). In M. R. Mehl & T. S. Conner (Eds.), *Handbook of research methods for studying daily life.* New York, NY: Guilford Press.

Mehl, M. R., Vazire, S., Holleran, S. E., & Clark, C. S. (2010). Eavesdropping on happiness: Well-being is related to having less small talk and more substantive conversations. *Psychological Science, 21,* 539–541.

Mehl, M. R., Vazire, S., Ramirez-Esparza, N., Slatcher, R. B., & Pennebaker, J. W. (2007). Are women really more talkative than men? *Science, 317,* 82.

Meier, B. P., & Robinson, M. D. (2004). Does quick to blame mean quick to anger? The role of agreeableness in dissociating blame and anger. *Personality and Social Psychology Bulletin, 30,* 856–867.

Mellor, D., Stokes, M., Firth, L., Hayashi, Y., & Cummins, R. (2008). Need for belonging, relationship satisfaction, loneliness, and life satisfaction. *Personality and Individual Differences, 45,* 213–218.

"Men or Women." (2008, August 25). Men or women: Who's the better leader? *Pew Research Center.* Retrieved from http://pewresearch.org/pubs/932/men-or-women-whos-the-better-leader

Mendes de Leon, C. F., Glass, T. A., Beckett, L. A., Seeman, T. E., Evans, D. A., & Berkman, L. F. (1999). Social networks and disability transitions across eight intervals of yearly data in the New Haven EPESE. *Journals of Gerontology: Series B: Psychological Sciences and Social Sciences,* 54B(3), S162–S172.

Mercer, C. H., Wellings, K., Macdowall, W., Copas, A. J., McManus, S., Erens, B., Fenton, K. A., & Johnson, A. M. (2006). First sexual partnerships—age differences and their significance: Empirical evidence from the 2000 British National Survey of Sexual Attitudes and Lifestyles ("Natsal 2000"). *Journal of Adolescent Health, 39,* 87–95.

Messman, S. J., Canary, D. J., & Hause, K. S. (2000). Motives to remain platonic, equity, and the use of maintenance strategies in opposite-sex friendships. *Journal of Social and Personal Relationships, 17,* 67–94.

Meston, C. M., & Buss, D. M. (2007). Why humans have sex. *Archives of Sexual Behavior, 36,* 477–507.

Metts, S. (1994). Relational transgressions. In W. R. Cupach & B. H. Spitzberg (Eds.), *The dark side of interpersonal communication* (pp. 217–239). Hillsdale, NJ: Erlbaum.

Metts, S. (2004). First sexual involvement in romantic relationships: An empirical investigation of communicative framing, romantic beliefs and attachment orientation in the passion turning point. In J. H. Harvey, A. Wenzel, & S. Sprecher (Eds.), *The handbook of sexuality in close relationships* (pp. 135–158). Mahwah, NJ: Erlbaum.

Metts, S., & Cupach, W. R. (1990). The influence of romantic beliefs and problem-solving responses on satisfaction in romantic relationships. *Human Communication Research, 17,* 170–185.

Meyer, D. R. (1999). Compliance with child support orders in paternity and divorce cases. In R. A. Thompson & P. R. Amato (Eds.), *The postdivorce family: Children, parenting and society* (pp. 127–157). Thousand Oaks, CA: Sage.

Michalski, R. L., & Shackelford, T. K. (2010). Evolutionary personality psychology: Reconciling human nature and individual differences. *Personality and Individual Differences, 48,* 509–516.

Michalski, R. L., Shackelford, T. K., & Salmon, C. A. (2007). Upset in response to a sibling's partner's infidelities. *Human Nature, 18,* 74–84.

Mickelson, K. D., Kessler, R. C., & Shaver, P. R. (1997). Adult attachment in a nationally representative sample. *Journal of Personality and Social Psychology, 73,* 1092–1106.

Mikulincer, M. (1998). Attachment working models and the sense of trust: An exploration of interaction goals and affect regulation. *Journal of Personality and Social Psychology, 74,* 1209–1224.

Mikulincer, M., & Shaver, P. R. (2005). Attachment theory and emotions in close relationships: Exploring the attachment-related dynamics of emotional reactions to relational events. *Personal Relationships, 12,* 149–168.

Mikulincer, M., & Shaver, P. R. (2007). A behavioral systems perspective on the psycho-dynamics of attachment and sexuality. In D. Diamond, S. J. Blatt, & J. D. Lichtenberg (Eds.), *Attachment and sexuality* (pp. 51–78). New York: The Analytic Press.

Mikulincer, M., Shaver, P. R., Sapir-Lavid, Y., & Avihou-Kanza, N. (2009). What's inside the minds of securely and insecurely attached people? The secure-base script and its associations with attachment-style dimensions. *Journal of Personality and Social Psychology, 97,* 615–633.

Milardo, R. M., Johnson, M. P., & Huston, T. L. (1983). Developing close relationships: Changing patterns of interaction between pair members and social networks. *Journal of Personality and Social Psychology, 44,* 964–976.

Miles, L. K. (2009). Who is approachable? *Journal of Experimental Social Psychology, 45,* 262–266.

Miller, G. E., & Chen, E. (2010). Harsh family climate in early life presages the emergence of a proinflammatory phenotype in adolescence. *Psychological Science, 21,* 848–856.

Miller, G., Tybur, J. M., & Jordan, B. D. (2007). Ovulatory cycle effects on tip earnings by lap dancers: Economic evidence for human estrus? *Evolution and Human Behavior, 28,* 375–381.

Miller, J. B., & Noirot, M. (1999). Attachment memories, models and information processing. *Journal of Social and Personal Relationships, 16,* 147–173.

Miller, J., Capezza, N., & Arriaga, X. (2008, February). *Implicit relationship beliefs and commitment to dating relationships.* Poster presented at the meeting of the Society for Personality and Social Psychology, Albuquerque, NM.

Miller, L. C., Berg, J. H., & Archer, R. L. (1983). Openers: Individuals who elicit intimate self-disclosure. *Journal of Personality and Social Psychology, 44,* 1234–1244.

Miller, M. A., & Rahe, R. H. (1997). Life changes scaling for the 1990s. *Journal of Psychomatic Research, 43,* 279–292.

Miller, P. J. E., Caughlin, J. P., & Huston, T. L. (2003). Trait expressiveness and marital satisfaction: The role of idealization processes. *Journal of Marriage and the Family, 65,* 978–995.

Miller, P. J. E., Niehuis, S., & Huston, T. L. (2006). Positive illusions in marital relationships: A 13-year longitudinal study. *Personality and Social Psychology Bulletin, 32,* 1579–1594.

Miller, P. J. E., & Rempel, J. K. (2004). Trust and partner-enhancing attributions in close relationships. *Personality and Social Psychology Bulletin, 30,* 695–705.

Miller, R. S. (1996). *Embarrassment: Poise and peril in everyday life.* New York: Guilford Press.

Miller, R. S. (1997a). Inattentive and contented: Relationship commitment and attention to alternatives. *Journal of Personality and Social Psychology, 73,* 758–766.

Miller, R. S. (1997b). We always hurt the ones we love: Aversive interactions in close relationships. In R. Kowalski (Ed.), *Aversive interpersonal interactions* (pp. 11–29). New York: Plenum.

Miller, R. S. (2001). Breaches of propriety. In R. M. Kowalski (Ed.), *Behaving badly: Aversive behaviors in interpersonal relationships* (pp. 29–58). Washington, DC: American Psychological Association.

Miller, R. S. (2008). Attending to temptation: The operation (and perils) of attention to alternatives in close relationships. In J. P. Forgas & J. Fitness (Eds.), *Social relationships: Cognitive, affective and motivational processes* (pp. 321–337). New York: Psychology Press.

Miller, R. S. (2009). Social anxiousness, shyness, and embarrassability. In M. R. Leary & R. H. Hoyle (Eds.), *Handbook of individual differences in social behavior* (pp. 176–191). New York: Guilford Press.

Miller, R. S., & Schlenker, B. R. (1985). Egotism in group members: Public and private attributions of responsibility for group performance. *Social Psychology Quarterly, 48,* 85–89.

Miller, R. S., & Simeon, J. R. (2011). *Relationship outcomes and attention to alternatives over time.* Manuscript submitted for publication.

Miller, S. L., & Maner, J. K. (2008). Coping with romantic betrayal: Sex differences in responses to partner infidelity. *Evolutionary Psychology, 6,* 413–426.

Miller, S. L., & Maner, J. K. (2010). Scent of a woman: Men's testosterone responses to olfactory ovulation cues. *Psychological Science, 21,* 276–283.

Miller, S. L., & Maner, J. K. (2011). Ovulation as a male mating prime: Subtle signs of women's fertility influence men's mating cognition and behavior. *Journal of Personality and Social Psychology, 100,* 295–308.

Miller, W. B., Sable, M. R., & Beckmeyer, J. J. (2009). Preconception motivation and pregnancy wantedness: Pathways to toddler attachment security. *Journal of Marriage and Family, 71,* 1174–1192.

Milletich, R. J., Kelley, M. L., Doane, A. N., & Pearson, M. R. (2010). Exposure to interparental violence and childhood physical and emotional abuse as related to physical aggression in undergraduate dating relationships. *Journal of Family Violence, 25,* 627–637.

Mills, J., Clark, M. S., Ford, T. E., & Johnson, M. (2004). Measurement of communal strength. *Personal Relationships, 11,* 213–230.

Miner, E. J., Starratt, V. G., & Shackelford, T. K. (2009). It's not all about her: Men's mate value and mate retention. *Personality and Individual Differences, 47,* 214–218.

Mirgain, S. A., & Cordova, J. V. (2007). Emotion skills and marital health: The association between observed and self-reported emotion skills, intimacy, and marital satisfaction. *Journal of Social and Clinical Psychology, 26,* 983–1009.

Mitchell, A. E., Castellani, A. M., Herrington, R. L., Joseph, J. I., Doss, B. D., & Snyder, D. K. (2008). Predictors of intimacy in couples' discussions of relationship injuries: An observational study. *Journal of Family Psychology, 22,* 21–29.

Mitchell, C. (2010). Are divorce studies trustworthy? The effects of survey nonresponse and response errors. *Journal of Marriage and Family, 72,* 893–905.

Mitchell, K., & Sugar, M. (2007, November 8). Annie's mailbox. *The Bryan-College Station Eagle,* A6.

Mitchell, K., & Sugar, M. (2008, January 24). Annie's mailbox. *The Bryan-College Station Eagle,* B2.

Mitchell, S. A. (2002). *Can love last? The fate of romance over time.* New York: Norton.

Mitnick, D. M., Heyman, R. E., Malik, J., & Smith-Slep, A. M. (2009). The differential association between change request qualities and resistance, problem resolution, and relationship satisfaction. *Journal of Family Psychology, 23,* 464–473.

Montoya, R. M. (2008). I'm hot, so I'd say you're not: The influence of objective physical attractiveness on mate selection. *Personality and Social Psychology Bulletin, 34,* 1315–1331.

Montoya, R. M., & Horton, R. S. (2004). On the importance of cognitive evaluation as a determinant of interpersonal attraction. *Journal of Personality & Social Psychology, 86,* 696–712.

Moore, M. M. (2010). Human nonverbal courtship behavior—A brief historical review. *Journal of Sex Research, 47,* 171–180.

Moore, T. M., Stuart, G. L., McNulty, J. K., Addis, M. E., Cordova, J. V., & Temple, J. R. (2008). Domains of masculine gender role stress and intimate partner violence in a clinical sample of violent men. *Psychology of Men & Masculinity, 9,* 82–89.

Moreland, R. L., & Beach, S. R. (1992). Exposure effects in the classroom: The development of affinity among students. *Journal of Experimental Social Psychology, 28,* 255–276.

Moreno, J. L. (1934). *Who shall survive? A new approach to the problem of human interrelationships.* Washington, DC: Nervous and Mental Disease Publishing.

Morgentaler, A. (2003). *The Viagra myth: The surprising impact on love and relationships.* San Francisco: Jossey-Bass.

Morin, R., & Cohn, D. (2008, September 25). Women call the shots at home; public mixed on gender roles in jobs. *Pew Research Center.* Retrieved from http://pewresearch.org/pubs/967/gender-power

Morris, W., & Kemp, B. (2011, January). *Do you take this marriage? Perceived choice over marital status affects stereotypes of single/married people.* Poster presented at the meeting of the Society for Personality and Social Psychology, San Antonio, TX.

Morrow, G. D., Clark, E. M., & Brock, K. F. (1995). Individual and partner love styles: Implications for the quality of romantic involvements. *Journal of Social and Personal Relationships, 12,* 363–387.

Morry, M. M. (2007). The attraction-similarity hypothesis among cross-sex friends: Relationship satisfaction, perceived similarities, and self-serving perceptions. *Journal of Social and Personal Relationships, 24,* 117–138.

Moskowitz, G. B. (2005). *Social cognition: Understanding self and others.* New York: Guilford Press.

Moss-Racusin, C. A., & Rudman, L. A. (2010). Disruptions in women's self-promotion: The backlash avoidance model. *Psychology of Women Quarterly, 34,* 186–202.

Muehlenhard, C. L., & Shippe, S. K. (2009). Men's and women's reports of pretending orgasm. *Journal of Sex Research, 46,* 1–16.

Mulac, A. (2006). The gender-linked language effect: Do language differences really make a difference? In K. Dindia & D. J. Canary (Eds.), *Sex differences and similarities in communication* (2nd ed., pp. 219–239). Mahwah, NJ: Erlbaum.

Muise, A., Christofides, E., & Desmarais, S. (2009). More information than you ever wanted: Does Facebook bring out the green-eyed monster of jealousy? *Cyberpsychology & Behavior, 12,* 441–444.

Murray, S. L. (2008). Realizing connectedness goals? The risk regulation system in relationships. In J. P. Forgas & J. Fitness (Eds.), *Social relationships: Cognitive, affective and motivational processes* (pp. 289–303). New York: Psychology Press.

Murray, S. L., Aloni, M., Holmes, J. G., Derrick, J. L., Stinson, D. A., & Leder, S. (2009). Fostering partner dependence as trust insurance: The implicit contingencies of the exchange script in close relationships. *Journal of Personality and Social Psychology, 96,* 324–348.

Murray, S. L., Bellavia, G. M., Rose, P., & Griffin, D. W. (2003). Once hurt, twice hurtful: How perceived regard regulates daily marital interactions. *Journal of Personality and Social Psychology, 84,* 126–147.

Murray, S. L., Griffin, D. W., Rose, P., & Bellavia, G. M. (2003). Calibrating the sociometer: The relational contingencies of self-esteem. *Journal of Personality and Social Psychology, 85,* 63–84.

Murray, S. L., & Holmes, J. G. (1999). The (mental) ties that bind: Cognitive structures that predict relationship resilience. *Journal of Personality and Social Psychology, 77,* 1228–1244.

Murray, S. L., Holmes, J. G., & Griffin, D. W. (1996). The self-fulfilling nature of positive illusions in romantic relationships: Love is not blind, but prescient. *Journal of Personality and Social Psychology, 71,* 1155–1180.

Murray, S. L., Holmes, J. G., & Griffin, D. W. (2000). Self-esteem and the quest for felt security: How perceived regard regulates attachment processes. *Journal of Personality and Social Psychology, 78,* 478–498.

Murray, S. L., Holmes, J. G., Griffin, D. W., Bellavia, G., & Rose, P. (2001). The mismeasure of love: How self-doubt contaminates relationship beliefs. *Personality and Social Psychology Bulletin, 27,* 423–436.

Murray, S. L., Holmes, J. G., MacDonald, G., & Ellsworth, P. C. (1998). Through the looking glass darkly? When self-doubts turn into relationship insecurities. *Journal of Personality and Social Psychology, 75,* 1459–1480.

Murray, S. L., Rose, P., Bellavia, G. M., Holmes, J. G., & Kusche, A. G. (2002). When rejection stings: How self-esteem constrains relationship-enhancement processes. *Journal of Personality and Social Psychology, 83,* 556–573.

Murstein, B. I. (1987). A clarification and extension of the SVR theory of dyadic pairing. *Journal of Marriage and the Family, 49,* 929–933.

Musick, K., & Meier, A. (2010). Are both parents always better than one? Parental conflict and young adult well-being. *Social Science Research, 39,* 814–830.

Myers, D. G., & Scanzoni, L. D. (2005). *What God has joined together? A Christian case for gay marriage.* New York: HarperCollins.

Myers, S. A., & Berscheid, E. (1997). The language of love: The difference a preposition makes. *Personality and Social Psychology Bulletin, 23,* 347–362.

Nardone, N., & Lewandowski, G. (2008, February). *The relation of self-expansion to well-being and relationship quality.* Poster presented at the meeting of the Society for Personality and Social Psychology, Albuquerque, NM.

National Center for Health Statistics. (2004, December). *Teenagers in the United States: Sexual activity, contraceptive use, and childbearing, 2002.* Retrieved from: http://www.cdc.gov/nchs/data/series/sr_23/sr23_024.pdf

National Center for Health Statistics. (2007, June 28). *Drug use and sexual behaviors reported by adults: United States, 1999–2002.* Retrieved from: http://www.cdc.gov/nchs/pressroom/07newsreleases/druguse.htm

Neff, L. A., & Karney, B. R. (2002). Judgments of a relationship partner: Specific accuracy but global enhancement. *Journal of Personality, 70,* 1079–1112.

Neff, L. A., & Karney, B. R. (2003). The dynamic structure of relationship perceptions: Differential importance as a strategy of relationship maintenance. *Personality and Social Psychology Bulletin, 29,* 1433–1446.

Neff, L. A., & Karney, B. R. (2004). How does context affect intimate relationships? Linking external stress and cognitive processes within marriage. *Personality and Social Psychology Bulletin, 30,* 134–148.

Neff, L. A., & Karney, B. R. (2005). To know you is to love you: The implications of global adoration and specific accuracy for marital relationships. *Journal of Personality and Social Psychology, 88,* 480–497.

Neff, L. A., & Karney, B. R. (2009). Compassionate love in early marriage. In B. Fehr, S. Sprecher, & L. Underwood (Eds.), *The science of compassionate love: Theory: research, and applications* (pp. 201–221). Chichester, England: Wiley-Blackwell.

Neighbors, C., Walker, D. D., Mbilinyi, L. F., O'Rourke, A., Edleson, J. L., Zegree, J., & Roffman, R. A. (2010). Normative misperceptions of abuse among perpetrators of intimate partner violence. *Violence Against Women, 16,* 370–386.

Nelson, L. D., & Morrison, E. L. (2005). The symptoms of resource scarcity: Judgments of food and finances influence preferences for potential partners. *Psychological Science, 16,* 167–173.

Newall, N. E., Chipperfield, J. G., Clifton, R. A., Perry, R. P., Swift, A. U., & Ruthig, J. C. (2009). Causal beliefs, social participation, and loneliness among older adults: A longitudinal study. *Journal of Social and Personal Relationships, 26,* 273–290.

Newcomb, T. M. (1961). *The acquaintance process.* New York: Holt, Rinehart & Winston.

Newman, M. L., Pennebaker, J. W., Berry, D. S., & Richards, J. M. (2003). Lying words: Predicting deception from linguistic styles. *Personality and Social Psychology Bulletin, 29,* 665–675.

Newport, F. (2008, April 4). Wives still do laundry, men do yard work. *Gallup Poll News Service.* Retrieved from http://www.gallup.com/poll/106249/Wives-Still-Laundry-Men-Yard-Work.aspx

Nezlek, J. B., & Leary, M. R. (2002). Individual differences in self-presentational motives in daily social interaction. *Personality and Social Psychology Bulletin, 28,* 211–223.

Nezlek, J. B., Richardson, D. S., Green, L. R., & Schatten-Jones, E. C. (2002). Psychological well-being and day-to-day social interaction among older adults. *Personal Relationships, 9,* 57–71.

Nezlek, J. B., Schütz, A., & Sellin, I. (2007). Self-presentational success in daily interaction. *Self and Identity, 6,* 361–379.

Noller, P. (1980). Misunderstandings in marital communication: A study of couples' nonverbal communications. *Journal of Personality and Social Psychology, 39,* 1135–1148.

Noller, P. (1981). Gender and marital adjustment level differences in decoding messages from spouses and strangers. *Journal of Personality and Social Psychology, 41,* 272–278.

Noller, P. (2006). Nonverbal communication in close relationships. In V. Manusov & M. L. Patterson (Eds.), *The Sage handbook of nonverbal communication* (pp. 403–420). Thousand Oaks, CA: Sage.

Noller, P., Feeney, J. A., Bonnell, D., & Callan, V. J. (1994). A longitudinal study of conflict in early marriage. *Journal of Social and Personal Relationships, 11*, 233–252.

Noller, P., & Vernardos, C. (1986). Communication awareness in married couples. *Journal of Social and Personal Relationships, 3*, 31–42.

North, R. J., Holahan, C. J., Moos, R. H., & Cronkite, R. C. (2008). Family support, family income, and happiness: A 10-year perspective. *Journal of Family Psychology, 22*, 475–483.

Norton, M. I., Frost, J. H., & Ariely, D. (2007). Less is more: The lure of ambiguity, or why familiarity breeds contempt. *Journal of Personality and Social Psychology, 92*, 97–105.

Nosko, A., Wood, E., & Molema, S. (2010). All about me: Disclosure in online social networking profiles: The case of Facebook. *Computers in Human Behavior, 26*, 406–418.

Notarius, C. I., Lashley, S. L., & Sullivan, D. J. (1997). Angry at your partner? Think again. In R. J. Sternberg & M. Hojjat (Eds.), *Satisfaction in close relationships* (pp. 219–248). New York: Guilford Press.

Oakman, J., Gifford, S., & Chlebowsky, N. (2003). A multilevel analysis of the interpersonal behavior of socially anxious people. *Journal of Personality, 71*, 397–434.

Oatley, K., Keltner, D., & Jenkins, J. M. (2006). *Understanding emotions* (2nd ed.). Malden, MA: Blackwell.

Oishi, S. (2010). The psychology of residential mobility: Implications for the self, social relationships, and well-being. *Perspectives on Psychological Science, 5*, 5–21.

Okimoto, T. G., & Brescoll, V. L. (2010). The price of power: Power seeking and backlash against female politicians. *Personality and Social Psychology Bulletin, 36*, 923–936.

Okonski, B. (1996, May 6). Just say something. *Newsweek, 131*, 14.

Olatunji, B. O., Lohr, J. M., & Bushman, B. J. (2007). The pseudopsychology of venting in the treatment of anger: Implications and alternatives for mental health practice. In T. A. Cavell & K. T. Malcolm (Eds.), *Anger, aggression, and interventions for interpersonal violence* (pp. 119–141). Mahwah, NJ: Erlbaum.

Olivola, C. Y., & Todorov, A. (2010a). Elected in 100 milliseconds: Appearance-based trait inferences and voting. *Journal of Nonverbal Behavior, 34*, 83–110.

Olivola, C. Y., & Todorov, A. (2010b). Fooled by first impressions? Reexamining the diagnostic value of appearance-based inferences. *Journal of Experimental Social Psychology, 46*, 315–324.

Oncale, R. M., & King, B. M. (2001). Comparison of men's and women's attempts to dissuade sexual partners from the couple using condoms. *Archives of Sexual Behavior, 30*, 379–391.

Orbuch, T. L. (2009). *5 simple steps to take your marriage from good to great.* New York: Delacorte Press.

Orbuch, T. L., & Brown, E. (2006). Divorce in the context of being African-American. In M. A. Fine & J. H. Harvey (Eds.), *Handbook of divorce and relationship dissolution* (pp. 481–498). Mahwah, NJ: Erlbaum.

Oriña, M. M., Wood, W., & Simpson, J. A. (2002). Strategies of influence in close relationships. *Journal of Experimental Social Psychology, 38*, 459–472.

Orr, A. (2004). *Meeting, mating, and cheating: Sex, love, and the new world of online dating.* Upper Saddle River, NJ: Reuters.

Orr, E. S., Sisic, M., Ross, C., Simmering, M. G., Arseneault, J. M., & Orr, R. R. (2009). The influence of shyness on the use of Facebook in an undergraduate sample. *CyberPsychology & Behavior, 12*, 337–340.

Orvis, B. R., Kelley, H. H., & Butler, D. (1976). Attributional conflict in young couples. In J. H. Harvey, W. J. Ickes, & R. E. Kidd (Eds.), *New directions in attribution research* (Vol. 1, pp. 353–386). Hillsdale, NJ: Erlbaum.

Ostovich, J. M., & Sabini, J. (2004). How are sociosexuality, sex drive, and lifetime number of sexual partners related? *Personality and Social Psychology Bulletin, 30*, 1255–1266.

O'Sullivan, L. F., Udell, W., Montrose, V. A., Antoniello, P., & Hoffman, S. (2010). A cognitive analysis of college students' explanations for engaging in unprotected sexual intercourse. *Archives of Sexual Behavior, 39*, 1121–1131.

O'Sullivan, M. (2008a). Deception and self-deception as strategies in short- and long-term mating. In G. Geher & G. Miller (Eds.), *Mating intelligence: Sex, relationships, and the mind's reproductive system* (pp. 135–157). New York: Erlbaum.

O'Sullivan, M. (2008b). Home runs and humbugs: Comment on Bond and DePaulo. *Psychological Bulletin, 134,* 493–497.

Oswald, D. L., & Clark, E. M. (2006). How do friendship maintenance behaviors and problem-solving styles function at the individual and dyadic levels? *Personal Relationships, 13,* 333–348.

Oswald, D. L., Clark, E. M., & Kelly, C. M. (2004). Friendship maintenance: An analysis of individual and dyad behaviors. *Journal of Social and Clinical Psychology, 23,* 413–441.

Oswald, D. L., & Russell, B. L. (2006). Perceptions of sexual coercion in heterosexual dating relationships: The role of aggressor gender and tactics. *Journal of Sex Research, 43,* 87–95.

Oswalt, S. B., Cameron, K. A., & Koob, J. J. (2005). Sexual regret in college students. *Archives of Sexual Behavior, 34,* 663–669.

Otto-Salaj, L. L., Traxel, N., Brondino, M. J., Reed, B., Gore-Felton, C., Kelly, J. A., & Stevenson, L. Y. (2010). Reactions of heterosexual African American men to women's condom negotiation strategies. *Journal of Sex Research, 47,* 539–551.

Overall, N. C., Fletcher, G. J. O., & Friesen, M. D. (2003). Mapping the intimate relationship mind: Comparisons between three models of attachment representations. *Personality and Social Psychology Bulletin, 29,* 1479–1493.

Overall, N. C., Fletcher, G. J. O., & Simpson, J. A. (2010a). Helping each other grow: Romantic partner support, self-improvement, and relationship quality. *Personality and Social Psychology Bulletin, 36,* 1496–1513.

Overall, N. C., & Sibley, C. G. (2008). Attachment and attraction toward romantic partners versus relevant alternatives within daily interactions. *Personality and Individual Differences, 44,* 1126–1137.

Overall, N. C., Sibley, C. G., & Travaglia, L. K. (2010b). Loyal but ignored: The benefits and costs of constructive communication behavior. *Personal Relationships, 17,* 127–148.

Owen, J., & Fincham, F. D. (2011). Effects of gender and psychosocial factors on "friends with benefits" relationships among young adults. *Archives of Sexual Behavior, 40,* 311–320.

Owen, P. R., & Laurel-Seller, E. (2000). Weight and shape ideals: Thin is dangerously in. *Journal of Applied Social Psychology, 30,* 979–990.

Padgett, P. M. (2007). Personal safety and sexual safety for women using online personal ads. *Sexuality Research & Social Policy, 4,* 27–37.

Paik, A. (2011). Adolescent sexuality and the risk of marital dissolution. *Journal of Marriage and Family, 73,* 472–485.

Palomares, N. A. (2009). Women are sort of more tentative than men, aren't they? How men and women use tentative language differently, similarly, and counterstereotypically as a function of gender salience. *Communication Research, 36,* 538–560.

Papp, L. M., Cummings, E. M., & Goeke-Morey, M. C. (2009a). For richer, for poorer: Money as a topic of marital conflict in the home. *Family Relations, 58,* 91–103.

Papp, L. M., Kouros, C. D., & Cummings, E. M. (2009b). Demand-withdraw patterns in marital conflict in the home. *Personal Relationships, 16,* 285–300.

Parks-Stamm, E. J., Heilman, M. E., & Hearns, K. A. (2008). Motivated to penalize: Women's strategic rejection of successful women. *Personality and Social Psychology Bulletin, 34,* 237–247.

Parrott, W. G., & Smith, R. H. (1993). Distinguishing the experiences of envy and jealousy. *Journal of Personality and Social Psychology, 64,* 906–920.

Patterson, M. L. (2011). *More than words: The power of nonverbal communication.* Barcelona, Spain: Aresta.

Paul, E. L., Wenzel, A., & Harvey, J. H. (2008). Hookups: A facilitator or a barrier to relationship initiation and intimacy development? In S. Sprecher, A. Wenzel, & J. H. Harvey (Eds.), *Handbook of relationship initiation* (pp. 375–390). Mahwah, NJ: Erlbaum.

Payne, J. W. (2006, January 8). Health risk indicator may be all in the belly. *Houston Chronicle,* G7.

Pearce, A. R., Chuikova, T., Ramsey, A., & Galyautdinova, S. (2010). A positive psychology perspective on mate preferences in the United States and Russia. *Journal of Cross-Cultural Psychology, 41,* 742–757.

Pearce, Z. J., & Halford, W. K. (2008). Do attributions mediate the association between attachment and negative couple communication? *Personal Relationships, 15,* 155–170.

Pease, A., & Pease, B. (2006). *The definitive book of body language.* New York: Bantam Books.

Pedersen, W. C., Miller, L. C., Putcha-Bhagavatula, A. D., & Yang, Y. (2002). Evolved sex differences in the number of partners desired? The long and the short of it. *Psychological Science, 13,* 157–161.

Peetz, J., & Kammrath, L. (2011). Only because I love you: Why people make and why they break promises in romantic relationships. *Journal of Personality and Social Psychology, 100,* 887–904.

Pelham, B. W., Carvallo, M., & Jones, J. T. (2005). Implicit egotism. *Current Directions in Psychological Science, 14,* 106–110.

Pennebaker, J. W., Dyer, M. A., Caulkins, R. J., Litowitz, D. L., Ackerman, P. L., Anderson, D. B., & McGraw, K. M. (1979). Don't the girls get prettier at closing time: A country and western application to psychology. *Personality and Social Psychology Bulletin, 5,* 122–125.

Peplau, L. A. (2003). Human sexuality: How do men and women differ? *Current Directions in Psychological Science, 12,* 37–40.

Peplau, L. A., & Fingerhut, A. W. (2007). The close relationships of lesbians and gay men. *Annual Review of Psychology, 58,* 405–424.

Peplau, L. A., Fingerhut, A., & Beals, K. P. (2004). Sexuality in the relationships of lesbians and gay men. In J. H. Harvey, A. Wenzel, & S. Sprecher (Eds.), *The handbook of sexuality in close relationships* (pp. 349–369). Mahwah, NJ: Erlbaum.

Perilloux, C., & Buss, D. M. (2008). Breaking up romantic relationships: Costs experienced and coping strategies deployed. *Evolutionary Psychology, 6,* 164–181.

Perilloux, C., Fleischman, D. S., & Buss, D. M. (2011). Meet the parents: Parent-offspring convergence and divergence in mate preferences. *Personality and Individual Differences, 50,* 253–258.

Perilloux, H. K., Webster, G. D., & Gaulin, S. J. C. (2010). Signals of genetic quality and maternal investment capacity: The dynamic effects of fluctuating asymmetry and waist-to-hip ratio on men's ratings of women's attractiveness. *Social Psychology and Personality Science, 1,* 34–42.

Perlman, D. (1989, August). *You bug me: A preliminary report on hassles in relationships.* Paper presented at the meeting of the American Psychological Association, New Orleans.

Perrett, D. (2010). *In your face: The new science of human attraction.* New York: Palgrave Macmillan.

Perrier, C., DeCourville, N., & Sadava, S. (2008, February). *Forgiving you makes us happy: The role of constructive communication and self-disclosure in the link between forgiveness, intimacy, and relationship satisfaction.* Poster presented at the meeting of the Society for Personality and Social Psychology, Albuquerque, NM.

Peter, J., & Valkenbug, P. M. (2007). Adolescents' exposure to a sexualized media environment and their notions of women as sex objects. *Sex Roles, 56,* 381–395.

Petersen, J. L., & Hyde, J. S. (2010). A meta-analytic review of research on gender differences in sexuality, 1993–2007. *Psychological Bulletin, 136,* 21–38.

Peterson, D. R. (2002). Conflict. In H. H. Kelley, E. Berscheid, A. Christensen et al. (Eds.), *Close relationships* (pp. 265–314). Clinton Corners, NY: Percheron Press.

Petronio, S. (2010). Communication privacy management theory: What do we know about family privacy regulation? *Journal of Family Theory & Review, 2,* 175–196.

Petronio, S., & Durham, W. T. (2008). Communication privacy management theory: Significance for interpersonal communication. In L. A. Baxter & D. O. Braithwaite (Eds.), *Engaging theories in interpersonal communication: Multiple perspectives* (pp. 309–322). Thousand Oaks, CA: Sage.

Pettijohn, T. F., II, & Jungeberg, B. J. (2004). *Playboy* playmate curves: Changes in facial and body feature preferences across social and economic conditions. *Personality and Social Psychology Bulletin, 30,* 1186–1197.

Picardi, A., Fagnani, C., Nisticò, L., & Stazi, M. A. (2011). A twin study of attachment style in young adults. *Journal of Personality.* DOI: 10.1111/j.1467-6494.2010.00707.x

Pillsworth, E. G., & Haselton, M. G. (2006). Women's sexual strategies: The evolution of long-term bonds and extrapair sex. *Annual Review of Sex Research, 17,* 59–100.

Pines, A. M. (1998). *Romantic jealousy: Causes, symptoms, cures.* New York: Routledge.

Pinquart, M. (2003). Loneliness in married, widowed, divorced, and never-married older adults. *Journal of Social and Personal Relationships, 20,* 31–53.

Pipitone, R. N., & Gallup, G. G., Jr. (2008). Women's voice attractiveness varies across the menstrual cycle. *Evolution and Human Behavior, 29,* 268–274.

Pittman, F. S., & Wagers, T. P. (2005). Teaching fidelity. *Journal of Clinical Psychology, 61,* 1407–1419.

Pitts, M. K., Smith, A. M. A., Grierson, J., O'Brien, M., & Misson, S. (2004). Who pays for sex and why? An analysis of social and motivational factors associated with male clients of sex workers. *Archives of Sexual Behavior, 33,* 353–358.

Place, S. S., Todd, P. M., Penke, L., & Asendorpf, J. B. (2009). The ability to judge the romantic interest of others. *Psychological Science, 20,* 22–26.

Planalp, S., & Benson, A. (1992). Friends' and acquaintances' conversations I: Perceived differences. *Journal of Social and Personal Relationships, 9,* 483–506.

Plaut, V. C., Adams, G., & Anderson, S. L. (2009). Does attractiveness buy happiness? "It depends on where you're from." *Personal Relationships, 16,* 619–630.

Pollmann, M. M. H., & Finkenauer, C. (2009). Investigating the role of two types of understanding in relationship well-being: Understanding is more important than knowledge. *Personality and Social Psychology Bulletin, 35,* 1512–1527.

Poortman, A. (2005). The mediating role of financial and time pressures. *Journal of Family Issues, 26,* 168–195.

Poortman, A., & Liefbroer, A. C. (2010). Singles' relational attitudes in a time of individualization. *Social Science Research, 39,* 938–949.

Poortman, A., & Lyngstad, T. H. (2007). Dissolution risks in first and higher order marital and cohabiting unions. *Social Science Research, 36,* 1431–1446.

Poortman, A., & Seltzer, J. A. (2007). Parents' expectations about childrearing after divorce: Does anticipating difficulty deter divorce? *Journal of Marriage and Family, 69,* 254–269.

Porter, S., & ten Brinke, L. (2008). Reading between the lies: Identifying concealed and falsified emotions in universal facial expressions. *Psychological Science, 19,* 508–514.

Porter, S., & ten Brinke, L. (2010). The truth about lies: What works in detecting high-stakes deception? *Legal and Criminological Psychology, 15,* 57–75.

Powers, S. I., Pietromonaco, P. R., Gunlicks, M., & Sayer, A. (2006). Dating couples' attachment styles and patterns of cortisol reactivity and recovery in response to a relationship conflict. *Journal of Personality and Social Psychology, 90,* 613–628.

Prager, K. J., & Roberts, L. J. (2004). Deep intimate connection: Self and intimacy in couple relationships. In D. J. Mashek & A. Aron (Eds.), *Handbook of closeness and intimacy* (pp. 43–60). Mahwah, NJ: Erlbaum.

Pratto, F., & Walker, A. (2004). The bases of gendered power. In A. H. Eagly, A. E. Beall, & R. J. Sternberg (Eds.), *The psychology of gender* (2nd ed., pp. 242–268). New York: Guilford Press.

Pressman, S. D., Cohen, S., Miller, G. E., Barkin, A., Rabin, B. S., & Treanor, J. J. (2005). Loneliness, social network size, and immune response to influenza vaccination in college freshmen. *Health Psychology, 24,* 297–306.

Previti, D., & Amato, P. R. (2003). Why stay married? Rewards, barriers, and marital stability. *Journal of Marriage and Family, 65,* 561–573.

Previti, D., & Amato, P. R. (2004). Is infidelity a cause or a consequence of poor marital quality? *Journal of Social and Personal Relationships, 21,* 217–230.

Priem, J. S., Solomon, D. H., & Steuber, K. R. (2009). Accuracy and bias in perceptions of emotionally supportive communication in marriage. *Personal Relationships, 16,* 531–552.

Prokosch, M. D., Coss, R. G., Scheib, J. E., & Blozis, S. A. (2009). Intelligence and mate choice: Intelligent men are always appealing. *Evolution and Human Behavior, 30,* 11–20.

Pronin, E., Lin, D. Y., & Ross, L. (2002). The bias blind spot: Perceptions of bias in self versus others. *Personality and Social Psychology Bulletin, 28,* 369–381.

Pronk, T. M., Karremans, J. C., & Wigboldus, D. H. J. (2011). How can you resist? Executive control helps romantically involved individuals to stay faithful. *Journal of Personality and Social Psychology, 100,* 827–837.

Proost, K., Schreurs, B., de Witte, K., & Derous, E. (2010). Ingratiation and self-promotion in the selection interview: The effects of using single tactics or a combination of tactics on interviewer judgments. *Journal of Applied Social Psychology, 40,* 2155–2169.

Puccinelli, N. M. (2010). Nonverbal communication competence. In D. Matsumoto (Ed.), *APA handbook of interpersonal communication* (pp. 273–288). Washington, DC: American Psychological Association.

Pulerwitz, J., Gortmaker, S. L., & DeJong, W. (2000). Measuring sexual relationship power in HIV/STD research. *Sex Roles, 42,* 637–660.

Purvis, J. A., Dabbs, J. M., Jr., & Hopper, C. H. (1984). The "opener": Skilled user of facial expression and speech pattern. *Personality and Social Psychology Bulletin, 10,* 61–66.

Putnam, R. D. (2000). *Bowling alone: The collapse and revival of American community.* New York: Simon & Schuster.

Quenqua, D. (2010, March 26). When couples fight on Facebook. *Houston Chronicle,* p. E6.

Ramirez, A., Jr. (2008). An examination of the tripartite approach to commitment: An actor-partner interdependence model analysis of the effect of relational maintenance behavior. *Journal of Social and Personal Relationships, 25,* 943–965.

Ramirez, A., Jr. & Zhang, S. (2007). When online meets offline: The effect of modality switching on relational communication. *Communication Monographs, 74,* 287–310.

Randall, A. K., & Bodenmann, G. (2009). The role of stress on close relationships and marital satisfaction. *Clinical Psychology Review, 29,* 105–115.

Randolph, M. E., Pinkerton, S. D., Bogart, L. M., Cecil, H., & Abramson, P. R. (2007). Sexual pleasure and condom use. *Archives of Sexual Behavior, 36,* 844–848.

Rashotte, L. S. (2002). What does that smile mean? The meaning of nonverbal behaviors in social interaction. *Social Psychology Quarterly, 65,* 92–102.

Rauer, A. J., Karney, B. R., Garvan, C. W., & Hou, W. (2008). Relationship risks in context: A cumulative risk approach to understanding relationship satisfaction. *Journal of Marriage and Family, 70,* 1122–1135.

Raven, B. H. (2001). Power/interaction and interpersonal influence: Experimental investigations and case studies. In A. Y. Lee-Chai & J. A. Bargh (Eds.), *The use and abuse of power: Multiple perspectives on the causes of corruption* (pp. 217–240). Philadelphia: Psychology Press.

Regan, K. V., Bartholomew, K., Kwong, M. J., Trinke, S. J., & Henderson, A. J. Z. (2006). The relative severity of acts of physical violence in heterosexual relationships: An item response theory analysis. *Personal Relationships, 13,* 37–52.

Regan, P. C. (1998). Of lust and love: Beliefs about the role of sexual desire in romantic relationships. *Personal Relationships, 5,* 139–157.

Regan, P. C. (2004). Sex and the attraction process: Lessons from science (and Shakespeare) on lust, love, chastity, and fidelity. In J. H. Harvey, A. Wenzel, & S. Sprecher (Eds.), *The handbook of sexuality in close relationships* (pp. 115–133). Mahwah, NJ: Erlbaum.

Regan, P. C. (2008). *The mating game: A primer on love, sex, and marriage* (2nd ed.). Thousand Oaks, CA: Sage.

Regan, P. C., & Atkins, L. (2006). Sex differences and similarities in frequency and intensity of sexual desire. *Social Behavior and Personality, 34,* 95–102.

Rehman, U. S., Gollan, J., & Mortimer, A. R. (2008). The marital context of depression: Research, limitations, and new directions. *Clinical Psychology Review, 28,* 179–198.

Reid, P. T., Cooper, S. M., & Banks, K. H. (2008). Girls to women: Developmental theory, research, and issues. In F. L. Denmark & M. A. Paludi (Eds.), *Psychology of women: A handbook of issues and theories* (2nd ed., pp. 237–270). Westport, CT: Praeger.

Reinhardt, J. P., Boerner, K., & Horowitz, A. (2006). Good to have but not to use: Differential impact of perceived and received support on well-being. *Journal of Social and Personal Relationships, 23,* 117–129.

Reis, H. T. (1986). Gender effects in social participation: Intimacy, loneliness, and the conduct of social interaction. In R. Gilmour & S. Duck (Eds.), *The emerging field of personal relationships* (pp. 91–105). London: Academic Press.

Reis, H. T. (1998). Gender differences in intimacy and related behaviors: Context and process. In D. J. Canary & K. Dindia (Eds.), *Sex differences and similarities in communication: Critical essays and empirical investigations of sex and gender in interaction* (pp. 203–234). Mahwah, NJ: Erlbaum.

Reis, H. T. (2002). Action matters, but relationship science is basic. *Journal of Social and Personal Relationships, 19,* 601–611.

Reis, H. T. (2009, May). *Perceived partner responsiveness as an organizing theme for the study of relation-ships and well-being.* Paper presented at the Texas Symposium on the Development of Close Relationships, Austin, TX.

Reis, H. T., & Aron, A. (2008). Love: What is it, why does it matter, and how does it operate? *Perspectives on Psychological Science, 3,* 80–86.

Reis, H. T., Clark, M. S., & Holmes, J. G. (2004). Perceived partner responsiveness as an organizing construct in the study of intimacy and closeness. In D. J. Mashek & A. Aron (Eds.), *Handbook of closeness and intimacy* (pp. 201–225). Mahwah, NJ: Erlbaum.

Reis, H. T., Caprariello, P. A., & Velickovic, M. (2011). The relationship superiority effect is moderated by the relationship context. *Journal of Experimental Social Psychology, 47,* 481–484.

Reis, H. T., & Gable, S. L. (2003). Toward a positive psychology of relationships. In C. L. M. Keyes & J. Haidt (Eds.), *Flourishing: positive psychology and the life well-lived* (pp. 129–159). Washington, DC: American Psychological Association.

Reis, H. T., Lin, Y., Bennett, M. E., & Nezlek, J. B. (1993). Change and consistency in social participation during early adulthood. *Developmental Psychology, 29,* 633–645.

Reis, H. T., Maniaci, M. R., Caprariello, P. A., Eastwick, P. W., & Finkel, E. J. (2011). Familiarity does indeed promote attraction in live interaction. *Journal of Personality and Social Psychology, 101,* 557–570.

Reis, H. T., Nezlek, J., & Wheeler, L. (1980). Physical attractiveness in social interaction. *Journal of Personality and Social Psychology, 38,* 604–617.

Reis, H. T., & Patrick, B. C. (1996). Attachment and intimacy: Component processes. In E. T. Higgins & A. W. Kruglanski (Eds.), *Social psychology: Handbook of basic principles* (pp. 523–563). New York: Guilford Press.

Reis, H. T., & Shaver, P. (1988). Intimacy as an interpersonal process. In S. Duck (Ed.), *Handbook of personal relationships: Theory, research, and interventions* (pp. 367–389). Chichester, England: Wiley.

Reis, H. T., Sheldon, R. M., Gable, S. L., Roscoe, J., & Ryan, R. M. (2000). Daily well-being: The role of autonomy, competence, and relatedness. *Personality and Social Psychology Bulletin, 26,* 419–435.

Reis, H. T., Smith, S. M., Carmichael, C. L., Caprariello, P. A., Tsai, F., Rodrigues, A., & Maniaci, M. R. (2010). Are you happy for me? How sharing positive events with others provides personal and interpersonal benefits. *Journal of Personality and Social Psychology, 99,* 311–329.

Reis, H. T., Wheeler, L., Spiegel, N., Kernis, M. H., Nezlek, J., & Perri, M. (1982). Physical attractiveness in social interaction: II. Why does appearance affect social experience? *Journal of Personality and Social Psychology, 43,* 979–996.

Rempel, J. K., Ross, M., & Holmes, J. G. (2001). Trust and communicated attributions in close relationships. *Journal of Personality and Social Psychology, 81,* 57–64.

Renninger, L. A., Wade, T. J., & Grammer, K. (2004). Getting that female glance: Patterns and consequences of male nonverbal behavior in courtship contexts. *Evolution and Human Behavior, 25,* 416–431.

Renshaw, K. D., Blais, R. K., & Smith, T. W. (2010). Components of negative affectivity and marital satisfaction: The importance of actor and partner anger. *Journal of Research in Personality, 44,* 328–334.

Repetti, R., Wang, S., & Saxbe, D. (2009). Bringing it all back home: How outside stressors shape families' everyday lives. *Current Directions in Psychological Science, 18,* 106–111.

Rhoades, G. K., Stanley, S. M., & Markman, H. J. (2009a). Couples' reasons for cohabitation: Associations with individual well-being and relationship quality. *Journal of Family Issues, 30,* 233–258.

Rhoades, G. K., Stanley, S. M., & Markman, H. J. (2009b). The pre-engagement cohabitation effect: A replication and extension of previous findings. *Journal of Family Psychology, 23,* 107–111.

Rhoades, G. K., Stanley, S. M., & Markman, H. J. (2010). Should I stay or should I go? Predicting dating relationship stability from four aspects of commitment. *Journal of Family Psychology, 24,* 543–550.

Rhodes, G. (2006). The evolutionary psychology of facial beauty. *Annual Review of Psychology, 57,* 199–226.

Rhodes, G., Harwood, K., Yoshikawa, S., Nishitani, M., & MacLean, I. (2002). The attractiveness of average faces: Cross-cultural evidence and possible biological basis. In G. Rhodes & L. A.

Zebrowitz (Eds.), *Facial attractiveness: Evolutionary, cognitive and social perspectives* (pp. 35–58). Westport, CT: Ablex.

Rhodes, G., Sumich, A., & Byatt, G. (1999). Are average facial configurations attractive only because of their symmetry? *Psychological Science, 10,* 52–58.

Rhodewalt, F., & Eddings, S. K. (2002). Narcissus reflects: Memory distortion in response to ego-relevant feedback among high- and low-narcissistic men. *Journal of Research in Personality, 36,* 97–116.

Richman, L. S., & Leary, M. R. (2009). Reactions to discrimination, stigmatization, ostracism, and other forms of interpersonal rejection: A multimotive model. *Psychological Review, 116,* 365–383.

Rick, S. I., Small, D. A., & Finkel, E. J. (2011). Fatal (fiscal) attraction: Spendthrifts and tightwads in marriage. *Journal of Marketing Research, 48,* 228–237.

Riela, S., Rodriguez, G., Aron, A., Xu, X., & Acevedo, B. P. (2010). Experiences of falling in love: Investigating culture, ethnicity, gender, and speed. *Journal of Social and Personal Relationships, 27,* 473–493.

Ridge, R. D, & Reber, J. S. (2002). "I think she's attracted to me": The effect of men's beliefs on women's behavior in a job interview scenario. *Basic and Applied Social Psychology, 24,* 1–14.

Riggio, H. R. (2004). Parental marital conflict and divorce, parent–child relationships, social support, and relationship anxiety in young adulthood. *Personal Relationships, 11,* 99–114.

Riggio, H. R., & Weiser, D. A. (2008). Attitudes toward marriage: Embeddedness and outcomes in personal relationships. *Personal Relationships, 15,* 123–140.

Riggle, E. D. B., Rostosky, S. S., & Horne, S. G. (2010). Psychological distress, well-being, and legal recognition in same-sex couple relationships. *Journal of Family Psychology, 24,* 82–86.

Rizkalla, L., Wertheim, E. H., & Hodgson, L. K. (2008). The roles of emotion management and perspective taking in individuals' conflict management styles and disposition to forgive. *Journal of Research in Personality, 42,* 1594–1601.

Roberts, B. W., Kuncel, N. R., Shiner, R., Caspi, A., & Goldberg, L. R. (2007). The power of personality: The comparative validity of personality traits, socioeconomic status, and cognitive ability for predicting life outcomes. *Perspectives on Psychological Science, 2,* 313–345.

Roberts, B. W., Kuncel, N. R., Viechtbauer, W., & Bogg, T. (2007). Meta-analysis in personality psychology. In R. W. Robins, R. C. Fraley, & R. F. Krueger (Eds.), *Handbook of research methods in personality psychology* (pp. 652–672). New York: Guilford Press.

Roberts, B. W., & Mroczek, D. (2008). Personality trait change in adulthood. *Current Directions in Psychological Science, 17,* 31–35.

Roberts, S. (2007, September 20). If you've been wed 25 years, you're in the minority. *Houston Chronicle,* p. A5.

Roberts, S. (2007, January 16). Majority of women now living without a husband. *Houston Chronicle,* pp. A1, A4.

Roberts, S. (2010, March 3). Want to raise the odds your marriage will last? Then try living apart. *Houston Chronicle,* p. A3.

Roberts, S. G. B., & Dunbar, R. I. M. (2011). The costs of family and friends: An 18-month longitudinal study of relationship maintenance and decay. *Evolution and Human Behavior, 32,* 186–197

Robertson, K., & Murachver, T. (2009). Attitudes and attributions associated with female and male partner violence. *Journal of Applied Social Psychology, 39,* 1481–1512.

Robillard, S. L., & Jarry, J. L. (2007, May). *Intrasexual competition for evolutionarily desirable men: The effect on women's eating behavior.* Poster presented at the meeting of the Association for Psychological Science, Washington, DC.

Robins, R. W., Caspi, A., & Moffitt, T. E. (2000). Two personalities, one relationship: Both partners' personality traits shape the quality of their relationship. *Journal of Personality and Social Psychology, 79,* 251–259.

Robins, R. W., Fraley, R. C., & Krueger, R. F. (2009). *Handbook of research methods in personality psychology.* New York: Guilford Press.

Robins, R. W., Mendelsohn, G. A., Connell, J. B., & Kwan, V. S. Y. (2004). Do people agree about the causes of behavior? A social relations analysis of behavior ratings and causal attributions. *Journal of Personality and Social Psychology, 86,* 334–344.

Rodgers, J. L., Nakonezny, P. A., & Shull, R. D. (1999). Did no-fault divorce legislation matter? Definitely yes and sometimes no. *Journal of Marriage and the Family, 61,* 803–809.

Rogers, S. J. (1999). Wives' income and marital quality: Are there reciprocal effects? *Journal of Marriage and the Family, 61,* 123–132.

Rogers, S. J. (2004). Dollars, dependency, and divorce: Four perspectives on the role of wives' income. *Journal of Marriage and the Family, 66,* 59–74.

Rohner, R. P., & Khaleque, A. (2010). Testing central postulates of parental acceptance-rejection theory (PARTheory): A meta-analysis of cross-cultural studies. *Journal of Family Theory & Review, 2,* 73–87.

Roisman, G. I. (2009). Adult attachment: Toward a rapprochement of methodological cultures. *Current Directions in Psychological Science, 18,* 122–126.

Roisman, G. I., Clausell, E., Holland, A., Fortuna, K., & Elieff, C. (2008). Adult romantic relationships as contexts of human development: A multimethod comparison of same-sex couples with opposite-sex dating, engaged, and married dyads. *Developmental Psychology, 44,* 91–101.

Rollie, S. S., & Duck, S. (2006). Divorce and dissolution of romantic relationships: Stage models and their limitations. In M. Fine & J. Harvey (Eds.), *Handbook of divorce and relationship dissolution* (pp. 223–240). Mahwah, NJ: Erlbaum.

Roloff, M., & Cloven, D. H. (1990). The chilling effect in interpersonal relationships: The reluctance to speak one's mind. In D. D. Cahn (Ed.), *Intimates in conflict: A communication perspective* (pp. 49–76). Hillsdale, NJ: Erlbaum.

Romero-Canyas, R., Anderson, V. T., Reddy, K. S., & Downey, G. (2009). Rejection sensitivity. In M. R. Leary & R. H. Hoyle (Eds.), *Handbook of individual differences in social behavior* (pp. 466–479). New York: Guilford Press.

Romero-Canyas, R., Downey, G., Berenson, K., Ayduk, O., & Kang, N. J. (2010). Rejection sensitivity and the rejection-hostility link in romantic relationships. *Journal of Personality, 78,* 119–148.

Ronay, R., & von Hippel, W. (2010). The presence of an attractive woman elevates testosterone and physical risk taking in young men. *Social Psychological and Personality Science, 1,* 57–64.

Rosenbaum, J. E. (2006). Reborn a virgin: Adolescents' retracting of virginity pledges and sexual histories. *American Journal of Public Health, 96,* 1098–1103.

Rosenbaum, J. E. (2009). Patient teenagers? A comparison of the sexual behavior of virginity pledgers and matched nonpledgers. *Pediatrics, 123,* 110–120.

Rosenberg, J., & Tunney, R. J. (2008). Human vocabulary use as display. *Evolutionary Psychology, 6,* 538–549.

Rosenfeld, M. J. (2010, April). *How couples meet and stay together.* Paper presented at the meeting of the Population Association of America, Dallas, TX.

Rosenthal, N. L., & Kobak, R. (2010). Assessing adolescents' attachment hierarchies: Differences across developmental periods and associations with individual adaptation. *Journal of Research on Adolescence, 20,* 678–706.

Rosenthal, R. (2006). Applying psychological research on interpersonal expectations and covert communication in classrooms, clinics, corporations, and courtrooms. In S. I. Donaldson, D. E. Berger, & K. Pedzek (Eds.), *Applied psychology: New frontiers and rewarding careers* (pp. 107–118). Mahwah, NJ: Erlbaum.

Ross, M. W. (2005). Typing, doing, and being: Sexuality and the Internet. *Journal of Sex Research, 42,* 342–352.

Ross, M., & Sicoly, F. (1979). Egocentric biases in availability and attribution. *Journal of Personality and Social Psychology, 37,* 322–336.

Rowatt, W. C., Cunningham, M. R., & Druen, P. B. (1999). Lying to get a date: The effect of facial physical attractiveness on the willingness to deceive prospective dating partners. *Journal of Social and Personal Relationships, 16,* 209–223.

Rowe, A., & Carnelley, K. B. (2003). Attachment style differences in the processing of attachment-relevant information: Primed-style effects on recall, interpersonal expectations, and affect. *Personal Relationships, 10,* 59–75.

Rubenstein, A. J., Langlois, J. H., & Roggman, L. A. (2002). What makes a face attractive and why: The role of averageness in defining facial beauty. In G. Rhodes & L. A. Zebrowitz (Eds.), *Facial attractiveness: Evolutionary, cognitive and social perspectives* (pp. 1–33). Westport, CT: Ablex.

Rubin, L. B. (1986). On men and friendship. *Psychoanalytic Review, 73,* 165–181.

Rubin, Z. (1973). *Liking and loving.* New York: Holt, Rinehart & Winston.

Rudman, L. A., & Fairchild, K. (2007). The F word: Is feminism incompatible with beauty and romance? *Psychology of Women Quarterly, 31,* 125–136.

Rudman, L. A., & Phelan, J. E. (2007). The interpersonal power of feminism: Is feminism good for romantic relationships? *Sex Roles, 57,* 767–799.

Rule, N. O., & Ambady, N. (2008). Brief exposures: Male sexual orientation is accurately perceived at 50 ms. *Journal of Experimental Psychology, 44,* 1100–1105.

Rusbult, C. E. (1987). Responses to dissatisfaction in close relationships: The exit-voice-loyalty-neglect model. In D. Perlman & S. Duck (Eds.), *Intimate relationships: Development, dynamics, and deterioration* (pp. 209–237). Thousand Oaks, CA: Sage.

Rusbult, C. E., Arriaga, X. B., & Agnew, C. R. (2001). Interdependence in close relationships. In G. J. O. Fletcher & M. S. Clark (Eds.), *Blackwell handbook of social psychology: Interpersonal processes* (pp. 359–387). Malden, MA: Blackwell.

Rusbult, C. E., Bissonnette, V. L., Arriaga, X. B., & Cox, C. L. (1998). Accommodation processes during the early years of marriage. In T. N. Bradbury (Ed.), *The developmental course of marital dysfunction* (pp. 74–113). New York: Cambridge University Press.

Rusbult, C. E., Drigotas, S. M., & Verette, J. (1994). The investment model: An interdependence analysis of commitment processes and relationship maintenance phenomena. In D. J. Canary & L. Stafford (Eds.), *Communication and relational maintenance* (pp. 115–139). San Diego: Academic Press.

Rusbult, C. E., Finkel, E. J., & Kumashiro, M. (2009). The Michelangelo phenomenon. *Current Directions in Psychological Science, 18,* 305–309.

Rusbult, C. E., & Martz, J. M. (1995). Remaining in abusive relationships: An investment model analysis of nonvoluntary dependence. *Personality and Social Psychology Bulletin, 21,* 558–571.

Rusbult, C. E., Van Lange, P. A. M., Wildschut, T., Yovetich, N. A., & Verette, J. (2000). Perceived superiority in close relationships: Why it exists and persists. *Journal of Personality and Social Psychology, 79,* 521–545.

Rusbult, C. E., Zembrodt, I. M., & Gunn, L. K. (1982). Exit, voice, loyalty, and neglect: Responses to dissatisfaction in romantic involvements. *Journal of Personality and Social Psychology, 43,* 1230–1242.

Rusbult, C. E., Zembrodt, I. M., & Iwaniszek, J. (1986). The impact of gender and sex-role orientation on responses to dissatisfaction in close relationships. *Sex Roles, 15,* 1–20.

Russell, D. W. (1996). The UCLA Loneliness Scale (Version 3): Reliability, validity and factorial structure. *Journal of Personality Assessment, 66,* 20–40.

Ruvolo, A. P., & Ruvolo, C. M. (2000). Creating Mr. Right and Ms. Right: Interpersonal ideals and personal change in newlyweds. *Personal Relationships, 7,* 341–362.

Rycyna, C. C., Champion, C. D., & Kelly, A. E. (2009). First impressions after various types of deception: Less favorable following expectancy violation. *Basic and Applied Social Psychology, 31,* 40–48.

Rydell, R. J., McConnell, A. R., & Bringle, R. G. (2004). Jealousy and commitment: Perceived threat and the effect of relationship alternatives. *Personal Relationships, 11,* 451–468.

Saad, L. (2007), May 29). Tolerance for gay rights at high-water mark. *Gallup Poll News Service.* Retrieved from: http://www.gallup.com/poll/27694/Tolerance-Gay-Rights-HighWater-Mark.aspx

Saad, L. (2010, May 25). American's acceptance of gay relations crosses 50% threshold. *Gallup Poll News Service.* Retrieved from http://www.gallup.com/poll/135764/Americans-Acceptance-Gay-Relations-Crosses-Threshold.aspx

Sabin, E. P. (1993). Social relationships and mortality among the elderly. *Journal of Applied Gerontology, 12,* 44–60.

Saffrey, C., & Ehrenberg, M. (2007). When thinking hurts: Attachment, rumination, and postrelationship adjustment. *Personal Relationships, 14,* 351–368.

Sagarin, B. J. (2005). Reconsidering evolved sex differences in jealousy: Comment on Harris (2003). *Personality and Social Psychology Review, 9,* 62–75.

Sagarin, B. J., Becker, D. V., Guadagno, R. E., Nicastle, L. D., & Millevoi, A. (2003). Sex differences (and similarities) in jealousy. The moderating influence of infidelity experience and sexual orientation of the infidelity. *Evolution and Human Behavior, 24,* 17–23.

Sagarin, B. J., Rhoads, K. V. L., & Cialdini, R. B. (1998). Deceiver's distrust: Denigration as a consequence of undiscovered deception. *Personality and Social Psychology Bulletin, 24,* 1167–1176.

Sagrestano, L. M. (1992). Power strategies in interpersonal relationships: The effects of expertise and gender. *Psychology of Women Quarterly, 16,* 481–495.

Sagrestano, L. M., Heavey, C. L., & Christensen, A. (2006). Individual differences versus social structural approaches to explaining demand-withdraw and social influence behaviors. In K. Dindia & D. J. Canary (Eds.), *Sex differences and similarities in communication* (2nd ed., pp. 379–395). Mahwah, NJ: Erlbaum.

Sahlstein, E. M. (2006). The trouble with distance. In D. C. Kirkpatrick, S. Duck, & M. K. Foley (Eds.), *Relating difficulty: The processes of constructing and managing difficult interaction* (pp. 119–140). Mahwah, NJ: Erlbaum.

Salovey, P., & Rodin, J. (1988). Coping with envy and jealousy. *Journal of Social and Clinical Psychology, 7,* 15–33.

Salska, I., Frederick, D. A., Pawlowski, B., Reilly, A. H., Laird, K. T., & Rudd, N. A. (2008). Conditional mate preferences: Factors influencing preferences for height. *Personality and Individual Differences, 44,* 203–215.

Salter, J. (2005, April 8). Look good? So does your paycheck. *Houston Chronicle,* p. D3.

Salvatore, J. E., Kuo, S. I., Steele, R. D., Simpson, J. A., & Collins, W. A. (2011). Recovering from conflict in romantic relationships: A developmental perspective. *Psychological Science, 22,* 376–383.

Sanchez, D. T., Crocker, J., & Boike, K. R. (2005). Doing gender in the bedroom: Investing in gender norms and the sexual experience. *Personality and Social Psychology Bulletin, 31,* 1445–1455.

Sanchez, D. T., Kiefer, A. K. & Ybarra, O. (2006). Sexual submissiveness in women: Costs for sexual autonomy and arousal. *Personality and Social Psychology Bulletin, 32,* 512–524.

Sandnabba, N. K., & Ahlberg, C. (1999). Parents' attitudes and expectations about children's cross-gender behavior. *Sex Roles, 40,* 249–263.

Sanford, K., & Grace, A. J. (2011). Emotion and underlying concerns during couples' conflict: An investigation of within-person change. *Personal Relationships, 18,* 96–109.

Sasaki, S. J., & Vorauer, J. D. (2010). Contagious resource depletion and anxiety? Spreading effects of evaluative concern and impression formation in dyadic social interaction. *Journal of Experimental Social Psychology, 46,* 1011–1016.

Sassler, S., & Miller, A. J. (2011). Waiting to be asked: Gender, power, and relationship progression among cohabiting couples. *Journal of Family Issues, 32,* 482–506.

Savin-Williams, R. C. (2001). *Mom, Dad, I'm gay: How families negotiate coming out.* Washington, DC: American Psychological Association.

Savin-Williams, R. C. (2005). *The new gay teenager.* Cambridge, MA: Harvard University Press.

Savin-Williams, R. C. (2006). Who's gay? Does it matter? *Current Directions in Psychological Science, 15,* 40–44.

Savitsky, K., Keysar, B., Epley, N., Carter, T., & Swanson, A. (2011). The closeness-communication bias: Increased egocentrism among friends versus strangers. *Journal of Experimental Social Psychology, 47,* 269–273.

Saxton, T. K., Burriss, R. P., Murray, A. K., Rowland, H. M., & Roberts, S. C. (2009). Face, body and speech cues independently predict judgments of attractiveness. *Journal of Evolutionary Psychology, 7,* 23–35.

Sayer, L. C. (2006). Economic aspects of divorce and relationship dissolution. In M. A. Fine & J. H. Harvey (Eds.), *Handbook of divorce and relationship dissolution* (pp. 385–406). Mahwah, NJ: Erlbaum.

Sbarra, D. A. (2006). Predicting the onset of emotional recovery following nonmarital relationship dissolution: Survival analyses of sadness and anger. *Personality and Social Psychology Bulletin, 32,* 298–312.

Sbarra, D. A., & Emery, R. E. (2005). The emotional sequelae of nonmarital relationship dissolution: Analysis of change and intraindividual variability over time. *Personal Relationships, 12,* 213–232.

Sbarra, D. A., & Nietert, P. J. (2009). Divorce and death: Forty years of the Charleston Heart Study. *Psychological Science, 20*, 107–113.

Schachner, D. A., & Shaver, P. R. (2002, June). *Attachment style and personality variables predict human mate poaching behaviors.* Paper presented at the meeting of the American Psychological Society, New Orleans, LA.

Schachter, S. (1959). *The psychology of affiliation: Experimental studies of the sources of gregariousness.* Stanford, CA: Stanford University Press.

Scharfe, E., & Cole, V. (2006). Stability and change of attachment representations during emerging adulthood: An examination of mediators and moderators of change. *Personal Relationships, 13,* 363–374.

Scharff, D. E., & de Varela, Y. (2005). Object relations couple therapy. In M. Harway (Ed.), *Handbook of couples therapy* (pp. 141–156). New York: Wiley.

Schindler, I., Fagundes, C. P., & Murdock, K. W. (2010). Predictors of romantic relationship formation: Attachment style, prior relationships, and dating goals. *Personal Relationships, 17,* 97–105.

Schlenker, B. R. (2003). Self-presentation. In M. R. Leary & J. P. Tangney (Eds.), *Handbook of self and identity* (pp. 492–518). New York: Guilford Press.

Schmitt, D. P. (2005a). Fundamentals of human mating strategies. In D. M. Buss (Ed.), *The handbook of evolutionary psychology* (pp. 258–291). Hoboken, NJ: Wiley.

Schmitt, D. P. (2005b). Sociosexuality from Argentina to Zimbabwe: A 48-nation study of sex, culture, and strategies of human mating. *Behavioral and Brain Sciences, 28,* 247–275.

Schmitt, D. P. (2008). Attachment matters: Patterns of romantic attachment across gender, geography, and cultural forms. In J. P. Forgas & J. Fitness (Eds.), *Social relationships: Cognitive, affective and motivational processes* (pp. 75–97). New York: Psychology Press.

Schmitt, D. P., & Buss, D. M. (2001). Human mate poaching: Tactics and temptations for infiltrating existing mateships. *Journal of Personality and Social Psychology, 80,* 894–917.

Schmitt, D. P., Couden, A., & Baker, M. (2001). The effects of sex and temporal context on feelings of romantic desire: An experimental evaluation of sexual strategies theory. *Personality and Social Psychology Bulletin, 27,* 833–847.

Schmitt, D. P., & Shackelford, T. K. (2003). Nifty ways to leave your lover: The tactics people use to entice and disguise the process of human mate poaching. *Personality and Social Psychology Bulletin, 29,* 1018–1035.

Schmitt, D. P., & the International Sexuality Description Project. (2003). Universal sex differences in the desire for sexual variety: Tests from 52 nations, 6 continents, and 13 islands. *Journal of Personality and Social Psychology, 85,* 85–104.

Schmitt, D. P., & the International Sexuality Description Project. (2004). Patterns and universals of mate poaching across 53 nations: The effects of sex, culture, and personality on romantically attracting another person's partner. *Journal of Personality and Social Psychology, 86,* 560–584.

Schneider, C. S., & Kenny, D. A. (2000). Cross-sex friends who were once romantic partners: Are they platonic friends now? *Journal of Social and Personal Relationships, 17,* 451–466.

Schonbrun, Y. C., & Whisman, M. A. (2010). Marital distress and mental health care service utilization. *Journal of Consulting and Clinical Psychology, 78,* 732–736.

Schutz, A. (1999). It was your fault! Self-serving biases in autobiographical accounts of conflicts in married couples. *Journal of Social and Personal Relationships, 16,* 193–208.

Schützwohl, A. (2005). Sex differences in jealousy: The processing of cues to infidelity. *Evolution and Human Behavior, 26,* 288–299.

Schützwohl, A. (2006). Sex differences in jealousy: Information search and cognitive preoccupation. *Personality and Individual Differences, 40,* 285–292.

Schützwohl, A. (2008a). Relief over the disconfirmation of the prospect of sexual and emotional infidelity. *Personality and Individual Differences, 44,* 666–676.

Schützwohl, A. (2008b). The intentional object of romantic jealousy. *Evolution and Human Behavior, 29,* 92–99.

Schwartz, P., & Young, L. (2009). Sexual satisfaction in committed relationships. *Sexuality Research & Social Policy, 6,* 1–17.

Schwarz, S., & Hassebrauck, M. (2008). Self-perceived and observed variations in women's attractiveness throughout the menstrual cycle—A diary study. *Evolution and Human Behavior, 29,* 282–288.

Schweinle, W. E., & Ickes, W. (2002). On empathic accuracy and husbands' abusiveness: The "over-attribution bias." In P. Noller & J. A. Feeney (Eds.), *Understanding marriage: Developments in the study of couple interaction* (pp. 228–250). Cambridge, England: Cambridge University Press.

Schweinle, W. E., Ickes, W., & Bernstein, I. H. (2002). Empathic accuracy in husband to wife aggression: The overattribution bias. *Personal Relationships, 9,* 141–158.

Scott-Sheldon, L. A. J., & Johnson, B. T. (2006). Eroticizing creates safer sex: A research synthesis. *Journal of Primary Prevention, 27,* 619–640.

Seal, D. W., Agostinelli, G., & Hannett, C. A. (1994). Extradyadic romantic involvement: Moderating effects of sociosexuality and gender. *Sex Roles, 31,* 1–22.

Secord, P. F. (1983). Imbalanced sex ratios: The social consequences. *Personality and Social Psychology Bulletin, 9,* 525–543.

Seder, J. P., & Oishi, S. (2010). *What a Facebook smile reveals about future happiness: Extent of smiling in college students' first-semester Facebook profile photos predicts subjective well-being, satisfaction with social life, and "school bonding" four years later.* Poster presented at the meeting of the Society for Personality and Social Psychology, Las Vegas, NV.

Sedikides, C., Campbell, W. K., Reeder, G. D., & Elliot, A. J. (1998). The self-serving bias in relational context. *Journal of Personality and Social Psychology, 74,* 378–386.

Sedikides, C., Oliver, M. B., & Campbell, W. K. (1994). Perceived benefits and costs of romantic relationships for women and men: Implications for exchange theory. *Personal Relationships, 1,* 5–21.

Seeman, T. E., Singer, B. H., Ryff, C. D., Love, G. D., & Levy-Storms, L. (2002). Social relationships, gender, and allostatic load across two age cohorts. *Psychosomatic Medicine, 64,* 395–406.

Segrin, C. (1998). Disrupted interpersonal relationships and mental health problems. In B. H. Spitzberg & W. R. Cupach (Eds.), *The dark side of close relationships* (pp. 327–365). Mahwah, NJ: Erlbaum.

Segrin, C., Taylor, M. E., & Altman, J. (2005). Social cognitive mediators and relational outcomes associated with parental divorce. *Journal of Social and Personal Relationships, 22,* 361–377.

Selcuk, E., Günaydin, G., Sumer, N., Harma, M., Salman, S., Hazan, C., Dogruyol, B., & Ozturk, A. (2010). Self-reported romantic attachment style predicts everyday maternal caregiving behavior at home. *Journal of Research in Personality, 44,* 544–549.

Selfhout, M., Denissen, J., Branje, S., & Meeus, W. (2009). In the eye of the beholder: Perceived, actual, and peer-rated similarity in personality, communication, and friendship intensity during the acquaintanceship process. *Journal of Personality and Social Psychology, 96,* 1152–1165.

Sellers, J. G., Woolsey, M. D., & Swann, W. B., Jr. (2007). Is silence more golden for women than men? Observers derogate effusive women and their quiet partners. *Sex Roles, 57,* 477–482.

Shackelford, T. K., & Goetz, A. T. (2007). Adaptation to sperm competition in humans. *Current Directions in Psychological Science, 16,* 47–50.

Shackelford, T. K., Goetz, A. T., Buss, D. M., Euler, H. A., & Hoier, S. (2005). When we hurt the ones we love: Predicting violence against women from men's mate retention. *Personal Relationships, 12,* 447–463.

Shackelford, T. K., Michalski, R. L., & Schmitt, D. P. (2004). Upset in response to a child's partner's infidelities. *European Journal of Social Psychology, 34,* 489–497.

Shadish, W. R., & Baldwin, S. A. (2005). Effects of behavioral marital therapy: A meta-analysis of randomized controlled trials. *Journal of Consulting and Clinical Psychology, 73,* 6–14.

Shaffer, D. R., Pegalis, L. J., & Bazzini, D. G. (1996). When boy meets girl (revisited): Gender, gender-role orientation, and prospect of future interaction as determinants of self-disclosure among same- and opposite-sex acquaintances. *Personality and Social Psychology Bulletin, 22,* 495–506.

Shaffer, D. R., Ruammake, C., & Pegalis, L. J. (1990). The "opener": Highly skilled as interviewer or interviewee. *Personality and Social Psychology Bulletin, 16,* 511–520.

Shah, J. (2003). Automatic for the people: How representations of significant others implicitly affect goal pursuit. *Journal of Personality and Social Psychology, 84,* 661–681.

Shannon, J. B. (Ed.). (2009). *Domestic violence sourcebook* (3rd ed.). Detroit, MI: Omnigraphics.

Shanteau, J., & Nagy, G. F. (1979). Probability of acceptance in dating choice. *Journal of Personality and Social Psychology, 37,* 522–533.

Sharp, E. A., & Ganong, L. H. (2000). Raising awareness about marital expectations: Are unrealistic beliefs changed by integrative teaching? *Family Relations, 49,* 71–76.

Shaver, P., Furman, W., & Buhrmester, D. (1985). Transition to college: Network changes, social skills, and loneliness. In S. Duck & D. Perlman (Eds.), *Understanding personal relationships: An interdisciplinary approach* (pp. 193–219). London: Sage.

Shaver, P. R., & Mikulincer, M. (2010). Mind-behavior relations in attachment theory and research. In C. R. Agnew, D. E. Carlston, W. G. Graziano, & J. R. Kelly (Eds.), *Then a miracle occurs: Focusing on behavior in social psychological theory and research* (pp. 342–367). New York: Oxford University Press.

Shaver, P. R., Murdaya, U., & Fraley, R. C. (2001). Structure of the Indonesian emotion lexicon. *Asian Journal of Social Psychology, 4,* 201–224.

Shepherd, R., & Edelmann, R. J. (2005). Reasons for Internet use and social anxiety. *Personality and Individual Differences, 39,* 949–958.

Sherkat, D. E., Powell-Williams, M., Maddox, G., & de Vries, K. M. (2011). Religion, politics, and support for same-sex marriage in the United States, 1988–2008. *Social Science Research, 40,* 167–180.

Shettel-Neuber, J., Bryson, J. B., & Young, L. E. (1978). Physical attractiveness of the "other person" and jealousy. *Personality and Social Psychology Bulletin, 4,* 612–615.

Shibazaki, K., & Brennan, K. A. (1998). When birds of different feathers flock together: A preliminary comparison of intra-ethnic and inter-ethnic dating relationships. *Journal of Social and Personal Relationships, 15,* 248–256.

Shimizu, M., Seery, M. D., Weisbuch, M., & Lupien, S. P. (2011). Trait social anxiety and physiological activation: Cardiovascular threat during social interaction. *Personality and Social Psychology Bulletin, 37,* 94–106.

Shrout, P. E., Herman, C. M., & Bolger, N. (2006). The costs and benefits of practical and emotional support on adjustment: A daily diary study of couples experiencing acute stress. *Personal Relationships, 13,* 115–134.

Sibley, C. G., & Overall, N. C. (2008). Modeling the hierarchical structure of attachment representations: A test of domain differentiation. *Personality and Individual Differences, 44,* 238–249.

Sillars, A. L. (1998). (Mis)understanding. In B. H. Spitzberg & W. R. Cupach (Eds.), *The dark side of close relationships* (pp. 73–102). Mahwah, NJ: Erlbaum.

Sillars, A., Smith, T., & Koerner, A. (2010). Misattributions contributing to empathic (in)accuracy during parent-adolescent conflict discussions. *Journal of Social and Personal Relationships, 27,* 727–747.

Simon, R. W., & Barrett, A. E. (2010). Nonmarital romantic relationships and mental health in early adulthood: Does the association differ for women and men? *Journal of Health and Social Behavior, 51,* 168–182.

Simon-Thomas, E. R., Keltner, D., Sauter, D., Sinicropi-Yao, L., & Abramson, A. (2009). The voice conveys specific emotions: Evidence from vocal burst displays. *Emotion, 9,* 838–846.

Simmons, C. A., & Lehmann, P. (2007). Exploring the link between pet abuse and controlling behaviors in violent relationships. *Journal of Interpersonal Violence, 22,* 1211–1222.

Simpson, J. A. (2007). Psychological foundations of trust. *Current Directions in Psychological Science, 16,* 264–268.

Simpson, J. A., Campbell, B., & Berscheid, E. (1986). The association between romantic love and marriage: Kephart (1967) twice revisited. *Personality and Social Psychology Bulletin, 12,* 363–372.

Simpson, J. A., Collins, W. A., Tran, S., & Haydon, K. C. (2007). Attachment and the experience and expression of emotions in romantic relationships: A developmental perspective. *Journal of Personality and Social Psychology, 92,* 355–367.

Simpson, J. A., & Gangestad, S. W. (1991). Individual differences in sociosexuality: Evidence for convergent and discriminant validity. *Journal of Personality and Social Psychology, 60,* 870–883.

Simpson, J. A., Gangestad, S. W., & Biek, M. (1993). Personality and nonverbal social behavior: An ethological perspective of relationship initiation. *Journal of Experimental Social Psychology, 29,* 434–461.

Simpson, J. A., Gangestad, S. W., & Lerma, M. (1990). Perception of physical attractiveness: Mechanisms involved in the maintenance of romantic relationships. *Journal of Personality and Social Psychology, 59,* 1192–1201.

Simpson, J. A., Ickes, W., & Blackstone, T. (1995). When the head protects the heart: Empathic accuracy in dating relationships. *Journal of Personality and Social Psychology, 69,* 629–641.

Simpson, J. A., Ickes, W., & Grich, J. (1999). When accuracy hurts: Reactions of anxious-ambivalent dating partners to a relationship-threatening situation. *Journal of Personality and Social Psychology, 76,* 754–769.

Simpson, J. A., Oriña, M. M., & Ickes, W. (2003). When accuracy hurts, and when it helps: A test of the empathic accuracy model in marital interactions. *Journal of Personality and Social Psychology, 85,* 881–893.

Simpson, J. A., Rholes, W. S., Oriña, M. M., & Grich, J. (2002). Working models of attachment, support giving, and support seeking in a stressful situation. *Personality and Social Psychology Bulletin, 28,* 598–608.

Simpson, J. A., Rholes, W. S., & Winterheld, H. A. (2010). Attachment working models twist memories of relationship events. *Psychological Science, 21,* 252–259.

Simpson, J. A., Wilson, C. L., & Winterheld, H. A. (2004). Sociosexuality and romantic relationships. In J. H. Harvey, A. Wenzel, & S. Sprecher (Eds.), *The handbook of sexuality in close relationships* (pp. 87–112). Mahwah, NJ: Erlbaum.

Simpson, J. A., Winterheld, H. A., Rholes, W. S., & Oriña, M. M. (2007). Working models of attachment and reactions to different forms of caregiving from romantic partners. *Journal of Personality and Social Psychology, 93,* 466–477.

Simpson, L. E., Doss, B. D., Wheeler, J., & Christensen, A. (2007). Relationship violence among couples seeking therapy: Common couple violence or battering? *Journal of Marital & Family Therapy, 33,* 270–283.

Sinclair, H. C., & Frieze, I. H. (2005). When courtship persistence becomes intrusive pursuit: Comparing rejecter and pursuer perspectives of unrequited attraction. *Sex Roles, 52,* 839–852.

Singh, D. (1993). Adaptive significance of female physical attractiveness: Role of waist-to-hip ratio. *Journal of Personality and Social Psychology, 65,* 293–307.

Singh, D. (1995). Female judgment of male attractiveness and desirability for relationships: Role of waist-to-hip ratio and financial status. *Journal of Personality and Social Psychology, 69,* 1089–1101.

Singh, D., Dixson, B. J., Jessop, T. S., Morgan, B., & Dixson, A. F. (2010). Cross-cultural consensus for waist-hip ratio and women's attractiveness. *Evolution and Human Behavior, 31,* 176–181.

Singh, D., & Luis, S. (1995). Ethnic and gender consensus for the effect of waist-to-hip ratio on judgment of women's attractiveness. *Human Nature, 6,* 51–65.

Singh, R., Yeo, S. E., Lin, P. K. F., & Tan, L. (2007). Multiple mediators of the attitude similarity-attraction relationship: Dominance of inferred attraction and subtlety of affect. *Basic and Applied Social Psychology, 29,* 61–74.

Slatcher, R. B. (2010). When Harry and Sally met Dick and Jane: Creating closeness between couples. *Personal Relationships, 17,* 279–297.

Slatcher, R. B., & Ranson, J. (2011, January). *Couples' emotion behaviors in everyday life: Links to relationship satisfaction and stability.* Poster presented at the meeting of the Society for Personality and Social Psychology, San Antonio, TX.

Slater, A., Bremner, G., Johnson, S. P., Sherwood, P., Hayes, R., & Brown, E. (2000). Newborn infants' preference for attractive faces: The role of internal and external facial features. *Infancy, 1,* 265–274.

Slater, P. E. (1968). Some social consequences of temporary systems. In W. G. Bennes & P. E. Slater (Eds.), *The temporary society* (pp. 77–96). New York: Harper & Row.

Sloan, D. M. (2010). Self-disclosure and psychological well-being. In J. Maddux & J. P. Tangney (Eds.), *Social psychological foundations of clinical psychology* (pp. 212–225). New York: Guilford Press.

Slotter, E. B., Finkel, E. J., DeWall, C. N., Pond, R. S., Jr., Lambert, N. M., Bodenhausen, G. V., & Fincham, F. D. (2011). *Putting the brakes on aggression toward a romantic partner: The inhibitory influence of relationship commitment.* Manuscript submitted for publication.

Slotter, E. B., Gardner, W. L., & Finkel, E. J. (2010). Who am I without you? The influence of romantic breakup on the self-concept. *Personality and Social Psychology Bulletin, 36,* 147–160.

Smith, A. E., Jussim, L., & Eccles, J. (1999). Do self-fulfilling prophecies accumulate, dissipate, or remain stable over time? *Journal of Personality and Social Psychology, 77,* 548–565.

Smith, C. A., Johnston-Robledo, I., McHugh, M. C., & Chrisler, J. C. (2010). Words matter: The language of gender. In J. Chrisler & D. McCreary (Eds.), *Handbook of gender research in psychology* (Vol. 1, pp. 361–377). New York: Springer.

Smith, C. V. (2007). In pursuit of "good" sex: Self-determination and the sexual experience. *Journal of Social and Personal Relationships, 24,* 69–85.

Smith, F. G., Jones, B. C., Little, A. C., DeBruine, L. M., Welling, L. L. M., Vukovic, J., & Conway, C. A. (2009). Hormonal contraceptive use and perceptions of trust modulate the effect of relationship context on women's preferences for sexual dimorphism in male face shape. *Journal of Evolutionary Psychology, 7,* 195–210.

Smith, G., Mysak, K., & Michael, S. (2008). Sexual double standards and sexually transmitted illnesses: Social rejection and stigmatization of women. *Sex Roles, 58,* 391–401.

Smith, L., Heaven, P. C. L., & Ciarrochi, J. (2008). Trait emotional intelligence, conflict communication patterns, and relationship satisfaction. *Personality and Individual Differences, 44,* 1314–1325.

Smith, S. J., Axelton, A. M., & Saucier, D. A. (2009). The effects of contact on sexual prejudice: A meta-analysis. *Sex Roles, 61,* 178–191.

Smith, T. W. (2006). Sexual behavior in the United States. In R. D. McAnulty & M. M. Burnette (Eds.), *Sex and sexuality, Vol. 1: Sexuality today: Trends and controversies* (pp. 103–131). Westport, CT: Praeger.

Smith, T. W., Cribbet, M. R., Uchino, B. N., Williams, P. G., MacKenzie, J., Nealey-Moore, J. B., & Thayer, J. F. (2011). Matters of the variable heart: Respiratory sinus arrhythmia response to marital interaction and associations with marital quality. *Journal of Personality and Social Psychology, 100,* 103–119.

Smith, T. W., Ruiz, J. M., & Uchino, B. N. (2004). Mental activation of supportive ties, hostility, and cardiovascular reactivity to laboratory stress in young men and women. *Health Psychology, 23,* 476–785.

Snyder, D. K. (2002). Integrating insight-oriented techniques into couple therapy. In J. H. Harvey & A. Wenzel (Eds.), *A clinician's guide to maintaining and enhancing close relationships* (pp. 259–275). Mahwah, NJ: Erlbaum.

Snyder, D. K., Baucom, D. H., & Gordon, K. C. (2007). *Getting past the affair: A program to help you cope, heal, and move on—Together or apart.* New York: Guilford Press.

Snyder, D. K., Castellani, A. M., & Whisman, M. A. (2006). Current status and future directions in couple therapy. *Annual Review of Psychology, 57,* 317–344.

Snyder, D. K., & Schneider, W. J. (2002). Affective reconstruction: A pluralistic, developmental approach. In A. S. Gurman & N. S. Jacobson (Eds.), *Clinical handbook of couple therapy* (3rd ed., pp. 151–179). New York: Guilford Press.

Snyder, D. K., Wills, R. M., & Grady-Fletcher, A. (1991). Long-term effectiveness of behavioral versus insight-oriented therapy: A four-year follow-up study. *Journal of Consulting and Clinical Psychology, 59,* 138–141.

Snyder, M. (1981). Seek, and ye shall find: Testing hypotheses about other people. In E. T. Higgins, C. P. Herman, & M. P. Zanna (Eds.), *Social cognition: The Ontario symposium* (Vol. 1, pp. 277–303). Hillsdale, NJ: Erlbaum.

Snyder, M. (1987). *Public appearances, private realities: The psychology of self-monitoring.* New York: W. H. Freeman.

Snyder, M., & Gangestad, S. (1986). On the nature of self-monitoring: Matters of assessment, matters of validity. *Journal of Personality and Social Psychology, 51,* 125–139.

Snyder, M., & Simpson, J. A. (1984). Self-monitoring and dating relationships. *Journal of Personality and Social Psychology, 47,* 1281–1291.

Snyder, M., & Simpson, J. A. (1987). Orientations toward romantic relationships. In D. Perlman & S. Duck (Eds.), *Intimate relationships: Development, dynamics, and deterioration* (pp. 45–62). Newbury Park, CA: Sage.

Snyder, M., & Swann, W. B., Jr. (1978a). Behavioral confirmation in social interaction: From social perception to social reality. *Journal of Experimental Social Psychology, 14,* 148–163.

Snyder, M., & Swann, W. B., Jr. (1978b). Hypothesis-testing processes in social interaction. *Journal of Personality and Social Psychology, 36,* 1202–1212.

Snyder, M., Tanke, E. D., & Berscheid, E. (1977). Social perception and interpersonal behavior: On the self-fulfilling nature of social stereotypes. *Journal of Personality and Social Psychology, 35,* 656–666.

Soler, C., Núñez, M., Gutiérrez, R., Núñez, J., Medina, P. Sancho, M., Álvarez, J., & Núñez, A. (2003). Facial attractiveness in men provides clues to semen quality. *Evolution and Human Behavior, 24,* 199–207.

Solomon, D. H., & Theiss, J. A. (2007). Cognitive foundations of communication in close relationships. In D. R. Roskos-Ewoldsen & J. L. Monahan (Eds.), *Communication and social cognition: Theories and methods* (pp. 117–140). Mahwah, NJ: Erlbaum.

Solomon, D. H., Weber, K. M., & Steuber, K. R. (2010). Turbulence in relational transitions. In S. W. Smith & S. R. Wilson (Eds.), *New directions in interpersonal communication research* (pp. 115–134). Thousand Oaks, CA: Sage.

Solomon, S. E., Rothblum, E. D., & Balsam, K. F. (2005). Money, housework, sex, and conflict: Same-sex couples in civil unions, those not in civil unions, and heterosexual married siblings. *Sex Roles, 52,* 561–575.

Sommer, K. L., & Rubin, Y. S. (2005). Role of social expectancies in cognitive and behavioral responses to social rejection. In K. D. Williams, J. P. Forgas, & W. von Hippel (Eds.), *The social outcast: Ostracism, social exclusion, rejection, and bullying* (pp. 171–183). New York: Psychology Press.

Sommer, K. L., Williams, K. D., Ciarocco, N. J., & Baumeister, R. F. (2001). When silence speaks louder than words: Explorations into the intrapsychic and interpersonal consequences of social ostracism. *Basic and Applied Social Psychology, 23,* 225–243.

Soons, J. P. M., Liefbroer, A. C., & Kalmijn, M. (2009). The long-term consequences of relationship formation for subjective well-being. *Journal of Marriage and Family, 71,* 1254–1270.

South, S. J., Trent, K., & Shen, Y. (2001). Changing partners: Toward a macrostructural-opportunity theory of marital dissolution. *Journal of Marriage and the Family, 63,* 743–754.

Southworth, C., Finn, J., Dawson, S., Fraser, C., & Tucker, S. (2007). Intimate partner violence, technology, and stalking. *Violence Against Women, 13,* 842–856.

Spain, J. S. (2011, January). *"White lies" in everyday life: A diary study of personality and daily deception.* Poster presented at the meeting of the Society for Personality and Social Psychology, San Antonio, TX.

Spielmann, S. S., Joel, S., & MacDonald, G. (2011, January). *Ex appeal: Substituting current partners and ex-partners to satisfy the need to belong.* Poster presented at the meeting of the Society for Personality and Social Psychology, San Antonio, TX.

Spielmann, S. S., MacDonald, G., & Wilson, A. E. (2009). On the rebound: Focusing on someone new helps anxiously attached individuals let go of ex-partners. *Personality and Social Psychology Bulletin, 35,* 1382–1394.

Spitzberg, B. H. (1999). An analysis of empirical estimates of sexual aggression, victimization, and perpetration. *Violence and Victims, 14,* 241–260.

Spitzberg, B. H., & Cupach, W. R. (2007). The state of the art of stalking: Taking stock of the emerging literature. *Aggression and Violent Behavior, 12,* 64–86.

Spitzberg, B. H., Cupach, W. R., & Ciceraro, L. D. L. (2010). Sex differences in stalking and obsessive relational intrusion: Two meta-analyses. *Partner Abuse, 1,* 259–285.

Sprecher, S. (1986). The relation between inequity and emotions in close relationships. *Social Psychology Quarterly, 49,* 309–321.

Sprecher, S. (2001). A comparison of emotional consequences of and changes in equity over time using global and domain-specific measures of equity. *Journal of Social and Personal Relationships, 18,* 477–501.

Sprecher, S. (2002). Sexual satisfaction in premarital relationships: Associations with satisfaction, love, commitment, and stability. *Journal of Sex Research, 39,* 190–196.

Sprecher, S., Barbee, A., & Schwartz, P. (1995). "Was it good for you, too?" Gender differences in first sexual intercourse experiences. *Journal of Sex Research, 32,* 3–15.

Sprecher, S., Christopher, F. S., & Cate, R. (2006). Sexuality in close relationships. In A. L. Vangelisti & D. Perlman (Eds.), *The Cambridge handbook of personal relationships* (pp. 463–482). New York: Cambridge University Press.

Sprecher, S., & Fehr, B. (2005). Compassionate love for close others and humanity. *Journal of Social and Personal Relationships, 22,* 629–651.

Sprecher, S., & Fehr, B. (2011). Dispositional attachment and relationship-specific attachment as predictors of compassionate love for a partner. *Journal of Social and Personal Relationships, 28,* 558–574

Sprecher, S., Fehr, B., & Zimmerman, C. (2007). Expectation for mood enhancement as a result of helping: The effects of gender and compassionate love. *Sex Roles, 56,* 543–549.

Sprecher, S., & Hendrick, S. S. (2004). Self-disclosure in intimate relationships: Associations with individual and relationship characteristics over time. *Journal of Social and Clinical Psychology, 23,* 857–877.

Sprecher, S., & Metts, S. (1999). Romantic beliefs: Their influence on relationships and patterns of change over time. *Journal of Social and Personal Relationships, 16,* 834–851.

Sprecher, S., Orbuch, T., & Felmlee, D. (2010, January). *Equity perceptions over time in marriage: Analyses of the Early Years of Marriage Project.* Poster presented at the meeting of the Society for Personality and Social Psychology, Las Vegas, NV.

Sprecher, S., & Regan, P. C. (1998). Passionate and companionate love in courting and young married couples. *Sociological Inquiry, 68,* 163–185.

Sprecher, S., Regan, P. C., & McKinney, K. (1998). Beliefs about the outcomes of extramarital sexual relationships as a function of the gender of the "cheating spouse." *Sex Roles, 38,* 301–311.

Sprecher, S., Schwartz, P., Harvey, J., & Hatfield, E. (2008). Thebusinessoflove.com: Relationship initiation at Internet matchmaking sites. In S. Sprecher, A. Wenzel, & J. Harvey (Eds.), *Handbook of relationship initiation* (pp. 249–265). New York: Psychology Press.

Sprecher, S., Treger, S., & Wondra, J. (2011, January). *Self-disclosure given versus received in initial acquaintance: Differential effects on liking, closeness, and enjoyment.* Poster presented at the meeting of the Society for Personality and Social Psychology, San Antonio, TX.

Srivastava, S., McGonigal, K. M., Richards, J. M., Butler, E. A., & Gross, J. J. (2006). Optimism in close relationships: How seeing things in a positive light makes them so. *Journal of Personality and Social Psychology, 91,* 143–153.

Stackert, R. A., & Bursik, K. (2003). Why am I unsatisfied? Adult attachment style, gendered irrational relationship beliefs, and young adult romantic relationship satisfaction. *Personality and Individual Differences, 34,* 1419–1429.

Stafford, L. (2003). Maintaining romantic relationships: A summary and analysis of one research program. In D. J. Canary & M. Dainton (Eds.), *Maintaining relationships through communication: Relational, contextual, and cultural variations* (pp. 51–77). Mahwah, NJ: Erlbaum.

Stafford, L. (2010). Geographic distance and communication during courtship. *Communication Research, 37,* 275–297.

Stafford, L., & Canary, D. J. (2006). Equity and interdependence as predictors of relational maintenance strategies. *Journal of Family Communication, 6,* 227–254.

Stafford, L., & Dainton, M. (1994). The dark side of "normal" family interaction. In W. R. Cupach & B. H. Spitzberg (Eds.), *The dark side of interpersonal communication* (pp. 259–280). Hillsdale, NJ: Erlbaum.

Stafford, L., & Merolla, A. J. (2007). Idealization, reunions, and stability in long-distance dating relationships. *Journal of Social and Personal Relationships, 24,* 37–54.

Stafford, L., Merolla, A. J., & Castle, J. D. (2006). When long-distance dating partners become geographically close. *Journal of Social and Personal Relationships, 23,* 901–919.

Stake, J. E., & Eisele, H. (2010). Gender and personality. In J. Chrisler & D. McCreary (Eds.), *Handbook of gender research in psychology* (Vol. 2, pp. 19–40). New York: Springer.

Stanik, C. E., & Ellsworth, P. C. (2010). Who cares about marrying a rich man? Intelligence and variation in women's mate preferences. *Human Nature, 21,* 203–217.

Stanley, S. M., Bradbury, T. N., & Markman, H. J. (2000). Structural flaws in the bridge from basic research on marriage to interventions. *Journal of Marriage and the Family, 62,* 256–264.

Stanley, S. M., Rhoades, G. K., Amato, P. R., Markman, H. J., & Johnson, C. A. (2010). The timing of cohabitation and engagement: Impact on first and second marriages. *Journal of Marriage and Family, 72,* 906–918.

Steiner-Pappalardo, N. L., & Gurung, R. A. R. (2002). The femininity effect: Relationship quality, sex, gender, attachment, and significant-other concepts. *Personal Relationships, 9,* 313–325.

Stephenson, K. R., Ahrold, T. K., & Meston, C. M. (2011). The association between sexual motives and sexual satisfaction: Gender differences and categorical comparisons. *Archives of Sexual Behavior, 40*, 607–618

Sternberg, R. J. (1987). *The triangle of love: Intimacy, passion, commitment.* New York: Basic Books.

Sternberg, R. J. (2006). A duplex theory of love. In R. J. Sternberg & K. Weis (Eds.), *The new psychology of love* (pp. 184–199). New Haven, CT: Yale University Press.

Sternglanz, R. W. (2004, June). *Exoneration of serious wrongdoing via confession to a lesser offense.* Paper presented at the meeting of the Society for Personality and Social Psychology, Austin, TX.

Stewart, A. J., Copeland, A. P., Chester, N. L., Malley, J. E., & Barenbaum, N. B. (1997). *Separating together: How divorce transforms families.* New York: Guilford Press.

Stickney, L. T., & Konrad, A. M. (2007). Gender-role attitudes and earnings: A multinational study of married women and men. *Sex Roles, 57*, 801–811.

Stillwell, A. M., Baumeister, R. F., & Del Priore, R. E. (2008). We're all victims here: Toward a psychology of revenge. *Basic and Applied Social Psychology, 30*, 253–263.

Stinson, D. A., Cameron, J. J., Wood, J. V., Gaucher, D., & Holmes, J. G. (2009). Deconstructing the "reign of error": Interpersonal warmth explains the self-fulfilling prophecy of anticipated acceptance. *Personality and Social Psychology Bulletin, 35*, 1165–1178.

Stinson, D. A, Logel, C., Holmes, J. G., Wood, J. V., Forest, A. L., Gaucher, D.,...Kath, J. (2010). The regulatory function of self-esteem: Testing the epistemic and acceptance signaling systems. *Journal of Personality and Social Psychology, 99*, 993–1013.

Stith, S. M., Smith, D. B., Penn, C. E., Ward, D. B., & Tritt, D. (2004). Intimate partner physical abuse perpetration and victimization risk factors: A meta-analytic review. *Aggression and Violent Behavior, 10*, 65–98.

Strachman, A., & Gable, S. L. (2006). What you want (and do not want) affects what you see (and do not see): Avoidance social goals and social events. *Personality and Social Psychology Bulletin, 32*, 1446–1458.

Strachman, A., & Impett, E. A. (2009). Attachment orientations and daily condom use in dating relationships. *Journal of Sex Research, 46*, 319–329.

Straus, M. A. (2008). Dominance and symmetry in partner violence by male and female university students in 32 nations. *Children and Youth Services Review, 30*, 252–275.

Straus, M. A., Hamby, S. L., Boney-McCoy, S., & Sugarman, D. B. (1996). The revised Conflict Tactics Scales (CTS2): Development and preliminary psychometric data. *Journal of Family Issues, 17*, 283–316.

Strong, G., & Aron, A. (2006). The effect of shared participation in novel and challenging activities on experienced relationship quality: Is it mediated by high positive affect? In K. D. Vohs & E. J. Finkel (Eds.), *Self and relationships: Connecting intrapersonal and interpersonal processes* (pp. 342–359). New York: Guilford Press.

Stroud, C. B., Durbin, C. E., Saigal, S. D., & Knobloch-Fedders, L. M. (2010). Normal and abnormal personality traits are associated with marital satisfaction for both men and women: An actor-partner interdependence model analysis. *Journal of Research in Personality, 44*, 466–477.

Stucke, T. S. (2003). Who's to blame? Narcissism and self-serving attributions following feedback. *European Journal of Personality, 17*, 465–478.

Stukas, A. A., Jr., & Snyder, M. (2002). Targets' awareness of expectations and behavioral confirmation in ongoing interactions. *Journal of Experimental Social Psychology, 38*, 31–40.

Subotnik, R. (2007). Cyber-infidelity. In P. R. Peluso (Ed.), *Infidelity: A practitioner's guide to working with couples in crisis* (pp. 169–190). New York: Routledge.

Sullivan, K. T., Pasch, L. A., Johnson, M. D., & Bradbury, T. N. (2010). Social support, problem solving, and the longitudinal course of newlywed marriage. *Journal of Personality and Social Psychology, 98*, 631–644.

Suls, J., & Martin, R. (2005). The daily life of the garden-variety neurotic: Reactivity, stressor exposure, mood spillover, and maladaptive coping. *Journal of Personality, 73*, 1485–1510.

Summers, R. F., & Barber, J. P. (2003). Therapeutic alliance as a measurable psychotherapy skill. *Academic Psychiatry, 27*, 160–165.

Sun, Y. (2001). Family environment and adolescents' well-being before and after parents' marital disruption: A longitudinal analysis. *Journal of Marriage and the Family, 63*, 697–713.

Sun, Y., & Li, Y. (2002). Children's well-being during parents' marital disruption process: A pooled time-series analysis. *Journal of Marriage and the Family, 64,* 472–488.

Sundie, J. M., Kenrick, D. T., Griskevicius, V., Tybur, J. M., Vohs, K. D., & Beal, D. J. (2011). Peacocks, Porsches, and Thorstein Veblen: Conspicuous consumption as a sexual signaling system. *Journal of Personality and Social Psychology, 100,* 664–680.

Sunnafrank, M., & Ramirez, A., Jr. (2004). At first sight: Persistent relational effects of get-acquainted conversations. *Journal of Social and Personal Relationships, 21,* 361–379.

Surra, C. A., & Longstreth, M. (1990). Similarity of outcomes, interdependence, and conflict in dating relationships. *Journal of Personality and Social Psychology, 59,* 501–516.

Swami, V., Greven, C., & Furnham, A. (2007). More than just skin deep? A pilot study integrating physical and non-physical factors in the perception of physical attractiveness. *Personality and Individual Differences, 42,* 563–572.

Swami, V., & IBP Project Members. (2010). The attractive female body weight and female body dissatisfaction in 26 countries across 10 world regions: Results of the International Body Project 1. *Personality and Social Psychology Bulletin, 36,* 309–325.

Swann, W. B., Jr. (1996). *Self-traps: The elusive quest for higher self-esteem.* New York: W. H. Freeman.

Swann, W. B., Jr., & Bosson. J. K. (2010). Self and identity. In S. Fiske, D. Gilbert, & G. Lindzey (Eds.), *Handbook of social psychology* (5th ed., Vol. 1, pp. 589–628). Hoboken, NJ: Wiley.

Swann, W. B., Jr., Bosson, J. K., & Pelham, B. W. (2002). Different partners, different selves: Strategic verification of circumscribed identities. *Personality and Social Psychology Bulletin, 28,* 1215–1228.

Swann, W. B., Jr., Chang-Schneider, C., & Angulo, S. W. (2008). Self-verification in relationships as an adaptive process. In J. V. Wood, A. Tesser, & J. G. Holmes (Eds.), *The self and social relationships* (pp. 49–72). New York: Psychology Press.

Swann, W. B., Jr., De La Ronde, C., & Hixon, J. G. (1994). Authenticity and positivity strivings in marriage and courtship. *Journal of Personality and Social Psychology, 66,* 857–869.

Swann, W. B., Jr., & Gill, M. J. (1997). Confidence and accuracy in person perception: Do we know what we think we know about our relationship partners? *Journal of Personality and Social Psychology, 73,* 747–757.

Swann, W. B., Jr., Hixon, J. G., Stein-Seroussi, A., & Gilbert, D. T. (1990). The fleeting gleam of praise: Cognitive processes underlying behavioral reactions to self-relevant feedback. *Journal of Personality and Social Psychology, 59,* 17–26.

Swann, W. B., Jr., & Pelham, B. (2002). Who wants out when the going gets good? Psychological investment and preference for self-verifying roommates. *Self and Identity, 1,* 219–233.

Swann, W. B., Jr., & Rentfrow, P. J. (2001). Blirtatiousness: Cognitive, behavioral, and physiological consequences of rapid responding. *Journal of Personality and Social Psychology, 81,* 1160–1175.

Swann, W. B., Jr., Rentfrow, P. J., & Gosling, S. D. (2003). The precarious couple effect: Verbally inhibited men + critical, disinhibited women = bad chemistry. *Journal of Personality and Social Psychology, 85,* 1095–1106.

Swann, W. B., Jr., Sellers, J. G., & McClarty, K. L. (2006). Tempting today, troubling tomorrow: The roots of the precarious couple effect. *Personality and Social Psychology Bulletin, 32,* 93–103.

Swann, W. B., Jr., Silvera, D. H., & Proske, C. U. (1995). On "knowing your partner": Dangerous illusions in the age of AIDS? *Personal Relationships, 2,* 173–186.

Tabak, B. A., McCullough, M. E., Luna, L. R., Bono, G., & Berry, J. W. (2011). Conciliatory gestures facilitate forgiveness and feelings of friendship by making transgressors appear more agreeable. *Journal of Personality.* DOI: 10.1111/j.1467-6494.2011.00728.x

Tafoya, M. A., & Spitzberg, B. H. (2007). The dark side of infidelity: Its nature, prevalence, and communicative functions. In B. H. Spitzberg & W. R. Cupach (Eds.), *The dark side of interpersonal communication* (2nd ed., pp. 201–242). Mahwah, NJ: Erlbaum.

Tanha, M., Beck, C. J. A., Figueredo, A. J., & Raghavan, C. (2010). Sex differences in intimate partner violence and the use of coercive control as a motivational factor for intimate partner violence. *Journal of Interpersonal Violence, 25,* 1836–1854.

Tanner, L. (2008, March 12). 1 in 4 girls has sex disease. *Houston Chronicle,* pp. A1, A6.

Tausczik, Y. R., & Pennebaker, J. W. (2010). The psychological meaning of words: LIWC and computerized text analysis methods. *Journal of Language and Social Psychology, 29,* 24–54.

Tavris, C. (1989). *Anger: The misunderstood emotion.* New York: Simon and Schuster.

Taylor, P. (Ed.). (2010). The decline of marriage and the rise of new families. *Pew Research Bureau.* Retrieved from http://pewsocialtrends.org/files/2010/11/pew-social-trends–2010-families. pdf

Teachman, J. (2008). Complex life course patterns and the risk of divorce in second marriages. *Journal of Marriage and Family, 70,* 294–305.

Tejada-Vera, B., & Sutton, P. D. (2010). Births, marriages, divorces, and deaths: Provisional data for 2009. *National Vital Statistics Reports, 58* (25). Hyattsville, MD: National Center for Health Statistics.

Tellegen, A., Lykken, D. T., Bouchard, T. J., Wilcox, K. J., Segal, N. L., & Rich, S. (1988). Personality similarity in twins reared apart and together. *Journal of Personality and Social Psychology, 54,* 1031–1039.

Tenney, E. R., Turkheimer, E., & Oltmanns, T. F. (2009). Being liked is more than having a good personality: The role of matching. *Journal of Research in Personality, 43,* 579–585.

Terhell, E. L., van Groenou, M. I. B., & van Tilburg, T. (2004). Network dynamics in the long-term period after divorce. *Journal of Social and Personal Relationships, 21,* 719–738.

Theodoridou, A., Rowe, A. C., Penton-Voak, I. S., & Rogers, P. J. (2009). Oxytocin and social perception: Oxytocin increases perceived facial trustworthiness and attractiveness. *Hormones and Behavior, 56,* 128–132.

Thibaut, J. W., & Kelley, H. H. (1959). *The social psychology of groups.* New York: Wiley.

Thomas, G., & Maio, G. R. (2008). Man, I feel like a woman: When and how gender-role motivation helps mind-reading. *Journal of Personality and Social Psychology, 95,* 1165–1179.

Thompson, S. C., & Kelley, H. H. (1981). Judgments of responsibility for activities in close relationships. *Journal of Personality and Social Psychology, 41,* 469–477.

Thornhill, R., & Gangestad, S. W. (2006). Facial sexual dimorphism, developmental stability, and susceptibility to disease in men and women. *Evolution and Human Behavior, 27,* 131–144.

Thornhill, R., & Gangestad, S. W. (2008). *The evolutionary biology of human female sexuality.* New York: Oxford University Press.

Thornhill, R., Gangestad, S. W., Miller, R., Scheyd, G., McCollough, J. K., & Franklin, M. (2003). Major histocompatibility complex genes, symmetry, and body scent attractiveness in men and women. *Behavioral Ecology, 14,* 668–678.

Thornton, A., Axinn, W. G., & Xie, Y. (2007). *Marriage and cohabitation.* Chicago: University of Chicago Press.

Thornton, A., & Young-DeMarco, L. (2001). Four decades of trends in attitudes toward family issues in the United States: The 1960s through the 1990s. *Journal of Marriage and the Family, 63,* 1009–1037.

Tice, D. M., & Baumeister, R. F. (1993). Controlling anger: Self-induced emotion change. In D. M. Wegner & J. W. Pennebaker (Eds.), *Handbook of mental control* (pp. 393–409). Englewood Cliffs, NJ: Prentice Hall.

Tjaden, P., & Thoennes, N. (2000). *Extent, nature, and consequences of intimate partner violence: Findings from the National Violence Against Women Survey.* Washington, DC: National Institute of Justice.

Tomlinson, J. M., Reis, H. T., Carmichael, C. L., & Aron, A. (2010, January). *Too much of a good thing? Curvilinear effects of perceived partner idealization on marital satisfaction.* Poster presented at the meeting of the Society for Personality and Social Psychology, Las Vegas, NV.

Tourangeau, R., & Yan, T. (2007). Sensitive questions in surveys. *Psychological Bulletin, 133,* 859–883.

Tracy, J. L., & Robins, R. W. (2008). The automaticity of emotion recognition. *Emotion, 8,* 81–95.

Tran, S., Simpson, J. A., & Fletcher, G. J. O. (2008). The role of ideal standards in relationship initiation processes. In S. Sprecher, A. Wenzel, & J. Harvey (Eds.), *Handbook of relationship initiation* (pp. 487–498). New York: Psychology Press.

Troy, A. B., Lewis-Smith, J., & Laurenceau, J. (2006). Interracial and intraracial romantic relationships: The search for differences in satisfaction, conflict, and attachment style. *Journal of Social and Personal Relationships, 23,* 65–80.

Tsai, F., & Reis, H. T. (2009). Perceptions by and of lonely people in social networks. *Personal Relationships, 16,* 221–238.

Tsapelas, I., Aron, A., & Orbuch, T. (2009). Marital boredom now predicts less satisfaction 9 years later. *Psychological Science, 20,* 543–545.

Tsapelas, I., Fisher, H. E., & Aron, A. (2011). Infidelity: When, where, why. In W. Cupach & B. Spitzberg (Eds.), *The dark side of close relationships II* (pp. 175–195). New York: Routledge.

Tucker, J. S., & Anders, S. L. (1998). Adult attachment style and nonverbal closeness in dating couples. *Journal of Nonverbal Behavior, 22,* 109–124.

Tucker, P., & Aron, A. (1993). Passionate love and marital satisfaction at key transition points in the family life cycle. *Journal of Social and Clinical Psychology, 12,* 135–147.

Turley, R. N. L., & Desmond, M. (2011). Contributions to college costs by married, divorced, and remarried parents. *Journal of Family Issues, 32,* 767–790.

Twenge, J. M. (2008). Social exclusion, motivation, and self-defeating behavior: Why breakups lead to drunkenness and ice cream. In J. Y. Shah & W. L. Gardner (Eds.), *Handbook of motivation science* (pp. 508–517). New York: Guilford Press.

Twenge, J. M. (2009). Status and gender: The paradox of progress in an age of narcissism. *Sex Roles, 61,* 338–340.

Twenge, J. M., Abebe, E. M., & Campbell, W. K. (2010). Fitting in or standing out: Trends in American parents' choices for children's names, 1880–2007. *Social Psychological and Personality Science, 1,* 19–25.

Twenge, J. M., & Campbell, W. K. (2010). Birth cohort differences in the Monitoring the Future dataset and elsewhere: Further evidence for Generation Me—commentary on Trzesniewski & Donnellan. *Perspectives on Psychological Science, 5,* 81–88.

Twenge, J. M., Catanese, K. R., & Baumeister, R. F. (2003). Social exclusion and the deconstructed state: Time perception, meaninglessness, lethargy, lack of emotion, and self-awareness. *Journal of Personality and Social Psychology, 85,* 409–423.

Tyler, J. M., Feldman, R. S., & Reichert, A. (2006). The price of deceptive behavior: Disliking and lying to people who lie to us. *Journal of Experimental Social Psychology, 42,* 69–77.

Ueno, K., Gayman, M. D., Wright, E. R., & Quantz, S. D. (2009). Friends' sexual orientation, relational quality, and mental health among gay, lesbian, and bisexual youth. *Personal Relationships, 16,* 659–670.

U.S. Census Bureau (2011). *The 2011 Statistical Abstract.* Retrieved from http://www.census.gov/compendia/statab/cats/international_statistics.html

Uysal, A., Lin, H. L., & Knee, C. R. (2010). The role of need satisfaction in self-concealment and well-being. *Personality and Social Psychology Bulletin, 36,* 187–199.

Vaaler, M. L., Ellison, C. G., & Powers, D. A. (2009). Religious influences on the risk of marital dissolution. *Journal of Marriage and Family, 71,* 917–934.

Valkenburg, P. M., & Peter, J. (2009a). Social consequences of the internet for adolescents: A decade of research. *Current Directions in Psychological Science, 18,* 1–5.

Valkenburg, P. M., & Peter, J. (2009b). The effects of instant messaging on the quality of adolescents' existing friendships: A longitudinal study. *Journal of Communication, 59,* 79–97.

van den Boom, D. C. (1994). The influence of temperament and mothering on attachment and exploration: An experimental manipulation of sensitive responsiveness among lower-class mothers with irritable infants. *Child Development, 65,* 1457–1477.

van der Linden, D., Scholte, R. H. J., Cillessen, A. H. N., te Nijenhuis, J., & Segers, E. (2010). Classroom ratings of likeability and popularity are related to the Big Five and the general factor of personality. *Journal of Research in Personality, 44,* 669–672.

Van Straaten, I., Engels, R. C. M. E., Finkenauer, C., & Holland, R. W. (2009). Meeting your match: How attractiveness similarity affects approach behavior in mixed-sex dyads. *Personality and Social Psychology Bulletin, 35,* 685–697.

Vandello, J. A., Bosson, J. K., Cohen, D., Burnaford, R. M., & Weaver, J. R. (2008). Precarious manhood. *Journal of Personality and Social Psychology, 93,* 1325–1339.

Vangelisti, A. L. (Ed.). (2009). *Feeling hurt in close relationships.* New York: Cambridge University Press.

Vangelisti, A. L., & Hampel, A. D. (2010). Hurtful communication: Current research and future directions. In S. Smith & S. Wilson (Eds.), *New directions in interpersonal communication research* (pp. 221–241). Thousand Oaks, CA: Sage.

Vannier, S. A., & O'Sullivan, L. F. (2011). Communicating interest in sex: Verbal and nonverbal initiation of sexual activity in young adults' romantic dating relationships. *Archives of Sexual Behavior.* DOI 10.1007/s10508-010-9663-7

Vasey, P. L., & VanderLaan, D. P. (2010). Avuncular tendencies and the evolution of male andro-philia in Samoan fa'afafine. *Archives of Sexual Behavior, 39,* 821–830.

Vazire, S. (2010). Who knows what about a person? The self-other knowledge asymmetry (SOKA) model. *Journal of Personality and Social Psychology, 98,* 281–300.

Vazire, S., & Mehl, M. R. (2008). Knowing me, knowing you: The accuracy and unique predictive validity of self-ratings and other-ratings of daily behavior. *Journal of Personality and Social Psychology, 95,* 1202–1216.

Veniegas, R. C., & Peplau, L. A. (1997). Power and the quality of same-sex friendships. *Psychology of Women Quarterly, 21,* 279–297.

Verhofstadt, L. L., Buysse, A., Ickes, W., de Clercq, A., & Peene, O. J. (2005). Conflict and support interactions in marriage: An analysis of couples' interactive behavior and on-line cognition. *Personal Relationships, 12,* 23–42.

Verhofstadt, L. L., Ickes, W., & Buysse, A. (2010). "I know what you need right now": Empathic accuracy and support provision in marriage. In K. Sullivan & J. Davila (Eds.), *Support processes in intimate relationships* (pp. 71–88). New York: Oxford University Press.

Veroff, J., Hatchett, S, & Douvan, E. (1992). Consequences of participating in a longitudinal study of marriage. *Public Opinion Quarterly, 56,* 315–327.

Vescio, T. K., Schlenker, K. A., & Lenes, J. G. (2010). Power and sexism. In A. Guinote & T. Vescio (Eds.), *The social psychology of power* (pp. 363–380). New York: Guilford Press.

Vincent, J. P., Weiss, R. L., & Birchler, G. R. (1975). Dyadic problem solving behavior as a function of marital distress and spousal vs. stranger interactions. *Behavior Therapy, 6,* 475–487.

Vincent, W., Peterson, J. L., & Parrott, D. J. (2009). Differences in African American and White women's attitudes toward lesbians and gay men. *Sex Roles, 61,* 599–606.

Vohs, K. D., & Baumeister, R. F. (2004). Sexual passion, intimacy, and gender. In D. J. Mashek & A. Aron (Eds.), *Handbook of closeness and intimacy* (pp. 189–199). Mahwah, NJ: Erlbaum.

Vohs, K. D., Catanese, K. R., & Baumeister, R. F. (2004). Sex in "his" versus "her" relationships. In J. H. Harvey, A. Wenzel, & S. Sprecher (Eds.), *The handbook of sexuality in close relationships* (pp. 455–474). Mahwah, NJ: Erlbaum.

Vohs, K. D., Finkenauer, C., & Baumeister, R. F. (2011). The sum of friends' and lovers' self-control scores predicts relationship quality. *Social Psychological and Personality Science, 2,* 138–145.

Vonofakou, C., Hewstone, M., & Voci, A. (2007). Contact with out-group friends as a predictor of meta-attitudinal strength and accessibility of attitudes toward gay men. *Journal of Personality and Social Psychology, 92,* 804–820.

Voracek, M., & Fisher, M. L. (2006). Success is all in the measures: Androgenousness, curvaceous-ness, and starring frequencies in adult media actresses. *Archives of Sexual Behavior, 35,* 297–304.

Vorauer, J. D., Cameron, J. J., Holmes, J. G., & Pearce, D. G. (2003). Invisible overtures: Fears of rejec-tion and the signal amplification bias. *Journal of Personality and Social Psychology, 84,* 793–812.

Vrij, A. (2006). Nonverbal communication and deception. In V. Manusov & M. L. Patterson (Eds.), *The Sage handbook of nonverbal communication* (pp. 341–359). Thousand Oaks, CA: Sage.

Vrij, A. (2007). Deception: A social lubricant and a selfish act. In K. Fiedler (Ed.), *Social communica-tion* (pp. 309–342). New York: Psychology Press.

Vrij, A., Edward, K., & Bull, R. (2001). Stereotypical verbal and nonverbal responses while deceiv-ing others. *Personality and Social Psychology Bulletin, 27,* 899–909.

Vrij, A., Granhag, P. A., & Porter, S. (2010). Pitfalls and opportunities in nonverbal and verbal lie detection. *Psychological Science in the Public Interest, 11,* 89–121.

Vrij, A., Paterson, B., Nunkoosing, K., Soukara, S., & Oosterwegel, A. (2003). Perceived advantages and disadvantages of secrets disclosure. *Personality and Individual Differences, 35,* 593–602.

Waas, G. A., & Graczyk, P. A. (1998). Group interventions for the peer-rejected child. In K. C. Stoi-ber & T. R. Kratochwill (Eds.), *Handbook of group intervention for children and families* (pp. 141–158). Needham Heights, MA: Allyn & Bacon.

Waite, L. J., & Joyner, L. (2001). Emotional and physical satisfaction with sex in married, cohabiting, and dating sexual unions: Do men and women differ? In E. O. Laumann & R. T. Michael (Eds.), *Sex, love, and health in America: Private choices and public policies* (pp. 239–269). Chicago: University of Chicago Press.

Waldron, V. R., & Kelley, D. K. (2008). *Communicating forgiveness.* Thousand Oaks, CA: Sage.

Wallace, H. M., Exline, J. J., & Baumeister, R. F. (2008). Interpersonal consequences of forgiveness: Does forgiveness deter or encourage repeat offenses? *Journal of Experimental Social Psychology, 44*, 453–460.

Waller, K. L., & MacDonald, T. K. (2010). Trait self-esteem moderates the effect of initiator status on emotional and cognitive responses to romantic relationship dissolution. *Journal of Personality, 78*, 1271–1299.

Waller, W. (1937). The rating and dating complex. *American Sociological Review, 2*, 727–734.

Waller, W. W., & Hill, R. (1951). *The family, a dynamic interpretation.* New York: Dryden Press.

Walster, E., & Walster, G. W. (1978). *A new look at love.* Reading, MA: Addison-Wesley.

Walster, E., Walster, G. W., Piliavin, J., & Schmidt, L. (1973). "Playing hard to get": Understanding an elusive phenomenon. *Journal of Personality & Social Psychology, 26*, 113–121.

Walther, J. B., & Ramirez, A., Jr. (2009). New technologies and new directions in online relating. In S. Smith & S. Wilson (Eds.), *New directions in interpersonal communication research* (pp. 264–284). Thousand Oaks, CA: Sage.

Wampold, B. E. (2007). Psychotherapy: The humanistic (and effective) treatment. *American Psychologist, 62*, 855–873.

Wang, H., & Wellman, B. (2010). Social connectivity in America: Changes in adult friendship network size from 2002 to 2007. *American Behavioral Scientist, 53*, 1148–1169.

Warburton, W. A., Williams, K. D., & Cairns, D. R. (2006). When ostracism leads to aggression: The moderating effects of control deprivation. *Journal of Experimental Social Psychology, 42*, 213–220.

Warren, M. (2010, July 16). Argentina legalizes same-sex marriage. *Houston Chronicle*, p. A5.

Waters, E., Merrick, S., Treboux, D., Crowell, J., & Albersheim, L. (2000). Attachment security in infancy and early adulthood: A twenty-year longitudinal study. *Child Development, 71*, 684–689.

Watson, D., & Humrichouse, J. (2006). Personality development in emerging adulthood: Integrating evidence from self-ratings and spouse ratings. *Journal of Personality and Social Psychology, 91*, 959–974.

Watson, D., Klohnen, E. C., Casillas, A., Simms, E. N., Haig, J., & Berry, D. S. (2004). Match makers and deal breakers: Analyses of assortative mating in newlywed couples. *Journal of Personality, 72*, 1029–1068.

Weaver, S. E., & Ganong, L. H. (2004). The factor structure of the Romantic Beliefs Scale for African Americans and European Americans. *Journal of Social and Personal Relationships, 21*, 171–185.

Weber, A. L. (1992). The account-making process: A phenomenological approach. In T. L. Orbuch (Ed.), *Close relationship loss: Theoretical approaches* (pp. 174–191). New York: Springer-Verlag.

Weber, A. L., & Harvey, J. H. (1994). Accounts in coping with relationship loss. In A. L. Weber & J. H. Harvey (Eds.), *Perspectives on close relationships* (pp. 285–306). Boston: Allyn & Bacon.

Weeden, J., & Sabini, J. (2007). Subjective and objective measures of attractiveness and their relation to sexual behavior and sexual attitudes in university students. *Archives of Sexual Behavior, 36*, 79–88.

Weeks, D. G., Michela, J. L., Peplau, L.A., & Bragg, M. E. (1980). The relation between loneliness and depression: A structural equation analysis. *Journal of Personality and Social Psychology, 39*, 1238–1244.

Weger, H., Jr. (2005). Disconfirming communication and self-verification in marriage: Associations among the demand/withdraw interaction pattern, feeling understood, and marital satisfaction. *Journal of Social and Personal Relationships, 22*, 19–31.

Wei, M., Russell, D. W., Mallinckrodt, B., & Vogel, D. L. (2007). The Experiences in Close Relationship Scale (ECR)-Short Form: Reliability, validity, and factor structure. *Journal of Personality Assessment, 88*, 187–204.

Weigel, D. J. (2008). A dyadic assessment of how couples indicate their commitment to each other. *Personal Relationships, 15*, 17–39.

Weisbuch, M., Ambady, N., Clarke, A. L., Achor, S., & Weele, J. V. (2010). On being consistent: The role of verbal-nonverbal consistency in first impressions. *Basic and Applied Social Psychology, 32*, 261–268.

Weiss, R. L., Birchler, G. R., & Vincent, J. P. (1974). Contractual models for negotiating training in marital dyads. *Journal of Marriage and the Family, 36,* 321–330.

Weiss, R. L., Hops, H., & Patterson, G. R. (1973). A framework for conceptualizing marital conflict, a technology for altering it, some data for evaluating it. In L. A. Hamerlynck, L. C. Handy, & E. J. Mash (Eds.), *Behavior change: Methodology, concepts and practice* (pp. 309–342). Champaign, IL: Research Press.

Weiss, R. S. (1973). *Loneliness.* Cambridge, MA: MIT Press.

Wells, B. E., & Twenge, J. M. (2005). Changes in young people's sexual behavior and attitudes, 1943–1999: A cross-temporal meta-analysis. *Review of General Psychology, 9,* 249–261.

Wendorf, C. A., Lucas, T., Imamoğlu, E. O., Weisfeld, C. C., & Weisfeld, G. E. (2011). Marital satisfaction across three cultures: Does the number of children have an impact after accounting for other marital demographics? *Journal of Cross-Cultural Psychology, 42,* 340–354.

Wenzel, A., & Emerson, T. (2009). Mate selection in socially anxious and nonanxious individuals. *Journal of Social and Clinical Psychology, 28,* 341–363.

Werking, K. (1997). *We're just good friends: Women and men in nonromantic relationships.* New York: Guilford Press.

Whalen, J. M., Pexman, P. M., & Gill, A. J. (2009). "Should be fun—not!" Incidence and marking of nonliteral language in e-mail. *Journal of Language and Social Psychology, 28,* 263–280.

Wheeler, J., & Christensen, A. (2002). Creating a context for change: Integrative Couple Therapy. In A. L. Vangelisti, H. T. Reis, & M. A. Fitzpatrick (Eds.), *Stability and change in relationships* (pp. 285–305). Cambridge, England: Cambridge University Press.

Wheeler, L., & Kim, Y. (1997). What is beautiful is culturally good: The physical attractiveness stereotype has different content in collectivistic cultures. *Personality and Social Psychology Bulletin, 23,* 795–800.

Wheeler, L., Reis, H., & Nezlek, J. (1983). Loneliness, social interaction, and sex roles. *Journal of Personality and Social Psychology, 45,* 943–953.

Whisman, M. A., Snyder, D. K., & Beach, S. R. H. (2009). Screening for marital and relationship discord. *Journal of Family Psychology, 23,* 247–254.

Whisman, M. A., Uebelacker, L. A., & Settles, T. D. (2010). Marital distress and the metabolic syndrome: Linking social functioning with physical health. *Journal of Family Psychology, 24,* 367–370.

Whitaker, D. J., Haileyesus, T., Swahn, M., & Saltzman, L. S. (2007). Differences in frequency of violence and reported injury between relationships with reciprocal and nonreciprocal intimate partner violence. *American Journal of Public Health, 97,* 941–947.

Whitaker, D. J., Le, B., & Niolon, P. H. (2010). Persistence and desistance of the perpetration of physical aggression across relationships: Findings from a national study of adolescents. *Journal of Interpersonal Violence, 25,* 591–609.

White, G. L. (1980). Inducing jealousy: A power perspective. *Personality and Social Psychology Bullein, 6,* 222–227.

White, G. L. (1981). Some correlates of romantic jealousy. *Journal of Personality, 49,* 129–147.

White, G. L., Fishbein, S., & Rutstein, J. (1981). Passionate love: The misattribution of arousal. *Journal of Personality and Social Psychology, 41,* 56–62.

Whitley, B. E., Jr. (1993). Reliability and aspects of the construct validity of Sternberg's Triangular Love Scale. *Journal of Social and Personal Relationships, 10,* 475–480.

Whitton, S. W., Schulz, M. S., Crowell, J. A., Waldinger, R. J., Allen, J. P., & Hauser, S. T. (2008). Prospective associations from family-of-origin interactions to adult marital interactions and relationship adjustment. *Journal of Family Psychology, 22,* 274–286.

Whitty, M. T., & Quigley, L. (2008). Emotional and sexual infidelity offline and in cyberspace. *Journal of Marital & Family Therapy, 34,* 461–468.

Whyte, W. F. (1955). *Street corner society: The social structure of an Italian slum.* Chicago: University of Chicago Press.

Widmer, E. D., Treas, J., & Newcomb, R. (1998). Attitudes toward nonmarital sex in 24 countries. *Journal of Sex Research, 35,* 349–358.

Wiederman, M. W. (2004). Methodological issues in studying sexuality in close relationships. In J. H. Harvey, A. Wenzel, & S. Sprecher (Eds.), *The handbook of sexuality in close relationships* (pp. 31–56). Mahwah, NJ: Erlbaum.

Wile, D. B. (1995). *After the fight: Using your disagreements to build a stronger relationship.* New York: Guilford Press.

Willetts, M. C., Sprecher, S., & Beck, F. D. (2004). Overview of sexual practices and attitudes within relational contexts. In J. H. Harvey, A. Wenzel, & S. Sprecher (Eds.), *The handbook of sexuality in close relationships* (pp. 57–85). Mahwah, NJ: Erlbaum.

Williams, K. D. (2001). *Ostracism: The power of silence.* New York: Guilford Press.

Williams, K. D. (2007). Ostracism. *Annual Review of Psychology, 58,* 425–452.

Williams, K. D., & Jarvis, B. (2006). Cyberball: A program for use in research on interpersonal ostracism and acceptance. *Behavior Research Methods, 38,* 174–180.

Williams, K. D., & Zadro, L. (2005). Ostracism: The indiscriminate early detection system. In K. D. Williams, J. P. Forgas, & W. von Hippel (Eds.), *The social outcast: Ostracism, social exclusion, rejection, and bullying* (pp. 19–34). New York: Psychology Press.

Williams, S. L., & Frieze, I. H. (2005). Courtship behaviors, relationship violence, and breakup persistence in college men and women. *Psychology of Women Quarterly, 29,* 248–257.

Williamson, I., & Gonzales, M. H. (2007). The subjective experience of forgiveness: Positive construals of the forgiveness experience. *Journal of Social and Clinical Psychology, 26,* 407–446.

Willis, J., & Todorov, A. (2006). First impressions: Making up your mind after a 100-ms exposure to a face. *Psychological Science, 17,* 592–598.

Wills, T. A., Weiss, R. L., & Patterson, G. R. (1974). A behavioral analysis of the determinants of marital satisfaction. *Journal of Consulting and Clinical Psychology, 42,* 802–811.

Wilson, T. D., & Gilbert, D. T. (2005). Affective forecasting: Knowing what to want. *Current Directions in Psychological Science, 14,* 131–134.

Winslett, A. H., & Gross, A. M. (2008). Sexual boundaries: An examination of the importance of talking before touching. *Violence Against Women, 14,* 542–562.

Wiseman, H., Mayseless, O., & Sharabany, R. (2006). Why are they lonely? Perceived quality of early relationships with parents, attachment, personality predispositions and loneliness in first-year university students. *Personality and Individual Differences, 40,* 237–248.

Wiseman, J., & Duck, S. (1995). Having and managing enemies: A very challenging relationship. In S. Duck & J. T. Wood (Eds.), *Confronting relationship challenges* (pp. 43–72). Thousand Oaks, CA: Sage.

Wickrama, K. A. S., Bryant, C. M., & Wickrama, T. K. A. (2010). Perceived community disorder, hostile marital interactions, and self-reported health of African American couples: An interdyadic process. *Personal Relationships, 17,* 515–531.

Wilcox, W. B., & Marquardt, E. (Eds.). (2010). *When marriage disappears: The new middle America.* The National Marriage Project. Retrieved from http://www.stateofourunions.org

Wildsmith, E., Schelar, E., Kristen-Peterson, K., & Manlove, J. (2010, May). Sexually transmitted diseases among young adults: Prevalence, perceived risk, and risk-taking behaviors. *Child Trends Research Brief.* Retrieved from http://www.childtrends.org/Files//Child_Trends–2010_05_01_RB_STD.pdf

Wiik, K. A., Bernhardt, E., & Noack, T. (2009). A study of commitment and relationship quality in Sweden and Norway. *Journal of Marriage and Family, 71,* 465–477.

Williams, K. M., Park, J. H., & Wieling, M. B. (2010). The face reveals athletic flair: Better National Football League quarterbacks are better looking. *Personality and Individual Differences, 48,* 112–116.

Williams, L. E., & Bargh, J. A. (2008). Experiencing physical warmth promotes interpersonal warmth. *Science, 322,* 606–607.

Williams, M. J., & Mendelsohn, G. A. (2008). Gender clues and cues: Online interactions as windows into lay theories about men and women. *Basic and Applied Social Psychology, 30,* 278–294.

Winston, R. (2002). *Human instinct.* London: Bantam Press.

Wirth, J. H., Sacco, D. F., Hugenberg, K., & Williams, K. D. (2010). Eye gaze as relational evaluation: Averted eye gaze leads to feelings of ostracism and relational devaluation. *Personality and Social Psychology Bulletin, 36,* 869–882.

Witt, E. A., Donnellan, M. B., & Orlando, M. J. (2011). Timing and selection effects within a psychology subject pool: Personality and sex matter. *Personality and Individual Differences, 50,* 355–359.

Witvliet, C. V. O., Worthington, E. L., Root, L. M., Sato, A. F., Ludwig, T. E., & Exline, J. J. (2008). Retributive justice, restorative justice, and forgiveness: An experimental psychophysiology analysis. *Journal of Experimental Social Psychology, 44,* 10–25.

Wojciszke, B., & Struzynska-Kujalowicz, A. (2007). Power influences self-esteem. *Social Cognition, 25,* 472–494.

Wolfinger, N. H. (2005). *Understanding the divorce cycle: The children of divorce in their own marriages.* New York: Cambridge University Press.

Women CEOs. (2010, May 3). Retrieved from http://money.cnn.com/magazines/fortune/fortune500/2010/womenceos/

Wood, A. M., Froh, J. J., & Geraghty, A. W. A. (2010). Gratitude and well-being: A review and theoretical integration. *Clinical Psychology Review, 30,* 890–905.

Wood, D., & Brumbaugh, C. C. (2009). Using revealed mate preferences to evaluate market force and differential preference explanations for mate selection. *Journal of Personality and Social Psychology, 96,* 1226–1244.

Wood, J. T. (2004). Monsters and victims: Male felons' accounts of intimate partner violence. *Journal of Social and Personal Relationships, 21,* 555–576.

Wood, W., & Eagly, E. A. (2007). Social structural origins of sex differences in human mating. In S. W. Gangestad & J. A. Simpson (Eds.), *The evolution of mind: Fundamental questions and controversies* (pp. 383–390). New York: Guilford Press.

Wood, W., & Eagly, A. H. (2009). Gender identity. In M. R. Leary & R. H. Hoyle (Eds.), *Handbook of individual differences in social behavior* (pp. 109–125). New York: Guilford Press.

Wood, W., & Eagly, A. H. (2010). Gender. In S. Fiske, D. Gilbert, & G. Lindzey (Eds.), *Handbook of social psychology* (5th ed., Vol. 1, pp. 629–667). Hoboken, NJ: Wiley.

Woolf, S. E., & Maisto, S. A. (2008). Gender differences in condom use behavior? The role of power and partner-type. *Sex Roles, 58,* 689–701.

Wortman, C. B., & Boerner, K. (2007). Beyond the myths of coping with loss: Prevailing assumptions versus scientific evidence. In H. S. Friedman & R. C. Silver (Eds.), *Foundations of health psychology* (pp. 285–324). New York: Oxford University Press.

Wright, C. N., Holloway, A., & Roloff, M. E. (2007). The dark side of self-monitoring: How high self-monitors view their romantic relationships. *Communication Reports, 20,* 101–114.

Wright, P. H. (1982). Men's friendships, women's friendships and the alleged inferiority of the latter. *Sex Roles, 8,* 1–20.

Xu, X., Aron, A., Brown, L., Cao, G., Feng, T., & Weng, X. (2011). Reward and motivation systems: A brain mapping study of early-stage intense romantic love in Chinese participants. *Human Brain Mapping, 32,* 249–257.

Yager, J. (1997). *Friendshifts: The power of friendship and how it shapes our lives.* Stamford, CT: Hannacroix Creek Books.

Yagil, D., Karnieli-Miller, O., Eisikovits, Z., & Enosh, G. (2006). Is that a "No"? The interpretation of responses to unwanted sexual attention. *Sex Roles, 54,* 251–260.

Yarkoni, T. (2010). Personality in 100,000 words: A large-scale analysis of personality and word use among bloggers. *Journal of Research in Personality, 44,* 363–373.

Yeagley, E., Morling, B., & Nelson, M. (2007). Nonverbal zero-acquaintance accuracy of self-esteem, social dominance orientation, and satisfaction with life. *Journal of Research in Personality, 41,* 1099–1106.

Yen, H. (2010, April 21). Gender gap in advanced degrees is vanishing. *Houston Chronicle,* p. A3.

Yen, H. (2010a, November 18). More believe marriage obsolete. *Bryan-College Station Eagle,* p. A3.

Yen, H. (2010b, September 24). More U.S. couples 'doubling up,' census shows. *Houston Chronicle,* p. A13.

Yoshimura, S. (2007). Goals and emotional outcomes of revenge activities in interpersonal relationships. *Journal of Social and Personal Relationships, 24,* 87–98.

Younger, J., Aron, A., Parke, S., Chatterjee, N., & Mackey, S. (2010). Viewing pictures of a romantic partner reduces experimental pain: Involvement of neural reward systems. *PLoS ONE, 5* (10), e13309.

Ysseldyk, R., Matheson, K., & Anisman, H. (2007). Rumination: Bridging a gap between forgivingness, vengefulness, and psychological health. *Personality and Individual Differences, 42,* 1573–1584.

Yu, E., & Liu, J. (2007). Environmental impacts of divorce. *Proceedings of the National Academy of Sciences, 104,* 20629–20634.

Yuan, J. W., McCarthy, M., Holley, S. R., & Levenson, R. W. (2010). Physiological down-regulation and positive emotion in marital interaction. *Emotion, 10,* 467–474.

Yucel, D., & Gassanov, M. A. (2010). Exploring actor and partner correlates of sexual satisfaction among married couples. *Social Science Research, 39,* 725–738.

Zaalberg, R., Manstead, A. S. R., & Fischer, A. H. (2004). Relations between emotions, display rules, social motives, and facial behaviour. *Cognition and Emotion, 18,* 183–207.

Zacchilli, T. L., Hendrick, C., & Hendrick, S. S. (2009). The Romantic Partner Conflict Scale: A new Scale to measure relationship conflict. *Journal of Social and Personal Relationships, 26,* 1073–1096.

Zadro, L., Arriaga, X. B., & Williams, K. D. (2008). Relational ostracism. In J. P. Forgas &J. Fitness (Eds.), *Social relationships: Cognitive, affective and motivational processes* (pp. 305–319). New York: Psychology Press.

Zadro, L., Williams, K. D., & Richardson, R. (2004). How low can you go? Ostracism by a computer is sufficient to lower self-reported levels of belonging, control, self-esteem, and meaningful existence. *Journal of Experimental Social Psychology, 40,* 560–567.

Zajonc, R. B. (2001). Mere exposure: A gateway to the subliminal. *Current Directions in Psychological Science, 10,* 224–228.

Zayas, V., Mischel, W., Shoda, Y., & Aber, J. L. (2011). Roots of adult attachment: Maternal caregiving at 18 months predicts adult peer and partner attachment. *Social Psychological and Personality Science, 2,* 289–297.

Zayas, V., & Shoda, Y. (2007). Predicting preferences for dating partners from past experiences of psychological abuse: Identifying the psychological ingredients of situations. *Personality and Social Psychology Bulletin, 33,* 123–138.

Zayas, V., Shoda, Y., & Ayduk, O. N. (2002). Personality in context: An interpersonal systems perspective. *Journal of Personality, 70,* 851–900.

Zechmeister, J. S., Garcia, S., & Vas, S. N. (2004). Don't apologize unless you mean it: A laboratory investigation of forgiveness and retaliation. *Journal of Social and Clinical Psychology, 23,* 532–564.

Zhang, F. (2009). The relationship between state attachment security and daily interpersonal experience. *Journal of Research in Personality, 43,* 511–515.

Zhang, F., & Parmley, M. (2011). What your best friend sees that I don't see: Comparing female close friends and casual acquaintances on the perception of emotional facial expressions of varying intensities. *Personality and Social Psychology Bulletin, 37,* 28–39.

Zhang, S., & Kline, S. L. (2009). Can I make my own decision? A cross-cultural study of perceived social network influence in mate selection. *Journal of Cross-Cultural Psychology, 40,* 3–23.

Zhang, Y., & Epley, N. (2009). Self-centered social exchange: Differential use of costs versus benefits in prosocial reciprocity. *Journal of Personality and Social Psychology, 97,* 796–810.

Zhang, Y., & Van Hook, J. (2009). Marital dissolution among interracial couples. *Journal of Marriage and Family, 71,* 95–107.

Zhaoyang, R., & Cooper, L. (2011, January). *For better or for worse? Unintended effects of dyadic diary study participation on close relationships.* Poster presented at the meeting of the Society for Personality and Social Psychology, San Antonio, TX.

Zhong, C., & Leonardelli, G. J. (2008). Cold and lonely: Does social exclusion literally feel cold? *Psychological Science, 19,* 838–842.

Zimmerman, D. H., & West, C. (1975). Sex roles, interruptions and silences in conversations. In B. Thorne & N. Henley (Eds.), *Language and sex: Difference and dominance* (pp. 105–129). Rowley, MA: Newbury House.

Zipp, J. F., Prohaska, A., & Bemiller, M. (2004). Wives, husbands, and hidden power in marriage. *Journal of Family Issues, 25*, 933–958.

Zuckerman, M., Koestner, R., & Alton, A. O. (1984). Learning to detect deception. *Journal of Personality and Social Psychology, 46*, 519–528.

Zurbriggen, E. L., & Morgan, E. M. (2006). Who wants to marry a millionaire? Reality dating television programs, attitudes toward sex, and sexual behaviors. *Sex Roles, 54*, 1–17.

Credits

Photo Credits TA1.1, Page 9: Buccina Studios/Getty Images; TA2.1, Page 48: © Punchstock/ Digital Vision; TA2.2a, Page 52: Ingram Publishing; TA2.2b, Page 52: © Flat Earth Images; TA3.1, Page 78: Little et al., 2002; Anthony Little (www.alittlelab.com); TA3.2, Page 79: Courtesy of Dr. Judith H. Langlois; TA3.3, Page 82: © Lars A. Niki; TA3.4, Page 93: Asia Images Group/Getty Images; TA4.1, Page 107: PhotoAlto/Veer; TA5.1a-d, Page 145: © Paul Ekman; TA5.4, Page 171: Getty Images; TA8.1, Page 248: © Comstock/PunchStock; TA13.1, Page 412: © Image Source/PunchStock; TA13.2, Page 419: © Image Source/PunchStock.

Chapter 1 Page: 3 Aron, A., Aron E. N., & Smollan, D. "Inclusion of other in the self scale and the structure of interpersonal closeness." JOURNAL OF PERSONALITY and SOCIAL PSYCHOLOGY, 63 (1992):597. **Page: 5** From "Prognostic importance of marital quality for survival of congestive heart failure" by James C. Coyne, Michael J. Rohrbaugh, Varda Shoham, John S. Sonnega, John M. Nicklas, & James A. Cranford. Reprinted from THE AMERICAN JOURNAL OF CARDIOLOGY 8, no. 5 (2001):526–539 with permission from Elsevier. **Page: 10** From UNDERSTANDING THE DIVORCE CYCLE: The Children of Divorce in Their Own Marriages, by N.H. Wolfinger, "The outcomes of cohabitation over time" p. 96. Copyright © 2005 Cambridge University Press. Reprinted with the permission of Cambridge University Press. **Page: 26** Sally Forth © 1995 King Features Syndicate. **Page: 31** "How My Partner Sees Me" Courtesy of Sandra Murray.

Chapter 2 Page: 43 "Schematic diagram of William Ickes's lab at the University of Texas at Arlington" Courtesy of William Ickes. **Page: 56** Hendrick, S.S. "A generic measure of relationship satisfaction" from JOURNAL OF MARRIAGE and THE FAMILY, 50 (1998): 94 Reprinted by permission of SAGE.

Chapter 3 Page: 72 "A student apartment building at MIT" from SOCIAL PSYCHOLOGY 9e by David Myers. Copyright © 1993 McGraw-Hill. Reprinted with permission. **Page: 83** "Women's probability of conception during the menstrual cycle" Courtesy of Jeffry Simpson.

Chapter 4 Page: 119 "Destiny and Growth Beliefs" Courtesy of C. Raymond Knee. **Page: 127** Swann, W. B., Jr., C. D L Ronde, & J. G. Hixon. "The marriage shift in self-verification" from "Authenticity and positivity strivings in marriage and courtship," JOURNAL OF PERSONALITY and SOCIAL PSYCHOLOGY, 66, (1994): 861. **Page: 133** Synder, M. and S. Gangestad, "The Self-Monitoring Scale" from "On the Nature of Self-Monitoring: Matters of Assessment, Matters of Validity," JOURNAL OF PERSONALITY and SOCIAL PSYCHOLOGY 51 (1986): 125–139.

Chapter 5 Page: 151 Zits © 2008 Zits Partnership King Features Syndicate. **Page: 168** Zits © 2007 ZITS Partnership King Features Syndicate.

Chapter 6 Page: 186 Gottman, J. M., & R.W. Levenson, "The arguments of couples at low and high risk of divorce" in "Marital processes predictive of later dissolution: Behavior, physiology, and health," JOURNAL OF PERSONALITY and SOCIAL PSYCHOLOGY, 63, no. 2 (1992): 221–233. **Page: 199** Mills, J.S., Clark, Ford, T.E., & Johnson, M. "Measurement of communal

Name Index

Abbey, A., 298
Abel, E. L., 145
Aber, J. L., 19
Abramson, A., 150
Acevedo, B. P., 263, 270
Achor, S., 150
Acitelli, L. K., 9, 134
Ackerman, D., 244–245, 250
Ackerman, P. L., 101
Adams, G., 87
Adams, K., 217
Afifi, T., 158
Afifi, T. D., 158, 349, 386
Afifi, W., 158–159
Afifi, W.A., 328, 332
Agnew, C. R., 3, 111, 175, 178,
  184, 205–208, 427, 434
Agostinelli, G., 285
Ahlberg, C., 26
Ahmetoglu, G., 269, 270
Ahrold, T. K., 288
Ahrons, C. R., 418–419, 422
Ainsworth, M. D. S., 14
Akalis, S., 225
Albrecht, S. L., 179
Albright, J. M., 288
Alessi, G., 358
Alexander, R., 32
Algoe, S., 432
Ali, L., 11
Al Issa, A., 147
Allan, G., 240
Allard, L. M., 264
Allen, A. B., 203
Allen, C. T., 382
Allen, E. S., 299
Allen, J. B., 375
Allen, K., 226
Allen, T. J., 29
Allik, J., 135
Alnwick, K. A., 134
Aloni, M., 196
Altman, I., 156
Álvarez, J., 82
Amato, P. R., 6, 9, 11, 183,
  195, 203, 204, 224, 225, 341,
  375–376, 393–396, 399, 405,
  407–408, 416, 420–421, 430
Ambadar, Z., 146

Ambady, N., 106, 145, 147, 148,
  150, 231
American Society of Plastic
  Surgeons, 86
Ames, D. R., 109, 110
Anders, S. L., 161
Andersen, P. A., 321
Andersen, S. M., 124
Anderson, D. B., 101, 327
Anderson, J. R., 193–194
Anderson, K. G., 289, 316
Anderson, K. J., 204
Anderson, M., 160, 193–194
Anderson, S. L., 87
Anderson, V. T., 37, 123
Andrews, P. W., 316
Andrzejewski, S. A., 135, 155
Angera, J. J., 136
Angulo, S. K., 165
Apostolou, M., 264
Archer, J., 74, 76, 381, 382, 385
Archer, R. L., 157
Argyle, M., 220
Ariely, D., 75, 88, 90, 293
Armstrong, C., 158
Aron, A., 3, 34, 61, 100, 113, 189,
  190, 249–252, 256, 258, 263,
  267, 269–271, 339, 430
Aron, E. N., 3, 190, 258
Arons, S., 79
Aronson, E., 90–91
Arriaga, X. B., 114, 175,
  205–206, 208, 378, 403
Arroyo, A., 232, 236
Asch, S. E., 108
Asendorpf, J. P., 28, 87, 135,
  233
Ash, J., 32
Asher, T., 121
Askari, S. F., 181, 368
Assad, K. K., 123
Atkins, D. C., 430
Atkins, L., 289
Atkinson, K., 292
Ault, L. K., 194
Aune, K. S., 190
Averill, J. R., 184
Axelson, S. J., 181
Axelton, A. M., 278

Ayduk, O. N., 36, 123
Ayres, M. M., 162

Baccus, J. R., 19, 88
Bach, G., 359–360
Bachman, G. F., 430
Bachman, J. G., 9, 333
Back, K. W., 41, 72
Back, M. D., 71, 128–129, 163
Badad, E., 147
Baehne, C. G., 146
Bailenson, J. N., 153
Bakeman, R., 159
Baker, L. R., 12, 233
Balchen, S., 89
Baldinger, A., 72
Baldwin, M. W., 19, 88, 125
Bale, C., 91
Balmer, R., 279
Balsam, K. F., 29, 276, 393
Bank, B. J., 229
Banks, K. H., 23
Bar, M., 106
Barbee, A. P., 77, 81, 152, 194
Barber, B. L., 293
Barber, J. P., 441
Barber, L. L., 187
Barber, N., 394, 407, 420
Barkin, A., 5
Barnes, R. D., 25
Barrett, A. E., 412
Barrett, L. F., 156, 158
Barry, R. A, 215
Barsade, S. G., 136
Bartell, D. S., 397, 407
Bartholomew, K., 15, 16
Bartz, J. A., 205
Baruch, A. T., 340
Basile, K. C., 381
Basow, S. A., 290
Bastian, B., 310
Battaglia, D. M., 410–411
Baucom, B. R., 349, 350
Baucom, D. H., 299, 436–438,
  441
Baucom, T. R., 315
Baumeister, R. F., 4, 6, 28, 171,
  184–185, 256, 269, 281, 290,
  307, 310, 345

Baxter, L. A., 37, 100, 160, 305, 329, 338, 339, 405, 409–410
Beach, S. R. H., 73–74, 99, 188, 333, 338, 357
Beal, D. J., 129
Beattie, G., 146
Beauchaine, T. P., 29, 276
Beck, F. D., 274
Beck, L. A., 197–198, 200, 205
Becker, D. V., 320
Becker, O. A., 98
Beckett, L. A., 226
Bélisle, J., 129
Bell, K. L., 324
Bellavia, G., 30–31
Bem, S. L., 23, 24, 239
Ben-Ari, A., 2, 194
Bennett, J. B., 181
Benson, A., 160
Bente, G., 147
Beougher, S. C., 284
Berant, E., 18
Berdahl, J. L., 26
Berenson, K., 123, 124
Berg, J. H., 157, 184
Berkenau, P., 135
Berkman, L. F., 5
Berman, J. S., 181
Bernhardt, E., 9
Bernieri, F., 134, 147
Bernstein, S., 202
Bernstein, W. M., 89
Berry, D. S., 99
Berscheid, E., 2, 76, 122, 183, 213, 251, 260–261
Besculides, M., 4
Bessel, D. R., 395, 407
Besser, A., 309
Bhullar, N., 27
Biblarz, T. J., 276
Biek, M., 152
Bieneck, S., 301
Biesanz, J. C., 121, 134
Birchler, G. R., 184
Birditt, K. S., 44, 346, 404
Birmingham, W. A., 148
Birnbaum, G. E., 290, 299
Birnie, C. J., 19
Bishop, P. J., 81
Bisson, M. A., 228
Bissonnette, V. L., 134
Blackhart, G. C., 429
Blais, R. K., 184
Blakemore, J. E. O., 256
Blanchard, V. L., 436
Blanch-Hartigan, D., 155
Blascovich, J. J., 55, 147, 225
Blehar, M. C., 14
Blekesaune, M., 417

Bleske, A. L., 315
Blickstein, I., 289
Blow, A. J., 283
Blozis, S. A., 81
Blumstein, P., 29, 282, 284–285, 296, 393
Bodenmann, G., 183, 260, 300, 400, 406, 408
Bodur, H. O., 129
Boerner, K., 169, 217
Bogaert, A. F., 299
Bogg, T., 27, 28, 65
Bohns, V. K., 216
Bolger, N., 109, 169, 217
Bond, C. F., Jr., 327
Bono, G., 334, 430
Boomsma, D. L., 238
Boon, S. D., 328
Booth, A., 9, 11, 183, 399, 404, 406
Booth-Butterfield, N., 160
Boothroyd, L. G., 101, 286–287
Boren, J. P., 148
Bornstein, R. F., 73
Bosco, J. S., 136
Bosson, J. K., 26, 28, 91, 178, 386
Bouchard, G., 368
Bouchard, T. J., Jr., 28, 33
Bowlby, J., 14
Boyd, C. H., 81
Boyes, A. D., 113
Boynton, M., 81
Brackett, M. A., 136
Bradbury, T. N., 9, 40, 47, 63, 116, 173, 193–194, 215, 387, 399, 400, 408
Bradford, S. A., 161
Bradney, N., 213
Bradshaw, S. D., 233, 293
Brady, S. E., 369
Braithwaite, S. R., 435
Brand, R., 289
Brandt, A. C., 149
Branje, S., 97, 158
Brase, G. L., 30, 94
Brashears, M. E., 231
Brassard, A., 299
Bratslavsky, E., 269
Bratton, J. L., 96
Braun, V., 295
Braver, S. L., 418, 420
Brehm, J. W., 100
Brehm, S. S., 100
Bremner, G., 77, 82
Brennan, K. A., 58, 96
Brescoll, V. I., 367
Brewer, G., 74, 76, 129, 324
Bridges, A. J., 288

Bridgstock, R., 78
Bringle, R. G., 313
Brinton, S., 94–95
Broady, E. F., 401
Brock, K. F., 263
Brock, R. L., 215, 217
Brody, L. R., 152, 153, 266
Broemer, P., 209
Broughton, R., 267
Brown, C. E., 146
Brown, E., 44, 53, 63, 77, 82, 407
Brown, J., 134
Brown, J. D., 147, 288
Brown, J. L., 58, 215
Brown, L., 270
Brown, N. R., 283
Browne, M. W., 236
Brownridge, D. A., 385
Bruce, J. W., 71
Brumbaugh, C. C., 124, 137
Brunell, A. B., 128, 158
Brunet, P. M., 163, 235
Brunson, J., 9
Bryant, A. N., 26, 375
Bryant, C. M., 18, 27, 404, 406
Buck, D. M., 158
Buckley, K. E., 307–309
Buckwalter, J. G., 98
Buhrmester, D., 221, 223
Bukowski, W. M., 221
Buller, D. B., 323
Bunde, M., 215
Burch, R. L., 289
Burdette, M. P., 3, 328, 329–331
Burger, J. M., 292
Burgoon, J. K., 323, 325, 326, 370–371
Burke, C. T., 169
Burkey, M., 81
Burleson, B. R., 155, 166, 300, 349, 350
Burnaford, R. M., 26
Burnette, J. L., 333
Burns, G. L., 87
Burns, L., 292
Burriss, R. P., 101, 150
Bursik, K., 120
Burt, D. M., 88, 101
Burt, M., 78
Busboom, A. L., 240
Busby, D. M., 355
Bush, A. L., 118
Buss, A. H., 232
Buss, D. M., 32–34, 71, 83, 84, 86, 89, 94, 95, 228, 264, 266, 280, 281, 312–314, 316–320, 322, 341, 343, 380–382, 415
Butts, A. M., 145
Butzer, B., 299

Buunk, A. P., 315
Buunk, B. P., 82, 101, 115, 202, 203, 246, 264, 313, 315, 427
Buysse, A., 216
Byers, E. S., 297–298
Byrne, D., 41, 51, 70, 92–93

Cable, D. M., 80
Cacioppo, J. T., 225, 236, 238, 240–241
Call, V., 269, 270, 281
Callan, M., 144
Cameron, J. J., 89, 123, 142–143, 325, 331
Cameron, K. A., 280
Campbell, A., 61
Campbell, J., 388
Campbell, L., 65, 177, 265, 286, 299, 340, 351
Campbell, S., 126
Campbell, W. K., 11, 115, 128, 176, 443
Canary, D. J., 22, 201, 202, 266, 337, 344, 346, 351, 358, 431, 433
Canevello, A., 219
Cann, A., 315
Cao, G., 249
Capezza, N., 119, 378
Caprariello, P. A., 32
Carey, B., 60
Carey, M. P., 293
Carli, L. L., 367
Carlsmith, K. M., 331
Carlson, E. N., 135
Carlström, E., 276, 277
Carmichael, C. L., 32, 113, 185
Carnelley, K. B., 120, 169, 205, 264, 416
Carnevale, P. J. D., 87
Carney, D. R., 106, 147, 370
Carothers, B. J., 375
Carpenter, J., 231
Carrère, S., 168, 203
Carrington, P. I., 87
Carstensen, L. F., 224, 225
Carstensen, L. L., 224, 225, 266
Carter, S., 98
Carter, S. C., 5, 260
Carter, S. J., 136
Carter, T., 142
Cartun, M. A., 113
Carvallo, M., 71, 92
Carver, C. S., 123
Carver, V. H., 130
Caryl, P. G., 91
Cascio, E. V., 158
Casillas, A., 99
Caspi, A., 27, 36, 65

Cassidy, J., 15, 57, 120, 161
Castellani, A. M., 158
Castro, F. N., 102
Catanese, K. R., 29
Cate, R. M., 202, 208
Catlett, J., 37
Caughlin, J. P., 25, 158, 184, 194, 350, 401
Caulkins, R. J., 101
Ceglian, C. P., 408
Centers for Disease Control and Prevention, 378
Chambers, J. R., 135
Chamorro-Premuzic, T., 269, 270
Chang-Schneider, C., 128, 389
Chantala, K., 23
Chaplin, W. F., 147
Charles, S. T., 224, 225
Chartrand, T. L., 76, 124, 152
Chatterjee, N., 250
Cheek, J. M., 232
Chen, E., 420
Chen, G. M., 164
Chen, H., 241, 263, 340, 377
Chen, S., 124
Cheng, C., 24
Cheng, C. M., 76
Cherlin, A. J., 7–9, 11, 64, 183
Chipperfield, J. G., 241
Chlebowsky, N., 233
Choi, N., 24
Chopik, W. J., 19
Chorost, A. F., 267
Christakis, N. A., 5, 61, 92, 228
Christensen, A., 349, 437–438
Christofides, E., 163
Chuikova, T., 102
Churchill, A. C., 196
Ciani, A. C., 277
Ciarrochi, J., 155, 178, 274, 371
Cillessen, A. H. N., 97, 134, 221
Civic, D., 291
Claffey, S. T., 203
Clanton, N. R., 147
Clark, A. P., 286
Clark, C. L., 58, 374
Clark, E. M., 263, 432
Clark, J. K., 134
Clark, L., 94–95
Clark, M. S., 2, 3, 76, 130, 197–200, 203, 205, 219
Clark, R. D., III, 46–48
Clarke, A. L., 150
Clarkwest, A., 408
Claxton, A., 195
Cleveland, H. H., 23
Clifton, R. A., 241
Clore, G. L., 70
Cloven, D. H., 339, 357

Coan, J. C., 4–5
Cobb, R. J., 19
Cody, M. J., 75, 152, 155
Cohen, D., 26, 118
Cohen, O., 290
Cohen, S., 5, 348, 416
Cohn, D., 367–368, 392
Cohn, E. S., 301
Cohn, J. F., 146
Cole, J. D., 134
Cole, T., 324
Cole, V., 19
Coleman, M., 392
Collins, N., 55
Collins, N. L., 120, 160, 216–218, 264, 310
Collins, W. A., 339
Coltrane, S., 203
Colvin, C. R., 106
Confer, J. C., 32, 33
Conger, R. D., 18, 27, 123
Conley, J. J., 28
Conley, T. D., 112, 274, 427
Connell, J. B., 114
Connelly, B. S., 134
Conner, B., 148
Constantinides, A., 79
Conway, C. A., 24, 84
Coontz, S., 394
Cooper, A., 288
Cooper, L., 62–63
Cooper, M., 91
Cooper, M. L., 66, 187, 293, 297
Cooper, S. M., 23
Copas, A. J., 280
Cope, V., 90–91
Cordova, A. G., 136
Cornelius, T. L., 358
Coss, R. G., 81
Costa, P. T., Jr., 27
Couch, L. L., 328–329
Cousins, A. J., 278
Cowan, G., 386
Coyne, J. C., 5
Coyne, S. M., 384
Crabtree, C. R., 81
Cranford, J. A., 5
Crary, D., 295
Crawford, M., 274
Crittenden, N., 155
Crocker, J., 28, 219
Cronk, L., 287
Cronkite, R. C., 215
Cross, S. E., 230, 351
Crouch, L. L., 3
Crouter, A. C., 25, 99
Crown, L., 302
Cuddy, A. J. C., 147
Cui, M., 18, 397

Cummings, E. M., 167
Cummins, R., 236
Cunningham, J. D., 19
Cunningham, M. R., 77, 81, 87, 91, 152, 194, 343
Cunradi, C. B., 386
Cupach, W. R., 24, 37, 342, 381
Cuperman, R., 93
Curtis, R. C., 90, 122
Custer, L., 413
Cutrona, C. E., 238, 241

Dabbs, J. M., Jr., 157
Daigen, V., 167
Dailey, R. M., 412–413
Dainton, M., 195
Dal Cin, S., 338
Daly, J. A., 132
Daneback, K., 288
Darley, J. M., 108–109
Davidson, J. K., 279
Davidson, R. J., 4–5
Davies, A. P. C., 317
Davies, M. S., 251
Davila, J., 19, 216
Davis, D., 264, 299
Davis, G. G., 196
Davis, K. E., 222, 381
Davis, K. W., 100
Davis, M., 128
Davis, P., 158
Davis, S. N., 203
Dawes, R. M., 185
Dean, G. O., 91
DeAndrea, D. C., 75, 164, 231
de Araujo Lopes, F., 102
Deaux, K., 23
De Bro, S. C., 373
DeBruine, L. M., 24, 84
Deci, E. L., 296
de Graaf, H., 280
DeGue, S., 300–301
De Jonge, C. R., 163
de Jong Gierveld, J., 236
DeLamater, J. D., 279
de la Mora, A., 238
Delaney, H. J., 101
De La Ronde, C., 127, 137
DeLillo, D., 300–301
della Cava, M. R., 231
Della Salla, S., 117
Denissen, J. J. A., 30, 97
Dennis, M. R., 193
Denrell, J., 106
Denton, W. H., 349, 350
DePaoli, J., 128
DePaulo, B. M., 15, 305, 323–326
Derlega, V. J., 155, 157, 158
Dermer, M., 250
Derous, E., 130

Derrick, J. L., 196
Desmond, M., 420
DeSteno, D. A., 312–314, 318
de Varela, Y., 439
de Visser, R. O., 302
De Vogli, R., 348
de Vries, K. M., 278
DeWall, C. N., 309–311
de Witte, K ., 130
Dewsbury, D. A., 269
Dhavale, D., 307
Diamond, L. M., 29, 61, 249–250
Dicke, A., 56
Diehl, M., 209
Diekman, A. B., 35
Diener, E., 5
Dijkstra, P., 101, 315
Dillow, M. R., 160
Dillworth, D., 101
Dindia, K., 22, 148, 157, 164, 320
Dion, K. K., 76
DiPaola, B. M., 351
Ditzen, B., 260
Dixson, A. F., 79, 81
Dixson, B. J., 79, 81
Dodge, B., 281
Dodge, K. A., 134
Dogruyol, B., 18
Doherty, W. J., 193
Dolan, C. V., 238
Donaghue, N., 202
Donahue, D., 434
Donnellan, M. B., 27, 47, 123
D'Onofrio, B. M., 420
Donovan-Kicken, E., 192
Dooley, T., 11
Doss, B. D., 9, 158, 195, 442
Doumas, D. M., 384
Douvan, E., 63
Dove, N. L., 184, 207
Dovidio, J. F., 143, 146
Downey, G., 37, 123, 185
Downs, A. C., 77
Downs, D. L., 132
Drigotas, S. M., 207
Driscoll, R., 100
Druen, P. B., 77, 81, 87
Drumm, P., 256
Duck, S., 410
Dunbar, N. E., 370–371
Dunbar, R., 129
Dunbar, R. J. M., 222
Dunham, B., 287
Dunleavy, K. N., 160
Dunn, M. J., 94–95
Duntley, J. D., 380–382
Dush, C. M. K., 6
Dutton, D. G., 251
Dweck, S., 91, 344
Dworkin, S. L., 297

Dyer, M. A., 101
Dykstra, P. A., 236, 240

Eagly, E. A., 23, 35, 95, 267, 432
Eaker, E. D., 357
Easton, J. A., 32, 33
Eastwick, P. W., 35, 42, 57, 86, 90, 96, 219, 315, 414
Ebbesen, E. B., 74
Ebel-Lam, A. P., 293
Eberhart, N. K., 6, 240
Eccles, J., 28, 123
Eckhardt, C. I., 377, 382, 386
Eddings, S. K., 128
Edelmann, R. J., 235
Edelstein, R. S., 19, 137
Edlund, J. E., 89, 319
Edwards, G. L., 293
Edwards, K. M., 177, 388
Edwards, R., 240
Egloff, B., 71, 128–129, 163
Ehlert, U., 260
Ehrenberg, M., 415
Eidelson, R. J., 118, 191, 357
Eisele, H., 26
Eisenberg, A. R., 339
Eisenberger, N. I., 5, 331
Eisikovits, Z., 299
Ekman, P., 326, 327
Elder, G. H., 18
Eldridge, K. A., 349
Elfenbein, H. A., 145
Elizur, Y., 159
Elliot, A. J., 81, 115
Elliott, S., 343
Ellis, A., 433
Ellis, B. J., 89, 177
Ellison, P. T., 82
Ellsworth, P. C., 30, 95
Ellyson, S. L., 146
Elsayegh, N., 204
Else-Quest, N. M., 279
Elwert, F., 5
Emerson, T., 89
Emery, B. C., 387
Emery, R. E., 414–415
Emmers, T. M., 148
Emmers-Sommer, T. M., 22, 266
Emmons, R. A., 128
Enke, A., 91
Enosh, G., 299
Epley, N., 135, 142, 189, 226
Epstein, N., 118, 357, 437
Erbert, L. A., 338, 339
Erchull, M. J., 181
Erens, B., 280
Erikson, E., 222
Ervin, C. E., 92
Esber, R., 256
Escoto, C., 278

Eshbaugh, E. M., 57, 283
Eskridge, W. N., Jr., 277
Essayli, J. H., 332
Etcheverry, P. E., 111, 208
Evans, D. A., 226
Exline, J. J., 61, 333

Fagnani, C., 18
Fagundes, C. P., 61, 88
Fairchild, K., 204
Falbo, T., 372, 374
Fallon, B. J., 202
Farina, A., 87
Farinelli, L., 201
Farley, S. D., 150, 370
Farris, C., 152, 298, 299
Farvid, P., 295
Fast, N. J., 368
Feeney, B. C., 57, 120, 205, 215,
    216, 218, 299, 309, 331
Fehr, B., 92, 189, 213–214, 220,
    222–224, 227, 228, 250, 256,
    260–261, 265, 267, 271, 333,
    339
Fein, E., 434
Feingold, A., 87
Feldman, R., 260
Feldman, R. S., 325
Feliciano, C., 85
Felmlee, D. H., 97, 102
Feng, T., 249, 251
Fenigstein, A., 283
Fenton, K. A., 280
Fenton-Voak, I. S., 260
Ferguson, M. J., 76
Ferguson-Isaac, C., 331
Fergusson, D. M., 378
Ferrara, M. H., 333
Festinger, L., 41, 72
Fetchenhauer, D., 101
Fielder, R. L., 293
Figueredo, A. J., 98
Finch, E., 381
Fincham, F. D., 115, 188, 228,
    333, 338, 344, 357, 397, 435
Fine, M. A., 413, 422
Finer, L. B., 278
Fingerhut, A., 29
Fingerman, K. L., 4, 225
Fink, B., 78, 83, 147
Finkel, E. J., 42, 57, 86, 90, 97,
    124, 315, 377, 382–383, 385,
    386, 428–429
Finkenauer, C., 133, 158
Firestone, R. W., 37
Firth, L., 236
Fischer, A. H., 145
Fischer, G., 292
Fischer, T. F. C., 240
Fischhoff, B., 292

Fishbein, S., 253
Fisher, H., 250, 267, 270
Fisher, H. E., 34
Fisher, M. L., 13, 79
Fisher, T. D., 283, 296
Fiske, S. T., 45, 257
Fitch, C. A., 364, 395, 407
Fitness, J., 328
Fitzgerald, C. J., 13, 102
Fitzpatrick, M. A., 154
Fitzsimons, G. M., 3, 124, 427
Flannagan, D., 213, 214
Fleischman, D. S., 32, 33, 264
Fleischmann, A. A., 322
Fletcher, G. J. O., 4, 23, 101, 102,
    112, 113, 126, 332
Flinn, M., 32
Florian, V., 220
Floyd, F. J., 159
Floyd, K., 148, 161, 166, 260
Flynn, F. K., 216
Foa, U. G., 367
Fokkema, T., 240
Follette, W. C., 200
Fong, G., 293
Ford, M. B., 216, 310
Ford, T. E., 198
Forest, A. L., 30
Forrest, J. A., 325
Forsyth, D. R., 113
Fortenberry, J. D., 281, 295
Foster, C. A., 128, 443
Foster, J. B., 143
Foster, J. D., 128, 317
Fowers, B. J., 414
Fowler, K. A., 386
Fox, A. B., 162
Fraley, R. C., 17, 19, 41, 124, 137,
    222, 274
Francesconi, M., 86
Franco, N., 37
Franiuk, R., 118, 119
Frankenhuis, W. E., 79
Franklin, M., 81
Frederick, D. A., 80, 101, 319
Freeman, B., 81
Freeman, J. B., 106
Frei, J. R., 214
French, J. R. P., Jr., 365
Friesen, M. D., 332, 333
Frieze, I. H., 57, 62, 258–259, 371,
    381, 386
Frost, J. H., 75
Fry, R., 367
Frye, N. E., 54, 117
Fugelstad, P. T., 131
Fugère, M. A., 278
Fuhrman, R. W., 213, 214, 228
Fujita, K., 217
Funder, D. C., 99

Fung, H. H., 224, 225
Fuqua, D. R., 24
Furman, W., 221
Furnham, A., 79
Furr, R. M., 135

Gable, S. L., 185, 187–188, 190,
    214–215, 218
Gabriel, B., 260
Gaddis, S., 129
Gaertner, L., 98
Gaetz, R., 89
Gagné, F. M., 112
Gagnon, J. H., 290
Gaines, S. O., Jr., 118, 353
Galinsky, A. D., 369
Gallup, G. G., Jr., 32, 80, 150,
    287
Galperin, A., 274
Galupo, M. P., 230
Galyautdinova, S., 102
Gambrill, E., 220
Gangestad, S. W., 34, 81–84, 94,
    133, 152, 285–287
Ganong, L. H., 117, 119
Gano-Phillips, S., 115
Gao, X., 263
Garcia, L. T., 300
Gardner, S., 408
Gardner, W. L., 376
Garris, C. P., 106
Garver-Apgar, C. E., 83, 287
Gassanov, M. A., 300
Gaucher, D., 30, 123
Gaulin, S. J. C., 80, 82
Gaunt, R., 93, 99
Gayle, B. M., 349
Geary, D. C., 33
Gephart, J. M., 434
Gerressu, M., 289
Giancola, P. R., 293
Gibson-Davis, C. M., 63–64
Gidycz, C. A., 302
Gifford, S., 233
Gilbert, D. T., 415
Gildersleeve, K., 81
Gill, M. J., 110, 132
Gill, S., 148
Gillath, O., 137, 325
Gillmore, M. R., 283
Gillum, J., 11
Gilovich, T., 114
Giordano, P. C., 213, 384
Givertz, M., 208
Gladue, B. A., 101
Glaser, R., 260
Glass, S. P., 430
Glass, T. A., 5, 226
Glasser, C. L., 85
Gleason, M. E. J., 217

Glenn, N. D., 11, 183, 407
Godbout, N., 384
Goel, S., 97
Goesling, B., 4
Goetz, A. T., 287
Goetz, C. D., 32, 33
Gohm, C. L., 5
Gold, M. S., 112
Goldberg, L. R., 27, 65
Goldman, B. M., 158
Gonsalkorale, K., 312
Gonso, J., 141–142
Gonzaga, G. C., 98, 251, 258, 274
Gonzales, J. E., 84
Gonzales, M. H., 334
Gonzalez, M., 61, 92
Goodfriend, W., 3, 178
Goodwin, P. Y., 392, 417
Goodwin, R., 118
Goodwin, S. A., 257
Gordon, A. K., 325
Gordon, A. M., 199, 209, 428
Gordon, C. L., 432
Gore, J. S., 351
Gormley, B., 384–385
Gosling, S. D., 46, 129
Gott, M., 300
Gottman, J. M., 44, 62, 141–142,
    166–168, 171, 172, 185, 186,
    203, 348, 351, 353, 357, 358,
    403, 406, 408, 435
Gottman, R. M., 266
Gouin, J., 5, 260, 348
Gover, A. R., 385, 386
Grace, A., 351
Graczyk, P. A., 221
Graham, C. A., 290
Graham, J. M., 190, 262
Graham, K., 385
Grammer, K., 78, 83, 152
Gramzow, R. H., 81
Graupmann, V., 256
Gray, J., 20, 434
Graziano, W. G., 71, 102, 340
Green, B. L., 26
Green, M. C., 320
Green, M. K., 231
Greenberg, A., 76
Greenberg, M. A., 413
Greene, J. O., 155
Greene, K., 155, 157
Greenstein, I. N., 203
Greiling, H., 34, 317
Greitemeyer, T., 81, 89
Grello, C. M., 291
Greven, C., 79
Grich, J., 205
Griffin, D. W., 30–32, 113
Griffit, W., 92

Grimshaw, G. M., 79, 81
Griskevicius, V., 6, 129
Gross, P. H., 108–109
Grote, N. K., 57, 198, 200, 203,
    258–259
Guberman, C., 292
Guéguen, N., 84
Guerrero, L. K., 150, 201, 312,
    313, 315, 320–321, 333, 430
Guichard, A. C., 216
Günaydin, G., 18
Guo, C., 263
Gupta, U., 267
Gurung, R. A. R., 27
Gustavsson, L., 94
Gute, G., 57, 283
Guthrie, M. F., 214
Gutiérrez, R., 82
Guttentag, M., 13–14
Guy, E. C., 30, 94

Haden, S. C., 331
Haerich, P., 278
Hagen, E. H., 382
Haig, J., 99
Haines, E. L., 23
Halatsis, P., 228
Hald, G. M., 48
Halford, W. K., 116, 120, 435
Hall, E. T., 148
Hall, J. A., 75, 106, 134, 135, 152,
    153, 155, 266, 370–371
Hall, J. K., 75, 155
Hallahan, M., 148
Hambaugh, J., 162
Hamermesh, D. S., 76
Hammen, C. L., 6, 240
Hammock, G., 202
Hampel A. D., 204, 329
Hampson, E., 155
Hancock, J. T., 327
Hannawa, A. F., 148
Hannett, C. A., 285
Hannon, P. A., 333
Hannover, B., 149
Hansel, C. A., 145
Hansen, G. L., 314, 315
Hansford, S. L., 229
Hanson, T. L., 417–418
Hanzal, A., 208
Harasymchuk, C., 189, 271, 339
Hardie, J. H., 63
Harinck, F., 351
Harkless, L. E., 414
Harknett, K., 13
Harma, M., 18
Harms, P. D., 28
Harold, G. T., 115
Harper, M. S., 291

Harris, C. R., 318
Harris, D. W., 65
Harris, M. J., 106
Hartnett, K., 283
Harvey, J. H., 291, 413, 422
Harway, M., 440
Harwood, J., 232, 236
Harwood, K., 78
Haselton, M. G., 81, 84, 101, 251,
    287, 298, 316, 324
Hashimoto, T., 263
Haslam, N., 310
Hassebrauck, M., 84
Hatchett, S., 63
Hatfield, E., 46–48, 200, 201, 244,
    246, 254, 263, 266
Haub, C., 7
Hawkins, A. J., 436
Hawkins, L. B., 131
Hawkley, L. C., 236, 238, 240, 241
Hayashi, Y., 236
Hayes, R., 77, 82
Haynes, O. M., 155
Hazan, C., 14, 18, 222
Hearns, K. A., 26
Heaton, T. B., 407
Heaven, P. C. L., 178, 274, 339
Hebl, M. R., 143
Hecht, M. L., 2, 270
Heffner, K. L., 348
Heider, F., 90
Heilman, M. E., 26
Heiman, J. R., 294, 296
Heine, S. J., 46
Heinrichs, M., 260
Hellmuth, J. C., 384–385
Helms, H. M., 25, 99, 376
Henderson, C. E., 422
Henderson, J., 4
Henderson, L., 234
Henderson, M., 220
Henderson, M. C., 353
Hendrick, B., 278
Hendrick, C., 56, 214, 259, 263
Hendrick, S. S., 56, 160–161, 166,
    214, 259, 263
Hendrie, C. A., 129, 324
Henline, B. H., 288
Henly, A. S., 142
Henning, K., 289
Henrich, J., 46
Henry, R., 397
Henton, J. M., 202
Heppner, W., 158
Herbenick, D., 281, 296
Herbst, K. C., 98
Herek, G. M., 29, 276
Herold, A. L., 370
Herrington, R. L., 158

Hershberger, S., 23
Hertenstein, M. J., 145, 148
Herz, R. S., 80
Hess, N. H., 382
Hesse, C., 148
Hetherington, E. M., 417
Heyman, R. E., 189
Higgins, J. A., 279, 280
Hile, S. N., 145
Hill, C. A., 256
Hill, K. M., 155
Hill, R., 181, 363
Hill, S. E., 315, 322, 331
Hill, W. L., 260
Hinchliff, S., 300
Hines, D., 293, 302
Hinsz, V. B., 82
Hira, S. N., 429
Hitsch, G. J., 80, 86, 88, 92, 94, 129
Hixson, J. G., 127
Hodges, S., 289
Hoff, C. C., 284
Hogg, F., 132
Høgh-Olesen, H., 48
Hohmann-Marriott, B., 9, 11, 99, 416
Hojjat, M., 331
Holahan, C. J., 215
Holland, R. W., 149
Hollems, D., 240
Holler, J., 146
Holleran, S. E., 164
Holley, S. R., 350
Holloway, A., 131, 219
Holman, T. B., 18, 354–355
Holmberg, D., 300
Holmes, J. G., 2, 3, 30–32, 112, 113, 123, 143, 167, 196, 203, 214, 293
Holmes, R., 145
Holt-Lunstad, J., 148
Holtzworth-Munroe, A., 155, 386
Home, S. G., 277
Honeycutt, J. M., 40
Hong, J., 88
Hood, K. B., 293
Hoppe, M. J., 283
Hopper, C. H., 157
Horan, S. M., 161
Horowitz, A., 217
Hortaçsu, A., 88
Horton, R. S., 97, 100
Houts, C., 5, 341, 358
Howard, E. S., 377
Howard, J. W., 185
Howard, M. D., 288
Howes, C., 221
Howland, M., 217

Hoyt, T., 301, 302
Hrebicková, M., 135
Hsueh, A. C., 9
Hubbard, J. A., 134
Hugenberg, K., 146
Hughes, S. M., 80, 150
Hugill, N., 147
Hui, B., 199
Human, L. J., 134
Humrichouse, J., 113
Hunt, M. M., 245
Hunter, S., 159
Hunt-Martorano, A. N., 189
Hurst, C., 76
Huston, T. L., 25, 100, 113, 224, 267, 341, 362, 401, 403
Hutton, S. B., 75, 155
Hyde, J. S., 21–22, 24, 274, 279
Hynes, K., 155

IBP Project Members, 80
Ickes, W., 25, 43, 65, 86, 93, 134, 136, 216, 232–233
Iemmola, F., 277
Igarashi, T., 12
Iida, M., 217, 218
Imamoglu, E. O., 195
Imhof, M., 148
Impett, E. A., 190, 199, 209, 294, 297, 299, 366, 428
Insko, C. A., 98
International Sexuality Description Project, 48
Inzlicht, M., 80
Iredale, M. E., 129
Ireland, M. E., 164
Isaacowitz, D. M., 224
Ivcevic, Z., 231
Ivey, M., 91
Iyengar, S. S., 86

Jackson, J. J., 28
Jackson, T., 263
Jacobson, N. S., 200, 437
Jacques-Tiura, A. J., 298, 299
Jalovaara, M., 407
Jaremka, L. M., 216
Jarry, J. L., 129
Jarvis, B., 311
Jarvis, M. O., 354
Jasienska, B., 82
Jayson, S., 7, 204, 402
Jemmott, J. B., 279
Jenkins, J. M., 251
Jenkins, N., 429
Jensen-Campbell, L. A., 102, 340, 385
Jessop, T. S., 79
Jöchle, W., 83

Joel, S., 4
John, O. P., 46
Johnson, A. E., 91
Johnson, A. M., 290
Johnson, B. T., 294
Johnson, D. R., 9, 11, 183
Johnson, K. L., 106, 148
Johnson, L. D., 9
Johnson, M., 198, 207
Johnson, M. D., 215
Johnson, M. P., 100, 224, 378–380, 382, 386
Johnson, S. M., 438–440
Johnson, S. P., 77, 81
Johnson, V., 298
Johnson, W., 28
Johnsson, J. L., 94
Joiner, T. E., Jr., 240
Jokela, M., 83
Jonason, P. K., 274, 317
Jones, B. C., 24, 84, 101
Jones, D., 77, 81
Jones, D. J., 99
Jones, D. N., 98
Jones, E. E., 130
Jones, J. M., 276, 430
Jones, J. T., 19, 71, 92
Jones, W. H., 3, 328–331
Jordan, B. D., 84
Jose, A., 9, 397, 407
Joseph, A., 349
Joseph, J. L., 158
Joyner, L., 296
Judge, T. A., 76, 80
Judice, T. A., 121
Jungeberg, B. J., 84
Jussim, L., 123

Kachadourian, L. K., 333
Kafetsios, K., 265
Kahneman, D., 184
Kaighobadi, F., 287, 380
Kalbfleisch, P. J., 370
Kalso, M., 136
Kambe, G., 60
Kammrath, L. K., 109, 110, 329, 344, 433
Kamphuis, J. H., 381
Kanazawa, S., 35
Kane, H., 55
Kane, H. S., 216
Kang, N. J., 123
Kanner, M., 204
Kantor, L. M., 279
Kaplan, R. M., 15
Kaplar, M. E., 325
Karney, B. R., 47, 54, 63, 88, 112, 116, 117, 122, 125, 194, 261, 399, 400, 408, 427

Karnieli-Miller, O., 299
Karremans, J. C., 79
Kashdan, T. B., 100
Kashy, D. A., 65, 216, 265, 324–325
Kath, J., 30
Katz, J., 301
Katz, S., 270
Kaufman, J., 61, 92
Kaul, M., 217
Kavanagh, P. S., 89
Kay, A. C., 3, 427
Kayser, D. N., 81
Kayser, K., 402
Keating, C. F., 129
Keelan, J. P. R., 125
Kellas, J. K., 412–414
Kellerman, J., 146
Kelley, D. K., 332
Kelley, H. H., 114, 175, 178, 196, 363
Kelly, E. L., 28
Kelly, K. M., 320, 321
Keltner, D., 145, 150, 199, 251, 368, 370
Kemp, B., 15
Kemper, D., 101
Kennedy, K. A., 344
Kenny, D. A., 65, 134, 240
Kenrick, D. T., 6, 26, 33, 34, 101, 129, 266
Kephart, W., 244
Kerkhof, P., 158
Kernis, M. H., 158
Kessler, R. C., 17, 184
Keysar, B., 142
Khaleque, A., 18
Kiecolt-Glaser, J. K., 5, 260, 349, 408
Kiefer, A. K., 296
Kilpatrick, S. D., 128, 134
Kim, H. K., 5
Kim, Y., 76, 348
Kimmel, A. J., 62
King, B. M., 294
King, R. B., 96
Kirby, D. B., 279
Kite, M. E., 23
Kjos, G. L., 74
Klapper, B., 295
Kleinke, C. L., 91, 146
Kline, S. L., 220, 263
Klohnen, E. C., 98, 99
Klusmann, D., 269, 289
Klute, M. M., 25, 99
Kluwer, E. S., 344
Knapp-Kline, K., 81
Knauper, B., 292
Knee, C. R., 118, 119, 158
Knobloch, L. K., 191–192, 314

Knoester, C., 399
Knöfler, T., 148
Knudson-Martin, C., 204
Kobak, R., 222
Koball, H. L., 4
Koch, E. J., 30
Koch, S. C., 146
Koeppel, L. B., 152
Koerner, A. F., 154
Koernez, A., 116
Kogan, A., 199
Konecni, V. J., 74
Konrad, A. M., 26
Koob, J. J., 280
Korn, M. S., 184, 207
Kornik, R., 292
Kouros, C., 167
Kouzakova, M., 153
Kowalski, R. M., 195, 232
Kozak, C., 95
Krahé, B., 301
Kraus, M. W., 124
Kraut, R. E., 147, 327
Kronick, R. G., 15
Kropp, J. P., 155
Krueger, R. F., 28, 41
Kruger, D. J., 13, 94, 102, 290, 313, 363
Kruger, J., 114, 163
Kruger, M. L., 145
Kruse, L., 146, 320
Kubacka, K. E., 158
Kuhle, B. X., 320
Kuijer, R. G., 203
Kumashiro, M., 338
Kuncel, N. R., 27, 65
Kunkel, A., 193, 295
Kunstman, J. W., 369
Kunz, P. R., 179
Kuppens, P., 135
Kurdek, L. A., 29, 193, 207, 208, 226, 403
Kurtz, J. E., 99
Kurzban, R., 85
Kusche, A. G., 30
Kwan, V. S. Y., 114
Kwang, T., 125
Lachance-Grzela, M., 368
Lackenbauer, S. D., 126
LaFlam, J., 231
Laird, J. D., 146
Laird, K. T., 80
Lakey, B, 217
Lakin, J. L., 129
Lam, A. G., 373
Lambert, N. M., 432
Lamberth, J., 92
Lamke, L. K., 288
Lammers, J., 369

Landers, A., 246
Lang, F. R., 224
Langhinrichsen-Rohling, J., 380, 382
Langlois, J. H., 78, 79
Langner, C. A., 368
Langston, C. A., 3
Langström, N., 276, 277
Lansford, J. E., 420
Larkey, L. K., 270
Larose, S., 240
Larrick, R. P., 385
Larson, C., 81
Larson, C. M., 287
Larson, J., 202
Larson, R., 222
Larson, R. W., 213
Lassek, W. D., 80, 82
Lauer, J. C., 259, 270, 443
Lauer, R. H., 259, 270, 443
Laumann, E. O., 290
Laurel-Seller, E., 84
Laurenceau, J., 156, 158
Laursen, B., 339
La Valley, A. G., 201
Lavee, Y., 2, 194
Lavery, D., 7, 392
Lavner, J. A., 193–194, 408
Lawrence, E., 217, 387
Le, B., 3, 184, 196, 207, 208
Leal, S., 326
Leaper, C., 162
Leary, M. R., 4–6, 28, 30, 41, 131, 132, 203, 215, 232, 234–236, 305–309, 311, 328
Lebovitz, E., 260
Leder, S., 196, 309
Ledermann, T., 65
Lee, E., 190
Lee, J. A., 262
Lee, L., 88
Leff, L., 397
Lehmann, P., 386
Lehnart, J., 28
Leigh, B. C., 283
Leitenberg, H., 289
Lemay, E. P., Jr., 76, 219
L'Engle, K. L., 288
Lennon, C. A., 363–364
Lenton, A. P., 86, 228
Leonardelli, G. J., 310
Leone, C., 131
Lepore, S. J., 413
Leslie, L. A., 100
Letzring, T. D., 128, 134
Leuschner, H., 147
Levenson, R. W., 44, 62, 167, 171, 185, 186, 266, 341, 350, 403

Lever, J., 295
Levin, L. A., 202, 228
Levine, A., 260
Levine, R., 263
Levine, T. R., 228, 326, 333
Levinger, A. C., 404
Levinger, G., 200, 203, 398, 404
Levitt, A., 187
Levitt, M. J., 37, 305
Levy, K. N., 320, 321
Levy-Storms, L., 215
Lewandowski, G., 190
Lewin, T., 12
Lewis, D. M. G., 32
Lewis, J., 146
Lewis, K., 61, 92
Lewis, T., 169
Lhutanen, R. K., 28
Li, N. P., 34, 101, 102
Li, Y., 420, 422
Liberman, R., 288
Liberman, V., 351
Lichtenfeld, S., 81
Lichtenstein, P., 276, 277
Lieberman, M. D., 5
Liebold, J. M., 386
Liefbroer, A. C., 15, 181
Light, K. C., 148
Lilgendahl, J. P., 413
Lin, A. J., 294
Lin, D. Y., 114
Lin, H. L., 158
Lin, P. K. F., 100
Lin, Y. W., 207
Linklater, W. L., 79, 81
Linville, P., 292
Linz, H., 106
Lipetz, M. F., 100
Lippa, R. A., 23, 29, 102, 289
Lipson, S. F., 82
Lishner, D. A., 318
Liss, M., 181
Litowitz, D. L., 101
Little, A. C., 24, 78, 84, 88, 101
Liu, H., 81
Liu, J., 419
Lloyd, S. A., 202, 339, 387
Löckenhoff, C. E., 224
Loewenstein, G., 88, 293
Logel, C., 30
Logue, E. M., 214
Lohr, J. M., 345
Lois, D., 98
Long, E. C. J., 136
Longmore, M. A., 213
Longstreth, M., 341
Lonsbary, C., 118, 119
Lopes, J., 183
Lopez, F. C., 384–385

Lorber, M. F., 385
Lorenzo, G. L., 134
Love, G. D., 215
Loving, T. J., 3, 5, 111, 160, 260, 348
Lucas, A., 63
Lucas, R. E., 182, 416–417
Lucas, T., 195
Luchies, L. B., 334, 429
Ludwig, T. E., 61
Luévano, V. X., 84
Luis, S., 85
Luke, M. A., 264
Luo, S., 57, 85, 95, 96, 98, 113, 133
Lupien, S. P., 235
Lussier, Y., 299
Lutfey, K. E., 295
Lutz, C. J., 217
Lutz-Zois, C. J., 98
Luxen, M. F., 82
Lydon, J. E., 19, 88, 112, 205, 208, 428
Lykins, A. D., 60
Lykken, D. T., 33, 408
Lyngstad, T. H., 407
Lynn, M., 86
Lyons, P. M., 77
Lyubomirsky, S., 432

MacDonald, G., 4, 30, 293, 341
MacDonald, K., 61, 260
MacDonald, T. K., 111, 293, 341, 415
MacDonald, T. M., 61, 260
Macdowall, W., 280
Mackey, S., 250
MacLean, I., 78
MacNeil, S., 297–298
Macrae, C. N., 134, 146
Madden, M., 12
Maddox, A. M., 288
Maddox, G., 278
Madey, S. F., 101
Magdol, L., 395, 407
Magee, J. C., 368
Mahoney, A. R., 204
Maier, M. A., 81
Maio, G. R., 134, 264
Maisel, N. C., 218
Maisto, S. A., 293, 373
Major, B., 87
Malarkey, W. B., 5, 260
Malik, J., 189
Malle, B. F., 114
Mallinckrodt, B., 58–59
Malouff, J. M., 27, 28
Maltby, J., 333
Maner, J. K., 84, 258, 311, 322, 369, 428

Manke, M. L., 2
Mann, S., 230
Manning, J. T., 78
Manning, W. D., 213
Mannix, L. M., 143
Mansson, S., 288
Manstead, A. S. R., 145
Manusov, V., 169, 413
Marcus, D. K., 77
Margolin, G., 437
Markey, C. N., 99–100, 289, 300
Markey, P. M., 99–100
Markman, H. J., 9, 10, 167–168, 170, 172, 207, 288, 332, 358–359, 435
Marks, J. P. G., 203
Marks, M. J., 274
Marquardt, E., 392, 394–395, 404, 407
Marshall, A. D., 25, 26, 155, 227, 228
Marshall, L. L., 388
Marston, P. J., 2, 270
Martin, J., 132, 169
Martin, R., 28
Martins, Y., 81
Martz, J. M., 178, 388
Mashek, D. J., 3
Masi, C. M., 241
Mason, M. F., 146
Mason, W., 97
Massar, K., 315
Mast, M. S., 134, 155, 371
Master, S. L., 5
Masters, W., 298
Matamoros, M., 213, 214
Mather, M., 7, 392
Mathes, E. W., 95
Matsumoto, D., 144
Matz, D. C., 82
Mayer, J. D., 136
McAdams, D. P., 413
McAndrew, F. T., 163
McBurney, D. H., 290
McCall, C., 55
McCarthy, E., 118
McClure, M. J., 88
McCollough, J. K., 81
McConnell, A. R., 386
McCornack, S. A., 327
McCrae, R. R., 27
McCullough, M. E., 128, 145, 331–333
McDaniel, S., 2
McDonald, D. W., 200
McEwan, B., 148
McEwan, T. E., 381
McFall, R. M., 152

McFarland, C., 117
McGonagle, K. A., 184, 339
McGraw, K. M., 101
McGue, M., 28
McHale, S. M., 25, 99
McHenry, P. C., 5
McHugh, M. C., 162
McKenna, K. Y. A., 75, 327
McKibbin, W. F., 380
McKinnish, T. G., 394, 404
McLeod, B. A., 328
McManus, S., 280
McMullen, A., 132
McNulty, J. K., 88, 115, 122, 194, 233, 296, 334, 357, 384–385
McPherson, M., 231
McQuinn, R. D., 184
Mealey, L., 78
Meana, M., 60
Mechanic, M. B., 387
Medina, P., 82
Meehan, J. C., 386
Meeus, W., 97, 280
Mehl, M. R., 43, 59, 135, 161–162
Meier, A., 420–421
Meier, B. P., 333
Meijer, S., 280
Mellor, D., 236
Mendelsohn, G. A., 114, 162
Mendes, W. B., 226
Mendes de Leon, C. F., 226
Men or Women, 367
Mercer, C. H., 280
Merolla, A. J., 75
Messman, S. J., 228
Meston, C. M., 280, 288
Metts, S., 24, 117, 266, 280, 328
Meyer, D. R., 418
Michael, R. T., 290
Michael, S., 274
Michaels, S., 290
Michalski, R. L., 35, 319
Michela, J. L., 240, 241
Mickelson, K. D., 17, 203
Mikulincer, M., 18, 95, 88, 120, 125, 264, 265, 299, 348
Milardo, R. M., 224
Miles, L. K., 219
Miller, A. J., 368
Miller, G., 84
Miller, G. E., 5, 420
Miller, J., 119
Miller, J. B., 120
Miller, K., 90, 122
Miller, L. C., 157, 160, 317
Miller, L. K., 232–234
Miller, M. A., 412
Miller, P. J. E., 25, 113, 114, 214

Miller, R., 81
Miller, R. S., 18, 77, 129, 132, 178, 184, 194–195, 205, 328, 337, 427
Miller, S. L., 84, 322
Milletich, R. J., 384
Mills, A., 289
Mills, J., 197, 198–199
Mills, R. D., 386
Milne, A. B., 134
Milroy, A., 287
Miner, E. J., 380
Minieri, A., 290
Minzer, A., 159
Mirenberg, M. C., 71, 92
Mischel, W., 19
Mitchell, A. E., 158
Mitchell, C., 57, 58
Mitchell, K., 196, 290
Mitchell, S. A., 268, 269
Mitnick, D. M., 351
Mochon, D., 90
Moffitt, T. E., 36
Moiduddin, E., 4
Montagne-Miller, Y., 152
Montoya, R. M., 88, 97, 100
Mooney, C. N., 128
Moore, M. M., 152
Moore, N. B., 279
Moos, R. H., 215
Moreland, R. L., 73–74
Moreno, J. L., 41
Morgan, B., 79
Morgan, E. M., 295
Morgan, M. J., 75, 155
Morgentaler, A., 273
Morin, R., 367–368
Morling, B., 147
Morris, M. L., 230
Morris, W., 15
Morrison, D. M., 283
Morrison, E. L., 84
Morrison, K. R., 9
Morrison, R., 91
Morrow, G. D., 263
Morry, M. M., 95, 230
Mortimer, A. R., 240
Moskowitz, G. B., 105
Moss-Racusin, C. A., 130
Möttus, R., 135
Moyer, A., 9
Mroczek, D., 27
Muehlenhard, C. L., 129, 324
Muise, A., 322
Mulac, A., 162
Mullin, L. L., 155
Murachver, T., 384
Murdock, K. W., 88
Murgain, S. A., 136

Murphy, M. J., 177
Murray, A. K., 150
Murray, S. L., 30–32, 112, 113, 196
Murstein, B. I., 96, 97
Musick, K., 420–421
Mutso, A. A., 184, 207
Myers, D. G., 276
Myers, S. A., 251
Myhr, L., 301
Mysak, K., 274

Nagy, G. F., 89
Nakamoto, M., 136
Nakonezny, P. A., 183
Naliboff, B. D., 5
Nantel, J., 129
Nardone, N., 190
National Center for Health Statistics, 280, 283
Neave, N., 78, 147
Neely, B., 217
Neff, A. A., 429
Neff, L. A., 88, 112, 125, 261, 400, 401, 427, 429
Neighbors, C., 384
Nelson, D., 41, 51, 92–93
Nelson, L. D., 84
Nelson, M., 147
Neta, M., 106
Neuberg, S. L., 6, 121
Newall, N. E., 241
Newcomb, R., 278
Newcomb, T. M., 92, 96
Newman, J. L., 24
Newman, M. L., 325
Newport, F., 368
Neyer, F. J., 28
Nezlek, J. B., 5, 130–132, 265
Nguyen, M., 9
Nicklas, J. M., 5
Niederhoffer, K., 91
Niehuis, S., 113
Niesta, D., 81
Nietert, P. J., 417
Nishitani, M., 78
Nistico, L., 18
Noack, T., 9
Noftle, E. E., 128
Noirot, M., 120
Noller, P., 153–155, 299, 357, 372
Norenzayan, A., 46
North, R. J., 215
Norton, A. T., 29, 276
Norton, M. I., 75
Nosko, A., 163
Notarius, C., 141–142, 346
Núñez, A., 82

Núñez, J., 82
Núñez, M., 82

Oakman, J., 233
Oatley, K., 251
O'Donnell, D., 91
O'Hair, D., 152
Oishi, S., 5, 145, 395
Okimoto, T. G., 367
Okonski, B., 169
Olatunji, B. O., 345
O'Leary, K. D., 9, 385
Olide, A., 144
Oliver, M. B., 176
Olivola, C. Y., 77, 107
Olson, J. E., 62
Olson, L. N., 158
Oltmanns, T. F., 93
O'Malley, P. M., 9
Omoto, A. M., 2, 213
Oncale, R. M., 294
Ones, D. S., 134
Orbuch, T. L., 44, 53, 63, 189, 271, 403, 407, 435
Oriña, M. M., 205, 368
Orlando, M. J., 47
Orr, A., 327
Orvis, B. R., 344
Ostovich, J. M., 286, 290
O'Sullivan, L. F., 292, 297
O'Sullivan, M., 326, 327
Oswald, D. L., 12, 301, 431–432
Oswalt, S. B., 280
Otto-Salaj, L. L., 294
Oveis, C., 199
Overall, N. C., 205, 265, 352, 428–429
Owen, J., 228
Owen, P. R., 84
Ozer, D. J., 99
Ozturk, A., 18

Padgett, P. M., 292
Palomares, N. A., 162
Papp, L. M., 167, 339, 341
Parish, A., 81
Park, J. H., 82
Park, N., 75, 155
Parke, S., 250
Parker, A. M., 76
Parks, M. R., 327
Parks-Stamm, E. J., 26
Parmley, M., 155
Parrott, D. J., 278, 312
Pasch, L. A., 215
Pataki, S. P., 130
Patel, L., 101
Patience, R. A., 82
Patrick, H., 118, 119

Patterson, G. R., 189
Patterson, M. L., 144, 153
Paul, E. L., 291
Pauley, P. M., 161
Pawlowski, B., 80
Payne, J. W., 82
Pearc, Z. J., 116
Pearce, A. R., 102, 120
Pearce, D. G., 143
Pease, A., 147, 149
Pease, B., 147, 149
Pederson, W. C., 317
Peetz, J., 329, 433
Pegalis, L. J., 157
Pelham, B. W., 71, 92, 126
Penke, L., 30, 87, 135
Pennebaker, J. W., 60, 101
Pennington, L. M., 81
Penton-Voak, H. S., 78
Peplau, L. A., 29, 112, 190, 240, 241, 284–285, 362, 366, 372, 374
Perella, A., 101
Perez, M., 100
Perilloux, C., 32, 264, 415
Perilloux, H. K., 82
Perlman, D., 184
Perrett, D. I., 78, 84, 88, 101
Perrier, C., 334
Perry, R. P., 241
Perry-Jenkins, M., 195
Peter, J., 163, 231, 288
Petersen, J. L., 21–22, 274
Peterson, D., 341–342, 346, 347, 356
Peterson, J. L., 278
Petrides, K. V., 79
Petronio, S., 158, 195, 338
Pettijohn, T. F., II, 84
Phelan, P. E., 204, 302
Phillips, J. B., 147
Picardi, A., 18
Piliavin, J., 90
Pillsworth, E., 81, 287
Pines, A. M., 323
Pinquart, M., 238
Pipitone, R. N., 150
Pittman, F. S., 430
Pittman, T., 130
Pitts, M. K., 290
Place, S. S., 135
Planalp, S., 160
Plant, E. A., 158
Plaut, V. C¦, 87
Poe, D. B., 147, 327
Pollmann, M. M. H., 133
Pomerantz, E. M., 118
Poore, J. C., 188, 251, 274
Poortman, A., 15, 73, 399, 407–408

Popp, D., 274, 287
Porter, S., 146, 326
Potter, J., 46
Pournajafi-Nazarloo, H., 260
Powell-Williams, M., 278
Powers, S. I., 348
Prager, K. J., 2
Pratto, F., 366
Pressman, S. D., 5
Preston, M., 283
Preti, G., 81
Previti, D., 399, 405, 408, 430
Priel, B., 309
Priem, J. S., 217
Prokosch, M. D., 81
Pronin, E., 114, 344
Pronk, T. M., 429
Proost, K., 130
Proske, C. U., 110
Proulx, C. M., 25, 99
Puccinelli, N. M., 142, 153
Pulerwitz, J., 293
Purvis, J. A., 157
Putcha-Bhagavatula, A. D., 317
Putnam, R. D., 183, 395
Pyszczynski, T. A., 250

Quenqua, D., 163

Rabin, B. S., 5
Radford-Davenport, J., 132
Rahe, R. H., 412
Rahman, Q., 276, 277
Ramirez, A., Jr., 12, 75, 106, 208, 209
Ramsey, A., 102
Randall, A. K., 183, 400, 406, 408
Randolph, M. E., 294
Ranson, J., 60
Rao, S. S., 402
Rapson, R. L., 244, 246
Rashotte, L. S., 150
Rauer, A. J., 406
Raven, B. H., 365–366
Realo, A., 135
Reber, J. S., 122
Reddy, K. S., 37, 123
Reece, M., 281
Reed, L. L., 146
Reeder, G. D., 115
Reeder, H., 2
Regan, P., 251, 267, 270, 275, 289, 377–378
Rehman, U. S., 240
Reichman, V., 148
Reid, P. T., 23
Reilly, A. H., 80
Reinhardt, J. P., 217

Reis, H. T., 2, 3, 25, 26, 32, 49, 73, 86, 87, 113, 158, 162, 164–165, 185, 187–188, 214–215, 218, 223, 228, 238, 239, 251, 427
Rempel, J. K., 214
Renninger, L. A., 152
Renshaw, K. D., 184
Rentfrow, B. J., 165
Reyna, N., 134
Rhoades, G. K., 10, 207, 288, 396–397
Rhodes, B. C., 150
Rhodes, G., 77–78, 217
Rhodes, J., 128
Rhodewalt, F., 128
Rholes, W. S., 117, 205, 265
Rich, S., 33
Richardson, D., 202
Richman, L. S., 311
Richmond, L. S., 202
Rick, S. I., 97
Ridge, R. D., 122
Riela, S., 263
Riggio, H. R., 398, 420
Riggle, E. D. B., 276
Riggs, M. L., 278
Righetti, F., 158
Rizkalla, L., 351
Robbins, M. L., 43, 59
Roberts, A. R., 77, 81
Roberts, B. W., 27, 28, 65
Roberts, L. J., 2, 302
Roberts, R. D., 136
Roberts, S., 7, 29, 194
Roberts, S. C., 150
Roberts, S. G. B., 222
Robertson, K., 384
Robillard, S. L., 129
Robins, R. W., 36, 41, 114, 145
Robins, S. C., 89
Robinson, M. D., 333
Robinson, M. E., 215
Robnett, B., 85
Rodgers, J. L., 183, 396
Rodin, J., 322
Rodriguez, G., 263
Roeder, U. R., 149
Roesch, S. C., 112
Rogers, P. J., 260
Rogers, S. J., 9, 11, 183, 394–396, 407
Roggman, L. A., 78, 79
Rohner, R. P., 18
Rohrbaugh, M. J., 5
Roisman, G. L., 16, 29
Rollie, S. S., 410
Roloff, M. E., 131, 339, 357
Romero-Canyas, R., 37, 123
Ronay, R., 129

Rooke, S. E., 27
Root, L. M., 61
Rose, P., 30
Rosen, L. D., 257
Rosen, S., 202
Rosenbaum, J. E., 279, 294
Rosenberg, J., 81
Rosenfeld, M. J., 75, 163
Rosenthal, A. M., 257
Rosenthal, N. L., 222
Rosenthal, R., 120–121, 147
Ross, L., 114
Ross, M., 57, 111, 117, 214
Ross, M. W., 288
Rostosky, S. S., 277
Rothblum, E. D., 29, 276
Rouby, D. A., 258
Rovine, M. J., 156, 158
Rowatt, W. C., 87
Rowe, A. C., 120, 260
Rowland, H. M., 101, 150
Ruammake, C., 157
Rubenstein, A. J., 78, 79
Rubin, H., 126
Rubin, L. B., 227
Rubin, Y. S., 312
Rubin, Z., 255, 266, 267
Rudd, N. A., 80
Rudman, L. A., 130, 204, 302
Ruggles, S., 364, 395, 407
Ruiz, J. M., 215
Rule, N. O., 106, 148
Runyan, T., 81
Rusbult, C. E., 3, 114, 134, 137, 175, 178, 206–209, 352–353, 388, 426–429
Russell, B. L., 301
Russell, D. W., 58–59, 237, 238
Russell, J., 62
Russell, V. M., 357
Ruthig, J. C., 241
Rutstein, J., 253
Ruvolo, A. P., 98
Ruvolo, C. M., 98
Ryan, R. M., 296
Rycyna, C. C., 332
Rydell, R. J., 314
Ryff, C. D., 215

Saad, L., 275–276
Sabin, E. P., 226
Sabini, J., 87, 286, 290, 320
Sacco, D. F., 146
Sacks, D., 132
Sadava, S., 299
Saffrey, C., 415
Sagarin, B. J., 89, 318, 319–320, 325
Sagrestano, L. M., 374

Sahlstein, E. M., 72, 75
Saigal, S. D., 42
Salman, S., 18
Salovey, P., 312, 318, 322
Salska, I., 80
Salter, J., 76
Salvatore, J. E., 348
Sanchez, D. T., 296, 297
Sancho, M., 82
Sanders, S. A., 281
Sandnabba, N. K., 26
Sandy, C. J., 46
Sanford, K., 351
Santelli, J. S., 279, 294
Sasaki, S. J., 236
Sassler, S., 368
Sato, A. F., 61
Sato, S., 263
Saucier, D. A., 278
Sauter, D., 150
Savin-Williams, R. C., 29, 159
Savitsky, K., 135, 142
Saxton, T. K., 150
Sayer, L. C., 418
Sbarra, D. A., 414–417
Scanzoni, L. D., 276
Schachner, D. A., 317
Schachter, S., 1, 4, 41, 72
Schaefer, H. S., 4–5
Schaer, M., 260
Schaller, M., 6
Scharfe, E., 19
Scharff, D. E., 439
Scharrer, E., 288
Scheib, J. E., 81
Scheier, M. F., 123
Scheinberger-Olwig, R., 301
Scheyd, G., 81
Schick, V., 281
Schilling, E. A., 184
Schindler, I., 88
Schlenker, B. R., 113, 114, 129
Schlessinger, L., 434
Schloerscheidt, A. M., 134
Schmidt, E. A., 163, 235
Schmidt, L., 90
Schmitt, D. P., 17, 30, 33, 48, 86, 95, 265, 266, 286, 317
Schmitt, J. P., 29
Schmukle, S. C., 71, 128–129, 163
Schneider, C. S., 240
Schneider, S., 434
Schneider, W. J., 439
Scholer, A. A., 110
Scholte, R. H. J., 97
Schreurs, B., 130
Schug, J., 144
Schutte, N. S., 27
Schutz, A., 115, 130

Schützwohl, A., 34, 312, 319–320
Schwartz, D., 134
Schwartz, P., 29, 269, 270, 282, 284–285, 290, 296, 393
Schwarz, S., 84
Schweinle, W. E., 136
Scott, A. M., 350
Scott, S., 3
Scott-Sheldon, L. A. J., 294
Seal, D. W., 286
Secord, P. F., 13–14
Seder, J. P., 145
Sedikides, C., 115, 176
Seeley, L. A., 376
Seeman, T. E., 215, 226
Seery, M. D., 235
Sefcek, J. A., 98
Segal, N. L., 33
Segers, E., 97
Segrin, C., 6, 208, 408
Seidman, G., 217
Selcuk, E., 18
Selfhout, M., 97
Sellers, J. G., 165
Sellin, I., 130
Seltzer, J., 399
Settles, T. D., 37
Shackelford, T. K., 35, 89, 287, 287, 315, 319, 380
Shaffer, D. R., 157, 165
Shah, J., 124
Shamblen, S. R., 194
Shannon, J. B., 381
Shanteau, J., 89
Sharp, E. A., 119
Shaver, P. R., 14–15, 17, 18, 58, 59, 88, 120, 125, 158, 164, 214, 223, 263–265, 299, 317, 348
Sheffield, D., 215
Sheldon, M. S., 66, 187
Shen, Y., 11, 183
Shepherd, R., 235
Shepperd, J. A., 30
Sherkat, D. E., 278
Sherwood, P., 77, 82
Shettel-Neuber, J., 321
Shibazaki, K., 96
Shih, K. Y., 203
Shimizu, M., 235
Shiner, R., 27, 65
Shippee, S. K., 129, 324
Shirinyan, D., 5
Shoda, Y., 19, 36, 388
Shoham, V., 5
Shook, N., 293
Shovelton, H., 146
Shrout, P. E., 217
Shull, R. D., 183
Sibley, C. G., 205, 265

Sicoly, F., 57
Sielky, K., 217
Sillars, A., 116, 132
Silver, M. E., 37
Silvera, D. H., 110
Simeon, J. R., 427
Simmons, C. A., 386
Simms, E. N., 99
Simo, M., 101
Simon, R. W., 412
Simon-Thomas, E. R., 150
Simpson, J. A., 3, 4, 23, 34, 36, 101, 112, 113, 117, 131, 136–137, 152, 177, 205, 214, 217, 221, 230, 244, 265, 285–286, 384, 428
Sims, C. L., 29, 276
Sinclair, H. C., 381
Sinclair, R. C., 283
Singer, B. H., 215
Singh, D., 79, 80, 85
Singh, P., 267
Singh, R., 100
Sinicropi-Yao, L., 150
Slatcher, R. B., 60, 156
Slater, A., 77, 82
Slater, P. E., 394
Sloan, D. M., 161
Slotter, E. B., 385, 414
Small, D. A., 97
Smith, A. E., 123
Smith, C. A., 24
Smith, C. V., 296
Smith, D. M., 121
Smith, F. G., 84
Smith, G., 274, 294, 357
Smith, L., 274, 294, 357
Smith, M., 132
Smith, R. H., 312
Smith, S. J., 277
Smith, S. M., 32
Smith, T., 116
Smith, T. W., 184, 215, 281, 348
Smith-Lovin, L., 231
Smith-Slep, A. M., 189
Smurda, J., 251
Snider, A. G., 113, 133
Snyder, D. K., 158, 430, 439–442
Snyder, M., 2, 108–109, 121–122, 131, 133, 213, 230
Snyder, M. L., 89
Solano, A. C., 264
Soler, C., 82
Solomon, D. H., 117, 191, 193, 217
Solomon, S. E., 29, 276, 343
Sommer, K. L., 310, 312
Song, H., 75, 155
Sonnega, J. S., 5
Soons, J. P. M., 182
South, S. J., 11, 183

Southworth, C., 381
Spain, J. S., 325
Spedale, D. R., 277
Spielmann, S. S., 4, 416
Spitzberg, B. H., 37, 282, 302, 316, 381
Sprecher, S., 117, 160–161, 166, 202, 203, 254, 261, 265–267, 269, 270, 274, 290, 319, 327
Springer, C. A., 328
Stacey, J., 276
Stackert, R. A., 120
Staebell, S. E., 181
Staeheli, J. C., 430
Stafford, L., 75, 195, 201, 202, 220, 431–432
Stake, J. E., 26
Stanik, C. E., 95
Stanley, S. M., 9, 10, 173, 207
Starratt, V. G., 287
Stazi, M. A., 18
Steele, J. L., 100
Stein, J. L., 147
Steiner-Pappalardo, N. L., 27
Stephens, B. O., 89
Stephenson, K. R., 288, 297
Sternberg, R. J., 246–247, 249, 267
Sternglanz, R. W., 332
Steuber, K. R., 193, 217
Stewart, A. J., 410, 418
Stickney, L. T., 26
Stillwell, A. M., 331
Stinson, D. A., 30, 89, 123, 125, 128, 196
Stith, D. A., 384
Stokes, M., 236
Stopfer, J. M., 129
Story, A., 205
Stowell, J., 5, 260
Strachman, A., 190, 218, 299
Straus, M. A., 377, 382
Streeter, S. A., 290
Strong, G., 190, 269, 271, 430
Stroud, C. B., 400–401
Strout, S. L., 13
Struzynska-Kujalowicz, A., 368
Stucke, T. S., 128
Stukas, A. A., Jr., 121
Subotnik, R., 288
Sugar, M., 196, 290
Suh, E., 5
Sullivan, K. T., 215
Suls, J., 28
Sumer, N., 18
Summers, R. F., 441
Sun, C., 288
Sun, Y., 420, 422
Sundie, J. M., 129
Sunnafrank, M., 106

Suppes, A., 109
Surra, C. A., 341
Sutton, P. D., 7–8, 392
Swami, V., 79, 84, 269, 270
Swann, W. B., Jr., 28, 91, 109, 110, 122, 125–128, 132, 137, 165, 178, 388
Swanson, A., 142
Swift, A. U., 241

Tabak, B. A., 333
Tafoya, M. A., 282, 316
Takai, J., 12
Talley, A. E., 187
Tan, L., 100
Tanha, M., 382, 388
Tanke, E. D., 122
Tanner, L., 278, 292
Tassinary, L. G., 148
Tatkow, E. P., 146
Tausczik, Y. R., 60
Tavris, C., 172, 345
Taylor, D. A., 156
Taylor, P., 7, 8
Taylor, S. E., 5
Teachman, J., 407
Teitler, J., 279
Tejada-Vera, B., 7–8, 392
Tellegen, A., 33
ten Brinke, L., 146, 326
te Nijenhuis, J., 97
Tenney, E. R., 93
Terhell, E. L., 418
Tesser, A., 99
Theiss, J. A., 117, 192
Theodoridou, A., 260
Thibaut, J. W., 175, 363
Thoennes, N., 377, 382
Thomas, G., 4, 101, 113, 134
Thomas, K., 220
Thompson, S. C., 114
Thornhill, R., 81–84, 94, 287
Thornton, A., 362
Thorsteinsson, E. B., 27
Thune, I., 82
Tice, D. M., 171, 345
Tjaden, P., 377, 382
Toczynski, A., 101
Todd, P. M., 87, 135
Todorov, A., 70, 77, 85, 106, 107
Tomlinson, J. M., 113
Tong, S. T., 75
Tourangeau, R., 58
Townsend, G. C., 78
Tracy, J. L., 145
Tran, S., 24, 101, 112
Treanor, J. J., 5
Treas, J., 278
Treat, T. A., 152

Trent, K., 11, 183
Troister, T., 126
Trussell, J., 279
Tsai, F., 32, 239
Tsapelas, I., 34, 189, 270, 271, 289
Tucker, J. S., 161
Tucker, P., 190, 267
Tunney, R. J., 81
Turkheimer, E., 93
Turley, R. N. L., 420
Tversky, A., 184
Twenge, J. M., 11, 26, 128, 274, 278, 310, 375, 395
Tybur, J. M., 84, 129
Tyler, J. M., 325

Uchino, B. N., 215
Udry, J. R., 23
Uebelacker, L. A., 37
Ueno, K., 230
Uller, T., 94
Umberson, D., 343
U.S. Census Bureau, 392
Uysal, A., 158

Vaaler, M. L., 407
Vainius, A. A., 81
Valentine, K. A., 101
Valkenburg, P. M., 163, 231, 288
Vanable, P., 58
van Aken, M. A. G., 30
van Anders, S. M., 155
van Baaren, R. B., 149, 152, 153
Vandello, J. A., 26
van den Boom, 18
VanderLaan, D. P., 277
van der Linden, D., 97
Vangelisti, A. L., 204, 305, 329
Van Hook, J., 96
van Knippenberg, A., 153
Van Lange, P. A. M., 3
Vannier, S. A., 297
Van Ryzin, M. J., 193
van Tilburg, T., 236
Van Vugt, M., 129
Vanwesenbeeck, I., 280
VanYperen, N. W., 202
Vasey, P. L., 277
Vazire, S., 129, 135
Veitch, R., 92
Veksler, A. E., 148
Venardos, C., 154
Veniegas, R. C., 362
Verhofstadt, L. L., 216
Verma, J., 263
Vernon, M. L., 264
Veroff, J., 63
Vescio, T. K., 377
Viechtbauer, W., 27, 65

Viken, R. J., 152
Vincent, J. P., 184
Vincent, W., 278
Voelz, Z. R., 240
Vogel, D. L., 58–59
Vohs, K. D., 29, 129, 281, 289, 290, 429
von Hippel, W., 129, 274
Vonofakou, C., 73, 230
Voracek, M., 79
Vorauer, J. D., 142–143, 236
Vrij, A., 150, 161, 323, 326
Vukovic, J., 24, 84

Waas, G. A., 221
Wade, T. J., 152
Wagers, W. P., 430
Waite, L. J., 296
Waldron, V. R., 332
Walker, A., 366
Wall, S., 14
Wallace, R. B., 238, 334
Wallen, A. S., 26
Waller, K. L., 415
Waller, N. G., 17
Waller, W. W., 181, 363
Walster, E., 76, 90, 251, 268–269, 434
Walster, G. W., 90, 268–269, 434
Walther, J. B., 12, 75
Walton, K. E., 28
Wampold, B. E., 441
Wang, H., 12
Warburton, W. A., 311, 328
Ward, D., 251
Warner, R. M., 136
Warren, M., 277
Waters, E., 14
Watson, D., 100, 113
Watts, D. J., 97
Waytz, A., 225
Weaver, J. R., 26
Weaver, S. E., 117
Webber, L., 228
Weber, A. L., 413
Weber, K. M., 193
Webster, G. D., 82, 158
Weeden, J., 85, 87
Weeks, D. G., 240, 241
Weele, J. V., 150
Wegener, D. T., 134
Weger, H., Jr., 349
Wei, M., 58–59
Weigel, D. J., 205, 431
Weisbuch, M., 150, 235
Weiser, D. A., 398
Weisfeld, C. C., 195
Weisfeld, G. E., 195
Weiss, R. L., 184, 189, 436–437

Weiss, R. S., 236
Weller, A., 260
Welling, L. L. M., 24, 84
Wellings, K., 280, 290
Wellman, B., 12
Wells, B. E., 274, 278
Welsh, D. P., 291
Wendorf, C. A., 195, 341
Weng, X., 249, 251
Wenzel, A., 89, 291
Werking, K., 224, 228–230
Wertheimer, V., 290
West, C., 370
West, L., 100
West, S. G., 102
West, T. V., 134
Westbay, L., 249
Western, D., 386
Whalen, J. M., 163
Wheeler, J., 437
Wheeler, L., 76, 164–165, 238
Whisman, M. A., 37
Whitaker, D. J., 99, 378, 386
Whitchurch, E., 135
White, G. L., 88, 253, 314
Whitley, B. E., Jr., 250, 270
Whitton, S. W., 207, 357
Wickham, R. E., 9
Wicklund, R. A., 89
Wickrama, K. A. S., 404
Widmer, E. D., 278, 283
Wiederman, M. W., 47, 57, 283
Wieling, M. B., 82
Wiersma, J., 57, 283
Wieselquist, J., 207
Wiik, K. A., 9
Wilcox, K. J., 33
Wilcox, W. B., 392, 394–395,
    404, 407
Wildsmith, E., 292
Wile, D. B., 171
Willemsen, G., 238
Willetts, M. C., 274, 281
Williams, K. D., 146, 167,
    310–312
Williams, K. M., 82
Williams, M. J., 162

Williams, S. L., 386
Williamson, I., 334
Willingham, B., 144
Willis, J., 70, 85, 106
Wills, T. A., 189
Wilmot, W. W., 160
Wilpers, S., 28, 233
Wilson, C., 260
Wilson, C. L., 287
Wilson, T. D., 415
Wimmer, A., 61, 92
Windschitl, P. D., 135
Winstead, B. A., 155, 157
Winston, R., 35
Winterheld, H. A., 117
Wirth, J. H., 146
Witt, E. A., 47
Wittenbraker, C. H., 155
Witvliet, C. V. O., 61, 334
Wobbes, T., 203
Woertman, L., 280
Wojciszke, B., 368
Wolfinger, N. H., 10
Women CEOs, 367
Wong, N. C. H., 190
Wood, D., 28
Wood, E., 163
Wood, J. T., 387
Wood, J. V., 30, 123
Wood, W., 23, 35, 95, 267, 432
Woolf, S. E., 293, 373
Woolsey, M. D., 165
Worthington, E. L., 61
Wortman, C. B., 169
Wosnitzer, R., 288
Wotman, S. R., 256
Wright, C. B., 131
Wright, P. H., 227
Wu, C., 77, 81
Wyden, P., 359–360
Wysocki, C. J., 81

Xu, X., 249, 251, 263
Yager, J., 223
Yagil, D., 299
Yan, T., 58
Yang, Y., 317

Yap, A. J., 147
Yarkoni, T., 164
Ybema, J. F., 203, 427
Yeagley, E., 147
Yeater, E. A., 301, 302
Yee, N., 153
Yen, H., 11, 367
Yeo, S. E., 100
Yopchick, J. E., 135
Yoshida, T., 12
Yoshikawa, S., 78
Yoshimura, S., 331
Young, J., 88
Young, L., 290
Young-DeMarco, L., 362
Younger, J., 250
Ysseldyk, R., 333–334
Yu, E., 419
Yu, X., 155
Yuan, J. W., 351
Yucel, D., 300

Zaalberg, R., 145
Zacchilli, T. L., 346, 356
Zadro, L., 310, 311
Zagoory-Sharon, O., 260
Zajone, R. B., 73
Zanna, M. P., 293
Zapp, D. J., 290
Zayas, V., 19, 36, 388
Zechmeister, J. S., 333
Zeifman, D., 222
Zhang, F., 19, 155
Zhang, G., 57, 85, 95, 113
Zhang, S., 75, 263
Zhang, Y., 96, 189
Zhaoyang, R., 62–63
Zhong, C., 310
Zimbardo, P., 234
Zimmerman, D. H., 370
Zimmerman, F., 146
Zimring, L., 132
Ziomkiewicz, A., 82
Zipp, J. F., 375
Zuckerman, M., 326
Zumbach, J., 146
Zurbriggen, E. L., 295

Subject Index

Abstinence education, 294
Acceptance
　degrees of, in relationships,
　　306
　relational value, 305–307
Accommodation, 353, 429
Accommodative behavior, 209
Active exclusion, 306
Active inclusion, 306
Active listening, 170
Actor/observer effects, 114–
　115, 343
Actual equity, 201–202
Actual sex differences, 20–22
Adolescence
　first sexual experience
　　during, 279–280
　friendship during, 221, 222
　parenting of, and
　　attachment style, 18–19
Advice support, 215
Affective component of
　friendship, 213
Affective reconstruction, 439
African Americans
　divorce and, 404
　marriage enrichment
　　program for, 63
Agape, 262
Age, 278. See also Adolescence;
　Elderly
　attraction and, 93–95
　conflict and, 340–341
　first sexual experience,
　　279–281
　love affected by, 265–266
　at marriage, divorce and,
　　406, 407
　sexual frequency and,
　　281–282
Agreeableness, 27
AIDS/HIV, 292
Alcohol myopia, 293
Alcohol use
　conflict and, 341
　as predictor of divorce, 408

Ambivalence, 306
Ancient Egypt, 245
Ancient Greece, 245
Androgyny
　communication and, 165
　instrumental and expressive
　　traits in, 23–24
　loneliness and, 238
Anger
　communication and,
　　171–172
　conflict and, 344, 345
Annie Hall (film), 290
Annoyances, cumulative,
　342–343
Anxiety over abandonment,
　16
Anxiety score, 58–59
Anxious-ambivalent
　attachment, 14
Apologies, 333
Approach motivation, 187
Approach processes, 188
Archives, 62
Arousal, 251–255, 269
Attachment
　in evolutionary sense of
　　love, 250
　four components of, 222
Attachment styles, 14–19
　accuracy of judging
　　partners and, 137
　attributions and, 115–116
　communication and, 164
　conflict and, 340, 348
　divorce and, 408
　forgiveness and, 333
　four categories of, 264–265
　hurt feelings and, 309
　interdependency and, 205
　jealousy influenced by, 315,
　　320
　learning and unlearning, 19
　love and, 264–265
　lying and, 325
　mismatched, 19

perception of partners and,
　120
　research assessing, 58
　response to conflict and, 353
　sexuality and, 299
　sexual orientation and, 29
　similarities in, 92–93
　speed-dates and, 88
Attitudes
　sexual, 274–278
　similarities in, 92
Attraction
　arousal and, 251–255
　dissimilarities, discovering,
　　95–97
　influencing dissolution of
　　relationships, 398–399
　physical appearance and,
　　74–91
　proximity and, 71–74
　reciprocity and, 89–91
　rewards and, 70–71
　sex differences, 101–102
　similarity and, 92–100
　to those we can't have,
　　100–101
　in Triangular Theory of
　　Love, 250
Attributional conflict, 344
Attributional processes
　conflict and, 343–344
　defined, 114–115
　made by happy and
　　unhappy couples, 116
　patterns, 113–116
Autonomy and connection
　tension, 338
Avoidance
　conflict and, 346
　of intimacy, 16
　processes, 188
Avoidance goal, 187
Avoidance score, 58–59
Avoidant style of attachment,
　14, 348
Avoiders, 353

Baby boomers, 12–13
Balance theory, 90–91
Barrier model of breakups, 398–399
Beauty. *See* Physical attractiveness
Behavioral approaches to marital therapy, 436–438
Behavioral couple therapy (BCT), 436, 437
Behavioral relationship maintenance mechanisms, 428–430
Behavior control, 364
Behavior description, 168
Beliefs about relationships, 117–120
  destiny and growth, 118
  difficulties in relationships and, 118–119
  dysfunctional, 117–118
  romanticism, 117
Belligerence, 167
Belong, need to, 4–6, 32–33, 236
Best friends, 223
Betrayal, 328–332
  coping with, 331–332
  examples of, 328
  getting away with, 332
  individual differences in, 329–330
  two sides to every, 330–331
Bias
  for beauty, 75–77, 83–84
  confirmation, 108
  self-serving, 57–58, 114–115, 343
  social desirability, 58
  truth, 326
  volunteer, 47
Big Five personality traits, 27–28
Bilateral style of power, 373–374
Birth control, used by teens, 278
Births out of wedlock, 7
Blirtatiousness, 165
Body, attractiveness in, 78–79
Body movement, 146–147

Caller ID, 12
Capitalization, in friendships, 214–215
Caring

attachment style and, 265
in intimate relationships, 2
on the Love Scale, 255
Casual sex, attitudes about, 47–48, 274–275
Cheating. *See* Infidelity
Child abuse, 386
Children
  of divorce, 397–398, 419–422
  friendship among, 221
  having without marriage, 7
  mother's influence on attachment styles of, 18–19
  predictors of divorce and, 407
  in single-parent homes, 8, 392
  temperament of, 18
Civil unions, 393, 397
Close connection, 236
Closedness and openness tension, 338
"Closing time effect," 101
Coding procedures (scientific observations), 60
Coercion, sexual,–302
Coercive power, 365
Cognitive-behaviorable couple therapy (CBCT), 437
Cognitive interdependence, 427
Cognitive relationship maintenance mechanisms, 427–428
Cohabitation, 396
  changes in, 6–7
  divorce and, 407
  success of marriage following, 8–11
"Cold shoulder," 310
Coming out, 159
Commitment, 204–209
  attachment style and, 265
  between best friends, 223
  cognitive relationship maintenance mechanisms for, 427–428
  as component of love, 247
  consequences of, 208–209
  in intimate relationships, 2, 3
  investment model of, 207
  obligation to, 204–205
  sex and, 281–282

three types of, 207–208
Communal aspect of friendship, 213
Communal relationships, 198–199, 376
  and exchange relationships compared, 198
Communal strength scale, 199
Communication, 141–174. *See also* Dysfunctional communication
  about sex, 297–299
  active listening in, 170
  attachment styles and, 164
  behavior descriptions used in, 168
  cautious, 159
  dysfunctional, 166–173
  error and misunderstanding in, 141–142
  gender differences in verbal, 161–166
  I-statements used in, 168
  miscommunication in, 166–168
  model of, 142
  nonverbal
  online, 163
  politeness and, 170–172
  respect and validation in, 172–173
  saying what we mean in, 168–169
  self-disclosure in, 155–158
  sympathy and concern, 169
  table talk, 141
  verbal, 155–166
Companionate love, 248, 249, 258–260
Comparison level (CL), 176–177, 179, 180, 182, 183
Comparison level for alternatives (CLalt), 177–180, 182–183, 364, 388n8
Compassionate love, 260–261
Complementarity, 99
Compromise, 356
Concern, communicating, 169
Condoms, 291–295, 373
Confirmation bias, 108
Conflict. *See* Interpersonal conflict
Conflict Tactics Scale, 377, 378
Connection with others, 236
Conscientiousness, 27

Constraint commitment, 208
Consummate love, 249
Contempt, 167
Contentment in relationships, 431–433
Convenience, proximity and, 72–73
Convenience sample, 45
Coolidge effect, 269
Correlational designs, 49–50, 52
Correlations, 49–50
Cosmetic surgery, 86
Costs
    interdependency and, 203–204
    of intimacy, 183–185
    relationship and, 191–192
    relationship satisfaction and, 183–191
    social exchange, 176
    as time goes by, 191–196
Counseling, premarital, 435–436
Counterpower, 365
Couples' reports, 63
Courtly love, 245
Criticism
    in communication, 167
    conflict and, 342
Cross-complaining, 167
Cross-sectional designs, 52
Cultural context of divorce, 404
Cultural influences, 6–14
    changes in, 6–14
    cohabitation and, 8–11
    divorce and, 394–395
    gestures and, 146–147
    individualism, 11
    physical attractiveness and, 81, 84–85
    sex ratio, 12–14
    sexual attitudes and, 277
    socioeconomic development and, 11–13
    sources of change in, 11–14
    technology and, 11–12
Cumulative annoyances, conflict and, 342–343
Cybersex, 288

Dark side of relationships, 36–37
Data, research
    analysis of, 64–66
    archival materials, 62

couples' reports, 63
    observational, 59–61
    paired, interdependent, 64–65
    physiological, 61
    self-report, 55–58
Dating, online, 75
Deceiver's distrust, 325
Deception
    defined, 323
    detecting a partner's, 326–328
Decoding, 153
Defensiveness, 167
Define the relationship, nonverbal communication and, 143
Demand/withdrawal pattern of conflict, 349–350
Demographic similarities, 92
Depression, loneliness and, 240
Derogation of tempting alternatives, 428
Designs, research
    correlational, 49–50, 52
    cross-sectional, 52
    developmental, 52–54
    experimental, 51
    longitudinal, 52–53
    retrospective, 53–54
Destiny beliefs, 118, 119
Devaluation, relational, 308, 328–329
Developmental research designs, 52–54
    cross-sectional, 52
    longitudinal, 52–53
    retrospective designs, 53–54
Dialectics, 338
Direct rewards, 70–71
Direct strategies of breaking up, 409
Direct style of power, 372
Direct tactics in conflict, 346, 351
Disillusionment model of breakups, 402
Dismissing style of attachment, 16–18
Display rules, 145
Dispositional influences on violence, 383
Dissimilarities
    decrease of, over time, 98
    discovering, 95–97

Dissolution of relationships. *See also* Divorce
    adjustments after, 412–414
    aftermath of, 412–422
    barrier model of, 398–399
    personal account of, 413
    premarital partners, 409–410
    process of breaking up, 408–412
    reasons for, 391
    relationship rules and, 405
    types of relationship and, 394–395
    typical script for, 411
    vulnerability-stress-adaptation model of, 399–401
Distal influences on violence, 383
Distress-maintaining attributions, 115–116
Divorce
    adjustment following, 414–417
    children of, 397–398, 419–422
    cohabitation and, 8–11
    comparison level for alternatives and, 179, 183
    cultural changes in, 7–8
    Early Years of Marriage Project on, 403–404
    energy/resource consumption and, 419
    finances and, 418
    high-risk vs. low-risk couples for, 185, 186
    PAIR Project, 401–403
    personal perception and, 404, 406
    predictors of, 398–408
    prevalence of, 392
    rates of, 7–8
    reasons for increase in, 394–396
    relationship with ex-spouses following, 418–419
    same-sex couples and, 397
    social networks and, 417–418
    specific predictors of, 405, 406
    steps to, 410–412

Domestic violence. *See* Violence in relationships
Domination, conflict ended with, 356
Dyadic phase of dissolution of relationships, 411
Dyadic withdrawal, 224
Dysfunctional beliefs, 117–118
Dysfunctional communication, 166–173
    active listening and, 170
    miscommunication, 166–168
    polite interaction and, 170–172
    respect and validation, 172–173
    saying what we mean and, 168–169

Early Years of Marriage (EYM) Project, 44, 53, 403–404
EARs (electronically activated recorders), 60
Economic hardship model of children of divorce, 420
Economies of relationships, 183–196
Egypt, ancient, 245
Elderly, the
    friendships of, 224–226
    loneliness in, 238
Electronically activated recorders (EARs), 60
E-mail, 163
Emergent distress model of breakups, 402
Emotional infidelity, 318–320
Emotional intelligence, 135–136
Emotional isolation, 236
Emotionally focused therapy (EFCT), 438–440
Emotional sharing, 227
Emotional support, 215, 217
Emotions
    facial expressions revealing, 144–146
    feigned expressions of, 146
    romantic love as an, 251
Empathic joining, 437
Empathy, 333
Empty love, 247, 249
Encoding, 153
Enduring dynamics model of breakups, 401, 403

Envy, jealousy vs., 312n3
Equality, in close relationships, 369
Equitable relationships, 200–203
Equity norm, 366
Eros, 262
Escalation, of conflict, 344, 346
Ethical issues in research, 62–63
Ethnicity, interethnic relationships, 96
Evolutionary perspectives
    on conflict, 343
    on cultural change, 35
    explaining patterns in relationships, 32–36
    on infidelity, 287, 289
    on jealousy, 316, 318–320
    on need to belong, 6, 32–33
    on parental investment, 33
    on physical attractiveness, 81–84
    sex differences in love and, 266
    on sexual selection, 32, 33
Excessive reassurance seeking, 240
Exchange relationships, 197–198
    and communal relationships compared, 198
Exit, response to conflict and, 352
Ex-lovers, friendship among, 239
Expectations
    of marriage, 394
    social cognition and, 120–123
Experience-sampling, 59
Experimental research designs, 51
Expert power, 365, 366
Expressive communication, 164–166
Expressive traits, 23–24, 26
Expressivity traits, 165, 166, 238
Extradyadic sex
    attitudes toward, 274–275
    cohabitation before marriage and, 8–11
    divorce and, 408

emotional infidelity vs., 318–320
evolutionary perspective on, 286, 289
gender and sexual orientation differences in, 283–284, 286
jealousy and, 318–319
jealousy and emotional vs. sexual, 318–320
sociosexuality and, 284, 286
Extraversion, 27, 28
Eye-tracking methodology, 60

Facebook, 12, 61, 231
"Face-to-face" friendships, 227
Facial expressions, 144–146
Facial features, attractive, 77–78
Facial symmetry, 82
Familiarity, attraction and, 73
Fantasy, 268
Fatal attraction, 97, 195
Fate control, 364
Fatuous love, 248, 249
Fearful style of attachment, 16–18
Female attractiveness, 77
Femininity, 23–24, 26
Feminism, 204
Fertility, 82, 94
Fight Effect Profile, 360
Fighting, 357–360
    benefits of, 357–360
    Fight Effects Profile, 360
    list of "don'ts" for, 358
    speaker-listener technique, 358, 359
Financial status, attraction and, 94–95
First impressions
    accuracy of perceptions and, 110–112
    confirmation bias, 108
    influence of, 106, 116–117
    influencing judgments of subsequent information, 109–110
    overconfidence in, 109–110
    physical attractiveness and, 74
    power of, 106
    primacy effect, 108
    stereotypes and, 106–107

Flirting, 152
Forgiveness, 61, 332–334, 430
Friendship-Based Love Scale, 258
Friendships, 212–243
    during adolescence, 221, 222
    after marriage, 224
    among ex-lovers, 239
    attributes of, 213–219
    best, 223
    during childhood, 222
    defined, 213
    difficulties in, 230–241
    early philosophers on, 41
    Facebook friends, 231
    gender differences in same-sex, 227–228
    importance of, 216
    individual differences on, 228–230
    between men and women, 229
    during midlife, 224
    networks of, and marital adjustment, 225
    during old age, 224–226
    proximity and, 71–74
    romances and, 212
    with romantic partners, 259
    romantic relationships vs., 213–214, 256
    rules of, 220
    self-monitoring and, 131–132
    in young adulthood, 222–224
"Friends with benefits," 229
Functional magnetic resonance imaging (fMRI), 61

Gay and lesbian relationships.
    See also Civil Unions
    attitudes about same-sex sexuality, 275–277
    causes of conflict, 343
    dissolution of relationships, 393
    equity in household tasks and, 203
    heterosexual couples vs., 29
    jealousy and, 320
    possible evolutionary origins of, 277

power styles of, 374
sexual communication by, 298
sexual frequency and, 282
Gay men. *See also* Gay and lesbian relationships
    coming out, 159
    expressivity in, 29
Gay rights, American attitudes on, 277
Gazing, 146
Gender differences
    conflict and, 349–350
    in control of power resources, 366–368
    expressive vs. instrumental traits, 23–24
    in friendships, 214
    interest in physical attractiveness, 83–84
    in intimate violence, 379, 381–382
    in loneliness, 238–240
    in nonverbal communication, 154–155
    in number of sexual partners, 283
    post-divorce finances and, 418
    power style and, 373–374
    in pressures to adhering to "proper" gender roles, 26–27
    response to jealousy, 320–322
    in same-sex friendships, 227–228
    sex differences vs., 22–24
    in social support, 215
    in targets of betrayal, 330
    touching and, 147–148
    in verbal communication, 161–166
Gender roles, 23
    divorce and, 395
    jealousy and, 315
    pressure on adhering to "proper," 26–27
    similarities in, 98–99
Genetics
    loneliness and, 238
    as predictor of divorce, 408
Gestures, 146–147
Good faith contracts, 437
Good gene hypothesis, 287

Grave-dressing phase of dissolution of relationships, 411
Greece, ancient, 245
Growth beliefs, 118, 119

Half-truths, 323
Handshaking, 147, 152
Health
    connections with others and, 4–5
    emotional support and, 215
    loneliness and, 238
Healthy Marriage Initiative, 63
Height, attractiveness and, 80
Heterosexual couples, same-sex couples vs., 29
High self-monitors, 131–132
High-tech role-playing, 55
History, 245–246
HIV/AIDS, 292
Homosexual relationships.
    See Gay and lesbian relationships
Hookups, 291
Hostile conflict style, 355
Household tasks, 98–99, 203, 396
How to Win Friends and Influence People (Carnegie), 219
Human nature
    influence on intimate relationships, 32–36
    need to belong, 4–6
HurryDate, 85
Hurt feelings, 307–310

I-cubed model, 382
Idealizing, of partners, 112–113
Idioms, 160
Illegitimate demands, 342
Illusion of unique invulnerability, 292
Immersive virtual environments (IVEs), 55, 153
Impelling influences, 382, 384
Impression management, 129–132
Inattention to alternatives, 427
Inclusion of Other in the Self Scale, 3

Income
 divorce and, 394–395
 height and, 80
Incompatability, gender
 differences and, 25
Indirect power, 372
Indirect rewards, 70, 71
Indirect strategies of breaking
 up, 409
Indirect style of power, 372
Indirect tactics in conflict,
 346, 351
Individual differences, 19
 betrayal, 329–330
 friendships, 228–230
 gender differences, 22–27
 loneliness and, 236, 238
 love, 263–267
 personality, 27–28
 self-esteem, 28–32
 sex differences, 20–22
 sexual orientation, 29
Individualism, 11, 394, 395
Inequity, 201
Infatuated love, 249
Infatuation, 246, 247
Infidelity. *See also* Extradyadic
 sex
 attachment style influences
  perceptions of, 321
 avoiding, 430
Informational power, 365,
 366
Ingratiation, 130
Inhibiting influences, 382
Initiator Style Questionnaire,
 349, 350
Insecure styles of attachment,
 16–17
 distress-maintaining
  attributions and, 115–116
 intimacy and, 264
 loneliness and, 238
 parenting and, 18–19
 speed-dating and, 88
Insight-oriented couple
 therapy (IOCT), 439–441
Instigating triggers, 382, 384
Instrumental communication
 skills, 164–166
Instrumental traits, 23–24, 26,
 165–166, 230
Integration with and
 separation from tension, 339
Integrative agreements, 356

Integrative behavioral couple
 therapy (IBCT), 437
Intensifying facial
 expressions, 145
Interdependence theory, 176
 businesslike emphasis of,
  183
 changes in comparison levels
  and comparison level for
  alternatives, 182–183
 comparison level, 176–177
 comparison level for
  alternatives, 177–179
 four types of relationships,
  179–182
 outcome, 176
 power, 363
 reasons for waning
  relationship satisfaction,
  192–194
Interdependency
 approach and avoidance
  motivations, 187–191
 attachment and, 205
 between best friends, 223
 commitment and, 204–209
 in communal relationships,
  198–199
 costs of intimacy and,
  183–185
 in equitable relationships,
  200–203
 in exchange relationships,
  197–198
 independence vs., 338
 in intimate relationships, 2
 nature of, 196–197
 power and, 181, 376–377
 relational turbulence model,
  191–192
 rewards and costs, 203–204
 social exchange, 175–183
Interdependent self-construal,
 230
Interdependent self-
 construals, 377
Interethnic relationships, 96
International Association for
 Relationship Research, 44
Internet
 cybersex, 288
 lying, 327
 ostracism on, 311
 used for observational
  research, 61

Interpersonal Betrayal Scale,
 330
Interpersonal conflict
 anger and, 344, 345
 attributions and, 343–344,
  346
 defined, 337–338
 demand/withdraw pattern
  in, 349–350
 dialectics causing, 338
 ending, 356
 engagement and escalation
  of, 344, 346, 348–349
 events instigating, 341–343
 evolutionary perspective,
  343
 fighting in, 357–360
 four different responses
  to, 352
 frequency of, 339–341
 influences correlated with
  amount of, 339–341
 negotiation and
  accommodation, 351–353
 possible courses of, 347
 types of couples in, 353, 355
Interpersonal distance,
 148–149
Interpersonal gap, 142
Interpersonal process model
 of intimacy, 158
Interrupting, 167, 370, 371
Intimacy
 attachment styles and, 264
 in childhood friendships, 221
 as component of love,
  246–247
 costs of, 183–185
 differences in need for, 229
 fear of, 37
 with friends, 212
 on the Love Scale, 255
 in men's vs. women's
  friendships, 229
 nature and importance of,
  2–6
Intimacy vs. isolation, 222
Intimate-mutual sharing, 223
Intimate partner violence
 (IPV), 378
 gender differences in, 379,
  381–382
Intimate relationships
 accuracy of perceptions in,
  132–138

Intimate relationships—*Cont.*
attachment styles and, 14–19
characteristics of, 2–4
cultural influences on, 6–14
dark side of, 36–37
dissolution of (*see* Dissolution of relationships)
early philosophers on, 41–44
gender differences in, 22–27
impression management in, 130–132
influence of interaction on, 36
mismatched attachment styles in, 19
need to belong in, 4–6
optimism about, 424–426
overview of, 424–426
personality differences in, 27–28
self-esteem's impact on, 28–32
sex differences and, 20–22
Intimate terrorism (IT), 379, 386
leaving a relationship with, 388–389
many facets of, 379
rationale for, 387
Intimate zone, 148
Intimidation, 130
Intoxication, safe sex and, 293
Investment model of commitment, 207, 426
Investments, in relationships, 178
Invisible support, 217
Isolation, 236
I-statements, 168–169, 171, 358
IVEs (immersive virtual environments), 55, 153

Jealousy
coping constructively with, 322–323
envy vs., 312n3
evolutionary perspective on, 316, 318–320
feeling defining, 312
people prone to, 313–315
reactive, 313
responses to, 320–322
rivals involved in, 315–316
for same sex affairs, 320
sex differences in reasons for, 318–319
for sexual vs. emotional infidelity, 318–320
suspicious, 313
traditional gender roles and, 315
Journal of Marriage and the Family, 44
Journal of Social and Personal Relationships, 44

Kansas State University, 92
Kitchen-sinking, 166
Knowledge
accuracy of perceptions based on, 134
between best friends, 223
in intimate relationships, 2

Laboratory setting, 54
Language, power expressed through, 370
Learned helplessness, 178
Legitimate power, 365, 366
Lesbians. *See also* Gay and lesbian relationships
coming out, 159
heterosexual women vs., 29
Liking, 247, 249
loving vs., 213
romantic love vs., 255
Liking Scale, 255
Listening, active, 170
Loneliness
depression and, 240
dull and negative attitude of lonely people, 240
emotional isolation, 236
explained, 236, 238
expressivity and, 238
gender differences in, 238–239
genetics and, 238
health and, 238
individual traits and, 238
overcoming, 240–241
self-esteem and, 238
social isolation, 236
UCLA Loneliness Scale, 236–237
with vs. without a romantic partner, 239–240

Long-distance relationships, 72–73, 75
Longitudinal designs, 52–53
Long-term mating strategies, 34
Love. *See also* Romantic love
age and, 265–266
attachment style and, 264–265
companionate, 248, 258–260
compassionate, 260–261
consummate, 249
courtly, 245
empty, 247, 249
fatuous, 248, 249
future of, 269–271
history of, 245–246
individual differences in, 263–267
intimacy and, 246–247
lust and, 291
passion and, 247–248
romantic, passionate, 251–258
sex differences and, 266–267
styles of loving, 261–263
through the passage of time, 267–271
Triangular Theory, 246–250
"Love is blind," 256
Love Scale, 255, 266–268
Low self-esteem, 238
Low self-monitors, 131–132
Loyalty, conflict and, 352
Ludus, as style of loving, 262
Lust, 250
Lying
in close and casual relationships, 323–325
detecting, 326–328
getting away with, 332
liar characteristics and, 325–326
online, 327

Machoism, 165
loneliness in men and, 238
response to conflict and, 352
Maintaining relationships. *See* Relationship maintenance mechanisms
Male attractiveness, 77–80
Male dominance in power, 366–367

Mania, 262
Marital Instability Over the Life Course project, 404
Marital interactions, as predictor of divorce, 408
Marital satisfaction
    average trajectory of, 193
    divorce and, 408
    dysfunctional communication and, 167–168
    nonverbal sensitivity and, 153–155
    reasons for waning, 192–194
    stereotyped gender roles and, 24–25
Marital therapy, 436–442
    common features of, 440–442
    core features of, 438
    emotionally focused, 438–439
    insight-oriented, 439–440
Marriage. *See also* Divorce
    in 1960, 6
    of African Americans, 63
    age at first, 6–8
    age of death and, 15
    attitudes, as predictor of divorce, 408
    attitudes toward sex without, 278
    balance of power in, 364–325, 367–368, 375–376
    changes in, 8–9
    cohabitation before, 8–11
    friendships after, 224
    high expectations of, 394
    history of romance and passion in, 245–246
    impoliteness in, 184
    inequity on household tasks and, 203–204
    prior, as predictor of divorce, 407
    research studies on, 44–45
    romantic love as reason for, 244
    romantic love decreasing after, 267
    sex without, 274–275
Marriage shift, 126–127
Masculinity, 23–24, 26
Massachusetts Institute of Technology, 72, 73
Masturbation, 290
Matching, 88, 93–95, 314

Mate-guarding, 380
Mate poaching, 317
Material support, 215, 217
Mate value, 89
Maximal exclusion, 306
Maximal inclusion, 306
Memories, 116–117
Men. *See also* Gender differences; Sex differences
    interest in physical attractiveness, 83–84
    jealousy of sexual infidelity by, 317, 318–319
    language style of, 370
    opening lines used by, 91
    rationale for violence, 387
    sexual double standard and, 274
    verbal communication styles, 162
Men Are From Mars, Women Are From Venus (Gray), 20, 434
Menstrual cycle, voice and, 150
Mental health, connections with others and, 5
Mere exposure, 73, 74
Meta-analyses, 65
Michelangelo phenomenon, 428
Middle Ages, 245
Midlife, friendship during, 224
Mimicry, 151–152
Mindreading, 166–167
Minimizing facial expressions, 145
Miscommunication, 166–168. *See also* Dysfunctional communication
Moral commitment, 208
Mothers, influence on attachment styles of children, 18–19
Motivation, accuracy of perceptions based on, 134
Mutuality
    dissolution of relationships and, 414
    in intimate relationships, 2–3

Narcissism, 128
National Institute of Justice, 377

National Violence Against Women Survey, 377
Natural research settings, 54
Natural selection, 32
Nature of commitment, 204–209
Nature of interdependency, 196–197
Need to belong, 4–6
    human nature and, 32–33
    loneliness and, 236
Negative affect, 167
Negative affect reciprocity, 171, 348
Negative self-concept, 127–128
Negative self-image, 126–128
Neglect, response to conflict and, 352
Negotiation, 346
Neuroticism, 27, 28
Neutralizing facial expressions, 145
No-fault divorce laws, 396, 407
Nonconscious social cognition, 124
Nonlove, 247, 249
Nonverbal communication, 143–155
    body movement, 146–147
    combining components of, 150–153
    facial expressions, 144–146
    flirting and, 152
    functions of, 144
    gazing, 146
    gender differences in, 154–155
    interpersonal distance, 148–149
    lying and, 326
    paralanguage, 150
    power expressed through, 370–371
    relationship satisfaction and misunderstanding in, 153–155
    touch, 147–148
Nonverbal sensitivity, 153–155, 370, 371–372
Normal curve, 21
Norm of equity, 366
Norm of reciprocity, 366
Norm of social responsibility, 366

Northwestern University, 42, 339
Novelty, 268

Observational studies, 59–62
Off-beam conversations, 166
Old age, friendship during, 224–226
Online communication, 12, 163
Online dating, 75
Online sex, 288
Opener Scale, 157, 164
Openness and closedness tension, 338
Openness to experience, 27, 28
Ostracism, 310–312
Other-oriented strategies of breaking up, 409
Outcome, 176, 177, 179, 182, 200
"Overbenefited," 201–203
Overconfidence, 109–110
Oxytocin, 61, 258

Paired, interdependent research data, 64–65
PAIR Project, 401–403
Paralanguage, 150, 151
Paraphrasing, 170
Parental conflict model of divorce, 420
Parental investment, 33
Parental loss model of divorce, 420
Parental stress model of children of divorce, 420
Parenthood
    attachment and, 18–19
    jealousy, infidelity and, 319–320
    with or without marriage, 7
    reactions to "coming out," 159
    relationships changing after, 195
    single-parent homes, 8
    working mothers and, 8, 394, 395, 407
Participant attrition, 53
Particularistic resources of power, 367
Passion
    attachment style and, 264–265

as component of love, 247–248
in marriage, history of, 246–247
romantic passionate love, 251–258
Passionate Love Scale, 254, 255
Passive exclusion, 306
Paternity uncertainty, 34, 316
Perceived partner responsiveness, 158, 218
Perceived similarity, 96
Perceived superiority, 209, 427
Perceiver ability, 135–136
Perceiver influence, 137
Perception checking, 170
Persevering indirectness, 410
Personal commitment, 207
Personal context of divorce, 404
Personal experience, research questions from, 44–45
Personality, 27–28
    attributes of, as predictor of divorce, 408
    conflict and, 339–340
    jealousy and, 315
    loneliness and, 238
    similarities in, 92–93
Personal phrase of dissolution of relationships, 411
Personal Relationships, 44
Pets, as friends, 226
"Phantom stranger" technique, 42
Physical attractiveness, 74–91
    assumptions about people with, 75–77
    bias for beauty, 75–77, 83–84
    of bodies, 79–80
    characteristics of, 77–78
    culture and, 84–85
    differences in notions of, 76
    evolutionary perspective on, 81–84
    facial symmetry and, 77–78
    height and, 80
    impact on interactions with others, 86–88
    impression management and, 132
    matching in, 88
    smell and, 80–81

Physical proximity, 71–72
Physiological measures, 61
Platonic love, 245
Play, relationship maintenance through, 429–430
Playing "hard to get," 90
Pluralistic ignorance, 293
Politeness, in communication, 170–172
Poor self-regard, 233
Pornography, 288
Positive illusions, 112, 427
Positive self-concept, 126
Post-dissolution relationships, 412–414
Posture, body, 147
Poverty, marital quality and, 394–395
Power, 362–377
    defined, 362
    gender differences in control of resources, 366–368
    and (in)dependence, 181
    indirect, 372
    inequities in, 293–294
    language expressing, 370
    nonverbal behavior expressing, 370–371
    outcome of, 375–376
    of proximity, 73–74
    sources of, 363–365
    styles of, 372–375
    two faces of, 376–377
    types of resources providing, 365
Pragma, as style of loving, 262
Premarital birth, as predictor of divorce, 407
Premarital counseling, 435–436
Premarital sex, attitudes toward, 274
Preoccupied style of attachment, 16, 17
Prevention and Relationship Enhancement Program (PREP), 435–436
Preventive relationship maintenance, 435–436
Previous research, research questions from, 44–45
Primacy effect, 108
Principle of lesser interest, 181, 363

Prior marriage, as predictor of divorce, 407
Privacy, in relationships, 158
Processes of Adaptation in Intimate Relationships (PAIR Project), 401–403
Proper Care and Feeding of Marriage, The (Schlessinger), 434
Proportional justice, 200
Providing information, nonverbal communication and, 143
Proximity, attraction and, 71–74
convenience and, 72–73
familiarity and, 73
power of, 73–74
Proximity seeking, 222
Psychological equity, 202
Public zone, 149
Purdue University, 92

Quid pro quid contract, 436–437

Race, divorce and, 407
Rape,–302
Ratings (scientific observations), 60
Reactance, 100
Reactive jealousy, 313
Reactivity, 60, 62
Rebuffs, conflict and, 342
Reciprocity, in self-disclosure, 157
Reciprocity norm, 366
Reconstructive memory, 117
Referent power, 365, 366
Regulating interaction, nonverbal communication and, 143
Rejection
degrees of, 306
hurt feelings, 307–310
ostracism, 307–312
relational value, 305–307
Rejection sensitivity, 123
Relational context of divorce, 404
Relational devaluation, 308, 328–329
Relational influences on violence, 383
Relational turbulence model, 191–192

Relational value, 305–307
Relationship Assessment Scale, 56
Relationship beliefs. *See* Beliefs about relationships
Relationship-enhancing attributions, 115
Relationship maintenance mechanisms, 208, 426–433
actions for staying content, 431–433
behavioral, 428–430
cognitive, 427–428
expressing gratitude for partner, 432
preventive, 435–436
Relationships, 200–203. *See also* Intimate relationships
approach and avoidance processes in, 188
avoiding infidelity, 430
ending (*see* Dissolution of relationships)
equality elements in, 369
exchange and communal differences, 198
gay and lesbian (*see* Gay and lesbian relationships)
importance of, 2–6
online, 12
repairing, 433–442
rewards-costs and, 191–192
romantic (*see* Romantic relationships)
rules for, 220
satisfaction in beginning, 191
Relationship satisfaction
equity and, 202–203
interdependence theory on degrees of, 179–182
perceived support and, 218–219
relational turbulence model on, 192
rewards-to-cost ratio for, 183–196
self-disclosure and, 160–161
sexual satisfaction and, 299–300
Relationship science. *See* Research, relationship
Relative resources of power, 367
Reliability, 55

Religion, divorce and, 407
Remarriage, 417
Repairing relationships, 433–442
advice from the media, 433–435
marital therapy, 436–442
preventive maintenance, 435–436
Representative sample, 45
Research, relationship, 40–69
archival materials for, 62
complexities of good, 66
correlational designs, 49–50
couples' reports used for, 63
current methods of, 42–44
developmental designs for, 52–54
ethical issues in, 62–64
experimental designs, 51
historical overview, 41–44
history of, 41–44
interpreting and integrating results of, 64–66
need for understanding, 40–41
observation data for, 59–61
participants for, 45–49
physiological measures for, 61
question development, 44–45
selecting a setting for, 54
self-report data for, 55–58
Respect
in communication, 172–173
in friendships, 214
Responsiveness, 214–215
in action, 219
perceived partner, 218
Resurrection phase of dissolution of relationships, 411
Retrospective designs, 53–54
Reward power, 365
Rewards
attraction and, 70–71
interdependence, 204
over time, 191–196
relationship satisfaction, 183–191
sex differences in evaluation of, 189
social exchange and, 176
Role-play, 54

Romance
  enhanced by fantasy, 268
  feminism's compatibility
    with, 204
  in marriage, history of,
    245–246
Romanticism, 117
Romantic love
  as an emotion, 251
  arousal, 251–255
  companionate love vs.,–261
  decreasing after marriage,
    267
  friendship vs., 213–214, 256
  involving passion, 251–258
  as reason for marriage, 244
  role of thoughts in, 255–258
  in Sternberg's Triangular
    Theory of Love, 249
  through the passage of
    time, 267–269
  in Triangular Theory of
    Love, 249
  unrequited, 260
Romantic relationships
  accuracy in predictions
    about, 110–112
  friendships vs., 213–214
  idealizing partners in,
    112–113
  self-verification on, 125–126
Romeo and Juliet effect, 100
*Rules: Time-Tested Secrets for
  Capturing the Heart of Mr.
  Right, The (Fein/Schneider),*
  434
Rules of friendship, 220
Rules of relationships, 221,
  405

Sacrifice, willingness to, 209,
  428
Safe haven, 222
Safe sex, 291–294
Same-sex friendships, 227–228
Same-sex relationships.
  See Gay and lesbian
  relationships
Same-sex sexuality, attitudes
  about, 275–277
Sarcasm, 150
Scales
  Commitment, 206
  Friendship-Based Love, 258
  Interpersonal Betrayal, 330

Loneliness, 237, 239
Love and Liking, 255
Measuring Communal
  Strength, 199
Passionate Love, 254, 255
Shyness, 232
Scenarios, 54
Schemas, 117–118
SCV perpetration, 383
Secrets, 158–161
Secure base, 222
Secure style of attachment, 14,
  16–19, 88
  intimacy and, 264
  perception of partners,
    120
  relationship-enhancing
    attributions and, 115
Self-bolstering, jealousy and,
  322–323
Self-concept, 125, 414
Self-control, 358, 429, 433
Self-Determination Theory,
  296
Self-disclosure, 155–158
  coming out, 159
  defined, 156
  example of, 155–156
  gender differences in, 164
  high openers, 157
  reciprocity in, 157
  relationship satisfaction,
    160–161
  social penetration theory,
    156–158
  taboo topics, 159–160
Self-enhancement, 125–127
Self-esteem, 125, 178
  based on rejections and
    acceptance, 306–307
  hurt feelings and, 309–310
  impact on intimate
    relationships, 28–32
  jealousy and, 314
  loneliness and, 238
  ostracism and, 311
Self-expansion, 414
Self-expansion model of
  human motivation, 190–191,
  258
Self-fulfilling prophecies,
  120–123
Self-monitoring, 86, 130–131,
  133, 228
Self-Monitoring Scale, 86

Self-oriented strategies of
  breaking up, 409
Self-promotion, 130
Self-regard, poor level of, 233
Self-reliance, jealousy and, 322
Self-reports, 55–58, 63, 66
Self-restraint, 429
Self-serving bias, 57–58,
  114–115, 343
Self-verification, 125–126
Sensitivity, nonverbal,
  153–155
Separation, ending conflict
  with, 356
Separation protest, 222
Sex differences
  in evaluation of relationship
    rewards, 189
  gender differences vs.,
    22–24
  in jealousy, 318–320
  judgments on relationships
    and, 135
  love and, 266–267
  in nonverbal
    communication, 153–155
  paralanguage, 150
  paternity uncertainty and,
    34
  reproductive potential, 33
  in sex drives, 289–291
  in sexual attitudes, 274
  stereotypes about, 20–22
  in what is desired in
    partners, 101–102
Sex drives, 289–290
Sex frequency, by age, 270
Sex ratio, 12–14, 396, 407
Sexual behavior,
  unwanted,–301
Sexual desire, 289–290
Sexual double standard, 274
Sexuality, 273–304
  adolescent friendships and,
    221–222
  age of first experience, 278,
    279–281
  attachment and, 299
  attitudes about, 274–278
  causes of conflict and, 343
  in committed relationships,
    281–282
  first experiences, 279–281
  frequency of sexual activity,
    281–282, 294–295

in homosexual vs. heterosexual relationships, 29
improving your sex life, 295
in the media, 295
numbers of sexual partners and, 283
online sex, 288
in opposite-sex friendships, 229
paternity uncertainty and, 34
power and, 363–364
problems with self-report research on, 57
research on, 47–49
safe sex, 291–294
satisfaction, 408
sex ratio and, 12–14
sexual coercion,–302
sexual satisfaction, 294–300
without love or commitment, 285, 286
Sexually transmitted infections (STIs), 292
Sexual orientation, 29
extradyadic sex and, 283–284
nonverbal behavior and, 148
sexual frequency and, 282
Sexual permissiveness, sex differences in, 22
Sexual selection, 32, 33
Sexual tension, among male/female friendships, 229
Sexual violation, 301
Shared activities, 227
Short-term mating strategies, 34
Shyness, 231–236
doing better with excuse for failure, 235
interpersonal effects of, 234
Shyness Scale, 232
"Side-by-side" friendships, 227
Silent treatment, 310
Similarity, 92–100
complementarity and, 99, 100
conflict and, 341
divorce and, 408
examples of, 92
importance of some over others, 98

opposites and attraction, 93–100
perceived vs. real, 97–98
types of, 92–93
Simulations, 54
Single, staying, 7, 15
Single-parent families, 392
Single-parent homes, 8
Singlism, 15
Situational couple violence (SCV), 379, 382–383
Situational influences on violence, 383
Smiling, 144
Sociability theme in friendship, 213
Social allergies, 342–343
Social cognition, 105–140
accuracy of perceptions, 132–138
attributional processes, 113–116
expectations, 120–123
first impressions, 106–112
idealizing romantic partners, 113
impression management, 129–132
memories and, 116–117
mistakes in, 111–112
nonconscious, 124
overview, 105
relationship beliefs, 117–120
self-perception and, 125–128
Social comparison
four types of relationships and, 179–182
in friendships, 215–218
Social desirability bias, 58
Social exchange, 175–183
comparison level and, 176–177
comparison level for alternatives, 177–179
defined, 175
outcome, 176
rewards and costs, 176
theories of, 175–176
Social isolation, 236
Social mobility, as predictor of divorce, 407
Social nature, 1
Social norms, 367
Social penetration theory, 156–158

Social phase of dissolution of relationships, 411
Social responsibility norm, 366
Social skills, 233
Social support, in friendships, 215–218
Social zone, 149
Sociocultural model, 266–267
Socioeconomic development, cultural changes and, 11–13
Socioeconomic status, divorce and, 404, 407
Socioemotional selectivity theory, 224–225
Sociometer, 28–29, 238
Sociosexuality, 285
Sociosexual Orientation Inventory, 285
Sociosexual orientations, 284
Solitary confinement, 1
Speaker-listener technique, 358, 359
Speed-dating, 42, 88, 90
Sperm competition, 287
Stability and change tension, 339
Stage of life, conflict and, 340
Stalking, 381
Statistically significant, 21, 64
Stepchildren, as predictor of divorce, 407
Stereotypes
about sex differences in intimate relationships, 20–21
first impressions and, 106–107
physical attractiveness, 76–77
power and gender, 367
Stimulus-value-role theory, 96, 97
Stonewalling, 167
Storge, as style of loving, 262
Street Corner Society (Whyte), 41
Stresses and strains in relationships, 305–334
betrayal, 328–332
deception and lying, 323–328
forgiveness, 332–334
hurt feelings, 307–310
jealousy (*see* Jealousy)

Stresses and strains in
   relationships—*Cont.*
   ostracism, 310–312
   pets and, 226
   relational value, 305–307
   stress as predictor of
      divorce, 408
Stress hormones, as predictor
   of divorce, 408
Stress spillover, 401
Structural improvement, 356
Styles of Loving, 261
Supplication, 130
Suspicious jealousy, 313
Symmetry, facial, 77–78, 82
Sympathy, communicating, 169

Taboo topics, 159–160
Talk table, 141
Technology. *See also* Internet
   cultural influences on
      relationships and, 12
   dating online and, 75
   for observational studies, 61
Teen birth rate, 279
Teen sex, as predictor of
   divorce, 407
Texting, 163
Therapy. *See also* Marital
   therapy
   behavioral approaches to,
      436–438
   coping with jealousy
      through, 322–323
Thought, romantic love and,
   255–258
Threatening perceptions,
   136–137
Tolerance building, 438
Touch, 147–148
"Trial marriage," 10
Triangular Theory of Love,
   246–250, 259
Trust
   between best friends, 223
   as a fluid process, 36
   in friendships, 214
   in intimate relationships, 2, 3

Truth bias, 326
UCLA Loneliness Scale, 237,
   239
"underbenefitted," 201
Unified detachment, 437
Unilateral style of power,
   373–374
Universalistic resources of
   power, 367
University of Arizona, 43
University of Michigan, 92, 341
University of Minnesota, 122
University of Texas, 43, 110
University of Virginia, 414
Unmarried birthrate, 7
Unrequited love, 260
Unwanted sexual behavior,

Validation, in communication,
   172–173
Validator conflict style, 353
Validity, 55
Value, relational, 305–307
Values, similarities in, 92
Vengeance, 333
Verbal communication, 155–166
   attachment styles, 164
   gender differences in,
      161–611
   instrumentality vs.
      expressivity, 164–166
   interpersonal model of
      intimacy, 158
   secrets, 158–161
   self-disclosure, 155–158,
      160–161, 164
   styles of, 162
Violence in relationships,
   377–389
   Conflict Tactics Scale, 377,
      378
   correlates of, 382–386
   gender differences in,
      381–382
   impelling influences, 382,
      384–385
   inhibiting influences, 382,
      385–386

instigating triggers, 382, 384
   intimate terrorism, 386
   leaving a relationship with,
      388–389
   mate-guarding and, 380
   prevalence of, 377–378
   rationales of, 387
   SCV perpetration, 383
   situational couple violence,
      382–383
   stalking, 381
   types of, 378–380
Violent resistance, 380
Visual Dominance Ratio
   (VDR), 146
Voice
   nonverbal communication
      through, 150
   response to conflict and, 352
Volatile couples, 353
Volunteer bias, 47
Vulnerability-stress-
   adaptation model of marital
   instability, 399–401
Waist-to-hip ratio (WHR), 79,
   82, 84, 85
Widowhood, 417
Women. *See also* Gender
   differences; Sex differences
   interest in physical
      attractiveness, 83–84
   language style of, 370
   opening lines used by, 91
   response to emotional
      infidelity, 317, 318–319
   sexual double standard
      and, 274
   verbal communication
      styles, 162
Working mothers, 8, 394, 395,
   407

XYZ statements, 169, 171

Yes-butting, 167
Young adulthood, friendship
   in, 222–224
Youth, attraction and, 93–95